Luxemburger Juristische Studien –
Luxembourg Legal Studies

edited by

Faculty of Law, Economics and Finance
University of Luxembourg

Volume 21

Carsten Ullrich

Unlawful Content Online

Towards a New Regulatory Framework
for Online Platforms

Nomos

Die Deutsche Nationalbibliothek verzeichnet diese Publikation in der Deutschen Nationalbibliografie; detaillierte bibliografische Daten sind im Internet über http://dnb.d-nb.de abrufbar.

The Deutsche Nationalbibliothek lists this publication in the Deutsche Nationalbibliografie; detailed bibliographic data are available on the Internet at http://dnb.d-nb.de

ISBN 978-3-8487-8315-1 (Print)
978-3-7489-2705-1 (ePDF)

British Library Cataloguing-in-Publication Data
A catalogue record for this book is available from the British Library.

ISBN 978-3-8487-8315-1 (Print)
978-3-7489-2705-1 (ePDF)

Library of Congress Cataloging-in-Publication Data
Ullrich, Carsten
Unlawful Content Online
Towards a New Regulatory Framework for Online Platforms
Carsten Ullrich
650 pp.
Includes bibliographic references and index.

ISBN 978-3-8487-8315-1 (Print)
978-3-7489-2705-1 (ePDF)

1st Edition 2021

Published by
Nomos Verlagsgesellschaft mbH & Co. KG
Waldseestraße 3–5 | 76530 Baden-Baden
www.nomos.de

Production of the printed version:
Nomos Verlagsgesellschaft mbH & Co. KG
Waldseestraße 3–5 | 76530 Baden-Baden

ISBN 978-3-8487-8315-1 (Print)
ISBN 978-3-7489-2705-1 (ePDF)
DOI https://doi.org/10.5771/9783748927051

Onlineversion
Nomos eLibrary

Preface

"...Proactively overseeing
Day-to-day operations
Services and deliverables
With cross-platform innovation
Networking, soon will bring, seamless integration
Robust and scalable, bleeding-edge and next-generation..."

Being a foreword to a scientific research work, source and background to this quote will obviously be explained, but I will do so at the end of my introductory words besides mentioning now already that it originates from a song. But the quote is very fitting to set the scene against which the Ph.D. thesis presented here was developed.

Platforms have completely changed, have shaped and are dominating the online environment. An environment that in 2000, when the regulatory approach towards platforms was defined for the area of the European Union with the E-Commerce Directive, was entirely different from what we experience today. In the words of above: through innovations brought by the emerging platforms, but even more, by not only allowing networking, but continuously expanding by benefitting from network effects, platforms have integrated all different kinds of services in a seamless manner – sometimes it is invisible to the users which services all belong to the same provider or are currently being used by them – and have become robust or, at least for the very large platforms, are in an entrenched market position. Which leaves us with the "next-generation" question from the above quote: after 20 years of watching this growth and fundamental change, it has become obvious and undisputed that platforms play a decisive role in the online user experience and, what's more, have become a key factor also in what can be regarded as a new public sphere for content dissemination and communication. And connected to that is the need for a new approach in regulating these actors, thereby giving up the longtime prevailing mantra of not "opening Pandora's box", meaning that any change to the E-Commerce Directive would lead to unexpected difficulties and fundamental discussions about readjusting regulation for the online environment overall. Indeed, we are now witnessing the beginning of a "next-generation platform regulation".

It is a lucky coincidence if an academic research project that starts out with the aim to analyse a status quo and derive conclusions about an improved future path, takes place exactly in alignment with the period when this is also debated in real. It is challenging because the project has to consider a steep increase in contributions to the debate, but rewarding because it offers potential for impact in the actual process. This is exactly what happened with *Carsten Ullrich*'s project on **"Unlawful Content Online – Towards a New Regulatory Framework for Online Platforms"**, the result of which we are happy to bring to a wider public attention by publication in the **„Luxemburger Juristische Studien – Luxembourg Legal Studies"** as volume 21 with Nomos as a publisher When he started end of 2016 it had become evident that the light touch regulation of platforms was being challenged, but that on short notice no new legislative framework would be proposed by the European Commission. And nearly on the day of the defence of his Ph.D. thesis mid-December 2020 the Commission put on the table two Proposals for Regulations, a Digital Services Act and a Digital Markets Act attempting at exactly creating a "new regulatory framework for online platforms". Obviously, this did not happen by coincidence but the research project was born out of the observation of the actual situation, the framing of a new doctoral training unit at the Department of Law of the University of Luxembourg (DTU REMS on regulatory enforcement in multi-level systems) and the background that *Carsten Ullrich* could bring to the project: having worked as manager for compliance and the notice-and-takedown operations of a large online platform he had the insights that allowed to shape the research in a way that promised practically applicable results. Nonetheless, the perfect timing at the end could not have been planned in advance, but offered and continues to offer the possibility of impacting the currently ongoing debate about how to best impose obligations on online platforms that increase their responsibility. Besides providing a thorough legal analysis based on some initial technical observations, this publication is finalized by developing a risk-based approach for due diligence obligations and is accompanied by concrete proposals for a standard concerning the removing and prevention of counterfeit on e-commerce platforms, which could serve as blueprint for application as a workable solution in practice.

More specifically, of this publication starts out in chapter 1 with explaining the background, the methodological approach and clarifying the key notions, while chapter 2 gives a summary overview of the socio-technical and economic role of platforms which are referred to as internet intermediaries. Chapter 3 details the emergence of rules about liability or – more precisely – exclusion of liability for intermediaries under specific situations and does so by presenting legislation and interpretation by courts in the United States of America, several EU Member States and further national approaches to internet regulation. In order to illustrate the difficulties in answering the question of liability in specific contexts, chapter 4 introduces several sectoral frameworks that each deal with the question in a different manner. Besides looking at responses to defamation that violates personality rights or hate speech and terrorist content that endangers public order, the analysis covers the protection of economic rights in the intellectual property setting. More importantly, the publication also draws attention to sectoral solutions which are not discussed a lot in the literature due to their highly specialized character but allow for insightful conclusions: the area of product and food safety regulation. This is then applied to case studies in those two areas to demonstrate the structures of enforcement and challenges in market surveillance in these sectors. Finally, the publication moves to discussing proposals on how to reform the issue of intermediary liability before presenting a well-argued and profound proposal for a co-regulation system relying on duty of care expectations to be fulfilled by the intermediaries based on harmonised technical standards. The conclusion allows for a first evaluation of the Commission proposal for a Digital Services Act (DSA), which *Carsten Ullrich* could add after his defence in order to offer an updated version of the thesis for publication.

Besides working on his Ph.D. thesis, his research also contributed to two studies on the need for reform of the E-Commerce Directive and platform regulation in the EU as well as a more detailed evaluation of the mentioned DSA proposal, which both are also available as open access publications with Nomos.[1] In the best possible way the research of the thesis that the reader will find after this foreword, contributed to those studies and in turn the work on those studies could then be used for the further development of the thesis. This is the type of exchange between academic research work and practical application that a Ph.D. supervisor – certainly I can say that for myself, but I think many will share this perception – can be happy

1 *Cole/Etteldorf/Ullrich*, Cross-Border Dissemination of Online Content – Current and Possible Future Regulation of the Online Environment with a Focus on the EU E-Commerce Directive, Schriftenreihe Medienforschung der Landesanstalt für Medien NRW (Band 81), Nomos 2020, https://doi.org/10.5771/9783748906438; *Cole/Etteldorf/Ullrich*, Updating the Rules for Online Content Dissemination – Legislative Options of the European Union and the Digital Services Act Proposal, Schriftenreihe Medienforschung der Landesanstalt für Medien NRW (Band 83), Nomos 2021, https://doi.org/10.5771/9783748925934.

to witness as it proves the added value of fundamental research. Its quality is also underlined by having been awarded the prestigious "Prix Rolf Tarrach“ of the Amis de l'Université du Luxembourg for the best Ph.D. thesis of 2020.

This leaves us with the open answer to the background of the musical quote at the beginning. Typically, for nearly every topic one can find a song that offers suitable titles or quotes that one can use as a reference in any type of publication. And in the case of introducing this publication of a thesis it was an obligation considering that *Carsten Ullrich* also has a passion and talent for music. One would think that "platform" is a common expression in lyrics and that it would be easy to find the appropriate quote. However, most platform-references concern either platform soles (of those types of boots that were especially popular in the 1970s) such as in *Dire Straits*' "Sultans of Swing" or they refer to platforms in train stations such as in numerous Bob Dylan songs or *Cream*'s "White Room". It took a more detailed research to find this one song "Mission statement", which by the way is in itself a fitting title in connection with a Ph.D. thesis as the research question could be regarded as the mission statement of a Ph.D. candidate, by *"Weird Al" Yankovic*. For those readers that are not very familiar with this artist (admittedly, I also only knew the artist, but not this specific song before I started the research), he is best known for his parodies of famous pop, folk and rock songs, for example on the same album of 2014 ("Mandatory fun", also a good motto for Ph.D. research which spans over several years and is easier to handle if it gives joy) a parody of *Robin Thicke's* "Blurred Lines" entitled "Word Crimes" (something that you will not find in this publication here). Thinking about it, it turned out to be a perfect match for a quote, even though the song may not have the same wide spread as the platforms you will be reading about in the following: the question of parody as an exception to exclusive rights of authors played an important role in the discussions on the introduction of a new form of platform responsibility with the Copyright in the Digital Single Market-Directive of the EU in 2019. And this is where Carsten Ullrich's thesis nicely ties together with the publications of previous Ph.D. students of mine in the „Luxemburger Juristische Studien – Luxembourg Legal Studies“ series: on "The Struggle in Online Copyright Enforcement – Problems and Prospects“ (Sandra Schmitz, vol. 8, 2015), on freedom of expression standards in the "Regulation of Sexualized Speech in Europe and the United States" (Lawrence Siry, vol. 6, 2016), "Reconstructing European Copyright Law for the Digital Single Market – Between Old Paradigms and Digital Challenges" (Bernd Justin Jütte, vol. 10, 2017) and "Implementing the EU

Audiovisual Media Services Directive – Selected issues in the regulation of AVMS by national media authorities of France, Germany and the UK" (Jenny Weinand, vol. 13, 2018) analysing a first important approach of the EU towards regulating a specific type of platforms, namely video-sharing platforms.

I am sure Carsten Ullrich's work will be a valuable read for you and hope it will receive the deserved attention, be an inspiration for future Ph.D. students as well as contribute to the further debate of a "next generation-regulatory framework for platforms". And I am happy that the author will himself continue to follow the discussions about implementing such new regulatory steps, but now again from the inside perspective of a platform that in the years to come will likely have to adapt to these new rules!

Dr. Mark D. Cole

Professor for Media and Telecommunication Law
University of Luxembourg and
Director for Academic Affairs
Institute of European Media Law (EMR)

Abridged Table of Contents

Table of Contents

Acknowledgements

It is impossible to mention all the people who have contributed, inspired and helped me to achieve this work over the last four years. First of all, my research mentor at the University of Luxembourg, Prof. Mark Cole, has been an invaluable support both on an academic and wider professional level. He provided for an open research environment and encouraged me to test and refine my ideas constantly through publications, conferences and workshops. Secondly, I would like to thank my other two research co-mentors, Prof. Elise Poillot and Prof. Herwig Hofmann, for their input and suggestions for improvements. This, and the various interactions I had with them over the last four years, helped in making this work what it is. I received other precious support and input during my research from the head of the Doctoral Training Unit on Enforcement in Multi-Level Regulatory Systems (DTU REMS I) at the University of Luxembourg, and Faculty Dean, Prof. Katalin Ligeti, but also from Prof. Joana Mendes, Prof. Jörg Gerkrath and the political science experts at the DTU, Prof. David Howarth and Prof. Robert Harmsen. Special thanks go to Dr. Andreas Heinz, who helped me design the survey questionnaire.

I am also deeply indebted to Assistant Professor Dr. Justin Jütte and Dr. Gavin Robinson for the time they spent on reviewing and commenting on earlier drafts of this work. The exchange and discussions with them were crucial to achieve important adjustments and improvements. They have also been of continued support and inspiration over my entire research work over the last four years.

This work would not have been completed without the constant, fruitful exchange and cooperation that took place in the research team of Prof. Cole, notably with Teresa Quintel, Dr. Annelies Vandendriessche, Angelica Fernandez, Juraj Sajfert, Dr. Sandra Schmitz and Dr. Andra Giurgiu. This statement can be extended to many other colleagues at the University, such as members of the DTU REMS I, Simona Demkova, Chrysa Alexandraki, Kelly Blount, Panagiotis Zinonos, Dr. Federico Bergamasco, Dr. Igor Tkalec, Ioannis Asimakopoulos, Dr. Dimitrios Kafteranis and other current and former colleagues, like Dr. Janine Silga, Dr. Julia Sinnig, Dr. Fatima Chaouche, Dr. Basak Baglayan or Dr. Hossein Nabilou, to name but a few.

Furthermore, I count myself lucky to have made the acquaintance of extremely dedicated and knowledgeable experts in national market surveillance and food safety authorities across several EU Member States as part of this research project. The interviews I conducted with them have provided me with empirical information that was crucial for the analysis and solution developed here. I am also grateful to the anti-counterfeiting organisation *REACT*, and particularly its managing director, Ronald Brohm, for giving me the opportunity to present, discuss, develop and test my ideas with the practitioners of his organisation.

Last, and by far not least, my family, above all my wife, my two children, my parents and my sister have provided me with inestimable encouragement and backup, not just over the last four years, but for far longer than that. Their support has been vital for the accomplishment of this work. This work is dedicated to them.

Abbreviations and Acronyms

AdCo	Administrative Cooperation Group (on market surveillance)
AG	Advocate General (of the Court of Justice of the European Union)
AML	Anti-Money Laundering
API	Application Programming Interface
AVMSD	Audiovisual Media Services Directive (2018/1808)
BGH	*Bundesgerichtshof* (Federal Court of Justice) (Germany)
CDA	Communications Decency Act (US)
CDPA	Copyright, Designs and Patents Act (UK)
CFREU	Charter of Fundamental Rights of the European Union
CJEU	Court of Justice of the European Union
CSA	*Conseil Supérieur de l'Audiovisuel* (Electronic Media Regulator) (France)
CSR	Corporate Social Responsibility
CTIRU	Counter-Terrorism Internet Referral Unit (UK)
DMA	Digital Markets Act COM(2020) 842 final (EU Proposal)
DMCA	Digital Millennium Copyright Act (US)
DSA	Digital Services Act COM(2020) 825 final (EU Proposal)
DSM	Digital Single Market
DSMD	Copyright in the Digital Single Market Directive (2019/790)
EEA	European Economic Area
ECD	E-Commerce Directive (2000/31)
ECHR	European Convention for the Protection of Human Rights and Fundamental Freedoms
ECtHR	European Court of Human Rights
EDD	Enhanced Due Diligence
EFSA	European Food Safety Authority
EMCD	Electromagnetic Compatibility Directive (2014/30)
ERGA	European Regulators Group for Audiovisual Media Services
EUTMD	Directive relating to trade marks (2015/2436)
EUTMR	EU Trade Mark Regulation (2017/1001)
FBA	*Fulfillment by Amazon*

FSA	Food Safety Authority
FSP	Fulfilment Service Provider
GAFAM	Google, Apple, Facebook, Amazon, Microsoft
GDPR	General Data Protection Regulation (2016/679)
GEMA	*Gesellschaft für musikalische Aufführungs- und mechanische Vervielfältigungsrechte* (Society for musical performing and mechanical reproduction rights) (Germany)
GiFTC	Global Internet Forum for Terrorist Content
GPSD	General Product Safety Directive (2001/95)
GRC	Governance, Risk and Compliance
HTML	Hypertext Mark-up Language
HTTP	Hypertext Transfer Protocol
IAP	Internet Access Provider
ICANN	Internet Corporation for Assigned Names and Numbers
ICSMS	Information and Communication System on Market Surveillance (EU)
Infosoc Directive	Directive on harmonisation of certain aspects of copyright and related rights in the information society (2001/29)
IoT	Internet of Things
IP	Intellectual Property
IPRED	Intellectual Property Enforcement Directive (2004/48)
IRU	Internet Referral Unit (Europol)
ISP	Intermediary Service Provider
ISSP	Information Society Service Provider
TCP/IP	Transmission Control Protocol/Internet Protocol
KPI	Key Performance Indicator
KYC	Know-Your-Customer
LCEN	*Loi pour la confiance dans l'économie numérique* (France)
MSA	Market Surveillance Authority
MSM	Multi-Sided Markets
MSR	Market Surveillance Regulation (2019/1020)
NetzDG	*Netzwerkdurchsetzungsgesetz* (Network Enforcement Act) (Germany)
NLF	New Legislative Framework
OTT	Over-The-Top (communication service)
P2B	Platform-to-Business Regulation (2019/1150)
P2P	Peer-to-Peer

SNEP	*Syndicat national de l'édition phonographique* (National Association of Phonographic Publishers) (France)
RAPEX	Rapid Alert System for Dangerous Non-Food Products
RED	Radio Equipment Directive (2014/53)
SIHD	Shared Industry Hash Database
TERREG	Proposal for a Regulation for preventing terrorist content online (EU)
TMG	*Telemediengesetz* (Germany)
TRIPS	Agreement on Trade-Related Aspects of Intellectual Property Rights
UCPD	Unfair Commercial Practices Directive (2005/29)
UGC	User Generated Content
URL	Uniform Resource Locator
WIPO	World Intellectual Property Organisation

Chapter 1 - Introduction

A. General background

It is by now commonplace that the information society and the internet are unprecedented in the way they have and will affect humankind.

> *"... almost like the weather, the flow of information defines the basic tenor of our times, the ambience in which things happen, and, ultimately, the character of a society. How and what you think depends on what information you are exposed to. ... We sometimes treat the information industries as if they were like any other enterprise, but they are not, for their structure determines who gets heard."*[2]

We now live in a society where connection to the internet has become for many an essential part of access to information and participation in social and economic life. Some countries have even started to declare access to the internet a fundamental right.[3]

As stated by *Castells*, knowledge and information generation have not only become direct sources of productivity but also have a direct effect on the productivity of information processing and knowledge creation itself, leading to a new technological paradigm.[4] This technology paradigm means that (information) technology today penetrates the "core of life and mind."[5]

Some go even further and say that we have been entering a new age in which the exchange of information and the digital traces left by our everyday lives, be it shopping, spare time activities, professional communication

---

2 Tim Wu, *The Master Switch: The Rise and Fall of Information Empires* (Atlantic 2012) 12.

3 For example in France: *Décision 2009-580 DC - 10 juin 2009 - Loi favorisant la diffusion et la protection de la création sur internet - Non conformité partielle* [2009] Conseil Constitutionnel CSCX0913243S, FR:CC:2009:2009580DC [12]; Greek Constitution, (Official English language translation of the Greek Constitution, Hellenic Parliament) 2008 para 5A; Electronic Communications Act (Estonia) (English Version) 2006 paras 69–70.

4 Manuel Castells, *The Rise of the Network Society* (2nd ed, Blackwell Publishers 2000) 17.

5 ibid 76.

or even our most private actions are surveyed constantly. Our behaviours and the "big data" gained from it are constantly analysed, predicted and influenced for commercial purposes. Moreover, this activity is currently in full swing of expanding to the offline world.[6]

Internet intermediaries are at a critical juncture of this digital information society. They enable individuals and organisations to find, exchange, share and produce information, to buy and sell products and services, to entertain, create and express themselves on the internet. We know these companies as search engines (*Google*), social networks (*Facebook*), user generated content or video sharing platforms (*YouTube*), online marketplaces (*Amazon, eBay*), content aggregators (*Booking.com, Reddit*) or sharing economy platforms (*Airbnb*), to name but a few. Being a critical layer of the internet, they exercise not only platform power, the power to connect, influence, amplify and disconnect user activity, but they have also built hugely profitable businesses through exploiting the data left by users on their platforms and elsewhere.[7]

The rise of these powerful actors and their influence has created controversies. It is increasingly accompanied by demands for stronger regulatory action and public accountability of these businesses, many of which have become global corporate behemoths. It would be an understatement to say that internet intermediaries, or online platforms, are subject to intense public debate. The concerns voiced over their business practices are manifold and fundamental. They range from allegations of privacy violations, abuse of market power, unfair commercial practices, allowing electoral manipulation, facilitating copyright piracy and counterfeit sales, promoting hate and violence, to more general claims of undermining democracy. At the heart of these problems lies a combination of the aforementioned essential function of online platforms in the information society and opaque business practices *vis-à-vis* platform users.

It is difficult to say whether the criticism is targeted more at the role of the most dominant platform businesses, like *Google, Apple, Facebook, Ama-*

---

6 Shoshana Zuboff, *The Age of Surveillance Capitalism: The Fight for the Future at the New Frontier of Power* (Profile Books 2019). Cathy O'Neil, *Weapons of Math Destruction: How Big Data Increases Inequality and Threatens Democracy* (Penguin Books 2016).

7 John Naughton, 'Platform Power and Responsibility in the Attention Economy' in Damian Tambini and Martin Moore (eds), *Digital dominance: the power of Google, Amazon, Facebook, and Apple* (Oxford University Press 2018) 382.

zon and Microsoft (the GAFAM),[8] or the responsibilities of internet intermediaries in general. What can be said is that there is currently a fully blown debate over the responsibility of online platforms for the content made available by them and for the way they manage and use the information collected on a massive scale from users.

This work focusses on one of the critical aspects mentioned above: the liability of online intermediaries for information, or content uploaded by users onto their platforms. It will do so by looking at the EU context. More precisely, this work will look at the current challenges of the framework of EU intermediary liability exemptions when it comes to preventing and removing unlawful content on online platforms.

This work attempts to answer two research questions:

1) Is the current legal framework regulating content liability exemptions of online platforms under the ECD still adequate when it comes to combating illegal content?
2) Are there alternative models for intermediary regulation that are better suited to include internet intermediaries in the fight against illegal content?

Unlawful content can take many forms: it can be copyright violating music and video clips, child pornography, counterfeits, illegal hate speech and incitements to violence, such as terrorist content, defamatory postings, or illegal and unsafe product offers.

The fact that unlawful content is a growing problem on the internet, including on "legal" platforms, can be witnessed by a flurry of regulatory activity by the European Commission and Member States in recent years. The European Commission's 2018 Recommendation on measures to effectively tackle illegal content online or the 2020 Digital Services Act Package are more recent prominent examples.[9] The 2018 Communication notes

---

8 The GAFA: Google, Apple, Facebook, Amazon; and, if including Microsoft, the GAFAM. Zuboff (n 5) ll 445–481 and Patrick Barwise and Leo Watkins, 'The Evolution of Digital Dominance' in Damian Tambini and Martin Moore (eds), *Digital dominance: the power of Google, Amazon, Facebook, and Apple* (Oxford University Press 2018) 21–25.

9 European Commission, 'Commission Recommendation of 1.3.2018 on Measures to Effectively Tackle Illegal Content Online, C(2018) 1177 Final' (European Commission 2018). European Commission, 'The Digital Services Act Package' (*Shaping Europe's digital future - European Commission*, 2 June 2020) <https://ec.europa.eu/digital-single-market/en/digital-services-act-package> accessed 4 November 2020.

that illegal content hosted on the internet remains a serious problem and it encourages online platforms to detect and remove unlawful content more proactively and effectively.[10] Meanwhile, the proposed Digital Services Act aims at defining increased obligations on digital services providers in order to address more effectively the problem of illegal content online.[11] These problems are not new, however. The EU noted the proliferation of illegal content on the internet consistently over the last 20 years.[12] As the platform economy thrives, internet penetration and connection bandwidth grow, and the online economy makes serious strides in transforming many areas of the offline world, this should not come as a surprise. Every new opportunity, especially one as vast as the digital revolution and the internet, also opens the door for abuse and new criminal activity. This is not made easier when considering that the internet has also challenged substantive law, for example on copyright.[13]

In the face of these breath-taking developments the legal framework has, until now, remained remarkably static. In the EU, the E-Commerce Directive[14] (ECD) has been regulating without change in this area since the year 2000. Drafted in the late 1990s and modelled largely on the US Communications Decency Act[15] (CDA) and the Digital Millennium Copyright Act (DMCA),[16] it offers online platforms far reaching exemptions from liability if they are neutral and purely technical, have no actual knowledge of illegal content and remove it expeditiously once notified of its existence.

10 European Commission, 'C(2018) 1177 Final' (n 8) paras 4–9.

11 European Commission, Proposal for a Regulation of the European Parliament and of the Council on a Single Market For Digital Services (Digital Services Act) and amending Directive 2000/31/EC, COM(2020) 825 final 2020 1.

12 European Commission, 'Online Services, Including e-Commerce, in the Single Market, A Coherent Framework to Boost Confidence in the Digital Single Market of e-Commerce and Other Online Services, Accompanying the Document, SEC(2011) 1641 Final' (European Commission 2012). Decision No 1151/2003/EC adopting a multiannual Community action plan on promoting safer use of the Internet by combating illegal and harmful content on global networks (OJ L 162).

13 Digital copies, mashups, sharing of content through linking or streaming have profoundly changed traditional copyright concepts. Bernd Justin Jütte, 'The EU's Trouble with Mashups: From Disabling to Enabling a Digital Art Form' (2014) 5 JIPITEC 172.

14 Directive 2000/31/EC of 8 June 2000 on certain legal aspects of information society services, in particular electronic commerce, in the Internal Market 2000 (OJ L 178).

15 Communications Decency Act 1996 (47 USC § 230) s 230.

16 The Digital Millennium Copyright Act 1998 (17 USC § 512).

These content liability exemptions have, however, come under progressive pressure over the last 10 years at least.[17] From the large variety of academic, policy and wider society sources, several arguments are commonly being put forward in favour of obliging internet platforms to take wider responsibilities for unlawful content on the internet:

- unlawful content keeps proliferating despite legislative efforts to motivate online platforms to do more to help preventing and removing it;
- many online platforms have become powerful corporations and have formidable financial means that they should better deploy for this purpose;
- platforms are not passive hosts any longer, but actively exploit (big) data and information, including illegal content, in order to make money;
- the technological means to prevent, detect and remove illegal content have improved significantly and online platforms are at the forefront in this area;
- due to their central position in the internet infrastructure, online platforms are technically best placed and have moral obligations to combat illegal content effectively.

In order to answer the first research question, this work will analyse these arguments by mapping out the regulatory landscape and the enforcement challenges related to the wide ambit of illegal content on online platforms.

17 As early as 2004: Lilian Edwards, 'The Changing Shape of Cyberlaw' (2004) 1 SCRIPT-ed 363, 364; Leonie Kempel and Patrick Wege, 'Die Haftung von Plattformbetreibern für „eigene Inhalte" – Welchen Einfluss hat ein Managementsystem auf den Umgang mit Haftungsrisiken?' in Nadine Klass, Silke von Lewinski and Henning Große Ruse-Khan, *Nutzergenerierte Inhalte als Gegenstand des Privatrechts: Aktuelle Probleme Des Web 2.0.* (Springer 2010); Patrick Van Eecke, 'Online Service Providers and Liability: A Plea for a Balanced Approach' (2011) 48 Common Market L. Rev. 1455 but also more explicitly in: D Friedmann, 'Sinking the Safe Harbour with the Legal Certainty of Strict Liability in Sight' (2014) 9 Journal of Intellectual Property Law & Practice 148.

It should be noted from the start that based on his prior research[18] and professional experience[19] the author advocates for enhanced, legally mandated responsibilities of online platforms to fight unlawful content. Yet, the current policy debate is less and less divided on *whether* platforms should have increased responsibilities rather than on *how* this should be achieved. This may lead critics to argue that, if there is mounting agreement on the need for reform, then why dissect the deficiencies of the current framework in such detail? The answer is that analysing the problems of the current intermediary liability system can provide useful lessons for a new regulatory model. In its last chapter before the conclusion, this work attempts to address this topic and respond to the second research question by exploring an adequate regulatory policy response. There are a variety of solutions debated currently. They range from self-regulatory approaches involving voluntary agreements by industry to more incisive regulatory interventions that see broad obligations imposed on online platforms. At the more extreme end, there are even considerations of subjecting the largest online platforms to tighter regimes along public utility regulation or even splitting them up.[20] Some of this appears to have been taken up at least

18 The author has outlined the arguments and a potential approach (based on technical standards) towards enhanced responsibilities for internet intermediaries first in his 2012 LLM Dissertation written at the University of Edinburgh: Carsten Ullrich, 'Online Intermediaries' Liability 2012: As the Digital Economy Comes of Age, Does the Industry Need to Take On More Responsibilities?' (Social Science Research Network 2012) SSRN Scholarly Paper ID 3594317 28–29 <https://papers.ssrn.com/abstract=3594317> accessed 22 July 2020, in further publications (see Bibliography), and most recently in Mark D Cole, Christina Etteldorf and Carsten Ullrich, *Cross-Border Dissemination of Online Content: Current and Possible Future Regulation of the Online Environment with a Focus on the EU E-Commerce Directive*, vol 81 (1st edn, Nomos 2020) 200–207

19 The author has worked for eight years as regulatory compliance, fraud detection and internal audit manager in a global internet company and managed, amongst others, operational notice and takedown and content removal processes for the company's EU marketplace and regulatory risk related to unsafe and non-compliant products.

20 Julie E Cohen, 'The Regulatory State in the Information Age' (2016) 17 Theoretical Inquiries in Law 369, 378–379; Lina M Khan, 'Amazon's Antitrust Paradox' [2017] The Yale Law Journal 96, 797–892; K Sabeel Rahman, 'Regulating Informational Infrastructure: Internet Platforms As The New Public Utilities' (2018) 2 Georgetown Law Technology Review 234; Frank Pasquale, 'Platform Neutrality: Enhancing Freedom of Expression in Spheres of Private Power' (2016) 17 Theoretical Inquiries in Law 487, 497–503. James Ball, 'How to Cut Big Tech down to Size' (25 January 2019) <https://www.prospectmagazine.co.uk/science-and-technology/how-to-cut-big-tech-down-to-size> accessed 19 August 2020.

partly by the EU Commission during the preparatory work for the new Digital Services Act (DSA) package.[21] This initiative aims to reform the current liability exemptions framework for online intermediaries under the ECD by supplementing it with additional obligations, but will also look to impose stricter regulatory measures on gatekeeper platforms to counteract anti-competitive effects.[22]

This work is the result of a doctoral research project. It aims to make a novel contribution in two aspects:

First, it will complement the current analysis of the regulatory landscape of enforcing against unlawful content *vis-à-vis* online platforms in two areas: product safety and food safety law. These areas have so far received very little attention in academic literature. It will be argued that the characteristics of product and food legislation and its specific enforcement landscape pose unique challenges in e-commerce. Nevertheless, they can provide useful lessons when constructing a new regulatory responsibility framework for online platforms.

Secondly, it will explore a regulatory model for content regulation and liability rules of online platforms, based on risk regulation and duty of care. This co-regulatory solution borrows from the *New Approach*, a system created by the EU in the 1980s, which relies on harmonised technical standards and which was initially used in product regulation.[23] It proposes the definition of public interests and fundamental rights which are harmed by unlawful content on online platforms. Online platforms, given their eminent role in contemporary society would be charged with responsibilities, along duties of care, in order to protect these public interests and values, while the current liability exemptions would be overhauled and reduced.

---

21 European Commission, 'The Digital Services Act Package' (n 8).

22 Laure Kayali, 'Brussels' Plan to Rein in Big Tech Takes Shape' *POLITICO* (30 September 2020) <https://www.politico.eu/article/digital-services-act-brussels-plan-to-rein-in-big-tech-takes-shape-thierry-breton-margrethe-vestager/> accessed 4 November 2020. The alleged anti-competitive effects of large gatekeeper platforms (the *GAFAM*) will not be in the focus of this work. However, the pre-dominance of these networks has a significant impact on the real power and sway of content management practices of these platforms and the availability of unlawful content. It will therefore play a role when analysing the enforcement challenges under the current ECD framework and when developing a reform proposal for intermediary responsibility.

23 Council Resolution 85/C 136/01 of 7 May 1985 on a new approach to technical harmonization and standards 2010; European Commission, 'New Legislative Framework - Growth' (*Growth*) <https://ec.europa.eu/growth/single-market/goods/new-legislative-framework_en> accessed 2 July 2020.

Harmonised technical standards would lay down the technical and procedural requirements which platforms need to implement in order to protect public interests.

B. Structure

Chapter 2 will provide a brief general overview of the history of the internet and its technical architecture. This technical background serves as a basis for charting the emergence of intermediaries as main power houses of the internet and the corporate world today. Internet intermediaries, or online platforms, sit at the top layer of the internet's content agnostic, distributed and open architecture. However, their rise to power has seen them invade, and successively capture, large parts of its infrastructure of servers and their connections.

The intermediary typology offered in this chapter will serve to visualise the spread of online platforms into almost all sectors of today's economies and the exchange of information between people. Finally, a description of new multi-sided platform dynamics and the power exercised by the leading players in this area today will underline the socio-technical and economic importance of internet intermediaries. This excursion is meant to create the context for the analysis of the challenges faced in regulating these players and obliging them to take on responsibilities that are commensurate with their economic power and societal significance.

Chapter 3 will start with an overview of the history of the emergence of the current legal system of internet intermediary liability. As online platforms have become an essential layer of today's web architecture, the discussion over internet regulation has become inseparable from the question of how to regulate internet intermediaries. Internet regulation, or internet law, is a wide and fluid term. From the variety of literature, it appears to encompass issues relating to the internet's infrastructure and content.[24] This would correspond to the basic function of the internet: transporting (via an infrastructure) digital information (content) from one piece of ter-

24 See for example: Jan Aart Scholte, 'Polycentrism and Democracy in Internet Governance' in Uta Kohl (ed), *The Net and the Nation State - Multidisciplinary Perspectives on Internet Governance* (Cambridge University Press 2017) 165.; Jacqueline D Lipton, *Rethinking Cyberlaw: A New Vision for Internet Law* (Edward Elgar Publishing 2015) 5.; Yochai Benkler, 'From Consumers to Users: Shifting the Deeper Structures of Regulation Toward Sustainable Commons and User Access' (2000) 52 Fed. Comm. L. J. 561, 576.

minal equipment to another.[25] The domain name system, communications protocols, the telecoms network, internet access providers, content servers and hosts, information stored and transmitted through the net, but also end devices, are typical components. Internet intermediaries are one part of this picture, although an increasingly prominent one.

On the other hand, internet regulation draws into its orbit all those legal areas which have been significantly influenced by the internet, such as data protection, copyright law, consumer protection, freedom of expression,[26] competition law, labour law or even more general legal concepts such as jurisdiction.[27]

This will be backed up by more general theoretical justifications for holding intermediaries accountable for the positive actions of others. These concepts had an impact on the first intermediary liability cases of the 1990s. They also served as a basis for the intermediary liability provisions in the EU and beyond. First, the current horizontal framework, set out by the ECD almost 20 years ago will be demonstrated. This will be compared to the regimes set up in the US, Australia, Canada, China and India. The analysis of the first three jurisdictions will chart out the different approaches that Western democracies have chosen towards regulating intermediaries. Meanwhile, the analysis of the Indian and Chinese frameworks serves as a reminder that the future of the internet will be significantly influenced by these emerging and most populous economies, which set different policy objectives.

The EU analysis will show how the pressures exerted on this framework have grown as the internet and online platforms have made massive strides into influencing our everyday lives and economic organisation. The ambiguous and controversial issues, which started to shine through already in the first years after the ECD's implementation, have only become more pronounced over time. Numerous case law from the last 15 years exposes significant problems with the application of the ECD when it comes to deciding,

25 Chris Reed, *Internet Law: Text and Materials* (2nd ed, Cambridge University Press 2004) 8.

26 Tatiana-Eleni Synodinou, *EU Internet Law: Regulation and Enforcement* (Springer Berlin Heidelberg 2017) v.

27 Dan Jerker B Svantesson, *Solving the Internet Jurisdiction Puzzle* (First edition, Oxford University Press 2017) 1–3.

- when an intermediary assumes liability for illegal content, i.e. when its intermediation activity is passive or active;
- when it can be assumed to have actual knowledge or control of the information it hosts;
- the scope of preventive activities that platforms can be obliged to perform, i.e. the demarcation line between a specific and a (prohibited) general obligation to monitor for unlawful content.

The case law discussed will draw from both EU and Member State judgements, but also refer, where appropriate, to case law of the European Court of Human Rights (ECtHR) and from outside Europe, such as the US, Canada, China and elsewhere.

Chapter 4 will offer a broad sectoral analysis of the variety of (unlawful) content hosted by platforms today. In the early days of the internet, legally controversial content related mainly to defamation, hate speech or child pornography, and was often communicated through newsgroups.[28] Even copyright infringing music file-sharing through peer-to-peer networks became a widespread and noticed phenomenon only after 2000.[29] It may not have played a role at all in the drafting phase of the ECD. By contrast, the kind of material hosted on Web 2.0 platforms today spans a much larger variety. The sectoral analyses will be structured in a similar, yet not identical way, for each type of unlawful content. Altogether seven subject matter areas will be treated: defamation, hate speech, terrorist content, copyright, trademark law, product safety and food safety.[30]

---

28 Lars Davies, 'Internet and the Elephant' (1996) 24 Int'l Bus. Law 151–159.

29 Pheh Hoon Lim and Louise Longdin, 'P2P Online File Sharing: Transnational Convergence and Divergence in Balancing Stakeholder Interests' (2011) 33 European Intellectual Property Review 2011 690.

30 An original plan to include child pornographic content and pharmaceutical products into the sectoral analysis was abandoned due to reasons of space and time. With regards to the ample legal literature on the fight against child pornography and child abuse online the following sources shall be recommended: Yaman Akdeniz, *Internet Child Pornography and the Law: National and International Responses* (Taylor & Francis Group 2008); Abhilash Nair, *The Regulation of Internet Pornography Issues and Challenges* (Routledge 2019). For further information on the fight against illegal and unsafe pharmaceutical products, see: Tim K Mackey, Phyo Aung and Bryan A Liang, 'Illicit Internet Availability of Drugs Subject to Recall and Patient Safety Consequences' (2015) 37 International Journal of Clinical Pharmacy 1076; OECD and European Union Intellectual Property Office, *Trade in Counterfeit Pharmaceutical Products* (OECD 2020) <https://www.oecd

First, the emergence of unlawful online content in each area will be sketched out. This will be followed by an analysis of EU-wide and national regulation of the sectoral subject matter. This analysis will expose differences in the more private law subject matter areas of defamation and hate speech, which lie within the national competency of Member States, as opposed to more mixed set-ups in the areas of copyright or terrorist content. The fully harmonised areas of trademark law and product and food regulation carry again different characteristics. The same can be said for the enforcement regimes, which in the areas that touch on public law, such as product, food regulation and terrorist speech are occupied by law enforcement and/or market surveillance authorities with a pronounced experience and approach in this area. By contrast, other sectoral regimes rely more on private law, contractual arrangements, where enforcement happens mainly through courts. The interaction of the specific sectoral regimes with the intermediary liability provisions of the ECD provides a first picture of disunity. On a second level, the interpretation of courts of the intermediary liability provisions have been varying since the inception of the ECD in 2000. The CJEU, as will be shown, had some, but arguably too little harmonising influence in this matter. The third factor of complexity is introduced by Member States. In some areas they have incorporated additional intermediary liability provisions into their substantive laws, while on a more general level, ordinary law principles of intermediary or secondary liability also interact in different ways with the ECD.

In a second step, the private enforcement practices of intermediaries in each of the sectors will be reviewed. Online platforms have charted ahead largely unimpressed by regulatory complexities and superimposed on users their own, often global standards of content regulation through their terms and conditions, or content policies. Whether and how these comply with local standards and policy objectives will be analysed in more detail. The rise of Web 2.0, social media, UGC platforms and online marketplaces added yet more complexity. The sheer volume, speed, interactivity and the increasing automation and opacity with which the global platforms manage and exploit user data for their commercial ends has made unlawful content almost endemic.

-ilibrary.org/governance/trade-in-counterfeit-pharmaceutical-products_a7c7e054-en> accessed 12 June 2020; Carsten Ullrich, 'Standards for Duty of Care? Debating Intermediary Liability from a Sectoral Perspective' (2017) 8 JIPITEC 111, 121–122;

The analysis will conclude with a review of sectoral regulatory initiatives at both national and EU level and how these relate to the wide liability protections enjoyed by Web 2.0 platforms under the ECD. The aim of Chapter 4 is to demonstrate the complexity and sheer size of the challenges at stake from a legal, technological and socio-economic point of view. This charting exercise will also reveal the multi-level regulatory character of the intermediary liability universe.

A purely sectoral approach towards enforcement, it might be argued, would not only be a missed opportunity, because it would prevent enforcers and legislators to learn from each other. Moreover, it would likely fail due to regulatory overload on both enforcers and businesses. Meanwhile, a one size fits all, rigid horizontal approach would not sufficiently take account of the different types of online platform business models.

Chapter 5 will introduce case studies which explore the challenges of effectively identifying and removing unlawful content from online platforms in two areas: non-food consumer products and food products. The choice of these two areas is deliberate. The challenges of enforcing copyright, trademarks, hate and defamatory speech and terrorist content have already been discussed more widely throughout academic literature, with copyright being a particularly well covered topic.[31]

By contrast, academic coverage of the challenges of enforcing product and food safety law online is patchy at best. Product and food safety regulation are complex, with an elaborate regulatory and enforcement regime. Product regulation is *New Approach* regulation. This is a highly technical, co-regulatory system, in which the public interest requirements are laid down in broad product directives, covering for example protective equipment, toys, radio equipment or medical devices. The implementation of these legal requirements in product design relies largely on voluntary harmonised technical standards, drawn up by industry and following a risk-based approach. Meanwhile, enforcement lies squarely within the hands of Member States, represented by a patchwork of national market surveillance authorities (MSAs). Food safety regulation operates on a similar basis, although not being part of the *New Approach*.

---

31 For example : Sandra VI Schmitz, *The Struggle in Online Copyright Enforcement: Problems and Prospects* (1. edition, Nomos 2015); Bernd Justin Jütte, *Reconstructing European Copyright Law for the Digital Single Market: Between Old Paradigms and Digital Challenges* (1. edition, Nomos; Hart Publishing 2017); João Pedro Quintais, 'Global Online Piracy Study' (Institute for Information Law (IViR), University of Amsterdam 2018); Christina Angelopoulos, *European Intermediary Liability in Copyright: A Tort-Based Analysis* (Kluwer Law International BV 2017).

The two case studies deal with the enforcement of product and food safety law on online platforms. They are based on 13 detailed and targeted interviews and survey results gained from both MSAs and food safety authorities (FSAs) across Europe, conducted over the period from November 2017 to March 2019. MSAs and FSAs shared the challenges they face when enforcing product legislation *vis-à-vis* online marketplaces and in e-commerce in general, in a national, European and global context. The feedback received confirms that a slow, highly fragmented, sectoral enforcement system is up against significant obstacles when facing the horizontal challenge of e-commerce. There is a general mismatch between the broad liability protections of online platforms and their potential usefulness and leverage in helping to keep unsafe and illegal products off the internet. Meanwhile, efforts to co-opt online marketplaces more into these efforts have so far hit against the wall of the ECD and its liability protections.

On the other hand, the *New Approach* regulation opens some interesting avenues with regards to intermediary liability. Products need to comply with mandatory technical specifications, which follow broad public interest criteria, defined by essential requirements in the law. Industry-designed and state-approved technical standards help economic actors to implement the mandatory technical specifications and provide an assumption of compliance. Could this also be a *modus operandi* for governing the responsibilities of internet intermediaries?

On a conceptual level, Chapters 2 to 5 are setting the foundations for advocating for a change in the current intermediary liability rules. Chapter 6 aims to propose such a regulatory framework. It will reopen the more general analysis of internet regulation of Chapter 2. First, an overview of a number of proposals to reform online intermediary provisions, made mainly by academics over recent years, will be discussed. The first such attempts were made as early as 2007, with the frequency of proposals increasing over the last five years. These reform proposals themselves testify for the broadly perceived and mounting need to reform the current regime. They all investigate a move from pure limited liability to broader responsibilities for reasons that should have become clear from the analysis provided in Chapters 3 to 5. Yet, the proposed regulatory tools and the intensity of regulation vary widely. They reach from self-regulatory approaches and co-regulation to partly more interventionist state involvement. This variety of approaches will set the scene for a more detailed analysis of the regulatory tools that may be appropriate for effectively regulating online platforms, with a view to stem the flow of unlawful content and activity that is a persisting problem on today's internet.

These tools will be put into the context of the cyclic nature of technological innovation, which is but an undercurrent of an increasing complexity of our societies over the last 200 years. The social fabric of our lives and societies is becoming more complex, and arguably that trend has only been amplified by globalisation and the information society revolution. These developments have been famously analysed by *Durkheim*[32] who, working in the middle of the second industrial revolution,[33] at the end of the 19th century, saw society and moral values overturned by mass urbanisation, mass production and the first means of mass communications. He called this state *anomie*. He noticed that the ever-progressing division of labour in capitalist society led to new, more specialised and denser professional, administrational and judicial functions, in which the state had a less and less central role as a rule setter.[34] New actors and relations fill the anomic state of modern societies with new normative values. His theory is today seen as a precursor to modern theories of governance and the emergence of co-regulatory systems.[35]

Policymakers are confronted by the regulatory challenges of the new technology paradigm of the information age.[36] The "jurisdictional puzzle" of the internet[37] and increasing demands on globally operating online platforms to provide transparency over their (algorithmic) content management decision, are just two illustrative issues.[38] In this multi-level regulatory environment, the legal norms are being formulated and enforced through hybrid systems of private and public ordering. Regulators rely increasingly on epistemic communities in the form of professional networks.[39] Content regulation on online platforms and its enforcement expose this multilevel regulatory and transnational maze in an exemplary way. This more theoretical discussion of different regulatory tools will

---

32 Émile Durkheim, *De la division du travail social (1873)* (Presses Électroniques de France 2013).

33 Castells (n 3) 33–38.

34 Durkheim (n 31) s 688.

35 Harm Schepel, *The Constitution of Private Governance: Product Standards in the Regulation of Integrating Markets* (Hart Pub 2005) 21.

36 Cohen (n 19)

37 Svantesson (n 26).

38 Kenneth A Bamberger, 'Technologies of Compliance: Risk and Regulation in a Digital Age' (2009) 88 Tex. L. Rev. 669, 688–689. He demonstrates the challenges of the state mandating and overseeing technical governance, risk and compliance systems (GRC) as part of risk regulation in tech industries.

39 Peter M Haas, 'Introduction: Epistemic Communities and International Policy Coordination' (1992) 46 International Organization 1.

serve as a reminder that the regulatory responses to the challenges posed by unlawful content on online platforms need to take these complexities into account. A regulatory solution will need to be specialised, technically flexible and scalable. It will need to answer the transnational challenges posed by the internet and globalisation. At the same time, it needs to be democratically accountable and transparent.

In the final part of Chapter 6, a co-regulatory framework of intermediary responsibility will be proposed, which attempts to respond to these demands. This system tries to apply the analysis made in the course of this work by moving away from the current liability exemption provisions to a more flexible, yet enhanced responsibility structure. Responsibility is more in line with contemporary forms of corporate governance. Responsibility is defined through broad public interest criteria which internet platforms would need to safeguard, given their important functions in today's society. In this sense, the proposal will apply features of the *New Approach* regulation discussed in the case studies. This work will go further and venture into describing the different risk management stages on a procedural level. A practical example of such a duty of care risk management standard will be showcased. This standard was developed in cooperation with *REACT*, an Amsterdam-based non-profit trade organisation that is dedicated to fighting counterfeiting. It covers the area of trademark infringements and lays down requirements that a responsible online marketplace would need to adopt in the prevention and fight against counterfeits and unsafe and illegal products. A detailed version can be found in ANNEX III. This system could eventually be incorporated into a technical standard, borrowing again from the *New Approach* and exploring a solution based on responsive regulation.[40] The standard would serve as a proof of compliance with the statutory responsibilities imposed on online platforms in the fight against illegal content or activity. It will be discussed whether this approach necessitates a change of the ECD, and what such a modification could look like. This discussion will also provide some brief comparative analysis and evaluation of the Digital Services Act package, which the Commission published in December 2020 and which coincided with the

40 Ian Ayres and John Braithwaite, *Responsive Regulation: Transcending the Deregulation Debate* (Oxford University Press 1992) chs 1, 4, where the authors describe how regulatory systems and government intervention should respond to specific market conduct, institutional and regulatory culture and history.

completion of this work.[41] This analysis was added during the final stages of preparing this work for publication in spring 2021.

C. Methodology

Chapter 2 gives an account of the emergence of internet intermediaries from an economic and socio-technical point of view. The research is descriptive for the historic and typological explanation of intermediaries. It is supplemented by an evaluative analysis of the position of internet intermediaries within modern society. The analysis relies mainly on a review of secondary legal sources from academia, policy makers and international organisations and from sources in neighbouring areas of law, such as economics (competition) and social sciences (history, sociology).

This descriptive approach is continued in Chapters 3 and 4. These Chapters deal with the emergence of the intermediary regulatory framework in the EU and the US and the sector specific legal provisions for most types of unlawful content found on online platforms. This descriptive approach is complemented by an analysis of the main failures and challenges of this current legal setup.[42] This part relies on a review of primary legal sources, namely case law and statutes, as well as secondary resources, such as doctrinal literature from academia and regulatory policy analysis from public institutions and industry.

This work focusses on the EU intermediary regulatory frameworks. It does not systematically pursue a comparative approach. However, it would be a serious miss if one failed to refer to the US when analysing internet intermediary regulation. The US was the first country to put in place laws dealing specifically with online intermediaries. This influenced other regulatory approaches worldwide. The analysis in Chapter 3 also includes comparisons with Australia, Canada, China and India. Some jurisdictions may offer potentially new and more effective approaches in legislation and enforcement. These differences in legislation and enforcement are also relevant when discussing the position of governments *vis-à-vis* large, globally

41 European Commission, 'The Digital Services Act Package' (n 8).

42 Descriptive research is used in the sense that it builds the ground for evaluative and conceptual argumentation in the latter parts of the work: see also Mark van Hoecke, 'Legal Doctrine: Which Method(s) for Which Kind of Discipline?' in Mark van Hoecke (ed), *Methodologies of legal research: which kind of method for what kind of discipline?* (Hart 2011) 18.

operating intermediaries as normative and executive powers in content regulation on a global scale.[43] Secondly, a discussion of the problems of applying the EU intermediary liability rules in reality would not be complete if it failed to highlight the varying interactions between EU Member States' national laws, legal approaches to secondary liability and the ECD. These differences play out at a horizontal level, when discussing doctrines of indirect liability in general, but also when looking at sectoral applications, in e.g. hate speech or copyright. For this reason, elements of a comparative analysis are included in Chapters 3 and 4. Every effort has been made to call out analysis across different jurisdictions and to offer summary outlines of main differences and commonalities.

Despite Brexit, which was decided shortly before the research for this work had started, abundant references to UK intermediary legislation and case law are made throughout this work. Both the horizontal analysis in Chapter 3 and the sectoral analysis in Chapter 4 include the UK, and England and Wales, in reviews of selected Member State case law and legislation at various points. The case studies in Chapter 5 also draw on feedback received from UK stakeholders. At the time of writing the UK was still part of the EU. Its law-making and its court rulings were influenced and determined by the ECD and various other EU acts and CJEU rulings. UK intermediary case law and national sectoral legislation, which includes specific obligations for internet intermediaries, is rich and varied. This has contributed to the diverse and multifaceted interpretations of the protections and obligations attributed to online intermediaries and their enforcement in the EU. Moreover, the UKs common law tradition has left a unique mark on the way online intermediary responsibilities and enforcement options have been approached in the EU. This singular influence is set to continue affecting EU policy making in this area. For all of these reasons, UK case law and legislation up to the end of 2020 have been included as an integral part of the analysis of EU online intermediary responsibilities *vis-à-vis* unlawful content.

The two case studies on the application of intermediary liability provisions in the areas of product safety and food safety in Chapter 5 follow a descriptive approach. They are based on a qualitative, pre-structured sur-

43 Luca Belli and Cristiana Sappa, 'The Intermediary Conundrum' (2017) 8 JIPITEC 183, 185–190.

vey,[44] conducted either in the form of personal interviews, held on location or by telephone, with market surveillance authorities across EU Member States, or by soliciting the completion of the survey sheet that was used during the personal interviews. The pre-structured survey imposes a set of common questions, thus allowing for empirical verification of certain assumptions. These interview questions were meant to incite interlocutors to expand in more detail on the practical enforcement challenges in their daily work. The template of the survey can be found in ANNEX I.

The pre-structured approach was deemed the most appropriate method because it allowed for a more in-depth and informal discussion while limiting the risk of interlocutors wandering off the topic. Secondly, the structured discussion also helped respecting the time accorded by the authorities, usually 2 – 3 hours. Third, it ensured comparability of the answers. The survey was constructed and verified using the methodology elaborated by *Jacob, Heinz and Décieux.*[45]

Chapter 6 uses conceptual analyses[46] in order to develop an alternative regulatory approach to online intermediary regulation. Building on the analysis in the previous chapters, the proposed framework is compared to the status quo in Europe and tested against moral, socio-economic and policy goals. The justifications for the proposed approach were derived from analysing primary legal sources in case law and secondary sources in academic research, but also from wider (non-legal) social science, namely sociology, economics and philosophy.

44 Harrie Jansen, 'The Logic of Qualitative Survey Research and Its Position in the Field of Social Research Methods' (2010) 11 Forum Qualitative Sozialforschung / Forum: Qualitative Social Research 4 <http://www.qualitative-research.net/index.php/fqs/article/view/1450> accessed 6 August 2019.

45 Rüdiger Jacob, Andreas Heinz and Jean Philippe Décieux, *Umfrage: Einführung in die Methoden der Umfrageforschung* (3., überarb. Aufl, Oldenbourg 2013).

46 Robert S Summers, 'The New Analytical Jurists' (1966) 41 New York University Law Review 861, 866–875. Mark van Hoecke (ed), *Methodologies of Legal Research: Which Kind of Method for What Kind of Discipline?* (Hart 2011) v.

D. Definitions, assumptions and limitations

1. Definitions

I. Internet intermediaries – intermediary service providers

The OECD defines internet intermediaries as entities that

> *"bring together or facilitate transactions between third parties on the Internet. They give access to, host, transmit and index content, products and services originated by third parties on the Internet or provide Internet-based services to third parties."*[47]

This simple and precise and definition appears to capture also the concept of intermediary service providers (ISP) under the EU's E-Commerce Directive (ECD).[48] Intermediary service providers (ISPs) are information society service providers (ISSPs) as per the Technical Standards and Regulations Directive,[49] which facilitate services that consist of the transmission of information[50] and storage (hosting) of information[51] for the service recipient. In other words, ISPs can be considered a sub-category of ISSPs. For example, an online retailer selling products on its own account would be considered an ISSP but not an intermediary service provider (ISP). By contrast, an online marketplace that lists offers from various sellers/retailers would be considered an ISP. Likewise, an online insurance agency or an online travel agency would be an ISSP but not an intermediary. However, an online price comparison engine for insurance services or a platform offering accommodation from third parties, such as hotels or private individuals, would be considered an ISP.[52]

The terms internet intermediary, online intermediary and intermediary service provider (ISP) will be used interchangeably in this work.[53]

---

47 OECD, 'The Economic and Social Role of Internet Intermediaries - DSTI/ICCP(2009)9/FINAL' (OECD 2010) 9.

48 Directive 2000/31 (ECD) s 4.

49 Directive 2015/1535/EU of 9 September 2015 laying down a procedure for the provision of information in the field of technical regulations and of rules on Information Society services 2015 (OJ L 241) Article 1 (1). See also Chapter 3

50 Directive 2000/31 (ECD) Articles 12, 13.

51 ibid Article 14.

52 For more detail see also Alfred Büllesbach (ed), *Concise European IT Law* (2nd ed, Kluwer Law International 2010) 696–698.

53 ISPs can therefore be considered a sub-category of ISSPs.

II. Online platforms

This work discusses the governance of online platforms. It should be stated from the outset that until the recent DSA proposal there was no legal agreed definition of online platforms.[54] The EU had until then refrained from attempting to create one, noting the variety of technological and business models and the fast-paced developments in this sector.[55] Notwithstanding this lack of a definition in law, there is ample literature within economics that offers definitions of platforms and online platforms. The economic discussion of platforms also deals with the particular aspects of two or multi-sided markets in the digital environment and how this affects rule-making as well as competition.[56]

For the purposes of this work, the term "online platform" refers to those ISPs that act as information hosts as specified under Article 14 (1) ECD.[57] More specifically, it refers to socially media and UGC networks, online marketplaces and sharing economy services as online platforms. Online platforms generally provide "infrastructure and enable interactions between suppliers and users for the provision of goods, services, digital content and information online."[58]

A typology of these different information hosts will be provided in Chapter 2.

ISP terminology	**Corresponding ECD Article**
internet intermediary/online intermediary, intermediary service provider (ISP)	Articles 12 – 14
internet access provider (IAP)	Article 12

54 Bertin Martens, 'An Economic Policy Perspective on Online Platforms' (Institute for Prospective Technological Studies 2016) Digital Economy Working Paper 2016/05 JRC101501.

55 European Commission, 'Commission Staff Working Document Online Platforms Accompanying the Document Communication on Online Platforms and the Digital Single Market SWD(2016) 172 Final' 2–3.

56 Michael L Katz and Carl Shapiro, 'Systems Competition and Network Effects' (1994) 8 Journal of Economic Perspectives 93. Kevin J Boudreau and Andrei Hagiu, 'Platforms Rules: Multi-Sided Platforms as Regulators' in Annabelle Gawer (ed), *Platforms, markets and innovation* (Paperback edition reprinted, Edward Elgar 2014).

57 First part of the first sentence: "…an information society service … that consists of the storage of information provided by a recipient of the service,…"

58 European Commission, 'Guidance on the Implementation/Application of Directive 2005/29/EC on Unfair Commercial Practices SWD(2016) 163' 121. European Commission DSA proposal (n 10) Article 2 (h).

caching service	Article 13
online/internet platform; online/internet host	Article 14

Table 1 - ISP terminology

III. Illegal versus unlawful content

The title of this work refers to *unlawful* content. It was originally planned to write about *illegal* content and activities on online platforms. This would have been in line with the wording in the ECD.[59] In everyday use both terms are often deployed synonymously. However, on closer observation *illegality* is a positive formulation, which defines forbidden actions.[60] Meanwhile, *unlawfulness* is a negative, non-exclusive term which refers to all acts disapproved by or against the law due to them being immoral or conflicting with public policy.[61] Other legal resources attribute both terms with the same meaning.[62] This is confirmed in everyday usage.[63] Given the above, *illegal* acts would refer to a finite number of defined acts, whereas the term *unlawful* can be assumed to include non-defined acts along defined (*illegal*) acts.

This becomes important when one considers the impact the internet and digitisation have made on society. While this work sides with the view that what is illegal offline should be illegal online, the internet and the intermediation practices of online platforms have led to new phenomena that are still being evaluated from a moral point of view. There are now more acts that, while not straightforwardly defined as illegal, may conflict with hitherto widely accepted ethics and morals. Moreover, some illegal acts may have become subject to a new moral re-evaluation by society.

---

59 Directive 2000/31 (ECD) Recitals 40, 44, 45, 46. 48 & Articles 14, 15.

60 'What Is UNLAWFUL? Definition of UNLAWFUL (Black's Law Dictionary)' (*The Law Dictionary*, 7 November 2011) <https://thelawdictionary.org/unlawful/> accessed 18 February 2019.

61 ibid.

62 The Cambridge Dictionary for example defines both terms as 'not allowed by law'. 'UNLAWFUL | Meaning in the Cambridge English Dictionary' <https://dictionary.cambridge.org/dictionary/english/unlawful> accessed 28 September 2020; 'ILLEGAL | Meaning in the Cambridge English Dictionary' <https://dictionary.cambridge.org/dictionary/english/illegal> accessed 28 September 2020.

63 The reasoning is complicated by the fact that illegal acts are also commonly seen as any act outside a given law, while in their strictest use this merely relates to explicitly defined acts outside the/a law.

Prominent examples can be the copyright infringing activities through peer-to-peer file sharing, the evolving jurisprudence on communication to the public on the internet in copyright law, or the public discussion on disinformation on social media, which is caused by the almost indiscriminate facilitation of massive amounts of content, products and advertisements through internet intermediaries. The term unlawful therefore seems to be corresponding better to the *Durkheimian* state of *anomie* that society today faces *vis-à-vis* certain business and information management practices in the digital economy.[64]

IV. Material content

This work deals with unlawful content hosted or shared on online platforms. For the purposes of this work, this is the kind of content or information which users or businesses upload to platforms for other users/businesses. This will be defined as *material* content. Subsequently, when talking about content or information uploaded to or hosted and shared on online platforms this will refer to the material content. Material content would be at the heart of an online platform's business model. For example, for *Facebook*, material content is all information, be it written text, sounds or moving images, which users upload and share with other users. Likewise, content posted by advertisers on *Facebook* would also be material content. On an e-commerce marketplace, such as *Amazon* or *Alibaba*, the material content would be all information related to and including products offered for sale by third parties, sponsored advertising or customer reviews.

This work uses the term *content* in an encompassing fashion, by relating to all material content or information hosted on online platforms, including speech, any type of media, but also listings of products and service offers.[65]

There are, however, other types of content or information on platforms. For example, ISPs are required to provide legal disclaimers, inform customers on the use of cookies or, depending on the kind of business, in-

64 Zuboff (n 5) ll 3398–3438; Jan Blommaert, *Durkheim and the Internet: On Sociolinguistics and the Sociological Imagination.* (Bloomsbury Publishing Plc 2018) ll 475–481.

65 This is similar to the approach by the Commission in its DSA Proposal: European Commission DSA proposal (n 10) Recital 12.

form and receive consent from users on the use of personal data. This ancillary information is not covered by the term material content in this work.

V. Unlawful activity and unlawful content/information

The liability protections of the ECD apply to illegal information and activity.[66] Unlawful activity, which comprises illegal activity, is usually related to the acts of offering or sharing unlawful information, services or products via the platform. This process usually involves uploading information to the platform. For example, in the context of e-commerce that activity would be the sale of a counterfeit product by a seller through an online marketplace. In the context of incitement to violence it would be the intentional act of uploading this kind of information onto an intermediary site and sharing it with other users. This work refrains from distinguishing between unlawful content and activity. The distinction may be relevant with regards to the sanctions incurred by the uploading user. For a platform's liability, or responsibility, it remains however legally irrelevant whether it is unlawful information or activity that occurred on the platform. It may have an impact on potential technical mitigation strategies in a risk-based compliance framework. But this will, where relevant, be discussed and called out in Chapter 4. For reasons of clarity and brevity unlawful content will therefore include unlawful activity.

VI. Harmful content

The limitation to unlawful content would imply that everything that is "legally allowed" on online platforms is out of the scope of this work. Policymakers and societal stakeholders in the EU and elsewhere have, however, repeatedly stated that harmful, contentious or offensive content that is not unlawful remains a problem on the internet, and on online platforms in particular. Typically, this concerns media content harmful to vulnerable groups, such as children, but also the spread of disinformation.[67]

66 Directive 2000/31 (ECD) Article 14 (1) (a).

67 Mark Bunting, 'Keeping Consumers Safe Online: Legislating for Platform Accountability for Online Content' (Communication Chambers 2018) 20–22, 26. European Commission, *A Multi-Dimensional Approach to Disinformation: Report of*

While certain information or (moving) images might be legal in general, they may become unlawful when exposed to children. Therefore, it is commonly the responsibility of the entity which makes this content available to the public to restrict or give users the opportunity to identify and suppress it. The recently recast Audiovisual Media Services Directive (AVMSD) has, for example, put such obligations in place for video sharing platforms (VSPs).[68] On the other hand, legal, but wrong or distorting information and news may acquire new meaning and significance in a social media environment of mass sharing and commenting. This may then have the potential to undermine societal values.[69] The EU is distinguishing its legislative approach on illegal content to that from "not necessarily illegal but potentially harmful" content.[70] Tackling the latter may indeed not warrant the same degree of urgency and also require a more careful balancing exercise with other fundamental rights, such as freedom of expression.[71] This work will only consider harmful or contentious content to the extent that it spills over into spheres of unlawfulness. The proposed solution to combat unlawful information online explored in the last chapter would, however, be adaptable to the management of this kind of content, subject to additional safeguards. In fact, it would be an integral part of a risk-based approach that a platform operator be able to understand the risk harmful (but legal) content poses in the context of its specific business model and the technology used.

---

the Independent High Level Group on Fake News and Online Disinformation (2018) 10–11.

68 Directive (EU) 2018/1808 of the European Parliament and of the Council of 14 November 2018 amending Directive 2010/13/EU on the coordination of certain provisions laid down by law, regulation or administrative action in Member States concerning the provision of audiovisual media services (Audiovisual Media Services Directive) in view of changing market realities 2018 (OJ L 303) Art. 28b.

69 Natali Helberger, Jo Pierson and Thomas Poell, 'Governing Online Platforms: From Contested to Cooperative Responsibility' (2018) 34 The Information Society 1, 7.

70 European Commission, 'Communication: Tackling Illegal Content Online Towards an Enhanced Responsibility of Online Platforms COM (2017) 555 Final' (2017) 6.

71 European Commission, 'Communication From The Commission To The European Parliament, The Council, The European Economic And Social Committee And The Committee Of The Regions Tackling Online Disinformation: A European Approach COM(2018) 236 Final' (European Commission 2018) 1 <https://eur-lex.europa.eu/legal-content/EN/TXT/?uri=CELEX:52018DC0236> accessed 19 July 2019.

VII. Platform users

Online platforms engage a number of different parties who partake in various ways in information and transactions hosted on their servers. In the context of this research, *users* means all businesses, consumers or other entities and parties which interact in some way or another with the platform, be it as, a) uploaders of content, sellers, advertisers (i.e. the "recipients of services" in the sense of the Technical Standards and Regulations Directive[72]); b) consumers and businesses downloading, purchasing or receiving or otherwise consuming content and products on online platforms, and c) other parties which engage with platforms by e.g. filing notice-and takedown requests of allegedly unlawful content to online platforms, or by requesting information or remedies in the exercise of their rights, and the like.

2. Assumptions

This being a predominantly legal analysis, no new empirical data on the availability and scale of unlawful content and activity promulgated through internet intermediaries will be provided here. It has been stated abundantly by governments, regulators, international organisations, academia and industry sources that, for all of their positive and beneficial contribution to contemporary society, online platforms are also seen as important conduits for the spread of unlawful content. This work will provide analysis and data from secondary sources where needed for the argumentation in order to substantiate this ongoing problem.

3. Limitations

I. Sanctions

Platforms which fall foul of their duties under the liability exemptions framework of the ECD are subject to sanctions imposed under national

72 Directive 2015/1535/EU of 9 September 2015 laying down a procedure for the provision of information in the field of technical regulations and of rules on Information Society services Article 1 (1) (b).

law.[73] These are typically non-criminal, secondary liability sanctions. Platforms which are found to be situated outside of the liability protections of Article 14 ECD because they are seen as active hosts which exercise control over the information,[74] would be directly liable for the tort or crime relating to the illegal information on their site. This may range from criminal sanctions in the case of terrorist content to civil sanctions in cases of IP infringements or defamation to name but a few. Given the variety of information, content and activity on platforms, this work cannot cover the sanction regimes of all the possible torts and crimes involved across the different Member States.

Moreover, the work will not attempt to sort out or redefine the complex and diverging national sanctions regimes relating to secondary liability for a platform's failure to comply with the ECD. This discussion focusses on the duties and responsibilities of online platforms in removing and preventing unlawful content. The solution proposed in this work will introduce a negligence based responsibility framework that aims to clarify and broaden the applicability of secondary liability, thus potentially limiting findings of primary liability. The design of a sanctions regime for secondary liability could be a fitting topic for further research in this area. Alternatively, it could be a unique chance to create a separate, free-standing sanctions regime that is directly attached to the new responsibilities of the framework proposed here.

II. Substantive law affecting online platforms

As mentioned above, the online platform landscape is diverse and constantly evolving. The current debate about the role of these businesses touches on many aspects. Unlawful content is just one part of this debate.

A discussion on unlawful content on internet platforms will invariably interface with these other legal aspects which are all linked to the various *fundamental rights* that are impacted by the activity of platforms and by any efforts to prevent and remove unlawful content. The most notable ones are human dignity,[75] the respect for private and family life,[76] the rights of chil-

73 Directive 2000/31 (ECD) Article 14 (3), 20.

74 ibid Recital 42.

75 Charter of Fundamental Rights of the European Union 2009 Article 1.

76 ibid Article 7.

dren,[77] the protection of personal data,[78] freedom of expression and information[79], the freedom to conduct a business[80] or the right to property.[81] The role of these fundamental rights is crucial when discussing liabilities, responsibilities and the regulation of online intermediaries in the fight against unlawful content. It deeply affects the balancing exercises of courts and the efforts of legislators when drawing up rules for online intermediaries. As overarching and encompassing principles they evoke a number of other, neighbouring substantive law areas that therefore become also relevant when discussing intermediary liability.

Data protection is a key concern as online platforms have made big data the substance of their business models. Big data is generated from the information users post, share and consume on the internet and from the services they offer to other users. It plays a role when talking about platforms' control over this data, which includes in many cases personal data. Control means that platforms collect, process and commercialise personal information on a massive scale. Could it be argued that the degree to which platforms exercise control from a data protection perspective influences the content liabilities of these platforms under the ECD, which only exempts passive hosts, with no control over the information they host? In addition to that, taming the flow of unlawful information on platforms will impact data protection where (algorithmic) content management decisions are made more transparent and where risk-based preventive content filtering involves processing of user data. It also plays a role when courts, law enforcement or other parties require the disclosure of the identity of service recipients that engage in allegedly infringing activities.

Consumer law is impacted when discussing the role of platforms that unwittingly facilitate the sale of counterfeits, pirated content, fake or unsafe consumer products or advertising for such products. The sections on trademarks, product and food safety will illustrate how e-commerce platforms impact on consumer protection objectives and how this affects commercial practices regulated under consumer law.

*Competition law a*nd abuse of market power become important when looking at the current dominance of a handful of large players in key on-

---

77 ibid Article 24.
78 ibid Article 8.
79 ibid Article 11.
80 ibid Article 16.
81 ibid Article 17.

line markets.[82] *Google, Amazon, Facebook, Apple* and *Microsoft (the "GAFAM")*, have all been subject to competition law cases at EU and global level regarding their activities. Meanwhile, traditional competition law approaches need to be adapted to the characteristics of multi-sided platforms.[83] The regulatory solution proposed at the end of this work will need to take account of a lopsided market structure in which a few large players could dominate and profit from a co-regulatory system at the expense of smaller players. As such, market competition concerns may have an influence on formulating new responsibilities, with large, systemic platforms that provide public goods being, for example, subject to stricter requirements.[84]

IT and cyber security will play a role when talking about transparency obligations of online platforms with regards to algorithmic decision-making, content management and other co-regulatory mechanisms as well as safeguarding user rights, such as privacy and other personality rights.

Other legal areas touched by digitisation and the emergence of online platforms are *copyright and trademark law, defamation law, incitement to violence, anti-terrorist law, the protection of minors, or product regulation.* Some of these areas are within the full competency of Member States while others are subject to shared competencies as per the EU treaties. This work cannot discuss the substance of these laws in detail, some of which are subject to intense debate due to the influence of the internet. It will however deal with substantive aspects of these laws where this touches on the roles and responsibilities of internet intermediaries. This will be done in Chapter 4.

---

82 see for example: Martin Moore and Damian Tambini (eds), *Digital Dominance: The Power of Google, Amazon, Facebook, and Apple* (Oxford University Press 2018).

83 OECD, 'Rethinking Antitrust Tools for Multi-Sided Platforms' (2018) <www.oecd.org/competition/rethinking-antitrust-tools-for-multi-sided-platforms.htm> accessed 30 July 2019.

84 Alexandre De Streel and Martin Husovec, 'The E-Commerce Directive as the Cornerstone of the Internal Market: Assessment and Options for Reform.' (European Parliament 2020) 45–46 <https://www.europarl.europa.eu/RegData/etudes/STUD/2020/648797/IPOL_STU(2020)648797_EN.pdf> accessed 2 November 2020; Ben Wagner, 'Free Expression? Dominant Information Intermediaries as Arbiters of Internet Speech' in Damian Tambini and Martin Moore (eds), *Digital dominance: the power of Google, Amazon, Facebook, and Apple* (Oxford University Press 2018) 220–221, 232–236.

Chapter 2 - The emergence of intermediaries on the internet – a socio-technical[85] review

A. *The early internet*

As *Wu* demonstrates in his book *The Master Switch*, the last 150 years have been characterised by successive waves of new information technologies of which many promised the dawn of a new age for society. The telegraph, telephone, radio and film all "*passed through a phase of revolutionary novelty and youthful utopianism*" that promised to change the lives of people forever.[86]

It does not come as a surprise that the internet, too, was hailed in the mid-1990s by its pioneers as a new utopian vision come true. *John Perry Barlow's* often cited *Declaration of Independence of the Cyberspace*[87] announced the construction of a new civilisation in cyberspace. He declared the internet a new social space, free from traditional government intervention, based on self-governance, arising out of "*ethics, enlightened self-interest, and commonwealth.*" *Barlow* conjured up a social contract in cyberspace, a new self-governance that would grow bottom-up, based on the norms of its users, regardless of where they are based in the world. *Post and Johnson* fleshed this vision out by arguing that regulation of the internet should be different from the laws of nation states. Cyberspace is a distinct place with unique characteristics, which defy the validity of legal rules from the "real world."[88] They pointed to independently operating self-government and enforcement mechanisms in cyberspace, such as banishing, technical protocols, netiquette and user education, operated by systems operators and

---

85 The term sociotechnical refers to the complex interactions that arise between technological systems (in this case information technology), society institutions and human beings. See also Roger Clarke and Marcus Wigan, 'The Information Infrastructures of 1985 and 2018: The Sociotechnical Context of Computer Law & Security' (2018) 34 Computer Law & Security Review 677, 678 and for the socio-technological paradigm in: Castells (n 3) 69.

86 Wu, *The Master Switch* (n 1) 5.

87 John Perry Barlow, 'A Declaration of the Independence of Cyberspace' (1996) <https://www.eff.org/cyberspace-independence> accessed 24 May 2019.

88 David R Johnson and David Post, 'Law And Borders- The Rise of Law in Cyberspace' (1996) 48 Stanford Law Review 1367.

users.[89] *Dyson* claimed that cyberspace would redraw the "*meaning of freedom,…, definition of property, nature of competition, sense of community.*"[90] He called for a new *Magna Carta* for the knowledge age.

Competition lawyers may partly agree when looking at today's multi-sided online platforms, but not necessarily in the sense inferred by *Dyson* at the time. The early internauts used the unique characteristics of the internet and its infrastructure to challenge the traditional legal authority of nation states, whose jurisdiction was bound by territory.[91] This was a time when the internet had 16 million users, most of them based in the Western industrialised world and belonging to a narrowly circumscribed "cyber elite."[92]

Others, like *Lessig* or *Winner*, put these views into perspective by underlining the interdependence of cyberspace and its inhabitants with the "real world." The fact that rules are not applicable to cyberspace does not mean that they should not have an effect or that the state should not have a legitimate interest to enforce them.[93] *Lessig* predicted an adaptation of law to cyberspace. States would get there by modifying the internet's architecture, read: its code, such as for example mandating encryption. Today we would add watermarking, content filtering or geo-blocking to this. Cyberspace would be zoned, boundaries created between illegal and permitted spaces and content, administered by "*technologies of control.*"[94] These technologies would not need to be 100% effective in order to be sufficiently dissuasive, daunting or frustrating for the average user. Harsher criticism comes from *Winner*. He sees cyber libertarians as propagators of a neoliberal ideology where "*ownership [of cyberspace] by the people*" means "*private ownership*", which peddles the interests of transnational communication businesses.[95]

In Europe, the debate over the regulation of cyberspace was less fierce. Most commentators at the time pointed to the need for traditional regu-

89 ibid 1388–1389.

90 Esther Dyson, 'Cyberspace and the American Dream: A Magna Carta for the Knowledge Age (Release 1.2, August 22, 1994)' (1996) 12 The Information Society 295, 296.

91 Joel Reidenberg, 'Governing Networks and Rule-Making in Cyberspace' (1996) 45 Emory Law Journal 911, 913.

92 Barney Warf, 'Alternative Geographies of Cyberspace' in Uta Kohl (ed), *The Net and the Nation State - Multidisciplinary Perspectives on Internet Governance* (Cambridge University Press 2017).

93 Lawrence Lessig, 'The Zones of Cyberspace' (1996) 48 Stanford Law review 1403.

94 ibid 1409.

95 Langdon Winner, 'Cyberlibertarian Myths and the Prospects for Community' (1997) 27 ACM SIGCAS Computers and Society 14, 16.

lation to adapt to the particular challenges of the digital environment, echoing *Lessig's* remarks. The debate focussed on the more hands-on theme of rights enforcement in cyberspace in the face of a number of emerging harms, such as defamation, child pornography, hate speech or copyright piracy. Self-regulation, standardisation,[96] international law principles *(jus cogens)*[97] or international legal harmonisation were seen as means to address these challenges.

Fast forward 25 years and it looks like the debate over the regulation of the internet and the involvement of the state is still led from the same angle. There are (still) those voices that call for a hands-off and largely self-regulatory approach towards resolving various legal problems on the internet. But there are also calls for a more robust intervention and regulation of companies operating on the internet. However, this observation only holds true on a superficial level. While the main strands of argument have indeed remained the same, the underlying socio-economic and regulatory dynamics of the internet have changed dramatically. This makes today's debate not necessarily less controversial, but much more eclectic, global and inherently less clear-cut.

A brief historic examination of the socio-technical and regulatory developments of the internet and intermediaries will help set today's debate into this new context.

B. The technical architecture of the internet

Although this work focusses on the EU regulatory space one cannot avoid but talking about the internet's US origins, both on a technological and economic level.

It may be seen as an irony: the internet, originally promoted by its most fervent advocates as a medium free from state intervention and subject only to free competition, came about thanks to decades of sustained funding

---

96 Caitriona Hegarty and Euan Cameron, 'Case for Minimal Regulation of Electronic Network Communications' 10th BILETA Conference Electronic Communications (1995) <https://www.bileta.org.uk/conference-papers/10th-annual-conference-1995/> accessed 3 January 2017.

97 Viktor Mayer-Schönberger and Teree E Foster, 'A Regulatory Web: Free Speech and the Global Information Infrastructure' (1997) 3 Mich. Telecomm. Tech. L. Rev 17.

by the US military and public research money.[98] *Castells* explains how in search for a communications system that could survive a nuclear attack, the development of a decentralised network of interconnected endpoint devices (usually computers) was funded in the 1950s. The aim was to transmit data without a centralised exchange system and largely independent of the underlying network infrastructure.[99] Financed initially mainly through the US Department of Defense's Advanced Research Project Agency (ARPA), it eventually drew in public institutions in government and Universities in a loosely structured and relatively open way.[100]

The main technical inventions which have been underpinning the extraordinary success of the internet originate from this time. They are still the internet's essential underlying technologies.

First, the invention of data packet switching in the 1960s allowed for a revolutionary new way to transmit data. This technology did not require the pre-allocation of bandwidth between end users (like in circuit switching), with its centralised system of exchanges. Instead, the information was broken down in smaller data packets and then sent in a distributed manner to the recipient. It made communication more resilient, due to the various routes data packets could take. It also ensured a more efficient and therefore timelier transmission of data than the circuit switching which prevailed in the telecommunications networks at the time.[101] This made it well suited for the real time transmission of data.[102]

Secondly, the famous layered structure of the internet was an engineering design choice that ensured additional resilience, flexibility and adaptability of the internet to various communication media. There are varying classifications of the functional layers that make up the internet.[103] The choice depends on the level of technical depth needed in a given context. In essence, each layer is responsible for a different function of the data transmission. Each of these functions is implemented through technical

98 Linda D Garcia, 'The Evolution of the Internet: A Socio-Economic Account' in Johannes M Bauer and Michael Latzer (eds), *Handbook on the economics of the internet* (Paperback edition, EE, Edward Elgar Publishing 2017) 533–537.

99 Castells (n 3) 45.

100 Garcia (n 97) 534.

101 W Richard Stevens and Kevin W Fall, *TCP/IP Illustrated. Volume 1, Volume 1,* (2nd edn, Addison-Wesley 2011) 4.

102 Garcia (n 97) 534.

103 Günther Knieps and Johannes M Bauer, 'The Industrial Organization of the Internet' in Johannes M Bauer and Michael Latzer (eds), *Handbook on the economics of the internet* (Paperback edition, EE, Edward Elgar Publishing 2017) 30.

protocols and the whole structure forms a suite or stack of protocols. Here, the most basic grouping of the internet into three layers shall be briefly explained.[104]

At the lowest level of the internet is the infrastructure or link layer (or physical network layer).[105] Protocols at this level ensure that the endpoint devices can link up to the internet via the chosen communication access channel, be it Ethernet, Wi-Fi, cable or cellular.[106]

From here, the protocols at the transport/network, or logical layer ensure that the information is transported and routed through the network to the end user. The Transmission Control Protocol (TCP) has since the 1970s become the standard protocol used to break-up information into data packets at source and reassemble them at the user end point.[107] It thus enables packet switching. According to *Huston*, TCP, which is today incorporated into billions of devices, has remained the "workhorse of the internet."[108]

The Internet Protocol (IP) ensures that the data packets are routed through the networks to their destination via a succession of network switches and routers.

Finally, as described by *Stevens and Fall*, the application layer integrates different ways of how the internet can be utilised. The most known applications are email, the File Transmission Protocol (FTP), peer-to-peer computing (P2P) or, indeed, the World Wide Web.[109]

This layered structure is a ground-breaking element of the internet. Data is successfully routed because each layer's protocol adds information that is essential for the routing process to the packets. This information is added to the data packets in the form of headers. The data packets form the actual content that needs to be transmitted (the payload). The payload is thus successively encapsulated with information on the internet uplink characteristics, sender and recipient details, data packet expiry, delivery quality, delays

---

104 For more detail see Barbara van Schewick, 'Internet Architecture and Innovation in Applications' in Johannes M Bauer and Michael Latzer (eds), *Handbook on the economics of the internet* (Paperback edition, EE, Edward Elgar Publishing 2017).

105 Knieps and Bauer (n 102) 30.

106 Stevens and Fall (n 94). The link up normally happens via the device's operating system and its network adapter.

107 Garcia (n 97) 536.

108 Geoff Huston, 'A Quick Look at QUIC' (2019) 22 The Internet Protocol Journal 2, 2.

109 Stevens and Fall (n 100).

and other transport information during the routing process.[110] These technical details will become important when content filtering and monitoring systems are being discussed later on.

Packet switching and the encapsulation of data, especially through the TCP/IP protocol suite, mean that the information can travel in a self-contained way, independent of the underlying physical network, devices or applications.[111] Through this set-up the internet could fully embrace and even accelerate the convergence of various communication channels (wireless, cable, fibre, GSM, etc,) that emerged over the coming years. In addition, this modular and decentralised structure would empower users[112] and companies to design a variety of innovative applications and services, which simply integrated on top of the internet's application layer. According to *Lessig* this end-to-end design principle is one of the most important factors behind the growth and innovation engendered by the internet.[113]

Meanwhile, the crucial TCP/IP protocols were open to the public, allowing for continuous modification, improvement and adaptation to operating systems and different infrastructures.[114] *Castells* describes, how in parallel to the ARPANET, a private computer counterculture ("hacker community") started to develop in the US and throughout the world since the 1970s.[115] Individuals started to connect their PCs through telephone lines, using modems, and communicating through newsgroups such as USENET. As ARPANET opened to public research networks, the sprawling computing community eventually adopted the TCP/IP protocol suites as a common standard for communication between PCs.[116]

Collins remarks that this technical set up of the internet explains to a large part the governance structure and subsequent regulatory approach to the internet.[117]

The controlled and subsidised opening of the internet to the academic research community and private networks may actually have been at the heart of the internet's success. *Wu* describes how the internet could sprout

---

110 ibid.

111 Wu, *The Master Switch* (n 1) 198.

112 Johnny Ryan, *A History of the Internet and the Digital Future* (Reaktion Books 2013) 16.

113 Lawrence Lessig, *Code: Version 2.0* (2. ed., Basic Books 2006) 44–45.

114 Garcia (n 97) 536; Castells (n 3) 47–49.

115 Castells (n 3) 50.

116 ibid 49–50.

117 Richard Collins, *Three Myths of Internet Governance: Making Sense of Networks, Governance and Regulation* (Intellect Books 2009) 60–62.

in a protected space, unbothered by the *"benign"* state-protected telecoms monopoly of AT&T in the US.[118] That monopoly successfully suppressed or delayed a number of other technological innovations for decades in the telecoms sector.[119] From 1995 onwards, the internet was carefully set afloat on the open market, equipped with a technical governance structure, which shall be discussed later.

Meanwhile, its adaptable structure facilitated the emergence of new internet intermediaries, which enabled users to access various new services on a global level, be it in order to communicate, search, create, share or store information, or buy and sell goods and services.

C. Internet intermediaries within the layered internet

Internet intermediaries locate, distribute and host information uploaded and shared by the internet's users.[120] From their humble beginnings in the mid-1990s they have seen a spectacular ascendance to become gatekeepers of the internet for consumers and businesses. They are now indispensable for the various activities that people perform through the internet.[121] Two elements have significantly helped their emergence in the early 1990: the invention of the world wide web and a dramatic increase in user take-up.

In 1990, the World Wide Web was conceived by a group of computer scientists around *Tim Berners-Lee* at the *Conseil européen pour la recherche nucléaire* (CERN) in Geneva. Its first key component is the Hypertext Markup Language (HTML), a format that allowed for a standard display of documents on the web, regardless of the underlying computer language. Secondly, the Hypertext Transfer Protocol (HTTP) enabled the communication of hypertext between servers. Finally, a standard address system, not just for the World Wide Web, but for a whole host of other applications, was created. The Uniform Resource Locator (URL), which appears in the

---

118 Wu, *The Master Switch* (n 1) 59.

119 ibid 107.

120 Lilian Edwards, 'The Fall and Rise Of Intermediary Liability Online', *Law and the Internet* (3rd ed, Hart Pub 2009) 47. See also section 1.4.1.

121 See for example: Natali Helberger, Katharina Kleinen-von Königslöw and Rob van der Noll, 'Regulating the New Information Intermediaries as Gatekeepers of Information Diversity' (2015) 17 info 50, 52; Mariarosaria Taddeo and Luciano Floridi, 'The Debate on the Moral Responsibilities of Online Service Providers', *The responsibilities of online service providers* (Springer Berlin Heidelberg 2016).

address bar of a web browser, referenced the resources stored on the internet in a standard way, thus making them easily findable.[122] Thanks to the invention of the World Wide Web, the foundations were laid for a broad usability of the internet. [123]

By the mid-1990s demand for individuals to connect and to exchange information had grown substantially across the world. The number of PCs connected to the internet had risen from around 300,000 in 1990 to 1 million two years later.[124] By 1995 an estimated 9 million users were on the internet, of which 75% in the US.[125] By that time, the commercial potential of the internet had become apparent. From 1995 onwards, the US Government-funded infrastructure of internet communication backbones was opened up to the private sector.[126] A handful of private investors started to roll out a fibre network of data cables which was to become the mainstay of data communication throughout the US, and globally. This is usually referred to as the "Tier 1" network. These private companies also dominated the "Tier 1" network in Europe, where internet up-take was initially slower than in the US.[127]

1. A typology of intermediaries

It is appropriate to give an overview of the type of internet intermediaries which have emerged over the last 25 years. There are several ways of classifying online intermediaries. However, the online intermediary business is diverse and evolving rapidly following the patterns of constant innovation in digital technologies and markets. A too rigid and fine-grained classification would inevitably be overrun by market developments. Meanwhile a broader classification risks not taking sufficient account of technical design and functional differences, which may become relevant when talking about liabilities and responsibilities of these intermediaries for unlawful content.

---

122 Castells (n 3) 50–51.
123 Ryan (n 111) 106–107.
124 ibid 94.
125 Mary Meeker, 'Internet Trends 1995' (Morgan Stanley 1996) 41 <https://www.bondcap.com/report/it95/> accessed 14 June 2019.
126 Garcia (n 97) 541.
127 Meeker (n 124) 35. Gartner, 'The International ISP Market: Evaluation and Selection Criteria (Archived)' (1998) Research Note R-06-3028 9.

EU law has classified ISPs according to their technical role in the information intermediation process, thus distinguishing between "mere conduit", "caching" and hosting.[128] *Rowland et. al.* et al take this typology further and identify intermediaries that facilitate:

- connectivity (internet access providers -IAP),
- navigation (e.g. search engines, peer-to-peer platforms),
- commercial and social networking (e.g. *Facebook, YouTube, Amazon, Skype*)
- traditional intermediation (e.g. online retailers, payment service providers (*PayPal*) etc)[129]

This classification progressively aligns with the degree of active involvement of the intermediaries in the online facilitation process. While this is a useful precision it may only really be practically applicable to internet access providers, whose commercial and technical purpose of connecting users to the internet has not changed over the last 25 years. However, it may be difficult to categorise navigation and commercial/social networking intermediaries according to the degree of (active) involvement in the facilitation process. Business models of these intermediaries and technical capabilities impacting the intermediation process have been evolving and it is exactly the degree of involvement of intermediaries in the facilitation process which has been subject to much controversy, including in front of courts. Secondly, the category of traditional intermediaries mentioned above does not correspond with the definition of intermediaries in the traditional legal understanding. For example, a retailer selling goods as a seller of record online would fall outside of the definition of an intermediary service provider (ISP) under EU law. *Amazon* would, for example, act as an intermediary under EU law for its marketplace activities, but as a "traditional" intermediary when selling goods as a retailer. The legal implications of both scenarios for liability differ significantly.

Peters and Johnson and *Ardia*[130] group intermediaries according to their functional role in facilitating or constraining speech into conduits, web hosts and search and application providers.

---

128 Directive 2000/31 (ECD) Article 14.

129 Diane Rowland, Uta Kohl and Andrew Charlesworth, *Information Technology Law* (4th ed, Routledge 2012) 71–73.

130 Jonathan Peters and Brett Johnson, 'Conceptualizing Private Governance in a Networked Society' (2016) 18 NCJL & Tech. 15, 41–58; David S Ardia, 'Free

Below a more pragmatic definition according to intermediary business model will be offered, which follows notably the approach by the OECD[131] and EU policy and legal documents such as the Guidance to the Unfair Commercial Practices Directive.[132] A search engine such as *Google* may have a similar array of technical possibilities as an online marketplace to structure (e.g. prioritise, personalise) the display of content on its website or monetise this information. In fact, e-commerce platforms or social media sites may even function as search engines for specific information, such as news or consumer products. A collaborative economy platform may be involved in facilitating payments in the same way as an e-commerce marketplace. Meanwhile, as will be shown below, many intermediaries have expanded beyond their original business model. They integrated horizontally by creating or acquiring other platform businesses in neighbouring markets. They also integrated vertically by expanding into services that impact structures beyond the web's application layer and extend into the internet's deeper infrastructure, or by integrating other downstream services (such as IT equipment manufacturing, logistics, financial services or advertising).

The typology offered below shall also help to demonstrate the quantum changes that the internet and internet intermediaries have undergone over the last 25 years.

2. Internet access providers

The first internet intermediaries emerged in the wake of the privatisation of the internet in the 1990s. Internet access providers (IAPs) connect individual households and businesses to the internet backbone.[133] Some of the larger Tier 1 backbone network owners also offered these internet access services in the European market (*WorldCom/UUNet, EUNet, PSINet*). In addition, post and telecommunication incumbents across EU Member States (*France Telecom, British Telecom, Deutsche Telekom, etc*) also offered internet

Speech Savior or Shield for Scoundrels: An Empirical Study of Intermediary Immunity under Section 230 of the Communications Decency Act' (2010) 43 Loyola of Los Angeles Law Review 373, 386.

131 OECD, 'The Economic and Social Role of Internet Intermediaries - DSTI/ICCP(2009)9/FINAL' (n 45) 10–15.

132 European Commission, 'UCP Directive Guidance' (n 57) 121–145.

133 also called internet service providers (ISPs). This term is not used here because of its confusion with information society service providers (IS(S)Ps)

access. Some of these national incumbents belonged initially to the Tier 2 network operators that sit between the Tier 1 and the local loop, which provides the internet connection for end users. With less extensive data cables these providers paid fees to pass some of their data through Tier 1 networks. Over time many of these incumbents became Tier 1 providers, as they expanded their backbones.[134]

Finally, a plethora of smaller Tier 3 IAPs, many without their own network, rented bandwidth from the larger operators and sold it on to customers. Hundreds of IAPs emerged over the 1990s in Europe and engaged in fierce competition.[135] Over the following years and especially in the aftermath of the dot.com crash in 2000 the IAP market thinned out significantly.

IAPs provide internet connectivity, but also other services such as email, file storage or web hosting. The larger Tier 1 and 2 players are exposed to all layers of the internet. IAPs are in a position to control the use of internet applications[136] and the access to the internet by users. They also run the servers which handle subscribers' information requests when they access the internet. IAPs are therefore essential for internet communication, because they own parts of the routing and switching infrastructure of the internet as well as the servers that respond to information requests by users.[137]

Some of the early IAPs were also information hosts in their own rights and some of them still are. *Demon Internet, CompuServe, AOL or BT Internet* hosted newsgroups and chatrooms on their servers through which users exchanged information, posted content or links. Much of the early case law on unlawful information on the internet deals with the role of these IAPs and their newsgroups in hosting and providing access to e.g. defamatory content.

Over time, other communication channels increasingly merged onto IP based systems. Cable networks and mobile telephone providers, or Wi-Fi operators have since also become IAPs.

The structure of the internet has become even more diverse. Today, communication does not need to involve the Tier 1 backbone any longer.

134 Rob Frieden, 'A Primer on Nctwork Neutrality' (2008) 43 Intereconomics 4, 10.
135 Gartner, 'The ISP Market - France' (1998) G0084758; Gartner, 'The ISP Market - Germany' (1998) G0084761; Gartner, 'The ISP Market - UK' (1998) G0084764.
136 David Clark and KC Claffy, 'Platform Models for Sustainable Internet Regulation' (2014) 4 Journal of Information Policy 463.
137 Ben Wagner, *Global Free Expression - Governing the Boundaries of Internet Content* (Springer Berlin Heidelberg 2016) 21; Meeker (n 124) ch 5.

Regional or national carriers are closely interconnected and internet traffic can pass through an indeterminable variation of connections. With the Web 2.0, large content providers emerged, which also invested in their own global backbones.[138] Meanwhile, the number of internet users accessing the internet has increased to 3.8 billion in 2018. [139] More than half of the world's population therefore need to make use of an IAP.

Due to this central position IAPs have been habitually called upon by damaged parties to stop, disable or prevent unlawful activity or access to unlawful information,[140] or to uncover internet users' physical address through locating the IP address.[141]

3. Search engines[142]

Imagine using the internet without a search engine. Search engines are such a crucial intermediary for our daily online activities that they are seen as gatekeepers not only to the internet, but to information in general.[143]

Soon after the World Wide Web, the first internet browsers emerged on the market in the early 1990s. *Mosaic*, *Netscape* and later the *Internet Explorer*, displayed web content in colour, with images and animations and offered the ability to click on hyperlinks to access content.[144] Due to better usability of the web, the number of pages and content stored on the internet soon proliferated. The number of websites grew from just 2,738 in

138 Esteban Carisimo and others, 'Studying the Evolution of Content Providers in IPv4 and IPv6 Internet Cores' (2019) 145 Computer Communications 54, 54.

139 Mary Meeker, 'Internet Trends 2019' 5 <https://www.bondcap.com/report/itr19/> accessed 14 June 2019.

140 *Tobias Mc Fadden v Sony Music Entertainment Germany GmbH, C-484/14* [2016] EU:C:2016:689 (CJEU); *Scarlet Extended SA v Société belge des auteurs, compositeurs et éditeurs SCRL (Scarlet Extended), C-70/10* [2011] EU:C:2011:771 (CJEU).

141 *Productores de Música de España (Promusicae) v Telefónica de España SAU, C-275/06* [2008] EU:C:2008:54 (CJEU) [30]. Jonathan Zittrain, *Jurisdiction* (Foundation Press 2005) 70–72.

142 Meta search engines or price comparison sites (like rentalcars.com, trivago.com or skyscanner.net) are included in this category.

143 see for example: Nicholas Diakopoulos and others, 'I Vote For—How Search Informs Our Choice of Candidate' in Damian Tambini and Martin Moore (eds), *Digital dominance: the power of Google, Amazon, Facebook, and Apple* (Oxford University Press 2018); Peters and Johnson (n 129) 55–56., Helberger, Kleinen-von Königslöw and van der Noll (n 120).

144 Ryan (n 111) 108.

1994 to 23,500 within one year. It reached the 1 million mark two years later. Today over 1.6 billion websites exist, of which over 200 million are active.[145]

There was therefore a clear need for search tools that helped users to find what they were looking for on the web. *Yahoo*, *Lycos*, *Excite* or *AltaVista* were some of the more known early movers that answered to that demand from the middle of the 1990s. A search engine would "crawl" the web for new, or changed web pages on a regular basis and then index the results. Users then received a selection of results drawn from that index, which corresponded to the terms they had entered into the engine's search bar.

Search engines therefore sit on top of the internet's application layer. Web search engines integrate with the World Wide Web application. This business is typically financed from advertising that is displayed with the search results. It is worth underlining that the search engine determines which results match best the user's search request. Its decision mechanism, or search algorithm, selects from the indexed content of the web those websites which appear to satisfy the user's information request. Initially, this selection was made simply by matching the words or phrases entered by the user with their appearance on indexed webpages. The most relevant sites would be the ones which contained the highest density of a users' search terms.[146]

This all changed with the arrival of *Google* in 1998. *Google's* search and display algorithm did not only rank results according to the density of user queries' text alone but also based on the 'relevance' of the website; which is measured by how often other web pages linked to it.[147] *AdWords*, the company's advertising program, works on a similar basis. Advertisers pay different prices for the same keyword depending on the relevance of their adverts in relation to the keyword, which is measured by click-through rates, i.e. how often users select the displayed ad link in order to access the advertised offers.[148] *Google* soon became the most successful search engine due its superior search results and its innovation in advertising models. As of

145 'Total Number of Websites - Internet Live Stats' <https://www.internetlivestats.com/total-number-of-websites/> accessed 19 June 2019.

146 Barwise and Watkins (n 7) 34.

147 Paško Bilić, 'Search Algorithms, Hidden Labour and Information Control' (2016) 3 Big Data & Society 1, 3.

148 Aysem Diker Vanberg, 'From Archie to Google - Search Engine Providers and Emergent Challenges in Relation to EU Competition Law' (2012) 3 European Journal of Law and Technology 18, 4.

2016, the search engine market was dominated by *Google*: in Europe over 90% of internet searches via static devices and over 95% of searches on mobiles devices were made using the *Google* search engine.[149] This dominance has remained unchallenged to this day.

Google and most other large search engines have in the meantime perfected the business of personalised search and advertisement by feeding users' behavioural data, collected through cookies, browsing history and other data collection activity into their business models. *Google* is in an advantageous position as it can draw on data from its numerous other prominent products and services, such as *Gmail*, the *Android* Operating System, the *Chrome* Browser or *YouTube.* In addition, it has agreements with third parties to capture more data in order to optimise its search and ad display algorithms.[150] Personalised advertising became the foundation of *Google's* extraordinary financial fortune.[151] Apart from *Microsoft's* Bing or *Yahoo* it may now be the only search engine that can afford to crawl the web on a more comprehensive basis.[152] Meanwhile, smaller search engine operators make use of the web bots of the leading players, which constantly inventorise the visible web. The arrival of the so-called Web 2.0 (discussed in more detailed below in the context of user generated content (UGC) platforms and social media), from the mid-2000s, heralded a data boon for search engines. With internet users being able to share and create content online via social media and content platforms, the amount of data available to horizontally integrated search engines belonging to *Google* or *Microsoft* skyrocketed. This allowed for further enhancements in personalised search and advertising, and hence revenue generation.

While in the early days there was a widespread assumption that search engines did not add their own bias to users' search results[153] that impartial-

---

149 *Commission Decision relating to proceedings under Article 102 of the Treaty on the Functioning of the European Union and Article 54 of the Agreement on the European Economic Area (AT39740 - Google Search (Shopping))* [2017] 58–73. This dominance has prevailed over the last 4 years with Google enjoying a global market share in the search engine market of 94.8% as of January 2020. Statista, 'Online Search Usage' (2020) 10.

150 Robert Epstein, 'Manipulating Minds' in Damian Tambini and Martin Moore (eds), *Digital dominance: the power of Google, Amazon, Facebook, and Apple* (Oxford University Press 2018) 299–300.

151 Zuboff (n 5) ch 3.

152 Epstein (n 149) 298.

153 see Vanberg (n 147) 3. who states that apart from the few overtly commercial search engines, such as Overture, which returned results based on the amount

ity is today far from being undisputed.[154] For example, *Google* was fined a record €2.42 billion by the European Commission in 2017 for abusing its dominant position and tweaking search results to the advantage of its own services.[155]

For the purposes of this work, it should be noted that the unique position of search engines in the intermediation of online information confers on them a decisive power to determine and potentially manipulate what content users may access. As will be shown in Chapter 4, search engines have also been playing a controversial role when it comes to making unlawful content, such as IP infringing, defamatory or terrorist material accessible to users.[156]

4. E-commerce platforms

The first companies which made use of the internet as a means of selling goods were retailers in their own right. Many of them were online bookshops. The first true e-commerce marketplace which acted as a commercial intermediary between sellers and buyers was *eBay*, launched as an auction marketplace in 1995. In China, *Alibaba* started its e-commerce marketplace in 1999. *Amazon*, which was founded as an online book retailer in the same year as *eBay*, opened itself to third party sellers in 2000. These first movers have remained the leading e-commerce marketplaces to this day.[157]

---

spent by advertisers on keywords, most other search engines returned results based purely on an "impartial crawler algorithm"

154 Bilić (n 146); Dirk Lewandowski, 'Is Google Responsible for Providing Fair and Unbiased Results?' in Mariarosaria Taddeo and Luciano Floridi, *The responsibilities of online service providers* (Springer Berlin Heidelberg 2016).

155 'European Commission - PRESS RELEASES - Press Release - Antitrust: Commission Fines Google €2.42 Bn for Abusing Dominance as Search Engine by Giving Illegal Advantage to Own Comparison Shopping Service' <http://europa.eu/rapid/press-release_IP-17-1784_en.htm> accessed 28 August 2018.

156 Pasquale (n 19) 494–503. And as evidenced by numerous court cases, such as *Google France, Google Inc v Louis Vuitton Malletier, C-236/08* [2010] EU:C:2010:159 (CJEU)

157 Amazon and Alibaba remain the most important online marketplaces by market capitalisation and by number of visitors. EBay, although somewhat declined in importance, remains among the top 3 online marketplaces in Europe. See: Meeker (n 102) 12; Ecommerce Foundation, 'European Ecommerce Report 2018 Edition' (2018) 22 <www.ecommercefoundation.org/reports> accessed 5 July 2018.

They were joined by numerous other marketplaces, operating across different regions of the globe, either specialised on certain product sectors or offering a wide range of consumer goods.

Growth in e-commerce has been outpacing traditional retail over the last 20 years and is expected to do so for the foreseeable future. As of 2018 worldwide e-commerce accounted for $2.86 trillion, or 15.1 % of total global retail sales, up from a share of 11.3% in 2016. Global e-commerce grew by 18% in 2018 compared to a 3.3% growth in total retail sales. Two thirds of these sales are being made by sellers on online marketplaces.[158] The data is similar for Europe where B2C e-commerce sales are forecast to grow by 13.5% in 2019 to €621 billion. In the UK, Germany and France online sales made up 17.5%, 15.2% and 10.0% of total retail sales, respectively, in 2017.[159] This growth even accelerated during the Covid 19 pandemic, as people relied even more on internet shopping.

E-commerce platforms, or online marketplaces, connect sellers with buyers via the World Wide Web and sit therefore also on top of the internet's application layer. Most commonly, platforms connect businesses or retailers (sellers) to consumers (B2C). Unlike search engines or IAPs, which answered to new demands of connectivity and information provision created by the World Wide Web, e-commerce marketplaces have significantly disrupted and eaten into already existing, traditional (retail) markets.[160] The ascendance of online marketplaces has impacted many established high street retailers, large or small. Many of them needed to downscale or transforms their business models and reconfigure their value chains along online supply chains, while others were forced out of business entirely.

Online marketplaces are a prime example of the internet's transformative influence on established, more traditional markets. For a start, the sheer variety of millions of products that even a medium sized online marketplace is able to display is unprecedented and cannot be matched by any physical retail outlet. Secondly, through e-commerce, consumers have been getting used to the convenience of home delivery. Thirdly, con-

---

158 All date on: Jessica Young | Jan 21 and 2019, 'Global Ecommerce Sales Grow 18% in 2018' (*Digital Commerce 360*) <https://www.digitalcommerce360.com/article/global-ecommerce-sales/> accessed 11 July 2019.

159 'Ecommerce in Europe' (*Ecommerce News*) <https://ecommercenews.eu/ecommerce-in-europe/> accessed 11 July 2019.

160 Johann J Kranz and Arnold Picot, 'Internet Business Strategies' in Johannes M Bauer and Michael Latzer (eds), *Handbook on the economics of the internet* (Paperback edition, EE, Edward Elgar Publishing 2017) 374.

sumers are able to shop products on a global scale, be it by accessing marketplaces "abroad" or by marketplaces integrating sellers from across the globe onto their platforms.

For sellers, the ubiquity of the internet means that even smaller businesses can now reach an international or even global audience directly. The story of the decline of the traditional corner shop is therefore often counterbalanced by that store now being able to sell globally online.

Meanwhile, e-commerce marketplaces have also reinforced the trend of the globalisation and digitisation of supply chains.[161] By cutting physical retail structures, sellers will be able to source and ship orders from anywhere in the world directly to the customer. As customer order fulfilment moves up in the supply chain, logistics has become one of the most important cost factors in e-commerce. The pressure for rationalisation engendered technological innovation in the form of business models that incorporate the Internet of Things (IoT), Big Data analytics and cloud computing.[162]

Entire logistics processes, from stock management, storage to delivery, are being transformed. Fast and customised delivery, inventory visibility, efficient returns management and order tracking have become a normal customer experience feature. New specialised logistics service intermediaries offer their services to sellers.[163] Larger marketplace have been offering their own fulfilment solutions in order to control customer experience and gain additional revenue from sellers.[164] Online marketplaces can therefore be considered as the first internet business that seriously disrupted parts of the "old economy."

This disruptive potential becomes apparent when one considers that there are currently over 7,000 online marketplaces and platforms operating in Europe.[165] Internet marketplaces are responsible for 56% of global cross-

161 Dieter Arnold (ed), *Handbuch Logistik* (3., neu bearb Aufl, Springer 2008) 532.

162 Ying Yu and Xin Wang, 'E-Commerce Logistics in Supply Chain Management' (2017) 117 Industrial Management & Data Systems 24.

163 Commonly called Fulfilment Service Providers (FSPs) or Third Party Logistics (3PL))

164 Amazon, Alibaba or JD.com all offer their own transportation and warehousing services to their sellers. Meanwhile, other platforms such as eBay offer their business sellers services with selected delivery companies.

165 'European Commission - PRESS RELEASES - Press Release - Digital Single Market: EU Negotiators Agree to Set up New European Rules to Improve Fairness of Online Platforms' Trading Practices' <https://ec.europa.eu/commission/presscorner/detail/en/IP_19_1168> accessed 17 July 2019.

border e-commerce. For example, in Europe 93% of sellers on eBay export their goods, as opposed to only 26% of companies that do not use online marketplaces for selling on the internet.[166] Meanwhile, on that marketplace, sellers listed over 1.8 billion products as of 2019.[167] On the largest e-commerce platform, *Amazon* marketplace, 2.5 million active sellers are offering their products. Two-thirds of them outsource their logistics, which includes warehousing, order fulfilment and customer returns to the company's *Fulfilment by Amazon (FBA)* service. Apart from reaping extra revenue and valuable inventory management data from sellers, *Amazon* has become one of the world's leading logistics companies.[168] Its marketplace alone has a share of 31.3% in the US online retail market and an estimated 27% in the German e-commerce market.[169] Sellers on these two Amazon marketplaces account for approximately 3% of the entire US and 4% of the entire German retail markets.[170] And this trend is to continue not only for the *Amazon* marketplace, where an estimated 540.000 new sellers have joined the platform in Europe in 2018 alone,[171] but also most e-commerce platforms.

With the advent of Web 2.0, online marketplaces have increasingly integrated a host of other intermediary services, from logistics to payments providers, and from advertising to financial services. This trend is reinforced by an explosion in customer product and seller reviews, not only in the form of text, but also as pictures and videos. In addition, purchase decisions are often shared through other platforms, usually social media. Meanwhile, multi-channel shopping via mobile devices or through voice recognition system has been growing rapidly. Finally, these platforms are

---

166 European Commission, 'Commission Staff Working Document Online Platforms Accompanying the Document Communication on Online Platforms and the Digital Single Market SWD(2016) 172 Final' (n 54) 13.

167 'EBay Research' (*Marketplace Pulse*) <https://www.marketplacepulse.com/research/eBay> accessed 17 July 2019.

168 'Amazon Research - Marketplace Pulse' <https://www.marketplacepulse.com/research/amazon> accessed 17 July 2019.

169 'Marketplaces Year in Review 2018' (Marketplace Pulse 2018) <https://www.marketplacepulse.com/marketplaces-year-in-review-2018> accessed 17 July 2019. 'Amazon Europe Cross-Border Sellers from UK, Germany, France, Spain, and Italy' (*Marketplace Pulse*) <https://www.marketplacepulse.com/amazon/europe-cross-border-sellers> accessed 17 July 2019.

170 Calculation based on data showing that the share of online retail in total retail sales was 10.0% for the US (Meeker (n 102) 20) and 15.1% in Germany.

171 'Marketplaces Year in Review 2018' (n 168).

open to developers so that their features can be integrated into other websites and systems.

Online marketplaces have therefor become true multisided platforms benefitting from important network effects.[172] Revenue and data are as much derived from sellers and buyers as from other integrated intermediaries which were attracted by the growth in website traffic in the first place, and now reinforce the power of these marketplaces.[173]

The rise of e-commerce marketplaces has also brought problems. The globalisation of retail via the internet has opened the door for unlawful activity, be it the global availability of counterfeit products, falsified medicines, and illegal, non-compliant or unsafe products. [174] Traditionally, enforcement in this area focussed on bulk and container shipments, which are a typical feature of established retail sourcing and distribution networks. EU customs and market surveillance enforcement concentrated on checking these shipments at the central entry points into the Union, such as major seaports or airports.

But as customers can now place orders on foreign marketplaces or through foreign sellers on local marketplaces, goods enter the jurisdiction increasingly as small consignments and parcels. They pass customs largely unchecked and undeclared. The number of small consignments arriving from outside the EU grew by almost 300%, from an estimated 29.8 million in 1999 to 114.8 million in 2013, which is in line with the rise in popularity of online shopping.[175] Customs, enforcement authorities and brand owners are simply overwhelmed. Enforcement is made more difficult by the fact that there is often no economic actor within the EU that can be

172 Barwise and Watkins (n 7) 27.

173 Martens (n 53) 8.

174 See for example: European Commission, 'Bringing E-Commerce Benefits to Consumers - Accompanying Document SEC2011_1640' (European Commission 2012) 40. OECD, 'Online Product Safety' (2016) OECD Digital Economy Papers 261 15–16, 27–28 <http://www.oecd-ilibrary.org/science-and-technology/online-product-safety_5jlnb5q93jlt-en> accessed 23 April 2018.; European Commission, 'Summary of Responses to the Public Consultation on the Evaluation and Modernisation of the Legal Framework for IPR Enforcement' (2016) 10, 41 <http://ec.europa.eu/DocsRoom/documents/18661> accessed 17 March 2017.; Hans-Georg Koch, 'Strategies against Counterfeiting of Drugs: A Comparative Criminal Law Study' in Christophe Geiger, *Criminal enforcement of intellectual property: a handbook of contemporary research* (Edward Elgar 2012) 353–355.

175 European Commission, *Assessment of the Application and Impact of the VAT Exemption for Importation of Small Consignments Final Report.* (European Commission 2015) 37–40

held responsible. Non-EU based sellers are outside the jurisdictional reach of public authorities and courts. Online marketplace operators, where based in the EU, or internet access providers, are the only entities which may be able to effectively stop the sales of unlawful products. These problems will be discussed in more detail in Chapter 4.

5. User generated content and social media platforms – the rise of Web 2.0

During its first 10 years, the commercial internet was used as a medium to search, consult and download information. Where possible, content or products were purchased through the content portals of IAPs. User live interaction was limited to chatrooms and newsgroups.[176] Intermediaries did not deliver content but merely facilitated user exchanges in a largely passive way.[177]

With the start of the new millennium and in the aftermath of the dot.com crash, the Word Wide Web and internet technology started to change, giving rise to the Web 2.0. The technological basis for the emergence of Web 2.0 rested mainly on advances in internet connection bandwidth and computing power.

This allowed for "applications that harness network effects to get better the more people use them."[178] New applications and business models invited users to create and upload content online, be it in the form of blogs, photos or video, and most importantly, share this content with other users.

The first social and professional networking or microblogging services, such as *MySpace*, *Facebook*, *LinkedIn* or *Twitter* all emerged between 2002 and 2006. User generated content sharing platforms - *YouTube, Flickr* or *Instagram* - also saw the light during the first decade of the new millennium.

These companies were founded on common business and design models, which are identified by *O'Reilly* as the core elements of the Web 2.0 era:[179]

---

176 Tarleton Gillespie, 'Platforms Are Not Intermediaries' (2018) 2 Georgetown Law Technology Review 198, 206.

177 Belli and Sappa (n 42) 190.

178 Collins (n 116) 40.

179 Tim O'Reilly, 'What Is Web 2.0: Design Patterns and Business Models for the Next Generation of Software' [2007] Communication & Strategies 17, 37.

They mobilise users to create, collaborate and shape the content and structures of the web. The exploitation of this user engagement leads to ever more sophisticated and personalised forms of advertisement, which is driven by users themselves, through their own interaction. Typical activities are tagging, liking, sharing, commenting or reviewing of photos, videos, text or other content created by professional or non-professional users, be it on social networking sites or UGC platforms.

This harnessing of "collective intelligence" goes hand in hand with the exercise of control over the unique data created by users' online interactions. These datasets get richer the more people use the service. This consolidation of consumer data opens new possibilities of personalised advertising and manipulation in order to keep users engaged on these platforms and maximise revenue.[180]

The race for data has facilitated a shift towards more nimble web applications, which utilise simple programming such as e.g. XML or JavaScript. Third party developers can easily integrate service features or ads from *Google Maps*, *Facebook*, *Instagram*, *Amazon* or *YouTube* into other websites. This allows for additional personalised and dynamic data and revenue generation across potentially millions of third part websites.

As a logical consequence over the fight for user data and traffic, Web 2.0 companies integrate across multiple types of end user devices and systems, from PC/Mac to mobile phones and smart TV applications or voice recognition systems. At the same time, they offer equally rich and interactive user experience across all of these devices.

Far from just integrating into the applications layer, these businesses have restructured the architecture of the World Wide Web from a "document retrieval tool"[181] to one of distributed applications and services.[182] They still utilise the platform design of the World Wide Web, but rather than

---

180 Roger Clarke, 'Web 2.0 as Syndication' (2008) 3 Journal of theoretical and applied electronic commerce research 40 <http://www.scielo.cl/scielo.php?script=sci_arttext&pid=S0718-18762008000100004&lng=en&nrm=iso&tlng=en> accessed 22 July 2019.

181 ibid 38.

182 Christopher T Marsden, 'Beyond Europe: The Internet, Regulation, and Multistakeholder Governance—Representing the Consumer Interest?' (2008) 31 Journal of Consumer Policy 115, 121.

answering and querying information, they manage and exploit the creation and the flow of data as it passes through their distributed systems.[183] The use pattern of the internet shifted from unidirectional access through IAPs towards interaction via platforms.[184]

The platform ecosystem of the internet has increased in complexity. As internet penetration, bandwidth, and technology convergence progress and new internet business models emerge, Web 2.0 intermediaries have become ever more powerful and indispensable. Social networking sites such as *Twitter, Instagram, Reddit or LinkedIn* have now hundreds of millions of active users. *Facebook* and *YouTube* are actively used by 2.7 billion and 2.3 billion people, respectively.[185] Meanwhile, the original division between social networking and user generated content sites has blurred. Social networks like *Facebook* or *LinkedIn* are as much hosts of photos, videos or other content as UGC sites *YouTube, DailyMotion*, *Pinterest* or *TikTok* are used for social interaction.

For a large part of internet users these Web 2.0 platforms have become the prime gateway of access to the internet: through them they participate in social interaction within their communities, receive and share news and, increasingly, search and shop for products. Altogether 3.96 billion people worldwide used social media and UGC platforms actively by July 2020, most of them through mobile devices.[186] Today, the average internet user spends 2.2 hours per day on these platforms.[187] Over 43% of US internet users stay up-to-date on daily news through *Facebook*, 21% by looking at *YouTube* and 12% on *Twitter*.[188] In Europe, of those users who access the internet for news, 22% rely on social media as a main source of information.[189] 57% of young people who use their mobile phone as a means to check the news first thing in the morning do so via social media apps.[190] These intermediaries have become so addictive and seemingly indispens-

183 O'Reilly (n 178) 34.

184 Wagner, *Global Free Expression - Governing the Boundaries of Internet Content* (n 136) 110.

185 Statista, 'Most Used Social Media 2021' (2021)

186 Statista, 'Social Media Usage Worldwide' (2020) 2–3.

187 Aleksandar S, 'How Much Time Do People Spend on Social Media in 2019?' (*Tech Jury*, 8 March 2019) <https://techjury.net/blog/time-spent-on-social-media/> accessed 23 July 2019.

188 Meeker (n 138) 179.

189 'Internet Users' Preferences for Accessing Content Online - Flash Eurobarometer 437' (European Commission 2016) 30.

190 Nic Newman, 'Reuters Institute Digital News Report 2019' (Reuters Institute, University of Oxford 2019) 55.

able that people have been calling the police when services such as *Facebook* or *YouTube* have faced local outages.[191]

A rapidly growing amount of data is created and replicated every day on the internet, be it through users' active participation or by passive navigation. While in 2013, 72 hours of new video were uploaded on *YouTube* every minute this had risen to 500 hours by August 2020.[192] *Facebook* users uploaded 147,000 photos every 60 seconds and *Instagram* recorded over 138,000 clicks per minute on ads posted by business profiles on their platform.[193] In 2010, people who connected to the internet had 208 digital data engagements per day (instances during which their presence on the net resulted in data). Thanks to an increase in time spent online this is set to rise to 4,900 such data engagements per day by 2025, one every 18 seconds.[194] This digital engagement means that for every person on earth, on average 1.7 MB of data are generated per second in 2020.[195]

As with the other intermediaries mentioned above, the ascendance of social media and UGC platforms has not come without problems. As regards unlawful content, the major challenges relate to copyright infringing content, material and activity harmful to children, and illegal speech, such as hate speech or terrorist content, that users upload, access or share via these platforms. These problems have become more prevalent over the last 15 years as the reach, day-to-day use, and variety and amount of content hosted and shared on these platforms grew.

Users may for example, intentionally or not, upload video or music which infringe the intellectual property rights of the owner, be they artists or commercial license holders such as record labels or film production companies. Violations are likely to happen as users, unaware of the complexities of copyright in a digital environment, incorporate popular excerpts or whole sets of music, images or film into their own creations, for example through sampling or mashups.[196] Since their inception, UGC

---

191 Sangeet Kumar, 'The Algorithmic Dance: YouTube's Adpocalypse and the Gatekeeping of Cultural Content on Digital Platforms' [2019] Internet Policy Review 11–12 <http://policyreview.info/node/1417> accessed 26 July 2019.

192 'Data Never Sleeps 2.0' (Domo 2014) <https://www.domo.com/learn/data-never-sleeps-2>; Statista, 'Social Media Usage Worldwide' (n 185) 29.

193 Statista, 'Social Media Usage Worldwide' (n 185) 29.

194 David Reinsel, John Gantz and John Rydning, 'The Digitization of the World from Edge to Core' (Seagate, IDC 2018) 13.

195 'Data Never Sleeps 6.0' (Domo 2018) <https://www.domo.com/learn/data-never-sleeps-6> accessed 23 July 2019.

196 Jütte (n 12).

platforms have been party to intellectual property disputes in many jurisdictions as users sought to share images, music or video without acquiring the necessary permissions under copyright.[197]

With regards to unlawful content, social media and UGC platforms have been identified as important conduits in the communication of child pornography, incitement to violence and terrorism,[198] defamatory speech or attempts to influence elections through disinformation and targeted advertising campaigns.[199] While IAPs and their newsrooms had some of these issues in the Web 1.0 era, the scale and complexity of the problem has escalated in the era of Web 2.0 platforms. This has led to the assertion that these platforms now control the flow of information online. Their business models and technologies, which are aimed at extracting data from users, lead to a degree of online manipulation that risks undermining the self-determination and autonomy of people.[200]

6. Sharing economy platforms

Sharing economy, or collaborative economy platforms emerged out of the Web 2.0. Like e-commerce platforms they belong to those intermediaries which disrupted and transformed already existing economic sectors. However, while e-commerce platforms uprooted traditional retail, sharing

---

197 For an early demonstration of the problem: Daithí Mac Síthigh, 'The Mass Age of Internet Law' (2008) 17 Information & Communications Technology Law 79. In Europe the court sagas of the German collective societies (GEMA) against *YouTube* is exemplary in this respect (*Haftung der Internetvideoplattform Youtube für rechtswidrige Uploads, 310 O 461/10* [2012] LG Hamburg 310 O 461/10, OpenJur 2012 36010.) It culminated in a currently pending reference to the CJEU (C-682/18). In France, early cases involving video sharing platform (VSP) *Dailymotion* are illustrative, such as *Christian, C, Nord Ouest Production v Dailymotion, UGC Images* (2007) (Unreported) (Tribunal de Grande Instance de Paris).In the US the key early reference is *Viacom International v YouTube* [2012] US Court of Appeals for the Second Circuit (Manhattan) 10-03270.

198 Great Britain and Media and Sport Department for Culture, *Online Harms White Paper.* (2019); European Commission, 'COM (2017) 555 Final' (n 69) 3–6. Danielle Keats Citron and Benjamin Wittes, 'The Problem Is Not Just Backpage: Revising Section 230 Immunity' (2018) 2 Georgetown Law Technology Review 21, 466–467.

199 Daniel Susser, Beate Roessler and Helen Nissenbaum, 'Technology, Autonomy, and Manipulation' (2019) 8 Internet Policy Review 22.

200 Michal Lavi, 'Evil Nudges' (2018) 21 Vanderbilt Journal of Entertainment and Technology Law; Susser, Roessler and Nissenbaum (n 198).

economy platforms transformed a variety of service sectors, which previously operated in comparatively closed, regulated environments. Another factor setting them apart from e-commerce marketplaces is that the transactions they facilitate often do not result in a transfer of material ownership,[201] but in a commercial sharing of resources, often between private individuals (referred to as P2P or C2C business models).

Sharing economy platforms suddenly subverted traditional business relationships between suppliers and consumers by allowing private individuals to compete with commercial suppliers. Individuals suddenly became "non-professional traders"[202] on service markets which previously faced a certain amount of entry barriers.

The most known examples are *Airbnb* in the holiday accommodation sector, and *Uber, Lyft* or *BlaBlaCar* in the transportation service market. Other rapidly developing sectors include the finance industry, especially crowdfunding platforms such as *Kickstarter*, marketplaces connecting private chefs with diners (*Eatro*), food delivery platforms (*Deliveroo*), second hand fashion marketplaces (*Vinted)*, or the sharing of parking space in inner cities (*JustPark*).

Like e-commerce and social media platforms, the new collaborative economy businesses exploit the opportunities offered by the new digital platform technologies and the Web 2.0: the possibility to join a seemingly unlimited number of suppliers in a structured way with a similarly wide customer base. New interactive web features such as online maps and geolocalisation, cloud computing[203] and the ease of online payments were all conducive to bypassing and innovating traditional market structures.

But collaborative platforms display some new features that set them apart from other online intermediaries. First, they capitalise on an already existing trend kicked off by the internet. Peer-to-peer exchange of information was at the very heart of early file sharing businesses such as *Napster* or *Kazaa*. Some theorists even see businesses such as *The Pirate Bay* as a model

---

201 Vassilis Hatzopoulos and Sofia Roma, 'Caring for Sharing? The Collaborative Economy under EU Law' (2017) 54 Common Market Law Review 81, 85.

202 Yolanda Martinez Mata, 'Bolkestein Revisited in the Era of the Sharing Economy' [2017] Revista Electrónica de Estudios Internacionales 3 <http://www.reei.org/index.php/revista/num33/notas/bolkestein-revisited-in-the-era-of-the-sharing-economy> accessed 12 September 2017.

203 Vassilis Hatzopoulos, *The Collaborative Economy and EU Law* (Hart Publishing 2018) 2.

of the collaborative economy, albeit an extreme version.[204] Collaborative platforms extend these habits into traditional sectors of the economy. Secondly, they also reflect a trend towards ecological consciousness and sustainability and a search for alternative economic models in the wake of the financial crisis of 2008.[205] They hark back to early day, more idealistic views of the internet as a liberalising force which redefines the way people interact socially and economically.[206]

Collaborative platforms have advanced most rapidly in the US, where they started to make an economic impact by the start of the 2010s. However, Europe has also seen rapid adoption of the sharing economy. The EU estimated that in 2018 the collaborative economy had resulted in transactions worth €28 billion and that it has the potential to add €572 billion to the EU economy in the future.[207]

On the flipside, these platforms challenge and potentially undermine established legal concepts and economic relations. While unlawful content appears to be less of a problem on these platforms, the blurring division between personal, commercial and charitable activities pose challenges to tax, labour and competition law.[208]

The legal challenge is that these platforms see themselves as intermediary service provider while the traditional economic actors, whose business are being disrupted, demand that they be regulated under specific sectoral regulation, e.g. as accommodation or transportation service providers.

The outcome of such a demand would depend on the degree of involvement of the collaborative platform in the provision of the underlying service, and in particular, whether the platform exercises decisive influence over the conditions under which it imparts that service.[209] In its *Uber* and

---

204 Davide Pellegrini and Francesca De Canio, *The New Social Game: Sharing Economy and Digital Revolution : Into the Change of Consumers' Habit* (Bocconi University Press 2017) 28–29.

205 Hatzopoulos (n 202) 3.

206 Wu, *The Master Switch* (n 1) 36., see also Section 2.1.1.

207 European Commission, 'Communication: A European Agenda for the Collaborative Economy - COM(2016) 356 Final' (European Commission 2016) 2.

208 For more detail: Hatzopoulos (n 202); Janelle Orsi, *Practicing Law in the Sharing Economy: Helping People Build Cooperatives, Social Enterprise, and Local Sustainable Economies.* (American Bar Association 2014) 28 <http://public.eblib.com/choice/publicfullrecord.aspx?p=1718422> accessed 25 July 2019.

209 *Asociación Profesional Élite Taxi v Uber Systems Spain SL, C-434/15* [2017] EU:C:2017:981 (CJEU) [39].

Airbnb rulings[210] the CJEU provided criteria and examples of which kind of platforms could be seen as falling under sector specific legislation, and which platforms were acting principally as ISSPs. This legal debate provides a good illustration of the increasingly complex involvement of online platforms in the intermediation process. The methodology employed by courts to assess the activities of collaborative platforms may be of benefit when evaluating other intermediaries and their responsibilities in the fight against unlawful content.

7. Messenger services, cloud platforms and other online intermediaries

There are numerous other intermediaries and platform business models. This sector is evolving dynamically and the border between different types of intermediaries is moving constantly.

Messenger service, such *WhatsApp, Facebook Messenger* or *Skype* may straddle the border between telecommunications services and information society services.[211] Most of these are now owned and integrated into larger platforms' ecosystems, such as those of *Microsoft* or *Facebook*. Messaging services converge as well with social media and user generated content (*Instagram, WhatsApp*).[212] At the same time, in-app e-commerce through services such as *WhatsApp* or *Instagram* is becoming more common.[213]

Peer-to-peer (P2P) intermediaries have evolved in line with legal and technological changes. Since their start at the end of the 1990s they were subject to claims of facilitating massive infringements in copyright by allowing for the sharing of protected works. Early P2P intermediaries such as *Napster* held indices that pointed users towards files that other users wanted to share. *Napster's* business model was successfully pursued and the company forced to put a stop to its P2P operations in 2001. Subsequently, P2P intermediaries successfully adapted their infrastructure and became more distributed. Modern P2P intermediaries divide the indexing labour.

---

210 *Uber* (n 170). *YA, AIRBNB Ireland UC, Hotelière Turenne SAS, Association pour un hébergement et un tourisme professionnel (AHTOP), Valhotel, C-390/18* [2019] ECLI:EU:C:2019:1112 (CJEU).

211 *Skype Communications Sàrl v Institut belge des services postaux et des télécommunications (IBPT), C-142/18* [2019] EU:C:2019:460 (CJEU).

212 European Commission, 'UCP Directive Guidance' (n 57) 142.

213 'How Conversational Commerce Is Changing E-Commerce' (*Content Harmony®*, 28 June 2016) <https://www.contentharmony.com/blog/conversational-commerce/> accessed 6 July 2020. Meeker (n 138) 316.

There are those that provide the torrent software with which users can index the content they would like to share. Others track user requests and connect users that seek to interchange files.[214] These intermediaries are far from obsolete and although legal challenges against them tend to be increasingly successful,[215] this is another story when it comes to closing them down operationally.

Cloud platforms have become important intermediaries in line with the Web 2.0 trend of interactivity and information sharing. They typically have a distinctive physical infrastructure element. Many boast their own data storage centres with servers, IT systems and physical network connections. Others may just rent network capacity from other infrastructure providers.[216]

It is an indispensable feature of the always-on environment that content and processing power are accessible to users at any time and at any place. The new collaborative nature of the web requires that multiple users have concurrent access to software, content or computing power. This paradigm shift has engendered a gradual move of computing power and storage from consumer end devices towards public cloud storage. End devices are in turn increasingly tethered and thin: many functionalities on mobile phones or other end devices are pre-configured and bound to the operating system's environment. In addition, many functions and applications work only when connected to the internet.[217] To illustrate the quantum change that constant connectedness has brought: in 2014 users shared "only"

214 Lilian Edwards and Charlotte Waelde, 'Online Intermediaries and Liability for Copyright Infringement', *WIPO Workshop Keynote Paper* (2005) 6–10 <https://papers.ssrn.com/sol3/papers.cfm?abstract_id=1159640> accessed 15 October 2019.

215 *Stichting Brein v Ziggo BV, XS4ALL Internet BV, C-610/15* [2017] EU:C:2017:456 (CJEU).

216 The most common services offered to consumers are data storage solutions (often classed as Software as a Service (SaaS), which comprises the entire suite needed for remote computing, from data storage and software to hardware and network capacity). B2B services comprise Platform as a Service (PaaS: offers operating systems, network and hardware as a service) and Infrastructure as a Service (IaaS: offers to run network and hardware on top of which companies can deploy there software and applications). Cesare Bartolini, Cristiana Santos and Carsten Ullrich, 'Property and the Cloud' (2018) 34 Computer Law & Security Review 358, 361–363.

217 David Lametti, 'The Cloud: Boundless Digital Potential or Enclosure 3.0?' [2012] Virginia Journal of Law & technology 219–220.

280,000 multimedia messages per minute via *Snapchat*.[218] Four years later 2.1 million "snaps" were shared every minute worldwide.[219]

It is estimated that by 2025 almost 50% of the world's data will be stored in the public cloud, compared to under 5% in 2010. By contrast, the percentage of data stored on consumer end devices will decline from over 60% to 20%, with the remainder being made up by enterprise cloud storage.[220] If one considers that the world's entire data sphere will rise from 33 Zettabytes in 2018 to 175 Zettabytes in 2025 [221] it becomes clear that public cloud solutions will become the common feature of user data storage.

UGC and social networks will store the exploding number of videos, music and photos on their own cloud servers. However, in the wake of Web 2.0 there are an increasing number of providers that offer cloud storage solutions to consumers for private document, photo, music or video storage. These services try to answer to the demand of consumers to collaborate and share content or to back up the content stored at home. Services such as *DropBox*, *Google Drive*, *Google Docs/Photos*, *Amazon Drive* or *Microsoft OneDrive* have become common services used by consumers.

The legal challenges here relate mostly to copyright over the content stored, collaboratively produced or modified and made available between users via these services.[222] Cloud services face therefore similar challenges as UGC platforms discussed above.[223]

It should be noted that the various industry and academic sources on this subject matter also mention other business models as internet intermediaries, namely mobile apps and app stores, online payment service providers, domain name registries and registrars, application platforms,

---

218 'Data Never Sleeps 3.0' (Domo 2015) <https://web-assets.domo.com/blog/wp-content/uploads/2015/08/15_domo_data-never-sleeps-3_final1.png> accessed 26 July 2019.

219 'Data Never Sleeps 6.0' (n 194).

220 Reinsel, Gantz and Rydning (n 193) 6.

221 ibid. 1 Zetabyte = 1 trillion Gigabytes = 10^{15} Megabytes

222 See, for example, on the unlicensed making available of cloud recorded TV *shift.tv, Urteil v 22042009, Az I ZR 216/06* [2009] GRUR 2009 845 (BGH); *VCAST Limited v RTI SpA, C-265/16* [2017] EU:C:2017:913 (CJEU). Or dealing with copyright protected content in general the recent referral to the CJEU C-683/18 (*Elsevier Inc.* v *Cyando AG*)

223 For a detailed analysis see: Martin Senftleben, 'Breathing Space for Cloud-Based Business Models' (2013) 4 JIPITEC. and Bartolini, Santos and Ullrich (n 215).

online advertising networks or webhosting services.[224] The categorisation offered here described the most common types of intermediaries from a socio-technical, economic and legal point of view. They are also the ones most commonly discussed in connection with unlawful content.

D. *Intermediary powerhouses*

1. Multi-sided platforms

The growth and diversification of the intermediary landscape over the last 25 years has been accompanied by vibrant merger and acquisitions activity. A handful of global intermediary "powerhouses" have emerged as a result, which prevail in their respective markets, or market segments, on a global scale.

These players have been capitalising on new characteristics of digital markets. First, the free and non-rivalrous nature of digital products[225] of using, for example, an internet search engine or a social network, helped attract a broad global user base. By building a strong, experience-based brand value,[226] partly due to being first movers, they created switching costs for consumers. In web-based markets these switching costs are often non-economic in nature (or low in economic terms)[227] as most of these services are offered for free and multi-homing remains possible.[228] Instead, the switching costs rest on other factors such as the power of direct network effects, attraction to the brand and its perceived quality, or more irrational behaviour, such as inertia.[229]

---

224 See for example different categorisations in: 'Roles and Responsibilities of Intermediaries: Fighting Counterfeiting and Piracy in the Supply Chain' 47 0 94 <https://iccwbo.org/publication/roles-responsibilities-intermediaries/> accessed 26 September 2017. OECD, 'The Economic and Social Role of Internet Intermediaries - DSTI/ICCP(2009)9/FINAL' (n 46) 9–15. European Commission, 'Online Platforms and the Digital Single Market Opportunities and Challenges for Europe COM(2016) 288 Final' 2.

225 Barwise and Watkins (n 7) 25.

226 ibid.

227 D Daniel Sokol and Jingyuan Ma, 'Understanding Online Markets and Antitrust Analysis' (2017) 15 Northwestern Journal of Technology and Intellectual Property 43, 50–52.

228 *Google (Search) EU Antitrust Procedure* (n 148) 67.

229 Renato Nazzini, 'Google and the (Ever-Stretching) Boundaries of Article 102 TFUE' (2015) 6 Journal of European Competition Law & Practice 301, 306–307.

Secondly, these online intermediaries operate as multi-sided markets (MSM). They are able to leverage their power and create indirect cross-market or network effects.[230] For example, a dominant position attained through a large active user base attracts more advertisers on to the platform.[231]

The important new element is that these intermediaries' have become enterprises that exploit their users' data in unprecedented ways, a practice which is now at the heart of their business model.[232] They not only derive advertising revenue from the data generated by a large and ever more interactive user community. This behavioural data is also processed with a view to constantly improve and personalise services thus reinforcing the existing network dynamics[233] and market hegemony.[234]

Today's large intermediaries have aimed at expanding diagonally across those markets that are, or could be connected to their own platforms. The aim is to channel as much additional web traffic as possible towards their core services in a bid to maximise data streams, exploitation of user data and therefore generate more revenue and reinforce market leadership.[235]

---

230 Sokol and Ma (n 226) 50.

231 Barwise and Watkins (n 7) 25.

232 Alexia Autenne and Élisabeth De Ghellinck, 'L'émergence et le développement des plateformes digitales : les enseignements de la théorie économique de la firme' (2019) XXXIII Revue internationale de droit économique 275, 287–288.

233 Damian Tambini and Martin Moore, 'Dominance, the Citizen Interest and the Consumer Interest (Conclusion)' in Damian Tambini and Martin Moore (eds), *Digital dominance: the power of Google, Amazon, Facebook, and Apple* (Oxford University Press 2018) 397–399. European Commission, 'Commission Staff Working Document Online Platforms Accompanying the Document Communication on Online Platforms and the Digital Single Market SWD(2016) 172 Final' (n 54) 21–22. and: Jacques Crémer, Yves-Alexandre de Montjoye and Heike Schweitzer, 'Competition Policy for the Digital Era - Final Report' (European Commission 2019) <http://ec.europa.eu/competition/publications/reports/kd0419345enn.pdf> accessed 31 July 2019.

234 However, some economists also call for caution against an overly dark and undifferentiated view of network effects and big data: David S Evans and Richard Schmalensee, 'Network Effects: March to the Evidence, Not to the Slogans' [2017] SSRN Electronic Journal <https://www.ssrn.com/abstract=3027691> accessed 31 July 2019.

235 Wagner, *Global Free Expression - Governing the Boundaries of Internet Content* (n 136) 104. For more detail on the new competition and regulatory policy challenges related to platforms in the web-based economy see: David S Evans, 'Competition and Regulatory Policy for Multi-Sided Platforms with Applications to the Web Economy' [2008] SSRN Electronic Journal <http://www.ssrn.com/abstract=1090368> accessed 30 July 2019. For example, *Google's* recent announce-

These new facets of online platforms mean that dominance and potential anti-competitive effects are difficult to assess with traditional economic antitrust tools.[236]

2. The leading players

The handful of leading players that have emerged to dominate the global intermediary landscape today are *Google, Amazon, Facebook, Apple* and *Microsoft*,[237] often referred to as the *GAFAM*. China, with its relatively closed and tightly controlled internet infrastructure may be the only other country, apart from the US, which has managed to create competing intermediaries which have started to expand massively on a global level, such as *Alibaba* or *Tencent*. By April 2020, the *GAFAM* and China-based *Alibaba* and *Tencent*, belonged to the 10 largest companies in the world by market capitalisation.[238]

A quick overview of the expansion of the *GAFAM* across global internet markets shall be given below.

I. Google (Alphabet)

Google's holding company *Alphabet* is centred around two core intermediary services. Apart from owning the world's most popular search engine,

---

ment to phase out the use of third party cookies in its *Chrome* browser in favour of its so-called "Privacy Sandbox" has been interpreted as a means to route even more activity and traffic data directly through its own "first party" tools and products. Elizabeth M Renieris, 'What Google's Privacy Sandbox Means for Internet Governance' (*Emerging Technology, Platform Governance - Centre for International Governance Innovation*, 19 March 2021) <https://www.cigionline.org/articles/what-googles-privacy-sandbox-means-internet-governance> accessed 1 April 2021.

236 See for more detail: OECD, 'Rethinking Antitrust Tools for Multi-Sided Platforms' (n 82) 55–64., Sokol and Ma (n 226). and Justus Haucap and Torben Stühmeier, 'Competition and Antitrust in Internet Markets' in Johannes M Bauer and Michael Latzer (eds), *Handbook on the economics of the internet* (Paperback edition, EE, Edward Elgar Publishing 2017).

237 Zuboff (n 5) l 2969. Barwise and Watkins (n 7); Giovanni Sartor, 'The Impact of Algorithms for Online Content Filtering or Moderation. Upload Filters' (European Parliament 2020) 14.

238 Statista, 'Biggest Companies in the World by Market Cap 2020' (2020)

the company acquired video sharing platform *YouTube* in 2006. Meanwhile, it has successfully built out its own cloud operations *Google Cloud* into the world's third largest professional cloud service by revenue.[239] *Google* also expanded in adjacent markets. Notably, its Android platform is the world's leading mobile operating system, with its own app store, *Google Play*. The *Google Chrome* browser is today the world's most used web browser.[240] *Gmail* and *Google Maps*, the consumer cloud services *Google Docs* and *Google Photos, the Google Shopping* marketplace and many other undertakings complete the picture of a company that is present in almost every sector of the internet economy. The ability to gather data through these services stands to benefit its two core activities *Google Search* and *YouTube*. They are considered to exert a key influence over content governance on large parts of the internet today.[241]

II. Amazon

Amazon is the global market leader in e-commerce. While an online retailer in its own right, it is the marketplace platform that has been responsible for generating an unprecedented degree of valuable user and sales data. Having 2.5 million sellers as competitors to its own retail operations on board means the company can cash in not only on seller fees but also on customer and market intelligence gathered from the sale of third-party products via its own site. The business intelligence and behavioural data generated through these activities is converted into money through advertising and by using it for improving its own product offers.[242] The *Amazon* search bar is today the world's most used search engine for product searches.[243] The company runs the world's leading enterprise cloud service *Amazon Web Services (AWS)*, which is used by a multitude of technology businesses and internet platforms as a computing and web hosting platform.

239 Meeker (n 138) 116.

240 'Browser Statistics' <https://www.w3schools.com/browsers/default.asp> accessed 1 August 2019.

241 Wagner, *Global Free Expression - Governing the Boundaries of Internet Content* (n 136) 104.

242 Khan (n 19) 781–782.

243 ibid 714.

This includes for example *Airbnb* or *Reddit*[244] and even *Amazon's* fiercest competitor in the video-on-demand market, *Netflix.* It has also been competing successfully for large-scale public-sector contracts across the world.[245] Apart from this, the company is amongst the leaders in music streaming, video-on-demand, voice-based commerce and has launched into entertainment content production.

III. Facebook

Facebook started in 2003 and is today the world's most popular social media network, with 2.7 billion active users by the end of 2020. By providing those users with the opportunity to upload images and video, it has also become one of the leading UGC platforms. It bought video sharing platform *Instagram* and messenger service *WhatsApp* in 2012 and 2014, respectively. *Instagram* and *WhatsApp* had 1.2 billion and 2.0 billion users by the end of 2020.[246] Facebook also started its own e-commerce marketplace in 2016, offering its user base to buy and sell goods and services privately or professionally.[247]

IV. Apple

Apple had started out as a hardware company. With the launch of its flagship product, the *iPhone,* in 2007 it successfully constructed an ecosystem of products, services and platforms. 20% of the world's 5 billion mobile phone users are using an iPhone and therefore Apple's *iOS* operating sys-

---

244 'Case Studies & Customer Success - Amazon Web Services (AWS)' (*Amazon Web Services, Inc.*) <https://aws.amazon.com/solutions/case-studies/> accessed 30 July 2019. The EU launched an antitrust investigation into these business practices: 'Antitrust: EC Opens Formal Investigation against Amazon' (*European Commission - European Commission*) <https://ec.europa.eu/commission/presscorner/detail/en/ip_19_4291> accessed 30 July 2019.

245 Norman Solomon, 'Why Amazon's Collaboration With the CIA Is So Ominous -- and Vulnerable' *HuffPost* (34:16 500) <https://www.huffpost.com/entry/why-amazons-collaboration_b_4824854> accessed 10 April 2020.

246 'Most Used Social Media 2021' (n 184).

247 Mary Ku, 'Introducing Marketplace: Buy and Sell With Your Local Community' (*About Facebook*, 3 October 2016) <https://about.fb.com/news/2016/10/introducing-marketplace-buy-and-sell-with-your-local-community/> accessed 11 November 2020.

tem.[248] Apple comprises its own web browser (*Safari*), music and video streaming service (*iTunes*) and an app store. While the *iPhone* was revolutionary, it also boosted sales of the *iTunes* music streaming service and the adoption of the app store. *Apple* constantly added new interactive products such as tablet computers, smart watches, and services, like mobile wireless payments, voice recognition, cloud services or video messaging services to its technology platform.[249] Due to their closed nature (*Apple* end devices are usually needed to download and consume content) the company's services are not normally cited as classical online intermediaries. However, the *Apple App* and *iTunes* stores offer third parties to upload and sell their content and can therefore be considered online intermediary services.

V. Microsoft

Microsoft's origins are in software, but it has turned into a true digital platform and data business over recent years. It reinvigorated its search engine *Bing*, making it the world's second most used general search engine.[250] This happened after substantial investment into search technology and data capture thus driving ad revenue.[251] *Microsoft* bought *Skype*, one of the most widely used messenger service with over 300 million users and is transforming it into a social messaging app.[252] In 2016, it bought the leading professional social network *LinkedIn*, with over 260 million active users. The company's *Azure* professional cloud service is the second largest by revenue worldwide behind *AWS*. It also offers a B2C cloud service, *OneDrive*, a web browser, *Microsoft Edge*, and owns the popular gaming brand *Xbox*, which includes interactive gaming and streaming. By virtue of having the most widely used PC operating system (*Windows*)[253] and pro-

248 'Mobile Operating System Market Share Worldwide' (*StatCounter Global Stats*) <http://gs.statcounter.com/os-market-share/mobile/worldwide> accessed 31 July 2019. 'Global Digital Report 2018' (Wearesocial 2018) 94 <https://wearesocial.com/blog/2018/01/global-digital-report-2018> accessed 23 July 2019.

249 Barwise and Watkins (n 7) 31–33.

250 *Google (Search) EU Antitrust Procedure* (n 148) 35.

251 Zuboff (n 5) l 2988.

252 'Skype Adds Snapchat-like AI Photo Effects to Its Mobile App' (*Engadget*) <https://www.engadget.com/2017/11/08/skype-photo-effects/> accessed 31 July 2019.

253 *Windows* is also an operating system for mobile devices, albeit far behind *Google's Android*, and *Apple's iOS*

ductivity software *(Office)* it aims to centralise the process of gathering data from user activities on its various platforms and services.[254]

3. From content to infrastructure control

Taken together, platforms and intermediary services, be it in e-commerce, social networking, video and image sharing, or internet search are used by a majority of the world's population on a daily basis. The world's six most popular websites by traffic volume belong to online platforms, namely search engines (*Google.com, Baidu*), social media and UGC platforms (*YouTube, Facebook, Instagram, Twitter*). Other intermediaries and platforms such as *Amazon, Reddit, Wikipedia, eBay, WhatsApp, LinkedIn, AliExpress, Tmall, Pinterest* and various *Google* country domain search sites are all amongst the top 50 webpages worldwide.[255]

Given their deep exposure to content and internet traffic, the leading players have expanded beyond simply sitting on top of the web application layer. The ongoing shift towards cloud-based content hosting, sharing, online transactions and on-demand entertainment via the systems of these intermediaries has triggered massive investments into physical infrastructure.[256]

All of the larger intermediary platforms have expanded their cloud operations by creating server farms, data centres and high speed data connections across the globe.[257] It is estimated that the leading platform corporations own several million data servers in hundreds of data centres worldwide in order to host content and process user requests and the related

254 Zuboff (n 5) 3036.

255 'Website Ranking: Top Websites Rank In The World - SimilarWeb' <https://www.similarweb.com/top-websites> accessed 1 August 2019.

256 Eli M Noam, 'From The Internet of Science to the Internet of Entertainment' in Johannes M Bauer and Michael Latzer (eds), *Handbook on the economics of the internet* (Paperback edition, EE, Edward Elgar Publishing 2017) 561–563.

257 See, for example, the statement that Google built its owns high-speed network infrastructure for the provision of its *Google Search* and *YouTube* services in *Google LLC v Bundesrepublik Deutschland, C-193/18* [2019] CJEU EU:C:2019:498 [22]. Or Jane Wakefield, 'Facebook Internet Cable "Circumference of Earth"' *BBC News* (15 May 2020) <https://www.bbc.com/news/technology-52676253> accessed 11 June 2020.

traffic data.[258] Today these leading companies control over 50% of the global cloud capacity.[259] Every time a user accesses or shares, and therefore replicates content, they are not only likely to retrieve it from an intermediary platform's server. Moreover, that information will also need to pass through critical interconnection or nodal points when it enters and leaves the realms of the platform's cloud storage and computing ecosystem.[260] The large internet intermediary players are today also the world's leading content providers. The demand for data storage, replication and transport generated by these companies' means they have moved towards the core of the internet by building infrastructures and conducting peering arrangements that parallel the Tier 1 networks.[261]

This marks a change from the former architecture of the web and suggests that intermediaries are increasingly affecting the basic infrastructure, or the core, of the internet.[262] This would confer on these intermediaries' powers to regulate the way content is managed not only on their platforms but also by exerting influence on data transmission. *Lessig's* famous assertion that in cyberspace "code is law"[263] and that the internet would become a zoned place has become therefore ever more real.

E. Summary: socio-technical and economic role of internet intermediaries

Internet intermediaries have seen a spectacular rise in importance over the last twenty-five years of the internet's history. The intermediary landscape has diversified and expanded. Initially, internet access providers were the main gatekeepers that enabled users to go online. However, with the commercial potential of the internet becoming apparent, more content being available and more people using the internet, the first information intermediaries started to emerge. Search engines and e-commerce marketplaces responded to the need to match the unprecedented amount of information

---

258 European Commission, 'Commission Staff Working Document Online Platforms Accompanying the Document Communication on Online Platforms and the Digital Single Market SWD(2016) 172 Final' (n 54) 7.

259 'Amazon Leads; Microsoft, IBM & Google Chase; Others Trail | Synergy Research Group' <https://www.srgresearch.com/articles/amazon-leads-microsoft-ibm-google-chase-others-trail> accessed 1 August 2019.

260 Lametti (n 216) 215–217.

261 Carisimo and others (n 137) 56–57.

262 ibid 55.

263 Lawrence Lessig, *Code and Other Laws of Cyberspace* (Basic Books 1999).

and services on the World Wide Web with the increase in demand for these contents.

Web 2.0 facilitated the sharing of content and the interaction of users online. This new interactivity spurred the emergence of social media networks, UGC platforms and sharing economy business platforms. The most successful intermediaries realised that interactivity brought unprecedented opportunities for capturing users' behavioural data. The more users engaged with the new platforms, shared and consumed content, purchased products and services, collaborated or just stayed online, the more behavioural data could be seized and analysed. This personalised data led to a boon in advertising revenue for these platforms. The successful platforms also used this data to lock in users by further personalising their services. As more content is created and moved online, the leading platforms invested in their own cloud and network infrastructure. These new, growing physical networks have come to rival the traditional physical infrastructure to the point that they now provide core parts of the internet's infrastructure.

The multi-sided platforms that have emerged display unique market dynamics, which are characterised by a tendency to create powerful network effects that can lead to market domination. They have created new markets and are fundamentally disrupting traditional markets. While the intermediary landscape remains vibrant and diverse, a small number of global online intermediaries dominate digital markets currently. These diagonally integrated super-platforms provide for search, information, retail and entertainment.

Today, for the majority of the world's population using the World Wide Web means using an internet platform, most probably one of the world's leading players. This is important in the context of the challenges that consumers and regulators face when dealing with unlawful content on the internet. This challenge is not only global in the sense that the internet is a global medium that cuts across jurisdictions, but also because the content is managed and governed by global corporate entities.

To be clear, this work does not focus on the problems of dealing with unlawful content on the world's dominating platforms, but rather with the general challenge of unlawful content facilitated by online intermediaries. However, their prominent position on the internet has made these large actors attractive targets for all kinds of illicit activity and unlawful content. Regulators approach these companies first when launching policy initiatives because of the comparatively high visibility of unlawful content on these platforms and because of their global presence.[264] These companies are also the defendants in high profile and influential court cases involving unlawful content on the internet.[265]

In the following chapter, the regulatory approaches towards the internet and content regulation will be demonstrated. After an introduction into online intermediary liability, an overview of the regulatory framework for intermediary liability in Europe, the US and some other jurisdictions will be given. This will be followed by a demonstration of key legal challenges that have arisen over the last twenty years with regards to the liabilities of internet intermediaries for unlawful content. The aim is to expose the evolving legal challenges in the light of the changes in the intermediary landscape, market and technological developments that were sketched out here.

---

264 European Commission, 'Code of Conduct on Countering Illegal Hate Speech Online - Results of the 3rd Monitoring Exercise - Fact Sheet | January 2018' (European Commission) <https://ec.europa.eu/newsroom/just/document.cfm?doc_id=49286> accessed 23 August 2018; 'European Commission - PRESS RELEASES - Press Release - Code of Practice against Disinformation: Commission Calls on Signatories to Intensify Their Efforts' <https://europa.eu/rapid/press-release_IP-19-746_en.htm> accessed 2 August 2019. Rowland, Kohl and Charlesworth (n 128) 73.

265 See for example *Viacom* (n 163); *Google France v Louis Vuitton* (n 123); *GEMA v YouTube, 310 O 461/10* (2012) openJur 2012, 36010 (LG Hamburg); *Opinion of Advocate General Szpunar on Eva Glawischnig-Piesczek v Facebook Ireland Limited, C-18/18* [2019] CJEU EU:C:2019:458. Although this is not entirely true for the area of trademarks where *eBay*, the then leading e-commerce marketplace, was in the focus of court cases.

Chapter 3 - Intermediaries and unlawful content – challenges in internet regulation

A. *The subject matter of internet governance*

Regulation of the internet has traditionally focussed on two major aspects: infrastructure and content.[266] Both shall be briefly discussed below.

1. Infrastructure

Consideration of internet regulation or internet governance goes back to the time when the internet still existed as a publicly funded, closed research project. Its release into the market during the 1990s happened out of a deeper appreciation, mainly by US public and academic stakeholders, that the internet could only fulfil its potential through commercial investment into physical infrastructure and exposure to creative market forces.[267]

As explained above, it is a unique design feature of the internet that it integrates and runs almost seamlessly on all underlying physical communication networks, as longs as those networks adopt the different layers of protocols. The term 'infrastructure' of the internet therefore refers to several features: first, there are the physical assets such as data centres, communication lines, exchange points or routers. In addition, this includes less tangible things such as technical standards, software programs or processes, e.g. the internet's protocols, communications standards, data storage or memory, and databases. Finally, end devices, e.g. mobile phones or PCs,

266 Scholte (n 23) 165; Panos Constantinides, Ola Henfridsson and Geoffrey G Parker, 'Introduction—Platforms and Infrastructures in the Digital Age' (2018) 29 Information Systems Research 381; Rolf H Weber, *Shaping Internet Governance: Regulatory Challenges* (Springer Berlin Heidelberg 2010) 4–5. Francesca Musiani, 'Alternative Technologies as Alternative Institutions: The Case of the Domain Name System' in Derrick L Cogburn and others (eds), *Turn to Infrastructure in Internet Governance* (Springer Nature 2016).

267 Castells (n 3) 69; Garcia (n 97) 541–543.

have become an ever more important element of the digital infrastructure.[268]

Given this heterogeneity, one of the first concerns was therefore to ensure that the technical interoperability of the internet's digital infrastructure remained intact once it was commercialised. A technical governance structure was therefore set up by the US Government over the 1980s, while the internet was still a publicly funded undertaking. The regulatory arrangement reflected the US Government's credo of self-regulation.[269] Institutions such as the Internet Corporation for Assigned Names and Numbers (ICANN), the Internet Engineering Task Force (IETF), the World Wide Web Consortium (W3C) or the Internet Society Internet (ISOC) are all private, not for profit organisations that control and decide on matters relating to the internet's address system or the technical standards behind protocols and data communication.

These organisations were set up in a way that allowed for participation by worldwide internet communities and decisions being made on a consensual basis. The role of states is usually limited to representative or advisory functions along with other interest and user groups, such as civil society or technical bodies.[270] For example, most states are represented on the Government Advisory Committee of ICANN, while a number of international organisations act as observers. Overall, there is a strong focus on broad, multi-stakeholder representation and technical expertise.[271] This system initially also coincided with the early internet pioneers' vision of an open and largely auto-regulated cyberspace.

---

268 Constantinides, Henfridsson and Parker (n 265) 381. This digital infrastructure is different to what is sometimes referred to as private infrastructure or platform control over internet infrastructure. That term relates to a platform's technology to manage content hosted on its servers. (See: Robert Gorwa, 'The Platform Governance Triangle: Conceptualising the Informal Regulation of Online Content' [2019] Internet Policy Review Fn 1. or Lina M Khan, 'Amazon—An Infrastructure Service and Its Challenge to Current Antitrust Law' in Damian Tambini and Martin Moore (eds), *Digital dominance: the power of Google, Amazon, Facebook, and Apple* (Oxford University Press 2018). and Francesca Musiani and Laura Denardis, 'Governance by Infrastructure' in Laura Denardis and others (eds), *Turn to Infrastructure in Internet Governance* (Springer Nature 2016) 5.

269 Collins (n 116) 52. Reidenberg (n 90) 921.

270 Weber (n 265) 39–72.

271 For example: 'ICANN Organizational Chart - ICANN' <https://www.icann.org/resources/pages/chart-2012-02-11-en> accessed 8 August 2019. '2016 W3C Internal Reorganization' <https://www.w3.org/2016/08/2016-reorg.html> accessed 8 August 2019.

These governance arrangements have been seen as an early manifestation of a move away from hierarchical regulation to network governance structures, in a bid to adapt to increasingly complex and globalised contemporary society.[272]

Nevertheless, the debate over the control of the infrastructure has also become more political as the economic and public role of the internet increased. The fact that the US was the only nation state that until recently exercised direct control over ICANN, the key organisation when it comes to maintaining the technical infrastructure of the internet, played a major part in this conflict.

The US relinquished its control over ICANN in 2016. It initiated a new governance structure which strengthened industry and civil society sector control and aimed to exclude control of any other state over ICANN. Some commentators have inferred that this change was helped by the fact that the world's leading online intermediaries, which facilitate, some might say control, access to content and growing parts of the digital infrastructure, are US corporations, that, at least up to 2016, shared wider US Government policy concerns.[273]

There is no space here to sketch the political power struggles that have taken place at an international level over the administration over the internet's root servers and the domain name system.[274] However, these developments are also seen as a consequence of the debate over content regulation spilling over into the area of infrastructure governance.[275]

As large internet platforms control significant spheres of the internet's content, leverage over the internet's neutral, content agnostic digital infrastructure is seen as an alternative means to influence or affirm power over the internet and its content flows. This is a specific feature of the open and modular structure of the internet. Content flows can be influenced by con-

---

272 Rolf H Weber', 'Future Design of Cyberspace Law' (2012) 5 Journal of Politics and Law 15, 5; Collins (n 116) 52.

273 Manuel Becker, 'When Public Principals Give up Control over Private Agents: The New Independence of ICANN in Internet Governance' [2019] Regulation & Governance rego.12250.

274 Nanette S Levinson and Meryem Marzowski, 'International Organizations and Global Internet Governance: Interorganizational Architecture' in Derrick L Cogburn and others (eds), *Turn to Infrastructure in Internet Governance* (Springer Nature 2016).

275 See for example: Kenneth Merrill, 'Domains of Control: Governance of and by the Domain Name System' in Derrick L Cogburn and others (eds), *Turn to Infrastructure in Internet Governance* (Springer Nature 2016).

trols over the digital infrastructure: the address system (disabling domains or IP addresses), via labelling/stamping of content at the logical layer (securing or identifying content through data packet header modification and encryption) or by physically controlling exchange points where traffic passes from one network provider or communication system to another.[276] For example, digital infrastructure governance organisations, like ICANN or downstream domain registration services, are increasingly called upon when it comes to fighting unlawful content.[277] By contrast, in other content systems, such as telecoms and television, control can be exerted by keeping networks closed.[278]

2. Content regulation = intermediary regulation?

In its very early days, internet regulation or governance was mainly concerned with digital infrastructure. This changed quickly as connectivity grew and diverse content started to circulate on the commercial web. Since the mid-1990s, cyber law researchers had already remarked on the potential of the internet to attract massive amounts of illegal content and activity and they debated on how to address this challenge.

Johnson & Post represented the cyber libertarian view of a distinct, autoregulated cyberspace in which users and engineers enforced agreed rules through systems operators, user conduct and public education.[279] *Lessig* contrasted this view by predicting that regulators would extend their influence towards the internet and its architecture. They would regulate web access to content by creating boundaries or zones through coding: an example used was the creation of technical protections of copyrighted material. Commercialisation of the web relies on property, *Lessig* argued. Property, in turn, relies on boundaries.[280]

---

276 Christopher T Marsden, *Internet Co-Regulation: European Law, Regulatory Governance and Legitimacy in Cyberspace* (Cambridge University Press 2011) 22–25.

277 Annemarie Bridy, 'Notice and Takedown in the Domain Name System: ICANN's Ambivalent Drift into Online Content Regulation.(Internet Corporation for Assigned Names and Numbers)' (2017) 74., *Coöperatieve Vereniging SNB-REACT UA v Deepak Mehta - C-521/17* [2018] EU:C:2018:639 (CJEU).

278 Marsden, *Internet Co-Regulation* (n 275) 23. This is somewhat undermined by the convergence of these systems with the internet, i.e. Voice over IP (VoIP)

279 Johnson and Post (n 87).

280 Lessig, 'The Zones of Cyberspace' (n 92) 1407–1410.

Without meaning to pre-empt, it should be mentioned that by the early 2000s illegal content on the internet had become a massive problem for policy makers.[281] This was exacerbated by the global spread of the internet, the first sprouts of Web 2.0 activity and the intermediation of content through platforms.[282]

Regulation of content that was facilitated by intermediaries moved gradually to the centre stage of internet regulation and has remained there since.[283] Given the rise of power of intermediaries, online platforms in particular, and the continued prominence of the problem of unlawful information, content regulation has become enriched with other areas of problematic platform dominance, such as competition and privacy law. In line with these more holistic concerns over the unfettered power of online platforms there has been a tendency to draw infrastructure regulation back into this equation.[284] Some commentators have advocated for overcoming the distinction between content and infrastructure regulation.[285] This should be kept in mind in the sectoral analysis of intermediary liability and of content regulation.

It has been a characteristic of content regulation since the internet's beginning that states were seeking to assert their jurisdiction more aggressively than in the area of infrastructure.[286] Unlawful content is defined and regulated differently across jurisdictions, be it hate speech, defamation, intellectual property infringments or terrorist material. The public policy objectives of states may be directly impacted when unlawful material is being accessed and shared by their populations. But the global and distributed nature of the internet's content and infrastructure mean that national en-

---

281 Christopher T Marsden, 'Co- and Self-Regulation in European Media and Internet Sectors: The Results of Oxford University's Study Www.Selfregulation.Info', *Self-regulation, Co-regulation, State Regulation* (OSCE 2004) 95 https://www.osce.org/fom/13844?download=true, or Uta Kohl, 'The Rise and Rise of Online Intermediaries in the Governance of the Internet and beyond – Connectivity Intermediaries' (2012) 26 International Review of Law, Computers & Technology 185, 204–205.

282 Francisco Javier Cabrera Blázquez, 'User-Generated Content Services and Copyright' (2008) 5 iris plus 1.

283 See for example: Hans J Kleinsteuber, 'The Internet between Regulation and Governance', *Self-regulation, Co-regulation, State Regulation* (OSCE 2004) <https://www.osce.org/fom/13844?download=true>. Kleinsteuber mentions internet regulation exclusively in the context of regulating content.

284 Musiani and Denardis (n 267) 5–6.

285 William J. Drake in: Weber (n 265) 6–7.

286 Scholte (n 23) 165.

forcement of content regulation is regularly frustrated. The problem is exacerbated as the internet becomes omnipresent in peoples' lives and, thanks to online platforms, indispensable throughout many parts of the world.

It can therefore safely be presupposed that, at least since the rise of the Web 2.0, internet regulation refers to a large extent to the content management practices of internet intermediaries.[287] These intermediaries are usually not in the first line of responsibility for the creation of unlawful content by their users. Without them, however, worldwide availability of content and its spread would be significantly hampered.

Given this indispensable role of intermediaries for the availability of content some commentators have come to define intermediary regulation as the very substance of cyberlaw today.[288] *Lessig's* assertion of the role of code as a quasi-regulator of user behaviour may still be valid. But this does not mean that law, cyberlaw specifically, is not needed to define and sanction unacceptable and unlawful user behaviour or content.[289]

As this work addresses the responsibilities of platforms *vis-à-vis* unlawful content (in the EU), it is necessary to review and analyse past regulatory efforts made in this area.

B. The emergence of internet intermediary liability

In the following, a brief overview will be given over the emergence of the internet intermediary regimes in the EU, the US and a number of other jurisdictions. Before this, it is appropriate to describe some general consideration of the role of intermediaries and their liabilities in the law. The different justifications for allocating liabilities to intermediaries and the varying types of liability that have developed under different legal systems are important elements that influence the regulation of these actors today.

---

287 Wagner, *Global Free Expression - Governing the Boundaries of Internet Content* (n 136) 104–118.

288 Jacqueline D Lipton, 'Law of the Intermediated Information Exchange' (2012) 64 Florida Law Review 33, 1338.

289 ibid 1342.

1. Justifications for internet intermediary liability in law

I. Moral justifications

Intermediaries, as entities that facilitate commercial and private interactions by third parties, have been existing since well before the internet. Classifieds newspapers, market halls that rent out stalls to traders, or financial service brokers are just some examples of such intermediaries. The discussion on internet intermediary liability is also informed by the doctrinal literature and case law from this pre-internet era. The moral arguments are strongly influenced by utilitarian thinking that can be traced back to *Mills:*

> "*To make any one answerable for doing evil to others, is the rule; to make him answerable for not preventing evil, is, comparatively speaking, the exception. Yet there are many cases clear enough and grave enough to justify that exception. In all things which regard the external relations of the individual, he is de jure amenable to those whose interests are concerned, and if need be, to society as their protector.*"[290]

According to *Mills* the "answerability" or liability of the agent arises out of a failure to act or prevent harm that is caused by one party to another. According to the utilitarian argument an agent would have a duty to act, even where it is against its own interests, when the harm caused leads to a net loss in happiness to society.[291]

On the other hand, following the *Kantian* logic of duty ethics, an intervening agent or intermediary would have a moral duty to act in a virtuous way, i.e. a way that is in line with its moral duties as an actor of society.[292] Under that approach an intermediary would be less likely to focus on the consequences of the harmful acts performed through them but rather be required to abstain from *any* harmful or non-virtuous behaviour.

Lawmakers have the opportunity to impose duties and responsibilities on intermediaries following these moral considerations. According to *Vedder*, content responsibilities imposed on internet intermediaries may be prospective or retrospective.[293] Prospective (moral) responsibilities would

---

290 John Stuart Mill, *On Liberty and Other Essays* (Digireads (2010 edition) 1859) 11.

291 ibid 84.

292 Thomas H Koenig and Michael Rustad, *Global Information Technologies: Ethics and the Law* (West Academic 2018) 67–68.

293 Anton Vedder, 'Accountability of Internet Access and Service Providers – Strict Liability Entering Ethics?' (2001) 3 Ethics and Information Technology 67, 68. Helberger, Pierson and Poell (n 68) 2.

impose duties and obligations on intermediaries aimed at preventing harm. Prospective responsibilities would be a precondition for being able to impose retrospective responsibilities. Retrospective, backward-looking or historic responsibilities would allocate blame to past actions of intermediaries.[294]

At least as regards internet intermediaries, prospective and retrospective responsibilities are reconcilable with utilitarian moral approaches.[295] In the former case, the intermediary's responsibilities are adjusted to their "ability to acquire, comprehend, and act upon socially relevant information."[296] This requires an impact estimation and would result in preventive responsibilities that create the largest net welfare or happiness. Retrospective considerations under a utilitarian scenario would adjust responsibilities to the negative impacts or harms caused, by for example attributing redemptive, retributive measures or by imposing deterrent measures to prevent similar harms in the future.[297]

Deontological approaches try to ascertain the agent's moral duties. In a forward-looking scenario, society would form a consensus view on the wider role of the agent, e.g. the expected moral behaviour of internet intermediaries, and define legal responsibility that correspond to that role.[298] *Yeung et. al.* refers to this as the 'role responsibility' when talking about ethics in artificial intelligence systems and robotics systems.[299] By contrast, retrospective responsibilities allow for verification of whether an intermediary has complied with the moral duties imposed on them in the first place (prospectively). This review would centre on the moral integrity of the agent and allows for balanced and contextual analysis.[300]

---

294 Helberger, Pierson and Poell (n 68) 11; Karen Yeung and Expert Committee on human rights dimensions of automated data processing and different forms of artificial intelligence (MSI-AUT), 'Responsibility and AI' (2019) Council of Europe study DGI(2019)05 48 <https://edoc.coe.int/en/artificial-intelligence/8026-responsibility-and-ai.html> accessed 11 November 2020.

295 Vedder (n 292) 68, 71–73.

296 Dan L Burk, 'Toward an Epistemology of ISP Secondary Liability' (2011) 24 Philosophy & Technology 437, 443.

297 Vedder (n 292) 69.

298 Derek E Bambauer, 'From Platforms to Springboards' (2018) 2 Georgetown Law Technology Review 15, 430.

299 Yeung and Expert Committee on human rights dimensions of automated data processing and different forms of artificial intelligence (MSI-AUT) (n 293) 51–53.

300 Vedder (n 292) 69–70.

The concept of prospective responsibility becomes important in the context of novel technologies and architectures deployed by digital platforms and the uncertainty over the harms they may cause. The debate centres on to what extent harms caused by platforms' own business models and systems were reasonably foreseeable. Meanwhile, retrospective, or historic responsibility would include measures that are taken *ex-post* in order to address and correct harms caused.[301]

II. Economic justifications

According to the cheapest cost avoider theory developed by *Coase* and *Calabresi*[302] liability should be allocated to the economic actor that is able to avoid a wrongdoing at the lowest cost. This cost comprises the economic investment of an entity into the prevention of unlawful activity as well as the external social costs and benefits of that intervention to society. Under this theory "a liability regime is optimal when it creates incentives to maximise the value of risky activities net of accident and precaution costs."[303] Meanwhile there is no unified view on whether a standard of strict, or primary liability, or a fault-based (secondary) liability standard would create the optimal incentives for a cheapest cost avoider.[304]

While originally not focussed on transactions that involve multiple parties, more recent research has looked at the problem of applying the cheapest cost avoider principle to multiple actor scenarios.[305] Intermediaries, or third parties, are drawn into this equation when they occupy positions that are central or indispensable for the activities in question. In this case they

301 Yeung and Expert Committee on human rights dimensions of automated data processing and different forms of artificial intelligence (MSI-AUT) (n 293) 59–68.

302 RH Coase, 'The Problem of Social Cost' (1960) 3 The Journal of Law and Economics 1; Guido Calabresi, *The Costs of Accidents: A Legal and Economic Analysis* (Yale University Press 1970).

303 Emanuela Carbonara, Alice Guerra and Francesco Parisi, 'Sharing Residual Liability: The Cheapest Cost Avoider Revisited' (2016) 45 The Journal of Legal Studies 173, 173.

304 Andrew F Tuch, 'Multiple Gatekeepers' (2010) 96 Virginia Law Review 1583, 1622.

305 Assaf Hamdani, 'Gatekeeper Liability' (2003) 77 Southern California Law Review 53; Tuch (n 303). In addition, the different components of the cheapest cost avoider, such as risk and the value of activities are also being "unpacked" in Carbonara, Guerra and Parisi (n 302) 173–201.

are also referred to as gatekeepers. Broadly speaking, gatekeepers are "... parties who sell a product or provide a service that is necessary for clients wishing to enter a particular market or engage in certain activities."[306]

Under the cheapest cost avoider principle an intermediary would be allocated with legal responsibilities and subsequent liabilities, if, in addition to their gatekeeping, role they have the capabilities to detect and prevent wrongdoings of their clients, or other contractual parties, at a reasonable cost.[307] This presupposes a certain element of control and knowledge of the gatekeeper over the activities of its client.

While there is little doubt today over the utility of enrolling gatekeepers in the fight against unlawful activity, there is much less clarity and agreement over the most efficient and adequate means of how to get it right. This has much to do with the fact that gatekeepers often possess superior knowledge over their clients' activities compared to regulators and have better technical and more effective means to gain such knowledge, evaluate the corresponding risks, and hand out sanctions.

The financial services sector, with its complex technical network of interdependent service intermediaries, such as accounting firms, insurers, rating agencies or auditors, has been an area of predilection for research in this area. This research has been spurred further by the *Enron* accounting scandals and the 2007 subprime financial crisis.[308] However, internet intermediaries have also moved into the focus of economic law theory on gatekeeper regulation, given their essential function as access providers to information and communication.[309]

Economic law theory is still in want of models to determine what kind of liabilities (strict, negligence- or knowledge based) are most effective in a given multiple-gatekeeper context. In addition, the cheapest cost avoider theory is also criticised for its inflexibility. The focus on identifying and ascribing liability to a cheapest cost avoider tends to overlook the opportunities that can be gained from establishing processes and mechanisms that reduce costs.[310] A collaboration of gatekeepers and economic actors and a split of legal responsibilities could result in such a reduction of costs. *Helman and Parchomovsky* and *Helberger et al* have explored this concept of co-

306 Assaf Hamdani (n 304) 58.

307 ibid 99.

308 Stavros Gadinis and Colby Mangels, 'Collaborative Gatekeepers' (2016) 73 Wash. & Lee L. Rev. 797, 812–815. Assaf Hamdani (n 304).

309 Assaf Hamdani (n 304) 99–108.

310 Lital Helman and Gideon Parchomovsky, 'The Best Available Technology Standard' [2011] Columbia Law Review 1194, 1212–1213.

operative responsibility or risk sharing in the area of content regulation and online intermediaries.[311] This involvement of multiple actors, however, is bound to add to the complexity that the cheapest cost avoider principle and economic regulation pose already for much more straightforward dual-actor scenarios. In addition, the unique characteristics of online platform markets have thrown further doubt on the application of economic regulation theories of risk-modelling and cost-benefit analysis to cyberspace.[312]

Courts and regulators in the US and the EU have nevertheless taken up the cheapest cost avoider principle as a justification for allocating liabilities to intermediaries, albeit not always in a consistent way.[313]

2. Primary and secondary liability

There are two possibilities of holding an intermediary liable for unlawful or harmful acts by third parties: primary or strict liability, and secondary liability.

The kind of liability that can be ascribed to intermediaries depends on the type of action or non-action (including non-performed duties and obligations) that justify the attribution of harm. A clear causal relationship between action/omission and the harm caused are a pre-condition for finding liability.[314] *Vedder* argues that this causal relationship is a characteristic of retrospective responsibility and therefore not necessary in finding liability for breach of a prospective duty.[315] An example here would be failure of an agent to comply with a statutorily imposed duty of care or compliance obligation in the absence of actual harm or damage caused by that shortcoming.

---

311 Helman and Parchomovsky (n 309); Helberger, Pierson and Poell (n 68).

312 Niva Elkin-Koren and Eli M Salzberger, 'Law and Economics in Cyberspace' (1999) 19 International Review of Law and Economics 553, 577–580; Cohen (n 19).

313 Graeme B Dinwoodie, 'Secondary Liability for Online Trademark Infringement: The International Landscape' (2014) 37 Columbia Journal of Law & the Arts 463, 499–501.

314 Augustin Waisman and Martin Hevia, 'Theoretical Foundations of Search Engine Liability' (2011) 42 International Review of Intellectual Property and Competition Law 785, 791.

315 Vedder (n 292) 68.

In many cases the borders between primary and secondary liability are fluent and far from clear-cut.[316] Consequently, findings of primary or secondary liability depend on the type of involvement, or the degree of relative responsibility of the actor in the causal chain of events which led to the breach or damage.

It is worth noting that the concept of (intermediary) liability discussed here does not mean contractual liability. Strict or primary liability refers generally to the extent to which an intermediary can be held responsible for the action of others, regardless of whether contracts are in existence or not.[317]

I. Primary liability for intermediaries

Primary or strict liability lies usually with the manufacturer, publisher or creator of a product, service or piece of work. However, in most legal systems this may be extended to other parties, such as intermediaries, if they introduce an additional risk into the issue at stake.[318]

For example, in EU product safety law, distributors have normally indirect, or secondary due care obligations to help ensure that only safe products are supplied to consumers.[319] Once, however, their activities directly affect the properties of a product, such as manipulation, repackaging or in-

---

316 Kohl (n 280) 191. Thibault Verbiest and others, 'Study on the Liability of Internet Intermediaries, Markt 2006/09/E' 54.

317 Without pre-empting the discussions made in this and the next Chapter, this is confirmed by the intermediary liability regime imposed by the ECD (Articles 12 – 15). It stipulates general liability conditions for the actions concerning third parties. However, failure to comply with these conditions may then trigger all sorts of liabilities, including contractual, administrational, tortuous, penal or civil liabilities. Patrick Van Eecke and Maarten Truyens, 'Legal Analysis of a Single Market for the Information Society (SMART 2007/0037) - Part 6 - Liability of Online Intermediaries' (European Commission 2011) 8–9 <https://ec.europa.eu/digital-single-market/en/news/legal-analysis-single-market-information-society-smart-20070037> accessed 4 February 2020; Etienne Montero, 'La responsabilité des prestataires intermédiaires sur les réseaux' [2001] Le commerce électronique européen sur les rails? : Analyse et propositions de mise en oeuvre de la directive sur le commerce électronique 273, 291.

318 Waisman and Hevia (n 313) 791.

319 Directive 2001/95/EC of 3 December 2001 on general product safety (OJ L 11) Article 5 (2).

appropriate handling, they become primarily liable for the safety of the product.[320]

In EU copyright law primary liability normally lies with the person who reproduces protected works without the permission of rightsholders.[321] However, primary liability may also lie with other parties that communicate and make available to the public protected works without seeking necessary permissions.[322] In *The Pirate Bay* ruling the CJEU found that an online platform, which merely indexed entertainment content available for download elsewhere, performed an act of communication to the public. It was therefore directly liable for facilitating the unauthorised peer-to-peer exchange of copyrighted protected works.[323]

The recently passed EU Copyright in the Digital Single Market Directive (DSMD) introduces direct copyright liability on online content-sharing platforms.[324] According to the EU legislator, the additional risk introduced by these intermediaries lies in the fact that: 1) they provide access to large amounts of copyright-protected content; 2) legal uncertainty exists as to whether these platforms perform copyright-relevant acts.[325]

II. Secondary liability

Secondary liability takes account of the fact that a party, although it had no direct part in an action, may still have had a degree of involvement that justifies the impositions of obligations to prevent or end unlawful activities.[326] Failure to fulfil these duties or obligations would then result in liabilities.

---

320 ibid Article 2 (f).

321 Directive 2001/29/EC of 22 May 2001 on the harmonisation of certain aspects of copyright and related rights in the information society 2001 (OJ L 167, 2262001) Article 2.

322 ibid Article 3.

323 *Stichting Brein II* (n 214) paras 38–43.

324 Directive (EU) 2019/790 of the European Parliament and of the Council of 17 April 2019 on copyright and related rights in the Digital Single Market and amending Directives 96/9/EC and 2001/29/EC (Text with EEA relevance.) 2019 (OJ L 130) Article 17. The term content –sharing platforms will be applicable to most UGC or social media platforms.

325 ibid Recital 61.

326 'What Is SECONDARY LIABILITY? Definition of SECONDARY LIABILITY (Black's Law Dictionary)' <https://thelawdictionary.org/secondary-liability/> accessed 13 August 2019.

a. Common law

In common law jurisdictions the concept of secondary liability has been further developed by courts, resulting in the distinction between vicarious and contributory liability.[327]

In vicarious liability an entity is held responsible for the infringing acts of agents over which it exerts control. Apart from the typical liability of the *respondeat superior* for the actions of its employees, this concept has been extended towards other principal-agency relationships in a commercial context.[328] Vicarious liability usually results in courts finding a faulted party strictly liable, regardless of whether the act was performed intentionally or not.

Contributory liability, by contrast, takes knowledge of the infringing activity as a yardstick. The contribution to infringement may happen by participation or by supplying the means to the unlawful activity. Typical cases here relate to the supplying of technology, capacity or advertisement for unlawful acts.[329] Where a party was found to have had knowledge over the unlawful activity or could have been expected to know about it as a reasonably responsible actor, this results in indirect liability and therefore a lesser degree of punishment compared to strict or primary liability. Likewise, courts may look at passive and active knowledge or negligence when determining contributory liability.[330]

Both vicarious and contributory liability

> *"...endorse a form of enterprise liability as a vehicle for creating obligations to police third-party behavior. The risk of liability is such that nearly all (lawful) services are compelled to shoulder a regulatory burden, and the ef-*

327 Alfred C Yen, 'Internet Service Provider Liability for Subscriber Copyright Infringement, Enterprise Liability, and the First Amendment' 88 The Georgetown Law Journal 63, 1872.

328 For example, dance hall operators for the unauthorised performance of music by music bands, or landowners for the unlawful activity of businesses being invited on their premises; more detail in: Burk (n 295) 439–440.

329 ibid 440.

330 Richard W Wright, 'Allocating Liability Among Multiple Responsible Causes: A Principled Defense of Joint and Several Liability for Actual Harm and Risk Exposure' 21 UC Davis Law Review 1141, 1159.

fect perceived by the consumer is a uniform marketplace where policing occurs."[331]

b. Civil law jurisdictions

In the EU, where most countries rely on a civil law legal system, the landscape of secondary liability rules is more disparate. The interplay between differing national secondary liability provisions and their application by courts on the one hand, and EU law on the other, result in a heterogeneous landscape regarding liabilities and remedies.[332] As an illustration, the secondary liability rules in three EU Member States will be briefly mentioned below.

In France, contributory liability is first regulated on a general level by the *Code Civil*.[333] Articles 1240 – 1241 impose civil liability in cases where harm is inflicted and where negligence has caused damage. Both articles are fault based and allow for the allocation of a wide range of civil remedies. The *Code Civil* imposes an intentionally wide obligation for compensation. This follows the civil law tradition of broadly protecting the individual rights of persons on the one hand, while ensuring adaptability of the law to changing circumstances in society on the other.[334] Apart from that, contributory liability can also be established through a duty to act established by statute.[335]

In Germany, contributory liability is expressed by the concept of "*Störerhaftung*" ("interferer liability") laid down in the German civil code

---

331 Matthew Schruers, 'Copyright, Intermediaries, and Architecture' in Francesca Musiani and others (eds), *Turn to Infrastructure in Internet Governance* (Springer Nature 2016) 110.

332 Dinwoodie (n 312) 485.

333 Code civil - Articles 1240 & 1241 (Code civil). Articles 1382 and 1383 prior to the 2016 reform of the Code Civil.

334 Karen Eltis, 'Can the Reasonable Person Still Be "Highly Offended" - An Invitation to Consider the Civil Law Tradition's Personality Rights-Based Approach to Tort Privacy' [2008] University of Ottawa Law & Technology Journal 199, 212–213.

335 For a more detailed description: Martin Vranken, 'Duty to Rescue in Civil Law and Common Law: Les Extremes Se Touchent' (1998) 47 International and Comparative Law Quarterly 934, 937–941. and Valérie Laure Benabou, 'Quelle(s) responsabilité(s) des intermédiaires techniques sur Internet?' (2006) 61 Annales des télécommunications 865.

(BGB).[336] This implies a wilful, causal contribution to the infringing act and the possibility of preventing the violation through a reasonable duty of care. It results in courts imposing injunctions, but usually not damages.[337] Outside of this, statutes may, like in France, provide for specific duties of care, subsequent tort liabilities and remedies (including damages). In Germany, as in other jurisdictions, the distinction between secondary, interferer style liability, and direct liability caused by abetting or contributing to an infringing act has become increasingly difficult to make.[338] This is due to the complex and often opaque involvement of online platforms in the information intermediation process. The distinction is made even more difficult by the fact that both liability concepts usually presuppose the violation of certain duties of care.[339]

Italian law applies secondary liability mainly in the form of vicarious liability following the *respondeat superior* doctrine. By contrast, contributory liability is less clearly expressed and would mainly be applied through the principles of joint or several liability (in the Italian Civil Code).[340]

Some authors have contrasted a broad approach towards contributory liability in civil law with a more rigid approach in common law. In the latter, they argue, a legal duty of care has never existed *per se.*[341] Precedence-based common law resulted in the development of categorised torts, each defined by specific criteria, to be verified by tests applied in courts.[342]

It is impossible to give a comprehensive overview of secondary liability rules across all Member States here. However, it can be safely assumed that standards of secondary liability that apply concepts of negligence through failure of applying a reasonable duty of care are in place throughout the

---

336 Bürgerliches Gesetzbuch Article 1004.

337 M Leistner, 'Structural Aspects of Secondary (Provider) Liability in Europe' (2014) 9 Journal of Intellectual Property Law & Practice 75, 79.

338 Thomas Hoeren and Viola Bensinger (eds), *Haftung Im Internet: Die Neue Rechtslage* (De Gruyter 2014) 395–396.

339 ibid 395.

340 Elisa Bertolini, Vincenzo Franceschelli and Oreste Pollicino, 'Analysis of ISP Regulation under Italian Law' in Graeme B. Dinwoodie (ed), *Secondary liability of internet service providers* (Springer Berlin Heidelberg 2017) 141–142. Codice Civile 1942 Article 2055.

341 Vranken (n 334) 935.

342 John DR Craig, 'Invasion of Privacy and Charter Values: The Common-Law Tort Awakens' (1997) 42 McGill Law journal 355, 363; Eltis (n 333).

EU Member States and other jurisdictions, albeit in different forms and with various types of sanctions.[343]

These considerations shall be kept in mind during the review of online intermediary case law in this and the next Chapter, and when discussing policy reactions and proposals for intermediary regulation.

As a general rule, secondary liability therefore hinges on two elements: 1) control of the agent over the other parties' activities and 2) knowledge of potential or actual breaches of law or injuries to other parties. In both cases, liability would be caused by failure to comply with obligations that could be reasonably expected from the agent given its degree of control and knowledge.[344] The active or passive involvement of the intermediary may be an additional vector to indicate the degree of liability. Control, knowledge, and active versus passive engagement are also the most controversial issues in the current debate over the duties and liabilities of online platforms for unlawful content, as will be explained later.

3. Early case law on internet intermediaries

In the 1990s, the internet and internet intermediaries were a new, technologically complex and rapidly expanding phenomenon. Unlawful content on the internet related mainly to defamation, hate speech or illegal pornographic material (including child pornography). Copyright cases were limited to violations of rights in images or literary works.[345] Issues with massive illegal downloading of music and videos through peer-to-peer file sharing or the sharing of such material through platforms did not arise before the start of the new millennium.

Nevertheless, the characteristics of the internet and digital technology already posed an entirely new regulatory challenge. Matters of jurisdiction, detection and enforcement became more complex. Originators of information could easily remain anonymous. Perpetrators could avoid law enforcement authorities through removal or relocation of content into other jurisdictions. Prosecuting consumers for accessing or downloading infringing

343 For a comprehensive overview by different EU jurisdictions and in the US regarding the liability of ISPs for third party content prior to the ECD, see: Gerald Spindler and Fritjof Börner (eds), *E-Commerce Law in Europe and the USA* (Springer 2002); Leistner (n 336) 89. and Verbiest and others (n 315) 22, 57.

344 Waisman and Hevia (n 313) 785.

345 Davies (n 27). Mayer-Schönberger and Foster (n 96).

material or products was likewise inefficient. Digitisation, in connection with the new nature of the internet, meant that copyrighted material could be multiplied, accessed and distributed widely, instantaneously and without loss in quality.[346]

When faced with these new legal challenges, courts responded in different ways. Many of these early cases dealt with IAPs which acted either as conduits or hosts for unlawful content, or both. They mostly ran newsgroups or bulletin boards through which their users shared information in texts and images. An illustration of cases prior to the creation of dedicated intermediary liability provisions gives a useful insight into the underlying diversity of legal approaches and interpretations of the roles and responsibilities of these new actors. Some basic controversies, such as whether intermediaries can be considered editors, what responsibilities they have in preventing unlawful activity, or the effect of their intermediation on substantive aspect of law governing the material in question, remain or have re-emerged as central liability issues.[347] This poses the question of whether the legal regimes that developed out of the cases discussed below have been fully effective and future proof. The following review shall also serve as an outline of key trends and the variety of possible ways of assessing and allocating liabilities and responsibilities for the new practices of information intermediation that emerged on the internet.

I. Case law in the EU

In Europe, many of these cases reflected a general perception that intermediaries should be made directly liable for unlawful content posted on their networks, in particular where they undertook efforts to monitor for infringing material or where they were notified of the potentially unlawful nature of content.

a. United Kingdom

In one of the first cases brought against an internet intermediary in Europe, an UK court found that the IAP *Demon Internet* was liable as a publish-

346 Hector L MacQueen and others, *Contemporary Intellectual Property: Law and Policy* (2nd ed, Oxford University Press 2011) 240–242.
347 Lipton (n 287) 1350.

er for defamatory content posted on one of its newsgroups.[348] The judge rejected the defendant's claim that they were *"merely owners of an electronic device through which postings were transmitted."* Instead, the defendant *"chose to store...postings within their computers."*[349] Having been found a publisher, the defendant had to pass the liability test of the 1996 UK Defamation Act,[350] which it failed because it did not react to notices received by the plaintiff concerning the defamatory nature of the content. It therefore did not take reasonable care and failed the knowledge test after receiving the notice. Regarding the knowledge test, the court called on a 1937 judgement[351] in which a golf club operator failed to remove defamatory content from one of its noticeboards. The case appears to construct a combination of vicarious and contributory liability, by combining elements of control and actual knowledge. The actual knowledge test was only applied once the defendant was found to be a publisher. The outcome of this case has been interpreted as obliging an IAP to monitor proactively for potentially unlawful information that passes through its system.[352]

The tendency of holding internet hosts liable for information posted on their sites was continued in the rulings of *Sir Elton John v Countess Joulebine*[353] and *Totalise v Motley Fool.*[354] In the former case the website provider was liable because they ought to have known that the information posted was privileged, and consequently released onto an online newsgroup under a breach of confidence. Meanwhile in *Totalise,* an IAP was ordered to disclose the identity of an anonymous user who had posted defamatory material.

---

348 *Godfrey v Demon Internet Limited* [1999] High Court Of Justice Queen's Bench Division 998-G-No 30, EWHC QB 244.

349 ibid 35.

350 Defamation Act 1996 c.31 1996 s 1.

351 *Byrne v Deane (1937)* 1 KB 818.

352 Charlie Wood and others, 'Great Britain' in Gerald Spindler and Fritjof Börner (eds), *E-commerce law in Europe and the USA* (Springer 2002) 291.

353 *Sir Elton John and others v Countess Joulebine and others [2001] MCLR 91* (Unreported).

354 *Totalise Plc v The Motley Fool Ltd & Anor [2001] EWHC 706 (QB) (19 February 2001)* (Unreported).

b. Germany

In Germany, the ISP *CompuServe* was initially successfully prosecuted for facilitating access to child pornographic material through its newsgroups.[355] In 1998, its managing director, *Felix Somm,* incurred criminal charges for facilitating the distribution of illegal materials and for failing to block access to them despite being notified of illegal content by German authorities. The decision was reversed one year later, noting that *CompuServe GmbH*, the German subsidiary of the US based group, did not have control over the information posted. Once it had gained knowledge, it was not in a position to physically remove the materials from the US-based servers. Meanwhile, existing German law at the time would have also protected *Somm* and the German subsidiary of *CompuServe Inc.* It was noted that the German laws were in compliance with the ECD, which was to become EU law one year later.[356]

In *CD Bench,* the Munich Upper Regional Court had to decide whether the operator of a File Transfer Protocol (FTP) server was liable for and had to stop and prevent the allegedly illicit download of software hosted on its system.[357] The FTP operator, a university, mirrored the content of seven software archives, containing around 40,000 pieces of software on its servers and offered unrestricted access to it. The Munich court first ruled that the University was not responsible for content hosted on its FTP server if it did not have any influence over that content. Secondly, it would only be liable if it had "positive knowledge", therefore presuming at least partial intent of the fact that it hosted illicit content. Thirdly, liability would then only arise if it was technically reasonable to prevent these downloads. The Munich Court saw control (influence) and knowledge as preconditions for liability. The most controversial issue was, however, whether it was reasonable to expect that the operator prevent downloads of illicit content. The Court answered in the negative. It found that in the absence of a technical solution a manual review of 40,000 software packets for infringing software was unreasonable. The technical and economic effort did not justify the limited effectiveness of the measures.[358] The assessment of the

355 *CompuServe* [1998] AG München 8340 Ds 465 Js 173158/95, MMR 1998, 429.

356 Lothar Determann, 'Case Update: German CompuServe Director Acquitted on Appeal' (1999) 23 Hastings International and Comparative Law Review 17, 123.

357 *CDBench, 6 U 5475/99* [2000] MMR 2000 617 (OLG München).

358 *CDBench, 6 U 5475/99* [2000] MMR 2000 617 (OLG München) [619]; Wulff-Axel Schmidt and Monika Prieß, 'Germany' in Gerald Spindler and Fritjof Börner (eds), *E-commerce law in Europe and the USA* (Springer 2002) 216.

proportionality of preventive measures was to be developed further by German courts in the years to come.

c. France

Union des étudiants juifs de France (UEJF) et La Ligue contre le racisme et l'antisémitisme (LICRA) v Yahoo Inc et Yahoo France[359] was one of the more high-profile early cases on the liability of internet intermediaries in the EU that took place prior to the enactment of the ECD. Decided in 2000, US ISP *Yahoo* was successfully prosecuted for making Nazi memorabilia, hosted on an auction site on its US servers, available for purchase to residents in France. The sale and possession of these materials is prohibited under the French penal code. The Paris court did not call into question *Yahoo.fr's* involvement in enabling the marketing of these goods by providing a link to the US site on *Yahoo.com* from its search engine. The judges ordered *Yahoo.com* in the US to disable access to the illegal memorabilia in question for users accessing the site from France. The judges found that it was possible to identify the country-of-origin of 70% of users from the IP address. An IP based block (geo-blocking) of France-based users would be technically possible and effective.

Meanwhile *Yahoo.fr* was ordered to warn all users of the illegality of these acts who, based on use of its search engine or other activity, were provided with a link to infringing material on *Yahoo.com*.[360] The decision concerning *Yahooo.com* was overturned by a US court five years later. The court rejected the notion that a French court should have a say over the regulation of speech in the US.[361]

The French law on liability for third party content received several iterations prior to the ECD. The above judgement reflects a situation of legal uncertainty at the time over the liability of IAPs and hosts for the material

---

359 *UEJF and Licra v Yahoo! Inc and Yahoo France* (2000) (Unreported) (Tribunal de Grande Instance de Paris).

360 For a detailed analysis see: Carolyn Penfold, 'Nazis, Porn and Politics: Asserting Control Over Internet Content' (2001) 2 The Journal of Information, Law and Technology <http://elj.warwick.ac.uk/jilt/01-2/penfold.html> accessed 2 October 2019.

361 *Yahoo! Inc v La Ligue Contre Le Racisme Et L'Antisemitisme* [2006] 9th Cir 2006 01-17424, 433 F.3d 1199.

hosted or referenced through their services.[362] While *Yahoo.com* was not incriminated for intentionally infringing acts, there was little question over it being liable for the sale of products offered by third parties in France. Likewise, *Yahoo.fr's* search engine and hosting services were ordered to warn users without any debate having taken place over the liability for the actions of third parties.

These uncertainties are also displayed in a 1999 case involving privacy and image rights of a fashion model, who had nude pictures of her posted on several websites.[363] Stocking images and making them accessible to others conferred on the four hosting providers in question professional diligence and duty of care obligations, which they had breached. Apart from clear terms and conditions that indicated the prohibition of illicit acts, the hosts would have had to prevent the availability of manifestly unlawful material on their sites. Putting in place an internal word search that was able to detect manifestly unlawful content was deemed as technically feasible and in line with principles of freedom of expression. Likewise, failure to notify and warn the editors of the existence of illicit material was a breach of professional duties. The court lamented on the lack of state regulation and nascent self-regulation in this area, which necessitated reference to the standards laid down in the Code Civil (the then Article 1382).

d. Italy

Italian judgements provide two conflicting interpretations on the liabilities of internet intermediaries for third party content.[364] This is certainly due to the less clearly expressed concept of contributory liability mentioned above,[365] combined with the new challenges posed by the internet. In a number of cases in the late 1990s Italian judges have, on the one hand, found that an IAP acted as an editor. It had therefore a duty to verify the

---

362 Isabelle Renard and Marie Amélie Barberis, 'France' in Gerald Spindler and Fritjof Börner (eds), *E-commerce law in Europe and the USA* (Springer 2002) 133.

363 *Madame L v les sociétés Multimania Production, France Cybermedia, SPPI, Esterel* (1999) (Unreported) (Tribunal de Grande Instance de Nanterre).

364 Massimiliano Mostardini, Luigi Neirotti and Massimo Travostino, 'Italy' in Gerald Spindler and Fritjof Börner (eds), *E-commerce law in Europe and the USA* (Springer 2002) 368–371.

365 Bertolini, Franceschelli and Pollicino (n 339) 141–145.

lawfulness of the content lest it be found guilty of negligent behaviour, thus causing contributory liability for facilitating illegal acts.[366]

By contrast, other decisions rejected the editor-analogy and added that it would be technically impossible for an IAP to check all the content it transmitted or hosted.[367] Commentators at the time also criticised the jurisprudence for not distinguishing between IAPs and hosting providers. Each business model results in different levels of control over content, which could be decisive for whether civil liability existed or not.[368]

e. Belgium

Belgium Courts have tended to find IAPs and internet hosts liable for third party content prior to the ECD. For example, a bulletin board was found responsible for copyright infringing material on its site and charged with monitoring the postings of its users' activities for further infringing material.[369] Likewise, an IAP was found responsible for providing access to illegal content on third party websites.[370] Courts found IAPs and hosting providers liable as contributors under tort, unfair competition, copyright and trademark law.[371]

The outcomes of the cases above offer an interesting diversity of approaches towards the liability of intermediaries. Intermediaries were occasionally charged with primary or strict liability for the acts performed by third parties. Where they were not found to be editors there does not seem to be a coherent line of argument over when vicarious or contributory liability would be attributed. This may have to do with the fact that secondary liability is differently construed in the different Member States. Secondly, it appears that there is a high degree of uncertainty over the level

---

366 see *Order of the Tribunal of Napoli on 8 August 1997*; *Order of the Tribunal of Roma on 22 March1999*; in: Mostardini, Neirotti and Travostino (n 339).

367 *Order of the Tribunal of Cuneo on 23 June 1997*; *Order of the Tribunal of Roma on 4 July 1998*; in: Bertolini, Franceschelli and Pollicino (n 317) 144; and in: Mostardini, Neirotti and Travostino (n 339) 369.

368 Mostardini, Neirotti and Travostino (n 363) 369.

369 *Cour d'Appel d'Anvers, 28 février 2002* (2002) (Unreported). in: Verbiest and others (n 315) 50.

370 *Cour d'Appel de Bruxelles, 13 février 2001* (2001) (Unreported); Benoit Michaux and Stefan Van Camp, 'Belgium' in Gerald Spindler and Fritjof Börner (eds), *E-commerce law in Europe and the USA* (Springer 2002) 56.

371 Michaux and Van Camp (n 369) 56.

of control and knowledge intermediaries have over the information on their systems. Thirdly, uncertainty exists over what standard of control and knowledge intermediaries should be expected to have from a moral, technical and legal standpoint.

These cases also reflect the relatively one-dimensional scope of the intermediary landscape at the turn of the millennium. The vast majority of legal challenges is directed at ISPs, which mainly act as infrastructure and communication network providers, and, in some, instances as hosting platforms for content and information.

II. Case in law in the US

A short overview of US case law provides a useful illustration of the commonalities and differences to the developments in the EU. In the US, the first cases on intermediary liability had emerged by the middle of the 1990s. This does not come as a surprise considering that the country was the pioneer in user adoption and commercialisation of the internet. Arguably, this precedence helped inform the legislator in its design of a regulatory framework for intermediary liability.

a. Cubby, Inc v CompuServe, Inc.

The earliest case involving the liability of an intermediary was *Cubby, Inc v CompuServe, Inc (Cubby)*,[372] which dealt with defamatory content and was decided in 1991. *CompuServe* was an early IAP that also ran an online information service in the form of an electronic library which contained over 150 special interest fora. One of these fora was dedicated to journalistic content and run and managed by a media company subcontracted by *CompuServe*. Defamatory content appeared on the forum in question, posted by a content provider working for the forum operator. The plaintiffs argued that *CompuServe* carried the defaming statements and was a publisher thus incurring a higher standard of liability than a distributor. *CompuServe* rejected the charges claiming it had no control over the entities responsible for the forum's content nor had it been notified of any defamatory statements.

372 *Cubby, Inc v CompuServe Inc,* (1991) 776 F. Supp. 135 (SDNY).

The New York judges reviewed *CompuServe's* business model and agreed, finding that it could only be judged by standards that apply to distributors of publications, but not editors. They likened *CompuServe* to a library or bookstore. Consequently, *CompuServe* was protected under the US Constitution's First Amendment which guarantees freedom of speech and freedom of press. The adequate liability standard applying to CompuServe was "whether it knew or had reason to know of the allegedly defamatory [...] statement."[373] However, no evidence was provided that substantiated that *CompuServe* was in a position to have this knowledge. The judges also rejected claims of vicarious liability. The media company running the news forum acted merely as an independent contractor of *CompuServe*, with all editorial control being delegated to the former. Likewise, the entity posting the comments had no contractual relationship whatsoever with *CompuServe*.

b. Stratton Oakmont v Prodigy Services Co.

Stratton Oakmont,[374] the plaintiff, was an investment firm that filed a libel claim for defamation against *Prodigy Services*, a computer network which hosted bulletin boards and had a subscriber base of 2 million users at the time. One of these boards carried defamatory statements against *Stratton*. The latter alleged that *Prodigy* acted as an editor of information and was therefore responsible for the defamatory comments made. *Stratton* rested its claim on the fact that *Prodigy* actively promulgated and enforced its content policies and used software to pre-screen publications for offensive content.

The judges agreed with the plaintiff. *Prodigy's* conscious choice to monitor and censor communication and invest in technology and staff to enable these activities made it an editor. The court also tried to disperse fears that this could motivate bulletin board hosts to abandon any control over communications lest they would incur full liability. Market demand, they presumed, would reward those providers that choose to police content and therefore risk higher exposure in order to offer value added services, such as a family-friendly communication environment, like *Prodigy's*.

---

373 ibid 141.
374 *Stratton Oakmont, Inc v Prodigy Services Co* (1995) 1995 WL 323710 (NY Sup Ct).

While described as irreconcilable with the *Cubby* ruling,[375] the judges in *Stratton* explicitly stated that they fully agreed with the principles in *Cubby*. However, while both *CompuServe* and *Prodigy* were seen as computer bulletin boards, it was the latter's conscious choice to "regulate" the content on its boards that exposed it to a higher standard of liability, which in this case was equal to editorial control. The judges may, however, have underestimated that the combined business risk of investing into content management and incurring higher liabilities could act as a serious deterrence for internet businesses at the time. Another way of reading it is, that a provider that engaged in good faith efforts to prevent illegal acts would incur higher liability than one that allowed all and every content to circulate unchecked on its systems. The decision was criticised on these grounds and had an important influence on the Communications Decency Act, which was to be passed one year later.[376]

c. Playboy Enterprises, Inc. v Frena

Copyright was another area that eventually moved into the limelight of courts due to the emergence of the internet and its intermediaries. The internet posed an existential challenge to copyright, since at its core it relies on the act of copying and sharing of information. As such, digitisation and the internet affect the substance of copyright law.

In *Playboy Enterprises, Inc. v. Frena*, the eponymous magazine charged the operator of a bulletin board, Mr. Frena, with copyright violation. Users of *Frena's* service could, for a fee, view, and up- and download photos to and from various directories stored on the bulletin board. *Playboy* held the copyright in some of these images and claimed that its rights were violated by the unauthorised sharing of these images. *Frena* contradicted this by stating that he was not aware of the images having been uploaded by its users and that he removed them once notified of their existence. The court found *Frena* directly liable for copyright infringement. It held that "intent

375 Bryan J Davis, 'Comment: Untangling the "Publisher" versus "Information Content Provider" Paradox of 47 u.s.c. § 230: Toward a Rational Application of the Communications Decency Act in Defamation Suits against Internet Service Providers' (2002) 32 New Mexico Law Review 75.

376 Citron and Wittes (n 197) 456–458; Felix T Wu, 'Collateral Censorship and the Limits of Intermediary Immunity' (2011) 87 Notre Dame Law Review 293, 313–317.

or knowledge is not an element of infringement, and thus even an innocent infringer is liable for infringement."[377]

d. Sega Enterprises, Ltd. v MAPHIA & Religious Technology Center v Netcom

This somewhat harsh judgement was toned down in *Sega Enters., Ltd. v. MAPHIA*[378] which concerned the distribution of copyright protected video games through a bulletin board operated by *Maphia*. In contrast to *Frena*, the courts found in *Sega* that the bulletin board operator was only liable for contributory infringement. *Maphia's* system was merely used by another party to commit the copyright breaches. The acts lacked therefore volition or causation, which would be necessary elements for a direct infringement claim to be successful.[379] In *Maphia*, the court applied reasoning from a previous ruling, *Religious Technology Center (RTC) v Netcom.*[380]

Netcom has been seen as establishing a line of argument that holds IAPs liable for contributory infringement in copyright disputes involving internet intermediaries.[381] The plaintiff *RTC* had asked IAP *Netcom* to stop a user on a bulletin board operated by another party on *Netcom's* system. The user had posted allegedly copyright infringing materials. However, *Netcom* refused to block access of the user, claiming this would unduly restrict other users on the Bulletin Board in question. It also claimed that it was impossible to pre-screen the postings of the user. Although technically possible, *Netcom* chose not to bring in filtering systems nor did it chose to archive or control traffic or content on its systems. The judges found that in the absence of control over the information passing through Netcom's system it would be an unduly broad construction of copyright to hold the company directly liable.[382] Therefore the important precedence this case established was that, no matter whether an intermediary proactively

377 *Playboy Enterprises, Inc v Frena* (1993) 839 F. Supp. 1552 (MD Fla) [1559].

378 *Sega Enterprises Ltd v MAPHIA* (1994) 857 F. Supp. 679 (Dist Court, ND Cal). & *Sega Enterprises Ltd v MAPHIA* (1996) 948 F. Supp. 923 (Dist Court, ND Cal).

379 *Sega Enterprises Ltd v. MAPHIA* (n 377) para 932.

380 *Religious Technology Center v Netcom On-Line Com* (1995) 907 F. Supp. 1361 (Dist Court, ND Cal).

381 Schruers (n 330) 110–112.

382 *Religious Technology Center v. Netcom On-Line Com.* (n 379) s 1372.

worked to prevent or investigate infringement claims, it would be subject to contributory infringement.[383]

The rulings of these early cases already demonstrate the diverse and fluid nature of facts and arguments involved when trying to pin down the obligations of intermediaries on the (new) internet. In the EU, distinct national traditions of secondary liability and varying interpretations of the role of the different internet intermediaries in hosting different kinds of unlawful content led to diverging rulings and calls for regulatory clarification.[384] In the US, a tendency of allocating certain protections against primary liability to these new intermediaries appeared to crystallise. However, the legal conditions for such outcomes were far from established.[385] Given the rising importance of the internet as a means for expression and as a commercial and economic factor, many countries in the world undertook to establish statutory rules for the obligations of online intermediaries. This will be discussed in the following section.

C. *Regulatory Frameworks of internet intermediary liability*

1. US

A discussion of intermediary liability law anywhere in the world would be incomplete without at least a short account of the US regulatory framework. Apart from its technical origins, the internet as a commercial endeavour also broke ground in the US. As shown above, this gave rise to the earliest legal disputes between new internet actors, users and rightsowners.

The need to codify the conditions under which internet intermediaries would be held liable arose out of several considerations. First, the US common law system of secondary liability, which would be applicable to the activities of internet intermediaries by default, is very complex. The different liability standards (e.g. contributory and vicarious liability) are applied in nuanced ways depending on the type of offense and legal area, varying between copyright, trademark or defamation law.[386] Given the rapidly de-

383 Schruers (n 330) 111.

384 As shown above in the case of: *Madame L. v. les sociétés Multimania Production, France Cybermedia, SPPI, Esterel* (n 362).

385 Andrej Savin, *EU Internet Law* (Second edition, Edward Elgar Publishing 2017) 152.

386 Salil K Mehra and Marketa Trimble, 'Secondary Liability of Intermediary Service Providers in the United States: General Principles and Fragmentation' in

veloping internet sector, this did not bode well for consistency of court rulings and predictability for this still volatile sector. Secondly, and partly as a result, the emerging internet intermediary industry had started to convince the legislator successfully that legally mandated limitations for content liability were necessary in order to safeguard the future of the internet.

Both in the US and the EU, intermediaries portrayed themselves as mere conduits and access providers. They stored files, web pages or email accounts for users and businesses on their servers. But they did not hold themselves to be content providers.[387] Indeed the early case law seemed to support this. Most early legal disputes concerned the likes of *CompuServe*, *Demon Internet*, *Yahoo* or *Netcom*. The emerging liability rules were influenced by these perceptions of online intermediaries.

I. Communications Decency Act 1996

The US decided for sectoral regulation of intermediary liability. The Communications Decency Act's Section,[388] which was put in place as section 230 of the Telecommunications Code in 1996, regulates the liabilities of "interactive computer services" for any offensive material.[389] This covers a broad array of claims, from defamation and discrimination to unfair competition.[390] The definition of an interactive computer service provider is sufficiently large to include any internet intermediary service that provides internet access and content storage and does not, at the same time, act as an information content provider. The CDA provides pure intermediaries with a blanket exemption from any liability over content provided by third parties. The famous "Good Samaritan" provision[391] exonerates internet intermediaries from being treated as a speaker or publisher, thus excluding primary liability for any information provided by another content provider. At the same time, it protects intermediaries from any secondary liability where these undertake voluntary measures in good faith, that aim to restrict the availability of offensive material and assist content providers

Graeme B. Dinwoodie (ed), *Secondary liability of internet service providers* (Springer Berlin Heidelberg 2017) 94–99.

387 Edwards, 'The Fall and Rise Of Intermediary Liability Online' (n 119) 60–61.

388 47 USC § 230. The detailed name 47 USC 230: "Protection for private blocking and screening of offensive material".

389 ibid 230 (c).

390 Ardia (n 129) 379.

391 47 USC § 230 s 230 (c).

in these efforts. This resulted in a broad safe harbour for the activities of internet intermediaries in the US. The protection does not, however, extend to any violation of US federal criminal statutes, such as for example material harmful to minors or content and communications relating to the sexual exploitation of children.[392]

The policy objectives of the CDA were clear: promote and protect a nascent and vibrant internet industry against liability risks during an essential phase of business expansion. The 2000 dot.com crash four years later was to serve as a reminder of the precariousness of many early internet business models. Still, policy makers wanted to encourage the industry to protect users, and especially children, against the worst excesses of unlawful, objectionable and offensive content on the internet. Conscious of the ambiguity of making decisions on speech and the broad protections afforded by the US Constitution in that respect, they therefore protected intermediaries against any mistakes when removing content as part of their good faith efforts. In addition, they wanted to assure that the knowledge accrued through voluntary content policing could not be turned against these intermediaries, as happened in the *Prodigy* case. The CDA was in line with the US Government's philosophy that regulation should be light touch and based on voluntary industry commitments.

No further analysis shall be given here of the effectiveness and consequences of this crucial piece of law on intermediary liability. Suffice it to state that it engendered a significant body of case law.[393] The majority of cases grapple with the rather blunt distinction between interactive computer services and content providers. Courts also felt compelled to investigate in more detail the degree of control and influence intermediaries had on content. The outcome of these inquiries would, of course, have an effect on the availability of the safe harbour defence. Case law appeared to become more frequent after 2003. This coincides with the emergence of Web 2.0 and the increasingly interactive and intrusive role of new types of intermediaries in the intermediation of content.

The debate over the CDA has become fiercer ever since. On one side of the spectrum it has been criticised as overshooting its target and intrusively regulating speech.[394] On the other side, the US Government's traditional

---

392 'Section 230 of the Communications Decency Act' <https://www.eff.org/issues/cda230> accessed 8 October 2019 (e) (1).

393 Ardia (n 129).

394 Raymond SR Ku and Jacqueline D Lipton, *Cyberspace Law: Cases and Materials* (2nd ed, Aspen Publishers, Inc 2006) 112–115.

hands off approach towards intermediaries is blamed for unduly protecting the practices of internet giants which have long ceased to be neutral intermediaries.[395] Yet others see the CDA as a guarantor of free expression on the internet.[396] However, while the broad anti-indecency provisions of the CDA had been successfully challenged by several court rulings,[397] the safe harbour passage of section 230 has remained largely intact. The only major change to this statute was made in 2018, when acts that facilitate sex trafficking were exempted from the protections offered by the CDA.[398] The US Government under President Trump moved to break, however, with this traditional light touch approach towards intermediary regulation. A review of the CDA by the US Congress, published in 2020, resulted in proposals that would see the current liability immunities being reduced significantly where it concerns content that relates to illegal drugs, child abuse, cyberstalking or terrorism.[399]

II. The Digital Millennium Copyright Act 1998

The DMCA[400] introduced a separate liability regime to the existing US Copyright code, targeting breaches of copyright committed via the internet. Section 512 DMCA, also called the safe harbour provisions, creates a somewhat higher standard of intermediary liability exemptions than compared to the CDA for speech violations. Section 512 creates four categories of intermediaries: a) service providers that merely transmit, route or transmit information – this would be IAPs under the typology offered in the previous chapter; b) services that cache information;[401] c) services that

395 Zuboff (n 5) ss 2015–2058.

396 'Section 230 of the Communications Decency Act' (n 391).

397 Amongst others by *Reno v American Civil Liberties Union* [1997] US Supreme Court 96-511, 521 US 844.

398 The Stop Enabling Sex Traffickers Act (SESTA) and Allow States and Victims to Fight Online Sex Trafficking Act (FOSTA) amend the CDA 47 USC § 230 (e) (5).

399 US Department of Justice's, 'Department of Justice's Review of Section 230 of the Communications Decency Act Of 1996' (2020) <https://www.justice.gov/ag/department-justice-s-review-section-230-communications-decency-act-1996> accessed 7 October 2020.

400 17 U.S.C. § 512.

401 Caching is an intermediary storage of information in hardware during the data transmission process on the internet, which happens for the sole purpose of retrieving future; similar information requests faster. It is a form of buffering.

store information at the request of a third party – these services are referred to as hosting services, and d) information location tools that link or refer users to another online location, i.e. search engines.[402]

All of these service providers need to act at the direction of third parties as a precondition in order to afford the safe harbours.[403] Information hosts and search engines have to meet a knowledge standard in order to avail themselves of (secondary) liabilities for copyright infringement. They must not have actual knowledge of infringing activity or must not be aware of any circumstances from which infringing activity is apparent. Once aware or in possession of such knowledge they need to remove infringing information or access to it expeditiously.[404] This "red flag" knowledge, which the company acquires in the course of its business, would need to stand a subjective and an objective test. The former would try to establish whether the intermediary had actual knowledge under the concrete circumstances. The objective test would then verify whether the knowledge was indeed "red flag" knowledge, i.e. whether to a reasonable person acting under the same circumstances the infringing nature of the activity would have been (blatantly) obvious.[405]

This test has become one of the more contentious issues. The exact circumstances of when the more complex and interactive intermediaries of today have actual, i.e. specific, knowledge of an infringing activity are notoriously difficult to establish by courts across the globe.

Knowledge can also be attained through notifications of a claim of infringement. The format, content and procedure for such notifications are laid down in detail under a notice-and-take-down process, which includes provisions for counter-claims.[406] The latter tries to limit the potential chilling effect from indiscriminate removal of content by intermediaries anxious to avoid liability. At the same time, intermediaries are freed from any liability against properly administered, but erroneous takedowns,[407] which

---

James Bottomley, 'Understanding Caching' [2004] Linux Journal <https://www.linuxjournal.com/article/7105> accessed 8 October 2019.

402 17 U.S.C. § 512 (a) - (c).

403 System caching services shall not be treated here in detail as there has been little controversy over their intermediary status and liabilities.

404 17 U.S.C. § 512 (c)(1) (A) - (C), (d) (1) (A) - (C).

405 'House of Representatives - Digital Millennium Copyright Act of 1998' (1998) Rept. 105–551 53.

406 17 U.S.C. § 512 c (3).

407 ibid (g)(1).

can be seen as an equivalent to the "Good Samaritan" protection afforded under the CDA.

Hosts can not avail themselves of these liability protections if they derive a direct financial benefit from infringing activities. The definition of direct financial benefit has become more difficult in the wake of Web 2.0 business models,[408] such as *YouTube*, which would "only" generate ad revenue from the display of copyright infringing content on its site.

Finally, the DMCA affords a limited array of injunctive relieves against intermediaries and does not allow for any monetary relief.[409]

Similar to recent initiatives to weaken the safe harbour protections of the CDA, the current US Government has also voiced its intention to roll back key protections afforded to internet intermediaries against copyright infringements conducted via their systems.[410] This will be mentioned in more detail in the section on copyright in Chapter 4.

III. Trademarks – The Lanham Act

Internet intermediaries have affected trademark law in several ways. First, cybersquatting concerns the registration and use of domain names that are confusingly similar to trademarks for abusive purposes. Secondly, since the rise of the commercial search engine, advertisers have used keywords of brands to display products of competitors to consumers. Thirdly, online marketplaces have been utilised by sellers offering imitations or counterfeits of successful, often prestigious, brands.

US trademark law (the Lanham Act)[411] had traditionally not dealt with secondary or indirect infringement. These kinds of conflicts are resolved by the owner of the mark, who directly pursues the infringer. Contributory liability in trademark infringement was only confirmed by the US Supreme Court in 1982.[412]

---

408 Rowland, Kohl and Charlesworth (n 128) 96.

409 17 U.S.C. § 512 (j).

410 'Section 512 of Title 17 - A Report of the Register of Copyrights' (United States Copyright Office 2020) <https://www.copyright.gov/policy/section512/> accessed 29 June 2020.

411 The Lanham (Trademark) Act 1946 (15 USC § 1051 et seq).

412 *Inwood Laboratories Inc v Ives Laboratories, Inc,* (1982) 456 U.S. 844 (United States Supreme Court). In: Jasmine Abdel-Khalik, 'Is EBay Counterfeiting?' in Hannibal Travis (ed), *Cyberspace law: censorship and regulation of the Internet* (Routledge 2013) 144;

As cybersquatting became more of a problem, the US passed the Anticybersquatting Consumer Protection Act (APCA)[413] in 1999 as an amendment of the Lanham Act. This statute charges domain name registrars and registries with liability for injunctive or monetary relief only where they fail to expeditiously comply with a court order concerning a fraudulent domain registration.

Apart from this, no specific statutory provision protects online intermediaries in trademark infringement cases. US courts have instead sought to apply direct infringement tests as well as the knowledge standard tests for contributory infringement in cases against search engines[414] or online marketplaces.[415] Both types of liability claims have generally been unsuccessful. Regarding contributory infringements, it is worth noting that, where online intermediaries acted on specific infringements notified by rightsowners, they were generally vindicated. US courts have applied a high bar to the standard of general knowledge over infringing activity.[416] It appears that for trademarks courts have arrived at similarly broad intermediary protections as in those guaranteed through the safe harbour provisions in the DMCA.

2. EU

I. Setting the scene for an intermediary liability framework

From 1996 the EU started to formulate a strategy aimed at capturing the opportunities of the internet and e-commerce for Europe. The 1996 Rolling Action Plan[417] and the 1997 Communication on "A European Initiative in Electronic Commerce"[418] brought together a number of separate

413 Anticybersquatting Consumer Protection Act (ACPA) (15 USC § 1125(d)).

414 *Rosetta Stone Ltd v Google, Inc* (2012) 676 F 3d 144 (4th Cir).

415 *Tiffany (NJ) Inc v eBay Inc* (2010) 600 F. 3d 93 (2nd Cir).

416 *Rosetta Stone Ltd. v. Google, Inc.* (n 413) para 163. *Tiffany (NJ) Inc. v. eBay Inc.* (n 414) para 107. And the detailed discussion of *Tiffany* in: Abdel-Khalik (n 411) 47–57.

417 European Commission, 'Communication from the Commission on" Europe at the Forefront of the Global Information Society: Rolling Action Plan", COM(96) 607 Final' (1996).

418 European Commission, 'Communication from the Commission: A European Initiative in Electronic Commerce, COM(97) 157 Final' (1997)

policy initiatives into a broad strategy.[419] It was aimed at promoting investments in technology and infrastructure, a favourable business environment, making a proactive impact on global cooperation and creating a coherent regulatory framework for e-commerce in the single market[420] as the EU entered the new millennium.

The EU had addressed the problem of illegal and harmful content on the internet in a separate Communication in 1996,[421] which recognised the variety of illegal and harmful content online and the need for innovative and differentiated legal and technological responses. This Communication acknowledges Member States' responsibility for applying their national laws to the new online environment but warned against diverging legal responses by national legislators. There was a risk that national solutions distorted competition, hampered the free movement of services and fragmented the internal market.[422]

The Commission did not appear to actively plan for an EU liability framework at that stage. It did, however, explore EU wide action as one policy option in conjunction with more industry self-regulation. It also encouraged Member States to come together and lay down minimum standards on criminal content.[423] However, it threatened with direct regulatory intervention should national legal solutions start to generate market fragmentation.

II. The E-Commerce Directive

a. General principles and scope

Two years after its Communication on illegal and harmful content on the internet, in December 1998, the Commission submitted a proposal for the

---

419 There were, for example, Information Society Initiatives on standardisation, education, illegal and harmful content, social and regional policy, infrastructure, market liberalisation, research and investment, and more.

420 European Commission, 'Communication from the Commission: A European Initiative in Electronic Commerce, COM(97) 157 Final' (n 417) 1–2.

421 European Commission, 'Communication from the Commission: Illegal and Harmful Content on the Internet, COM(96) 487 Final' (1996) <https://core.ac.uk/reader/5078710> accessed 9 October 2019.

422 ibid 4–5.

423 ibid 24–25.

ECD.[424] The ECD finally became EU law on 8 June 2000 as *Directive 2000/31 on certain legal aspects of information society services, in particular electronic commerce, in the Internal Market*. Based on the objectives in the European Initiative on Electronic Commerce, it approximates EU Member States' laws in several areas, one of which being the liability exemptions accorded to internet intermediaries. The additional areas include national provisions of information society service providers, the establishment of service providers, commercial communications, electronic contracts, code of conducts and the cooperation between Member States.[425]

The preoccupation to remove cross-border obstacles within the single market could serve as one explanation for the broad horizontal regime the ECD sought to establish. The shared legislative competence of the Directive is derived from Articles 47(2), 55 and 95 of the EC Treaty, now corresponding to Articles 53 (1), 62 and 114 of the Treaty of the Functioning of the European Union (TFEU).[426] Article 53 concerns provisions aimed at persons that want to take up and pursue activities as self-employed persons. It allows the EU to issue directives aimed at stipulating conditions for the mutual recognition of professional qualifications under the freedom of establishment. Article 62 provides shared competences in the area of the provision of services. Finally, Article 114 confirms the remit of the ECD as a legal instrument adopted as part of the shared, and therefore limited, competence of the EU as detailed in Article 4 (2) TFEU.

Accordingly, the Directive rests on the principle of proportionality and therefore pursues a minimum harmonisation approach. This means it lays down only measures that are strictly needed for the operation of the internal market and the safeguard of general interest principles, particularly the protection of minors, human dignity, consumers and public health.[427] The Commission tried to avoid overregulation.[428] This is underlined by commitments in the ECD to light touch regulatory intervention, specifically the use of self-regulatory measures. Article 16 and 17 of the ECD emphasise the promotion and creation of voluntary codes of conduct by industry,

---

424 European Commission, Proposal for a European Parliament and Council Directive on certain legal aspects of electronic commerce in the internal market 1999 [1999/C 30/04].

425 Directive 2000/31 (ECD) Article 1 2.

426 Treaty on the Functioning of the European Union (Consolidated versions of the Treaty on European Union and the Treaty on the Functioning of the European Union 2016) 2016 (OJ C 202).

427 Directive 2000/31 (ECD) Recital 10.

428 Büllesbach (n 51) 295.

professional and consumer associations, as well as the use of out-of-court settlement procedures.[429]

The ECD seeks to create a harmonised regulatory environment for information society service providers (ISSPS). ISSPs had been defined under the Technical Standards and Regulations Directive in 1998 as "any service normally provided for remuneration, at a distance, by electronic means and at the individual request of a recipient of services."[430]

ISSPs' activities are regulated by the country-of-origin principle. The country-of origin-principle in Article 3 (1) obliges Member States to ensure that ISSPs comply with the laws of the Member State in which they are established throughout the territory of the EU. The non-discrimination principle in Article 3(2) precludes Member States from restricting the freedom to provide information society services from any other Member State.[431] This means that services covered by the ECD will only need to follow the rules of the Member State in which they are established. This straightforward use of the country-of-origin principle can be attributed to the EU's desire to establish a regulatory framework for electronic commerce that is harmonised.[432]

On the other hand, the impracticalities of the strict country-of-origin rule come to the fore when courts need to enforce certain decisions, such as for example information requests against ISSPs, including online intermediaries. National or local authorities are, strictly speaking, required to approach the EU jurisdiction where the entities are established, even where subsidiaries may exist in their own country.[433] This may cause additional administrative burdens. The country-of-origin principle in the ECD

429 Directive 2000/31 (ECD) Articles 16 and 17.

430 Directive 98/48/EC of the European Parliament and of the Council of 20 July 1998 amending Directive 98/34/EC laying down a procedure for the provision of information in the field of technical standards and regulations 1998 (OJ L 217) Article 1 2. (a). This was later amended by Directive 2015/1535/EU of 9 September 2015 laying down a procedure for the provision of information in the field of technical regulations and of rules on Information Society services.

431 Directive 2000/31 (ECD) Article 3 1. & 2.

432 Rowland, Kohl and Charlesworth (n 128) 268–269.

433 *Auskunftsanspruch über persönliche Daten von Nutzern einer Onlineplattform wegen des Verdachts der Zweckentfremdung von Wohnraum* [2017] VG Berlin 6 Kammer 6 L 162.17, DE:VGBE:2017:07206L162170A at 33 - 39. In this case, brought against a local branch of *AirBnB*, Berlin authorities were denied an information disclosure order. The administrative court of Berlin applied the ECD's country-of-origin principle by ruling that the order would need to be filed against *AirBnB's* EU seat of establishment in Ireland.

has therefore been seen as encompassing a conflict of law rule because it directs towards the law of the seat of establishment of the ISSP.[434]

The country-of-origin principle applies to the coordinated field of law defined in Article 2. It covers only matters that are inevitably linked to taking up and pursuing the activities of an ISSP. This would be matters relating to authorisation and qualifications, the behaviour of the service provider, the quality of content, including advertising and contracts, and the liability of ISSPs. Other requirements related to the delivery of goods as such and to services provided offline are excluded.[435] Recital 21 provides an explanation of this exclusion by making it clear that the scope of the coordinated field relates to the online activities of ISSPs. It underlines this delineation with a list of excluded requirements relating to tangible goods. This includes safety standards, labelling obligations, liability for goods and requirements relating to the delivery or the transport of goods, including the distribution of medicinal products. By drawing this line, the EU appears to have been alert to the risk that rules set for online service providers could eventually pervade areas outside the scope of the ECD. This could be the case for business services that feature an electronic component, but whose substance is governed by rules to which the EU Treaties allocate a different level of competency.

The *Ker-Optika* case is a good example for the dangers that the EU perceived from blurring the functional scope of ISSPs and the boundaries of the coordinated field.[436] The CJEU ruled that a national provision which prohibited the sale of contact lenses via the internet due to public health concerns was invalid. It distinguished provisions covering the *sale* of contact lenses via the internet from those that governed the *supply* of these products. The former activity was clearly under the remit of the ECD's coordinated field while the latter fell outside its scope.[437] Restricting the online sale of these goods in order to safeguard the legitimate public health interests relating to the supply was deemed disproportionate.

It should be kept in mind that the ECD was drafted in the late 1990s and that legislators, like most other people, were unlikely to predict the emergence of platforms such as *Facebook, YouTube, Airbnb* or video-on-demand services such as *Netflix*.

434 Büllesbach (n 51) 306.

435 Directive 2000/31 (ECD) Article 2 (h) (i) (ii).

436 *Ker-Optika bt v ÀNTSZ Dél-dunántúli Regionális Intézete*, C-108/09 [2010] EU:C:2010:725 (CJEU)

437 ibid 23–30.

However, as e-commerce and the online platform economy have been evolving, further conflicts are programmed. Beyond the iterations of the CJEU in defining the status of newer sharing economy platforms like *Uber*[438] and *Airbnb*,[439] challenges may also arise in the area of product and intermediary liability. A clear delineation of on- and offline activities, it seems, may become more difficult in the future in view of the fact that e-commerce increasingly happens via online marketplaces and platforms whose true involvement in the transaction is not clear.[440] For example, the strict circumscription of the coordinated field to online activities leads to the situation that mandatory product labelling requirements for products sold online would be excluded, while the display of product labels in online advertising would not.[441]

Moreover, over recent years EU consumer and product law have been adapted in several areas to include, e.g. new labelling rules for online sales[442] or the classification of online marketplaces as professional traders.[443] This trend is likely to blur the borders between on- and offline rules even further.

b. The liability (exemptions) of intermediaries

The liability of intermediaries is addressed in Section 4, Articles 12 – 15 of the ECD. The 1996 Communication on Illegal and Harmful content on the internet had still favoured an industry-led, auto-regulatory approach. By late 1998 this had changed. For one, it did not appear that the emerging intermediary sector managed to come up with its own rules. Secondly, and

---

438 *Uber* (n 208).

439 *Opinion of Advocate General Szpunar on YA, AIRBNB Ireland UC, Hotelière Turenne SAS, Association pour un hébergement et un tourisme professionnel (AHTOP), Valhotel, C-390/18* [2019] ECLI:EU:C:2019:336 (CJEU).

440 European Commission, 'UCP Directive Guidance' (n 57) 122–127.

441 Rowland, Kohl and Charlesworth (n 128) 269.

442 For example, the Energy-labelling and Toys Safety Directives require that specific product information (warnings, energy efficiency classification) is made visible to consumers, which includes online sales: Regulation (EU) 2017/1369 of 4 July 2017 setting a framework for energy labelling and repealing Directive 2010/30/EU 2017 (OJ L 198) Article 5 (1) (a); Directive 2009/48/EC of 18 June 2009 on the safety of toys 2009 (OJ L 170) Article 11 (2); European Commission, 'Toy Safety Directive 2009/48/EC - An Explanatory Guidance Document Ref. Ares(2016)1594457' 42–43.

443 European Commission, 'UCP Directive Guidance' (n 57) 122–123.

as has been shown earlier, contradictory rulings by EU Member States' courts, including diverging interpretations of whether and how intermediaries should be made liable for third party content, had emerged over the second half of the 1990s. Thirdly, with the CDA (1996) and the DMCA (1998), the US had charged ahead with two key acts that regulated the liability exemptions of intermediaries .

Contrary to the US' sectoral approach, the EU chose a horizontal framework to regulate the liability protections of online intermediaries. It applies to all information society services (ISSPs) that act as intermediary service providers (ISPs). This latter term is, however, not clarified by the ECD. Instead, the EU creates three separate types of ISPs, which are defined through Articles 12 – 14 of the ECD.

It should be underlined that the intermediary liability regime introduced though the ECD favours a fault-based, secondary liability regime, that relies on negligence[444] and is outside of the remit of contractual liability. In fact, the ECD expressly excludes laws that apply to contractual obligations relating to consumer contracts.[445] However, the negligence bar, as will be seen, is substantial, affording intermediaries comfortable protections against liability.

Mere conduits

The first type of intermediaries are "mere conduits" of information, specified in Article 12 (1). Mere conduits relay information via a communication network or provide access to it. They would typically be the IAPs that provide individuals with an internet connection. A mere conduit would need to fulfil three conditions in order to be exempted from liability for the content it transmits. Mere conduits must not: initiate the transmission, select its receiver and select or modify the information contained in the transmission.

Article 12 (2) provides further clarification by specifying that this activity includes the transient storage of information where that storage takes place entirely as part of the transmission process. This means the information may not be kept for longer than reasonably necessary for the transmis-

444 Giancarlo Frosio and Sunimal Mendis, 'Monitoring and Filtering: European Reform or Global Trend?' [2019] Center for International Intellectual Property Studies Research Paper No. 2019-05 29, 4–6.

445 Directive 2000/31 (ECD) Recital 55.

sion.[446] Where content is being modified this must happen purely out of technical necessity during the transmission process.

The above means in essence, that a mere conduit is understood as not being an editor of the information it transmits. According to Recital 42, it needs to acts in a purely technical, automatic and passive nature[447] in order to avail itself of any content responsibility. In other words, by the same Recital, the conduit does not have either control or knowledge of the information transmitted.

These liability exemptions do not preclude courts or authorities of Member States to issue injunctions, such as in the form of orders aimed at terminating or preventing an infringement. Recital 45 specifies that these orders can be injunctions aimed at any infringement and that they include the removal and the disabling of access. Again, failure to respond to such orders would result in liability. In the area of the internet and mass communication, the intervention of the mere conduit or IAP is technically the most straightforward and, arguably, easiest way for an authority or court to interfere with the communication. Given that the conduit acts more like a neutral carrier, similar to a parcel or postal service, the justifications for marshalling the support of the IAP are likely to be justified by the cheapest cost avoider rationale rather than moral principles. As will be seen later on, there have been numerous cases in which courts and authorities have been seeking to enlist the services of IAPs to remove, stop and prevent unlawful content and activity.

The IAP landscape has also undergone diversification since the early days of the internet. With the spread of wireless internet and portable devices, new mere conduits have emerged. Wi-Fi access providers and wireless telecommunication service providers are IAPs in their own right. Public Wi-Fi networks are a feature of everyday life. These services are run by all kinds of businesses, from retailers, restaurants or coffee shops, hospitals, schools and universities, airports and transportation services to public authorities. This poses additional enforcement challenges also in this area.[448]

Caching

Caching is the process of automatic, intermediate and temporary storage of information as it travels the internet. This act is not restricted to specific services or part of a business model. Rather it is an essential technical activ-

---

446 ibid Article 12 (2).
447 ibid Recital 42.
448 *Mc Fadden* (n 139).

ity that aims at economising data traffic. Data packets are copied and forwarded at various connection points of the internet. At the end points of a communication, copies of popular web pages are often stored longer than needed for the actual transmission processes. They can then be called up when requested repeatedly so as to reduce data traffic on the network. The storage done through caching is therefore essentially the same as the transient storage covered under Article 12 (2), just that the storage is prolonged for the reasons explained. This provision was drawn up to protect the users and providers at the end points of a communication from being found liable for temporarily stored, cached content on their devices.[449]

In order to qualify for the liability exemptions attached to cached content the provider must meet five conditions:[450] They must a) not modify the cached content, b) comply with conditions on access to the information. This can be understood as meaning that, for example, if the cached content is paid content, the provider may not unduly access it or derive money from it. In addition, c) the information must be regularly updated according to industry standards, d) the provider must not interfere with technology that measures the use of the information (i.e. web statistics) and e) they will need to remove or disable access to cached content as soon as they gain knowledge of the fact that the source information was removed due to a court or authority order. This is meant to prevent that unauthorised content remains on the internet in the form of cached copies.

Courts or authorities may impose injunctions to require caching intermediaries to terminate or prevent an infringement.[451] In practice, this provision has however not posed any significant problems.

Hosting services

Article 14 defines hosting services as intermediaries that store information provided by a recipient of the service. The latter is the third party, such as for example a content uploader, advertiser or seller, that uses the hosting providers' service in order to post, share or sell content, service or product offers. The difference to the other two categories of intermediaries is that the storage that is provided by hosting services constitutes the actual service. The duration of the storage is decided by the third party, the recipient

449 Arno R Lodder and Andrew D Murray (eds), *EU Regulation of E-Commerce: A Commentary* (Edward Elgar Publishing 2017) 49.
450 Directive 2000/31 (ECD) Article 13 (1) (a) - (e).
451 ibid Article 13 (2).

of the service, and therefore not transient. The hosting service relies therefore on the recipient using an IAP to access the internet in the first place.[452]

In line with this deeper involvement, the bar for a full exemption from liability is higher than for IAPs and caching services. For this threshold to be met the following two conditions have to be fulfilled:

> *"a) the provider does not have actual knowledge of illegal activity or information and, as regards claims for damages, is not aware of facts or circumstances from which the illegal activity or information is apparent; or*
> *b) the provider, upon obtaining such knowledge or awareness, acts expeditiously to remove or to disable access to the information"*[453]

Failure to meet these requirements would imply negligence on the part of the intermediary and confer liability. This liabilityw is broad and horizontal. It can be evoked by the legal provisions that govern the illegal information and activity that the intermediary failed to act upon, be it copyright or trademark violations, IP infringements, unfair commercial practices, hate speech or other illegal content, or unfair competition.[454]

According to Article 14 (2) the hosting services provider is not eligible for the liability exemptions if it exerts authority or control over the recipient of the service, i.e. the party that requests the storage.

Article 14 (1) and (2) address therefore the two most prominent criteria for secondary liability: knowledge and control. Actual knowledge implies all liabilities, including criminal, while awareness of facts and circumstances confers civil liability.[455]

While courts and national authorities may impose injunctions to terminate or prevent infringements, like for conduits and caching services, Member States also have powers to establish procedures for information hosts that lay out how illegal content must be removed or made inaccessible.[456]

Hosting services make up a large variety of intermediaries today. This includes search engines, social media and UGC platforms, online marketplaces and cloud services, which have all been classified as hosting services on numerous occasions at Member State and EU level. This is a far cry

---

452 Büllesbach (n 51) 331.
453 Directive 2000/31 (ECD) Article 14 (1) (a) - (b).
454 Van Eecke and Truyens (n 316) 9.
455 Rowland, Kohl and Charlesworth (n 128) 86; Lodder and Murray (n 448) 50.
456 Directive 2000/31 (ECD) Article 14 (3).

from the more monochrome intermediary landscape from before the turn of the millennium, when IAPs, some of them hosting their newsrooms, a limited number of search engines, or the very first e-commerce marketplaces, such as eBay, ruled the scene.

No monitoring obligation

Article 15 (1) limits the possibility of Member States to oblige intermediary service providers to terminate or prevent infringements. When requiring intermediaries to prevent infringements, Member States must ensure that this is not done in a way that would oblige the service provider to monitor for illegal activity or information on a general basis or to actively search for indications of such activity. This prohibition applies to all categories of intermediaries covered by the ECD in Articles 12 – 14.

For one, this limitation is absolutely necessary for filling the neutrality condition with meaning. Were intermediaries obliged to monitor internet traffic on a general manner in order to identify and prevent illegal information, they would inevitably gain actual knowledge and acquire a degree of control that disqualifies them from immunity.[457]

Secondly, at the time when the ECD was drafted, there was a concern that more onerous obligations to proactively scrutinise the rapidly growing volume of internet traffic could pose a barrier for the development of the young internet economy.[458] A threat of liability resulting from such obligations could lead to new, innovative start-ups needing to invest undue amounts of resources into the prevention and removal of potentially illegal information. This view is supported by the EU's first implementation report of the ECD of 2003. Recognising the unsatisfactory state of filtering technology at the time, Article 15 was to protect internet intermediaries against being required to manually checking potentially millions of websites, which would pose a disproportionately high burden.

Thirdly, the 2003 report also mentions that an obligation to monitor for illegal activity and information on a general basis would result in the removal of legal content and therefore come into conflict with freedom of speech.[459] In addition, this kind of obligation could also lead to an undue

457 Büllesbach (n 51) 333.

458 *Savin*, EU Internet Law, p. 161-162.

459 European Commission, 'First Report on the Application of Directive 2000/31/EC of the European Parliament and of the Council of 8 June 2000 on Certain Legal Aspects of Information Society Services, in Particular Electronic Commerce, in the Internal Market' (2003) COM(2003) 702 final 14 fn 73.

interference with the fundamental right to privacy.[460] This would be the case if an intermediary needed to identify data of users that uploaded content, such as IP, email addresses, or user names, as part of its general monitoring efforts. Later case law at EU level underlined the role of Article 15 (1) as a safeguard for these fundamental rights.[461]

The scope of Article 15 (1)'s limiting capacity *vis-à-vis* the power of courts and authorities to impose injunctions in order to prevent specific infringements[462] has been another controversially debated feature of the ECD's liability framework.[463] From a legal point of view the controversy concentrated on the reach of specific, preventive injunctions that were effective while remaining proportional in the sense required by Article 15 (1).[464] On a more technical level, the argument turned around finding measures, such as filtering systems, that responded to injunctions targeted at preventing a particular type of illegal activity or information but did not result in the entire web traffic needing to be monitored by the intermediary.[465]

Art. 15 (2) ECD imposes two additional obligations on intermediaries. Member States may provide that public authorities be informed by intermediaries of illegal activities. In addition, the latter can be forced by authorities to provide them with the identity of service recipients with whom they have concluded service agreements. This passage was clarified by the CJEU in *Promusicae*. According to the CJEU, Member States need to balance fundamental rights (in this case intellectual property) and privacy when they design legal frameworks that deal with the communication of users' personal data.[466]

---

460 *Büllesbach (ed.)*, Concise European IT Law, p. 333.

461 Particularly in *Belgische Vereniging van Auteurs, Componisten en Uitgevers CVBA (SABAM) v Netlog NV, C-360/10* [2012] EU:C:2012:85 (CJEU); and *Scarlet Extended* (n 133).

462 As provided for in Recital 47 ECD.

463 Commission, SEC(2011) 1641 Final, supra (fn. 11) para. 47–51.

464 *L'Oréal (UK) Ltd v eBay International AG, eBay Europe SARL, eBay (UK) Ltd and others, C-324/09 [2011] EU:C:2011:474 (CJEU) para. 141; Eva Glawischnig-Piesczek v Facebook Ireland Limited, C-18/18 [2019] CJEU EU:C:2019:821 paras 41 - 46*

465 *Nolte/Wimmers*, in: GRUR 16(2014), p. 16, 21-23; *Valcke/Kuczerawy/Ombelet*, Did the Romans Get it Right? What Delfi, Google, eBay, and UPC TeleKabel Wien Have in Common, p. 11.

466 *Promusicae* (n 140) paras 65–68.

3. Comparing the EU and US intermediary liability frameworks

The EU framework was clearly inspired by earlier US efforts. Articles 12 – 15 ECD draw from both the CDA and the DMCA. The division into functional types of intermediaries is obviously borrowed from the DMCA.[467] Nevertheless, the ECD does not provide a separate classification for search engines, which has caused separate problems due to the unique function and nature of these intermediaries. This will be discussed in more detailed in this chapter, but also, as relevant, in the sectoral analysis of Chapter 4. The knowledge standard that defined the availability of immunities in the ECD for information hosts (Article 14 (1)) is virtually identical to that of the DMCA for information hosts and search engines.[468] Both frameworks are essentially based on utilitarian arguments that favoured wide immunities out of concerns over the viability of new intermediaries' business models and the promotion of new economic actors and innovation.[469]

However, the ECD also offers important differences to the US system. The ECD's intermediary liability provisions are generally considered more rigid than those of the US.[470] The EU applies the stricter conditions of liability immunities used in the US under the DMCA for copyright violations to all content areas. There are also some specific procedural options that are absent from some or all of the sectoral pieces in the US. For example, the CDA does not provide for any court orders or injunctions targeted at preventing infringements,[471] nor does it give authorities the option to oblige online intermediaries to provide information on illegal activity or the identity of service recipients.[472] EU Member States may define reason-

---

467 17 U.S.C. § 512 (a) - (d).

468 ibid.

469 Koenig and Rustad (n 291) 148–149; Marcelo Thompson, 'Beyond Gatekeeping: The Normative Responsibility of Internet Intermediaries' (2016) 18 Vanderbilt Journal of Entertainment & Technology Law 783, 786–787; Giancarlo F Frosio, 'Why Keep a Dog and Bark Yourself? From Intermediary Liability to Responsibility' (2018) 26 International Journal of Law and Information Technology 1, 32. This is also evident from the CDA in 47 USC § 230 (b) (1) - (2), the ECD, in Recital 2, and the policy document that sets out the motivations for the ECD liability framework: European Commission, 'Communication from the Commission: Illegal and Harmful Content on the Internet, COM(96) 487 Final' (n 420) 7.

470 Savin (n 384) 148; Rowland, Kohl and Charlesworth (n 128) 93.

471 Directive 2000/31 (ECD) Articles 13 (2) & 14 (3) .

472 ibid Article 15 (2).

able duties of care for intermediaries, which is an option that is not explicitly provided for in the US.

At the same time the ECD is also less specific.[473] For example, there are no detailed provisions on formats and procedures for notice requests and for counterclaims, such as those available under the DMCA).[474] Instead, these procedures are left to Member States to regulate according to their national laws.[475] The ECD also does not offer any protections for "Good Samaritans" that voluntarily engage in identifying and removing illegal content.

These differences may be explained by three reasons:

1) The more rigid EU approach towards intermediary liability is in line with an overall more interventionist stance when it comes to regulating economic actors. It should be kept in mind that in the drafting phase of the ECD varying national views on intermediary liability had to be accommodated. Different opinions on the meaning of "actual knowledge", the preventive obligations of intermediaries and the cooperation with authorities, as well as how far the remit of the EU went in prescribing liability conditions and expressing itself on sanctions, had to be reconciled.[476]
2) The lack of detail may be explained by the constitutional set up of the EU. The ECD needs to comply with the principle of subsidiarity. In areas where the EU has no exclusive competency, its remit is therefore limited to measures where Union level intervention would be more effective.[477] The ECD operates in the area of shared competency with the Member States. Consequently, it harmonises only in areas where it is absolutely necessary for the smooth operation of the internal market.
   The failure to spell out more detailed notice requirements and to formulate sanctions can arguably be attributed to this minimum harmonisation approach.[478] In addition, and as stated above, secondary liability systems are deeply rooted in the legal traditions of civil and private law

473 Edwards, 'The Fall and Rise Of Intermediary Liability Online' (n 119) 74.
474 17 U.S.C. § 512 (c) (3) & (g) (3).
475 Directive 2000/31 (ECD) Article 14 (3).
476 European Union Council, 'Progress Report - E-Commerce Directive - 8891/99' (1999) 150–153.
477 Treaty on European Union (Consolidated versions of the Treaty on European Union and the Treaty on the Functioning of the European Union 2016) 2016 Article 5 para 3.
478 Büllesbach (n 51) 295. Van Eecke and Truyens (n 316) 41 fn 227.

systems within Member States.[479] Further harmonisation would have impinged on the competencies of Member States to regulate in civil criminal matters concerning defamation[480] or hate speech.[481] Areas such as copyright fall under shared competency. They limit EU intervention to aspects that concern commercial and internal market matters only.[482]

Any sectoral intervention related to unlawful content on the internet and intermediary liability at EU level would therefore need to be restricted to areas where the EU has at least shared competency. The ECD thus takes the function of a framework directive as regards intermediary lability protections and the activities of ISSPs at the content layer in general.[483]

3) Finally, it can be added that the EU wanted to ensure that its framework plugged into global efforts to regulate the internet and the information society. Recital 60 states the need for simple and clear rules that are consistent with international efforts in order to avoid EU companies being placed at a competitive disadvantage.[484] This Recital can also serve as proof and explanation for why the ECD was influenced so clearly by the DMCA and the CDA.[485]

---

479 Dinwoodie (n 312) 484; Benabou (n 334) 468–469.

480 Savin (n 384) 126–30; 'Out of Balance - Defamation Law in the European Union: A Comparative Overview for Journalists, Civil Society and Policymakers' <http://legaldb.freemedia.at/wp-content/uploads/2015/05/IPI-OutofBalance-Final-Jan2015.pdf> accessed 3 December 2020.

481 Jon Garland and Neil Chakraborti, 'Divided by a Common Concept? Assessing the Implications of Different Conceptualizations of Hate Crime in the European Union' (2012) 9 European Journal of Criminology 38, 43–47.

482 Treaty on the Functioning of the European Union (Consolidated versions of the Treaty on European Union and the Treaty on the Functioning of the European Union 2016) Articles 118 & 207. Matthias Cornils, 'Designing Platform Governance: A Normative Perspective on Needs, Strategies, and Tools to Regulate Intermediaries' (Algorithm Watch 2020) 16–20, 80–82.

483 Andrej Savin, 'Regulating Internet Platforms in the EU - The Emergence of the "Level Playing Field"' (2018) 34 Computer Law & Security Review 1215, 1223.

484 Directive 2000/31 (ECD) Recitals 58 - 60.

485 Sophie Stalla-Bourdillon, 'Sometimes One Is Not Enough! Securing Freedom of Expression, Encouraging Private Regulation, or Subsidizing Internet Intermediaries or All Three at the Same Time: The Dilemma of Internet Intermediaries' Liability' (2012) 7 Journal of International Commercial Law and Technology 22, 157.

4. Other jurisdictions

In the following a brief overview of a number of intermediary liability regimes elsewhere in the world will be given. Legislators around the world have been facing similar challenges, and borrowed from each other's frameworks, when adopting intermediary liability rules. The US and EU have served as the most common reference points for regulation elsewhere in the world.

However, the examples also show that there are notable differences and nuances when it comes to evaluating the roles of internet intermediaries and their responsibilities. These differences may be due to a variety of factors, such as specific legal and socio-cultural traditions, institutional set-ups or economic policy priorities. It should be added that the examples below relate solely to regulatory frameworks and, to some extent, court decisions . They do not provide any detail on the nature of regulatory cooperation between government and industry and the use of regulatory tools, such as self- or co-regulation.

I. Australia

Australia introduced general horizontal liability exemption rules for online intermediaries in 1999 by amending its Broadcasting Services Act of 1992. According to this, internet hosts and internet service providers will not be liable for content hosted or transmitted by them if they have not been aware of its nature. Furthermore, these intermediaries are protected from any obligation that would require them to monitor, enquire about or keep records of content hosted or transmitted.[486] The minister in charge may provide for exemptions to these rules by legislative acts. These general rules go even beyond the simplicity and broad protections offered by the US' CDA. However, the fuzziness of the requirement of "awareness" as opposed to the legally more tried and tested, although also still fluid, concept of "(actual) knowledge" as a condition for finding liability has been criticised.[487] Commentators think that beyond the rather clear act of being put on notice by a third party, the protections for intermediaries could range

486 Broadcasting Services Act 1992 Schedule 5, Clause 91.

487 Peter Leonard, 'Safe Harbors in Choppy Waters Building a Sensible Approach to Liability of Internet Intermediaries in Australia.' (2010) 3 Journal of International Entertainment & Media Law 221.

from extremely weak to very strong. In the former case, awareness would include knowledge of the mere possibility that hosted material was unlawful. In the latter, it would just cover cases of actual knowledge of the unlawful nature of specific information.[488] The absence of any safe harbour protections or notice-and-takedown obligations only adds to this ambiguity.

The rules were originally conceived with regards to objectionable content on the internet. However, their applicability to all kinds of content and related offences has been established through Australian case law. The degree of active involvement of the intermediary seems to be a common departure point for courts in determining (the degree of) awareness that would eventually lead to liability according to the very general provisions in the Australian Broadcasting Services Act.[489] However, based on the specific precedence and doctrine which developed for various torts under Australia's common law system, courts have developed different tests. As a result, a diverging and quite heterogeneous landscape of intermediary liability has emerged which applies different standard according to the legal area and violation concerned.[490]

On the one hand, an overarching impression of uncertainty and even incoherence may arise when looking at the Australian intermediary liability framework. On the other hand, this crowded landscape may reflect the diversity of the intermediary scene and the types of torts that are characteristic for content regulation on the internet. The heterogeneity may as well reflect a legal system that adapts to the reality.

Australia adapted its copyright law in 2000 to provide for instances where a carrier provides facilities that are used by another person for copyright protected acts. In such circumstances the carrier cannot be seen to "authorise" such acts.[491] However, the practical significance of this provision has been questioned as well.[492]

More recently, the Australian Government introduced legislation that obliges online platforms to report and remove "abhorrent violent materi-

---

488 ibid.

489 Kylie Pappalardo and Nicolas Suzor, 'The Liability of Australian Online Intermediaries' (2018) 40 Sydney Law Review 31, 485.

490 For a detailed account see: Pappalardo and Suzor (n 488).

491 Communications, 'Copyright Amendment (Digital Agenda) Act 2000' <https://www.legislation.gov.au/Details/C2004A00702/Html/Text, accessed 3 January 2020 ss 39B, 112E, and also ss 36 (1A), 101 (!a).

492 'Copyright Act 1968 (Cth) | Wilmap' <https://wilmap.law.stanford.edu/entries/copyright-act-1968-cth> accessed 3 January 2020.

al" expeditiously once they have become aware of it. This law has an extraterritorial reach in that it applies to all intermediaries globally that make material available for access in Australia.[493] The law was put in place following the live transmission of the terrorist attacks in Christchurch, New Zealand, on the social media platform *Facebook Live* in March 2019.

II. Canada

Canada stands somewhat apart from the EU and the US in that it has no statutes in place that deal specifically with the liability (exemptions) of online intermediaries. Being a common law jurisdiction, with a notable exception for the Province of Quebec, rules have developed largely out of case law, borrowing heavily from precedence that relies on cases concerning distributors in the offline world.[494] They are combined with specific common law rules related to defamation and libel.[495] Like in other jurisdictions around the world, Canadian and provincial courts have applied the concepts of (actual) knowledge, negligence and control found in secondary liability theory. For example, in *Crookes v. Newton* the Supreme Court of Canada established without difficulty that the posting of hyperlinks on an intermediary's server did not constitute an act of publication on behalf of the intermediary.[496] Even more, this ruling has been construed as meaning that there are intermediary acts (on the internet) that are so passive that immunity exists no matter whether knowledge of the illegality of the act exists or not.[497]

---

493 'Criminal Code Amendment (Sharing of Abhorrent Violent Material) Act 2019' <https://www.legislation.gov.au/Details/C2019A00038/Html/Text, http://www.legislation.gov.au/Details/C2019A00038> accessed 3 January 2020; Australian Government, Attorney-General's Department, 'Sharing of Abhorrent Violent Material Act - Fact Sheet' <https://www.ag.gov.au/Crime/federal-offenders/Documents/AVM-Fact-Sheet.pdf> accessed 3 January 2020.

494 Corey Omer, 'Intermediary Liability for Harmful Speech: Lessons from Abroad' 28 Harvard Journal of Law & Technology [illegible].

495 Emily Laidlaw, 'Notice-and-Notice-Plus: A Canadian Perspective Beyond the Liability and Immunity' in Giancarlo F Frosio (ed), *The Oxford Handbook of Intermediary Liability Online* (Oxford University Press 2019) 3–5 <https://ssrn.com/abstract=3311659> accessed 6 August 2019.

496 *Crookes v Newton* [2011] Supreme Court of Canada 33412, 3 SCR 269; Omer (n 493) 307–308.

497 Omer (n 493) 307.

Generally speaking, the fact that a notice has been received, and how it has been processed by the intermediary, will also play a role when deciding on liabilities. Many provincial laws have specific conditions for notices. However, they rely on press law in the offline world. Their applicability to online intermediaries is not entirely clear.[498]

Only in 2012 did Canada introduce a legal framework that specifically includes provisions for intermediary liability. However, this is restricted to the area of copyright. The Copyright Modernization Act of 2012 categorises intermediaries similar to the approach in the EU into network services (i.e. IAPs), caching and hosting services.[499] Copyright owners may notify intermediaries of infringing content. Like in the US, but unlike the EU, the form and content of such notices are clearly defined by the law.[500] However, intermediaries are only obliged to forward these notices to the uploader within 30 days of receipt and keep a copy. This so-called Notice-and-Notice regime means an internet service provider is not required to judge on the request received and is also not in a position of actual knowledge regarding the content in question. It does however require search engines to delete caches of notified content that has been removed by uploaders.[501] Whether this regime would also be practical for other kinds of unlawful content, such as defamatory or terrorist speech, is a subject of discussion.[502] This supposedly light touch approach to intermediary liability is somewhat relativised by the 2017 judgement in *Equuestek*. The Canadian Supreme forced *Google* to delist search results that linked to pages of a company that infringed *Equuestek's* trademark rights on a worldwide basis.[503]

498 ibid 306.

499 Copyright Modernization Act 2012 (SC 2012, c 20) s 31.1., for more detail see: Federica Giovanella, 'Online Service Providers' Liability, Copyright Infringement, and Freedom of Expression: Could Europe Learn from Canada?' in Mariarosaria Taddeo and Luciano Floridi, *The responsibilities of online service providers* (Springer Berlin Heidelberg 2016) 234–237.

500 S.C. 2012, c. 20 s. 41.25.

501 Employment and Social Development Canada, 'Notice and Notice Regime' (*gcnws*, 17 June 2014) <https://www.canada.ca/en/news/archive/2014/06/notice-notice-regime.html> accessed 20 December 2019.

502 Laidlaw (n 494).

503 *Google Inc v Equustek Solutions Inc* [2017] Supreme Court of Canada 36602, 1 SCR 824.

III. China

China started in 2000 to introduce horizontal provisions aimed at regulating the liability protections for online intermediaries. These fairly general provisions provide that internet service providers must not reproduce, post or disseminate illegal information and stop the transmission of the information once they become aware of it.[504] Largely based on the US DMCA, they did not, however, provide for any safeguards against the possibility of imposing general monitoring obligations,[505] nor did they differentiate between different types of intermediaries. Courts applied these rather broad rules and developed them through case law, mainly in the area of defamation and copyright. As a result, a distinct fault-based regime developed, which focussed on imposing strict liability on intermediaries depending on their involvement in the act of dissemination. Courts eventually adopted a lighter approach by tying liability to the receipt of and reaction to a notice before moving to a broader knowledge-based liability. Under the latter approach Chinese courts have recently moved to finding fault with intermediaries where they "should have known" about illegal content on their servers.[506] Broadly speaking, this means the courts have looked into duties of care that can be reasonably expected of such intermediaries relating to the detection and removal of unlawful information.

In 2010, China passed a horizontally applicable Tort Liability law, which solidifies the fault–based standard for intermediary liability by taking knowledge as a yardstick.[507] China supplemented these horizontal rules with online intermediary liability provisions specifically relating to copyright. First introduced in 2000, they were last revised in 2012 in order to bring in place safe harbours and clarify that ISPs are not obliged to monitor on a general basis for infringing information.[508] The safe harbours mainly apply to ISPs that react to notices and to those that can prove that infringing information was outside of what they "should have

504 Qian Tao, 'Legal Framework of Online Intermediaries' Liability in China' (2012) 14 info 59, 59–60.

505 Jie Wang, 'Development of Hosting ISPs' Secondary Liability for Primary Copyright Infringement in China – As Compared to the US and German Routes' (2015) 46 IIC - International Review of Intellectual Property and Competition Law 275, 278.

506 Tao (n 503) 60–62.

507 Q Tao, 'The Knowledge Standard for the Internet Intermediary Liability in China' (2012) 20 International Journal of Law and Information Technology 1, 2–3.

508 Wang (n 504) 279–280.

known" given the circumstances at hand. The Chinese law puts down a set of indicative criteria which relate to the role of the platform in the transmission process, its business model, its notice processes and its preventive activities.[509] Courts have further interpreted these criteria and applied so - called "red flag" tests, not only in copyright cases, but also in areas such as defamation or counterfeiting.

Overall, a distinctive approach has developed, which, although borrowing heavily from the US and the EU, appears to apply more qualified and onerous duty of care obligations to online platforms, which includes the use of automated preventive tools. As a result, the Chinese intermediary liability system can generally be seen as stricter than that of the US and the EU. At the same time, it may have developed more elaborate tests and methodologies on how to assess intermediaries' duty of care. However, outside the area of copyright the rather general provisions have led to courts applying homegrown approaches towards duty of care,[510] which combine doctrines from its own civil law system with that of various other jurisdictions, mainly in the US and EU.[511]

IV. India

India introduced rules for liability exemptions of internet intermediaries in Section 79 of the Information Technology Act in 2000. These rules were originally very general. They stated that network service providers shall not be liable for any third party information if they can prove that they had no knowledge of its unlawful character and applied due diligence to prevent any offences. The rules were amended in 2008 by more specific provisions that appear to be referring at least partly to the ECD. The amended section 79 now introduces a categorisation similar to Articles 12 – 14 of the ECD by exempting intermediaries that provide access to communication systems over which data is transmitted, temporally stored or hosted.[512] A passivity condition introduces the requirement that those intermediaries do not initiate, select or modify the data transmitted, or select its receiver.[513]

---

509 ibid 286.

510 INTA Anticounterfeiting Committee China Subcommittee, 'Online Counterfeiting Issues and Enforcement in China (CT20)' (International Trademark Association 2015) 10

511 Tao (n 503) 60, 67.

512 Information Technology (Amendment) Act, 2008, s. 79 (2) (a).

513 ibid (2) (b).

That wording is almost identical to Article 12 (1) ECD. Importantly, however, subsection (2) (c) makes the liability exemption also dependent on due diligence obligations identified in the Act and additional guidelines that may be issued by the government. Meanwhile, the liability exemptions would not apply if the intermediary had abetted, aided or induced the unlawful acts and, upon receiving actual knowledge, did not act expeditiously to remove or disable access to that material.[514]

The Indian Government passed more detailed guidelines on the due diligence obligations of internet intermediaries in 2011.[515] These guidelines specify amongst others that online intermediaries need to publish their rules and conditions of use clearly to users and inform them of the fact that various types of unlawful information must not be communicated through their systems. Intermediaries are obliged to remove unlawful information of which they have gained actual knowledge within 36 hours. That knowledge can be obtained through notification by third parties or through the intermediary's own investigative activity. In addition, the intermediary must have in place IT security measures to protect its information and network integrity.

Despite borrowing notably from the ECD's provisions in Articles 12 – 14, the Indian intermediary liability framework has been seen as imposing more onerous obligations, and subsequent liability risks, on internet intermediaries than for example the US or the EU.[516] It relies heavily on due diligence obligations as a precondition for avoiding liabilities for passive internet intermediaries, without however distinguishing between different kinds of intermediaries.[517] In addition, the Indian laws lack any limitations on the scope of due diligence obligations, notably the kind of limitations that prohibit general monitoring obligations, such as provided in Article 15 ECD.

This more hawkish stance on internet liability *vis-à-vis* intermediaries has been confirmed in case law. For example, in *Louboutin v Bajaj*, the French trademark owner successfully sued Indian e-commerce market-

---

514 ibid (3).

515 Information Technology (Intermediaries Guidelines) Rules, 2011, GSR 314(E) Rule 3.

516 Rishabh Dara, 'Intermediary Liability in India: Chilling Effects on Free Expression on the Internet' [2011] SSRN Electronic Journal 2–4 <http://www.ssrn.com/abstract=2038214> accessed 2 January 2020.

517 ibid 3.

place *Davey.com* for violating its trademark right.[518] The court ruled that the due diligence obligations imposed on internet intermediaries by Indian Law were broad and far-reaching. A strict word-by-word application of the law with regards to notifying and informing sellers of the inadmissibility of unlawful acts through terms and conditions was not sufficient. Given the involvement of the marketplace in the sale and transaction, the due diligence specified under Indian law would extend to enforceable contracts between seller and platform and further measures to assure the authenticity of products sold.[519] Meanwhile, the Delhi court also offered detailed criteria to determine when an online marketplace can be seen as playing an active role in the intermediation process, making it subject to enhanced due diligence requirements and reduced protections from liability.[520]

The intermediary liability conditions of the Information Technology Act and the Intermediary Guidelines, apply horizontally, with the exception of copyright. The Copyright (Amendment) Act 2012 exempts any intermediary that stores works in a transient or incidental way during the process of electronic transmission or communication to the public. Likewise, the act of providing access through links to works during such process, where not expressly forbidden by the rightsholder, shall also not constitute a violation of copyright.[521] The NTD regime requires intermediaries to disable access to content for 21 days after receipt of a written notice. Any longer lasting removal will need to be achieved through a court order. The procedural details of the notice-and-takedown regime are specified through statutory Copyright Rules.[522] They regulate the content and format of notices, reaction times and information obligations. However, they do not provide for specific counter-notice procedures.

This description of the various intermediary liability frameworks demonstrates that at the outset, many jurisdictions around the globe had chosen similar legal approaches when tackling the occurrence of unlawful content and activity on the internet. With the notable exception of Canada, many international regimes were influenced by the CDA and the DMCA, the pioneering US acts in that respect. At a closer look, the regimes

518 *Christian Louboutin Sas v Nakul Bajaj & Ors on 2 November, 2018* [2018] High Court of Delhi CS COMM - 344/2018.

519 ibid paras 70, 82; Pratik Dixit, 'Liability of Indian E-Commerce Websites for Trade Mark Infringement by Sellers' (2019) 14 Journal of Intellectual Property Law & Practice 424.

520 *Christian Louboutin Sas v Nakul Bajaj & Ors on 2 November, 2018* (n 517) para 56.

521 Copyright (Amendment) Act, 2012, s. 52 (b) (c).

522 Copyright Rules 2013, GSR 172(E) Rule 75.

portrayed here offer some important differences. *Savin* distinguishes between three intermediary liability regimes: those allocating full liability to intermediaries, an early option now abandoned by most jurisdictions across the globe; the US model of generous liability immunities, and an EU style model that ties stricter conditions to the immunity of intermediaries.[523] Moreover, the EU has favoured a horizontal model that imposes identical liability immunity conditions regardless of the type of infringement, an approach also initially embraced by Australia, China and India. The US meanwhile selected a model that allocates levels of protections by type of infringement (i.e. speech acts, copyright, trademarks).

It appears that of the frameworks discussed above, those of the US and the EU are the only ones that have stayed relatively static over the last 20 years. All other jurisdictions have seen major changes and amendments that have generally lowered the bar for intermediary liability. This trend has usually been accompanied by a sectorisation of rules, with copyright being a main target of stricter intermediary obligations. This sectoral adjustment may be relevant for current EU initiatives to reform the ECD. Notably India and China have recently emerged with more elaborate duty of care obligations, partly by weakening certain safeguards that are upheld in other jurisdictions. These newer systems and the experiences gained from their application may provide valuable insights for the EU's current efforts. Meanwhile, even the current US system has been subject to political initiatives that aim at imposing higher barriers to immunity on online intermediaries.

The section also demonstrates that over the last 10 years at least, intermediary liability rules appear to diverge on an international level, partly as a response to specific cultural, political and economic pressures,[524] and partly due to the particularities of national legal systems. The remainder of this chapter and the sectoral analysis of Chapter 4 will show that similar pressures exist within the EU.[525] Arguably, the EU, as a political and economic union, is more compelled to countering these diverging trends at

523 Savin (n 384) 146–147.

524 Thomas Poell, David Nieborg and José Van Dijck, 'Platformisation' (2019) 8 Internet Policy Review 8–9 <http://policyreview.info/node/1425> accessed 28 January 2020.

525 European Commission, 'SEC(2011) 1641 Final' (n 11) 26–20; Cornils (n 481) 76–79. Alexandre de Streel and others, *Moderation of Illegal Content Online: Law, Practices and Options for Reform.* (EU Publications Office 2020) 19 <https://data.europa.eu/doi/10.2861/831734> accessed 7 October 2020.

Member State level. Meanwhile, this makes the challenges of drafting new laws that are consistent with international rules even more difficult.

D. Enforcement challenges in internet intermediary liability

1. Emerging challenges - EU reviews of the ECD

The ECD obliged the Commission to re-evaluate its intermediary liability framework by 2003 and within a time frame of every two years thereafter. An emphasis was put on review of the need to adapt the categorisation of intermediaries and the necessity to harmonise NTD procedures.[526]

I. The 2003 and 2007 ECD evaluations

The first review of the ECD in 2003, however, found that there was no sufficient experience yet on the practical application of Articles 12–14. The few court rulings available by that time on the matter of intermediary liability had taken place prior to Member States implementing the ECD into their national laws.[527] The 2003 ECD application report also found no grounds that justified regulatory intervention in the areas of NTD and the categorisation of internet intermediaries.

In 2007, the European Commission published two reports that evaluated the implementation of the ECD and its impact. While one of these reports evaluated the economic impact of the ECD,[528] the other one, by *Verbiest et al*, specifically looked into the transposition and the practical application of the intermediary liability exemptions regime by Member States.[529] The first study found that many internet intermediaries at the time welcomed the provisions of Articles 12 -15 ECD as providing legal certainty for their business models. However, it also pointed out two areas of ambiguity. Firstly, intermediaries were unsure how far they could stretch their own voluntary preventive efforts against unlawful activity and

526 Directive 2000/31 (ECD) Article 21.

527 European Commission, 'First Report on the Application of Directive 2000/31/EC' (n 458) 13 fn 71.

528 Dr Claus Kastberg Nielsen and others, 'Study on the Economic Impact of the Electronic Commerce Directive' (DG Internal Market and Services, European Commission 2007).

529 Verbiest and others (n 315).

content. While there was no obligation to generally monitor all information, it remained unclear in how far voluntary efforts to monitor web traffic for unlawful content could lead to liabilities in cases were the intermediary detected content or missed to detect content. Secondly, this study found that legal uncertainty existed as to whether search engines were within the scope of Articles 12 – 15 ECD.[530]

Verbiest et al noted in the second study a number of emerging problems when it came to the practical application of the intermediary liability provisions by courts, particularly those concerning host providers covered by Article 14 ECD. First, the study indicated uncertainty over the terms "actual knowledge" and "aware(ness) of facts or circumstances from which the illegal activity or information is apparent", which are both conditions that determine the liability of intermediaries.[531] There was a lack of understanding over the level of knowledge required to make it "actual" knowledge. The question centred around knowledge of specific content *and* its unlawful character versus knowledge that was created from automated activity of computer software, such as databases or monitoring tools, or through negligent ignorance.[532] The conditions under which such actual knowledge or awareness could be established, varied according to definitions, specific tests and doctrines relating to knowledge and awareness in Member States' legal systems. Lastly, it was not clear when an intermediary service provider could be considered to have been put on notice and incurred liability after failing to act appropriately, as the ECD did not establish common procedural requirements in that area. These uncertainties led to a fear that intermediaries would be pressured into becoming private judges over the legality of content and speech.[533]

Furthermore, the study identified potential problems that courts had in reconciling obligations arising from injunctions aimed at preventing specific violations with the preclusions of general monitoring. The study points to specific court cases in Germany, Austria, Italy, Sweden, Belgium, the Netherlands and the UK where the permissibility and scope of so-called stay-down orders against both IAPs and host providers was controversially debated. The orders concerned unlawful content and activity in

530 Nielsen and others (n 527) 16–22.

531 Directive 2000/31 (ECD) Article 14 (1); Verbiest and others (n 315) 36–47.

532 Verbiest and others (n 315) 36–37.

533 ibid 41–42.

the areas of terrorist speech, child pornography and intellectual property law.[534]

Finally, the study noted the emergence of newer Web 2.0 intermediaries. These new types of intermediaries were referred to as content aggregators, such as video-sharing platforms and the first social media sites. The report noted the potential for legal controversy over the role of these players in the intermediation process and the availability of the liability exemptions of Article 14 ECD.[535]

Overall this study provides a comprehensive and detailed insight into how Member States' courts tried to interpret the rules laid down by Articles 12 – 15 ECD and their national implementations. The different legal traditions and doctrines, combined with different degrees of understanding of the new, technically complex and rapidly evolving intermediation models gave a glimpse of the problems that were to come.

II. The 2012 public consultation

The EU's 2012 public consultation on the application of the ECD shows that the initial frictions of 2007 had developed into fully blown legal problems: the staff working document accompanying the consultation states that "a wide variety of stakeholders face a high degree of regulatory uncertainty about the application of the intermediary liability regime of the E-Commerce Directive."[536] Apart from the issues mentioned in the 2007 study, the diverging assessments on the kind of intermediaries covered by Art. 12–14 of the ECD had moved to centre stage. By that time, new Web 2.0 intermediaries had grown into sizeable actors of the internet and information economies. Video-sharing platforms and social networks' business models increasingly relied on the commercialisation of user data. They reaped the first benefits from network effects as they emerged into multi-sided platforms. In addition, e-commerce marketplaces and collaborative economy platforms were starting to disrupt more traditional offline sectors of the economy, such as high street retail, travel, accommodation and transportation services.

The problem of unlawful content and illegal activity, meanwhile, persisted and the ECD's liability framework did not provide for an effective

---

534 ibid 48–71.

535 ibid 102–104.

536 European Commission, 'SEC(2011) 1641 Final' (n 11) 25.

and consistent enforcement against this. The 2012 stakeholder consultation exposed four main problem areas: 1) the definition of intermediary activities in Articles 12 to 14 ECD; 2) the conditions for the availability of the safe harbour in Articles 12 to 14 ECD; 3) the unclear and fragmented nature of NTD procedures; 4) the general monitoring prohibition in Article 15 and its relation to specific, preventive injunctions.[537] A plethora of national court rulings with diverging and even contradictive interpretations serve as a testimony to the ineffectiveness and ambiguities of the ECD's liability provisions. The matter was aggravated by differing transpositions of this Directive into national laws. More detail on this will be provided in the following section.

However, in its evaluation exercise of the E-Commerce Action Plan, the Commission followed the pleas of intermediaries and user representations, which had constituted the majority of stakeholders that had participated in this exercise, and refrained from any attempts to reform the ECD's liability framework.[538]

III. Reviews and initiatives under the Digital Single Market policy

Five years later, the Commission found that unlawful content on the internet, and on online platforms, had not just persisted but actually continued to proliferate. At the same time, it noted the ascendance of online platforms to gatekeepers, which held sway over large parts of the internet's ecosystem, governing access to information and content.[539] Further stakeholder consultations conducted in 2016 had revealed a divided opinion over the fitness of the then over 15-year-old liability framework to effectively address the problem of unlawful content in the Web 2.0 era of multisided online platforms. A synopsis report of the 2016 consultation showed that rightsholders and notice providers were largely at odds with it, citing the above voiced legal unclarities as persisting and in need of adjustment.

537 ibid 25–26.

538 European Commission, 'E-Commerce Action Plan 2012-2015, State of Play 2013, SWD(2013) 153 Final' (2013) 17.

539 European Commission, 'Communication on the on the Mid-Term Review on the Implementation of the Digital Single Market Strategy - A Connected Digital Single Market for All COM(2017) 228 Final' (2017) COM(2017) 228 final 7–8; European Commission, 'COM(2016) 288 Final' (n 223) 2.

Intermediaries themselves, user organisations and content-uploaders were largely satisfied with the provisions.[540]

In view of this divided picture the EU vowed to "maintain the existing intermediary liability regime while implementing a sectoral, problem-driven approach to regulation."[541] The Commission would focus on a review of intermediary liability responsibilities in the area of copyright and audiovisual media services.[542] It would step up efforts to encourage platforms to take more responsibility through self-regulatory measures. That sectoral focus, however, implicitly meant that the overarching horizontal liability provisions in Articles 12 – 15 ECD would remain unchanged. In the wake of the sectoral reviews in copyright and audiovisual media services a number of other sectoral initiatives sprang up or were re-enforced, which all dealt with the responsibilities of intermediaries, and hosting services in particular.[543] These initiatives will be discussed in more detail in the sectoral reviews of Chapter 4.

The Commission confirmed its sectoral approach in a 2017 Communication and a 2018 Recommendation both aimed at tackling illegal content online.[544] Both initiatives acknowledged the link between sectoral enforcement at EU level, directed at the various kinds of unlawful content, from hate speech and disinformation to intellectual property violations and illegal and unsafe products. At the same time, they affirm an emerging con-

---

540 European Commission, 'Synopsis Report on the Public Consultation on the Regulatory Environment for Platforms, Online Intermediaries and the Collaborative Economy' (European Commission 2016) 15–21 <https://ec.europa.eu/digital-single-market/en/news/results-public-consultation-regulatory-environment-platforms-online-intermediaries-data-and> accessed 29 March 2017.

541 European Commission, 'COM(2016) 288 Final' (n 223) 9.

542 ibid.

543 'Code of Conduct on Countering Illegal Hate Speech Online' (2016) <http://ec.europa.eu/justice/fundamental-rights/files/hate_speech_code_of_conduct_en.pdf> accessed 9 March 2017; 'Memorandum of Understanding on the Online Sale of Counterfeit Goods, 2016' <http://ec.europa.eu/DocsRoom/documents/18023/attachments/1/translations/> accessed 17 March 2017; European Commission, 'Memorandum of Understanding on Online Advertising and Intellectual Property Rights' (2018) <https://ec.europa.eu/docsroom/documents/30226> accessed 26 June 2020; European Commission, 'COM(2018) 236 Final' (n 70); European Commission, 'Product Safety Pledge Voluntary Commitment of Online Marketplaces with Respect to the Safety of Non-Food Consumer Products Sold Online by Third Party Sellers' (European Commission 2018) For a summary overview see: European Commission, 'COM (2017) 555 Final' (n 69) 2–3.

544 European Commission, 'COM (2017) 555 Final' (n 69); European Commission, 'C(2018) 1177 Final' (n 8).

sensus that internet intermediaries, notably online platforms, should step up their efforts, and take on more responsibilities in the fight against unlawful content.

The articulation of enhanced responsibilities for platforms appears to have arisen out of public consultations. It took a more concrete form as stakeholders called for the definition of duties of care that internet intermediaries would need to commit to in the removal but also the prevention of unlawful content. The imposition of duties of care is, at least theoretically, an option offered by Recital 48 of the ECD.

On the side of the EU, the concept of duty of care has not been explored further. There remain different understandings of the concept of duty of care, which some stakeholders, notably intermediaries, tend to see as more voluntary commitments, often entirely targeted at *ex-post* activities in the form of NTD procedures and transparency reports. On the other side of the spectrum, damaged parties would see these duties of care extend to statutory obligations that include proactive measures aimed at identifying and preventing harms and violations.[545]

While enhanced responsibilities for internet intermediaries where increasingly discussed by the EU at least since 2016, it has remained unclear if and how they would be reconciled with the broad protections offered by the ECD.

In July 2019, the new European Commission president-elect, *Ursula von der Leyen*, announced that under her presidency in 2019 – 2024 the EU would draft a Digital Services Act (DSA) in a bid to overhaul the ECD. The aim would be to "*upgrade our liability and safety rules for digital platforms, services and products, and complete our Digital Single Market.*"[546] A leaked note of the European Commission's Digital Single Market Strategic Group confirmed that such an Act would finally look at reforming Europe's horizontal liability framework for intermediaries.[547] Amongst others, that draft confirmed that online platforms are increasingly subject to diverging liability rules across Member States. These differing rules are partly due to diverging interpretations by national courts on the liability provisions of the ECD. This, in turn, is owed to outdated provisions of the ECD, which has

---

545 European Commission, 'Synopsis Report on the Regulatory Environment for Platforms' (n 539) 19–20.

546 Ursula von der Leyen, 'A Union That Strives for More - My Agenda for Europe. Political Guidelines for the next European Commission 2019 - 2024' 13.

547 The leaked note is available under 'Digital-Services-Act-Note-DG-Connect-June-2019.Pdf' <https://cdn.netzpolitik.org/wp-upload/2019/07/Digital Services-Act-note-DG-Connect-June-2019.pdf> accessed 7 January 2020.

been overrun by new platform economy business models, technologies and socio-technical realities. Over the year 2020, the Commission's plans for a new DSA were further elaborated and supplemented by a public consultation. Published on 15 December 2020, the focus of the proposed DSA is on providing an enhanced set of obligations in addition to the existing intermediary liability exemptions regime of the ECD, and a specific regime for so-called large gatekeeper platforms.[548] The details of this original proposal will be evaluated briefly in the relevant sectoral sections and in Chapter 6. A more in-depth analysis has been published elsewhere since.[549] In addition, the DSA package will undoubtly be subject to intense negotiations, with further changes being made during the EU policy making process during 2021. It may only be finally adopted during 2022 or later.

IV. Main legal challenges of the ECD inhibiting enforcement against unlawful content

The EU's reviews of the framework of intermediary liability exemptions and its practical application since 2003 reflect a number of distinct problems. The EU, however, was not alone with this. More than that, these reviews were an expression of even more intense discussion on this matter in society at large, in academic, industry and civil society circles over the last 15 years. As early as 2004, *Edwards* remarked that there was a fundamental change under way in the intermediary landscape, with the emergence of content aggregators (search engines, price comparison sites) and P2P file sharing. The new roles that these intermediaries would play in the of exchange information online may lead lawmakers to substantially review existing liability rules for these players.[550] Five years later, she stated that Articles 12 – 15 of the ECD were desperately in need of review.[551] On the academic side, the debate has advanced further with a variety of proposals that aim at reforming today's intermediary liability framework to varying degrees. Many of these debates are linked to specific content areas, such as

548 European Commission, 'The Digital Services Act Package' (n 8).

549 For example: Mark D Cole, Christina Etteldorf and Carsten Ullrich, *Updating the Rules for Online Content Dissemination: Legislative Options of the European Union and the Digital Services Act Proposal* (Nomos 2021).

550 Edwards, 'The Changing Shape of Cyberlaw' (n 16) 364.

551 Edwards, 'The Fall and Rise Of Intermediary Liability Online' (n 119) 87.

hate and terrorist content, disinformation, copyright, trademarks or child abuse material. An overview of these proposals will be given in Chapter 6.

To summarise, a number of vectors can be identified that have contributed to challenging the original intermediary liability provisions of the ECD, but also other intermediary liability frameworks around the world:

a) technological advances: the rise of Web 2.0 interactivity, mobile internet, technology convergence, data storage and connection capacity;
b) business innovation: big data exploitation, e-commerce, collaborative economy platforms, online streaming, user-generated content platforms;
c) user behaviour: growth in internet use across the world population and by time spent per user on the internet;
d) socio-economic importance of internet intermediaries: indispensable for the operation of the internet (content and infrastructure gatekeepers), enablers of information exchange/speech conduits, amongst the most valuable and powerful corporations worldwide.

These tendencies are interconnected: for example, technological advances in data storage, bandwidth or wireless applications directly impact business models and user behaviour.

Three main problem areas have crystallised out of the plethora of legal issues that have been generated by the above changes.[552]

1) the neutrality/passivity condition for non-liable online intermediaries;
2) the meaning of actual knowledge;
3) the preventive obligations of intermediaries.

These three problems will be analysed in more detail in the following section. The analysis shall first serve as a basis for developing a deeper understanding of underlying legal and technological factors that shape consider-

---

552 The following publications shall serve as examples for more detailed discussions of these problems: Zuboff (n 5) ll 1997–2050; Rowland, Kohl and Charlesworth (n 128) 85–92; Martens (n 53) 33–35; Peggy Valcke, Aleksandra Kuczerawy and Pieter-Jan Ombelet, 'Did the Romans Get It Right? What Delfi, Google, EBay, and UPC TeleKabel Wien Have in Common' in Mariarosaria Taddeo and Luciano Floridi, *The responsibilities of online service providers* (Springer Berlin Heidelberg 2017) 11–16; Georg Nolte and Jörg Wimmers, 'Wer Stört? Gedanken Zur Haftung von Intermediären Im Internet – von Praktischer Konkordanz, Richtigen Anreizen Und Offenen Fragen' (2014) 16 GRUR.

ations over internet intermediary liability today. Secondly, it demonstrates the challenges of enforcing against unlawful content on the internet in an exemplary manner. Finally, it shall also be useful when discussing options for alternative regulatory frameworks in the last chapter.

The analysis below also highlights the multi-dimensional and multi-layered nature of the problems at hand. Should a legal analysis of the enforcement problems be approached by looking at the different categories or business models of intermediaries, or should it start from the type of infringement, violation or harm at hand, i.e. defamation, terrorist content, copyright. Certain types of unlawful content have typically been connected with specific types of intermediaries: defamation with social networks, trademark infringements and product safety with e-commerce marketplaces, copyright with UGC platforms, hate speech with social media and UGC platforms. Search engines may be the only type of intermediary where almost all types of infringement would be apparent. In Chapter 4, each legal challenge will be analysed according to how it played out in case law. The CJEU's mixed success in providing clarification will also be discussed.

It should be mentioned that these problems are not restricted to the EU. Legal systems across the world have had to grapple with essentially the same questions when it comes to unlawful content online. With that in mind, the following detailed analysis of the main challenges of the ECD's liability framework will be supplemented with case law from jurisdictions outside the EU where this helps to illustrate possible alternative approaches.

2. ECD intermediary liability – the main challenges through case law

The availability of the hosting defence had originally been discussed mainly in light of the intermediary business models in questions. Courts' assessments of the active or passive role was necessarily tied to the activity of the intermediary and the kind of content hosted – be it product offers, news and comments, or entertainment. Therefore, the analysis of the first challenge, determining the neutral status of intermediaries, will be done from the angle of different intermediary business models.

Once courts established that intermediaries qualified for the liability exemptions of the ECD, they applied the specific conditions of that regime. Actual knowledge of unlawful information or activity is one central condition for liability. However, courts have had marked difficulties in interpreting this requirement in a consistent fashion throughout the EU.

Where intermediaries are found to have actual knowledge of illegal content or activity, they are obliged to remove or disable access to it. Very quickly, however, the Sisyphean task of purely reactive blocking and removal of illegal content on the internet became clear. Rightsowners and damaged parties made use of the option given under the ECD to apply for preventive injunctions of already notified violations. Soon, the scope of these preventive injunctions broadened and hit the limitations imposed by Article 15 ECD that prohibits the imposition of general monitoring duties. This conflict is a technical as well as a legal one and shall be discussed as the third legal challenge of the ECD.

I. The neutrality of internet intermediaries

The premise that intermediary actors with no knowledge or control over third parties and their actions are free from liability for these acts is a basic concept of secondary liability. By contrast, secondary liability may be attributed when those intermediaries are found to play a more active part in the intermediation process, which would imply an involvement that confers a certain level of control and/or knowledge. Neutrality, or passivity, is therefore a precondition for the availability of the liability exemptions under the ECD. Recital 42 refers to the "*mere technical, automatic and passive role*" of intermediaries and Articles 12 (1), 13 (1) and 14 (1) provide the basis of this principle.

Establishing the (degree of) passivity or neutrality of intermediaries is a central test that courts in the EU have applied in order to decide whether the liability immunities of the ECD are available. In the two extreme scenarios a provider is either so actively involved in the intermediation process that they would be considered an editor or publisher of information, which could even lead to conferring primary liability. On the other hand, a totally neutral host would be assessed with regards to compliance with the conditions set out under Articles 12 – 14 in order to qualify for the exemptions from intermediary liability.

During the first years of the ECD there seemed to be little controversy for courts in deciding on the availability of the immunity protections for intermediaries. The type of business models in the focus of litigation were IAPs, blog portals or P2P file sharing networks. Mere conduits or IAPs have, in general, never had to fear that the protection of the ECD would not be available to them. The controversies in the application of the ECD relate mainly to internet hosts and can be linked to the rise of new types of

Web 2.0 intermediaries, such as information location tools (search engines), UGC or social media platforms, and e-commerce marketplaces.[553]

a. Search engines

Unlike in the US intermediary liability provisions, the ECD does not offer a separate classification for search engines. National courts came therefore initially to diverging outcomes when considering the categorisation of internet search engines. Courts in Germany, UK, Belgium and France classed these actors respectively as information hosts (Article 14 ECD),[554] mere conduits (Article 12)[555] or as editors and therefore not eligible for the protections of the ECD.[556]

These divergences were eventually put to bed by the CJEU ruling in *Google France*, which established criteria according to which a search engine could be considered an active or passive host.[557] The rightsholders of the French luxury product group *LVMH* claimed that *Google* asserted control over the content of its web search results by assisting clients in using the AdWords service: *Google* drafted the commercial text next to the ad link and suggested keyword combinations to ameliorate the effectiveness of the displayed adverts. Those ads were displayed in the form of "sponsored links" that led to websites that offered fakes of products, for which *LVMH* enjoyed trademark protection.

The highest EU court ruled that a search engine operator, whose search engine matched user requests with keywords or a combination of keywords selected by advertisers, which then led to search results being displayed, did not play an active role. By contrast, where the operator created the advertising message that appeared next to sponsored links and assisted in the selection of the advertising keywords to improve the relevance of the sponsored links, this may indicate such an active role and lead to a de-

553 European Commission, 'SEC(2011) 1641 Final' (n 11) 26–30; Waisman and Hevia (n 313) 797–800.

554 *Vorschaubilder* [2010] BGH I ZR 69/08, MMR 2010 475; *Jean-Yves Lafesse et autres v Google et autres* (2009) (Unreported) (Tribunal de grande instance de Paris, 3ème chambre).

555 *R v Rock and Overton*, [2010] Gloucester Crown Court T20097013,

556 *Copiepresse et al v Google Inc* [2007] Brussels Court of First Instance 7964. For more detail on these cases see: European Commission, 'SEC(2011) 1641 Final' (n 11) 27.

557 *Google France v Louis Vuitton* (n 155) para 143.

nial of the classification as a hosting service under Article 14 ECD.[558] The outcome did confirm that search engines, when they remain passive, would be classified as host providers under the ECD. However, it did not solve the problem of the general availability of the hosting defence for search engines, because the CJEU said that national courts would need to assess based on the concrete facts at hand whether the criteria it had laid down as guidance did indeed apply.

The guidance delivered by the CJEU translated into largely favourable rulings for *Google's* search engine operations. Judges either accorded the hosting privileges or tried to circumvent the tricky questions of deciding on the active role of the search engine.[559] However, some courts still found *Google's* search engine as too active for deserving the host status of the ECD, in particular when looking at the company's *Autocomplete* or *Suggest* functionality.[560] Today, many of the large e-commerce or social media platforms, such as *Amazon* or *Facebook* own search engines in their own right. For these search engines, questions of liability have been assimilated into the hosting liability of the platform into which they are integrated.[561]

b. E-commerce marketplaces

i. National case law

E-commerce marketplaces belonged to the first intermediaries that started to affect the real economy in a sense that they competed directly with traditional brick and mortar high street retailers. While providing access to millions of products at an international level, they also acted as product search engines, utilising data from clients, customers and sellers alike for personalised advertising and expansion into adjacent markets.[562]

558 ibid 115–119.

559 Jacques Larrieu, Christian Le Stanc and Pascale Tréfigny-Goy, 'Droit Du Numérique Juillet 2010 - Août 2011' Recueil Dalloz 2011 2363.

560 *Google France c/ Syndicat Français de la Literie* (2010) (Unreported) (Cour d'appel de Paris Pôle 5); *Olivier M c/ Prisma Presse, Google* (2011) (Unreported) (Tribunal de Grande instance, Paris, 17eme chambre).

561 See for example *Cosmetic Warriors Ltd & Anor v amazon.co.uk Ltd & Anor* (2014) [2014] EWHC 181 (Ch).

562 *Amazon*, for example, is known for its aggressive expansion into private label products, logistics and web hosting services, payment, product insurance and consumer credit services. These services benefit from competitive intelligence

Early cases against marketplaces mainly focussed on *eBay*. In France, courts have held *eBay's* activities as consisting of hosting, publishing and of brokering. In 2008, *eBay* was found by a Paris court to provide its sellers with tools to set up their own stores and promotional activity, send commercial reminders and run a "Power Seller" program. These activities were all geared towards increasing sales and subsequently *eBay's* commissions. This conferred on it a "very active" role within the sales process. In line with its active involvement, *eBay* had a general obligation of supervision to prevent the sales of obviously counterfeit products, which took place on a massive scale. It could not benefit from the hosting defence for merely technical service providers under the ECD. The court also defined some of these preventive measures, such as for example verifying the identity of sellers and requiring sellers to prove the authenticity of their products.[563] This view was shared by the *Tribunale de Grande Instance de Troyes* in *Hermès International v Feitz*.[564] By contrast, a 2009 decision by the *Cour de Cassation*, France's supreme appeals court, held that *eBay* was a mere technical service provider. Its auction service fell therefore under the hosting liability privileges of the ECD. It only had to act if it acquired knowledge of manifestly illegal activity or information.[565] In another decision concerning the trademark rights of *L'Oréal*, the *Tribunal de Grande Instance of Paris* dissociated eBay's hosting activities and the making available of sales offers from its promotional activities that accompanied sales offers on the site. While the former were purely technical and indispensable activities for the function of an online marketplace, the latter were going beyond this and could therefore not qualify for the liability protections afforded to hosts.[566] This would in effect mean that the content liabilities would differ within the business activities of the same marketplace.

that is gathered from the behavioral data of clients of the multiple markets served by that company. Similarly, *eBay* has early expanded into classifieds and ticket sales, and for a time owned payment service *PayPal*.

563 *SA Louis Vuitton Malletier v eBay Inc and eBay International* [2008] 2010 ETMR 10 (Tribunal de Grande Instance de Paris, France) [188–189, 193].

564 *Hermès International v Feitz* [2009] Tribunal de Grande Instance de Troyes RG 06/02604. In : *L'Oreal SA v eBay International AG* (2009) E.T.M.R. 53 (High Court of Justice (Chancery Division)) [941].

565 *DWC v eBay France, eBay Europe* [2009] Cour de cassation, Chambre commerciale, Paris 08-11.672.

566 *L'Oréal SA c eBay France SA* [2009] Tribunal de Grande Instance de Paris RG 07/11365.

Belgian courts, on the other hand, have had less difficulty in qualifying e-commerce marketplaces as information hosts under the ECD. In *Lancôme v eBay* a Brussels court held that *eBay's* activities fell within the protections of Article 14 ECD.[567]

In Germany, courts were more concerned with the way in which the marketplace platform had 'appropriated' the content of the seller. In *Internetversteigerung I*, a case decided in 2004, the Federal Court of Justice (BGH) assessed that online marketplaces did not exercise any responsibility for the sales offers stored by them on behalf of third parties and that the hosting privileges of Article 14 took effect.[568] This line was continued in the *Internetversteigerung II* and *III* cases of 2007 and 2008.[569] The judgement also extended to (allegedly trademark infringing) advertisements, because these contents were not owned by the marketplace. German courts therefore appear to have looked strictly at whether content is stored on behalf of a third party and also took account of the fact that that storage occurred through the use of automated tools. The nature of the ancillary activities did not affect the classification as hosts under Article 14 ECD, as was done for example in the assessments of some French courts. However, these liability protection would not extend to injunctions.[570]

Marketplaces in the UK had a more difficult time to find refuge under the wings of the Article 14 protections for hosts. In one of the probably most high-profile cases, *L'Oréal* brought an action against e*Bay*, alleging, amongst others, that the latter could not avail itself of the hosting defence because its activities were going beyond mere technical and passive interventions. Again, it was claimed that *eBay* participated more actively in the sales process by organising and taking a part in the creation of information, namely advertising. Moreover, it promoted the sales offers and provided sponsored links to infringing products. Judge *Lord Arnold* voiced a preference for the arguments provided by claimant *L'Oréal* and agreed with the latter that *eBay* could have done more to prevent the sale of infringing goods via its site. However, he also noted the varying assessments and judgements concerning the liability of intermediaries across the EU.

---

567 *Lancôme v EBay, A/07/06032* (2008) (Unreported) (Tribunal de commerce de Bruxelles); *L'Oreal SA v. eBay International AG* (n 546) para 941.

568 *Internetversteigerung I (Rolex v Ricardo.de), Az I ZR 304/01* (2004) GRUR 2004, 860 (BGH) [863].

569 *Internetversteigerung II (Rolex v Ricardo.de)* [2007] BGH I ZR 35/04, JurPC-Web-Dok. 0108/2007; *Internetversteigerung III (Rolex v Ricardo.de), Az I ZR 73/05* [2008] MIR06/2008 (BGH).

570 *Internetversteigerung II (Rolex v Ricardo.de)* (n 568) para 19.

The interpretation of Article 14 ECD was far from clear and required clarification by the CJEU.[571]

ii. EU case law

The CJEU attempted to provide that clarification in one of its most influential rulings in the area of intermediary liability.[572] Apart from the question at hand, the CJEU's *L'Oréal v eBay* judgement also provided guidance on two other key ambiguities of the liability exemptions regime: actual knowledge and the preventive obligations of e-commerce marketplaces. In addition, the ruling gave clarification in the area of trademark law. An online marketplace operator, it said, did not make use of trademarks in the course of business where these trademarks were attached to goods sold by third parties via its website.[573]

L'Oréal had complained against repeated sales of perfumery products that infringed its trademark rights via the *eBay* marketplace. Of those products, some were counterfeits, but the majority were so-called grey imports and product samples, which were not destined for retail sales, but were nevertheless available via *eBay.* The French company also denounced the fact that *eBay* assisted the infringing sellers in the marketing of their products by selecting keywords in *Google's AdWords* program to display sponsored links on *Google's* search results pages to sales offers on its platform. These activities, it claimed, made *eBay* directly liable for violating *L'Oréal's* trademark rights. Failing that, *eBay* should at least be subject to an injunction aimed at preventing any future infringements of the trademarks in question.

The question about trademark liability and the availability of injunctions turned on the point of whether *eBay* could claim protection under the hosting provider defence of the ECD. The proceedings from the referring court demonstrated that the availability of the hosting defence for *eBay*'s activities was disputed and not clearly deductible from the text of

571 *L'Oreal SA v. eBay International AG* (n 563) paras 940–941. Further clarification was sought on whether sponsored links to infringing goods constituted trademark violations and the scope of relief available to trademark owners against intermediaries under IPRED 2004/48.

572 *L'Oréal v eBay* (n 463)

573 ibid 98–105.

the ECD.[574] The court therefore asked the CJEU whether *eBay's* activities were covered by the scope of Article 14 ECD. [575]

Like in *Google France*, the CJEU referred this question back to the referring national court for assessment based on the facts at hand. It provided, however, some indicative criteria to help national courts along in their assessments. The CJEU found that *eBay's* activities of setting the terms of service for sellers, storing the offer, providing general information to consumers and being remunerated did not impinge on the neutral role of an online marketplace. Assisting the seller by, e.g. optimising the display and promotion of offers, however, would point towards an active involvement of the marketplace and therefore the loss of the liability exemption.

iii. Application of CJEU rulings

Unfortunately, the referring UK court in *L'Oréal v eBay* never got the chance to apply the guidance provided by the CJEU. The case was settled out of court in 2014.[576] Notwithstanding the guidance provided by the CJEU, it remains disputed whether these rulings have brought the clarity sought. The judgement was very soon applied by various courts. However, despite the indicative criteria, national courts have assessed the role of e-commerce marketplaces in different ways, developing their own methodologies. Given the wealth of business models and functionalities, the constantly evolving nature of e-commerce, distinctive national legal traditions and different levels of awareness of technical detail, this is hardly surprising. National judges have therefore continued to this day to interpret the role of online marketplaces and the availability of the hosting defence in Article 14 ECD in different ways, which shall be illustrated in the following.

France

In 2012, a Paris appeals court, by referring to the CJEU's *L'Oréal v eBay* judgement, denied the marketplace the hosting provider status. It found

574 *L'Oréal SA v. eBay International AG* (n 563) paras 436–443.

575 *L'Oréal v eBay* (n 463) para 50 (9).

576 William Horobin And Greg Bensinger, 'L'Oréal, EBay Settle Dispute Over Counterfeit Goods' *Wall Street Journal* (15 January 2014) <https://www.wsj.com/articles/l8217or233al-eBay-settle-dispute-over-counterfeit-goods-1389816939> accessed 14 January 2020.

that through its "power seller" programme, *eBay* had actively promoted and assisted sellers in the sale of their products. These activities, the Paris court said, did go beyond mere storage of information. Indeed, *eBay* derived a direct profit from both the data stored and the goods sold. *EBay* hosted sales offers in order to support its principal activity of promoting products for its clients.[577] The French Supreme Court came to a similar result in 2012 when it confirmed decisions against *eBay* by lower instances in 2008 and 2010, brought by the *Luis Vuitton* owners *LVMH*. In this judgement, the French Supreme Court found that *eBay* provided the entirety of its sellers with information to help optimise their sales offers and the description and definition of their products. The marketplace was found guilty of selling counterfeit products and charged to pay EUR1.7 million to *LVMH*.[578]

By contrast, in 2012 the *Tribunal de grande instance de Paris* held in *Maceo*[579] that *eBay's* aforementioned promotional activities were solely aimed at improving and facilitating the searchability of offers. *EBay*'s technical design choices provided sellers with the opportunity to better structure, promote and market their products via its marketplace. That activity did, however, not mean that *eBay* selected and made decisions regarding the information that was put on its site. It did, therefore, not result in an active role of *eBay* in a sense that it had gained knowledge and control over information. Deriving an economic benefit from this activity did also not preclude *eBay's* classification as a hosting service. This outcome was confirmed in the same year in *Groupement des brocanteurs de Saleya v eBay's*. In an almost directly opposed reading of the CJEU judgement in *L'Oréal v eBay*, the *Cour d'appel de Paris* said that the optimisation of the presentation of offers, where it was automated and did not result in a modification of the content, could be considered as part of the technical service provided by the host.[580]

In the following years *Amazon, Alibaba* or *CDiscount* joined the ranks of *eBay* and appeared in front of French courts, again with varying results. The Chinese e-commerce behemoth *Alibaba* was denied the hosting

---

577 *eBay International v Burberry Ltd et autres* (2012) (Unreported) (Cour d'appel de Paris Pôle 5, Chambre 12).

578 *eBay Inc, eBay International v LVMH et autres* [2012] Cour de cassation (Surpeme Court) Chambre commerciale, financière et économique 11-10.508.

579 *Maceo v eBay International AG*, (2012) (Unreported) (Tribunal de grande instance de Paris, 3ème chambre, 1ère section).

580 *Groupement des brocanteurs de Saleya, CBA / eBay France et Ing* (2012) (Unreported) (Cour d'appel de Paris Pôle 5, chambre 1).

provider privilege in 2017.[581] The judges deemed that certain of its functionalities, e.g. a premium seller programme or structuring of the display of sellers and offers, visibly favouring Chinese sellers, corresponded to a specific commercial interest of the marketplace. *Alibaba* gave itself the appearance of a hosting service, while in reality it was an editor of information, playing an active role. It was found liable for offering counterfeit products and for unfair commercial practices. Meanwhile, French competitor *CDiscount*[582] was accorded the hosting provider status in a counterfeit action brought by apparel brand *Jansport* in 2019. The *Tribunal de Grande instance Paris* found that *CDiscount's* professional seller programme, the opportunity given to sellers to personalise and promote their offers, and to take part in a specific logistics program were either purely automated services, independent from the actual information stored, or did not lead to an active knowledge over the content. In a case concerning selective distribution agreements brought against *Amazon* and *Samsung*,[583] the former marketplace was also accorded the host status of Article 14 ECD. The *Cour de Cassation* mentioned *obiter dictum* that the claimant had failed to demonstrate that *Amazon* played an active role by offering: sellers to market their products internationally, i.e. on other *Amazon* country sites; payment services, notably cheque and bank card payments processing; product delivery, and to deal with problems arising during order fulfilment.

Germany

In 2011, a regional court in Stuttgart was one of the first to apply the CJEU ruling in Germany. It found that respondent *eBay* did not qualify for the host provider privilege because it had played an active role by promoting the offers of trademark infringing perfume products, owned by the applicant *Coty*.[584] This view was confirmed in the BGHs judgements in *Kinder-*

---

581 *Lafuma Mobilier v Alibaba et autres* (2017) (Unreported) (Tribunal de Grande instance, Paris).

582 *Jansport Apparel v Cdiscount* (2019) (Unreported) (Tribunal de Grande instance, Paris, 3ème chambre - 2ème section).

583 *Concurrence v Amazon services Europe, Samsung Electronics France* [2017] Cour de cassation - Chambre commerciale, financière et économique - 14-16.737, FR:CCASS:2017:CO01027.

584 *Coty Germany GmbH v eBay International AG (No1)*, [2011] LG Stuttgart, 17 Zivilkammer 17 O 169/11, [2012] ETMR 19 [46].

hochstühle II and *III*, of 2013 and 2015.[585] In this case *eBay* had selected keywords, relating to a brand of toddlers' high chairs in the *Google's AdWords* program. The search results from *Google* led to a list of offers that corresponded to a keyword search on *eBay's* platforms. This list included offers that infringed the trademark of the claimants, the owners of the brand of high chairs that corresponded to the keywords. In a direct application of *L'Oréal v eBay*, the BGH ruled that although the resulting product offer list was dynamic and automatic, *eBay* had an active role where it selected and booked *AdWords* campaigns on behalf of those sellers. It rejected *eBay's* argument that this service was purely automated and merely served as a neutral, supporting activity to the sale of goods undertaken by the sellers.[586] Meanwhile, the provision of automated tools aimed at creating and displaying product offers, sending promotional emails to customers and the option to manage sales transactions and payments did not lead to an active role of the marketplace.[587]

A regional court in Stuttgart applied the BGH's *Kinderhochstühle III* ruling in a case brought in 2018 against *Alibaba* by *Calvin Klein*. It added that offering different language versions of product detail pages and the existence of a buyer protection program by the platforms were also not sufficient for making *Alibaba* an active intermediary that had appropriated third party content.[588]

By contrast, marketplace *Amazon* was found liable for reproducing product images on its marketplace platform, because of the active role it played in selecting these images, which were uploaded by its sellers.[589] The claimant, who manufactures *Davidoff* perfumes, had a selective distribution agreement with *Amazon* and uploaded product images on that plat-

585 *Kinderhochstühle im Internet II, I ZR 216/11* [2013] MIR 2013 Dok 077 (BGH); *Kinderhochstühle im Internet III* [2015] BGH I ZR 240/12, 144/2015 JurPC Web-Dok.

586 *Kinderhochstühle im Internet III* (n 584) paras 85, 94–95. The same claimant had been less successful in 2012 in the Netherlands against the *eBay* subsidiary *Marktplaats (Stokke Nederland BV v Marktplaats BV* [2012] Gerechtshof Leeuwarden 107.001.948/01, NL:RBZLY:2007:BA4950. The Leeuwarden court ruled under virtually identical circumstances that, based on the CJEU criteria in *L'Oréal v eBay*, *Marktplaats* took a neutral position and was protected by Article 14 ECD.

587 *Kinderhochstühle im Internet III* (n 584) paras 81–82.

588 *Beeinträchtigung der Herkunftsfunktion einer Marke trotz Fälschungshinweises (Parfume Made in China)* [2018] LG Stuttgart, 17 Zivilkammer 17 O 928/13, GRUR-RS 2018, 20582 [53].

589 *Wiederholungsgefahr, 16 O 103/14* [2016] LG Berlin, 16 Zivilkammer DE:LGBE:2016:0126.16O103.14.0A, BeckRS 2016, 10918.

forms for the marketing of its products. A competing seller, who rightfully distributed similar products on *Amazon*, was allocated the same product images for its detail pages. The image selection was done through an algorithm deployed by *Amazon* and used for selecting the most suitable product images. The *Davidoff* licence holders complained. *Amazon* retracted the pictures but failed to make a cease-and-desist declaration. The marketplace argued that the selection of pictures was fully automated, giving its staff neither knowledge nor control over the decision over which images were allocated to an offer. The Berlin court found that it did not matter whether the selection process was done manually or algorithmically, as long as it was done by *Amazon* itself. By selecting the pictures *Amazon* "cut the decision chain between the seller and the picture." *Amazon* went therefore beyond being a purely neutral intermediary. Although this decision has been appealed, it remains remarkable as it somewhat counteracts a previous trend, at least in Germany, according to which marketplaces have not been found liable for erroneously or otherwise modifying product descriptions or price recommendations of sellers due to the fully automated nature of this activity.[590]

Finally, the ongoing challenges on assessing the role of today's intermediaries can be seen from the recent CJEU ruling in *Coty v Amazon.*[591] In this case the perfume manufacturer claimed that *Amazon's* activities as a marketplace operator in conjunction with its logistics service for sellers, *Fulfillment by Amazon (FBA)*, went beyond a merely neutral role. The vertically integrated activities, through which grey market goods sold by third party sellers were offered and shipped to customers, led to *Amazon* making use of *Coty's* marks in the course of business, thus constituting violations of its trademark. This view was not shared by the CJEU, which also partly contradicted the assessment offered by the AG.[592] The CJEU looked at *Amazon's* marketplace operations and its fulfilment service individually. Each of these services taken in isolation were intermediary activities for

590 Bernhard Knies, 'Amazon Haftet Für Urheberrechtsverletzungen Seiner Verkäufer' (*new-media-law.net*, 9 June 2016) <https://www.new-media-law.net/amazon-haftet-fuer-urheberrechtsverletzungen-seiner-verkaeufer/> accessed 17 January 2020; *Haftung für falsche UVP-Angabe bei Amazon* [2015] OLG Köln 6 W 29/15, openJur 2016, 3226.

591 *Coty Germany GmbH v Amazon Services Europe Sàrl and others, C-567/18* [2020] EU:C:2020:267 (CJEU).

592 *Schlussanträge des Generalanwalts Manuel Campos Sánchez-Bordona, Coty Germany GmbH gegen Amazon Services Europe Sàrl und andere, C-567/18* [2019] EU:C:2019:1031 (CJEU).

which case law had confirmed that they did not make use of trademarks in the course of business. It implied that marketplace operations would need to be examined under Article 14 ECD, while the storage activities fell under Article 11 IPRED.[593] This case serves as a fitting example over the difficulties of assessing the status of online intermediaries in the dynamically evolving platform economy.[594] It also demonstrates the challenges of the current ECD framework, which looks at liability and the regulation of intermediaries by applying a rather narrow neutral/passive dichotomy. This appears to be oddly out of place with current realities. Online platforms have for some time started to expand into and transform more traditional "physical" activities of the wider economy and integrated them into other business models. This makes the distinction between electronic and non-electronic services which the ECD relies on in its functional scope for regulating ISSPs all the more challenging. This judgement will be analysed in more detail in the trademarks section of Chapter 4.

UK

UK courts applied the CJEU ruling of *L'Oréal v eBay* in *Cosmetic Warriors v Amazon*.[595] *Cosmetic Warriors* is the owner of the *Lush* cosmetics brand and brought *Amazon* to court for trademark infringements. Using an autocomplete functionality, *Amazon* customers' searches were completed with *Lush* product names and suggestions, resulting in the display of competing sales offers, which did not bear the *Lush* trademark. These products were either sold by Amazon itself or by third party sellers on its marketplace, some of them also utilising the *Amazon FBA* logistics service. Applying *L'Oréal v eBay*, the English court had relatively little difficulty in finding Amazon's activity "much more than merely use in a service consisting of enabling its customers to display on its website signs corresponding to trade marks."[596] Although the display of products sold and shipped by third party sellers may not be infringing use, the list of search results was mixed with those products that were sold by *Amazon* itself and those sold by third-part sellers using the e-commerce giant's fulfilment service *FBA*. For the latter two categories *Amazon* clearly engaged in commercial communication to pro-

593 *Coty v Amazon (FBA)* (n 590) para 49.
594 Carsten Ullrich, 'Déjà vu Davidoff – The German Federal Court of Justice Refers Another Case Brought by Coty Dealing with Trade Marks in e-Commerce to the CJEU' (2019) 14 Journal of Intellectual Property Law & Practice 5.
595 *Cosmetic Warriors v Amazon* (n 560).
596 ibid 57.

mote its own activities. This reading is remarkable because it somewhat pre-confirms the opinion of the CJEU's AG Campos Sánchez-Bordona in *Coty v Amazon.* The AG had indicated that the fulfilment and marketplace activities of Amazon, seen jointly, could be seen as active involvement and trademark use.[597]

The rulings above show that courts in Europe have to this day had marked difficulties in evaluating the role of marketplaces in the intermediation process. The technical architecture, supporting services (promotional activities, sales optimisation, payment and logistics services) and the changes in business models have caused veritable headaches to judges. E-commerce marketplaces are therefore a fitting example of the changing nature of online intermediaries. Over the last 10 years at least, e-commerce marketplaces have engaged in online marketing activities (on site, advertising on third party sites), have built sophisticated search engine functionalities, integrated other intermediary service providers (payment, third party logistics), offered their ancillary services (buyer insurance, logistics services), and diversified their product choice (integrating own products, international/global selling). As a result, courts have continued to struggle when pinning down the role of e-commerce marketplace in the intermediation process and the availability of the ECD's hosting defence, even in the wake of the supposedly clarifying rulings by the CJEU.

iv. US developments

US courts, by contrast, have been more consistent in according the liability protections to these internet intermediaries. In the earlier cases of *Stoner,*[598] *Hendrickson*[599] and *Tiffany*[600] the courts confirmed that intermediary *eBay*, who was the defendant in all three cases, qualified for the protections offered to internet intermediaries under the CDA, the DMCA and the Lanham Act, respectively. Thus, in *Hendrickson*, a case involving the sale of pirated video DVDs, the judges had no doubt that *eBay* qualified for the safe

---

597 *AG Opinion, Coty v Amazon (FBA)* (n 591) paras 59–62.

598 *Randall Stoner v EBay Inc, et al* [2000] Sup Ct Ca Civ. No. 305666, (Unreported).

599 *Hendrickson v eBay* [2001] CD Cal CV 01-0495 RJK (RNBx) (C.D. Cal. 2001), 165 F. Supp. 2d 1082.

600 *Tiffany (NJ) Inc v eBay Inc* (2010) 600 F. 3d 93 93 (2nd Cir).

harbour provisions offered by the DMCA.[601] Similarly in *Tiffany*, the jewellery maker complained against the massive sale of counterfeits on *eBay*, which infringed its trademark. Here, the availability of protections against secondary infringements by intermediaries under the Lanham Act were confirmed.[602] More recently, the very narrow interpretation of (secondary) liability was confirmed for the new type of e-commerce marketplaces.[603] In *Milo Gabby v Amazon*,[604] a pillow manufacturer brought *Amazon* to court over the repeated sale of "knock-off" versions of its products. The company argued that at least for those sellers using the *FBA* service the marketplace acted as a seller with enhanced liability for the products on offer. The Court found, however, that *Amazon* did not take ownership of the goods through its FBA service, and that "even if Amazon were to take title under the Fulfillment by Amazon agreement, it would do so only to dispose of the product, not to sell it."[605] This is in marked contrast to the view of the platform's involvement by the CJEU's AG in *Coty v Amazon*, but also the UK judgement in *Cosmetic Warriors v Amazon*.

c. UGC platforms and social networks

Social media and UGC platforms' new interactive and immersive qualities when it comes to the dissemination of information have already been introduced in Chapter 2. Similar to e-commerce marketplaces, courts have grappled with problems in according these intermediaries the immunity status as hosting providers under Article 14 ECD. The variety of potentially unlawful content spread via these sites is much larger than compared to e-commerce marketplaces. UGC and social media sites have been in the focus for their involvement in the spread of copyright infringing content,

---

601 According to the US' DMCA 17 U.S.C. § 512 (c) (1), intermediaries will merely not have to have actual knowledge of unlawful activity, do not directly benefit financially from it and remove such content expeditiously once notified of it.

602 Andrew Lehrer, 'Tiffany V. EBay: Its Impact And Implications On The Doctrines Of Secondary Trademark And Copyright Infringement' (2012) 18 Boston University Journal of Science & Technology Law 32, 389–400.

603 R Bruce Rich and David Ho, 'Sound Policy and Practice in Applying Doctrines of Secondary Liability Under U.S. Copyright and Trademark Law to Online Trading Platforms: A Case Study' (2020) 32 Intellectual Property & Technology Law Journal 15, 9–10.

604 *Milo & Gabby LLC v Amazon.com* [2017] Fed Cir 2016-1290, 693 F. App'x 879.

605 ibid.

hate and terrorist speech, defamatory content, and child abuse material as well as counterfeits or illegal products.

i. National case law

France

In France, the early social networking site *MySpace's* was seen as a publisher of content, thus forfeiting the hosting provider liability protection under the ECD.[606] In this 2007 case, the *Tribunal de Grande instance de Paris* found that *MySpace* had structured the design of user accounts pages and displayed dynamic adverts from which it generated revenue. These activities inferred control and knowledge of the information stored.[607] Consequently, *MySpace* was found directly liable for copyright infringement and obliged to prevent uploads of illegal (copyright infringing) content. It is interesting to note that under similar circumstances *Dailymotion*, a French video sharing platform (VSP) was found to be a host provider in 2010. In that case the judges argued that making available a pre-structured design and providing tools for classifying content was a pure technical necessity for the act of hosting under *Dailymotion's* business model.[608] Already in 2007, when a film producer sued the platform for copyright infringements and parasitic conduct, had this VSP been accorded the status of a host provider.[609] Nevertheless, the French judges still refused to accord *Dailymotion* the liability protections. Because its (hosting) business model relied on the infringing activity by its users, it was inevitable that it had actual knowledge of these unlawful acts.[610] This approach was confirmed in a case against *Google Video* in 2008.[611]

---

606 *Jean Yves L dit Lafesse v Myspace* (2007) (Unreported) (Tribunal de grande instance de Paris).
607 ibid., see also : Angelopoulos, 2009, p. 3
608 *Roland Magdane et autres v Dailymotion* (2010) (Unreported) (Cour d'appel de Paris Pôle 5, chambre 1). Under the judgement's heading: *Sur la nature du service offert par la société Daily Motion*
609 *Christian, C., Nord Ouest Production v Dailymotion, UGC Images* (n 196). Under Chapter « DISCUSSION Sur la nature de l'activité exercée par la société Dailymotion et sa responsabilité ».
610 See also the discussion in: Christina Angelopoulos, 'Filtering the Internet for Copyrighted Content in Europe' (2009) 4 iris plus 12.
611 *Flach Film et autres v Google France, Google Inc* (2008) (Unreported) (Tribunal de commerce de Paris 8ème chambre).

The tendency of granting UGC sites the status of hosts under the ECD was somehow disrupted by the French Supreme Court's 2010 ruling in *Tiscali Media*.[612] Despite agreeing that *Tiscali* was not a publisher of the personal pages that they assisted users in creating, the company engaged in more than mere technical activities required of a hosting provider. For example, *Tiscali* offered to place advertisements on the personal pages of their users, including on pages containing copyright infringing content. By benefitting from this activity, *Tiscali* became more than a simple technical host of information and took over a responsibility for the unlawful content.[613]

Germany

By contrast, German courts were less hesitant initially in qualifying UGC services as host provider. The test to determine the active /neutral role corresponded to an evaluation of whether the platform had appropriated ("*sich zu Eigen Machen*") the content hosted on behalf of a third party.[614] This line was established by the BGH in *Marion's Kochbuch.*[615] *Marion's Kochbuch* was an internet portal that made cooking recipes uploaded by users publicly available. The portal was found taking possession of the content by verifying it for completeness and accuracy before sharing it amongst its users. In addition, the portal providers had obtained rights to monetarise the content, including marketing it to third parties. In the following *Rapidshare* and *GEMA v YouTube* cases,[616] the application of hosting provider privileges caused markedly less headaches to the German courts. In an ongoing saga of several cases for a period of over 10 years, *GEMA*, the German music authors and publishers' rights association, claimed that *YouTube* engaged in infringing acts by making works publicly available without having received the authorisation for it. The Hamburg court distinguished this case from *Marion's Kochbuch*. Notably, *YouTube* did not need to check uploaded content for its correctness before sharing

612 *Télécom Italia (Tiscali) v Dargaud Lombard, Lucky Comics* (2010) (Unreported) (Cour de cassation 1ère chambre civile).

613 See also: Tobias Bednarz, 'Keyword Advertising before the French Supreme Court and beyond - Calm at Last after Turbulent Times for Google and Its Advertising Clients?' (2011) 42 International Review of Intellectual Property and Competition Law 641, 653–655.

614 Nolte and Wimmers (n 551) 20–21.

615 *Marion's Kochbuch* [2009] BGH I ZR 166/07, MIR 2010, Dok. 082.

616 *RapidShare II* [2012] OLG Hamburg 5 U 87/09, MMR 2012, 393; *GEMA v YouTube* (n 264).

it. Activities such as structuring or categorisation of content did not result in *YouTube* having editorial or active control.[617] Likewise, the fact that *YouTube* exploited third-party content economically, through sub-licencing and advertising, was insignificant. Users were offered the possibility to withdraw the permission for this activity at any time.[618]

Italy

In Italy, courts went yet a slightly different way in determining the availability of the hosting defence for UGC platforms, notably *YouTube*. Faced with the complexities of the activities of these platforms they developed the concept of "active hosting providers." This may also reflect an attempt to fit the new activities of Web 2.0 platforms to the categories of intermediary liability available through Italian national law.[619] Thus, in 2011, the VSPs *IOL* and *Yahoo!* were classified this way. The determining factors were that they carried advertising on detail pages that contained infringing content; that they reserved themselves the right to edit or modify uploaded content; and that they provided an internal search engine functionality. Moreover, they were themselves engaged in uploading content. In the end they were seen as hosts, albeit with an active role, and therefore directly at fault for copyright infringements.[620] The latter judgement was overturned in 2015 when the appeals court disapproved of the active hosting provider category and ruled that the service in question was neutral.[621] Finally, in 2019, the Italian Supreme Court qualified the previous rulings by affirming the active hosting provider doctrine of the Italian judiciary. It pointed out a number of activities that can be seen as indicative for active behaviour of the hosting service, such as indexing, selecting, filtering, organising, promoting or aggregating content. An active host would lose the protections of Article 14 ECD. However, the previous appeals court had correctly ruled that *Yahoo* was passive.[622]

---

617 *GEMA v YouTube* (n 264) para B V 2 a bb.

618 ibid B V 2 b.

619 See Ch 3. B. 2. II. b

620 *Reti Televisive Italiane S.pA v Italia On Line S.r.l* [2011] Court of Milan 3821/11; *Reti Televisive Italiane S.pA v Yahoo! Italia S.r.l and Yahoo! Inc,* (2011) (Unreported) (Court of Milan). In: E Bonadio and M Santo, 'Court of Milan Holds Video Sharing Platforms Liable for Copyright Infringement' (2012) 7 Journal of Intellectual Property Law & Practice 14.

621 Giulio Coraggio, 'Internet Litigation.' (2015) 21 IP Litigator 25.

622 *Reti Televisive Italiane SpA v Yahoo! Inc and Reti Televisive Italiane SpA v Yahoo! Inc* [2019] Court of Appeal of Milan 7708/19 and 7709/19. In: Eleonora Rosati,

In the same vein, VSP *YouTube* was qualified as a passive host in 2017, with its indexing and content organisation activities being seen as not altering the content itself.[623] Its competitors *Dailymotion* and *Vimeo* were, meanwhile, seen as active hosts two years later, and not in a position to make use of the liability protections of the ECD. In the latter case, the fact that *Vimeo* had set up its own search engine, categorised and indexed content uploaded by users, and linked the display of advertisings to user searches all confirmed its active character.[624] *Facebook* also forfeited the hosting privilege entirely as a result of being held directly responsible for copyright infringing acts.[625]

UK

In the UK defamation case of *CG v Facebook*, a Northern Irish appeals court accorded the social network the immunities of Article 14 implicitly and without any further test of its activities.[626] In contrast to cases involving e-commerce marketplaces, this appears to be a common line in UK jurisprudence on social media platforms.[627] At least, however, the hosting provider status of UGC sites and social media platforms is not challenged

---

'Italian Supreme Court Clarifies Availability of Safe Harbours, Content of Notice-and-Takedown Requests, and Stay-down Obligations - The IPKat | Diigo' (*The IPKat*, 20 March 2019) <https://ipkitten.blogspot.com/2019/03/italian-supreme-court-clarifies.html> accessed 23 January 2020.

623 *Delta TV v Google and YouTube* [2017] Turin Court of First Instance (Tribunale di Torino) No. 1928, RG 38113/2013. In: Eleonora Rosati, 'Italian Court Finds Google and YouTube Liable for Failing to Remove Unlicensed Content (but Confirms Eligibility for Safe Harbour Protection)' (*The IPKat*, 30 April 2017)

624 *Mediaset v Dailymotion* [2019] Rome Court of First Instance 14757/2019; In: ibid. *Reti Televisive Italiane S.p.a (RTI) v Vimeo* [2019] Tribunale di Roma 623; in: Ernesto Apa and Bassini, 'Court of Rome Rules Vimeo Liable for Copyright Infringement' [2019] iris Newlsetter 50.

625 *Mediaset v Facebook* [2019] Rome Court of First Instance 3512/2019. In: Eleonora Rosati, 'Facebook Found Liable for Hosting Links to Unlicensed Content' (*The IPKat*, 21 February 2019) <http://ipkitten.blogspot.com/2019/02/facebook-found-liable-for-hosting-links.html> accessed 23 January 2020.

626 *CG v Facebook Ireland Ltd & Anor* [2016] 2016 NICA 54 (Court of Appeal in Northern Ireland) [53]. See also for more detailed discussion: Lorna Woods, 'When Is Facebook Liable for Illegal Content under the E-Commerce Directive? CG v. Facebook in the Northern Ireland Courts' (*Inforrm's Blog*, 28 January 2017) <https://inforrm.org/2017/01/28/when-is-facebook-liable-for-illegal-content-under-the-e-commerce-directive-cg-v-facebook-in-the-northern-ireland-courts-lorna-woods/> accessed 23 January 2020

627 *J20 v Facebook Ireland Ltd* [2012] High Court Of Justice In Northern Ireland Queen's Bench Division COL10121 [48].

by the courts. In *Galloway v Frazer* the Northern Irish court declined to settle this particular matter without being specifically asked, and examined *Google's* conduct practically under the premise that it was a hosting provider.[628]

ii. EU case law

The first, and so far, only attempt by the CJEU at a clarification on the availability of the hosting defence for social networks site came from the *Netlog* case in 2012.[629] *Netlog* was a Belgian social media network, which was brought to court by the Belgian association of music authors and rightsholder (*SABAM*). *SABAM* tried to impose an injunction forcing *Netlog* to stop the unauthorised sharing of music for which it owned the copyright. The CJEU found no difficulty in according the hosting provider status to the social network, noting that "it is not in dispute that the owner of an online social networking platform - such as Netlog - stores information provided by the users of that platform, relating to their profile, on its servers."[630] One had to wait until the recent *Facebook*[631] ruling to see the CJEU pronounce itself on the availability of the hosting defence for a social networking platform. In that judgement the CJEU, however, just said that it was common ground that *Facebook* provided a service that qualified for protection under the hosting provider regime of the ECD. A small glimpse of doubt is, however, gleaned from AG Szpunar's Opinion on this case. He remarks curiously and seemingly in passing that the assessment of the referring court accorded *Facebook* the status of a hosting provider *"irrespective of the doubts that one might have in that regard."*[632]

It seems the *CJEU* did not want to trouble itself with this potentially thorny issue. Another explanation may be that, since in *Google France* and *L'Oréal v eBay* the CJEU had referred the detailed assessment on the neutral/passive role on the platform back to national courts, it did not want to pronounce itself further without being specifically asked.

628 *Galloway v Frazer, Google Inc (YouTube) and Ors* [2016] Northern Ireland Queen's Bench Division HOR979, [2016] NIQB 7 [7].
629 *SABAM v Netlog* (n 460).
630 ibid 27.
631 *Eva Glawischnig-Piesczek v Facebook Ireland Limited, C-18/18* (n 463).
632 *Opinion of Advocate General Szpunar on Eva Glawischnig-Piesczek v Facebook Ireland Limited, C-18/18* (n 264) para 30.

That chance will however present itself in the future. There are currently two referrals by the Austrian and German Supreme Courts in front of the CJEU which aim to establish clarity on the availability of the hosting defence for the VSP *YouTube*.[633] The plaintiffs seek guidance on whether various activities of *YouTube* conferred on it an active role, outside of the hosting provider status of the ECD. These activities consist, amongst others of: providing users with the possibility to search, flag and comment on videos, making advertising and licencing revenue from the shared content, structuring content, such as by sorting and ranking, as well as recommending clips to users. It appears logic that any decision taken for the UGC site *YouTube* would have repercussions on the activities of social networks like *Facebook*, through which also various types of content are being shared, recommended and advertised on a similarly massive scale.

This hands-off approach by the CJEU was confirmed in the *SNB-REACT* ruling. The Estonian Court of Appeal in Tallinn had asked the CJEU whether internet registries and registrars could qualify for the ECD's liability protections.[634] The case was brought by *REACT*, an industry association that defends trademark owners' rights, against a provider which offered services for rental and registration of IP addresses. This service had registered 38,000 IP addresses and domain names which were in violation of *REACT* members' trademark rights. The CJEU stated, however, that first it was for the referring court to determine whether IP address rental and registration services fulfilled the criteria of an ISSP. Secondly, that court would also need to assess that the service met the detailed criteria of Articles 12 – 14 ECD, including the decision which kind of intermediary these services would be. The court cited almost *ad verbatim* its iterations in *Google France* and *L'Oréal v eBay*.

---

633 Request for a preliminary ruling from the Bundesgerichtshof (Germany) lodged on 6 November 2018 — LF v Google LLC, YouTube Inc, YouTube LLC, Google Germany GmbH (Case C-682/18) (CJEU); Request for a preliminary ruling from the Oberster Gerichtshof (Austria) lodged on 1 July 2019 — Puls 4 TV GmbH & Co KG v YouTube LLC and Google Austria GmbH (Case C-500/19) (CJEU).

634 *Coöperatieve Vereniging SNB-REACT U.A. v Deepak Mehta - C-521/17* (n 276) paras 47–52.

II. The intermediary's actual knowledge of illegal acts

a. Defining actual knowledge

Online intermediary service providers that act merely technical and passive will qualify for the liability exemptions offered by Articles 12 – 14 ECD. Caching and hosting services will not be liable for any illegal information or activity that they had no actual knowledge of.[635] Once they obtain that knowledge they need to remove the information expeditiously or block access to it. An additional condition applies to hosting providers. They must not be aware of facts and circumstances from which illegal information or activity is apparent.[636] Mere conduits, by contrast, only need to respond to court or administrative orders to terminate or prevent infringements.[637]

As mentioned above, throughout common and civil law systems knowledge has been used as a condition to determine fault and subsequent liability of intermediaries. Not all Member States did, however, transpose the actual knowledge requirement of the ECD literally into their national laws. The Netherlands merely refer to liability only where an intermediary knew of unlawful acts or activity or could have been reasonable expected to know. The Czech Republic and Spain tie actual knowledge directly to the receipt of a notice. Germany and Portugal just refer to knowledge, instead of actual knowledge.[638]

But even where Member States did follow a word-by-word transposition of the ECD, courts still risked at coming to different interpretations of actual knowledge. As concluded by Judge Arnold in the *Newzbin* case "the interpretation of the requirement of 'actual knowledge'... is primarily a matter of domestic law, albeit within the framework created, and the constraints imposed, by European law."[639]

Courts faced notable problems when trying to establish the circumstances under which an intermediary could be presumed to have attained actual knowledge that would trigger an obligation to act. This question is linked first to the definition of actual knowledge. In the UK case of *Newzbin*, for example, it was found that actual knowledge was related to

---

635 Directive 2000/31 (ECD) Article 14 para 1 (a) (b), Article 13 para 1..

636 Ibid. Article 14 para 1 (a).

637 *Mc Fadden* (n 139) paras 63–65.

638 Verbiest and others (n 315) 34–35. European Commission, 'SEC(2011) 1641 Final' (n 11) 32–37.

639 *Twentieth Century Fox Film Corp & Ors v British Telecommunications Plc* [2011] 2011 EWHC 1981 Ch (High Court of Justice Chancery Division) [202].

the extent to which a service provider knew about particular persons being involved in particular restricted acts, involving particular copyrighted works.[640] This reasoning implies that actual knowledge is linked to subjective knowledge of the service provider of infringing activity. This reading is confirmed by German case law, where actual knowledge has been interpreted as knowledge of specific unlawful acts or content by a human being. By contrast, general awareness of illegal activity cannot be equated to actual knowledge.[641]

The requirement of awareness of facts and circumstances indicating illegal activity, which may result in pecuniary damages, if not addressed,[642] is likened to the tort of gross negligence. This can also be "objective knowledge", or facts, which a person or actor in comparable circumstances should or could have been expected to be aware of. Another early consensus that arose from national court rulings was that intermediaries were supposed to attain actual knowledge or actionable awareness where it concerned manifestly illegal information or activity. However, the definition of manifestly illegal content varies by country. While there is little difference nationally over the manifestly illegal nature of child pornographic content, it appears that courts have applied different knowledge standards when it came to less obvious areas such IP law or defamation.[643]

b. Obtaining actual knowledge

Following jurisprudence at national and EU level there are usually three ways of how an intermediary service provider may obtain actual knowledge. First, through notification by an authority or court. Secondly, the notice can be given by an allegedly damaged party, such as an IP rightsholder or a defamed person. The third method has been much more controversially discussed. It relates to an intermediary being aware of facts or circumstances that indicate illegal activity and thus being obliged to act under the ECD.[644]

640 ibid 148.
641 Verbiest and others (n 315) 37.
642 Directive 2000/31 (ECD) Article 14 (1) (a).
643 Verbiest and others (n 315) 36–41.
644 European Commission, 'SEC(2011) 1641 Final' (n 11) 33.

i. Court or authority orders

Orders from a court or an authority may be the most obvious way for an intermediary to gain such actual knowledge. This is because the intermediary would not need to engage in his own assessment of whether the notified content is indeed illegal under the laws of the respective jurisdiction. Spain, for example, defined in its national transposition of the ECD the term actual knowledge explicitly as only relating to such instances where a competent authority has declared such content illegal and notified the intermediary.[645] While this may be the safest way to avoid mistakes and erroneous or over-cautious blocking of legal content, it is questionable that this would be an effective way of dealing with the vast amounts of illegal content. In addition, it may relieve intermediaries of any duty at all and therefore render the knowledge requirement superfluous.[646]

ii. Notice-and-Takedown

Notification by private third parties can be seen as the standard procedure under the current ECD regime, and under intermediary liability regimes worldwide, of providing intermediary service providers with actual knowledge of illegal content or activity. This procedure is globally known as notice-and-takedown (NTD) or notice-and-action (NA). Upon receipt of a notice, it is the responsibility of the intermediary to decide on the claim's veracity. The safe harbour protection would apply if the online intermediary removes or disables access to the notified unlawful content or activity.[647] The US intermediary provisions of the DMCA operate on the same principle for hosting services and for search engines.[648]

Unlike US law, the ECD does not lay down requirements for the process and format of NTD requests. This means that the details required to put an intermediary on actionable notice vary across Member States. The latter may or my not regulate these details through their national laws for hosting providers established in their jurisdiction.[649] The EU has set out in the

---

645 Thibault Verbiest and others, 'Study on the Liability of Internet Intermediaries, Markt 2006/09/E - Country Report Spain - Executive Summary' 2; Rowland, Kohl and Charlesworth (n 128) 86.

646 Rowland, Kohl and Charlesworth (n 128) 86.

647 Directive 2000/31 (ECD) Article 13 (1) (e), 14 (1) (b).

648 17 U.S.C. § 512 c (1) (A) (iii), d (1) (c).

649 Directive 2000/31 (ECD) Article 14 (3).

ECD that measures to formalise NTD should rely on self-regulation, such as codes of conducts.[650]

Some Member States have decided to implement such requirements through national or soft law provisions. Most of the time, these processes did not follow the broad horizontal remit of the ECD, but were put in place for specific content sectors, such as copyright, or child abuse content, or for only certain types of intermediaries. According to a 2012 European Commission study, nine Member States had implemented NTD procedures in their national laws.[651] Sweden and Portugal had put in place horizontal NTD frameworks for hosting providers that covered any type of infringement. However, only in Portugal does compliance with the procedures set out in the NTD framework protect intermediaries explicitly from liabilities. Finland, France, Hungary, Lithuania, the UK and Spain have put NTD procedures in place for copyright violations. Germany put in place notification procedures for child pornographic material and the UK for terrorist content. The requirements on the format and content of notices under these national regimes, for example, whether it should contain an URL, a description of the violation, a proof of authority, varied widely, as did the time limits set for reacting to a notice or for filing counterclaims. More recently, Germany and France have introduced or proposed laws aimed at codifying notification and removal procedures for hate speech on social media and UGC platforms.[652]

In addition, in many Member States, industry led, self - regulatory procedures have been set up, which are aimed at formalising NTD in specific sectors. In Austria, Belgium, Denmark, France, Germany, the Netherlands and the UK, industry and trade associations have set up code of conducts for their members concerning the reporting and removing of unlawful content.[653] Some of the more well-known industry led projects in the area of notifying and removing child abuse content on the internet are the

650 ibid Recital 40, Article 16 (1).

651 European Commission, 'SEC(2011) 1641 Final' (n 11) 137–140.

652 Gesetz zur Verbesserung der Rechtsdurchsetzung in sozialen Netzwerken 2017 (BGBl I S 3352 (Nr 61)); Laetitia Avia, Proposition de loi visant à lutter contre la haine sur internet.

653 Verbiest and others (n 315) 110–115. Swiss Institute of Comparative Law, 'Study on Filtering, Blocking and Take-down of Illegal Content on the Internet' (Council of Europe 2015) 796–800 <https://www.coe.int/en/web/cybercrime/news/-/asset_publisher/S73WWxscOuZ5/content/study-on-filtering-blocking-and-take-down-of-illegal-content-on-the-internet> accessed 4 February 2020.

UK's *Internet Watch Foundation* and Germany's *Association for Voluntary Self-Regulation of Digital Media Service Providers (FSM)*.[654]

In the absence of any guiding procedures in national law on NTD, courts have also stepped in and decided on a case by case basis whether notices where sufficient to confer actual knowledge of the existence of illegal content. For example, in 2007, a Belgian judge specified the details of a copyright infringement notice and the time limit for reaction in a case involving the intermediary *Google News*.[655] Until as recent as 2019, Italian and French courts have given guidance on the level of detail required for notices in copyright and trademark infringement that would give intermediaries actual knowledge.[656]

Meanwhile, larger, global, often US-based online platforms that determine the intermediary landscape of today have put in place their own notification systems on their platforms.[657] These are largely based on the more detailed US legal requirements, as for example set out by the DMCA. They are adapted, where necessary, to local requirements. In the absence of any fixed rules, these systems have become the quasi standard for NTD.

The meaning of "expeditious" removal of unlawful information is less of a contested issue. With the incredible surge in NTD requests that many of the larger platforms receive today, especially in the area of copyright, these activities are by now largely automated and operationalised. Where the public interest is at a higher stake, such as for terrorist content, the EU and Member States have started to formulate more onerous review and removal timelines.

---

654 'Our Members' (*IWF*) <https://www.iwf.org.uk/become-a-member/join-us/our-members> accessed 4 February 2020; 'FSM | About Us' <https://www.fsm.de/en/about-us> accessed 4 February 2020.

655 *Copiepresse et al v. Google Inc* (n 555).

656 For Italy: Eleonora Rosati, 'Italian Supreme Court Clarifies Availability of Safe Harbours, Content of Notice-and-Takedown Requests, and Stay-down Obligations - The IPKat | Diigo' (*The IPKat*, 20 March 2019) <https://ipkitten.blogspot.com/2019/03/italian-supreme-court-clarifies.html> accessed 23 January 2020; for France: *Jansport Apparel v Cdiscount* (Tribunal de Grande instance, Paris, 3ème chambre - 2ème section).

657 'How to Report Things on Facebook | Facebook Help Center' <https://www.facebook.com/help/181495968648557/> accessed 4 February 2020; 'Amazon.de - Mitteilung an Amazon.de Über Eine Rechtsverletzung' <https://www.amazon.de/report/infringement?> accessed 4 February 2020; 'Copyright Infringement Notification - YouTube' <https://www.youtube.com/copyright_complaint_form> accessed 4 February 2020; 'Signaler les comportements inappropriés' <https://help.twitter.com/fr/safety-and-security/report-abusive-behavior> accessed 5 February 2020.

CJEU guidance on this matter has not been overly helpful. In *L'Oréal v eBay*, the EU's highest court simply stated that for a notification to eventually lead to awareness of illegal information or activity, it must be sufficiently precise and adequately substantiated. Whether that was the case in a given situation was a matter for national courts to decide upon.[658]

The resulting patchwork of notification and removal standards across the EU has been recognised as a barrier to the effective and transparent removal of unlawful information on online platforms, including by the European Commission.[659] For one, the current situation still leads to varying interpretations of the level of detail needed in a notification that leads to actual knowledge. Secondly it obliges intermediaries operating across Member States to comply with various notification standards, which runs counter to the original aim of the ECD to establish clear and general rules that regulate the activities of ISSPs.[660] Thirdly, it hinders the establishment of EU wide, consistent and transparent notification procedures that are not only effective, but also safeguard fundamental rights, such as freedom of expression, privacy, the right to exercise a business and intellectual property. This is important because of intermediaries' role as "private judges" over the legality of content, especially in cases where content is not manifestly or obviously unlawful. Notorious areas in this respect are exemptions provided in copyright or borderline speech that may be differently regulated by national laws.[661]

The latter problem is accentuated by the emergence of mass notifications in certain areas, such as IP rights. Major platform operators, such as *YouTube*, or *eBay* have been responding to this with automated takedown systems which have been found to lead to over-blocking and chilling effects on freedom of expression, while at the same time not adequately protecting IP rights.[662] These problems are even more apparent with regards to voluntary measures taken by platforms to prevent illegal information,

658 *L'Oréal v eBay* (n 463) paras 121–122.

659 European Commission, 'C(2018) 1177 Final' (n 8) Recitals 11, 12.

660 Directive 2000/31 (ECD) RECITAL 7.

661 European Commission, 'SEC(2011) 1641 Final' (n 11) 45–46. Sebastian Felix Schwemer, 'Trusted Notifiers and the Privatization of Online Enforcement' (2019) 35 Computer Law & Security Review 105339.

662 Lilian Edwards, 'With Great Power Comes Great Responsibility?: The Rise of Platform Liability' in Lilian Edwards (ed), *Law, policy, and the Internet* (Hart 2019) 272–277. Jennifer M Urban, Joe Karaganis and Brianna L Schofield, *Notice and Takedown in Everyday Practice* (American Assembly 2016).

which will be discussed below and in the relevant content subject matter sections of Chapter 4.

The European Commission did not identify any immediate need for the establishment of EU wide NTD procedures in the ECD evaluation exercises of 2003 and 2007. Following feedback received from a 2010 public consultation, which substantiated the problems outlined above,[663] the European Commission committed, as part of its Digital Agenda for Europe, to "adopt a horizontal initiative on notice and action procedures" subject to an impact assessment.[664] From 2016 to 2018 the Commission then committed to reviewing the need for formal notice and action procedures, however, with a view to do this on a sectoral level.[665] These intentions were accompanied by a number of EU Codes of Conduct and Memoranda of Understanding[666] aimed at establishing sectoral standards for the identification and removal of unlawful content. These will be discussed in the next chapter.

Finally, in its 2018 Recommendation, the Commission provided a number of general minimum procedural recommendation on NTD in order to safeguard fundamental rights. This covers information requirements to content providers and counter notice procedures, but does not go into further detail on the information that a notice should contain. The proposed Digital Services Act (DSA) now proposes for the first time legally binding procedural requirements for NTD for hosting services, and enhanced procedural obligations for the new category of online platforms.[667]

It is important to state that throughout the EU and its Member States, policy makers see NTD as a central element by which online intermediaries will receive actionable knowledge of unlawful information and activity. This is despite the growing importance attached to voluntary, proactive investigations on the part of online platforms. However, the nature of NTD has also been enriched by collaborative technology. User engage-

---

663 European Commission, 'SEC(2011) 1641 Final' (n 11) 39–46.

664 European Commission, 'A Coherent Framework for Building Trust in the Digital Single Market for E-Commerce and Online Services, COM(2011) 942 Final' (European Commission 2012) 11–15.

665 European Commission, 'COM(2016) 288 Final' (n 223) 8–9; European Commission, 'COM(2017) 228 Final' (n 538) 9.

666 'Memorandum of Understanding on the Sale of Counterfeit Goods over the Internet, 2011' <https://perma.cc/DF6M-JNJ8> accessed 29 June 2020; 'Memorandum of Understanding on the Online Sale of Counterfeit Goods, 2016' (n 542); 'Code of Conduct on Countering Illegal Hate Speech Online' (n 542).

667 European Commission DSA proposal (n 10) Articles 14, 17 and 19.

ment, for example through trusted flaggers or trusted notifier systems has received increasing policy attention, although there are reservations about these newer models of NTD.[668] At the same time, the relevance of NTD motivated content removals appears to decline in importance. Today, proactive and automated, artificial-intelligence-based detection systems, such as *Google's Content ID* software for copyright infringements, or *Facebook's* software to detect terrorist content, make up over 98% of all removals on these platforms.[669]

iii. Awareness of illegal activity or information

National interpretations

Awareness of facts and circumstances from which illegal activity is apparent is another unclear and hotly debated issue.[670] For truly passive hosts there would appear to be no other way of receiving indications of the apparent illegal nature of information or conduct other than being notified of it by users or other stakeholders. According to some Member States' early interpretations, mere awareness of illegal activity would constitute objective, general knowledge and therefore not trigger liabilities. Meanwhile, the absence of awareness of facts that indicate unlawful activity is in some Member States interpreted as absence of gross negligence, and related to more specific knowledge.[671]

In an early German decision, an e-commerce marketplace was absolved from that gross negligence. The existence of past trademark violations and of general indications over the occurrence of sales of counterfeits via the platform did not constitute facts that made the existence of specific illegal activities apparent. It also precluded an obligation on behalf of the online marketplace to seek more concrete information, because this would violate

---

668 European Commission, 'C(2018) 1177 Final' (n 8) Recital 29, paras 25-27; Schwemer (n 660).

669 'Press - YouTube' <https://www.youtube.com/about/press/> accessed 4 June 2020; Facebook, 'Community Standards Enforcement Report - Terrorist Propaganda' (2019) <https://transparency.facebook.com/community-standards-enforcement#terrorist-propaganda> accessed 28 April 2020. This will be discussed in more detail under the private enforcement sections of the sectoral analysis in Chapter 4.

670 Directive 2000/31 (ECD) Article 14 (1) (a).

671 For example in Germany, Austria and Italy: Verbiest and others (n 315) 37–43; Kempel and Wege (n 16) 101.

Article 15 ECD.[672] This judgement was escalated up to the BGH as *Internetversteigerung II.* The BGH contrasted the earlier rulings and found that an online intermediary can be made liable for future, similar infringements under certain circumstances, such as past infringements that point towards the danger of future violations.[673]

An additional dimension is added when courts tie the question of the awareness of the intermediary over facts and circumstances pointing to illegal acts to the degree to which information is manifestly illegal. Thus, courts in France found that hate speech and racist content were more likely to provide clear indications of illegal activity. In Belgium, this was the case for child pornographic content. In Austria this also included defamatory content, according to the aforementioned EU study by *Verbiest et al.* By contrast, IP violations impose a higher barrier of manifest illegality due to the complex nature of these rights. However, in the French *Dailymotion* case of 2007, the Paris court found that the VSP's architecture and technology was aimed at maximising content sharing between users.[674] The company should have been aware that the success of its business model, which relied on maximising advertising revenue, necessarily included the sharing of copyright protected content. The court concluded that *Dailymotion* had knowledge of the fact that infringing videos would be shared via its sites. It could not offload its responsibility to the users, whom it had equipped with the means to committing these infringements.

The above rulings show the complicated and ambiguous nature of intermediaries' obligations: should an awareness of past infringements and/or manifestly illegal content constitute a reason for the intermediary to become more alert, or risk conscious? Would this then imply a higher likelihood of being aware of and discovering specific instances of unlawful activity, or should the prohibition of any "general obligation to actively to seek facts or circumstances indicating illegal activity" as of Article 15 (1) ECD, be interpreted strictly, i.e. regardless of the illegal nature and the history of infringements? Article 15 was originally put in place to protect the emerging intermediary sector from detrimental economic and legal burdens that could have endangered the open development of the internet. However, the situation had started to change towards the end of the 2010s, when some of the above rulings were made.

---

672 *Markenrechtsverletzung durch Onlineauktion* [2002] LG Düsseldorf 4a O 464/01 [126].

673 *Internetversteigerung II (Rolex v Ricardo.de)* (n 568) 510.

674 *Christian, C., Nord Ouest Production v Dailymotion, UGC Images* (n 196).

CJEU clarification

The CJEU's first iteration on the issue comes again from *L'Oréal v eBay*. The court clarified that awareness of facts or circumstances "on the basis of which a diligent economic operator should have identified the illegality in question" constituted actionable knowledge.[675] Failure to remove or prevent access to any unlawful information that it discovered as part of its reasonable due diligence would trigger liability. This includes investigations undertaken on the intermediary's own initiative.[676]

It is important to note that the CJEU did not go the route of previous national rulings and provide indications on the significance of the obviousness of illegality or the history of violations. Rather, it went beyond and suggested that, though passive information hosts may not have general knowledge of unlawful activity, to a diligent economic operator specific illegal acts could become apparent.[677] *L'Oréal v eBay* was the first time that the CJEU confirmed the existence of more general duties for an online platform that go beyond the reactive obligations established through NTD. The diligent economic operator principles formulated in *L'Oréal v eBay* are comparable to duties of care, which Member States may oblige hosting providers to apply under the ECD,[678] or, arguably, even broader principles of (corporate) responsibility and ethics.[679] Again, it is up to Member States to formulate these principles. Nevertheless, the diligent economic operator concept for intermediaries was taken up by the European Commission as a confirmation that voluntary proactive measures may lead to actual knowledge.[680] It was also taken over into the new (Copyright) Digital Single Market Directive (DSMD). The DSMD essentially applies diligent operator principles to evaluate online content-sharing service providers' (OCSSPs) best efforts to prevent unauthorised works being made available through their systems)).[681] National courts have also adopted this guidance, not only in the area of e-commerce and trademarks,[682] but also for cases involving defamation.[683]

675 *L'Oréal v eBay* (n 463) para 120.

676 ibid 122.

677 Valcke, Kuczerawy and Ombelet (n 551) 108–109.

678 Directive 2000/31 (ECD) Recital 48.

679 Valcke, Kuczerawy and Ombelet (n 551) 114.

680 European Commission, 'COM (2017) 555 Final' (n 69) 12.

681 DSMD 2019/790 Recital 66. Although the platforms covered in this provision are already outside the scope of the ECD.

682 *Maceo v. eBay International AG*, (n 578). under Chapter « Discussion »

683 *CG v Facebook* (n 625) para 72.

This is one of the more problematic aspects of the ECD's liability regime. It actually discourages platforms from (openly) engaging in voluntary measures to prevent and detect illegal content, as any failure to act expeditiously on its removal may result in liabilities. It may lead to the paradox situation that platforms are incentivised not to be too curious about their clients' activities lest they could "stumble upon" and therefore become aware of concrete incidences of unlawful activity. The introduction of the diligent economic operator concept in intermediary liability can be seen as an attempt to formulate some reasonable, positive duties in the absence of any statutory encouragement for voluntary measures, although the effects may not be the same.

The US "Good Samaritan" provisions in the CDA and the DMCA protect those intermediaries that voluntarily engage in good faith measures to prevent unlawful content against any charges for negligent behaviour.[684] However, even that provision is increasingly criticised as counter-productive when it comes to unlawful material on the internet.[685]

The *L'Oréal v eBay* ruling has also been criticised for potentially conflicting with the ECD's Article 15, which prohibits the imposition of general monitoring obligations. Intermediaries may be nudged into monitoring more broadly for illegal activity in order to be seen as diligent economic operators.[686] However, this may be too simplistic as an interpretation. Whether the broad prohibition of general monitoring obligations does indeed stand in the way of diligence principles will be discussed below.

The awareness standard of "red flag" knowledge in the US and China

In the US, the same concept of awareness of facts and circumstances exists for intermediaries under copyright law,[687] but not for violations under the CDA. It was the intention of US lawmakers to establish the existence of this awareness through a "red flag" test.[688] This test has a subjective ele-

684 47 USC § 230 (c) (2); 17 U.S.C. § 512 (g) (1).

685 Zuboff (n 5) l 2040; Danielle Keats Citron and Benjamin Wittes, 'The Internet Will Not Break: Denying Bad Samaritans Section 230 Immunity' (2017) University of Maryland Francis King Carey School of Law Legal Studies Research Paper No. 2017-22 14–15 <https://papers.ssrn.com/sol3/papers.cfm?abstract_id=3007720> accessed 18 September 2017; Dr Melanie Smith, 'Enforcement and Cooperation between Member States' (European Parliament 2020) 32.

686 Savin (n 384) 161.

687 17 U.S.C. § 512 (c) (1) (A) (ii), (d) (1) (B) (ii).

688 'House of Representatives - Digital Millennium Copyright Act of 1998' (n 404) 53–54.

ment of establishing the concrete facts and circumstances, and an objective element that determines whether for a reasonable person acting under these subjective circumstances the unlawful activity would have been apparent. The interpretation is meant to be relatively strict, with liability limited to specific incidences of blatantly visible unlawful acts. The red flag test, it appears, establishes a higher standard of "should have known" knowledge than that of the diligent economic operator.

US Courts have indeed exercised considerable restraint in finding intermediaries liable under this test. The final judgement in *Viacom v YouTube*[689] ended a six-year litigation battle in which the entertainment giant claimed $1 billion in damages for unauthorised broadcasts of videos. *YouTube* was acquitted on all counts and held not responsible for uploads by its users, nor obliged to monitor its site for unauthorised uploads even though it had received indications that some of these could contain infringing material. Red flags would only be found in cases of blindness to specific, identifiable infringements. The court overruled an earlier judgement which had found *YouTube* liable because it was wilfully blind to specific infringing acts and aware of massive infringements on its site.[690] This narrow interpretation of a red flag is confirmed by *Corbis v Amazon*, which was about the availability of copyright infringing images through sites owned by the e-commerce giant. The court laid down that a red flag existed when the infringing nature of content would be obviously "apparent from even a brief and casual viewing" of the website. In other words, such a flag must be "brightly red indeed – and be waving blatantly in the provider's face – to serve the statutory goal of making infringing activity… apparent."[691] Indeed, such a red flag is therefore difficult to prove under US law. It depends on whether in the course of its normal business the intermediary became aware of the unlawfulness of specific acts. Meanwhile, *Corbis v Amazon* confirms that mere notifications of infringing activity would not confer knowledge of other infringements, nor that awareness of suspicious activity amounted to red flags.[692]

Chinese courts appear to apply their red flag knowledge standard in a more hawkish way.[693] Contrary to the US, this standard is seen in conjunc-

689 *Viacom International v YouTube* [2013] US District Court for the Southern District of New York No. 07 Civ. 2103, 2013 WL 1689071.

690 *Viacom 2012* (n 196).

691 David Nimmer, *Copyright: Sacred Text, Technology, and the DMCA* (Kluwer Law International 2003). In: Wang (n 504) 280.

692 Burk (n 295) 442.

693 Tao (n 506) 15–16.

tion with more expansive duty of care obligations.[694] Chinese courts have considered "should know" circumstances, such as a combination of high popularity of content (established through the number of downloads and the release date) and the way this content is sorted, recommended or commercially exploited (i.e. through advertising) as giving indications of red flags. In addition, they consider factors such as the business model, or the way the intermediary deals with infringement notices and the proactive measures it has in place. If, under the combined consideration of all these circumstances, the platform should have been aware of obviously infringing activity, or even the risk thereof, then a red flag would exist. In essence, the more a platform is involved in the hosting of highly popular and commercially valuable content, the more it is at risk of discovering red flags for unlawful activity on its site.[695] Since Chinese intermediary provisions do not have any protections against general monitoring obligations, courts have been less inhibited to considering more expansive interpretations of red flag knowledge.

III. The preventive obligations of intermediaries

The largely reactive duties of intermediaries with regards to the removal of unlawful content created conflicts early on. Once uploaded, it is notoriously difficult, if not impossible, to delete or remove information from the internet. As users can often be anonymous or easily disguise their identity, repeat uploads or sharing of banned content require little extra effort. Fighting the almost endemic repeat uploads and proliferation of unlawful content in a more effective manner would, however, imply that the reactive duties be complimented by preventive efforts. Intermediaries, as the gatekeepers to and hosts of this information are obvious targets for this, on a technical and economic level, but also on moral and legal grounds.

The ECD opens the door for courts and authorities to require online intermediaries to terminate and prevent infringements.[696] However, the scope of injunctions to prevent infringements soon turned out to be problematic in view of the limitations imposed by Article 15 ECD.

Naturally, damaged parties had an interest to ensure that information that was removed once through an NTD request did not reappear, but

694 Wang (n 504) 308.
695 ibid 284–286.
696 Directive 2000/31 (ECD) Articles 12 (3), 13 (2), 14 (3).

stayed-down permanently. This has remained one of the most difficult and seemingly unsurmountable problems until today. The legal answer to this were stay-down orders, which aim at ensuring that, once a piece of notified content was removed, it was successively blocked by the intermediary from reappearing. In addition, courts and authorities sought to widen the scope of these preventive injunctions by obliging intermediaries to not only block the same, but also similar infringing content, or even a broad, unspecified range of future infringements.[697]

Intermediaries saw themselves very soon on the defensive and claimed that these preventive injunctions conflicted with Article 15 ECD.[698] They argued that these injunctions imposed *de facto* general monitoring obligations on them, because they would force them to monitor their entire traffic to identify the content covered by the injunction. Indeed, at least in some earlier cases (discussed below), it was argued that even more specific stay-down orders would necessitate a general monitoring of traffic. On the other side, those demanding preventive injunctions reasoned that orders aimed at preventing specific content only necessitated a closely circumscribed monitoring or filtering. This would be in compliance with the ECD's Article 15 and in the spirit of Recital 47 which specified that monitoring obligations in a specific case cannot be prevented. These conflicts were addressed in Member States' courts with varying methodologies and results.

Matters were not made easier by the fact that the ECD does not define the term general monitoring. Meanwhile, content and data recognition, filtering and analytics technologies have become more effective, less intrusive and scalable, which also impacted this debate.[699]

A further point of complication is introduced by Recital 48, which gives Member States the option to require hosting providers to apply "duties of care, which can reasonably be expected from them and which are specified by national law in order to detect and prevent certain types of illegal activi-

---

697 As, for example, in *Scarlet Extended* (n 139).

698 On the motivations behind Article 15 ECD see above in this chapter

699 Christina Angelopoulos, *European Intermediary Liability in Copyright: A Tort-Based Analysis* (Kluwer Law International BV 2017) 473–474; Lilian Edwards and Michael Veale, 'Slave to the Algorithm? Why a 'Right to Explanation' Is Probably Not the Remedy You Are Looking For' (2017) 16 Duke Law & Technology Review 18, 82. Lorna Woods, 'The Carnegie Statutory Duty of Care and Fundamental Freedoms' [2019] Carnegie UK Trust 11 <https://www.carnegieuktrust.org.uk/publications/doc-fundamental-freedoms/> accessed 2 March 2020.

ties."[700] This requirement could, on the one hand be interpreted as conflicting with the limitations imposed by Article 15 ECD.[701] On the other hand, this passage could be seen as unwittingly causing the well-meant intention to encourage the application of more encompassing notions of responsibility to amplify the divergence between national intermediary liability practices. The tort law based negligence that underpins duty of care does not call up identical normative concepts and applications nationally. A look at the different translations of the duty of care referred to in Recital 48 may give a glimpse of this. While in German, Recital 48 refers to *Sorgfaltspflicht* (which can be literally translated into duty of care), the French version speaks of *précautions*, and the Italian version points to *dovere di diligenza* (diligence duties). For Germany, the direct link has been made between the concept of *Sorgfaltspflicht* (although referring to its iteration in the *L'Oréal v EBay* ruling),[702] and the German law "interferer liability" that has been widely applied in national intermediary liability cases.[703] For France, however, no such clear link between the concept of *précautions* and the broad formulations of the *Code Civil's* civil liability Articles 1240 and 1241 can be made. In fact, *van Dam* suggests that the French concept of *faute* in the Code Civil refers to negligence simply as a lack of a certain standard of care, but does not impose a *duty* of care.[704] The reference to *précautions* in the ECD may therefore not add any value other than 'permitting' French courts to apply their broad secondary law concepts. A similar observation can be made for Italy, where, as explained in the previous chapter, secondary liability rules are more linked to vicarious liability.

It should be noted that the difficulties of pinning down preventive duties concern mainly information hosts. However, IAPs had also been early in the focus of courts due to their central function of enabling access to the internet. Injunctions against IAPs would normally concern the disabling or filtering of locations on the internet (DNS/IP/URL based) or of content by restricting certain applications (i.e. P2P systems). Court injunctions against host providers, on the other hand, focus more on identifying and

700 Directive 2000/31 (ECD) Recital 48.

701 Gerald Spindler, Fabian Schuster and Katharina Anton (eds), *Recht Der Elektronischen Medien: Kommentar* (2. Aufl, CH Beck 2011) 1511. (see also supra fn 724)

702 *L'Oréal v eBay* (n 463) para 124.

703 Jan Bernd Nordemann, 'Haftung von Providern im Urheberrecht Der aktuelle Stand nach dem EuGH-Urteil v. 12. 7. 2011 – C-324/09 – L'Oréal/eBay' GRUR 2011 977, 978–879.

704 CC van Dam, *European Tort Law* (Second edition, Oxford University Press 2013) paras 302–1.

preventing unlawful content hosted on their sites. For the legal argumentation at hand the difference shall not be important as the basic conflict between specific and general infringement prevention poses the same normative legal problems.

a. National case law

i. France

In the French cases brought against *Google Video* in 2007[705] it was found that the company had an obligation to monitor and prevent every re-upload of content that had been previously notified. *Google* was charged with copyright violation for every upload that re-occurred. It had originally argued that for each (re-)upload a separate NTD request would have to be filed. Meanwhile, *Dailymotion* was explicitly denied the protections of Article 15 ECD because, according to the court, it had induced its users to uploading infringing material. This meant the VSP had actual knowledge of its site being used for infringing activities and therefore needed to monitor its traffic for illegal content before upload by its users.[706] French courts continued to apply notice-and-stay-down obligations in a number of cases directed at *Google Video*. The company was denied the protections of the ECD because it failed to disable future uploads of once notified copyright protected content.[707]

In a trademark case that set *eBay* against *L'Oréal* a Paris court found that the marketplace had fulfilled its obligations as an intermediary, which consisted of ensuring that its activities did not facilitate illicit acts. These activi-

705 *Christian, C., Nord Ouest Production v Dailymotion, UGC Images* (n 196). *SARL Zadig Productions, Jean-Robert Viallet et Mathieu Verboud v Sté Google Inc et AFA* (2007) (Unreported) (Tribunal de grande instance de Paris).

706 *Christian, C., Nord Ouest Production v Dailymotion, UGC Images* (n 196) see under « DISCUSSION - Sur la nature de l'activité exercée par la société Dailymotion et sa responsabilité ».

707 Catherine Jasser, 'Recent Decisions of the Paris Court of Appeal: Towards an Extra Duty of Surveillance for Hosting Providers?' (*Kluwer Copyright Blog*, 29 March 2011) <http://copyrightblog.kluweriplaw.com/2011/03/29/recent-decisions-of-the-paris-court-of-appeal-towards-an-extra-duty-of-surveillance-for-hosting-providers/> accessed 17 February 2020. Aleksandra Kuczerawy, *Intermediary Liability and Freedom of Expression in the EU: From Concepts to Safeguards* (Intersentia 2018) 234–235. See for example: *Google Inc v Les Films de la Croisade, Goatworks Films* (2010) (Unreported) (Cour d'appel de Paris Pôle 5, chambre 2).

ties consisted, amongst others, in contractual clauses, information targeted at advertisers and sellers, notification tools for unlawful content, an IP right protection programme (*VeRo*), dedicated staff and key word searches aimed at identifying counterfeit products.[708] Any further obligations would be in conflict with Article 15 ECD. The ruling implies that certain proactive prevention measures, that may even go beyond repressing specific repeat infringement, were seen as adequate and in compliance with Articles 14 and 15 ECD. From 2012, this practice however was somewhat qualified when the French Supreme Court ruled that in order to "prevent any new upload of the infringing videos, without even being informed of it by another notification, which is nevertheless required for them [Google] to be effectively aware of its illegal nature" would amount to a general obligation to monitor for illicit content.[709]

ii. Italy

Italian courts initially offered differing readings of the interplay between authorised specific and prohibited general preventive obligations.[710] In a legal battle stretching several years between *Google's YouTube* service and *Delta TV*, a Turin court confirmed in 2017 an earlier decision by another Italian court.[711] It obliged the VSP to prevent any future uploads of copyright infringing content that it had removed due to earlier NTD requests by deploying its *Content ID* software. As a "new generation" hosting service it needed to take over enlarged responsibilities, which would be in line with the "duty to act" in order to prevent illegal activities, provided for in Recital 40 ECD.[712] By contrast, in a parallel ongoing dispute between *RTI*, a private Italian broadcaster, and *Yahoo!*, the Milan court overturned previous instances and found that *Yahoo!* was not obliged to ensure that once removed unlawful content stayed down as this would require it to monitor

708 *L'Oréal SA c eBay France SA* (n 565).

709 *Google Francev Bac films* [2012] Cour de cassation, Première chambre civile 11-13.669, FR : CCASS : 2012 : C100831; (translation by author) see also: Amélie Blocman, 'Pas d'obligation générale de surveillance du réseau, rappelle la Cour de cassation' [2013] iris plus.

710 Giancarlo F Frosio, 'The Death of No Monitoring Obligations' (2017) 8 J. Intell. Prop. Info. Tech. & Elec. Com. L. 199, 205–206.

711 *Delta TV v Google and YouTube* (n 622).

712 Frosio, 'The Death of No Monitoring Obligations' (n 709) 206.

its site in a general fashion.[713] This decision was then overturned by the Italian Supreme Court, which found that stay-down obligations were specific and therefore in line with the provisions of the ECD, and did not mean the VSP needed to monitor its service in a general way.[714] In Italy, dynamic blocking injunctions have also been successful. For example, in 2017, Italian publisher *Mondadori* succeeded in bringing action against several internet service providers for copyright infringement and required them to go beyond blocking the domain names identified in the original injunction.[715] The perpetrating platform changed its domain names dynamically and redirected traffic to the servers where infringing material was hosted, a common practice to subvert blocking activities. *Mondadori* requested that the providers identify and block all future domain names (hence dynamic blocking) that directed to the infringing platform in question. In this decision, the eligibility of these measures was judged mainly from the IP Rights Enforcement Directive (IPRED), and especially the guidance document of the European Commission, which will be discussed later in the copyright section of Chapter 4.[716] However, the court also found that the dynamic injunction did not constitute a general monitoring obligation, if the right holder provided a list specifying the new domain names that needed to be blocked.[717]

---

713 *Yahoo! Italia S.r.l and Yahoo! Inc, v Reti Televisive Italiane S.pA* (2015) (Unreported) (Court of Appeal of Milan). Mario Berliri, 'The Court of Appeal of Milan Rules on Yahoo's Liability with Respect to Copyright Infringement' (*Global Media and Communications Watch*, 25 February 2015) <https://www.hlmediacomms.com/2015/02/25/the-court-of-appeal-of-milan-rules-on-yahoos-liability-with-respect-to-copyright-infringement/> accessed 18 February 2020.

714 *Reti Televisive Italiane SpA v Yahoo! Inc and Reti Televisive Italiane SpA v Yahoo! Inc.* (n 621); Rosati, 'Italian Supreme Court Clarifies Availability of Safe Harbours, Content of Notice-and-Takedown Requests, and Stay-down Obligations - The IPKat | Diigo' (n 621).

715 *Arnoldo Mondadori Editore SPA, v Fastweb SPA and others* [2018] Tribunale di Milano 51624/2017. In: Eleonora Rosati, 'Milan Court Issues Dynamic Blocking Injunction against Italian ISPs - The IPKat' (*The IPKat*, 25 August 2018) <https://ipkitten.blogspot.com/2018/08/milan-court-issues-dynamic-blocking.html> accessed 18 February 2020.

716 European Commission, 'Guidance on Certain Aspects of Directive 2004/48/EC of the European Parliament and of the Council on the Enforcement of Intellectual Property Rights, COM(2017) 708 Final'.

717 Rosati, 'Milan Court Issues Dynamic Blocking Injunction against Italian ISPs - The IPKat' (n 714).

iii. Germany

German courts developed rather intricate ways of defining the proactive obligations of internet intermediaries. The *BGH* confirmed the legality of stay-down orders as early as 2004 in *Internetversteigerung I*, and then later in *Internetversteigerung II and II in* 2007 and 2008.[718] In these cases, the *BGH* found that not only did e-commerce marketplace *Ricardo.de* (and later *eBay*) had to ensure the stay-down of specific offers of trademark infringing *Rolex* watches. Moreover, following the specific infringement notifications, it had a duty to prevent the offer of all clearly noticeable trademark infringements relating to the *Rolex* brand in general, including associated brands and model numbers.[719] This duty is part of the German civil law doctrine for intermediaries known as *Störerhaftung ("interferer liability")*.[720] The *BGH* confirmed that this preventive activity could involve the use of automated means, such as filter software, which detected, with the help of specific search criteria, potentially infringing offers. These would need to be verified manually.[721] Possible indicative criteria for violations of the claimant's brand could be price points or concrete indications that the products in questions were imitations. These duties of care were acceptable as long as they did not endanger the business model of the marketplace operator.

Commentators had initially seen this ruling as in conflict with Article 15 ECD, because these relatively broad duties risked creating a general surveillance infrastructure.[722] The BGH toned down its approach somewhat in *Kinderhochstühle I*. This case dealt with the counterfeit sales of baby high chairs via the *eBay* marketplace. *EBay* had checked the product images of over 6,400 alleged counterfeit offers on its site by non-automated means to find less than 0.5% of those offers actually infringing.[723] The *BGH* ruled that imposing these measures was disproportionate and went beyond a rea-

718 *Internetversteigerung I (Rolex v Ricardo.de), Az. I ZR 304/01* (n 567); *Internetversteigerung II (Rolex v Ricardo.de)* (n 568); *Internetversteigerung III (Rolex v Ricardo.de), Az. I ZR 73/05* (n 568).

719 *Internetversteigerung III (Rolex v Ricardo.de), Az. I ZR 73/05* (n 568) para 55.

720 Urs Verweyen, 'Grenzen der Störerhaftung in Peer to Peer-Netzwerken' [2009] MMR 590, 590. This duty of care is called reasonable due diligence ("zumutbare Prüfpflicht").

721 *Internetversteigerung II (Rolex v Ricardo.de)* (n 568) 47.

722 Gerald Spindler, 'BGH-Urteil (U. v. 19.4.2007 - I ZR 35/04) Internetversteigerung II - Anmerkung' [2007] MMR 511; Nordemann (n 702) 980.

723 *Kinderhochstühle im Internet, I ZR 139/08* [2010] MIR 122010 (BGH) [41].

sonable duty of care as it endangered the company's business model. In the absence of any reliable automated means to filter for infringing products, the intermediary was not required to do more. The BGH also considered the fact that the brand owner was given the opportunity to search for infringing offers through participation in *eBay's VeRo* programme. Under these circumstances, it was not justified to ask the platform operator to engage in more onerous preventive duties than the brand owner. It has been argued that, on a practical level, this balance may not hold for other areas of unlawful content or activity (outside trademarks), such as defamatory or copyright infringing material.[724] The application of the horizontal liability principles on different areas of unlawful content shall be discussed in the next chapter.

Meanwhile, in the area of trademarks, the use of automated image and text recognition software, targeted at preventing infringements similar to already notified content seems to have entered standard reasoning of German courts. It includes limited manual checks, mainly aimed at updating filter software. The intermediary would, however, be protected against identifying infringements that are based on substantial variations in text or images and subsequent failure of the filtering software to recognise the violation. Such violations would have to be notified to the intermediary first.[725]

This line of argument was applied in copyright disputes between rightsholders and platforms, such as the aforementioned *YouTube v GEMA* saga. Here, the use of the *Content ID* file recognition software, supplemented by manual checks on the part of the intermediary, was explicitly seen as belonging to the mandatory duty of care of *YouTube*. This development is a result of similar case law adjustments over the previous years, which saw a move from more onerous manual and automatic filtering duties, although in the area of file sharing,[726] to rejecting the necessity of excessive manual checks in order to prevent future infringements.[727] Considering defamatory comments, search engines would also be subject to reasonable preventive measures once they were notified and had received proof of unlawful comments. However, given the importance of search engines for the opera-

724 Gerald Spindler, 'Präzisierungen Der Störerhaftung Im Internet Besprechung Des BGH-Urteils „Kinderhochstühle Im Internet"' [2011] GRUR 101, 107.

725 *Beeinträchtigung der Herkunftsfunktion einer Marke trotz Fälschungshinweises (Parfume Made in China)* (n 587) paras 83–84.

726 *Sharehoster II* [2009] OLG Hamburg 5 U 111/08, openJur 2009, 1105.

727 *RapidShare II* (n 615).

tion the internet, preventive duty of care measures would need to be decided on a case-by-case basis.[728]

iv. UK

The approach to balancing the proactive duties of internet intermediaries is yet different in the UK. In *L'Oréal v eBay*, the existence of a filtering programme could not be counted against the intermediary and they could not be obliged to do more by law. However, the UK court was unclear about the remit of the measures *eBay* could be forced to take according to Article 11 IPRED with regards to preventing future infringements and in light of the limitations imposed by Article 15 ECD. It asked the CJEU for guidance, which eventually resulted in a key ruling, discussed above and below.[729]

By contrast, the UK is considered the jurisdiction within the EU that has most widely adopted live (and dynamic) web blocking orders into practice.[730] In *Newzbin,* the High Court endorsed the use of targeted and narrow web blocking orders against IAP *British Telecom* in order to block access to the sites and services of *Newzbin*. The site had already been charged previously with giving access to and hosting copyright infringing content. The measures were found both as in compliance with Article 15 ECD and as proportional with regards to balancing copyright with the fundamental rights of freedom of expression of *Newzbin*, its users and *BT*.[731] They subsequently led to a wave of similar requests by rightsholders. Eventually, they also covered trademarks.[732] Dynamically modified live blocking orders are now also a common practice in the fight against live streaming of popular sports events, such as football matches.[733] In essence, rightsholders have

728 *Haftung des Suchmaschinenbetreibers für geschlossene rechtswidrige Äußerungen* [2014] LG Hamburg 324 O 660/12, openJur 2014, 26809 [87–88].

729 *L'Oreal SA v. eBay International AG* (n 563) paras 375, 464–465.

730 Edwards, 'With Great Power Comes Great Responsibility?: The Rise of Platform Liability' (n 661) 283.

731 *Newzbin* (n 638) 161–162, 199–201.

732 *Cartier International AG & Ors v British Sky Broadcasting Ltd & Ors [2016]* [2106] England and Wales Court of Appeal (Civil Division) A3/2014/3939 & A3/2014/4238, EWCA Civ 658.

733 *The Football Association Premier League Ltd v British Telecommunications Plc & Ors* [2017] 2017 EWHC 480 Ch (England and Wales High Court (Chancery Division)).

with success tried to force ISPs to adopt a filtering and blocking technology called *Cleanfeed*, developed by *BT*. *Cleanfeed* was originally set up to act on child pornographic content identified by the *Internet Watch Foundation (IWF)*.

Much of the national jurisprudence by EU Member States, decided after 2011, appears to draw on the guidance given in the first intermediary liability rulings of the CJEU.[734] Yet, despite the supposedly clarifying character of the CJEU's jurisprudence, the above trends still show that national courts continued to come to different interpretations on the scope of proactivity that can be required of internet intermediaries.[735] This can be attributed to several, interdependent reasons. First, different legal traditions may have different impacts on how the proactive obligations for (internet) intermediaries under criminal and civil provisions are interpreted. Secondly, the CJEU's interpretation of EU law in preliminary rulings is handed back to national courts for implementation. As part of this procedure, the CJEU often requires a separate assessment of the matter based on the facts at hand, which may limit the unifying character of these rulings, given differing national legal traditions. Thirdly, the fact that even within Member States decisions may vary (e.g. France, Italy), testifies to the technically complex and fast-moving nature of internet intermediary liability as well as the mounting pressure on courts and policymakers to act in the face of the aggravating problem of unlawful content.[736]

Preventive obligations outside the EU

In the US, the DMCA and the Lanham Act provide for injunction aimed at preventing repeat or future infringements in the area of copyright and trademarks.[737] In the area of copyright, intermediaries are also barred from interfering with any technical measures used by rightsowners to identify and protect copyrighted works. Meanwhile, no such legal provisions exist for other areas of unlawful online content covered by the CDA. This statue

---

734 Such as *Google France v Louis Vuitton* (n 155); *L'Oréal v eBay* (n 463); *SABAM v Netlog* (n 460); *Scarlet Extended* (n 139).

735 'Copyright Protection On Digital Platforms: Existing Tools, Good Practice And Limitations - Report By The Research Mission On Recognition Tools For Copyright-Protected Content On Digital Platforms' (Conseil Superieur de la Propriete Litteraire et Artistique (CSPLA), Ministère de la Culture 2017) 9 <https://perma.cc/5A6F-4VDJ> accessed 21 April 2021.

736 Van Eecke (n 16); Valcke, Kuczerawy and Ombelet (n 551).

737 17 U.S.C. § 512 (i) (1) (A); 15 U.S.C.§ 1114 (2) (B).

does not allow for any remedies against interactive computer services.[738] In addition, the DMCA, like the ECD, shields intermediaries from any obligation to proactively monitoring its service or seeking facts indicating infringing activity.[739]

An obligation to prevent repeat infringements in the area of IP is the maximum that US courts have been requiring from intermediaries as regards proactive measures.[740] The "Good Samaritan" protections merely encourage the development of self-regulatory and voluntary enforcement practices between platform operators and rightsholders.[741] Content stay-down obligations have so far not been enforced against intermediaries in the US. However, pressures exist to introduce these kinds of obligations, especially in the area of copyright.[742]

Stay-down orders and obligations to monitor more proactively for infringing activity have, however, been imposed throughout other jurisdictions in the world, such as Australia, India, China, Japan or South Korea, to name but a few.[743] With regards to India and China, this can partly be explained by an absence in the law of any Article 15 ECD style limitation that prohibits general monitoring duties. As detailed above, there has been a focus on developing more proactive, duty of care style, monitoring obligations in these jurisdictions. This concerns both once notified infringements (stay-downs), but also broader efforts to prevent specific types of infringements. These trends can now also be observed worldwide across virtually all types of unlawful content and activity.[744]

---

738 Mehra and Trimble (n 385) 104.

739 17 U.S.C. § 512 (m).

740 *Perfect 10, Inc v CCBill, LLC* [2007] 9th Cir 04-57143, 04-57207, 488 F3d 1102 [27–29]; *Corbis Corp v Amazon Inc* [2004] US District Court, WD Washington (Seattle) No. CV03-1415L., 351 F.Supp.2d 1090 [1102–1103].

741 Rich and Ho (n 602) 8–9.

742 Evan Engstrom and Nick Feamster, 'The Limits of Filtering: A Look at the Functionality & Shortcomings of Content Detection Tools' (Engine 2017) 8–10 <https://www.engine.is/the-limits-of-filtering> accessed 3 March 2020; Urban, Karaganis and Schofield (n 661) 60–62.

743 Dan Jerker B Svantesson, 'Internet & Jurisdiction Global Status Report 2019' (Internet & Jurisdiction Policy Network 2019) 73–128, 142–146.

744 ibid 142.

b. CJEU and ECtHR case law

i. L'Oréal v EBay (C-324/09)

The problem of the permissible proactive duties of internet intermediaries under the ECD was addressed for the first time in *L'Oréal v EBay*. This case confirmed that an injunction against an intermediary to prevent future intellectual property infringements must not result in the monitoring of all content. This would be irreconcilable with the ECD and IPRED Article 3. The latter stipulates that any measures and remedies to protect IP rights must be proportionate, provide for safeguards against abuse and must not create barriers to trade. However, these measures must also be effective and dissuasive. If the hosting provider failed to take on its own initiative measures aimed at preventing infringements of the same kind by the same seller, a court would have the power to impose such measures.[745] This is somewhat commensurate with earlier German case law in e.g. *Internetversteigerung I – II*. The CJEU can be credited for confirming that hosting providers are obliged to be more than just reactive notice recipients when it comes to preventing unlawful activity. Some commentators have seen a possible contradiction between Article 15 and Recital 48 ECD. The latter gives Member States leeway in imposing reasonable duties of care on hosting providers.[746] However, *L'Oréal v eBay* confirmed at the highest EU level that stay-down orders did not amount to a general monitoring duty on behalf of the intermediary. Whether a permissible proactive duty went beyond stay-down orders is a matter for interpretation of the term "the same kind of infringements." That interpretation however is up to national courts. As shown above, this has indeed led to differing approaches and interpretations. Arguably, the clarification by the CJEU therefore opened up new threats of national diversion in the conditions that govern intermediary liability.

The CJEU also said in *L'Oréal v eBay* that an e-commerce marketplace may be ordered to make identification of its customer-sellers easier so that damaged parties can profit from their right to an effective remedy. This should be balanced with other rights as laid down in *Promusicae,* an earlier

745 *L'Oréal v eBay* (n 463) para 141.

746 Rosa Julià-Barceló and Kamiel J Koelman, 'Intermediary Liability in the E-Commerce Directive: So Far so Good, but It's Not Enough' (2000) 16 Computer Law & Security Review 231, 232. Spindler, Schuster and Anton (n 700) 1511; Lodder and Murray (n 448) 53.

CJEU ruling about the right of copyright holders to receive personal data from an IAP about users that allegedly infringed copyright.[747] This can also be interpreted as justifying additional due diligence measures that may be required from platforms.[748] Moreover, the term prevention of further infringements "by the same seller"[749] implies a certain amount of monitoring on behalf of the platform of parties that are repeatedly found to engage in unlawful acts. This would suggest that customer-sellers on online marketplace would need to go through a verification or identification process. Allowing anonymity with regards to the economic activity of selling could arguably be interpreted as a lack of diligence on behalf of the marketplace operator, according to this ruling. Finally, *L'Oréal v eBay* introduced the diligent economic operator principle. According to this, a hosting provider, in this case an online marketplace operator, could lose its immunity protections under Article 14 (1) ECD if it ignored indications of illegal activity that a diligent economic operator should have been aware of. This includes the receipt of notifications of illegal activity or information, but also situations where the marketplace had uncovered such unlawful activity or information following its own proactive investigation.[750] With the diligent economic operator concept and the requirements to prevent future infringements of the same kind by the same seller and make identification of customer-sellers easier, the CJEU formulated for the first time duties of care style responsibilities for online intermediaries that go beyond pure reactive obligations. It should be remembered that the ECD gives Member States the option of applying duties of care through national legal systems.[751] In this respect, *L'Oréal v eBay* is probably one of *the* landmark cases in EU intermediary liability jurisprudence.

ii. Scarlet Extended (C-70/10) & Netlog (C-360/10)

While *L'Oréal v eBay* explored the permissible scope of specific, preventive injunctions and proactive duties of intermediaries in the light of the prohi-

747 *L'Oréal v eBay* (n 463) paras 142–143; *Promusicae* (n 140).

748 Carsten Ullrich, 'A Risk-Based Approach towards Infringement Prevention on the Internet: Adopting the Anti-Money Laundering Framework to Online Platforms' (2018) 26 International Journal of Law and Information Technology 226, 243.

749 *L'Oréal v eBay* (n 463) para 141.

750 ibid 122.

751 Directive 2000/31 (ECD) Recital 48.

bition to impose general monitoring obligations, *Scarlet Extended* and *Netlog*[752] clarified the reach of broader preventive injunctions under Article 15 ECD. The Belgian association of music authors and rightsholder (SABAM) filed charges against IAP *Scarlet* and the social networking site *Netlog*, a hosting provider.

SABAM tried to prevent alleged copyright infringements of musical works in its repertoire committed by users of both companies' services by imposing an obligation on both intermediaries to prevent the unauthorised making available of works. In *Scarlet Extended*, the rights management organisation *SABAM* argued that the IAP was best placed to take technical measures to stop copyright infringements of its subscribers through the use of P2P services. *SABAM* first successfully achieved an order by a Belgian court that *Scarlet* filter and block on a permanent basis all P2P traffic by its users which was aimed at sharing works in SABAM's repertoire. The IAP, however, appealed claiming that such an order resulted in a *de facto* general monitoring obligation because it would require it to screen its entire traffic for P2P transmissions. In addition, this measure was not proven to be effective and would negatively impact the company's network operation. Furthermore, it would be in contravention of Article 15 ECD and, lastly, violate EU law on the protection of personal data and the secrecy of communications.[753]

In *Netlog*, *SABAM* demanded that the social network prevent its users to share works under the license of SABAM and asked for damages for any delays in complying with this order. Similar to *Scarlet Extended*, *Netlog* argued that this would result in a *de facto* general monitoring of its users' activities and breach the same EU law provisions as detailed in *Scarlet Extended*.

Both cases were argued by the CJEU essentially on the same lines, but concerning two types of intermediaries: *Scarlet*, a mere conduit, and *Netlog*, a hosting provider. The referring questions of the Belgian courts went beyond asking for guidance on whether the measures required by *SABAM* were in contravention of Article 15 ECD. They also asked whether they were permitted under the Infosoc Directive and IPRED, read in conjunction with the ECD, data protection, secrecy of communication legislation

752 *Scarlet Extended* (n 139); *SABAM v Netlog* (n 460).

753 *Scarlet Extended* (n 139) paras 23–26.

and EU Fundamental Rights.[754] The Infosoc Directive and IPRED allow for the imposition of injunctions against intermediaries, but require at the same time that any such measures are effective, proportionate and dissuasive, and, regarding IPRED, are not unnecessarily complicated or costly.[755]

In both cases the CJEU ruled that *SABAM's* orders would have required the IAP (*Scarlet*) to filter all electronic communications, and the hosting provider (*Netlog*) to filter all information stored on its service. These orders would have applied indiscriminately to all users, on a preventative basis, at the exclusive expense of the service and for an unlimited period. The CJEU judged that this would amount to an obligation to monitor its traffic on a general basis. They were therefore in violation of Infosoc Directive, IPRED, the applicable fundamental rights and Article 15 ECD. In the cases at hand, the fundamental rights of the freedom to conduct a business, the right to protection of personal data and the freedom to receive or impart information were outweighing the right to intellectual property.[756]

Scarlet Extended and *Netlog* defined the limits of Article 15 ECD[757] and also performed a clarifying balancing exercise between EU law and fundamental rights, given the specific filtering injunctions demanded by rightsholder *SABAM*. This ruling provided useful guidance on when a preventive injunction would generate effects that are in violation of EU law. It also implied, however, that adequately designed filtering injunctions may indeed be possible. This issue was first dealt with by the CJEU in *UPC Telekabel.*[758] It is worth mentioning, however, that the CJEU ruled in that case, which involved specific blocking injunctions against Austrian IAP *UPC*

754 Directive 95/46/EC of the European Parliament and of the Council of 24 October 1995 on the protection of individuals with regard to the processing of personal data and on the free movement of such data 1995 (OJ L 281) 46; Directive 2002/58/EC of the European Parliament and of the Council of 12 July 2002 concerning the processing of personal data and the protection of privacy in the electronic communications sector (Directive on privacy and electronic communications) 2002 (OJ L 201) 58; European Convention for the Protection of Human Rights and Fundamental Freedoms 1950 Articles 8 & 10.

755 Directive 2001/29 (Infosoc Directive) Article 8; Directive 2004/48/EC of 29 April 2004 on the enforcement of intellectual property rights Articles 3, 11.

756 *Scarlet Extended* (n 139) paras 53–54; *SABAM v Netlog* (n 460) paras 51–52.

757 Stalla-Bourdillon, 'Sometimes One Is Not Enough! Securing Freedom of Expression, Encouraging Private Regulation, or Subsidizing Internet Intermediaries or All Three at the Same Time: The Dilemma of Internet Intermediaries' Liability' (n 484) 173.

758 *UPC Telekabel Wien GmbH v Constantin Film Verleih GmbH, Wega Filmproduktionsgesellschaft mbH, C-314/12* [2014] EU:C:2014:192 (CJEU).

Telekabel, solely in respect of the Infosoc Directive, and did not follow the AG Opinion's deliberations, which included an assessment of the compatibility with Article 15 ECD.[759]

This opens the question whether a proportionality assessment involving fundamental rights needs to be done in the context of Article 15 ECD. Traditional reading of *Scarlet Extended* and *Netlog* sees Article 15 ECD strongly impacted by a fair balancing exercise of fundamental rights.[760] However, despite of the references between Infosoc, IPRED and the intermediary liability provisions of the ECD, the actual fundamental rights balancing exercise is conducted in the context of the proportionality provisions of IPRED's Article 3 (1).[761] This makes sense as any balancing exercises pertaining to the prevention of certain types of unlawful content should be made primarily with regard to the fundamental right attached to that content,[762] and not in respect of a broad, horizontal prohibition of general monitoring. Concerning IP rights, the IPRED Guidance confirms that the act of general monitoring prohibited by Article 15 would also fail the proportionality requirements of IPRED's Article 3 (1). Therefore, Article 15 does not seem to play a direct role, or indeed be necessary for an effective fundamental rights balancing that assesses the scope of injunctions.[763] The question is then, if the absence of Article 15 would prevent a successful fundamental right balancing exercise also beyond the area of IP rights. In addition, if a court's balancing exercise would find that more proactive prevention measures are justified under certain circumstances, e.g. facilitat-

---

759 *Opinion of Advocate General Cruz Villalón UPC Telekabel Wien GmbH v Constantin Film Verleih GmbH, Wega Filmproduktionsgesellschaft mbH, C-314/12* [2011] EU:C:2013:781 (CJEU) [77–78]. This judgement will also be dealt with in the Chapter on the interface between copyright and intermediary liability. (p.xxx)

760 Giovanni Sartor, 'Providers Liability: From the ECommerce Directive to the Future - IP/A/IMCO/2017-07' (2017) 17–18.

761 Ullrich, 'A Risk-Based Approach towards Infringement Prevention on the Internet' (n 747) 230. *Scarlet Extended* (n 139) paras 41–53, 48; *SABAM v Netlog* (n 460) paras 39–51, 46.

762 Such as the IPRED 2004/48 for IP rights, and, in addition, Infosoc 2001/29 for copyright, or, for incitement to violence by national and EU law (e.g. Council Framework Decision 2008/913/JHA of 28 November 2008 on combating certain forms and expressions of racism and xenophobia by means of criminal law 2008 (OJ L)

763 European Commission, 'Guidance on Certain Aspects of Directive 2004/48/EC of the European Parliament and of the Council on the Enforcement of Intellectual Property Rights, COM(2017) 708 Final' (n 715) 16–21.

ed by technology, then Article 15 ECD could theoretically still prevent this outcome.[764]

While it is not contested here that excessively broad, preventive filtering obligations are likely to violate fundamental rights, it is suggested that the ECD's Article 15 is not needed for an effective proportionality assessment. As demonstrated by the national case law, the problem of clearly distinguishing between prohibited general and permitted specific monitoring obligations has persisted to this day, despite the clarifications that the CJEU was supposed to give.

Problems with defining general monitoring at a technical level

The approaches in *Scarlet Extended* and *Netlog* imply that, in light of technological improvements in filtering and content recognition, preventive injunctions that are seen unfeasible at a certain point of time, could be considered proportionate in the future. Filtering technologies are now used more widely by online intermediaries, making content checking less costly and intrusive.[765] At the same time, these technologies have improved in accuracy and processing capacity.[766] Less intrusive filtering methods, such as shallow packet inspection, could potentially lie outside the scope of general monitoring.[767] Monitoring, in this context, denotes the act of proactively analysing user activity and content in search for any unlawful information or activity. Filtering systems partly use the results of monitoring in that they act on the identified content by either blocking or removing it. Filtering can be done by humans or through automated sys-

---

764 Ullrich, 'A Risk-Based Approach towards Infringement Prevention on the Internet' (n 747) 230.

765 See for example the development of private and public content recognition technologies, such as *Google's ContentID*, Mircosoft's *PhotoDNA*, British telecom's *Cleanfeed* system, the *AudibleMagic* or INA Signature the French Institut National de l'Audiovisuel Institut National de l'Audiovisuel, 'Ina-Signature: Protégez et Gérez Vos Contenus' <https://www.ina-expert.com/content/download/2103/44165/version/latest/file/1> accessed 5 March 2018. There are also a number of solutions by other companies targeted at helping rightsowners to identify copyright protected content on platforms, offered by e.g. Gracenote or MarkMonitor.

766 Sartor (n 236) 63. An overview of the content recognition solutions in the area of terrorist content and copyright protection will be given in Chapter 4.

767 Angelopoulos (n 30) 473–474.

tems, while monitoring is ensured through technical tools.[768] Algorithmic decision making is now routinely used by online platforms in both the distribution and the monitoring and filtering of internet content. This does, however, not mean that personal data will necessarily be processed. For example, a system that just matches content against a database of hashes, embedded metadata or watermarks does not need to analyse underlying user details or activity data.[769] The EU itself has suggested that filtering technology that is absolutely effective and available at no cost would make Article 15 unnecessary.[770] In the end, a lot depends also on defining "general monitoring", which, unfortunately, the EU lawmaker has not ventured to do. Meanwhile, the CJEU has also not established any clear methodology to distinguish lawful, specific prevention from prohibited general monitoring.[771] The lack of clarity on this has been noted many times.[772] This contributes to rendering Article 15 problematic and potentially less relevant in its application today.

iii. Mc Fadden (C-484/14)

This case focussed on the permissible scope of measures taken by a public Wi-Fi operator to prevent and deter copyright infringing activities by its users over its network.[773] The operator was a shop owner who ran a Wi-Fi network that gave free and unprotected internet access to people in the vicinity of the shop. A user of this free network committed copyright infringing acts by making music available free of charge to the general public. The rightsholder notified the violation to the Wi-Fi operator and subsequently filed claims for damages, an injunction against the infringement and reimbursement of notice costs. The operator, *Mc Fadden*, claimed exemption from liability on the grounds of Article 12 (1) ECD, as a mere conduit for internet access.

---

768 C Angelopoulos and others, 'Study of Fundamental Rights Limitations for Online Enforcement through Self-Regulation' (Institute for Information Law (IViR), University of Amsterdam 2015) 6–9.

769 Woods, 'The Carnegie Statutory Duty of Care and Fundamental Freedoms' (n 698) 11; Edwards and Veale (n 698) 82–83.

770 European Commission, 'SEC(2011) 1641 Final' (n 11) 50.

771 Sartor (n 236) 60.

772 Nolte and Wimmers (n 551) 21–23. Friedmann (n 16) 148, 152–155; Valcke, Kuczerawy and Ombelet (n 551) 109–110; Angelopoulos (n 30) 100–107.

773 *Mc Fadden* (n 139).

The CJEU was asked first for confirmation whether the Wi-Fi operator was indeed a mere conduit under the ECD's Article 12, and secondly, whether it was obliged to prevent future infringements of the work in question. The court was also asked about the adequacy of certain measures to prevent such infringements, notably: the termination of connections; installing password protected access; and monitoring all traffic via the network. The latter measure was predictably found to be in violation of Article 15 (1) ECD. Meanwhile, requiring the Wi-Fi operator to terminate the connection was deemed a disproportionate interference with the operator's business compared to the copyright interest at stake. Password protection of access to the Wi-Fi service was, however, deemed an adequate means. It would force users to reveal their identity and was therefore more likely to be an effective deterrent against unlawful use of the service.[774]

With this ruling the CJEU confirmed the validity of preventive measures, such as customer identification, as adequate for the prevention of unlawful activity, at least where intellectual property rights are concerned. It also provided some indication on the preventive measures that an IAP could be expected to take under the ECD. This can be contrasted to the ruling in *UPC Telekabel*, which justified the scope of preventive, blocking injunctions solely through the Infosoc Directive 2001/29. Taken together with the ruling in *L'Oréal v eBay*, this can be seen as a further step to formulating reasonable duty of care requirements for online intermediaries for certain kinds of unlawful content and activity.[775]

iv. The ECtHR rulings in Delfi v Estonia & MTE v Hungary

While the European Court of Human Rights' (ECtHR) jurisprudence is not binding for the CJEU, the ECtHR still rules on the European Convention of Human Rights (ECHR) to which all EU Member States have acceded. The provisions of the ECHR are recognised as general principles of EU law[776] and the CJEU has also acknowledged the ECHR as guidelines in the application of EU law.[777] The ECtHR may therefore bring cases against EU

774 ibid 90–98.

775 Ullrich, 'A Risk-Based Approach towards Infringement Prevention on the Internet' (n 747) 243–244.

776 Treaty on European Union (2007) Article 6 (3).

777 *J Nold, Kohlen- und Baustoffgroßhandlung v Commission of the European Communities*, C-4/73 [1974] EU:C:1974:51 (CJEU) [13]. In: Alina Kaczorowska, *European Union Law.* (Taylor and Francis 2013) 414.

Member States when they apply EU law and the CJEU does consider the rulings of the ECtHR.

Delfi[778] is a popular Estonian online news portal which offered its users the opportunity to comment anonymously on the news articles published on its site. One news article attracted a series of defamatory and insulting comments from readers against which the addressee of these comments filed an NTD request and claimed damages. While *Delfi* took down the abusive comments immediately, it refused to pay the damages. After regional and appeals courts in Estonia classed *Delfi* as an editor and ordered it to pay the damages, and after the Estonian Supreme Court refused to hear the case, the company went to the ECtHR claiming violation of its right to freedom of press and expression. Although the ECtHR did not come down decisively on *Delfi's* role as a provider of a comments function, it distinguished *Delfi* from bulletin boards or social media platforms. Due to its size, its editorial ownership of the news articles and the economic interest in providing reader comments, its role was more seen as that of an editor.[779] Despite of this, the ECtHR recognised the auxiliary character of *Delfi's* comments function. The judges conceded that its duties and responsibilities regarding that comment function may be different from that of a traditional publisher.[780] This is a useful analysis. It somehow sidelines the more cumbersome, and increasingly artificial, distinction between active and passive intermediaries of the CJEU and acknowledges the more differentiated role of internet intermediaries. In a certain sense, this assessment can be seen as coming close to the "active intermediary" standard developed by Italian courts.

The ECtHR considered the economic interest of the news portal and the measures that *Delfi* had in place to moderate and prevent certain types of comments. Notably, it had put in place terms and conditions, a notice-and-takedown system, automatic word filters and editorial actions by portal administrators.[781] However, despite of this, it noted, *Delfi* still failed to limit the dissemination of hate speech and speech inciting violence. Given the severity of comments at issue *Delfi* needed to do more to prevent and remove obviously unlawful comments. The need to be more proactive in this matter outweighed concerns over the protection of the fundamental

778 *Delfi AS v Estonia* [2015] ECtHR (Grand Chamber) 64569/09.

779 ibid 110–117.

780 ibid 113.

781 ibid 155.

right to freedom of speech.[782] The judgement was widely criticised for putting an undue weight on the policing role of intermediaries to the detriment of freedom expression.[783] Others speculated that the same outcome would have been reached had the case been judged by the CJEU under the ECD's liability regime. *Delfi* would likely have been found falling foul of the diligent economic operator standard.[784] If the latter is true, then the *Delfi* judgement offers a useful mini step towards establishing a standard of responsibility for comments functions of commercial news portals *vis-à-vis* defamatory speech.

The ECtHR applied this approach in *MTE*,[785] which concerned the alleged failure of a non-commercial, self-regulatory body of Hungarian internet content providers and the consumer protection section of a commercial news portal to remove and prevent defamatory speech. Both parties appealed a ruling by the Hungarian courts that allegedly deprived them of their intermediary liability protections. The ECtHR first found that the comments in question were not obviously unlawful. The comments also concerned the commercial reputation of companies as opposed to the personal reputation of private individuals in *Delfi*. In this context, the NTD system of the applicants, their terms and conditions and the employment of content moderators was sufficient to afford them protection against liability for comments by users.[786] By not taking these circumstances into account and by failing to perform a balancing exercise, the domestic courts had violated the applicants' freedom expression, guaranteed by Article 10 of the ECHR.[787] This ruling shows the malleability of due diligence obligations depending on the nature of comments and the character of the intermediary involved. Specific proactive monitoring, seen appropriate for the *Delfi* portal, may not be adequate for other types of content and intermediaries.

---

782 Valcke, Kuczerawy and Ombelet (n 551) 152–162.

783 Frosio, 'The Death of No Monitoring Obligations' (n 709); Martin Husovec, 'General Monitoring of Third-Party Content: Compatible with Freedom of Expression?' (2016) 11 Journal of Intellectual Property Law & Practice 17.

784 Valcke, Kuczerawy and Ombelet (n 551) 113.

785 *Magyar Tartalomszolgáltatók Egyesülete and Index.hu zrt v Hungary* [2016] ECtHR (Fourth Section) 22947/13.

786 ibid 81.

787 ibid 88.

v. Eva Glawischnig-Piesczek v Facebook Ireland (C18/18)

In this case, brought against *Facebook*, the CJEU had the opportunity to refine its jurisprudence on the scope of preventive activity that is allowed under the ECD.[788] It was asked whether the world's largest online social network could be compelled to identify and delete defamatory comments that were posted repeatedly against an Austrian politician and former Member of Parliament. The politician demanded that the scope of a stay-down order concerning defamatory comments against her person be extended to cover equivalent comments. Following the confirmation of the validity of such an order against *Facebook* by a Higher Court in Austria, the social network appealed the ruling to the Austrian Supreme Court. *Facebook* claimed that such an order would require the network to monitor the entirety of its traffic and therefore violate Article 15 ECD, which prohibited the imposition of general monitoring obligations on intermediary service providers. The Austrian Supreme Court referred the case to the CJEU for further clarification.

The CJEU ruled in October 2019 that *Facebook* could in fact be forced to implement stay-down orders for identical comments that were made by *any* user of the social media site against the Austrian politician. Moreover, *Facebook* could be compelled to identify and prevent equivalent defamatory comments from the *same* user under the condition that any variation in the nature of the remarks did not necessitate that *Facebook* engage in a new, independent assessment. The CJEU judged that such an order was proportionate if the original injunction contained enough specific elements that allowed *Facebook* to identify the equivalent defamatory nature of the comments without engaging in an independent assessment. Such elements would be: the name of the person concerned by the infringement, the circumstances under which the infringement was determined and an indication of content equivalent to that already declared illegal. The implication by the court was that the specificity of the injunction would allow *Facebook* to deploy automated search tools. This specificity also ensured that the intermediary would not be obliged to monitor its network on a general basis for unlawful content or activity.[789] By implication, requiring the intermediary to assess anew every uploaded comment with regard to its potentially equivalent meaning would be excessive.

788 *Eva Glawischnig-Piesczek v Facebook Ireland Limited, C-18/18* (n 463).
789 ibid 45–47.

The decision has been viewed as backing the use of automatic filtering software and weakening the liability protections of Article 14 of the ECD.[790] On the other hand, it could also be argued that this reasoning continues the line of certain rulings in Germany, where the use of automated content recognition tools was explicitly endorsed, while a reliance on manual reviews was rejected as imposing a too high burden on the intermediary. It is, however, interesting that the CJEU appears to compare the independent assessment, read: human involvement, to the general monitoring obligation rather than judging it merely as excessive. This suggests that, rather than a direct endorsement of automated tools, the CJEU considers that automated software would lower the burden on the intermediary to effectively enforce this somewhat broader injunction. Arguably, in the absence of such technology it would be unthinkable to compel intermediaries to suppress unlawful content that contains equivalent wording. This argument appears to be in accordance with the European Commission's more recent move to support the use automated filtering systems in order to detect and prevent specific infringements.[791]

In his Opinion, the Advocate-General usefully distinguished between intermediaries' preventive efforts in the area intellectual property, such as in *L'Oréal v EBay*, and in defamation cases, like the one at hand. Given the nature of intellectual property, it was justified to restrict the mandatory preventive efforts by intermediaries in this area to new infringements of the same kind of the same rights.[792] By contrast, defamatory acts are rarely repeated in exactly the same way, by using precisely the same terms for the same type of offense. This justified a seemingly broader formulation of a preventive injunction.[793] However, applying this broader scope to all users would amount to a general monitoring obligation. The intermediary would become an active censor and loose its neutral character.[794]

---

790 Daphne Keller, 'Filtering Facebook: Why Internet Users and EU Policymakers Should Worry about the Advocate General's Opinion in Glawischnig-Piesczek' (*Inforrm's Blog*, 7 September 2019) <https://inforrm.org/2019/09/08/filtering-facebook-why-internet-users-and-eu-policymakers-should-worry-about-the-advocate-generals-opinion-in-glawischnig-piesczek-daphne-keller/> accessed 25 October 2019.

791 European Commission, 'COM (2017) 555 Final' (n 69) 14–15.

792 *Opinion of Advocate General Szpunar on Eva Glawischnig-Piesczek v Facebook Ireland Limited, C-18/18* (n 264) paras 68–69.

793 ibid 70.

794 ibid 73.

The broad horizontal focus of the ECD may be a problem in the context of this more differentiated case law arising out of the CJEU and Members States. As demonstrated, the reach of preventive obligations is likely to depend on the type of violations at stake and the business model of the platform operator. Balancing acts could result in different results, contingent on the type of interests involved in protecting e.g. personality rights, intellectual property rights, public security or consumer protection interests. Accordingly, the reach of proportional preventive duties could vary for hate speech, trademark violations, defamation, copyright infringements, child abuse or illegal products. Some of the larger online or social media platforms may be confronted with all of these problems at once and require differentiated responses, safeguards and technologies depending on the type of content involved. The monolithic design of the ECD seems ill-fitted to provide that level of flexibility.

3. Summary of legal challenges of the ECD

The above discussion has illustrated the complex challenges of establishing effective remedies and legal enforcement mechanisms for unlawful activity and content on online intermediaries under EU law. The specific legal framework of the ECD, set up to deal with the liabilities of mere conduits and information hosts in the intermediation of information exchanges, has been subject to serious tests. Originally set up to protect the new enablers and facilitators of communication via the internet against undue burdens and interference in the dissemination of content, it is now increasingly seen as outdated, inflexible and morally unjustified. Three paramount legal challenges have been identified that hinder an effective fight against the ongoing and diverse problem of unlawful content.

I. Summary: The availability of the ECD protections

The requirement of the "mere technical, automatic and passive" intermediary service is troubled in its application to modern-day online platforms. Indeed, this assessment is one of the most difficult to make when having to determine the availability of the liability exemptions for online platforms. The variety of platform business models, the fervency with which content is shared and the opaqueness of content dissemination and manipulation practices have made a clear-cut assessment almost impossible. However, the decision is a key one. Under the current ECD provisions, it determines the availability of generous liability exemptions. An intermediary that qualifies as a neutral actor is subject to secondary liabilities at most. If not, however, it may face the full blow of primary liability under the relevant legal provisions that govern the content in question under national or EU law.

Meanwhile, there will likely be other, newer digital platform services, for which the application of the current hosting service definition may prove similarly difficult to judge. For example, the position of mobile web portals, cloud services, collaborative or participatory platforms or IoT platforms are just some examples.

The availability of the hosting defence has been discussed by judges, lawmakers and other specialists mainly in relation to the distinct business activities (e-commerce, content sharing, access provision), specific service features (advertising, fulfilment, comment function), technical features and content management practices (sorting, display, recommendation). These considerations would in the widest sense correspond to the complex architecture/infrastructure and design choices of platform operators.[795] Online platforms today assert almost exclusive control and power over these design choices. Most of these choices are aimed at maximising data capture, engaging multiple market actors and steering user behaviour towards more interaction and tenure on the platform.[796] The above deliberations have shown that it is by now more than doubtful that the current distinction between passive and active platforms can hold. Given how today's digital platforms govern user interaction, they have almost exclusively ceased to be "merely technical" actors in the original sense of the meaning 20 years ago.[797] Consequently, and in the absence of clear legal rules, courts in EU members continue to struggle with coming to coherent decisions in that matter. Moreover, looking for such a decision may be missing the point and hinder the formulation of effective rules that are adapted to fight unlawful content online.

It has been argued that the creation of new intermediary service provider categories in the ECD could be a way to clarify the availability of

795 Lorna Woods, 'The Duty of Care in the Online Harms White Paper' (2019) 11 Journal of Media Law 6, 13–15. Poell, Nieborg and Van Dijck (n 523).

796 Poell, Nieborg and Van Dijck (n 523). Olivier Sylvain, 'Intermediary Design Duties' (2018) 50 Connecticut Law Review 203.

797 Zuboff (n 5); Martens (n 53); Pasquale (n 19); Helberger, Pierson and Poell (n 68).

the ECD's Article 14 for new Web 2.0 platforms.[798] However, this approach risks to be overtaken by developments in the markets, possibly even before the necessary legal changes are put in place. It could also undermine the technology-neutral direction of the ECD. An alternative way could be to scrap the distinction between neutral and active intermediaries altogether. As has been shown, this assessment requires deeper technical and operational understanding of the platform models at hand. This is often not available in the courtroom nor would it be practical to enshrine more detailed criteria into the law. Why pursue this question when it has become clear that for most of today's Web 2.0 platforms, the data and content generated by user interaction, is at the heart of their business models? It generates massive profits, which even leads these actors to actively steer user behaviour. The neutrality claims of many of these intermediaries sit rather uncomfortably with the intrusive nature of their activities and the profits generated from user data. It appears that this way of thinking has found its way into the European Commission. The early version of a leaked preparatory document of the future "Digital Services Act" gives up on insisting on a distinction between active and passive hosts.[799] Unfortunately, this thinking has not prevailed in the formulation of the DSA proposal published in December 2020. As will be suggested further below, the availability of the intermediary liability exemptions should be rather tied to broader technical and design considerations of platforms.[800]

II. Summary: The knowledge standard

The assessment of actual knowledge of infringing activity and content is closely tied to the above question of neutrality. A purely neutral host under the current framework would hardly be in a position to gain knowledge of unlawful content other than by being notified of it. The US intermediary liability framework clearly follows this line in the most consequent fashion. In the EU, however, judges across Member States and the CJEU could not help but assessing the knowledge requirement in light of the increasingly immersive activities of Web 2.0 intermediaries. This was

798 European Commission, 'Synopsis Report on the Regulatory Environment for Platforms' (n 539) 16 fn 500.

799 'Digital-Services-Act-Note-DG-Connect-June-2019.Pdf' (n 546).

800 See also: Sylvain (n 795); Lorna Woods and William Perrin, 'Online Harm Reduction – a Statutory Duty of Care and Regulator' (Carnegie UK Trust 2019).

certainly helped along by the fact that there are no common requirements for NTD procedures and no explicit protections for "Good Samaritans." Jurisprudence in the EU culminated in the diligent economic operator standard and the consideration of "should have known" knowledge in *L'Oréal v eBay*. Actual knowledge of unlawful activities could be gained from proactive activities or even awareness of certain facts and circumstances. Meanwhile, diverging approaches towards determining actual knowledge have persisted, again, due to the complex nature of today's intermediaries, but also due to the different national legal cultures and approaches of dealing with secondary or intermediary liability. These diverging approaches have resulted in an uneven enforcement landscape and legal uncertainty with regards to the obligations of intermediaries *vis-à-vis* unlawful content.

The question of actual knowledge of unlawful information of today's more complex and globally operating platforms touches on deeper questions of corporate epistemology[801] in a business organisation: how is information that resides in a company's infosphere, its systems, documents and people, managed? At what stage can knowledge and therefore potential liability be inferred?[802] This problem is not unique to internet intermediaries but it exists across various areas of economic life, where it is addressed through standards of corporate responsibility.[803] The question acquires a new significance when seen in conjunction with the discussion about the gatekeeping roles of internet intermediaries for information exchange in today's society.[804] Is a strict qualification of actual knowledge still appropriate or would broader concepts that incorporate constructive knowledge and corporate responsibility be more apt today?[805] The question shall be discussed in more detail in Chapter 6, where an approach towards a new responsibility framework will be explored.

801 Burk (n 295) 451–453.
802 Burk (n 296), who borrows his approach from Floridi's concept of information ethics and the concept of infosphere: Luciano Floridi, 'Information Ethics: On the Philosophical Foundation of Computer Ethics' (1999) 1 Ethics and Information Technology 33.
803 Burk (n 295); Helberger, Pierson and Poell (n 68).
804 Taddeo and Floridi (n 120).
805 Valcke, Kuczerawy and Ombelet (n 551) 113.

III. Summary: Specific versus general monitoring

Finally, establishing when a specific monitoring or prevention obligation becomes a general one has been another tricky point. It took Member States considerable time to acknowledge more generally that stay-down orders did not result in general monitoring obligations. Meanwhile, the reappearance of once notified content throughout the internet remains a problem. This is also helped along by the nature of the internet and digital information exchange as a succession of copying instances. The ongoing wide availability of unlawful content has led to calls by legislators and enforcers for enlisting online intermediaries more proactively in this battle. Soon the attempt to ask intermediaries to prevent unlawful information beyond the suppression of already notified material hit the wall of Article 15 ECD. This provision was originally set up to protect the new intermediary sector against undue burdens of manually reviewing information that they transmitted or stored, and to shield them against attempts to use them as censors. However, with their rise in importance and with improved filtering and surveillance technologies, pressure mounted on intermediaries to broaden their preventive monitoring.

The ECD did not provide enough clarity in this respect. Courts have struggled to find the dividing line between general and specific monitoring. They developed different approaches, which, predictively, led to differing interpretation on the permitted proactive obligations of online intermediaries. It appears that the terms of specific and general monitoring are moving targets, driven mainly by technological change. Proactive measures that 15 years ago would have necessitated significant manual correction and *de-facto* general monitoring may today be less intrusive, more targeted and effective.[806] Thanks to advances in content recognition, data inspection and analytics they could today be seen as "specific", reasonable and proportional.[807]

The CJEU attempted to define the scope of more proactive, but specific monitoring obligations (*L'Oréal v eBay*, *Facebook*) and distinguish them from excessively broad monitoring duties (*Scarlet Extended, Netlog*). However, it appears that the CJEU relied in its fundamental rights balancing exercises on the safeguards provided for in the sectoral legal provisions specific to the content involved. In that sense, Article 15 ECD may have in-

---

806 Woods, 'The Carnegie Statutory Duty of Care and Fundamental Freedoms' (n 698) 11; Edwards and Veale (n 698) 82–83.

807 Friedmann (n 16) 152–153.

deed become an empty shell.[808] Preventive obligations change in proportion with technological progress and the type of violation and harms involved. The scope of permitted monitoring should not be limited by a diffuse concept of "generality" but rather be determined by proportionality that is derived from balancing the unlawful acts with the specific fundamental rights involved. The futile quest over the dividing line between general and specific monitoring duties of intermediaries has impeded the more important task of defining proportional and effective proactive obligations for online intermediaries in the fight against unlawful content.

808 Sophie Stalla-Bourdillon, 'Internet Intermediaries As Responsible Actors? Why It Is Time to Rethink the E-Commerce Directive as Well.' in Mariarosaria Taddeo and Luciano Floridi, *The responsibilities of online service providers* (Springer Berlin Heidelberg 2016) 287 .

Chapter 4 - Sectoral frameworks and the E-Commerce Directive – the enforcement gaps

A. *Introduction*

Chapter 3 provided an overview of the horizontal framework of intermediary liability at EU level. On the one hand, the legal challenges of the ECD that hinder an effective enforcement against unlawful content arose out of technological and socio-economic changes related to the internet. On the other hand, these challenges are further complicated by the diversity of unlawful content online. The sectoral provisions that govern different areas of content are to a large extent under the competency of Member States, the EU having only indirect or peripheral influence. Exceptions may be the AVMSD, the Infosoc Directive, the new (Copyright) Digital Single Market Directive (DSMD) or the EU consumer protection and product regulation *aquis*.[809] However, some of these provisions only relate to certain aspects of the content in question. Furthermore, the EU exercises peripheral influence in content regulation where EU constitutional principles are at stake. These are mainly the free movement principles[810] and fundamental rights, such as freedom of expression and others protected by the ECHR and the CFREU.[811] The EU also uses soft law instruments for protecting these principles in certain areas of online content regulation, such as codes of conduct or memoranda of understanding. These shall be explored in more detail in the respective content Sections.

Content regulated by Member States' laws may fall under civil and/or criminal law provisions. This may differ between Member States, as much as normative consideration on unlawful content, their enforcement and sanction mechanisms differ. Consequently, there are variations in the application of sectoral content regulation between Member States and this has an influence on the interaction with EU law, and specifically the intermediary liability provisions contained in the ECD. To make matters more

809 Savin (n 384) 115.

810 Treaty on the Functioning of the European Union (Consolidated versions of the Treaty on European Union and the Treaty on the Functioning of the European Union 2016) Articles 49, 54, 114.

811 These are usually: ECHR Articles 8, 10; CFREU Articles 7, 8, 11, 16, 17.

complex, the ECD provisions may coexist with specific rules for intermediaries set out in sectoral provisions and with the general rules applied to secondary or intermediary liability through the ordinary law in Member States. The interplay between these various intermediary liability frameworks is complex. As will be shown, national courts tend to prioritise constitutional and national ordinary law principles over EU law.[812] This may partly explain the limited success of the ECD in harmonising online intermediary liability exemption conditions.

This chapter will also demonstrate how the arrival of the internet and online intermediaries has influenced the substantive matter of sectoral law. For example, in copyright the very reliance of the internet on constant copying as a means of "transporting" information and the revolutionary nature of dematerialised, digital copying have gone to the very substance of that law itself. The more detailed analysis of case law in the area of digital copyright and internet intermediaries aims to demonstrate the technical and legal complexities of new intermediation practices on the internet. UGC, content sharing or hyperlinking have all challenged courts, both in the application of copyright law and intermediary liability provisions. Have online intermediaries through which content is shared, become more than just intermediaries in this process? Substantive trademark law, on the other hand, has been less powerfully affected by the trend of digitisation, especially where it concerns the activities of online intermediaries. Only since recent have the vertically integrated activities of online marketplaces started to be seen as affecting the scope of trademark protection directly. However, the superior economic interests at stake in this area have triggered an equally powerful policy debate over the role and responsibilities of online marketplaces. The discussion in this area will dedicate more detail to the various policy initiatives, which started as early as 2011 with the Memorandum of Understanding on the Sale of Counterfeit Goods over the Internet.[813]

In the cases of defamation, hate speech and terrorist material online, the role of intermediaries in amplifying or spreading content or in nudging users to communicate in certain ways may still not make them liable authors with primary responsibility. But could the new quality of facilitation and manipulation of information exchange confer new, extended responsibilities and liabilities on these intermediaries, and if yes, which? In general,

812 Benabou (n 334) 880; Kohl (n 280) 192.

813 'Memorandum of Understanding on the Sale of Counterfeit Goods over the Internet, 2011' (n 665).

the liability of (online) intermediaries in the different content sectors is dependent on the type of content and the specific legal traditions pertaining to secondary or intermediary liability.

Finally, in the area of product and food safety the rise of e-commerce conducted through intermediaries has led to significant enforcement challenges. Online marketplaces and other intermediaries are not the originators of unsafe, non-compliant or illegal products. But do the increasingly vertically integrated activities of e-commerce intermediaries, which may offer advertising, marketing, payments, logistics or financial services to sellers and consumers, affect their responsibilities for the legality of products sold? As lawmakers extend labelling, information and registration requirements onto products sold online and their sellers, does this also affect the obligations of e-commerce marketplaces, which are offering their platforms to thousands or even millions of sellers from across the world?

If this is not difficult enough, then each content sector also engages different fundamental rights. Different unlawful activities and content types may cause different kinds of harms and trigger the public interest in a variety of ways. This may lead to different balancing exercises and outcomes, at both Member State level and by content type, when determining the scope of the responsibilities accorded to online intermediaries. The patchwork of enforcement methods and standards applied against unlawful content can be seen as yet another challenge to the establishment of an effective and predictable common intermediary responsibility framework.

A number of central questions arise out of this heterogeneous picture: Are the ECD's general, horizontal provisions flexible enough to address each sector's and Member State's specific interpretations on the legal protections and responsibilities of online intermediaries? Are there overarching online intermediary principles and characteristics that would justify a horizontal approach to intermediary liability? If yes, how deep should new, horizontally applied principles and responsibilities reach into sectoral frameworks. Should sectoral frameworks be primarily structured by legal area, the harm caused, or by the type of intermediary, or a combination of all?

It is the aim of this chapter to contrast the different sectoral enforcement frameworks of unlawful content and draw conclusions. Given the broad scope of this work, these sectoral overviews can be but introductory and selective. Each sectoral area will be analysed by giving an outline of the legal provisions and competencies at Member State and at EU level. Where relevant, examples will be used to highlight the differences in the substantive laws of the Member States and the impact on enforcement on the internet. The discussion aims to evaluate the suitability of the current ECD's liability exemption rules and their national transposition in effectively protecting rights at sectoral level and fighting unlawful activity in the specific area. This analysis will include case law, technological trends and developments in private enforcement by platforms, such as the use of filtering or content recognition. Finally, policy trends and developments will be critically reviewed.

This chapter will be a demonstration of how the complex multi-level regulatory set up of the EU has amplified the enforcement problems of the broad, profound and fast transformations caused by the internet. It aims to complement the description of the horizontal legal challenges of the intermediary liability framework described in the previous chapter. These two chapters will serve as a backdrop for the development of a new intermediary responsibility framework, which will be attempted in Chapter 6.

B. *Personality rights and public order: defamation, hate speech and terrorist content*

1. Defamation

I. Defamation online - background

Together with copyright infringements, defamatory comments belong to the earliest unlawful activities that involved the liability of intermediaries on the internet. Unrestricted online speech was a major achievement of cyberspace for the early Libertarian utopians of the internet. It also influenced early perceptions of cyberspace as a borderless and open medium.[814] As the internet commercialised and became more popular in daily use, however, this free speech ethos created more and more conflicts. Online defamation or libels became more frequent. Comments posted by users against or about others on news servers or bulletin boards[815] or carried through internet access providers[816] caused the first significant legal chal-

---

814 Edwards, 'The Fall and Rise Of Intermediary Liability Online' (n 119) 51. see also Chapter 2 A

815 Such as the previously discussed *Cubby* (n 371); *Godfrey v Demon Internet Limited* [1999] High Court Of Justice Queen's Bench Division 1998-G-No 30, EWHC QB 240.

816 *Bunt v Tilley & Ors* (2006) [2006] EWHC 407 (QB) (England and Wales High Court Queen's Bench Division).

lenges in courts against the new intermediaries of the internet. Apart from pursuing the actual authors, the complaining parties also went after online intermediaries. They claimed that they were either liable for the defamatory comments as publishers, or that they were negligent as transmitters in failing to remove or prevent unlawful statements.

There are ongoing legal discussions on the role online intermediaries play in defamation via the internet. *Oster*, for example, discusses in relation to common law jurisprudence the view that, if publication is interpreted as an act of communication, then any internet intermediary that participates in this act, simply by virtue of providing the technical facilities, could be seen as a publisher. He notes the basic flaws of the concept of passive intermediary in this context.[817] That view could then be extended to any unlawful acts facilitated in that way by an internet intermediary, putting the intermediary firmly in the chain of responsibility.[818] Under common law rules, online intermediaries, be they IAPs or hosting providers, could seek defences as innocent disseminators of (defamatory) information. Introducing this knowledge element moves the tort of defamation closer to liability for negligence and the exercise of reasonable care.[819] Others, however, define publication more narrowly as acts that confer editorial responsibility and tie the liability of intermediaries for defamatory content to whether they are publishers, subject to strict liability.[820]

In the US, early online defamation cases have contributed to the formulation of the current framework that regulates intermediaries' liability exemptions under the CDA. This Act's almost unfettered immunities of online intermediaries against defamatory content reflect the robust and far reaching free speech protections under the US Constitution's First Amendment.[821] This means that the rights to privacy or protection of personal data succumb more often than not to the right of free speech, which in turn means that intermediaries are less required to intervene in the availability of content.

This balance is somewhat different in the EU. *Pollicino et al* have pointed towards almost diametrically opposite assessments in Europe and the US

817 Jan Oster, 'Communication, Defamation and Liability of Intermediaries' (2015) 35 Legal Studies 348, 354–356, 358. In that context, the "passivity test" under Articles 12 (1) – 14 (1) should rather become a "mere dissemination" test. (358)

818 Benabou (n 334) 871.

819 Oster (n 816) 357.

820 Lipton (n 23) 120.

821 Oster (n 816) 351. Omer (n 493) 301–304.

when dealing with the impact of the internet on fundamental rights:[822] In *Reno v ACLU* the US Supreme Court stressed the importance of encouraging freedom of speech enabled by the internet and assumed that government would be more likely to censor than to promote that freedom. It called therefore for a broad protection of internet intermediaries from liability for third party speech.[823] In Europe, however, the ECtHR stressed, notably in *Shtekel v Ukraine* and in *KU v Finland*, the new risks and harms that content and communications on the internet posed to the fundamental right of privacy. This, it said, outweighed the risk to freedom of expression. Policies regulating the internet had to be adjusted to this new technology in order to adequately protect all fundamental rights.[824]

Although the above cases were judged by the ECtHR, which has no jurisdiction over EU law, many of the ECHR rights and freedoms have been taken over into the CFREU. This includes the two freedoms which are most commonly engaged when dealing with (online) defamation cases: the freedom of expression and the right to a private life. Both have found their way into the online intermediary jurisprudence of the CJEU at several occasions. Given the specific European and EU values, the CJEU, the ECtHR and national courts have traditionally accorded a more measured emphasis to the freedom of speech right than in the US. Consequently, that right has traditionally been restricted more widely by the right to privacy[825] and other rights, such as the protection of personal data[826].

II. The legal framework of defamation in the EU

Apart from the fundamental rights principles, the EU influence on defamation law comes mainly from three areas:[827] the determination of ju-

822 Oreste Pollicino and Marco Bassini, 'Free Speech, Defamation and the Limits to Freedom of Expression in the EU: A Comparative Analysis (Ch. 21)' in Andrej Savin and Jan Trzaskowski, *Research Handbook on EU Internet Law* (Edward Elgar Publishing 2014) 351–352.

823 *Reno v. American Civil Liberties Union* (n 396) para 855. In: Pollicino and Bassini (n 821) 531.

824 *Editorial Board of Pravoye Delo and Shtekel v Ukraine* [2011] ECtHR (Fifth Section) 33014/05 [63] and *KU v Finland* [2008] ECtHR (Fourth Section) 2872/02 [49]. In: Pollicino and Bassini (n 821) 531.

825 A prominent example being *Delfi* (n 777).

826 *Google Spain v AEPD and Mario Costeja González, number C-131/12* [2014] EU:C:2014:317 (CJEU) [97].

827 Savin (n 384) 130.

risdiction in cases that involve international defamation on the internet,[828] the choice of law[829] and, where applicable, the intermediary liability provisions of the ECD. Matters of jurisdiction are probably the most hotly discussed legal issue in online defamation today. There is by now ample jurisprudence by the CJEU that has attempted to interpret the Brussels I regulation in the online context.[830] This subject shall not be treated here. However, the ongoing discussions and disputes on this particular issue just illustrate how much defamation is a transnational phenomenon and how much the internet has influenced this problem.

By contrast, the substantive legal provisions on defamation are not harmonised across the EU and remain under Member States' national competencies. Given different legal and cultural traditions, these substantive provisions may vary considerably. In most Member States defamation may still incur criminal charges, including prison sentences that vary between one and 96 months. However, there is a marked overall trend to decriminalise this offence. In practice, civil sanctions for defamatory acts have become the norm.[831] Defamation law can serve as a useful example for a study on how harmonised framework rules for intermediary liability exemptions interact with national sector laws that may vary significantly not only with regards to normative aspects, but also procedural set-ups and sanction regimes.

---

828 Regulation (EU) No 1215/2012 on jurisdiction and the recognition and enforcement of judgments in civil and commercial matters 2012 Article 7.

829 Regulation (EC) No 864/2007 of the European Parliament and of the Council of 11 July 2007 on the law applicable to non-contractual obligations 2007 (OJ L 199). Although this applies only to tort law conflicts.

830 For an overview: Emeric Prévost, 'Study on Forms of Liability and Jurisdictional Issues in the Application of Civil and Administrative Defamation Laws in Council of Europe Member States' (2019) Council of Europe study DGI(2019)04.

831 'Out of Balance - Defamation Law in the European Union: A Comparative Overview for Journalists, Civil Society and Policymakers' (n 479) 7–11. Savin (n 384) 126.

III. Defamation, online intermediaries and the ECD in national law

a. UK

The UK's 2013 Defamation Act[832] deals directly with online intermediaries. In other Member States, the various general principles of third party liability would be engaged when defamation-related claims arise against internet intermediaries.

Article 5 (2) of the UK Defamation Act creates a defence for a website operator that can show that it has not posted the defamatory speech on its site. This can be likened to the conditions governing the availability of the hosting defence in Article 14 (1) ECD, which requires that an intermediary service provider stores information at the request of a service recipient, and that that recipient does not act under the authority of the host.[833] This defence is unavailable when the claimant could not identify the originator of the post and when the claimant provided the website host with a notice and the host failed to respond to that notice.[834] Furthermore, the Act defines the content of a valid notice of complaint and opens up the possibility to specify procedural requirements through separate regulations, such as response times for notices and provisions on dealing with the identity of the originator.[835]

These provisions have been described as making the immunities of the ECD redundant.[836] While the Defamation Act indeed appears to impose conditions that are congruent with Article 14 ECD, it can also be argued that it makes use of the options provided in the ECD for Member States to formulate additional provisions for NTD or for duties of care. The Defamation Act provisions are indeed more detailed than those of the ECD. Regarding duties of care, the fact that the website operator only has a defence if the claimant was able to identify the originator of the defamatory comments (and reacts to notices), may incite the operator to put systems in place that discourage or ban anonymity.[837] Anonymity is to this day one of the major problems of dealing effectively with defamation and

832 Defamation Act 2013 c. 26.
833 Directive 2000/31 (ECD) Article 14 (2).
834 Defamation Act 2013 c. 26 Article 5 (3).
835 ibid Article 5 (5) (6).
836 Kohl (n 280) 192–193.
837 Alex Mills, 'The Law Applicable to Cross-Border Defamation on Social Media: Whose Law Governs Free Speech in "Facebookistan"?' (2015) 7 Journal of Media Law 1, 28.

other unlawful speech acts.[838] However, this defence has apparently rarely, if ever, been used by intermediaries during its more than five years of existence. Website operators may find this provision too complicated and unattractive compared to other available defences.[839]

UK case law shows that courts can rely on several legal sources when determining the liability (exemptions) of intermediaries in defamation cases: ordinary law, represented by common law concepts of innocent dissemination or knowing involvement in publication,[840] the aforementioned Defamation Act and the ECD, as transposed by the 2002 Electronic Commerce Regulations.[841] While in most cases online intermediaries have rarely been found directly liable for defamatory comments, UK judges tend to look first at the common law and nationally based provisions before making use of the EU law.[842]

In *Bunt v Tilley*,[843] the claimant Mr. Bunt brought proceedings against several IAPs alleging they were responsible for defamatory comments made on a blog that was communicated using the IAPs' services. The judge looked first and foremost at the common law defence of innocent dissemination and concluded that the IAPs were entirely passive. This meant they did not need any other defences, such as for example provided by the 1996 Defamation Act or the 2002 Electronic Commerce Regulations.[844] Nevertheless, in examining these statutes the judge found that these additional defences would also have been valid.

Tamiz v Google, decided six years later, deals with defamatory content on a blog hosted by *Google*. The claimant alleged that *Google* was liable for the defamatory comments by failing to remove them in a timely manner. The case was heard by the same judge who sat in *Bunt v Tilley*, and decided using the same methodology, coming to an identical conclusion. *Google* did not act as a publisher according to common law principles and therefore

838 Omer (n 493) 319–320.

839 Wilson Brett, 'Defamation Act 2013: A Summary and Overview Six Years on, Part 2, Sections 4 to 14 –' (*Inforrm's Blog*, 30 January 2020) <https://inforrm.org/2020/01/30/defamation-act-2013-a-summary-and-overview-six-years-on-part-2-sections-4-to-14-brett-wilson-llp/> accessed 13 March 2020.

840 *Bunt v Tilley & Ors* (n 815) paras 17, 23.

841 The Electronic Commerce (EC Directive) Regulations 2002 Articles 17 - 19.

842 Kohl (n 280) 192–193, 197.

843 *Bunt v Tilley & Ors* (n 815).

844 ibid 37.

did not need a defence under the other two statutes.[845] However, it would have been accorded such defences under the 1996 UK Defamation Act and, alternatively, under protections afforded to hosting providers under the 2002 Electronic Commerce Regulations. The appeals court agreed in principle that *Google* would not be a primary or secondary publisher under the common law principle of innocent dissemination. However, for the five weeks that elapsed between notification and removal the company would have associated or made itself responsible for the comments and thus be seen as a publisher.[846] Since the case was struck out because of triviality the court did not see a need to look into the potential availability of immunities under the Electronic Commerce Regulations.

Finally, in the more recent case of *Galloway v Frazer & Others,*[847] a Northern Irish politician brought an action against *YouTube* alleging that the VSP was responsible for publishing defamatory videos about him. *Google* sought the protections of the Article 14 ECD hosting provider immunities for its *YouTube* service. The judge in this case again mentioned the possibility of *Google* to seek protection under common law, the 1996 Defamation Act and the EU-law-based 2002 Electronic Commerce Regulations. Finding that *"while there are striking similarities between these different defences, there are obvious differences"* the court looked first at the common law protections applied in preceding cases.[848] It judged that the reasonable time to react to a notice had been overstepped. 23 days was perceived as too long given the gravity of the allegations. Therefore, the common law concept of knowing interference in the publication applied for the time between notification and removal. The remainder of the judgement seems to indicate consideration of the 1996 Defamation Act, which requires that a website operator must have no knowledge or reason to believe that they contributed to a defamatory publication for it to have a defence. The finding that *Google* did not react swiftly enough given the serious and alarming nature of the comments may also indicate reference to the 2002 Electronic Commerce Regulations, which require an expeditious removal after notification.[849]

845 *Tamiz v Google Inc Google UK Ltd* [2012] England and Wales High Court (Queen's Bench Division) HQ11D03178, [2012] EWHC 449 (QB) [39].

846 *Tamiz v Google Inc* [2013] England and Wales Court of Appeal (Civil Division) A2/2012/0691, [2013] EWCA Civ 68 [34–36].

847 *Galloway v Frazer, Google Inc (YouTube) and Ors* (n 627).

848 ibid 67.

849 ibid.

In all three cases the hierarchy and relationships between the available defences are ambiguous. Moreover, the harmonising element of the ECD is not at all visible. The UK judges may, understandably, be more interested in finding the most appropriate and effective provisions to deal with the legal conflict at hand, rather than establish a hierarchy of the available legal defences. If, however, common law doctrines exist in conjunction with national provisions on defamation and the latter include specific provisions for online intermediaries, EU law may indeed be perceived as redundant in litigation practice.[850] This applies even more where the EU law leaves considerable room of interpretation and lies outside of national legal traditions and customs. It should be said that the newer 2013 Defamation Act has alleviated some of this disaccord with the 2002 Electronic Commerce Regulations, which however, appears to be scarcely used in practice.

b. France

In France, the delict of defamation is defined through the 1881 Press Law.[851] This law is used for determining whether a remark or publication qualifies as defamatory. The law is more geared towards responsibilities of press publication in a pre-digital world, as it envisages civil and criminal sanctions mainly against the authors, editors and directors of publication.[852] In 1982, the law on audiovisual communication[853] introduced communication to the public by audiovisual means into the 1881 Press Law, tying responsibilities to the same parties. Finally, when France adopted the ECD through its 2004 *Loi pour la confiance dans l'économie numérique* (LCEN) it extended the rules of the 1982 law to electronic communications. This added the intermediary liability protections[854] to all infractions covered by the French Press law, including defamation, but also incitement to violence, hate and discrimination.

---

850 With Brexit this has now indeed become a mere theoretical point. However, it still serves as a good example of the complex interplay between national and EU intermediary rules.

851 Loi du 29 juillet 1881 sur la liberté de la presse Articles 29 - 35.

852 Renard and Barberis (n 361) 130–133.

853 Loi n° 82-652 du 29 juillet 1982 sur la communication audiovisuelle 1982 Article 93-3.

854 Loi n° 2004-575 du 21 juin 2004 pour la confiance dans l'économie numérique 2004 (2004-575) Article 6.

While the main defences of this law target primarily editors and publishers, there is also the more generally available defence of *prescription* which stipulates that a defamatory act can only be complained against within three months after which it was committed. This extends to internet publications and may constitute an additional defence for intermediaries in France. It has been differently interpreted by French courts. Earlier judgements saw internet publications, due to their characteristic of allowing for unlimited re-publications, as constant and successive offences. Consequently, the prescription period of three months started when such publication ceased, which questions the adequacy of this defence for internet publications.[855] Another court stipulated that the prescription period started anew with each modification of an internet address.[856] Finally, later judgements appear to concur that the prescription period starts with first publication, a date which is easily established from the server logs of internet hosts, or at the date when a judicial summons is delivered to the registry of a court.[857]

A glimpse on the interaction between the ordinary law defences on contributory liability in the *Code Civil*[858] and the defences available through French press law, and *inter alia*, the hosting immunities provided by the LCEN, can be gained from the above-mentioned case of *Les Editions R. v Google France.*[859] A claimant brought an action against *Google Search's* autosuggest functionality, which associated his name with the term *escroc ("crook").* First, the court rejected the claims for defamation and public injury according to the Press Law: the action had passed the prescription period of 3 months. Secondly, the autosuggestion function was seen as protected by the freedom to impart and receive information. Thirdly, the court also denied the claimant the parallel application of the *Code Civil* if this concerned an action that the claimant had already targeted by invok-

---

855 *Carl L v Raphaël M, Thierry M et Réseau Voltaire* (2000) Unreported (Tribunal de Grande Instance de Paris 17ème chambre, Chambre de la presse).

856 *Jean-Louis C v Ministère public, la Ligue internationale contre le racisme et l'antisémitisme (Licra), la Ligue française pour la défense des droits de l'homme et du citoyen, le Mouvement contre le racisme et pour l'amitié entre les peuples (Mrap) et l'Union des étudiants juifs de France (Uejf)* (1999) Unreported (Cour d'appel de Paris 11ème chambre correctionnelle, section A). For this and the judgement in (n. 790) see also : Renard and Barberis (n 361) 131.

857 *Les Editions R v Google France, Google Inc* (2013) Unreported (Tribunal de grande instance de Paris 17ème chambre civile).

858 Code Civil - Articles 1240 & 1241.

859 *Les Editions R. v Google France, Google Inc.* (n 856).

ing the French Press Law. Invoking the *Code Civil* in this way was seen as a means to circumvent the procedural obligations of the French Press Law. Considering that a successful claim for defamation and public injury would have engaged the hosting provider protections of the LCEN/ECD, then it can be argued that the *Code Civil's* contributory liability provisions and the LCEN are mutually exclusive for defamation cases. Meanwhile, a case against *Wikimedia France*, where this association was charged with deleting a Wikipedia page with defamatory remarks, was struck out by the Paris appeals court because the claimants failed to call on the appropriate provisions of the French Press Law. The court reminded the claimants that alleged abuses of the freedom of expression, including against intermediaries, could only be repaired by the 1881 Press Law, and not by the *Code Civil*.[860]

It appears therefore that defamatory acts or any acts sanctioned under the French Press law that involve online intermediaries, would automatically disqualify the (joint) use of the *Civil Code* and the LCEN provisions concerning online intermediaries. Meanwhile "neighbouring" offences such as denigration would allow for the engagement of the LCEN and the Code Civil.[861] For these acts, broader contributory liability rules of the French *Code Civil* and the bespoke online intermediary protections of the LCEN) coexist and are not mutually exclusive but rather apply in a cumulative manner.[862]

c. Germany

In Germany, defamatory acts are covered by Article 323 of the German civil code (BGB),[863] which imposes damage reparation on those who violate the life, body, health, property or other rights of others. The most common unlawful acts committed online that fall under this provision are violations of personality rights, such as defamatory acts, denigration or statements of false facts.[864] It should be noted that the wide formulation of this Article also opens the door to further liabilities. False or inciting state-

860 *Monsieur X et la société Z v Wikimedia France* (2014) Unreported (Cour d'appel de Paris, Pôle 2 – Chambre 7).
861 *M X et Nouvelles de l'annuaire Français v Qwant* (2020) Unreported (Cour d'appel de Paris, pôle 1, chambre 3).
862 Benabou (n 334) 880–881.
863 BGB Article 323 - Schadensersatzpflicht.
864 Hoeren and Bensinger (n 337) 4.

ments may also engage product liabilities or infringe the right to conduct a business. These claims however are usually not directly invoked by claimants.[865] Meanwhile, defamatory comments may also be punishable under the German criminal code. Articles 187 makes libel and slander of defamatory comments punishable with up to 5 years imprisonment. Articles 185 and 186 make "neighbouring" offences such as insult and malicious gossip subject to a maximum of two and one year imprisonment, respectively.[866] In German practice, the *Telemediengesetz (TMG)* which transposes the ECD into German law[867] acts like a filter before any responsibilities according to the civil and penal codes are being allocated.[868] Courts would therefore look first at the qualification of the online intermediary in question as a host or mere conduit and then apply concepts of interferer ("*Störer*") liability in view of the applicable sectoral provision of the unlawful act.

With regards to defamatory comments this means that once qualified as an online intermediary under the *TMG*, German courts apply the interferer liability doctrine. The BGH decided in its *Blogspot* judgement that a *Google*-owned blog portal only needed to fulfil its due diligence obligations once it had been notified of defamatory comments. However, the BGH acknowledged that it may be difficult for a host provider to determine the legal nature of defamatory content. A host provider would only need to act, if the notification was detailed and specific enough in order to affirm its illegality without difficulty, i.e. without detailed legal and factual analysis.[869] Once, however, the illegal nature of the content had been established it had not only an obligation to remove it, but also to prevent future violations of this kind.[870] It should be noted that the relatively formalised procedure to determine and apply interferer liability means that German courts can draw from jurisprudence in other legal areas, such as violations

865 ibid 4–5.

866 Strafgesetzbuch Article 185 - 186.

867 Telemediengesetz Articles 7 - 10.

868 Hoeren and Bensinger (n 337) 19; Spindler, 'Präzisierungen Der Störerhaftung Im Internet Besprechung Des BGH Urteils „Kinderhochstühle Im Internet"' (n 723) 107. This statement, however, needs to be qualified for copyright infringements, where courts lately tend to establish first whether the intermediary engages in direct violations of copyright, thus sidelining the verification of the hosting provider status.

869 *Verantwortlichkeit eines Hostproviders für einen das Persönlichkeitsrecht verletzenden Blog-Eintrag (Blogspot)* [2011] BGH VI ZR 93/10, GRUR 2012, 311 [25 0 27].

870 ibid 24.

of trademark rights or protection of minors. While this makes for a conceptually unified and predictable approach[871] it has also been criticised as being disproportionate. Applying duty of care *modus operandi* from, for example, the area of economic rights (such as IP) may not take account of the specific balancing exercises needed in the area of online speech.[872] The fear would be that automated infringement prevention technologies e.g. from the area of counterfeit prevention online, be applied directly to the area of defamation, leading to an undue restriction of speech and expression online.

d. Differences in assessing the manifestly illegal nature of defamation

Due to the different normative evaluations of national defamation laws, there are also differences at national level in determining when and if defamatory speech is manifestly illegal. This in turn may have an influence on the presumed knowledge after notification and the expectation of proactive duties according to the diligent economic operator concept.

Austrian courts have repeatedly held that defamatory comments are manifestly illegal and could therefore be more straightforwardly determined by intermediaries following a notification.[873] In the *Facebook* case judged by the CJEU, the Austrian court of first instance explained its preventive injunctions with the argument that the social network had failed to remove clearly obvious unlawful comments after being notified.[874] In the same vein, Belgian courts have ruled incontestable defamatory comments as manifestly illegal.[875]

Meanwhile, German, French, Dutch or UK courts have been less straightforward, with at times contradictory assessments regarding the manifestly illegal nature of defamatory comments.[876] In the *Blogspot* judgement the BGH said that a host provider could not always be expected to identify defamatory comments as clearly unlawful. It would need to rely on specific notifications and statements from involved parties to help it de-

871 Swiss Institute of Comparative Law (n 652) 286.

872 Spindler, 'Präzisierungen Der Störerhaftung Im Internet Besprechung Des BGH-Urteils „Kinderhochstühle Im Internet"' (n 723) 107.

873 European Commission, 'SEC(2011) 1641 Final' (n 11) 34. Van Eecke and Truyens (n 316) Chapter 6 18.

874 *Glawischnig-Piesczek v Facebook*, [2016] Handelsgericht Wien 11 CG 65/16 w - 17.

875 European Commission, 'SEC(2011) 1641 Final' (n 11) 35.

876 Verbiest and others (n 315) 51–61, 100.

cide whether to remove or retain the comments in question.[877] Earlier decisions by German courts have been less indicative on this matter.[878] French courts have also absolved host providers from needing to investigate whether comments posted on *YouTube* against an apparel retailer constituted defamation. In this case, defamation did not necessarily constitute a manifestly unlawful act.[879] By contrast, in the UK *Google* was faulted for failing to identify notified content concerning an MP as clearly defamatory.[880]

The ECtHR has implied in its *Delfi* ruling that defamation constituted clearly unlawful speech, putting it on the same footing with hate speech and incitement to violence. It found that liability of intermediaries for such speech was an effective remedy for protecting the personality rights of the persons targeted by this kind of unlawful speech.[881] The assessment of the clearly unlawful nature of the comments posted on the *Delfi* website played a role when finding the company guilty of failing to remove and prevent this kind of content.

The expectations on online intermediaries to determine the unlawful nature of speech notified to them differ across the EU. On the one hand, it appears excessive to enlist private intermediaries in content decisions that affect fundamental rights, especially when there is no clear-cut case over the nature of the content. Private actors are ill fitted to make decisions that should be reserved to regulators and judges. Today's online platforms are more often than not driven by commercial interests that aim at maximising revenue from online content and that influence content management decisions. On the other hand, in the face of the ongoing flood of unlawful speech on the internet, what choice exists other than involving these essential communication intermediaries more proactively in this fight? This will become even clearer when looking at other, more harmful, types of unlawful content. The ECD has not been helpful in finding a common EU approach to making the intermediary liability exemptions provide an effective remedy for violations of personality rights.

---

877 *Blogspot* (n 868) paras 25–27.

878 Hoeren and Bensinger (n 337) 29.

879 *H&M Hennes & Mauritz Logistics GBC France et H&M Hennes & Mauritz AB v Google Inc, Youtube* (2013) Unreported (Tribunal de grande instance de Paris).

880 *Galloway v Frazer, Google Inc (YouTube) and Ors* (n 627) para 67.

881 *Delfi* (n 777) para 67.

e. Defamation and the interactive, social web

Before the rise of Web 2.0 intermediation, defamatory acts were almost entirely restricted to postings on newsgroups or bulletin boards that were accessed by other users. Social media, UGC intermediaries and personalised web navigation have added a new dimension to not only defamatory acts but all sorts of unlawful content. The specific challenges of the interactive web with regards to defamation law and intermediary liability shall be briefly lined out.

Search engines have developed Autocomplete or Suggest functions with the aim to accurately predict searches conducted by users. Social networks and UGC platforms direct user attention. They manipulate the dissemination of information through recommender functionalities, targeted filtering or pre-defined personalisation choices of how to engage with content.[882] These functionalities are based on conscious architectural design choices by todays' online intermediaries aimed at maximising attention, amplifying messages selectively and personalising the user experience.[883] This is ultimately done for nothing else than business reasons:[884] Advertising revenue is linked to the ability to optimise microtargeting of users while at the same time maximising the circulation of and exposure to content. Although most of these nudging mechanisms remain opaque and subtle, they are powerful and put in question the role that these platforms play in the publication process.

Would a search engine that suggests an association of a defamatory remark with a specific search term be a mere passive host or actually provide its own content and become liable as a publisher?[885] In Germany, the BGH saw that *Google Search* provided its own content when suggesting additional words in order to complete a users' search. The autocomplete functionality did not qualify as mere conduit, caching or hosting activity.[886] Nevertheless, the BGH chose not to apply direct publisher liability but resorted to *interferer liability*, charging *Google* with failure to apply duties of care that would also apply to a hosting provider after being notified of the search suggestion's unlawful nature. It appears that the BGH took account

882 Lavi (n 199).

883 Oster (n 816) 351. Lavi (n 199) 64.

884 Anupam Chander and Vivek Krishnamurthy, 'The Myth of Platform Neutrality' (2018) 2 Georgetown Law Technology Review 17, 404.

885 Oster (n 816) 359.

886 *Verantwortlichkeit des Betreibers einer Suchmaschine mit Suchwortergänzungsfunktion* [2013] BGH VI ZR 269/12, 108/2013 JurPC WebDok [20].

of the fact that the autocomplete function rested on an algorithm which, while producing the unlawful association, was not intentionally designed to violate the rights of others. However, *Google* would need to take measures to prevent that its software violates the personality rights of others.[887] What appears to be important is that the BGH recognised the active nature of this intermediary service and refused to apply the intermediary liability immunities of the ECD. *Oster,* by contrast, argues that such a function would make search engine providers content owners.[888]

Other nudging mechanisms of social media or UGC platforms mentioned above have scarcely been the subject of intermediary liability considerations as yet. In *Facebook,* the CJEU noted the risk inherent in social networks that *"information which was held to be illegal is subsequently reproduced and shared by another user."* This and the availability of automated search tools and technologies arguably influenced its decision to confirm *Facebook's* proactive duties to prevent the spread of defamatory remarks as adequate. Meanwhile, users that "Like" defamatory remarks on *Facebook* have been found as potentially being liable for defamation. However, *Facebook's* own involvement in providing a medium and the architecture for amplifying defamatory remarks in this way was not discussed in this recent Swiss case.[889] The role of these architectural nudges is more than just neutral: the intermediary facilitates the generation of content that it prefers on its platform. The use of automated content management tools that rely on big data only exacerbates that activity. In that context, a truly neutral design or provision of technical infrastructure may not exist,[890] or may indeed have never existed since the ascendance of Web 2.0. May greater liabilities for (evil) nudges, whose content management practices cause severe harm, be justified?[891]

IV. Summary and outlook

An authoritative, EU wide interpretation of the obligations of online intermediaries in the fight against defamatory speech comes from the CJEU's

887 ibid 26.

888 Oster (n 816) 359.

889 André Müller, 'Wegen Facebook-Likes verurteilt | NZZ' *Neue Zürcher Zeitung* (29 May 2017) <https://www.nzz.ch/zuerich/aktuell/bezirksgericht-zuerich-wegen-facebook-likes-verurteilt-ld.1298231> accessed 24 March 2020.

890 Lavi (n 199) 28–32. Chander and Krishnamurthy (n 883).

891 Lavi (n 199) 71–82.

Facebook ruling. First, it appears that online intermediaries like *Facebook* can safely rely on the hosting provider protections as long as national courts determine it this way. The removal duties after notification remain reasonably clear, yet the decision on the manifestly illegal nature that will stir intermediaries into action lie again with national courts. On the preventive obligations, it appears that a diligent operator in a defamation scenario would need to prevent the identical comment from any user on its network, and similar comments only from the user at fault. The implication is that, following a sufficiently specific and detailed notification, automated tools could be tuned in a way that allow for an effective prevention of the same and similar comments without manual intervention. Manual intervention, on the other hand, would not only be seen as too onerous, but also as coming close to a (prohibited) general monitoring obligation. Whether this provides enough clarity for intermediaries in future defamation cases is open to question. First, the determination of the hosting provider status may be thwarted by other provisions in national defamation laws. Secondly, an active provider may be subject to differing obligations according to national systems, which may not even foresee such a hybrid role (e.g. like France but unlike Germany). Thirdly, the CJEU's *Facebook* guidance on hosting providers duties may still undergo assessment of the various national secondary liability rules. All this makes for rather disparate applications of the intermediary liability rules in the EU with regards to defamatory speech online.

Given its largely private law nature and the national competencies of Member States on defamation, there have been no specific policy actions at EU level. However, given the ongoing salience of the issue a more coordinated policy at EU level may indeed be beneficial for the protection of EU citizens.[892] The border between defamatory remarks, hate speech and incitement to violence is often fluid. In the face of the incessant continuation of defamatory comments, but mainly because of its more extreme iterations, the EU and Member States have stirred into policy action over recent years. At national level notably Germany, France and the UK have passed national laws in the area of hate speech and disinformation that may also cover certain defamatory acts. These shall be treated in the next section in more detail.

892 Savin (n 384) 142.

2. Hate speech

I. The phenomenon of hate speech on Web 2.0

The ever-growing connectivity of people worldwide through social media and UGC platforms did not remain unexploited by extremists and populists. Recent negative events around the world, such as the 2008 financial shock, migrant crises, terrorist attacks, environmental disasters or the Covid 19 pandemic have been widely exploited by these people to spread their extreme views via the internet. The internet allows for the sort of information intermediation that would appear to provide a fertile ground for the spread of extreme, polarising and hateful speech. The sheer scale of publications on the internet makes their identification and categorisation frustratingly cumbersome. Digital publication is instantaneous, global in its reach, notoriously difficult to eradicate and can be multiplied and shared endlessly. Most speech is hosted by a handful of intermediaries which connect "communities" of hundreds of millions, or even billions of users. It is distributed through content management practices that are little understood outside the corporate realm of these intermediary platforms. Speech on these networks is published with virtually no editorial control.[893] Last but not least, hate speech online is facilitated also by the relative ease with which a speaker can obscure their identity and post anonymously.

Hard data on the global spread of hate speech is difficult to come by due its elusive nature and different definitions of the phenomenon at national level. However, various national and regional statistics and reports testify to the rising influence of hate speech online and its negative impact on open and democratic societies. Hate crimes in general are also thought to be widely underreported.[894] This has a lot to do with the fact that the loud-

---

893 Catherine O'Regan, 'Hate Speech Online: An (Intractable) Contemporary Challenge?' (2018) 71 Current Legal Problems 403, 416–417.

894 Iginio Gagliardone and others, *Countering Online Hate Speech* (UNESCO 2015) 13; Daniel Geschke and others, '#Hass Im Netz - Der schleichende Angriff auf unsere Demokratie' (Institut für Demokratie und Zivilgesellschaft (IDZ) 2019) <http://www.das-nettz.de/publikationen/hass-im-netz-der-schleichende-angriff-auf-unsere-demokratie> accessed 3 April 2020; Laetitia Avia, Karim Amellal and Gil Taïeb, 'Renforcer La Lutte Contre Le Racisme et l'antisémitisme Sur Internet - Rapport à Monsieur Le Premier Ministre' (2018) 10–11 <https://www.gouvernement.fr/rapport-visant-a-renforcer-la-lutte-contre-le-racisme-et-l-antisemitisme-sur-internet> accessed 21 April 2021. 'State of Hate 2020 - Far Right Terror

est, vilest and most extreme speakers usually intimidate those with measured views and respectful and tolerant debating cultures. It also leads to the latter withdrawing from the debate, seemingly leaving the field to the "haters" and extremists and thus causing chilling effects to freedom of speech. In addition, there is a proven link between the spread of hate speech via social networks, on the one hand, and radicalisation of certain parts of society and acts of violence against minorities or certain groups of society, on the other. Its impact is particularly grave and dangerous for young people and minors.[895] Hate speech has become a hotly debated issue for politicians and societies, and, together with fake news, has, according to *Edwards*, become one of the "two new horsemen of the infocalypse"[896] over the last decade.

Despite an almost global recognition of the problem there is no internationally agreed definition of hate speech. The variety of definitions and legal instruments on the subject appear to target most commonly speech that is xenophobic and racist.[897] However, most people today, and indeed many legal instruments, would also include all sorts of speech that discriminates and incites to hatred and violence against people on the basis of their gender, sexual orientation, a disability, age, religion, social, political and other characteristics. Another common characteristic is that hate speech is based on unsubstantiated, distorted or false facts.[898]

Goes Global' (HOPE not hate 2020) <https://www.hopenothate.org.uk/wp-content/uploads/2020/02/state-of-hate-2020-final.pdf> accessed 9 April 2020.

895 Philip Brey, Stéphanie Gauttier and Per-Erik Milam, *Harmful Internet Use. Study Part II, Part II,* (European Parliament, European Parliamentary Research Service 2019) 18 <http://www.europarl.europa.eu/RegData/etudes/STUD/2019/624269/EPRS_STU(2019)624269_EN.pdf> accessed 6 April 2020; Geschke and others (n 893); Avia, Amellal and Taïeb (n 893) 12.

896 Edwards, 'With Great Power Comes Great Responsibility?: The Rise of Platform Liability' (n 661) 286.

897 Alisdair A Gillespie, 'Hate and Harm: The Law on Hate Speech' in Andrej Savin and Jan Trzaskowski (eds), *Research Handbook on EU Internet Law* (Edward Elgar Publishing 2014) 490.

898 Savin (n 384) 140.

II. The legal framework of hate speech

a. Fundamental rights at stake

Like in the area of defamation, hate speech online engages different, at times conflicting fundamental rights. On the one side of the spectrum is the right to freedom of expression which is broadly protected both under the CFREU and the ECHR.[899] This covers controversial and borderline speech that may disturb, offend or shock, because its toleration is a necessity for the existence of an open and democratic society.[900] On the other side, incitement to hatred and violence may affect the dignity, equality and safety of the targeted persons.[901] Different legal instruments, that commonly rely on international human rights standards, may spell out these rights in a variety of ways. For the EU, they are guaranteed through the CFREU in Articles 1, 6, 7, 10, or Title III, which, respectively, protect human dignity and guarantee the freedom to security, and private and family life, conscience and religion and equality to everyone. Under the ECHR and the ECtHR case law this may involve for example the protected right to a private life (Article 8)[902] or the prohibition of discrimination (Article 14).[903] It should also be remembered that hate speech itself may have a chilling effect on freedom of speech. Both the CFREU and the ECHR have abuse of rights provisions which may be triggered where the borders of freedom of expression are overstepped.[904]

Under the EU legal and cultural tradition hate speech is therefore always subject to a balancing exercise of various fundamental rights with the right to freedom of expression. Freedom of expression is therefore no absolute right and restrictions to its exercise must be limited to what is strictly necessary for the general interest.[905] In the US, by contrast, freedom of speech enjoys a much more blanket protection and asserts itself more readily over potential violations of privacy, personal integrity and dignity and other rights. This also means that online speech that is prohibited in the EU, or its Member States, may be admissible in the US. An early demonstration of these differences in the scope of freedom of speech online can be seen

899 Articles 11 and 10, respectively
900 *Handyside v The United Kingdom* [1976] ECtHR (Plenary) 5493/72 [49].
901 Gagliardone and others (n 893) 27.
902 *Delfi* (n 777); *MTE* (n 784).
903 *Handyside* (n 899).
904 Such as in *Delfi* (n 777) para 136.
905 CFREU Article 52 (1); ECHR Article 10 (2).

from the famous *Yahoo* case in the US and France which was discussed in Chapter 2.[906]

b. EU regulation

Without going into exhaustive detail on the international framework set up in the fight against hate speech online, some key provisions concerning the EU shall be mentioned briefly. The EU became more actively involved in political initiatives concerning hate speech since the 1990s. The Amsterdam Treaty started a process of gradual expansion of the EU's focus beyond a purely economic union. The 1996 Joint Action to combat racism and xenophobia[907] was a first step to coordinate judicial cooperation and encourage Member States to criminalise hate speech. In the following years the EU Treaties included specific commitments to ensuring equality and combating discrimination. Article 10 TFEU defines the fight against *"discrimination based on sex, racial or ethnic origin, religion or belief, disability, age or sexual orientation"* as an aim when the Union defines and implements its policies. To this end, the EU enacted the 2008 Framework Decision to combat racism and xenophobia by means of criminal law.[908] While this instrument does not specifically address hate speech crimes online, it can be seen as the main existing means of the EU to fight hate speech where it concerns racist and xenophobic expressions. This also reflects a general position that no distinction should be made between on- and offline hate crimes.[909]

Racist and xenophobic speech online is, however, targeted through the 2003 Additional Protocol to the Convention on Cybercrime, whose signature is not obligatory for EU Member States.[910] The main thrust of these instruments is to achieve that Member States criminalise hate crime acts,

906 *UEJF and Licra v. Yahoo! Inc. and Yahoo France* (n 358); *Yahoo! Inc. v. La Ligue Contre Le Racisme Et L'Antisemitisme* (n 360). see Chapter 3

907 Joint Action 96/443/JHA to combat racism and xenophobia 1996 (OJ L185).

908 Council Framework Decision 2008/913/JHA of 28 November 2008 on combating certain forms and expressions of racism and xenophobia by means of criminal law 2008 (OJ L 328).

909 Gillespie, 'Hate and Harm: The Law on Hate Speech' (n 896) 496–497.

910 Additional Protocol to the Convention on Cybercrime, concerning the criminalisation of acts of a racist and xenophobic nature committed through computer systems 2003 (European Treaty Series - No189). By the time of writing 24 Member States had signed the Protocol and 17 had ratified it.

apply aggravated and standard minimum penalties, enhance international judicial cooperation, clarify jurisdictional issues and regulate the interaction with fundamental rights. The substantive provisions on hate speech crimes, their definition and enforcement remain in the hands of Member States. The broad definitions of hate speech and the relatively broad discretion given to implementing the Framework Decision means that thresholds for criminalising hate speech vary across Member States.[911]

The ECD is another key tool at EU level, as it attempts to harmonise the liability exemptions of the intermediaries through which hate speech is shared and amplified. As will be shown below, the uneven application of these liability immunities also plays out when looking at the interpretations at national level on how internet intermediaries may be utilised in the fight against hate speech. However, it is important to note that Member States, in line with the exceptions provided by the Treaties, may divert from the country-of-origin principle and restrict an ISSP from another Member State to provide services where public policy objectives, which includes the fight against incitement to hatred, are being impacted.[912] Meanwhile, according to Recital 10 ECD, any EU action must ensure a high level of protection of general interest objectives, in particular the protection of minors and human dignity. The significance of hate speech as a crime that may affect Member States' public interest and the mandate of the EU to act in the fight against hate speech, given the Treaty objectives, give both parties strong reasons to act. The ECD's choice of action in this area are self-regulatory codes of conduct. Article 10 (e) ECD encourages the Commission and Member States to create industry codes of conduct regarding the protection of minors and human dignity.

i. The EU Code of Conduct on illegal hate speech online

In 2016, the European Commission brought major internet companies that operate online platforms to the table, in order to conclude such a self-regulatory agreement. The Code of Conduct on countering illegal hate

911 Teresa Quintel and Carsten Ullrich, 'Self-Regulation of Fundamental Rights? The EU Code of Conduct on Hate Speech, Related Initiatives and Beyond' in Bilyana Petkova and Tuomas Ojanen (eds), *Fundamental rights protection online: the future regulation of intermediaries* (Edward Elgar Publishing 2020) 204.

912 Directive 2000/31 (ECD) Article 3 (4).

speech online[913] builds on the 2008 Framework Decision. It makes the link between the need for an effective application of criminal laws on hate speech, as envisaged by the Framework Decision, and the necessity of online intermediaries to act expeditiously when notified of unlawful hate speech. The Code was a result of EU actions following the March 2016 terror attacks in Brussels. This also underlines the public policy and security aspects of hate speech spread online.

The internet companies commit to review and remove the majority of illegal hate speech within 24 hours of receipt of a valid notification. The code also encourages the IT companies involved to educate users, provide flagging and reporting tools as well as commit resources aimed at the efficient removal of notified content. The companies also commit to have in place internal rules or community guidelines that prohibit hate speech and to review any notifications first according to these guidelines, and secondly, where necessary, according to national law. This is remarkable as it indeed elevates the internal rules of these companies to quasi law, a status that they may already enjoy more discretely given their massive global reach. However, this confirms a more worrying development of public actors outsourcing the enforcement of the law to private companies, without little or no democratic oversight.[914]

The fundamental rights balancing exercises required under EU law are complex. The exercise is made more complex by the variation in national laws. For one, these kind of content decisions can only be operationalised to a certain extent. It remains then open how accurate these decisions are given the time limit of 24 hours. Whether they result in overblocking is another question, however. A doubt can be raised about whether a soft instrument like this code would really pressure these companies to overblock content and traffic, the lifeblood of their business. Secondly, it is of concern that these decisions are put in the hands of private companies whose content management policies are often deeply rooted in US American and often more Libertarian free speech values[915] that may not fit with Euro-

---

913 'Code of Conduct on Countering Illegal Hate Speech Online' (n 542). The initial participants YouTube, Facebook, Twitter and Microsoft have since been joined by Instagram, Google+, Dailymotion, Snap and Jeuxvideo.com

914 Article 19, 'Responding to "Hate Speech": Comparative Overview of Six EU Countries' (2018) 14 <https://www.article19.org/wp-content/uploads/2018/03/ECA-hate-speech-compilation-report_March-2018.pdf> accessed 20 August 2018; Quintel and Ullrich (n 910) 206.

915 Danielle Keats Citron, 'Extremist Speech and Compelled Conformity' (2018) 93 NOTRE DAME LAW REVIEW 43, 3.

pean values. It is likely that in order to avoid the quagmire of ruling on a patchwork of national hate speech laws across the globe, social media platforms apply more uniform standards that escape closer scrutiny.

An EU assessment of the regular transparency reports issued by social media companies as part of the Code of Conduct shows increases in the removal rates of notified content from 28% in 2016 to 72% in 2019 and in the 24-hour turnaround time from 40% to 89%. Meanwhile the amount of notifications has been rising continuously. For example, *Facebook* reported an increase in removed hate speech postings from 3.3 million during the last quarter of 2018 to 4 million in the first quarter of 2019.[916] Other measures that social media companies reportedly improved under the Code include processes for trusted flaggers of hate speech, the involvement of civil society in notifying and determining unlawful content, as well as appeals procedures. This all has led the Commission to claim that the Code has become an industry standard.[917]

The Code stays squarely within the limits of the ECD by trying to formalise ex-post standards of content notification and removal that are mainly focussing on the quantitative aspect of takedowns. No commitment is made to bringing transparency into the decision-making processes of these companies, the appeals procedures or the reporting on decision accuracy. There is also no commitment to actions that would improve the prevention of abusive and unlawful behaviour on these platforms in the first place as the worrying trend of an increase in hate speech online continues despite the existence of the Code. There are by now a number of proposals and projects that look at introducing more proactive responsibilities for the prevention of unlawful activities, which shall be discussed in Chapter 6. The narrative of the Code being a "reactive" industry standard rather fits the ethos of the big internet players, which have traditionally rejected any government intervention that interferes with their operating models.[918]

The Code clearly demonstrates the fix the EU finds itself in with regards to the ECD. The Commission may well be wanting to impose more far reaching responsibilities on online platforms. But the main competencies

---

916 European Commission, 'Assessment of the Code of Conduct on Hate Speech Online - State of Play (Information Note) - 12522/19' (European Commission 2019).

917 European Commission, 'How the Code of Conduct Helped Countering Illegal Hate Speech Online - Factsheet' (2019).

918 Stephen Kinsella, 'Twitter Cannot Keep Hiding Behind Blanket Anonymity' (*Inforrm's Blog*, 6 April 2020) <https://inforrm.org/2020/04/07/twitter-cannot-keep-hiding-behind-blanket-anonymity-stephen-kinsella/> accessed 9 April 2020.

in this regard lie with Member States. The substantive rules on hate speech, the participation in the Cybercrime Convention's Additional Protocol and the ECD allocate the decisive powers to Member States. Under the ECD, the role of the Commission is restricted to encouraging, together with Member States, the creation of codes of conduct. Meanwhile, the formulation of NTD procedures, the imposition of measures to prevent an infringement (in Article 14 (3)) or the application of duties of care (Recital 48) remain in Member States' hands.

The next, more assertive efforts in the EU's strategy to fight the surge of hate content online were its 2017 Communication and the 2018 Recommendation, both aimed at tackling illegal content online. While broader in their sectoral scope, these instruments allocate particular attention to the fight against hate speech, especially in connection with terrorist content.[919] The Commission mentions the progress made through the Code of Conduct in removing and acting on notified illegal hate speech, but also says that unlawful content, including hate speech, remains a serious problem. These two documents provide the first clearer iterations that advocate for the use of proactive detection and removal measures on the side of platforms in the fight against hate speech, and other types of illegal content. Importantly, the Commission puts forward that proactive and automated detection and removal tools would not automatically lead to the loss of the hosting provider immunities under the ECD (Article 14). Moreover, they could be performed in compliance with the general monitoring prohibitions in Article 15 ECD.[920] The latest assessment report of the Code of Conduct also summarises the proactive and automated detection activities undertaken by *Twitter*, *Facebook* and *YouTube*. For the latter two companies, 65% and 87% of removed unlawful content had been picked up by software. All content identified in this way was allegedly reviewed by humans before being removed.[921] The Communication also mentions that a more aligned approach to fighting unlawful content online, which ties together separate efforts across Member States by content type and type of platform, would be beneficial for the fight against unlawful content in general. Nevertheless, sector specific differences would be appropriate and

919 European Commission, 'COM (2017) 555 Final' (n 69) 20; European Commission, 'C(2018) 1177 Final' (n 8) Recital 4.

920 European Commission, 'C(2018) 1177 Final' (n 8) Recitals 24 - 27.

921 European Commission, 'Assessment of the Code of Conduct on Hate Speech Online - State of Play (Information Note) - 12522/19' (n 915) 6–7.

justified.[922] However, since the Recommendation no further rules specific to the combat of hate speech have been issued at EU level.

ii. The AVMSD and the DSA proposal

In the area of media policy, the EU included video-sharing platforms (VSPs) in the scope of the recently recast Audio-Visual Media Services Directive (AVMSD). VSPs now have an obligation to "*take appropriate measures to protect … the general public from programmes, user-generated videos and audiovisual commercial communications containing incitement to violence or hatred.*"[923] In addition, VSPs have to protect minors from programs that could harm their development and prevent programs that contain content the dissemination of which constitutes a criminal offence. This concerns terrorist content, child pornographic material and racist and xenophobic hate covered under the 2008 Framework Decision. It means that VSPs that operate in the EU, such as *YouTube*, *Vimeo*, *DailyMotion* or *Twitch,* but also social media platforms that host video content (e.g. *Facebook, Instagram*) will fall under this Directive.

The AVMSD includes a list of concrete protective measures that VSPs may have to take. These are mainly targeted at users, such as providing clear terms and conditions as to non-permissible content, giving users the opportunity to rate and flag content, providing parental control measures or establishing age verification systems. Which of these measures are appropriate, needs to be determined by the VSP after consideration of the type of content, its potential harm and the type of users and their vulnerabilities as well as by considering the general interest.[924] This, however, would require VSPs to engage in a more detailed risk assessment process as to the specific harms that their business model and content may cause. Such an obligation is a useful step in imposing a degree of responsibility and duty of care on VSPs with regards to the prevention of hate speech content. Member States are required to be in a position to assess the appropriateness of the protective measures taken by VSPs.[925] This can be seen as a useful starting point to establish procedures for accountability of these

---

922 European Commission, 'COM (2017) 555 Final' (n 69) 5–6.
923 AVMSD 2018/1808 Article 28b (1) (b).
924 ibid Article 28b (3).
925 ibid Article 28b (5).

platforms with regards to the measures taken to protect users from hate speech.

Member States may impose stricter requirements. However, they need to follow the intermediary liability framework of the ECD (Articles 12 – 15). The EU warns in particular against any measures that would be in conflict with the general monitoring prohibition of Article 15 ECD, such as requiring VSPs to install upload filters.[926] It also encourages the use of co-regulation to put in place these protection measures. It tasks the European Regulators Group for Audiovisual Media Services (ERGA) with coordinating these measures as well as providing technical advice on regulatory matters in the area of hate speech. [927]

The AMVSD foresees more concrete and proactive measures for VSPs in protecting users against hate speech than what is currently in place for others types of content at EU level. The involvement of the public sector in assessing and supervising the implementation of measures against hate speech constitutes a new step. But the measures are necessarily limited by the ECD's intermediary liability provisions. They do not contain more formalised NTD procedures or detail on the scope of proactive detection measures for hate speech. In addition, the imposition of anti-hate speech measures for one type of content or platform business model, as opposed to the whole sector, may create further fragmentation of the already dispersed intermediary liability landscape in the EU.

The AVMSD needs to be transposed into Member State laws by September 2020. It will be interesting to see how ERGA, Member States' supervisory authorities and VSPs engage in the setup and assessment of protective measures against hate speech (and other regulated content). The arrangements set out in the AVMSD are a first steps towards a co-regulatory structure, and may well be more fitting to create true industry standards than the purely self-regulatory Code of Conduct on hate speech.

The EU's 2020 DSApackage proposes to place enhanced obligations on intermediary service providers. This would also cover actions against illegal hate speech. While the DSA proposal would not be the appropriate vehicle for aligning national provisions of illegal hate speech, it proposes a set of harmonised obligations for intermediaries that target the fight against hate content, where it is illegal under national law. Very large online platforms (VLOPs), in particular, would have to put in place specific risk management systems to address systemic risks related to illegal content, including

926 ibid Article 28b (3).
927 ibid Article 28b (4), Recital 58.

hate speech.[928] The DSA proposal complements sectoral rules, such as those imposed by the AVMSD. The latter would now persist as *lex specialis* for VSPs under the new horizontal provisions of the proposed DSA.[929] The implementation of these new obligations, which will be touched on again in Chapter 6, would be supported through voluntary codes of conduct. The DSA draft specifically refers to the EU Code of Conduct on illegal hate speech as a basis on which new self-regulatory codes of conduct could be based. While the code would remain voluntary in nature, non-participation of a VLOP, where specifically invited to participate by the Commission, could be counted negatively against the platforms when the fulfilment of its new obligations under the DSA is being evaluated.[930] While the enhanced due diligence obligations of the proposal would bring platforms to take more responsibilities in the fight against illegal hate speech, the choice of continuing to rely on largely self-regulatory measures for their implementation is open to debate. As has been shown, self-regulation has proven to be less effective in bringing in place effective and comparable processes in the fight against illegal hate speech. In addition, these kind of initiatives need to be accommodated by already existing measures at national or sectoral level, as for example, the German *Netzwerkdurchsetzungsgesetz (NetzDG)*,[931] discussed below, or the AVMSD.[932]

c. Member States

National differences persist in the legal definition of hate speech, the setup of these offences within the legal system and its enforcement and sanction regimes. The border between other kinds of illegal material, such as defamation or terrorist content, may be fluid and Members States may draw the dividing line differently. They may accord different priorities to acts of hate crime, which is, for example, visible from vastly differing efforts and methodologies to collect data on these offences. Depending on the historical experiences and cultural traditions of countries, they may vary in their focus on crimes against certain minority groups. For example, Islamophobic, Anti-Semitic, right wing extremism or homophobic itera-

928 European Commission DSA proposal (n 10) Recital 57, Articles 26, 27.
929 ibid Recital 9.
930 ibid Recitals 67 - 69.
931 NetzDG.
932 Cole, Etteldorf and Ullrich (2021) (n 548) 193.

tions may be given different levels of priority.[933] There are also marked differences in the way hate speech offences are treated through various provisions of Member States' criminal, civil and administrative laws.[934] Meanwhile, progress on a consistent treatment of hate crimes through legislation as agreed under the 2008 Framework Decision has been slow and uneven.[935] This is not the place for a detailed analysis of hate speech laws across EU Member States. However, a short overview of the situation in the UK, France and Germany shall demonstrate that the national differences are also played out in the way hate speech is tackled in the online environment. Moreover, the inconsistencies in the enforcement of these crimes is exacerbated by the heterogenous understanding and application of online intermediary liability provisions.[936]

i. England and Wales

In the UK, hate speech is mainly regulated through criminal law by the Crime and Disorder Act and the Public Order Act. These Acts target behaviour that abuses or insults people on racial or religious grounds and that stirs up racial hatred and hatred on grounds of religion and sexual orientation.[937] Hate speech is also regulated through several civil law provisions under the Protection from Harassment Act and the Equality Act, which is aimed at protecting users of services or premises as well as employees.[938]

Hate speech via electronic communications and the media is covered by the 2003 Communications Act, with the media regulator OFCOM taking control in this area. This Act punishes the senders of offending communications. On a general basis, the 2002 Electronic Commerce Regulations impose obligations on social media platforms to react to notified hate content along the lines of the EU intermediary liability framework. But unlike the Defamation Act, the Crime and Disorder Act and the Public Order

---

933 Garland and Chakraborti (n 480) 43–47.

934 Article 19 (n 913).

935 Garland and Chakraborti (n 480) 44.

936 Kyriaki Topidi, 'Words That Hurt (2): National and International Perspectives on Hate Speech Regulation' [2019] SSRN Electronic Journal 29–30 <https://www.ssrn.com/abstract=3488718> accessed 6 April 2020.

937 Crime and Disorder Act 1998 subsections 31, 32; Public Order Act 1986 sections 18, 19, 21, 28 & 29B, C, D, E; O'Regan (n 892) 419.

938 Protection from Harassment Act 1997; Equality Act 2010; Article 19 (n 913) 25.

Act, or any other of the instruments mentioned above, do not contain any specific provisions for website operators or internet intermediaries. The new ambiguities and dynamics of unlawful speech online have primarily focussed on an adaption of enforcement guidelines and, through case law, on actions against the originators of the hateful comments. For example, the Crown Prosecution Service adapted its guidelines on prosecuting cases involving communications sent via social media in 2016 to include more speech crimes. However, the effectiveness of these measures in tackling hate speech online has been questioned.[939] The occurrence of hate crimes via social media has not stopped to grow in the UK. Meanwhile, the murder of MP Jo Cox, during the Brexit campaign, and the 2017 terror attacks in Manchester and London shifted the focus of policy makers eventually towards the responsibilities of social media platforms in this battle.[940]

In 2016, the Malicious Communications (Social Media) Bill was tabled for discussion in the UK Parliament. This instrument sought to oblige social media platforms to prevent and filter threatening speech. It proposed that non-filtered access would only be available for users that had provided proof that they were over 18 years of age. Supervision of this Act would have been allocated to the UK media and telecoms regulator, OFCOM.[941] The Bill contained no cross reference to the liability framework as transposed by the 2002 Electronic Commerce Regulations. However, the Bill fell due to the 2017 General Elections and was not further pursued.

In July 2016, the UK Parliament also announced an inquiry into hate crime and its violent consequences, which included an analysis of the role of social media companies in addressing hate crimes and illegal content online. The subsequent report on abuse, hate and extremism online found that, after taking evidence from *Google*, *Twitter* and *Facebook*, social media platforms were "shamefully far from taking sufficient action to tackle illegal and dangerous content."[942] Apart from failure to remove and prevent

939 Sandra Schmitz and Gavin Robinson, 'Das NetzDG Und Die CPS Guidelines Zur Verfolgung Strafbarer Inhalte In Sozialen Medien', *Recht 4.0 - Innovationen aus den rechtswissenschaftlichen Laboren* (OlWIR Verlag für Wirtschaft, Informatik und Recht 2017) 11–12.

940 ibid 9–12.

941 Parliamentary Counsel, Malicious Communications (Social Media) Bill 2017 [HC Bill 44].

942 House of Commons, Home Affairs Committee, 'Hate Crime: Abuse, Hate and Extremism Online' (2017) Fourteenth Report of Session 2016–17 21 <https://publications.parliament.uk/pa/cm201617/cmselect/cmhaff/609/60902.htm> accessed 14 April 2020.

notified hate speech and terrorist content it also found that the companies failed to have adequate processes in place to protect their users from harm caused by this unlawful speech. This included inconsistent and haphazard interpretation and enforcement of their own community standards but also a lack of using technology to proactively tackle hate speech.[943] The Parliamentarians passed several recommendations aimed at making online platforms more accountable for countering hate speech online. They recommended a comprehensive overhaul of the entire regulatory framework on hate speech and extremism in order to make it fit for the realities of the digital age.[944] However, the report does not contain any separate assessment of the ECD liability provisions or how the recommendation would fit into these provisions.

It appears that, like in the area of defamation, the interplay between national and EU-based provisions on intermediary liability and the responsibilities of online intermediaries is not clear. Meanwhile, the concerns over the perceived failure of social media platforms to tackle hate speech online have been incorporated into a more general Online Harms Reduction Regulator (Report) Bill in January 2020.[945] This Bill proposes to task the current regulator OFCOM with developing recommendations that impose statutory duties of care on online platform service operators to prevent harms to users. These duties would relate to a specified list of unlawful acts which includes hate speech and discrimination.[946]

ii. Germany

Hate crimes are pursued under several provisions of the German Criminal Code (*StGB*) that include, but are not limited to, insult, libel, slander, public provocation to commit offences, sedition, coercion, threats and the use of symbols of unconstitutional organisations.[947] The latter prohibits for ex-

943 ibid 23–24.

944 ibid 24.

945 Lord McNally, Online Harms Reduction Regulator (Report) Bill [HL] 2020 [HL Bill 22]. This Bill follows the recommendations of the UK Government's Online Harms White Paper (Great Britain and Department for Culture (n 190)), which is based on proposals developed by the UK Carnegie Trust and Woods and Perrin (n 799).

946 Lord McNally Online Harms Reduction Regulator (Report) Bill [HL] (n 944) Article 2A (4)(c) (d).

947 Geschke and others (n 893) 15.

ample the use of the swastika, and other symbols of the Nazi regime, including the Nazi salute. While many of these offences may be easily identifiable as unlawful, the border to defamatory comments, for which the manifestly illegal character is less obvious, remains fluid.[948] Up until 2018 there were no provisions that dealt specifically with hate speech online. The legal obligations of platforms with regards to hate speech were discharged through the *TMG*, the German law transposing the intermediary liability framework of the ECD. This is supplemented by the interferer liability doctrine, which allocates responsibilities along duties of care and negligence principles to social media intermediaries. According to this, the duties of removal of notified unlawful content are complemented by obligations to prevent the re-upload and sharing of removed content. These measures should be reasonable with regards to their technical and economic feasibility, as well as with regards to their impact on the right to freedom of expression.[949]

However, the proactive duties of internet hosts with regards to hate speech differ according to the business model. According to a recent BGH judgement,[950] internet search engines have less attenuated proactive duties with regards to the prevention of once notified (hate speech) content. The claimants in this case had tried to enjoin *Google* from preventing the display of comments that infringed their personality rights and bring the company to install a word filter to that effect. Search engines had clear duties with regards to manifestly illegal notified content, such as incitement to violence, child pornography, hate speech or clearly defamatory content. Nevertheless, with regards to defamation and hate speech, the border was less clear, especially for search engines. They could not be expected to validate the legality of the comments as they typically lacked the contextual information.[951] Imposing proactive duties of care on the line of social media platforms would endanger the business model of search engine operators and, as a consequence, the usability of the internet.[952] This statement of

948 Bernd Holznagel, 'Das Compliance-System Des Entwurfs Des Netzwerkdurchsetzungsgesetzes' [2017] ZUM 2017 615, 618.

949 *Haftung eines sozialen Netzwerkes für durch Dritte hochgeladene ehrverletzende Inhalte, 11 O 2338/16 UVR* [2017] GRUR-RS 2017 103822 (LG Würzburg) [108–110, 119, 124].

950 *Zur Prüfungspflicht des Betreibers einer Internet-Suchmaschine bei Persönlichkeitsrechtsverletzungen* [2018] BGH VI ZR 489/16, GRUR 2018, 642.

951 ibid 35–37.

952 ibid 34.

the BGH is in itself a glaring proof of the power of commercial intermediaries over the accessibility of information on the internet.[953]

Like elsewhere in Europe, the spread of unlawful hate content became a more pressing problem over the last five years and grew into a matter of public interest. In Germany, this phenomenon was fuelled in the wake of the migration crisis in 2015 and further accentuated in the run-up to the Federal elections in 2017. The German government initiated a national code of conduct with *Facebook, Google* and *Twitter* at the end of 2015.[954] This *Task Force against Illegal Hate Speech* contained essentially the same commitments as the EU wide code of conduct one year later. The social media companies committed to remove manifestly illegal, notified content within 24 hours and to invest in dedicated resources (staff, processes). However, the government's monitoring report, published in March 2017, still found that the complaints management and removal processes agreed under the *Task Force* fell short of the original commitments. Two of the three participating networks were still not deleting the majority of illegal content notified to them.[955]

The NetzDG

As a consequence, in June 2017, the German Federal Government brought in a law which codified obligations of social media networks with regards to the removal of unlawful content.[956] The law has become known as the *Netzwerkdurchsetzungsgesetz* (Network Enforcement Act) (*NetzDG*). It was the first national regulatory initiative in Europe aimed at tackling the rise of hate speech on the internet directly.

---

953 Gerhard Wagner, 'Haftung von Plattformen Für Rechtsverletzungen (Teil 1)' [2020] GRUR 2020 329, 331.

954 Bundesministeriums der Justiz und für Verbraucherschutz, 'Together against Hate Speech - Ways to Tackle Onl Ine Hateful Content Proposed by the Task Force against Illegal Online Hate Speech' (2015)

955 jugendschutz.net, 'Löschung rechtswidriger Hassbeiträge bei Facebook, YouTube und Twitter - Ergebnisse des Monitorings von Beschwerdemechanismen jugendaffiner Dienste' (Bundesministerium für Justiz und Verbraucherschutz, Bundesministerium für Familie, Senioren, Frauen und Jugend 2017) <https://www.fair-im-netz.de/SharedDocs/Downloads/DE/News/Artikel/03142017_Monitoring_jugendschutz.net.pdf?__blob=publicationFile&v=3> accessed 22 September 2020.

956 NetzDG.

The *NetzDG* has since been widely analysed and commented on and shall therefore be discussed only briefly.[957] It applies to all ISSPs that operate profit-oriented platforms, which are set up to share content between users or with the public. In addition, it concerns only those social networks which do not have editorial responsibility for the content shared. Platforms with less than two million registered users in Germany are exempt from the complaints, takedown and reporting obligations imposed under this law.[958] The *NetzDG* defines certain provisions of the German criminal code according to which content is unlawful and therefore actionable by the social media platforms. This includes, amongst others, acts that threaten public order and security, such as incitement to hatred or violence against national, ethnic or religious groups, including sedition, depictions that glorify cruelty, or violence against humans, and severe defamation of religious or ideological organisations.

The law obliges social media platforms to have a complaints management system in place for content that has been notified to them as unlawful.[959] That complaints management system includes processes to deal with notified content. Manifestly illegal content will need to be removed within 24 hours and other unlawful content within seven days of reception (with some exceptions).[960] The staff dealing with complaints, or notices, under the *NetzDG* need to receive training on a regular basis. The operation of the complaints management system needs to be checked on a monthly basis by the company management.[961] The platform may involve co-regulatory institutions (i.e. usually set up by civil society and industry) in the decision-making process on notices. In addition, the social media operators need to publish bi-annual reports on their compliance with the law. These reports must contain, amongst others, data on the amount of complaints, removals, turnaround times, information procedures to notifiers and users

---

957 Schmitz and Robinson (n 938); Gerald Spindler, 'Internet Intermediary Liability Reloaded' (2017) 8 JIPITEC 166; Wolfgang Schulz, 'Regulating Intermediaries to Protect Privacy Online – the Case of the German NetzDG', *Personality and Data Protection Rights on the Internet, Forthcoming* (2018) <https://ssrn.com/abstract=3216572> accessed 27 August 2018. Thomas Wischmeyer, '"What Is Illegal Offline Is Also Illegal Online": The German Network Enforcement Act 2017' in Bilyana Petkova and Tuomas Ojanen (eds), *Fundamental rights protection online: the future regulation of intermediaries* (Edward Elgar Publishing 2020).

958 NetzDG para 1 (2).

959 ibid 3.

960 ibid 3 (2).

961 ibid 3 (4).

from whom the content originated, and explain the process and organisation of their complaints management system in Germany.[962]

In essence, the *NetzDG* fixes the non-binding measures previously agreed by the 2015 *Task Force*. It focusses on *ex-post*, reactive content removal procedures for hate postings that violate German law. In its current form, it lays out the procedural detail of obligations that internet hosts have already under the ECD.[963]

The *NetzDG* has been criticised mainly on two grounds: 1) The law outsources the decision-making process over illegal hate speech to private actors and imposes potentially more restrictive national standards on content available worldwide. This could lead an undue restriction of speech worldwide.[964] In addition, private companies may be ill fitted to make decisions on the legality of speech with respect to all fundamental rights involved and in difficult contextual situations.[965] 2) The complexity of the verification process, coupled with tight removal deadlines and the threat of hefty fines would lead to over-blocking of content by social media platforms and an overzealous application of automated content filtering.[966] An argument voiced in contrast is that the regulated platforms have little commercial interest to over-enforce. Overzealous blocking would eventually reduce user traffic, popularity[967] and deprive these platforms of valuable advertising revenue. Secondly, social media networks already regulate speech through their private content policies, which are detached from legal standards and public interests. The new law would help to realign the content policies of social media networks to public interest principles. If society deems social media networks so important that their content removals affect freedom of expression, then they should also be held responsible for the protection of other rights.[968]

962 ibid 2.

963 Quintel and Ullrich (n 910) 219.

964 Citron (n 914) 7; 'Germany: Removal of Online Hate Speech in Numbers – Kirsten Gollatz, Martin J Riedl and Jens Pohlmann' (*Inforrm's Blog*, 23 August 2018) <https://inforrm.org/2018/08/24/germany-removal-of-online-hate-speech-in-numbers-kirsten-gollatz-martin-j-riedl-and-jens-pohlmann/> accessed 27 August 2018.

965 Schulz (n 956) 8.

966 'EU Action Needed: German NetzDG Draft Threatens Freedom of Expression' (*EDRi*, 23 May 2017) <https://edri.org/eu-action-needed-german-netzdg-draft-threatens-freedomofexpression/> accessed 27 August 2018.

967 Schmitz and Robinson (n 938) 8.

968 jugendschutz.net, 'Stellungnahme von jugendschutz.net zum Entwurf eines Gesetzes zur Verbesserung der Rechtsdurchsetzung in sozialen Netzwerken

An analysis of the early transparency reports published in 2018 by *Google (YouTube), Twitter* and *Facebook* show that none of the platforms removed more than 50% of the content notified.[969] Meanwhile, the number of notifications received under the *NetzDG* varied significantly. While *Twitter* and *Google* received each in excess of 250,000 notifications, *Facebook* reported just over 1,000. However, the deletion of manifestly illegal content within 24 hours reached over 95% for *Twitter* and *Google*, and 70% for *Facebook.* A proof of systematic over or under blocking could not be established. Despite the transparency reports, the actual decision-making process on an operational level remains shrouded in anonymity. It is evident from the transparency reports that the networks will increasingly apply automated software proactively - during content upload and through ongoing site monitoring - in order to flag potentially unlawful content for human review.[970] How and to what extent these companies have already moved to fully automated removals is, however, unclear. Indications by *Facebook* show that automated removals take place for hate speech content that receives high risk scores, while in other instances this software flags controversial hate speech for final human review.[971]

Meanwhile, *Facebook* received a fine of EUR 2 million from the German Government (currently under appeal) because of allegedly insufficient reporting and opaque complaints procedures. The over 1,000 complaints reported under the *NetzDG* were in stark contrast to the several millions of hate speech removed under the company's Community Standards.[972]

(NetzDG)' 2–3 <https://www.bmjv.de/SharedDocs/Gesetzgebungsverfahren/Stellungnahmen/2017/Downloads/03172017_Stellungnahme_jugendschutz.net_RefE_NetzDG.html> accessed 22 September 2020.

969 Medienanstalt Hamburg/Schleswig-Holstein, 'MA HSH - Auswertung von Transparenzberichten Nach NetzDG' (Medienanstalt Hamburg/Schleswig-Holstein 2019) <https://www.ma-hsh.de/infothek/publikationen/ma-hsh-auswertung-der-transparenzberichte-nach-netzdg.html> accessed 16 April 2020.

970 Google, 'Removals under the Network Enforcement Law – Google Transparency Report' <https://transparencyreport.google.com/netzdg/youtube?hl=en> accessed 16 April 2020.

971 Facebook, 'Community Standards Enforcement Report - Hate Speech' (2019) <https://transparency.facebook.com/community-standards-enforcement#hate-speech> accessed 16 April 2020.

972 'BfJ - Pressemitteilungen -Aktuell- - Bundesamt Für Justiz Erlässt Bußgeldbescheid Gegen Facebook' <https://www.bundesjustizamt.de/DE/Presse/Archiv/2019/20190702.html?nn=3451902> accessed 16 April 2020; Facebook, 'Community Standards Enforcement Report - Hate Speech' (n 970).

In December 2019, the German Government published a bill to fight right wing extremism and hate crimes, which intends to change some provisions of the *NetzDG*. It proposes to oblige social media platforms to report certain types of extreme hate speech to law enforcement authorities.[973] On 1 April 2020, the government announced further changes to the *NetzDG* aimed at making it easier for users to get social networks to disclose the data of hate speech perpetrators.[974] It proposes to introduce mandatory counterclaims procedures and oblige social media networks to provide more detail and comparative data in their transparency reports. Social media companies would also need to report more about the basic features and the scope of automated content removal tools, such as training data used, verification procedures and the extent to which scientific and research communities have assisted in the evaluation process.[975] This small detail of the draft is, however, significant and innovative. It may be a start for achieving more transparency and public scrutiny over the automated tools and decision-making procedures of these platforms. It may also provide a counter-balance to the risk of unchecked state influence on social media platforms.[976] The bill testifies to the unsatisfactory results in some areas of the current *NetzDG*. Extremist and hate speech on the internet are an ongoing phenomenon, which was linked to several right wing and extremist terror attacks in Germany in 2019 and 2020.[977]

The new *NetzDG* would also incorporate the changes demanded by the AVMSD (Articles 28a and 28b) with regards to the risk management activities of video sharing platforms in the fight against extremist and child abuse material.

Despite its potential shortcomings, this a useful step to formulate and codify *ex post,* reactive duties of care and a level of public scrutiny that is probably unique in this area. It could be an important element towards

---

973 Christina Etteldorf, 'Bill to Combat Right-Wing Extremism and Hate Crime' [2020] iris Newlsetter <http://merlin-int.obs.coe.int/article/8802> accessed 16 April 2020; Bundesministerium für Justiz und Verbraucherschutz, Entwurf für ein Gesetz zur Bekämpfung des Rechtsextremismus und der Hasskriminalität 2019.

974 Bundesministerium für Justiz und Verbraucherschutz, Entwurf eines Gesetzes zur Änderung des Netzwerkdurchsetzungsgesetzes 2020.

975 ibid Article 2 (2).

976 Human Rights Watch, 'Germany: Flawed Social Media Law' (*Human Rights Watch*, 14 February 2018) <https://www.hrw.org/news/2018/02/14/germany-flawed-social-media-law> accessed 16 April 2020.

977 Such as the murder of district commissioner Walter Lübcke on 2 June 2019, and extremist terror attacks in Halle (2019) and Hanau (2020).

building more comprehensive and transparent risk management obligations for online platforms in the fight against unlawful content.

iii. France

France regulates the substantial provisions on hate speech through the French Press Law of 1881 and the criminal code (*Code Pénal*) . The 1881 Press Law's Article 24 makes incitement to hatred and violence based on a person or group's ethnic, racial or religious characteristics a criminal offence. This text was amended in 1990 by adding Article 24 *bis* and Article 32, which make the denial of crimes against humanity, such as the holocaust, a criminal offence.[978] The criminal code punishes similar hate speech acts when committed through private communications, which also applies to electronic communications. The respective passage of the criminal code was amended several times over the last 20 years in order to increase the scope and penalties for racist acts. In addition, the dissemination of images linked to criminal acts was also made punishable with maximum five years imprisonment and a fine of EUR 75,000, thus adapting it to better target acts of cyberbullying and harassment.[979] This arsenal is completed by the LCEN, which transposes the ECD into French Law.

The French Press Law and the criminal code punish the originators or publishers of hate speech acts. The normative differences to other jurisdictions and the impact on expression on the internet have been vividly demonstrated in the *Yahoo* case described above.[980] Within France, the application of hate speech provisions has also not gone without problems: striking the balance between freedom of expression and hate speech, and the more procedural aspects, that may be less adapted to the online environment, are cases in point.[981] The intricate procedural requirements of the French Press Law and its interplay with the LCEN were already described in the section on defamation. This also applies to hate speech acts.

978 Topidi (n 935) 16; Christiane Féral-Schuhl, *Cyberdroit 2018/19 - 7e ed.: Le droit à l'épreuve de l'internet* (Edition 2018-2019, Dalloz 2018) chs 713-Atteintes aux libertés individuelles713.122. Textes.

979 Code pénal Articles 222-33, 222-33-2, 222-33-3, 227-24; Féral-Schuhl (n 977) chs 713-Atteintes aux libertés individuelles713.122. Textes. Agnès Granchet, 'Réseaux sociaux, médias en ligne et partage de contenus : le temps de la responsabilité et de la régulation' [2020] Legipresse 93.

980 See Chapter 3

981 Topidi (n 935) 15.

Like elsewhere in Europe, France has witnessed a surge of hate speech promulgated through social media.[982] The successive attempts to amend the substantive provisions of hate speech laws may be one indication of the continuous efforts of the law maker in that respect. Court cases involving intermediaries have focussed on the obligations of host providers. For example, *Twitter* was found guilty as a host provider under the LCEN of not providing an easily visible and accessible system of notification of unlawful content to its users and for failing to communicate data of users that had posted anti-Semitic content.[983] The courts also confirmed that hosting providers only needed to remove notified content that was manifestly illegal without waiting for a court or authority. Manifestly illegal content was defined as child pornographic material, denial of crimes against humanity and incitement to racial hatred.[984]

A series of grave extremist terror attacks since 2015 brought the role of social media platforms in the incitement to extremist violence and hatred increasingly into the public debate.[985] In 2018, the MP *Laetitia Avia*, published a report aimed at stepping up efforts to combat racism and anti-Semitism on the internet.[986] The report proposed new obligations on social media platforms to remove hate speech. The proposal takes the German *NetzDG* and notably its 24-hour removal target for manifestly illegal hate speech as well as its steep sanctions as an example.[987] On 20 March 2019, *Laetitia Avia* and a number of other Parliamentarians introduced a bill to combat hate content on the internet to the National Assembly (the *Loi Avia*).[988] The bill was adopted into law after a second reading by the *Sénat*, the French upper house of Parliament, on 28 February 2020. By inserting a new Article (Article 6.2.) into the LCEN, social media platforms would be obliged to remove or make inaccessible, manifestly illegal content notified to them. The law defines manifestly illegal content, by referring to specific provisions in the 1881 French Press Law and the criminal

982 Avia, Amellal and Taïeb (n 893) 12–13.
983 *L'Union des Etudiants Juifs de France (UEJF) v Twitter* (2013) (Unreported) (Cour d'appel de Paris Pôle 1, chambre 5). The action in thsi case was based on the LCEN in conjunction with civil procedural rules.
984 *Rose B v JFG Networks* (2013) (Unreported) (Cour d'appel de Paris Pôle 1, chambre 2).
985 Avia, Amellal and Taïeb (n 893).
986 ibid.
987 ibid 5, 20–22.
988 Laetitia Avia Proposition de loi visant à lutter contre la haine sur internet (n 651).

code.[989] Like the *NetzDG*, the manifestly illegal content includes terrorist propaganda and the dissemination of child pornographic material along hate speech. The law introduces a new delict of non-removal of notified content. The maximum fine for platforms that are in contravention of the new law is EUR20 million, or 4% of global turnover, whichever is the higher amount.[990] The bill does not define any exemptions or thresholds for the application of the law, but asks the *Conseil d'État*, the French Government's legal advisory body, to determine such thresholds by decree.

The law obliged platforms, amongst others, to withdraw all terrorist and child pornographic content notified by authorities within one hour. Platforms would also need to withdraw any manifestly illegal content notified by other persons within 24 hours.[991] Other procedural obligations include the provision of standardised and easily accessible notification systems for unlawful content. Platforms need to acknowledge the receipt of a notification, confirm the date and time of the receipt, inform the notifiers of the course of action taken and the reasons behind any decision, such as removal or no action. Content uploaders shall be informed of any removal, the reasons for it and the possibilities of contesting the decisions. They shall also be given a warning that the publication of manifestly illegal content is subject to civil and criminal sanctions.[992] Abusive notifications would be punishable with up to one year of imprisonment and a fine of EUR15,000.[993]

The *Conseil supérieur de l'audiovisuel (CSA)*, France's audio-visual media regulator is given powers to oversee the reporting obligations of platforms, the administration of fines and to coordinate best practice sharing, and co-operation between social media platforms.[994] In the area of preventive measures, the efforts focus on education about the issue of hate speech online. But the law also foresaw the creation of an observatory on online hate speech under the aegis of the *CSA*. This observatory should unite civil society, researchers, social media platforms and administrators to monitor and discuss emerging issues in hate speech online and preventive efforts.[995]

It is true that the French bill was similar to the *NetzDG* in that it focussed mainly on procedural, *ex-post* measures of notices and takedown.

---

989 ibid Article 1 (II).
990 ibid Article 4 (I).
991 ibid Article 1 (I, II).
992 ibid Article 2 (II).
993 ibid Article 1 (II).
994 ibid Article 4.
995 ibid Article 7.

However, there are some important differences. By charging the *CSA* with overseeing and developing transparency reporting procedures, corrective actions, sanctions and with leading wider cooperation efforts between stakeholders and industry in the fight against hate speech, the proposal goes more in the direction of co-regulation than the *NetzDG*.

The CSA has already been tasked with a similar mandate in the recently passed law against disinformation online.[996] It is also the regulator responsible for implementation of the AVMSD, which now covers VSPs. France appears to put the CSA at the heart of a future co-regulatory system aimed at establishing transversal principles of content regulation on online platforms, and applying them in a differentiated way to the various content sectors and platform operating models.[997]

In May 2020, 60 French Senators brought a challenge to this law in front of France's Constitutional Council, the *Conseil Constitutionnel*. They complained that, notably the one hour and 24 hour withdrawal obligations and the severity of fines imposed contravened several provisions of the ECD, such as Article 3 on the freedom to provide services and Articles 14 and 15 on the liabilities of online intermediaries. They also violated the fundamental rights of freedom of expression and to receive information.[998] On 18 June 2020, the *Conseil Constitutionnel* vindicated the concerns of the Senators by declaring large parts of the law unconstitutional and in contravention of, amongst others, the ECD and its French implementation, the LCEN.[999] The short reaction times accorded to platforms did not take account of the legal complexities related to the legality of certain content and the amount of notifications that platforms receive. Combined with the threat of high fines, this would incite platforms to withdraw content without due consideration, thus impacting freedom of expression and information. In its current form, only two substantial provisions have been retained: Article 2, which spells out the detail of the content and format of a

996 LOI n° 2018-1202 du 22 décembre 2018 relative à la lutte contre la manipulation de l'information 2018 (2018-1202) Articles 11 & 12.

997 Roch-Olivier Maistre, 'Point d'étape Vers Un Nouveau Modèle de Régulation Des Plateformes' [2019] Legipresse 459.

998 Groupe Les Republicains, 'Saisine CC – PPL Avia lutte contre les contenus haineux sur internet' <https://www.conseil-constitutionnel.fr/sites/default/files/as/root/bank_mm/decisions/2020801dc/2020801dc_saisine.pdf>.

999 *Décision n° 2020-801 DC du 18 juin 2020, Loi visant à lutter contre les contenus haineux sur internet* [2020] Conseil Constitutionnel 2020-801.

notice, and Article 16, which nominates the *CSA* as the body to host and supervise the creation of the observatory for online hate speech.[1000]

III. Private regulation of hate speech

Social media platforms and UGC platforms have been constantly refining the enforcement of their own content standards or community policies. This is in their own interest. The maximum of (profitable) content engagement can only be achieved when abusive, extreme and illegal behaviour does not put off too many users. Meanwhile, removing too much content may dent user trust and advertising revenue.[1001] From an economic perspective, platforms may only have an interest to remove those kinds of extreme content that lead to a net loss in user traffic and "behavioural surplus."[1002]

Each platform may have its own balance and policy approach depending on the market and the operational model that it has carved out for itself. Consequently, some of them may be more prone than others to attracting and amplifying extreme speech, including hate comments that stray into unlawful territory.[1003] What all of these profit-orientated social media and UGC platforms have in common is that the revenue is highest when the information platform meets the expectations of a maximum of users.[1004] This is the case when the content hits the nerve of the user, leading to increased sharing with like-minded people on the platform and prolonged engagement in front of the screen. That "hitting the nerve" and the occasional virality of a piece of content happen all too often when fringe or more extreme news and opinions are voiced that outrage and confirm own opinions and views.[1005]

The content management practices and policies of platforms are ultimately geared towards the mechanisms that generate additional financial revenue. The community policies and the algorithms that govern the cre-

1000 LOI n° 2020-766 du 24 juin 2020 visant à lutter contre les contenus haineux sur internet | Legifrance 2020 (2020-766)

1001 Kate Klonick, 'The New Governors: The People, Rules, and Processes Governing Online Speech' (2018) 131 Harvard Law Review 1599, 1627–1628.

1002 Zuboff (n 5) l 2053.

1003 For a detailed analysis of how this manifests itself in platform architecture and content moderation policies see: Lavi (n 199).

1004 Klonick (n 1000) 1627.

1005 Chander and Krishnamurthy (n 883) 404.

ation and spreading (or not) of content are designed in order to create an environment conducive to advertisers. The right type of content is that which draws a maximum of user attention and which corresponds to the desired target audience of advertisers on a given social network or a section thereof.[1006] Corporate and ethical values and respect of the law may also influence the formulation of content policies.[1007] However, the real weight of ethical and normative corporate values and their application in day-to-day content management is open to debate.[1008]

It is increasingly uncontested that the content management policies of a small number of dominant platforms, which reach hundreds of millions and even billions of people worldwide, create a private regulatory regime for online speech with little accountability.[1009] With regards to hate speech, it may be a challenge for a globally operating network on the internet to respect and comply with the patchwork of different national standards and values, especially since each piece of content is accessible globally. These platforms are under constant pressure to operationalise content management policies on the one hand, and reacting to increasing pressures from regulators to enforce national hate speech standards on the other. A social network platform would try to balance the legal risk of non-compliance in certain jurisdictions against the efficiency loss incurred through adapting global operating procedures to national specificities, while safeguarding its revenue generation. This does not bode well for open and transparent content management practices, and may be harmful to wider public interests where these platforms are gatekeepers of internet content. Companies like *Facebook* or *Google* have, arguably, become more important as actors in regulating content and expression than states.[1010]

Social media platforms want to keep regulators and civil society organisations at bay and prefer self-regulating. Any fundamental debate about

---

1006 Fernando Bermejo, 'Online Advertising as a Shaper of Public Communication' in Rikke Frank Jørgensen (ed), *Human Rights in the Age of Platforms* (The MIT Press 2019) 131 <https://direct.mit.edu/books/book/4531/Human-Rights-in-the-Age-of-Platforms> accessed 28 May 2020.

1007 Which are also called Community Standards (Facebook), Content Policies (Reddit) , Community Policy (LinkedIn), Terms of Service (Google) or Rules and Policies (Twitter)

1008 Zuboff (n 5) l 2056; Citron (n 914) 6–8. Wagner, 'Free Expression? Dominant Information Intermediaries as Arbiters of Internet Speech' (n 83) 233–234.

1009 Wagner, *Global Free Expression - Governing the Boundaries of Internet Content* (n 136) 54.

1010 ibid 116.

the transparency of enforcement processes, the values and risks underlying certain business practices and architectures, such as live-streaming, content amplification algorithms or targeted advertisement may backfire on revenue. This is also meant to obscure the fact that content moderation, by these self-professed passive platforms, is an active selection process of what is and what is not publicly available to users. Reams of borderline and straightforwardly illegal texts, images and videos need to be reviewed, judged, and then removed or allowed by armies of content moderation workers across the globe, or as is increasingly the case, by automated software.[1011]

Social media platforms have reacted to the growing volume and diversity of content online and the mounting pressure of regulators in two ways.

First, they have changed their content policies and the internal content moderation guidelines with increasing frequency.[1012] Content policies are adapted to public opinion, or following user trends, and less strictly enforced if it involves commercially more valuable content types or service recipients. With the overarching objective to derive money from content, the enforcement of these policies is therefore often inconsistent, or even contradictory, if seen from a legal and ethical standpoint. Essential standards of transparency and accountability succumb to changing internal enforcement priorities that are dictated by financial preoccupations.[1013] Secondly, regulatory initiatives are pre-empted by commitments to deploy more staff, build internal oversight boards and use automated removal tools and artificial intelligence.[1014] This may speed up certain removal processes of hate speech and unlawful content, but also make the content management policies even more opaque.

1011 Tarleton Gillespie, *Custodians of the Internet: Platforms, Content Moderation, and the Hidden Decisions That Shape Social Media* (Yale University Press 2018) 120–125.

1012 Klonick (n 1000) 1639.

1013 Sarah T Roberts, *Behind the Screen: Content Moderation in the Shadows of Social Media* (Yale University Press 2019) 95–104.

1014 MacKenzie F Common, 'Fear the Reaper: How Content Moderation Rules Are Enforced on Social Media' [2020] International Review of Law, Computers & Technology 1, 11. Robert Gorwa, 'As Platforms Rely Less on Human Content Moderators, What's at Stake?' (*Centre for International Governance Innovation*, 31 March 2020) <https://www.cigionline.org/articles/platforms-rely-less-human-content-moderators-whats-stake> accessed 22 April 2020; Richard Waters, 'Facebook's Attempt to Prove Impartiality Looks Doomed to Failure' *Financial Times* (22 August 2019)

In parallel to that, there is a determined move to employ fully automated systems that proactively identify and remove unlawful hate speech. This has been demonstrated in the sections on the EU Code of Conduct on hate speech and the *NetzDG*. This proactivity may serve online platforms as a pacifier to regulators, which seek to impose enhanced responsibilities and obligations on platform. On the other hand, these internal content management tools pre-empt more profound investigations and verifications from outside parties as to the standards applied when deciding which content can stay up and which needs to be taken down. The sheer number of automated takedowns and the technical nature of these processes make it difficult to retrace content decisions by platforms without having access to data. The additional benefit for platforms is that these tools can easily incorporate but also mask the frequent changes in content policies and their internal enforcement. Public authorities are placed in the dilemma between welcoming what might appear as a helping hand in enforcing the law, on the one hand, and seeing the actual decision-making process over removals of hate speech moving beyond their sphere of influence, on the other. Meanwhile, the discrepancy between the relatively few notifications received though notifiers and the huge number of automated removals confirms the tendency of online platforms acting as largely unsupervised private regulators of speech and information on the internet that are in direct competition with nation states.[1015]

IV. Summary and outlook

Given the influence of social media platforms as speech regulators, national governments and the EU have first tried to get these companies to enforce their own content policies consistently and transparently. This was mainly attempted through codes of conduct. At a second level, the adherence to national standards, already fixed into law, has been adapted to the specificities of the internet, e.g. in France, Germany and the UK. These efforts are a good start to achieve a more effective and transparent removal of

---

1015 Mariarosaria Taddeo and Luciano Floridi, 'The Debate on the Moral Responsibilities of Online Service Providers' (2016) 22 Science and Engineering Ethics 1575, 1593; Uta Kohl and Carrie Fox, 'Introduction: Internet Governance and the Resilience of the Nation State' in Uta Kohl (ed), *The Net and the Nation State Multidisciplinary Perspectives on Internet Governance* (2017) 12–14; Belli and Sappa (n 42) 189–190.

notified unlawful content. However, they will arguably do little in bringing more light into risky content management practices that are responsible for the ongoing massive availability of hate speech online in the first place. While at least in Germany, there is no conclusive evidence of systematic over or under blocking following the *NetzDG*, it cannot be denied that these kind of systems continue to outsource the complex enforcement of fundamental rights to private actors. The current efforts may therefore not be enough to ensure accountability for content management decisions that affect freedom of expression, human dignity and democratic order.

The crux is that social media platforms are not responsible as editors for content and can generally claim immunity under the ECD's intermediary liability conditions. Consequently, only reactive procedural duties, NTD or information and transparency requirements, have been imposed on these companies under the national laws mentioned above. But, as has been demonstrated, the new mechanisms of social media clearly give these actors more than just a merely technical and passive role in the information intermediation process.

Rather than just regulating *ex post* mechanisms or curtailing the market imbalances or dominance of certain social media platforms, harmful content management and business practices need to be regulated more systematically. Platform business models and design choices for algorithms and nudging systems that promote or amplify hate speech and other harms need to be openly assessed from a moral and ethical public interest standpoint.[1016] This, however, means imposing prospective obligations along more systemic content governance and risk management mechanisms, which the current legal framework of the ECD prohibits.

The UK appears to incorporate more holistic prospective and retrospective responsibilities of platforms regarding hate speech into the wider reform of online platform responsibilities under the Online Harms Reduction Regulator (Report) Bill. These efforts will ultimately be pursued outside of the EU jurisdiction over the coming years.

France has chosen to task the *CSA* with oversight of both *ex-post* content removal and transparency obligations, as well as more forward-looking societal research, dialogue and best practice sharing in the fight against hate speech online. The *CSA* appears to emerge as a central platform (co-)regulator with competencies that might eventually extend towards establishing

1016 Karine Favro and Célia Zolynski, 'De la régulation des contenus haineux à la régulation des contenus (illicites)' [2019] Legipresse 461. Woods, 'The Duty of Care in the Online Harms White Paper' (n 794).

more forward-looking risk management obligations on platforms in the fight against hate speech and other types of unlawful content. Too onerous *ex-post* withdrawal obligations are clearly out of place. But whether this remains relevant in the context of the automated proactive content removal systems deployed by most large platforms remains to be seen. The new responsibilities of the *CSA* are one of the few parts that were left intact after the *Conseil Constitutionnel* struck down most other provisions of the *Loi Avia*.

Germany intends to toughen the *ex-post* procedural and transparency obligations of social media networks with its new *NetzDG*. Like France, it also wants to shed more light on the mechanisms that govern the identification and removal of hate speech. However, the institutional regulatory structure to support this is less defined and less holistic.

Both approaches are likely to provide valuable insights for a future regulatory framework at EU level for content moderation and intermediary responsibility as envisaged by the European Commission under the future Digital Services Act.[1017] So far, the European Commission has not attempted to tackle the issue of hate speech online through legislation. It remains to be seen whether and how the future DSA would address this particular issue in its final version. The current proposal contains useful, enhanced obligations that would also apply to the removal and prevention of illegal hate speech. It remains, however, questionable whether the choice of accompanying the enhanced obligations with, so far ineffective industry self-regulation may bring the results hoped for. Meanwhile, the decision of the *Conseil Constitutionnel* on the *Loi Avia* should be a warning shot over the red lines that EU lawmakers need to navigate when they draft the DSA.[1018]

1017 'Digital-Services-Act-Note-DG-Connect-June-2019.Pdf' (n 546).

1018 Jean-Sébastien Mariez and Laura Godfrin, 'Censure de La « loi Avia » Par Le Conseil Constitutionnel : Un Fil Rouge Pour Les Législateurs Français et Européens ?' [2020] Dalloz actualité 29 juin 2020.

3. Terrorist content

I. Background

Over 370 people were killed in the EU by terrorist attacks between 2010 and 2018.[1019] Besides of this invaluable human loss, the negative impact of terrorism on the EU's GDP is estimated at EUR180 billion between 2004 and 2016.[1020] In the long term, terrorism, poses a substantial threat to the values of democratic societies and the freedoms, rights and security of its citizens.[1021]

Terrorist groups have early caught on to the opportunities of the internet and digital communications and exploited them to their advantage. The internet already played a key role in the preparation of the 9/11 terror attacks in New York.[1022] In many ways the internet, with its global reach, ease of access, low degree of regulation, increasing means of free encryption, and above all, its anonymity, has become an ideal medium for terrorist purposes. With the emergence of Web 2.0 and social media, the use of the internet by terrorists has expanded even more.[1023] Apart from the logistical coordination of attacks, the internet is used for: psychological warfare and propaganda, by subtle and manipulative communication through social media; for recruitment and mobilisation, including through closed groups and on social media platforms; data mining and virtual training; and for financing. Online fund-raising activities include the soliciting of donations, the sale of drugs, counterfeits or other illegal goods through the Darknet and e-commerce marketplaces.[1024] The European Commission has estimated in 2017 that approximately 10,500 hosting providers were established in Europe, and another 10,000 in the US and Canada that targeted

1019 Wouter van Ballegooij and Piotr Bakowski, *The Cost of Non-Europe in the Fight against Terrorism: Study* (European Parliament, European Parliamentary Research Service 2018) vii–ix; European Union Agency for Law Enforcement Cooperation, *European Union Terrorism Situation and Trend Report 2019.* (2019) 8. a combination of European Parliament and Europol data.

1020 Ballegooij and Bakowski (n 1018) vii–ix.

1021 European Council, 'European Counter Terrorism Strategy 14469/4/05 REV 4' (2005) para 1.

1022 Allison Miller and Yannis A Stivachtis, 'Investigations of Terrorist Cases Involving the Internet' in John R Vacca (ed), *Online terrorist propaganda, recruitment and radicalization* (2020) 172.

1023 Gabriel Weimann, *Terrorism in Cyberspace: The next Generation* (Woodrow Wilson Center Press 2015) 27–29.

1024 ibid 29–39.

EU users. 150 of these hosting providers were abused for terrorist propaganda. Other reports show 400 platforms being used by *Daesh* for terrorist crimes.[1025] Thanks to the internet, terrorist organisations could expand their international networks substantially. International cooperation on a judicial as well as institutional level is therefore of key importance to effectively combat terrorism.

II. Legal framework against terrorism online – EU and Member States

Due to its effect on national security the fight against terrorism is primarily within the competency of Member States in the EU.[1026] The definition of terrorist offences are therefore down to national law. On a global international level, however, agreement over the definition of terrorism and the scope of terrorist crimes differ. Similar to hate speech, the view on what is extremist and terrorist content may vary, depending on cultural, geographic, historic, temporal and subjective influences.[1027] These differences play out at the political level: one man's terrorist may be another's freedom fighter.[1028] It is therefore no surprise that the UN has as yet failed to come to a consensus definition of terrorism and terrorist entities.[1029] Notwithstanding these differences, there is some consensus amongst liberal democracies over how to define terrorist actors and terrorist offences.[1030] The EU adopted a common position on what it considers terrorist persons and en-

1025 European Commission, 'Commission Staff Working Document - Impact Assessment - Proposal for a Regulation of the European Parliament and of the Council on Preventing the Dissemination of Terrorist Content Online - SWD(2018) 408 Final' (European Commission 2018) 6–8.

1026 Treaty on European Union (Consolidated versions of the Treaty on European Union and the Treaty on the Functioning of the European Union 2016) Article 4 (2). Allocates Member States with sole responsibility for national security issues.

1027 Donald Holbrook, 'Designing and Applying an "Extremist Media Index"' (2015) 9 Perspectives on Terrorism 57, 58. For more detail: Bruce Hoffman, *Inside Terrorism* (Columbia University Press 2017) 1–44 <https://columbia.degruyter.com/view/title/541544> accessed 23 September 2020.

1028 Boaz Ganor, 'Defining Terrorism: Is One Man's Terrorist Another Man's Freedom Fighter?' (2002) 3 Police Practice and Research 287, 290–295.

1029 Chris Meserole and Daniel Byman, 'Terrorist Definitions and Designations Lists - What Technology Companies Need to Know' [2019] Royal United Services Institute for Defence and Security Studies 4.

1030 ibid 4–5.

tities, and terrorist acts.[1031] It has produced a list of terrorist entities and persons that are subject to restrictive measures, which covers mainly the freezing of funds and financial assets and special police and judicial cooperation.[1032] This list is updated every six months.[1033] The 2017 EU Terrorism Directive provides a minimum list of offences that Member States need to define as terrorist crimes under their national laws.[1034] This section will be based on this common understanding of terrorist acts and actors as developed through EU law and agreements reached by the Council of Europe.[1035] It shall, however, be kept in mind that for globally operating online platforms the varying legal interpretations and terrorist entity definitions across the world complicate the task of identification and removal of such content.

Terrorist content and hate speech are often treated closely together, at least where these crimes are committed via the internet. For example, the EU Code of Conduct on Illegal hate speech[1036] makes a link to terrorist acts and propaganda. The *NetzDG* and the *Loi Avia* both include terrorist crimes, such as incitements to terrorist acts or terrorist propaganda within their scope.[1037] Unlike defamation, and, to a lesser extent, hate speech, terrorist content is usually more *prima facie* illegal. *Holbrook*, for example, establishes an extremist media index according to which terrorist iterations would fall under extremist speech that openly supports and incites political violence.[1038] Further clarity would be gained where these iterations are made by social media users that identify with or are linked to designated terrorist entities.[1039]

1031 Council Common Position of 27 December 2001 on the application of specific measures to combat terrorism 2001 (OJ L 344) Article 1 (2, 3).

1032 ibid Articles 2 - 4.

1033 For the latest update at the time of writing: Council Decision (CFSP) 2020/1132 of 30 July 2020 updating the list of persons, groups and entities subject to Articles 2, 3 and 4 of Common Position 2001/931/CFSP on the application of specific measures to combat terrorism 2020 (OJ L 247).

1034 Directive (EU) 2017/541 on combating terrorism 2017 (OJ L 88) Articles 3 - 12.

1035 Council of Europe - Convention on Cybercrime 2001; Council of Europe - Convention on the Prevention of Terrorism 2005.

1036 'Code of Conduct on Countering Illegal Hate Speech Online' (n 542).

1037 NetzDG Article 1 (3). covers as illegal acts linked to terrorist crimes under the German Criminal Code (Articles 89a, 90, 129a, 129b), Laetitia Avia Proposition de loi visant à lutter contre la haine sur internet (n 651) Article 1 (II). refers to the French Criminal Code Article 421-2-5

1038 Holbrook (n 1026) 58–60.

1039 Meserole and Byman (n 1028) 3.

Member States have densified anti-terrorist legislation over the last thirty years, especially where it involves internet and communications systems. France, for example, has continuously adapted its criminal laws by creating new terrorist offenses or raising penalties in line with successive terror attacks. It included terrorist propaganda committed via the internet in its criminal code, and regular user visits to jihadist websites to its Domestic Security Code.[1040] A series of anti-terrorist laws on cybersecurity have imposed data retention obligations on telecommunications operators and IAPs, or given authorities enlarged surveillance powers to collect, monitor and intercept communications data.[1041]

The UK has also continuously adapted its counter-terrorism legislation by making successive changes to the Public Order Act and the Terrorism Act. The scope of terrorist offences has gradually been widened and surveillance, search and censorship powers were stepped up.[1042] The UK Terrorism Act, for example, introduced police powers to request that electronic service providers withdraw terrorist material directly within two working days, bypassing judicial oversight. However, that provision has been virtually unused due to existing informal and voluntary cooperation between law enforcement and social media platforms in this particular area of content, mainly through the Counter Terrorism Internet Referral Unit (CTIRU) set up by the police.[1043] Nevertheless, this demonstrates the potential indirect coercive power of statutory measures that aim at enforcing national security objectives. The CTIRU, set up in 2010, aims to identify terrorist content regulated under the 2000 and 2006 Terrorism Acts. It refers or notifies these pieces of content to online service providers for removal.[1044] It should be noted that these referrals are not equal to official

1040 Céline Castets-Renard, 'Online Surveillance in the Fight Against Terrorism in France' in Tatiana-Eleni Synodinou and others (eds), *EU internet law: regulation and enforcement* (Springer Berlin Heidelberg 2017) 388–389.

1041 ibid.

1042 Thomas J Holt, Joshua D Freilich and Steven M Chermak, 'Legislation Specifically Targeting the Use of the Internet to Recruit Terrorists' in John R Vacca (ed), *Online terrorist propaganda, recruitment and radicalization* (2020) 131; Clive Walker and Maura Conway, 'Online Terrorism and Online Laws' (2015) 8 Dynamics of Asymmetric Conflict 156, 163–166.

1043 UK Parliament, 'Lords Hansard Text for 23 Sep 2013 (Pt 0001)' (2013) <https://publications.parliament.uk/pa/ld201314/ldhansrd/text/130923w0001.htm#wa_st_3> accessed 27 April 2020.

1044 'Counter-Terrorism:Written Question - 30893' (*UK Parliament*) <https://www.parliament.uk/business/publications/written-questions-answers-statements/written-question/Commons/2016-03-14/30893/> accessed 27 April 2020.

public authority or judicial orders, but constitute normal notifications under the ECD's NTD system. The CTIRU had identified and referred over 300,000 pieces of alleged terrorist content between 2010 and 2018, which were removed by the platforms concerned.[1045]

The tightening of online surveillance, stop and search, and access powers in the area of counter-terrorism online give more serious cause for concern over fundamental rights protections. Not only are the freedoms of respect for private and family life and protection of personal data of the targeted persons affected, but also those of their families, other contacts and indeed, anyone subject to state-ordered online surveillance.[1046] The more secretive and informal nature of cooperation between platforms and national authorities only adds to the existing opacity of content management decisions of these companies.[1047]

With the international and borderless nature of terrorism on the internet, police authorities, national intelligence and prosecution services need to exchange information and coordinate action increasingly fast. International cooperation therefore becomes crucial for the effective battle against terrorist acts on a national level. International cooperation on anti-terrorism measures was intensified after the 9/11 terror attacks in New York. Today, nineteen international agreements and instruments exist under the UN auspices to fight terrorism on an international level.[1048] However, the UN instruments have had only a limited impact on the international fight against terrorism on the internet. This is mainly due to the obstacles of cooperation between Western nations and other states, whose proposed restrictions are often perceived by the former as violating democratic principles.[1049] The Financial Action Task Force (FATF) is another international forum that is dedicated to the fight against terrorism. Initially set up to combat money laundering, its mandate was extended in 2001 to include the fight against terrorist financing.[1050] The 2001 Convention on Cyber-

---

1045 THERON Francois, 'Terrorist Content Online' (European Parliament 2020) Members' Research Service PE 649.326. 'Together We're Tackling Online Terrorism' (*Counter Terrorism Policing*, 19 December 2018) <https://www.counterterrorism.police.uk/together-were-tackling-online-terrorism/> accessed 23 September 2020.

1046 Castets-Renard (n 1039) 394.

1047 Citron (n 914) 26–27.

1048 Ballegooij and Bakowski (n 1018) 10.

1049 Walker and Conway (n 1041) 166.

1050 FATF, 'What We Do - Financial Action Task Force (FATF)' <https://www.fatf-gafi.org/about/whatwedo/> accessed 24 September 2020.

crime and its 2003 Additional Protocol are the first measures at European level aimed at establishing tools and cooperation processes in the fight against terrorist acts committed through computer systems.[1051]

The EU has a shared competency to regulate in matters that foster coordination and cooperation between Member States in the Area of Freedom, Justice and Security, thanks to its enlarged mandate following the 2009 Lisbon Treaty.[1052] It has a responsibility to ensure a high level of security as per Article 67 (3) TFEU. TFEU Articles 82 (1) (2) and 83 (1) allow it to propose legislation in the area of judicial cooperation and Article 87 with regards to police cooperation. Article 75 TFEU confers powers on the EU when it comes to combating the financing of terrorism. Where the fight against terrorism touches on the functioning of the internal market the EU can legislate based on Article 114 TFEU.[1053]

The EU has noted the potential of the internet for political radicalisation and the need to coordinate Member States' actions to prevent misuse of the web for terrorism since at least 2005, with the publication of its Counter Terrorism Strategy.[1054] It updated this strategy in 2015 with the Agenda on Security and made the fight against terrorism and cybercrime a priority.[1055] The EU has since brought in place a series of institutional arrangements and legal instruments aimed at supporting the fight against terrorism and cybercrime. The European Union Agency for Law Enforcement Cooperation (*Europol*) and the European Union Agency for Criminal Justice Cooperation (*Eurojust*) have been set up to support Member States in cross-border investigations, prosecutions, law enforcement and providing intelligence on serious crimes, including terrorism. Investigations and prosecutions of terrorist offences at EU level have been strengthened through joint investigations teams, European arrest warrants and the ex-

---

1051 Walker and Conway (n 1041) 12., Council of Europe - Convention on Cybercrime 2001; Additional Protocol to the Convention on Cybercrime, concerning the criminalization of acts of a racist and xenophobic nature committed through computer systems.

1052 Treaty on the Functioning of the European Union (Consolidated versions of the Treaty on European Union and the Treaty on the Functioning of the European Union 2016) Article 4 (2) (j).

1053 Ballegooij and Bakowski (n 1018) Annex A, p. 112 - 114.

1054 European Council (n 1020) paras 9, 13.

1055 European Commission, 'The European Agenda on Security - COM(2015) 185 Final' (2015) ch 3.

change of criminal records. A number of information systems and databases facilitate cross-border access of data for law enforcement.[1056]

These cooperation measures are also aimed at keeping track of the increasing speed with which terrorist organisations act through the internet. The 2017 Directive on combatting terrorism obliges Member States to criminalise the distribution, regardless of whether on- or offline, of material that constitutes a public provocation to commit terrorist offences.[1057] Member States also need to ensure that terrorist content online is removed, or access to it blocked promptly, and subject to transparent procedures. This should happen with respect to the provisions of the ECD.[1058] *Europol's* Internet Referral Unit (IRU), established in 2015, supports the identification, flagging assessment and referral of terrorist content online for removal by online platforms. In addition, it supports Member States in monitoring and provides investigative capabilities regarding terrorist content online. Between July 2015 and 2018 it had identified close to 88,000 pieces of content and referred over 85,000 for action to online service providers, achieving a removal rate of 84.8%.[1059]

It should be noted that these efforts relate mainly to *ex-post* actions and law enforcement. The EU has also committed to developing counter-narratives and stepping up educational efforts such as developing inter-cultural dialogue and social inclusion in a bid to oppose the radicalisation of society.[1060] Meanwhile, the efforts to include social media platforms on any proactive technical measures to combat terrorist content on their systems are restricted to voluntary actions.[1061] At this stage, government actions towards social media platforms are limited to national level efforts that are often less transparent. It is not clear in how far hosting providers are informally involved in working with governments proactively to prevent terror-

---

1056 Ballegooij and Bakowski (n 1018) 16–17. Teresa Alegra Quintel, 'Interoperability and Law Enforcement Access to Personal Data. Data Protection Rights of Third Country Nationals in the Light of the CJEU's Case Law' [2018] Europarättslig tidskrift 7–8

1057 Directive (EU) 2017/541 on combating terrorism Article 5.

1058 ibid Article 21, Recital [illegible]

1059 European Union Agency for Law Enforcement Cooperation (n 1018) 76.

1060 European Commission, 'Radicalisation Awareness Network' (*Migration and Home Affairs - European Commission*, 6 December 2016) <https://ec.europa.eu/home-affairs/what-we-do/networks/radicalisation_awareness_network_en> accessed 28 April 2020.

1061 European Commission, 'The European Agenda on Security COM(2015) 185 Final' (n 1054) ch 3.3.

ist content online. The EU contributes with capacity building and judicial and law enforcement cooperation to fight terrorist crimes on the internet.

III. Private regulation of terrorist content and technological developments

As in other areas, the EU has initiated self-regulatory projects with social media platforms to fight terrorist content online. Following on from the 2015 Agenda on Security the European Commission set up the EU Internet Forum, a self-regulatory structure, bringing together *Europol*, hosting providers and the European Parliament in a bid to establish "a joint, voluntary approach based on a public-private partnership to detect and address harmful material online."[1062] The initial membership from the industry, *Ask.fm, Facebook, Google, Microsoft* and *Twitter*, has now grown to over 20 hosting providers, and includes social media and UGC platforms, cloud providers, content management systems and messaging services. This private-public initiative has so far worked in different areas.

First, the industry members committed to participating in the EU's Civil Society Empowerment Programme that aims at developing counter narratives to terrorism on social media and UGC sites. This plugs into existing efforts of companies such as *Google, Facebook* and *Twitter* to post alternative messages and counter-adverts on pages that contain potentially extremist and terrorist content.[1063]

Secondly, the member companies are also the forum of choice for referrals by *Europol*'s IRU. Under this process, the participating platforms had removed 61% of referred content during the first half of 2018, with the "big four" (*Facebook, Microsoft, Twitter and YouTube*) removing between 90% and 100%. The majority of companies, however, did not manage to remove content within one hour of notification, an objective of the IRU in order to effectively prevent potential sharing and multiplication across the internet.[1064]

1062 European Commission, 'EU Internet Forum: Bringing Together Governments, Europol and Technology Companies to Counter Terrorist Content and Hate Speech Online' (*European Commission - European Commission*, 12 March 2015) <https://ec.europa.eu/commission/presscorner/detail/en/IP_15_6243> accessed 28 April 2020.

1063 Citron (n 914) 28–29.

1064 European Commission, 'Terrorist Content Regulation Proposal - Impact Assessment' (n 1024) 135.

Thirdly, the Forum also set up a shared industry hash database (SIHD) for terrorist content that allows its members to prevent the reappearance of content identified by one platform on other ones. In 2017, *Facebook, Google, Twitter* and *Microsoft* founded for this purpose the Global Internet Forum for Terrorist Content (GifTC). Through this initiative they pool resources and develop solutions to combat terrorist content online in cooperation with civil society and governments around the globe. As of 2019, the GifTC had another 5 members: *Amazon*, *DropBox*, *Pinterest*, *LinkedIn* and *WhatsApp*, while the Hash Sharing Consortium of the SIHD counted *Reddit*, *Snap*, *Verizon* and *Ask.fm* amongst its participants.[1065]

The hash database relies on technology that assigns a numerical value - hash codes or digital fingerprint - to images.[1066] Terrorist content identified by participants is hashed and may be enriched with metadata, such as the type of content, the terrorist group or the company that hashed and shared the content with the SIHD.[1067] According to GifTC, the SIHD contained over 200,000 hashes by 2019. Participants will be able to use the hashed content in order to identify and remove matching content that already exists or is uploaded to their systems where it breaches their policies. The particular technology used relies on perceptual hashing. The fingerprints are calculated based on certain characteristic features of the content. This method is more resistant to marginal modifications and allows for detection according to commonly identified characteristics or traits (of terrorist content), rather than exact matches. This technology is also closely related to mechanisms used in deep learning systems that aim to proactively detect content features.[1068] The exact processes and methods relating to the hash database and the way content is shared and used remain rather secretive, which is partly understandable given the highly sensitive techniques involved. Nor is it clear to what extent content hash-filtered during upload will be removed automatically or is subject to human review for a final decision.[1069]

1065 'GifCT' <http://www.gifct.org> accessed 28 April 2020.

1066 Brian A Jackson and others, *Practical Terrorism Prevention: Reexamining U.S. National Approaches to Addressing the Threat of Ideologically Motivated Violence* (RAND 2019) 83.

1067 Robert Gorwa, Reuben Binns and Christian Katzenbach, 'Algorithmic Content Moderation: Technical and Political Challenges in the Automation of Platform Governance' (2020) 7 Big Data & Society 205395171989794, 8.

1068 ibid 4.

1069 ibid 8.

Meanwhile, GifTC members have also increasingly engaged in the proactive, automated detection and blocking of terrorist content. As stated, the technology of perceptual hashing lends itself to the use in predictive content identification and classification. *Facebook*, for example, noted in its latest Community Standards Enforcement report that, for Q3 2019, 98% of terrorist content that it removed was detected by its own automated systems. Altogether, over 5.2 million pieces of content were removed, both by its own systems and through user notifications. Meanwhile, 205,300 pieces of content were restored again, of which 32,400 after an appeal.[1070] This makes for an overall decision accuracy rate of 96%.[1071] It is not exactly clear to what degree human reviewers at *Facebook* are involved in reviewing content decisions made by automated systems, but it appears that the exclusive use of these tools is increasing. Nevertheless, the company continues to beef up its army of content reviewers. The number of content reviewers employed or subcontracted by *Facebook* around the globe has risen to 15,000 by end November 2019.[1072]

Similar developments can be reported for *Twitter* and *YouTube (Google)*,[1073] and as a rule, for any larger online platform operator, which all use automated systems to detect and remove terrorist content, albeit to varying degrees. It should, however, not be forgotten that even with constantly improving detection tools, a content identification accuracy of 99% still means that the real number of falsely identified content is enormous.[1074] It can be safely assumed that it would be in the reputational and financial interest of any social media platform to contain the number of erroneous decisions by introducing human reviews.

1070 Facebook, 'Community Standards Enforcement Report - Terrorist Propaganda' (n 668).

1071 If one were to take the so-called reinstate rate as a measure for decision accuracy. Isabelle van der Vegt and others, 'Shedding Light on Terrorist and Extremist Content Removal' [2019] Royal United Services Institute for Defence and Security Studies 7.

1072 'Facebook's AI Wipes Terrorism-Related Posts' *BBC News* (29 November 2017) <https://www.bbc.com/news/technology-42158045> accessed 28 April 2020. Facebook, 'Understanding the Community Standards Enforcement Report' (November 2019) <https://transparency.facebook.com/community-standards-enforcement/guide> accessed 28 April 2020.

1073 Omi Hodwitz, 'Rule-of-Law and Respect for Human Rights Considerations' in John R Vacca (ed), *Online terrorist propaganda, recruitment and radicalization* (2020) 74. In addition see the regular transport reports on the enforcement of these companies' own community guidelines

1074 van der Vegt and others (n 1070) 8–9.

Smaller platforms, on the other hand, may not have the resources to develop and maintain automated software systems. Research and cooperation on automated removal systems has also been a focus area of the GifTC.[1075] It appears that the larger players share their respective technologies, such as *Microsoft's PhotoDNA* or *Google's Content Safety API*, which were developed originally to spot and remove child abuse material. These technologies may even assist smaller players.[1076] Nevertheless, human review of potential terrorist content still appears to be important. Larger platforms may use it in parallel to automated systems, while smaller players are more likely to rely on it exclusively.[1077] This does not necessarily disadvantage these latter companies, as content reviews can be scaled by other means than matching software. Behavioural patterns may, for example, also give useful clues about the propensity of content for being unlawful, e.g. terrorist.[1078] This can be supplemented by other risk management approaches.

Despite internet platforms rubbing elbows in self-regulatory circles like the GifTC, the criteria and processes by which terrorist content is defined vary across different platforms. For a start, the definition of terrorist content varies on a normative basis between the different companies.[1079] Globally operating platforms then also face varying and at times contradicting definitions and understandings of terrorist activity across jurisdictions. They often do not understand how to incorporate specific terrorist or sanctions lists issued by governments, civil society or academia, in their content policies.[1080]

Secondly, the internal enforcement procedures, ranging from content moderation procedures to the use of automated tools, appeals procedures through to the yardsticks for measuring efficacy and decision accuracy of identification and removal processes, vary. This may be due to several factors: different contextual situations of speech on platforms, varying business models of these platforms, different resource allocations or simply in-

---

1075 Gorwa, Binns and Katzenbach (n 1066) 9.

1076 Citron (n 914) 23; Gorwa, Binns and Katzenbach (n 1066) 8. Facebook mentions in its company blog that it utilises Microsoft and Google technology: Antigone Davis and Guy Rosen, 'Open-Sourcing Photo- and Video-Matching Technology to Make the Internet Safer' (*About Facebook*, 1 August 2019) <https://about.fb.com/news/2019/08/open-source-photo-video-matching/> accessed 29 April 2020.

1077 van der Vegt and others (n 1070) 6–7.

1078 ibid 4–7.

1079 Citron (n 914) 22.

1080 Meserole and Byman (n 1028).

dividual company cultures, such as the fervency with which US-style free speech values are being pursued.[1081]

The next striking observation is that there is a considerable variance between platforms' enforcement systems of their own content standards and their policies with regards to notified terrorist propaganda. This extends to the referrals processes in place with *Europol* and national enforcement authorities. The low volume of referrals from IRUs (compared to platforms own enforcement actions), the relatively low removal rate and the closed nature of the GifTC's operations, point to the existence of parallel systems of terrorist content removals on these platforms.[1082] The IRU referrals processes stand in stark contrast to *Facebook* et al's sophisticated, scaled and fast enforcement of their own content policies. This reinforces arguments that these platforms, and not authorities, are acting as the *de facto* regulators in content regulation.[1083] Real states, meanwhile, face difficulties in getting these platforms to address the public interest concerns related to unlawful content.[1084]

Yet, concerns over the transparency and power of platforms' own content enforcement policies are as salient as concerns over a too intimate and closed relationship between law enforcement and platforms. In how far, however, social media intermediaries have really become global enforcers of stricter EU speech standards is less clear.[1085] Platforms appear more to enforce their own policies based on carefully concealed internal operational guidelines.[1086] They adapt to situations outside these terms and policies in a more haphazard and inconclusive manner. This points towards the dominance of economic reasons and cultural speech standards of their managers,[1087] to the detriment of compliance with local laws and public interests. In the end, Member States' IRU referrals are being decided against the private terms and conditions of these platforms and not against the legal norms that apply in the respective country. The exact power rela-

1081 Klonick (n 1000); van der Vegt and others (n 1070).

1082 van der Vegt and others (n 1070) 9

1083 Uta Kohl, *The Net and the Nation State - Multidisciplinary Perspectives on Internet Governance* (Cambridge University Press 2017) 12. Taddeo and Floridi (n 120) 1593; Belli and Sappa (n 42) 189–190.

1084 Ben Wagner, 'Governing Internet Expression: How Public and Private Regulation Shape Expression Governance' (2013) 10 Journal of Information Technology & Politics 389, 399.

1085 Citron (n 914) 29–30.

1086 Klonick (n 1000) 1635–1650.

1087 Zuboff (n 5) l 2012; Klonick (n 1000) 1644–1645.

tions between the state and platforms in these self-regulatory initiatives are far from clear and warrant further study.[1088]

All of this shows that the content removal processes of online platforms, in general, and in the case of hate speech and terrorist propaganda, in particular, are in dire need of more transparency. This concerns both the decisions taken by companies on their own account and those taken after referrals from authorities. But the current regulatory framework in the EU, does not provide for any mandate to prescribe more holistic content management obligations that comply with standards of transparency, accountability and corporate responsibility that are commensurate with the status of online platforms today.

IV. EU regulation

a. Proposal of a Regulation for preventing terrorist content online

In 2018, the European Commission introduced a proposal for a regulation aimed at preventing the dissemination of terrorist content online (TERREG).[1089] With this proposal, the Commission intends to tighten measures that it had urged Member States to take against the spread of terrorist propaganda in its Recommendation on tackling illegal content online, made only six months earlier.[1090] Although broadly addressing any type of unlawful content, that document contained specific recommendations on combating terrorist material.

The TERREG proposal's impact assessment notes that despite the self – regulatory efforts and progress made (e.g. through the EU Internet Forum), the security threat posed by terrorist content spread through hosting platforms remained considerable. It states as main problems the continued abuse of hosting service providers, particularly smaller ones, for these purposes and the inefficacy of preventing this content to spread and reappear across platforms.[1091] It identifies four problem drivers, which have also

1088 Gorwa (n 267) 13.

1089 European Commission, Proposal for a regulation on preventing terrorist content online, COM(2018) 640 final 2018.

1090 European Commission, 'C(2018) 1177 Final' (n 8).

1091 European Commission, 'Terrorist Content Regulation Proposal - Impact Assessment' (n 1024) 7–10. OECD, 'Current Approaches to Terrorist and Violent Extremist Content among the Global Top 50 Online Content-Sharing Services', vol 296 (2020) OECD Digital Economy Papers 296 6–7 <https://www.oe

been discussed above: 1) the legal fragmentation facing hosting providers under, *inter alia*, the ECD: this includes variations in NTD systems, procedural differences in removal orders, the parallel existence of informal removal procedures (e.g. the UK), different level of duties of care, national specificities in the imposition of transparency obligations regardless of the place of establishment of the ISSP.[1092] 2) Member States have difficulties in establishing effective relations with many, mostly smaller, platform operators.[1093] 3) and 4) relate to ineffective or uneven implementation of systems to detect and remove terrorist content, and their intransparency *vis-à-vis* users and public authorities. The Commission remarked that IRU referrals were not actioned fast enough, preventive efforts varied across platforms and automated systems lacked safeguards and transparency, which impacted user rights negatively.[1094]

The proposed TERREG has a number of important elements. First, it provides a broad overarching definition of terrorist content.[1095] Secondly, it obliges platforms to remove content notified under a court or authority removal order within one hour and act expeditiously on the assessment of referrals from authorities.[1096]

The proposal imposes for the first time the application of duties of care on hosting providers,[1097] suggests a procedural and transparency framework for the removal of content[1098] and specifies the use of proactive mea-

---

cd-ilibrary.org/science-and-technology/current-approaches-to-terrorist-and-violent-extremist-content-among-the-global-top-50-online-content-sharing-services_68058b95-en> accessed 19 March 2021. 'Analysis: ISIS Use of Smaller Platforms and the DWeb to Share Terrorist Content – April 2019 - Tech Against Terrorism' (29 April 2019) <https://www.techagainstterrorism.org/2019/04/29/analysis-isis-use-of-smaller-platforms-and-the-dweb-to-share-terrorist-content-april-2019/, accessed 19 March 2021.

1092 European Commission, 'Terrorist Content Regulation Proposal - Impact Assessment' (n 1024) 10–12.

1093 ibid 13–16.

1094 ibid 13–17.

1095 European Commission COM(2018) 640 final (n 1088) Article 2 (5).

1096 ibid Articles 4 & 5.For a detailed analysis of these parts of the proposal see: Gavin Robinson, 'The European Commission's Proposal for a Regulation on Preventing the Dissemination of Terrorist Content Online' [2018] eucrim - The European Criminal Law Associations' Forum <https://eucrim.eu/articles/commission-proposal-regulation-preventing-dissemination-terrorist-content-online/> accessed 6 April 2020.

1097 European Commission COM(2018) 640 final (n 1088) Article 3, Recital 12.

1098 ibid Articles 4, 8, 9, 10, 11.

sures by hosting providers, using a risk management approach.[1099] It was amended during the negotiation process with the European Parliament and the Council. The version discussed here was voted by the plenary in April 2019,[1100] before the European elections in September that year. Under the current version the hosting providers' duties of care specifies that they need to protect users from terrorist content in a diligent, proportionate and non-discriminatory way, and with due regard to fundamental rights.[1101] The European Parliament inserted language specifying that any such duties should not amount to a general obligation to monitor content. This can be seen as a reminder of the prohibition in Article 15 ECD.

Obligatory proactive measures under a proposed Article 6 have been turned into voluntary specific measures in the current European Parliament version. Again, the respect of the principles laid down in the ECD and the new AVMSD are being recalled. Any measures need to be proportionate and correspond to the risk and level of exposure to terrorist content and the fundamental rights involved. Member States have, however, the option of imposing specific measures on those hosting providers, which have received substantial numbers of removal orders. Substantial numbers are not defined in the proposal. The Commission's suggestion in Recital 19 to derogate from the sacrosanct Article 15 (1) of the ECD in exceptional circumstances was rejected by the Parliament. It would have allowed Member States to potentially impose obligations on hosting providers to monitor their systems on a general basis and proactively seek illegal information in situations of overriding public security concerns. The European Parliament held that this would result in a dramatic shift in intermediary liabilities and an excessive impact on fundamental rights.[1102]

The proposed reactive duties provide a procedural framework aimed at transparent and accountable content removal processes and reporting.[1103]

1099 ibid Article 6, Recital 16 & 19.

1100 European Parliament, 'Report on the Proposal for a Regulation of the European Parliament and of the Council on Preventing the Dissemination of Terrorist Content Online - A8-0193/2019' (2019) PE 632.087v02-00 <https://www.europarl.europa.eu/doceo/document/A-8-2019-0193_EN.html> accessed 30 April 2020. During the time of writing the Council and the European Parliament reached a political compromise on this proposal on 10 December 2020, which, however, maintains the key changes proposed by the European Parliament in the 2019 version analysed here. At the time of writing, the political compromise version was in the final stages of adoption.

1101 ibid Article 3.

1102 ibid Opinion of the Committee on Culture and Education (iii).

1103 European Commission COM(2018) 640 final (n 1088) Articles 8, 9, 10, 11.

Article 9 asks providers that use automated tools to have safeguards in place that ensure the appropriateness of content decisions, especially with regards to fundamental rights. Such safeguards would be, for example, verification procedures and human oversight. The European Parliament version of April 2019 enhances user rights by imposing more detailed remedies in cases of content removals, such as explanations from the platform about the removal and more detailed appeals procedures.[1104] However, the obligation to publish annual transparency reports has been limited to only those platforms that were subject to removal orders for authorities or courts. The providers concerned would need to publish annual accounts on the detection, identification and removal of content. They also have to detail their efforts to prevent the re-upload of content, especially where automated means are used, state the numbers of content removals following an order, and the numbers and outcomes of complaints following a removal.[1105]

The TERREG proposal is probably the most far reaching effort by the EU legislator so far to regulate the framework conditions for online intermediaries in the prevention of unlawful content. It may be no surprise to see the proposed emergency cancellation of the general monitoring prohibition of Article 15 (1) ECD being rolled back by the European Parliament. However, the original attempt of the Commission may be a demonstration of the interpretational problems this 20-year-old provisions causes in today's social media platforms environment. The obligatory use of automated tools to prevent terrorist content has been toned down to a voluntary encouragement of specific measures. However, the option to impose specific (read: proactive) measures has been kept for those riskier platforms that have received removal orders from Member States' courts or authorities and where the latter determine that the current measures are not sufficient. The transparency obligations for those platforms that deploy specific measures and that are subject to removal orders may go a certain way towards more accountability and openness. However, the proposal lacks a more solid institutional substructure at an EU level that would accompany, supervise and drive the implementation of consistent accountability and risk management structures. Although it requires Member States to nominate a functionally independent authority for issuing removal orders, overseeing specific measures of hosting providers and imposing penalties, the level of cooperation between them in order to build consistent struc-

1104 European Parliament (n 1099) Articles 10, 11.
1105 ibid Article 8.

tures and processes is not further specified.[1106] By contrast, the AVMSD which also foresees the application of proactive measures following a risk-based approach, puts in place an EU wide regulatory body (ERGA) to accompany and supervise this process. This may be more effective in the medium term. As it stands now, the partly far-reaching specific measures and transparency obligation on platforms in the proposed regulation risk fizzling out without an EU wide institutional framework that forces coherent and unified reporting and accountability standards.

b. Regulation 2019/1148 on marketing and use of explosives precursors[1107]

In 2019, the EU enacted a new regulation that imposes due diligence operation on online marketplaces in the fight against the unlicensed sale of chemicals that can be used to fabricate explosives for terrorist attacks.[1108] This Regulation does not cover digital content related to terrorism as covered above. However, it shall be included here, and not in a later section on unsafe products, because of the potential use of these substances for terrorist acts. The Regulation falls therefore into the wider context of the misuse of the internet and online intermediaries for terrorism-related crimes and the hams to public security covered in this section.

According to the European Commission "explosives precursors are chemical substances habitually used for legitimate purposes, but that can also be misused to manufacture homemade explosives."[1109] Explosives precursors can be, just to give two examples, sulphuric acid, which is widely used in industry but also in agriculture; or ammonium nitrate, which is

1106 ibid Articles 9 (a), 12, 13, Recital 37.

1107 Regulation (EU) 2019/1148 of the European Parliament and of the Council of 20 June 2019 on the marketing and use of explosives precursors 2019 (OJ L 186).

1108 See also: Anja Hoffmann and Alessandro Gasparotti, 'Liability for Illegal Content Online - Weaknesses of the EU Legal Framework and Possible Plans of the EU Commission to Address Them in a "Digital Services Act"' (cep | Centre for European Policy 2020) 21 .

1109 European Commission, 'Counter Terrorism and Radicalisation - Protection' (*Migration and Home Affairs - European Commission*, 6 December 2016) <https://ec.europa.eu/home-affairs/what-we-do/policies/counter terrorism/protection_en> accessed 26 August 2020.

used as a fertiliser.[1110] In the Impact Assessment for this Regulation, the European Commission notes that, amongst other problems with the enforcement of registration and verification duties regarding the sale of these substances, explosive precursors have continued to be available for purchase by terrorists in the EU partly due to a shift towards e-commerce, where restrictions were applied less diligently.[1111] It states that precursors used in the fabrication of explosives that were deployed in recent terrorist attacks in the EU had been purchased online. The anonymity and the difficulty of tracing customers in transactions conducted via online marketplaces, the problems in detecting the products in question and identifying suspicious transactions pose a new security threat.[1112]

While adding new substances to the restricted substances list and tightening overall registration, licensing, verification, detection and reporting obligations of economic operators, the Regulation now also includes online marketplaces in its scope. It acknowledges the central role of online marketplaces in online transactions and the availability of regulated explosive precursors, but stops short of qualifying online marketplaces as economic operators.[1113] The obligations imposed on online marketplaces are therefore lighter than for economic operators. The former are not required to pass on information on the acquisition and possession of restricted precursors along the supply chain or assure that their staff are adequately trained.[1114] They also do not need to apply customer verification processes, such as identity checks or requesting evidence of the intended use of the substances sold.[1115]

However, online marketplaces would need to ensure that users (in this case sellers) that offer regulated explosives precursors on their platforms are aware of their obligations and support them in their compliance with verification duties.[1116] Online marketplace will have, nevertheless, the same obligations as economic operators when it comes to detecting and re-

1110 European Commission, 'Commission Staff Working Document - Impact Assessment - Proposal for a Regulation of the European Parliament and of the Council on the Marketing and Use of Explosives Precursors - SWD(2018) 104 Final' (European Commission 2018) 93–94.

1111 ibid 10–12.

1112 ibid 91.

1113 Regulation (EU) 2019/1148 of the European Parliament and of the Council of 20 June 2019 on the marketing and use of explosives precursors Recital 15.

1114 ibid Article 7.

1115 ibid Article 8.

1116 ibid Articles 7 (3) & 8 (5).

porting suspicious transactions.[1117] These detection measures shall be appropriate, reasonable and proportionate and adapted to the specific environment. Recital 16 of the Regulation clarifies that the obligations imposed on online marketplace shall not lead to a general monitoring obligation, but remain specific to the detection and reporting of suspicious transactions. Online marketplaces that have reasonable detection procedures in place shall not be liable for any transactions that they fail to pick up. When it comes to reporting suspicious transactions, the regulation provides five (non-exhaustive) indicators that would trigger a notification to the authorities. Two of these indicators appear to be relevant for online marketplaces: reporting may be triggered when customers buy quantities or combinations of products that are uncommon for legitimate use, and where customers use unusual payment methods, such as cash.[1118]

The detection and reporting obligations take account of the fact that most online marketplaces today widely collect and utilise data on consumer purchases, browsing behaviour, seller sales and marketing analytics. They are indeed in a central position, not just when it comes to facilitating the availability and marketing of products, but also where market intelligence about the supply and demand of products is concerned. The reporting obligations remind of existing obligations in the area of anti-money laundering, where financial institutions, including electronic payment services or electronic money institutions, have already suspicious transaction monitoring and reporting obligations. Most online marketplaces integrate payment services into their platforms. Where they do not offer their own payment service, like *AmazonPay* or *AliPay*, they integrate other service providers such as *PayPal*, *GooglePay*, major credit cards or other providers into their platforms. Some elements of transaction monitoring under these obligations, or under existing internal fraud detection processes, should therefore be familiar to most online marketplaces. Subsidiaries of *Amazon*, *Rakuten*, *eBay* or *AliExpress* are all registered as banks, payment institutions or electronic money institutions in the EU.[1119]

1117 ibid Article 9.

1118 ibid Article 9 (1). Note that some online marketplace like *eBay* or *CDiscount.com* offer cash and/or cash on delivery as payment methods: 'Artikel Bezahlen' (*eBay*) <https://www.eBay.de/help/buying/paying-items/artikel-bezahlen?id=4009> accessed 26 August 2020; 'Cdiscount.com Payment' (*CDiscount*) <https://www.cdiscount.com/payment/paymentinfo.html> accessed 26 August 2020.

1119 For further detail see the section on trademarks in this Chapter.

Meanwhile, the requirement to ensure that sellers are aware of their obligations under the Regulation and to help them in their efforts to put in place customer verification measures, takes advantage of the gatekeeping functions of today's online marketplaces. First, marketplaces are able to put detailed information and qualification processes in place when they onboard sellers on their platforms. This can very well include specific education and information processes. These processes can be narrowed down to product categories and certain seller characteristics. This will be shown in more detail in the section on consumer protection, the case studies in Chapter 5 and the example of a duty of care standard for economic harms provided in Chapter 6 and ANNEX III. Secondly, online marketplace can indeed provide additional leverage when it comes to customer verification. They provide the technical facilities for marketing, sale, transactions and customer communication. In order to buy through an online marketplace, customers would normally need to be registered or create an account on the marketplace. Online marketplaces are able to insert additional customer verification processes into the transaction chain, or offer sellers the option for integrating these steps into their own transactions. Finally, online marketplaces also have the ability to check and audit compliance with these procedures.

Smaller marketplaces may indeed not be well equipped to comply with all of these obligations to the same extend as larger operators. But it can be argued that, as diligent economic operators, smaller marketplaces that choose to include more highly regulated, risky product categories on their platform would still have to be aware of the potential harm that could be caused by selling these products. This also exposes the gap in the current online intermediary liability framework of the ECD. An almost blanket exemption absent any 'actual knowledge' fits uncomfortably with the wide reach of activities of today's online marketplaces and other online intermediaries.

The regulation also appears to provide a procedural framework for enforcement and supervision. It tasks Member States with facilitating cooperation and exchange of information between law enforcement, national supervisory authorities, economic operators, online marketplaces and representatives of the sectors that use regulated explosives precursors. The European Commission will need to provide guidance on measures that online marketplaces may adopt under the Regulation. Meanwhile national authorities will need to inspect and control effective compliance.[1120]

Overall, the regulation goes a significant way in imposing enhanced responsibilities on online marketplaces that appear to fit into a wider due diligence or duty of care framework. These obligations appear adequate and commensurate with the gatekeeping function of today's online marketplaces. On the other hand, it stops short of qualifying online marketplaces as economic operators. Arguably, this is a missed opportunity. The crucial position of online marketplaces when it comes to seller and customer onboarding and transaction monitoring extends into other aspects, such as online product information (e.g. online labelling and warning requirements). Here too, they may affect essential requirements relating to the product itself. Secondly, by making money from the sale of these products, either through a commission on sales, seller fees or advertisements related to the online offer, online marketplace clearly have a financial interest in the transactions of explosive precursors. In the area of copyright and trademarks this has been a determining element for courts in allocating primary liability to online intermediaries. The procedural framework for effective implementation and compliance, however, is closer to traditional state regulation. Whether it provides space for defining more detailed due diligence criteria through active participation of economic operators and marketplace operators remains to be seen. A co-regulatory approach may be possible though the commitment to a wider stakeholder dialogue in Article 10 (3). Opening these circles to civil society and/or regular reporting would certainly be a safeguard against the risk of scope creep in the detection and reporting obligations imposed on online marketplaces and economic operators.

Like in the area of hate speech, new horizontal due diligence obligations under the DSA proposal would apply without prejudice to the proposed TERREG and to Regulation 2019/1148 on explosives precursors,[1121] thus confirming the *lex specialis* status of the latter. Potential overlaps or conflicts could arise between orders to act against illegal content under the current DSA proposal[1122] and removal orders by law enforcement authorities for terrorist content under the proposed Regulation on terrorist content online. While under the DSA proposal these illegal content removal

1120 Regulation (EU) 2019/1148 of the European Parliament and of the Council of 20 June 2019 on the marketing and use of explosives precursors Articles 1- - 12.

1121 European Commission DSA proposal (n 10) Article 1 (5), Recitals 9, 10.

1122 ibid Article 8, Recital 30.

orders are part of the liability exemption conditions, failure to implement removal orders under the Regulation are subject to penalties.[1123] Secondly, the implementation of the traceability obligations that online marketplace will have *vis-à-vis* traders on their platforms under the proposed DSA[1124] could significantly help in the execution of the information, detection and reporting requirements on the sale of explosive precursors under Regulation 2019/1148.

V. Summary and outlook

In December 2020, the European Council announced a provisional agreement with the European Parliament in the negotiation of the TERREG.[1125] The compromise appears to retain the key provisions set out in the version analysed above. It confirms the notion of duties of care and specific measures that hosting service providers exposed to terrorist content would need to take under a risk-based approach, although in a toned down version. It bolsters, however, the overall safeguards to protect fundamental rights when platforms use specific and automated tools to detect and remove terrorist content. Notably, it specifies that hosting providers should be under no obligation to use such automated tools.[1126] It also keeps the scope of the transparency obligations. Nevertheless, this latest compromise refrains from defining more tangible specific measures and from creating stronger institutional and procedural structures at EU level. The proposed Regulation goes in the right direction in proposing additional responsibilities for social media platforms in the fight against terrorist content. It re-

---

1123 European Commission, European Parliament legislative resolution of 17 April 2019 on the proposal for a regulation of the European Parliament and of the Council on preventing the dissemination of terrorist content online (COM(2018)0640 – C8-0405/2018 – 2018/0331(COD)) Article 18 (1).

1124 European Commission DSA proposal (n 10) Article 22.

1125 Council of the EU, 'Terrorist Content Online: Council Presidency and European Parliament Reach Provisional Agreement' (10 December 2020) <https://www.consilium.europa.eu/en/press/press-releases/2020/12/10/terrorist-content-online-council-presidency-and-european-parliament-reach-provisional-agreement/> accessed 15 March 2021.

1126 Council of the EU, 'Proposal for a Regulation of the European Parliament and of the Council on Preventing the Dissemination of Terrorist Content Online - Analysis of the Final Compromise Text with a View to Agreement 2018/0331(COD) - 12906/20' <https://data.consilium.europa.eu/doc/document/ST-12906-2020-INIT/en/pdf> accessed 15 March 2021 Article X, Recital 16, 19.

mains unclear, however, how these proposed platform responsibilities would be supervised, checked and enforced. It remains to be seen how the additional due diligence obligations of the DSA proposal will interact with this draft Regulation.

Regulation 2019/1148 on marketing and use of explosives precursors imposes relatively broad verification, detection and reporting obligations on online marketplaces for the sale of explosive precursors. These measures are a direct response to a shift of the availability of these products through online marketplaces and the increased risk of this channel being used by terrorists to procure components for explosives. They take account of the central gatekeeping role of online platforms in e-commerce by imposing specific detection and reporting obligations and asking platforms to assist sellers in their compliance efforts. The measures remind of existing duties under EU anti-money laundering legislation. This raised standard of responsibility is accompanied by a procedural framework under the auspices of the European Commission and national authorities. While encouraging stakeholder cooperation and exchange of information, the measures would gain in transparency if the circle was opened to wide society participation and regular reporting obligations. Overall, the obligations imposed on marketplace operators would be bolstered through the due diligence obligations on the traceability of traders that are proposed in Article 22 of the DSA draft.

Self-regulatory efforts, by contrast, have gone only a limited away to appease public security concerns in this respect. Platforms have developed and shared technical know-how in the fight against the terrorist threat online that appears to bypass enforcement authorities. The mass of their referrals is filed against the private content policies of these platforms rather than legal provisions. This current practice entrenches the position of these platforms as quasi regulators of speech that follow privately set standards and rules, be it in the area of defamation, hate speech or terrorist content. It should be noted, however, that the interactive and participative role of social media platforms is less controversially discussed in the area of terrorist content online than for violations in the areas of defamation and hate speech. Rather than challenging the role of platforms as potential editors of terrorist content, national law makers have defined specific crimes that relate to dissemination of this material via electronic media. While this rules out the allocation of primary responsibilities to platforms as terrorist speech editors, it does pose the question what dissemination actually means in the age of social media and content sharing. This touches directly on the roles and responsibilities of social media platforms for hosted and shared content, which is the centrepiece of their business model.

It is submitted here that without widening and consolidating the general responsibilities of these platforms under current EU intermediary liability rules, the efforts of the proposed Regulation will remain piecemeal and do little to effectively address public security concerns. A redraft of these intermediary liability exemption or responsibility provisions would have the advantage of redefining the wider moral and normative responsibilities of social media platforms. This would then provide a basis for defining procedural obligations in the area of terrorist content online and supplement them with an institutional regulatory framework to supervise and enforce these obligations.

C. Economic rights: intellectual property

4. Copyright

I. Copyright and the information society

Copyright disputes have affected internet intermediaries since the early days of the commercial web. This is not surprising. Conflicts in copyright are imputed by the very nature of the internet, in which information is not sent in the traditional way, but where every transmission is an act of copying. The sender will not lose the information sent, as much as the addressee will not be its sole proprietor. Meanwhile, numerous copies, both transient and permanent, are being made at network interconnections and servers that lie along the globally dispersed communication channels.[1127]

Social networking, UGC sites or P2P systems facilitate the sharing (read: copying) of content at an unprecedented speed and to an audience with global reach that cuts across (almost) any jurisdiction. This is bound to conflict with the territorial and proprietary characteristics of copyright.[1128] Users, far from just consuming copyright protected works, are now engag-

1127 James J Marcellino and Melise Blakeslee, 'Fair Use in the Context of a Global Computer Network–Is a Copyright Grab Really Going On?' (1997) 6 Information & Communications Technology Law 137.

1128 H Bosher and S Yeşiloğlu, 'An Analysis of the Fundamental Tensions between Copyright and Social Media: The Legal Implications of Sharing Images on Instagram' (2019) 33 International Review of Law, Computers & Technology 164, 165.

ing in copyright relevant acts by uploading, sharing, modifying or reusing content at a massive scale. These acts have become commonplace and normal. People upload personal content enhanced by their favourite music tracks on *Facebook*. Musicians sample, create and share covers or remixes of songs on *YouTube* or *SoundCloud*. Users modify or replicate images of personalities, buildings or objects on social messaging apps, such *Instagram*, *TikTok* or *Snapchat* or web blogs.

For the Web 2.0 platforms, this user interaction is of course the mainstay of their business. It generates valuable user data and the advertising revenue that they have been thriving on. The undisputed benefit of the new exchange and creation of content for cultural and socio-economic enrichment has, however, been accompanied by more detrimental behaviours. Illegal downloading, P2P file sharing, streaming, or unauthorised sharing or reusing of content are the more common behaviours that remain widespread as of today.[1129] Some of these activities happen simply out of user ignorance over the intricacies of copyright law, or, like piracy, may also be due to a lack of legal offers on the market.[1130] Others are linked to organised crime.[1131] Some users and operators also challenge the entire concept of copyright or advocate for a significant reduction in its scope of protection.[1132] Some followers of these ideas, like the operators of *The Pirate Bay* P2P file sharing system, would intentionally disregard copyright regulations.[1133]

Online intermediaries have been in the main line of fire over their role in facilitating what rightsholders perceive as massive unauthorised distribution and communication of protected works. Music labels, film producers, copyright collecting societies and authors have lamented over substan-

---

1129 Tatiana-Eleni Synodinou, 'Copyright Law: An Ancient History, a Contemporary Challenge' in Andrej Savin and Jan Trzaskowski (eds), *Research Handbook on EU Internet Law* (Edward Elgar Publishing 2014) 98.

1130 Red Points, *Millennials and Piracy - Behaviour, Trends and Future Planning* (2016) <https://meet.redpoints.com/lp-203-ebook-millennials-and-piracy/> accessed 7 May 2020. João Pedro Quintais and Joost Poort, 'The Decline of Online Piracy: How Markets – Not Enforcement – Drive down Copyright Infringement' (2019) 34 American University International Law Review 807.

1131 EUIPO and Europol, 'Intellectual Property Crime Threat Assessment' (2019) 27–29.

1132 Michele Boldrin and David K Levine, *Against Intellectual Monopoly* (Cambridge Univ Press 2010). Shelly Warwick, 'Is Copyright Ethical? An Examination of the Theories, Laws and Practices Regarding the Private Ownership of Intellectual Work in the United States' [1999] B.C. Intell. Prop. & Tech. F.

1133 *Stichting Brein II* (n 214) para 45.

tial revenue losses and the erosion of their business models over the last 15 years.[1134] They have pursued not only the originators of unauthorised sharing and exploitation of works but also online intermediaries, internet access or hosting providers, in order to enlist them in their cause to prevent and remove infringing content.[1135] This battle has been going on despite of disagreement over the real economic damage caused by copyright violations and valid arguments over traditional publishers' failure to adapt to the internet age.[1136]

Some of the first cases in intermediary liability have dealt with these substantive challenges that rightsowners owners have faced when their works were shared and copied though bulletin boards or file sharing services without authorisation.[1137] Since then, copyright has probably become the most prominently analysed and debated content area in the context of intermediary liability, both from a policy and from an academic perspective.[1138]

This is due to several reasons. First, copyright, as an intellectual property right rests on a careful balance between potentially conflicting interests: while the property rights of the author are protected as a fundamental right,[1139] they are not absolute. They may be restricted by other fundamental rights and legitimate interest, such as the right to freedom of expres-

1134 For data see for example: Frontier Economics, 'The Economic Impacts of Counterfeiting and Piracy - Report Prepared for BASCAP and INTA' 38. This reports estimates the value of digital piracy film, music and software at $213 billion in 2015.

1135 Kristofer Erickson and Martin Kretschmer, 'Analyzing Copyright Takedown of User-Generated Content on YouTube' [2018] JIPITEC 75, 78–79; Edwards, 'With Great Power Comes Great Responsibility?: The Rise of Platform Liability' (n 661) 281–285.

1136 Quintais, 'Global Online Piracy Study' (n 30) 23–27.

1137 See Chapter 3 see for example the cases of *Playboy Enterprises, Inc v Frena* (1993) 839 F. Supp. 1552 (MD Fla); *Sega Enterprises Ltd v MAPHIA* (1994) 857 F. Supp. 679 (Dist Court, ND Cal); *CDBench, 6 U 5475/99* [2000] MMR 2000 617 (OLG München). *Madame L. v. les sociétés Multimania Production, France Cybermedia, SPPI, Esterel* (n 362). It should be mentioned that the weight accorded to different rights varies between the US (Anglo-Amercian) and the European Continental traditions, especially were moral rights and copyright exemptions are concerned. MacQueen and others (n 345) 44–45.

1138 Carsten Ullrich, 'Standards for Duty of Care? Debating Intermediary Liability from a Sectoral Perspective' (2017) 8 JIPITEC 111, 114.

1139 CFREU Article 17 (2).

sion, the right to privacy,[1140] cultural interest and the freedom to conduct a business.[1141]

After bulletin boards and file sharing applications, the upcoming Web 2.0 intermediaries accelerated the use of new creative and communicative practices. Collaborative creation, mashups, linking and sharing would all be less popular and prevalent had it not been for the likes of *YouTube, Facebook, DailyMotion, Instagram or Google Search,* and thousands of other information hosts, including filesharing services. Online intermediaries have spurred the mass consumption of content and the mass participation of users in new content creation and sharing, providing ground-breaking new means for expression and cultural value. This has shaken the balance that copyright has sought to establish. The complex and intricate protections of copyright and their exceptions and limitations, became suddenly relevant for large swathes of the population in their daily use, as they interact via online platforms. This has led to consumer confusion and insecurity.[1142]

Secondly, intermediaries as hosts of third-party content and gatekeepers to the internet portray themselves as mere middlemen in order to minimise liabilities for the content they host. In reality, however, not only have they massively profited from their central position. Their content management decisions influence and steer user behaviour towards more interaction and tenure on the platform, inciting more communication and content creation. As explained already, this is done first and foremost for commercial reasons to create traffic, data, advertising and sales. The controversial question is whether these more intrusive platform business models interfere more directly in the substance of copyright.

Thirdly, copyright is primarily an economic right. As mass entertainment and media have spread increasingly through the internet and digital communications, online platforms have eaten into the cake comfortably enjoyed by established media and entertainment companies for decades. Despite being relative newcomers, *Google* and *Facebook* alone have been upsetting worldwide media advertising markets within less than a decade, diverting ad spend revenue away from TV and print media. While, for example in the US, traditional media (TV, print and radio) attracted 81% of advertising spending in 2010, their share had fallen to 49% within a span

---

1140 *Promusicae* (n 140).

1141 MacQueen and others (n 345) 243–244. *SABAM v NetlogShtekel* (n 460) para 51; *Scarlet Extended* (n 139) para 53.

1142 Bosher and Yeşiloğlu (n 1127) 166–179.

of only eight years.[1143] Established media rightsowners have repeatedly claimed that this shift happened on the back of unlicensed or unlawful content shared freely by internet platform users. The ensuing economic battle has played out in major litigations, lobbying campaigns and policy initiatives worldwide. Copyright has therefore influenced significantly overall intermediary liability approaches as well as the way how online platforms today regulate content, both from a legal as well as a technological perspective.[1144]

The evolving adjustments of substantive copyright law to the internet era will not be fully recounted here.[1145] This section will focus on copyright where it touches on the role and responsibilities of online intermediaries, by paying attention to IAPs and hosting providers.

II. International law and EU set-up

Copyright law is partly harmonised through EU legislation. The starting point for this has to be sought at a global level. The 1996 WIPO Internet Treaties[1146] adapted copyright law to the digital age by supplementing the Berne and Rome Conventions that protect the authors of literary and artistic works and the rights of performers and producers, respectively.[1147] Most importantly, the WIPO Internet Treaties grant authors the public communication and distribution rights. The WIPO Copyright Treaty Article 11 also authorises the application of technical protection measures to copyright works. The provisions of the WIPO Treaties were transposed into EU law by the Infosoc Directive in 2001. This Directive is the first instrument that introduced a horizonal harmonisation of core aspects of copyright law.[1148] The EU competency to act in his area rests on today's Article 114 TFEU, which allows the EU to approximate national laws where this serves the establishment and functioning of the internal mar-

1143 Meeker (n 138) 22.

1144 Cornils (n 481) 17; Helman and Parchomovsky (n 309) 1195.

1145 For in-depth analyses see: Jütte (n 30); Schmitz (n 30); Synodinou, 'Copyright Law: An Ancient History, a Contemporary Challenge' (n 1128).

1146 WIPO Copyright Treaty (WCT) 1996 Articles 6 - 8 ; WIPO Performances and Phonograms Treaty (WPPT) 1996 Articles 6 - 8.

1147 Berne Convention for the Protection of Literary and Artistic Works 1886; Rome Convention for the Protection of Performers, Producers of Phonograms and Broadcasting Organisations 1961.

1148 Jütte (n 30) 111–113.

ket.[1149] This underlines the economic dimension and motivations behind copyright.[1150]

On the one hand, the Infosoc Directive harmonises the core economic aspects of copyright through the rights of distribution and reproduction and the communication and making available to the public.[1151] National legal disputes and ambiguities of these rights and their application to the internet have been consistently harmonised at EU level, either through CJEU intervention or though EU policy action, especially where it concerns the rights of communication to the public and making available.[1152] Internet intermediaries enter into the frame of this discussion through the practices of hyperlinking and direct content hosting and sharing.

On the other hand, Member States are left with a margin of implementation when it comes to exceptions and limitations of copyright as per Article 5 of the Infosoc Directive. The exceptions provide for flexibility where copyright would conflict with other legitimate uses that are in the public interest or protect fundamental rights. The exceptions and limitations to the reproduction and communications rights in Article 5 Infosoc Directive are of special relevance to the internet and its intermediaries. It provides an exhaustive list of optional exceptions and limitations and one mandatory exception. For example, Member States are allowed to exempt the distribution of copies and the communications to the public from authorisation where this: happens for research and teaching purposes; concerns current economic or political news reporting, political speeches, and is part of quotations or criticisms, parody or caricature. Although the CJEU has stipulated that the exceptions, where implemented by national law, have an autonomous (unified) meaning under EU law,[1153] their voluntary character has resulted in a *de facto* fragmentation of copyright law.[1154]

1149 Directive 2001/29 (InfoSoc Directive) Recitals 1 - 3.

1150 Savin (n 384) 176.

1151 Directive 2001/29 (InfoSoc Directive) Articles 2 - 4.

1152 Tatiana-Eleni Synodinou, 'Directive 2001/29/EC on the Harmonisation of Certain Aspects of Copyright and Related Rights in the Information Society' in Arno R Lodder and Andrew D Murray (eds), *EU regulation of e-commerce: a commentary* (Edward Elgar Publishing 2017) 66–75.

1153 Laid down for the parody exception by the CJEU in *Johan Deckmyn and Vrijheidsfonds VZW v Helena Vandersteen and Others, C-201/13* [2014] EU:C:2014:2132 (CJEU). As mentioned by: Synodinou, 'Directive 2001/29/EC on the Harmonisation of Certain Aspects of Copyright and Related Rights in the Information Society' (n 1151) 80.

1154 P Bernt Hugenholtz, 'Why the Copyright Directive Is Unimportant and Possibly Invalid Hugenholtz' (2000) 22 European Intellectual Property Review 499,

The exceptions play a key role in protecting user rights but also in giving certainty to authors and rightsholders.[1155] Not making them equally applicable in all Member States has therefore been seen as signalling a certain carelessness for the public interest aspects of copyright compared to the economic preoccupations of rightsowners.[1156] The exhaustive list of exceptions makes for a certain inflexibility with regards to new uses of works engendered by e.g. UGC platforms. It has been notoriously difficult for online platforms and for users to understand exceptions like parodies, review or criticism, or political use as they apply to new forms of UGC, such as mashups, remixes and parodies. This is made even more complex when these exceptions do not apply consistently across all Member States.[1157]

The role of intermediaries in copyright law is addressed by Article 8(3) of the Infosoc Directive. This offers rightsholders the option to apply for injunctions against intermediaries that are used by a third party to infringe copyright or related rights. IPRED complements this by providing for the availability of injunctions against intermediaries in Articles 9 (1) and 11, as per the Infosoc Directive. However, IPRED and the Infosoc Directive both apply without prejudice to the liability provisions formulated under the ECD.[1158] The ECD therefore ties in with IP legislation and can be seen as supplementary to copyright law, similar to the provisions of data protection law.[1159] Any injunctions against intermediaries have to be in respect of the principles laid down in the ECD, specifically those that prohibit the imposition of general monitoring obligations. Meanwhile, the procedural and administrational detail of the injunctions and sanctions that intermediaries can be subjected to are regulated by national law.

501; Lucie Guibault, 'Why Cherry-Picking Never Leads to Harmonisation: The Case of the Limitations on Copyright under Directive 2001/29/EC' (2010) 1 JIPITEC 55.

1155 Christophe Geiger and Francisca Schönherr, 'Limitations to Copyright in the Digital Age' in Andrej Savin and Jan Trzaskowski (eds), *Research Handbook on EU Internet Law* (Edward Elgar Publishing 2014) 114.

1156 Savin (n 384) 193.

1157 Jütte (n 12); Erickson and Kretschmer (n 1134).

1158 Directive 2004/48 (IPRED) Article 2 (3); Directive 2001/29 (InfoSoc Directive) Recital 16.

1159 Synodinou, 'Copyright Law: An Ancient History, a Contemporary Challenge' (n 1128) 97–98.

III. Copyright enforcement and online intermediaries

a. Enforcement at Member State level

Member States have used the liability provisions of the ECD in conjunction with the intermediary enforcement options available under the Infosoc Directive and IPRED in order to enlist intermediaries in the fight against copyright infringements. But the Infosoc Directive and IPRED leave the conditions and modalities of such injunctions to Member States' national laws.[1160]

Therefore, the application of the ECD in the area of copyright is characterised by the generally diverging legal attitudes towards intermediary liability and the various remedies available through national laws. The disparate nature of the application of the liability provisions and the enforcement *vis-à-vis* intermediaries in copyright infringement cases has been analysed in great detail.[1161] Ample case law has been building up over the last 20 years to support this research. Intermediary liability in copyright can be seen as a showcase example for the fragmented and ambiguous landscape of enforcement against IAPs and hosting providers in Europe.[1162] A large part of the cases used to demonstrate the enforcement challenges of the ECD in Chapter 3 deal with unlawful acts in the area of copyright. This section will provide an overview by drawing on the rich literature on the subject.

As in other sectoral areas, some Member States, like for example the UK (when it was still in the EU), chose to look at intermediary liability conditions through specific provisions in their copyright or other statutes. Meanwhile, others, such as Germany, apply their civil law doctrine of *Störerhaftung* directly to intermediaries in copyright infringement cases.

1160 Directive 2001/29 (InfoSoc Directive) Recital 59; Directive 2004/48 (IPRED) Recital 23. Martin Husovec, 'Injunctions against Innocent Third Parties': (2013) 4 JIPITEC 14. Eleonora Rosati, 'Intermediary IP Injunctions in the EU and UK Experiences: When Less (Harmonization) Is More?' (2017) 12 Journal of Intellectual Property Law & Practice 338, 22.

1161 See for example in the following works: Angelopoulos (n 30); Schmitz (n 30); NaNM van Eijk and others, 'Moving Towards Balance: A Study into Duties of Care on the Internet' (Social Science Research Network 2010) SSRN Scholarly Paper ID 1788466 <https://papers.ssrn.com/abstract=1788466> accessed 13 May 2020. Graeme B Dinwoodie, 'A Comparative Analysis of the Secondary Liability of Online Providers' in Graeme B. Dinwoodie (ed), *Secondary liability of internet service providers* (Springer Berlin Heidelberg 2017).

1162 Angelopoulos (n 30) 177.

In the UK, judges have tried to approach intermediary liability in copyright through the legal instrument of authorisation under section 16 of the Copyright, Designs and Patents Act (CDPA)[1163] or, alternatively, the common low doctrine of joint tortfeasance. By contrast, English courts have rarely made use of the tort of negligence, which would eventually lead to defining reasonable duties of care.[1164] This would be in line with the relative unease of common law jurisprudence with broader principles for positive obligations.[1165] The possibility of injunction against intermediaries involved in copyright infringements, provided for by Article 8(3) IPRED, was established by section 97A of the CDPA in 2003. It gives courts the power to grant an injunction against an ISSP, where the latter has actual knowledge of being used by someone else to infringe copyright. Actual knowledge is established through a notice which must contain the name and address of the sender and details of the infringement.[1166]

In France, the actions of intermediaries in copyright infringements are regulated through the aforementioned Article 6 of the LCEN. Injunctions against intermediaries are possible through the *Code de la Proprieté Intellectuelle (CDI)*Article L336-2 which was amended in 2006 in response to the Infosoc Directive.[1167] In parallel to these provisions, French courts make use of the *Code Civil's Articles 1240 and 1241* that deal with third party liabilities[1168]

Germany regulates the civil liabilities of infringers in Art 97 of the Law on Copyright and Related rights.[1169] As regards intermediaries that are found to qualify for the exemptions of the ECD, the German law applies its interferer liability doctrine, which relies on negligence-based considerations but will only result in the imposition of injunctions, and not dam-

1163 Copyright, Designs and Patents Act 1988 c.48.

1164 Angelopoulos (n 30) 94–120.

1165 See Chapter 3

1166 Copyright, Designs and Patents Act 1988 c.48 s 97 A.

1167 LOI n° 2006-961 du 1er août 2006 relative au droit d'auteur et aux droits voisins dans la société de l'information. See also the explanation in the judgement *SNEP v Microsoft France et Microsoft Inc* (2016) (Unreported) (Tribunal de grande instance de Paris).with respect to search engine Bing

1168 *Jean-Yves Lafesse et autres v Google et autres* (n 553); *Roland Magdane et autres v Dailymotion* (n 607). where the relevant Articles of the *Code Civil* were still 1381 and 1382

1169 Gesetz über Urheberrecht und verwandte Schutzrechte Article 97.

ages.[1170] Since 2008, intermediaries can also be ordered to disclose information about the identity of an infringer. [1171]

Both France and the UK also introduced additional legislation targeted at users, which criminalises illegal downloads. This was an answer to the surge in P2P filesharing witnessed in the first decade of the millennium. This will be covered in the following section.

It should also be noted that some Member States chose to regulate NTD requirements for copyright infringements through their national laws. Finland, France, the UK, Spain and Hungary have such regulations in place, while Portugal and Sweden have horizontal NTD statutory requirements which cover copyright.[1172] The Netherlands have a voluntary code of conduct for an NTD system in place.[1173] The nature of the statutory NTD processes varies, with some countries applying it to all intermediaries, while others only cover IAPs or hosting providers. The procedural requirements also vary widely. Since a notice is seen as the principal means for establishing actual knowledge of unlawful content or activity under the ECD, this variety alone is bound to lead to different intermediary knowledge, and hence, liability conditions. The application of intermediary liability rules developed differently for IAPs and different types of hosting providers, with varying consequences for the obligations and liabilities imposed by courts and national statutes.[1174]

b. Enforcement against IAPs – blocking and filtering injunctions

IAPs have very early been in the focus of rightsowners and authorities when it comes to stopping or preventing the availability of copyright infringing material on the internet. Right from the start of the P2P filesharing wars of the early 2000s they were the enforcers of choice of rightsholders against the elusive and distributed architecture of *Grokster*, *eDonkey*,

---

1170 Spindler, 'Präzisierungen Der Störerhaftung Im Internet Besprechung Des BGH-Urteils „Kinderhochstühle Im Internet"' (n 723) 103.

1171 Olla Polzin und Rolf Schwartmann, 'Sharehoster Und Andere Host-Provider' in Thomas Hoeren and Viola Bensinger (eds), *Haftung im Internet: die neue Rechtslage* (De Gruyter 2014) 382.

1172 European Commission, 'SEC(2011) 1641 Final' (n 11) 137–140.

1173 Quintais and Poort (n 1129) 843.

1174 Nicolas Jougleux, 'The Role of Internet Intermediaries in Copyright Law Online Enforcement' in Tatiana-Eleni Synodinou and others (eds), *EU internet law: regulation and enforcement* (Springer Berlin Heidelberg 2017) 285–286.

Kazaa, The Pirate Bay and other P2P services.[1175] Their central, gatekeeping position means that they are ideal enforcement targets when it comes to filtering or blocking content unlawfully accessed through or shared by other service providers, such as P2P services, or by private users. At the same time, this technical and infrastructural command has a direct impact on important rights and freedoms. Access to the internet is increasingly regarded as a fundamental right linked to the freedom to receive and impart information and to participate in (the information) society. User traffic data and IP data requested by rightsholders or authorities in the pursuit of illegal downloaders impact the data protection and privacy rights, and for ISPs, the freedom to conduct a business.[1176]

The mere conduit exemption for liability under Article 12 ECD limits IAPs' obligations to the more reactive actions of stopping or preventing infringements following a court or administrative order, which are handed down as injunctions. Rightsholders across the EU, but also worldwide, tried to use these injunctions to oblige IAPs to install systems that would filter or block IP addresses, DNS names, URLs, or data packets, or a combination of these, in order to end copyright infringing activity.[1177] The battles over finding the right balance of the adequate scope of these injunctions took place against the backdrop of the changing technical architecture of P2P services and their business models, and of mounting evidence of infringing use. On the other side, concerns over the impact on fundamental rights by forcing IAPs into potential censorship roles grew in parallel with the importance of the internet and the expansion of its user base. The ECD allows for preventive injunctions against IAPs in Article 12 (3), but prohibits them as soon as they become general monitoring obligations. Meanwhile, IPRED and the Infosoc Directive demand that any inunctions, including against intermediaries, are effective, proportionate and dissuasive.[1178] In addition they must be fair, equitable, not unnecessarily complicated or costly, do not create barriers to trade and provide safeguards against abuse.[1179]

1175 Edwards, 'With Great Power Comes Great Responsibility?: The Rise of Platform Liability' (n 661) 281.

1176 Christophe Geiger and Elena Izyumenko, 'The Role of Human Rights in Copyright Enforcement Online: Elaborating a Legal Framework for Website Blocking' (2016) 3 American University International Law Review 45, 52–54.

1177 Schmitz (n 30) 546–556.

1178 Directive 2004/48 (IPRED) Article 3 (2); Directive 2001/29 (InfoSoc Directive) Article 8 (1).

1179 Directive 2004/48 (IPRED) Article 8.

National courts have grappled notably with the scope of preventive injunctions. Different approaches with varying outcomes developed out of Member States' jurisprudence. This has been demonstrated as one of the major horizontal challenge in Chapter 3. It is owed to procedural and administrative aspects of injunctions being left to Member States' varying national law and the by now familiar differences in the legal traditions on intermediary law. The CJEU eventually had to step in and give authoritative guidance on the scope of such injunctions by balancing the rights concerned.

The CJEU judgements, despite referring mostly to IAPs, give some useful guidelines in the search for more holistic intermediary responsibilities of hosting providers, where it concerns copyright protection. First, the CJEU specified in its *Promusicae* judgement that Member States are not required to impose an obligation on IAPs that user data be disclosed to rightsholders in order to effectively protect copyright.[1180] This case dealt with a Spanish rightsowner that had asked the ISP *Telefónica de España* to disclose the identities and physical addresses of internet subscribers who had used the P2P filesharing service *Kazaa* in order to exchange copyright protected works. Secondly, *Scarlet Extended* established that a preventive injunction could not oblige an IAP to filter the traffic of all of its customers in order to identify and block file sharing traffic of copyright infringing materials for an unlimited period of time.[1181] Thirdly, in *UPC Telekabel*, although solely basing itself on the Infosoc Directive and not on the ECD, the CJEU allowed an injunction that ordered an IAP to block their customers' access to a website with infringing material, but left the design of the specific measures to the IAP. The IAP would also be freed of any sanctions for breaching the order if it showed that it took all reasonable measures to comply, even when the measures could be circumvented by some users.[1182] Finally, in *Mc Fadden* the CJEU confirmed that a free of charge Wi-Fi hotspot operator could be qualified as an IAP where that service is used for advertising of the goods or services offered.[1183] It was reasonable to expect that such an IAP secured its network against copyright infringing use by installing password protected access.[1184] Requiring users to give up total

1180 *Promusicae* (n 140) para 70.
1181 *Scarlet Extended* (n 139) paras 40, 47.
1182 *Telekabel* (n 757) para 64.
1183 *Mc Fadden* (n 139) para 43.
1184 ibid 99.

anonymity when using the hotspot was deemed a proportionate and effective measure.

The rulings would appear to sketch the contours of a responsibility or duty of care framework within the tight limits of the ECD, IPRED and the Infosoc Directive in the area of copyright. On one side, obliging IAPs to install broad monitoring systems that would cover all user traffic for an unlimited time in the search for copyright infringing material could be seen as disproportional. On the other side, *UPC Telekabel* offered the possibility that an intermediary define the most adequate means for complying with an injunction if this meant that it took all reasonable measures that could be expected of it. It has been criticised that this was a *de facto* outsourcing of fundamental rights balancing exercises to a private entity.[1185] By contrast, it could also be argued that this is a characteristic of a duty of care system. It forces the intermediary to thoroughly consider and weigh the measures it implements, because they are accountable for their decision. It promotes therefore responsible action along the concept of *bonus pater familias* or duty of care,[1186] similar to the "diligent economic operator" standard formulated in in *L'Oréal v EBay* regarding trademarks.[1187] Meanwhile, *Mc Fadden* would vindicate the establishment of processes that seek to establish a user's identity before they join an online network that allows for content downloading and sharing. This appears to be in line with risk management processes that would align the due diligence measures of an actor to the risk of the business model.[1188]

Others have, however, argued that these rulings did little to harmonise intermediary liability provisions in copyright cases.[1189] The cases referred were specific to national legal systems. The consistent delegation of the balancing exercises back to national courts did little to harmonise these provisions, considering the national differences in the nature and application of injunctions.[1190] Meanwhile, as concerns *UPC Telekabel*, some Member States, like the UK, Netherlands or Italy, may not allow for broad injunctions the finetuning of which would lie with the economic operator.

1185 Geiger and Izyumenko (n 1175) 91–92.
1186 Valcke, Kuczerawy and Ombelet (n 551) 109–112.
1187 *L'Oréal v eBay* (n 463) paras 120–124.
1188 Ullrich, 'A Risk-Based Approach towards Infringement Prevention on the Internet' (n 747) 242–244.
1189 Jougleux (n 1173) 282–286.
1190 Angelopoulos (n 30) 72.

Other countries, like France and Austria, may, however, have less problems in accepting such broad injunctions.[1191]

The enforcement methods against IAPs for illegal file sharing and downloads vary significantly across Member States. In the Netherlands, Spain and the UK for example, injunctions against IAPs to block or remove infringing content are the most commonly used enforcement tools.[1192] The UK stand out as one of the world's most aggressive pursuers of blocking injunctions in the fight against pirate sites. In the UK, the scope of these injunctions has broadened following the *Newzbin* judgement.[1193] They can now cover dynamic injunctions, which target mainly illegal live streaming sites, where URL addresses can be added to the injunctions after the court order has been issued.[1194] In Poland and France, enforcement has focussed on individual users, with France also looking at IAPs to block and filter unlawful traffic. In Germany and Sweden, privately administered cease-and-desist systems appear to be a popular means of enforcement, targeted mainly at users.[1195]

Some EU Member States have introduced administrative enforcement measures, also known as graduated response systems, to go after users who engage in illegal downloading or sharing of content. Enforcement against users means that the IAP is enlisted in helping administrative authorities to pursue infringers at some stages of the process. IAPs are needed to disclose the identity of the IP address subscriber,[1196] issue warning messages and suspend internet access of users who have repeatedly downloaded and shared copyright infringing content, notably through P2P systems.[1197] In

---

1191 Geiger and Izyumenko (n 1175) 92–95.

1192 João Pedro Quintais, 'Global Online Piracy Study Legal Background Report' (Institute for Information Law (IViR), University of Amsterdam 2018) 86–88.

1193 See Chapter 3. *Newzbin* (n 638).

1194 Edwards, 'The Fall and Rise Of Intermediary Liability Online' (n 119) 283–284.

1195 Quintais, 'Global Online Piracy Study Legal Background Report' (n 1191) 85–88. For a detailed description of the cease-and-desist system works in Germany see: Sandra Schmitz and Thorsten Ries, 'Three Songs and You Are Disconnected from Cyberspace? Not in Germany Where the Industry May "Turn Piracy into Profit"' (2012) 3 European Journal of Law and Technology 14.

1196 Usually done through a court order and, following the *CJEU's Promusicae* judgement, only possible where national laws allow for such disclosure in case of copyright infringements. See also: Sandra VI Schmitz, *The Struggle in Online Copyright Enforcement: Problems and Prospects* (1. edition, Nomos 2015) 219–221.

1197 Angelopoulos (n 30) 148.

2006, France proposed its infamous HADOPI Law[1198] which criminalised the acts of illegal file downloading. The obligations imposed on IAPs were outside of the provisions of the intermediary liability framework, but they illustrate the strategic position of IAPs in the online communication chain. In France, it took three years and two legislative rejections before this law was eventually adopted.[1199] HADOPI2 introduces a graduated response system consisting of three strikes against users who illegally download content from the internet. The successive sanctions would lead to a suspension of internet access (a measures which was revoked in 2013) and fines depending on the volume of downloads. The effectiveness of the HADOPI laws has been debated. While the increase in court cases, warning letters and emails appear to have had some impact on the volume of illegal downloads,[1200] there are doubts over its effectiveness. The impact on the general availability of illegal offers remains disputed, while technical circumvention measures continue to evolve[1201] and enforcement costs appear to be high.[1202] Other concerns centre around fundamental rights such as privacy, freedom of speech and the presumption of innocence.[1203] The UK tried to introduce such a graduated response system through the 2010 Digital Economy Act. This was, however, never adopted in its original version. It was eventually watered down into a private warning systems system that allows copyright owners to pursue repeat infringers legally.[1204] A similar private scheme exists in Ireland.[1205]

1198 LOI n° 2009-1311 du 28 octobre 2009 relative à la protection pénale de la propriété littéraire et artistique sur internet 2009 (2009-1311).

1199 For a detailed account see : Emmanuel Derieux and Agnès Granchet, *Lutte Contre Le Téléchargement Illégal: Lois Dadvsi et Hadopi* (Lamy 2010).

1200 Quintais, 'Global Online Piracy Study' (n 30) 28.

1201 Schmitz (n 30) 236–240.

1202 Rebecca Giblin, 'Beyond Graduated Response' in Susy Frankel, Daniel J Gervais and New Zealand Centre of International Economic Law (eds), *The evolution and equilibrium of copyright in the digital age* (Cambridge University Press 2014) 86–90.

1203 Derieux and Granchet (n 1198) 195–197. Christophe Geiger, 'The Rise of Criminal Enforcement of Intellectual Property Righs...and Its Failure in the Context of Copyright Infringements on the Internet' in Susy Frankel, Daniel J Gervais and New Zealand Centre of International Economic Law (eds), *The evolution and equilibrium of copyright in the digital age* (Cambridge University Press 2014) 134–137.

1204 Quintais, 'Global Online Piracy Study Legal Background Report' (n 1191) 65.

1205 Gerard Kelly, 'A Court-Ordered Graduated Response System in Ireland: The Beginning of the End?' (2016) 11 Journal of Intellectual Property Law & Practice 183.

Overall, the measures to stop copyright infringement through issuing blocking and filtering injunctions at IAP level can be assessed as showing mixed success. For one, these are mostly reactive measures, which take time, a crucial disadvantage in the internet age, and can be circumvented. Except for the UK, where dynamic injunctions allow for a certain adaptability, especially in the case of illegal live streaming, this is a piecemeal approach. But given the fundamental rights at stake in asking internet gatekeepers to monitor, filter and block content, and disclose user information, judicial oversight is needed. This and the different setup of injunctions within national, legal systems means that the use of IAPs in the fight against copyright breaches varies significantly between Member States. The European Commission sought to clarify the situation through its 2017 Guidance on IPRED. It took note of the fact that some members, namely the UK, Ireland and Belgium, provided for dynamic injunctions through their legal systems. While IPRED did not expressly provide for these measures, it conceded that they can be effective to prevent continued infringements provided they include the necessary safeguards.[1206] That document also clarified that ordering *"excessively broad, unspecific and expensive filtering"* would hit the barriers of Article 3 (1) IPRED, the general monitoring prohibition of Article 15 (1) ECD and applicable fundamental rights. It confirmed and summarised the guidance provided through its case law in *Scarlet Extend*, *Netlog*, *L'Oréal v eBay* and *UPC Telekabel*.[1207]

c. Content hosting, sharing and the road towards primary liability

Hosting providers are the kind of intermediary that third parties use directly to share content. The rise of Web 2.0 was the main trigger for rightsowners shifting attention from IAPs to P2P file sharing services, search engines, social media and UGC platforms. The likes of *The Pirate Bay*, *eMule*, *Grokster*, *Google Search*, *Bing*, *YouTube*, *DailyMotion*, *Instagram* or *Facebook* have enabled an unprecedented surge in interactive, global, mass sharing of images, video and music. Given the economic importance of IP rights, most of the controversies and legal challenges against intermediaries in the fight against unlawful content have been played out in this area. These

1206 European Commission, 'Guidance on Certain Aspects of Directive 2004/48/EC of the European Parliament and of the Council on the Enforcement of Intellectual Property Rights, COM(2017) 708 Final' (n 715) 21.

1207 ibid 20.

rights are exercised by a powerful industry with the money and vested interest in bringing court challenges and in influencing policy. By contrast, defamation and hate speech on the internet mostly concern private parties, which have naturally fewer means to go to court and fight legal battles.

Rightsowners have challenged the legal assumptions on which online platform business models were built: no primary liability due to their intermediary role; an exemption from secondary liability due to their neutral, content agnostic character that relies on third party notifications for stopping unlawful acts.

The national idiosyncrasies that relate to the responsibilities of information hosts under Article 14 ECD in copyright cases will not be recounted in detail here. This section will focus on the role that these actors play in the substance of copyright. This is inevitably linked to some of the challenges to the neutral intermediary status, on the one hand, and the particular characteristics of digital copyright, on the other. It has a resulted in a gradual shift in jurisprudence from allocating secondary liability to finding hosting providers directly liable for copyright infringements. This development will be analysed in the following.

Web 2.0 intermediaries have been challenged in three main areas: unlawful file sharing though P2P systems; hyperlink sharing, mainly through search engines, and content sharing through UGC and social media platforms.

P2P file sharing and hyperlinking

Early file sharing services often boasted their own centralised file index and even hosted content themselves, practices which were early on doomed for failure. The prime example here is *Napster,* whose central file index conferred on it a level of control that made it relatively easy to prove actual or constructive knowledge of infringing activity. The business eventually collapsed when forced to police its content in order to stop infringing use. The crux for the judges was that the service "turned a blind eye to detectable acts of infringement for the sake of profit."[1208] In this US judgement, *Napster's* business model fell under the narrowly applied 'red flag' or wilful blindness standard and was denied protection under the DMCA's

1208 *A&M Records, Inc v Napster, Inc* [2001] United States Court of Appeals for the Ninth Circuit 00-16401, 00-16403, 239 F.3d 1004 [69].

safe harbour. Of course, not every P2P file sharing service derives benefits from infringing activity to the same degree as Napster did. Many of these services have perfectly legitimate uses until today. Still, following this early judgement, file-sharing services, such as *Grokster* or *BitTorrent*, have adapted their architecture and now provide different, unconnected software for tracking and for sharing activities. The idea is that a decentralised and distributed architecture would disperse suspicions over knowledge or control of the service over the data stored or indexed by its users.

At least in Europe this has met with mixed success. In a 2003 Dutch case, P2P software provider *Kazaa* was still cleared from any copyright infringement accusation. The service just provided file exchanging software, which was used for both legitimate and illegitimate acts. Users alone would engage in copyright infringing acts, but not *Kazaa*.[1209] It should be kept in mind that file sharing service providers have been classified as hosting service providers under Article 14 of the ECD. This was confirmed notably by a rush of cases brought against file sharing networks in Germany between 2007 and 2012.

Initially, German courts had found filesharing services secondary liable as interferers for failing to prevent massive copyright infringements that were facilitated by their business models.[1210] They eventually changed this interpretation and applied the jurisprudence developed by the BGH and the CJEU on the liability of online marketplaces as intermediaries under the ECD in a number of so-called *Sharehoster* cases.[1211] This resulted in services like *Rapidshare* or *eDonkey* being charged with proactive duties to prevent the repeated making available of links to infringing content, which the courts recognised as a frequent practice.[1212] This line was confirmed by the BGH in 2012,[1213] with a later qualification that certain sharehoster activities promoted infringing use of their services, through e.g. offering

1209 *Vereniging Buma, Stichting Stemra v KaZaA BV* (2003) [2004] E.C.D.R. 16 (Hoge Raad).

1210 *Störerhaftung des Webhosters* [2007] LG Köln 28 O 15/07, MMR 2007, 806; *Rapidshare I* [2008] OLG Hamburg 5 U 73/07, MMR 2008, 823; *Sharehoster II* (n 725).

1211 *RapidShare II* (n 615). German jurisprudence unites all sorts of filehosting and sharing services under the concept of Sharehoster, including cloud services and P2P systems.

1212 ibid 401–402. *Verantwortlichkeit eines Sharehoster-Dienstes für die rechtswidrige Zugänglichmachung urheberrechtlich geschützter Filme* [2010] OLG Düsseldorf I-20 U 166/09, openJur 2009, 1105; see also: Urs Verweyen, 'Grenzen der Störerhaftung in Peer to Peer-Netzwerken' [2009] MMR 590.

1213 *Alone in the Dark* [2012] BGH I ZR 18/11, GRUR 2013, 370.

users anonymity, providing premium accounts for enhanced download bandwidth or loyalty points for users with high amounts of downloads.[1214] Those services would have enhanced verification and infringement prevention duties.

In other Member States, filesharing services were also denied the safe harbour defences under the ECD. In Sweden and Finland, file sharing services *The Pirate Bay* and *Finreactor* lost their safe harbour protection due to the blatantly illegal character of their services.[1215] In Spain, by contrast courts appear to have historically exempted these services from liability either because they saw them as mere software providers or because their activity was protected by the intermediary liability provisions of the ECD.[1216] This trend to assess P2P services as intermediaries was halted by the 2014 CJEU ruling in *Svensson*, which found that hyperlinking was an act of communication and required the author's consent where a new public was being targeted.[1217] Following this judgement, a P2P streaming website was criminally charged for copyright infringements in Spain.[1218] Meanwhile, France has rarely pursued P2P services directly, but chose to go after users or IAPs in the first place.

The *Svensson* ruling was the start of a series of judgements that sought to define different circumstances of hyperlinking on both editorial websites and intermediary sites. In *Bestwater, GS Media* and *Filmspeler* the CJEU developed its line on hyperlinking by introducing duty of care elements notably on commercial websites and intermediaries that posted hyperlinks to copyright protected material.[1219] The CJEU confirmed its broad interpretation of the Infosoc Directive Article 3, which eventually offered no alterna-

---

1214 *Haftung eines Sharehosters als Störer* [2013] BGH I ZR 79/12, ZUM-RD 2013, 565 [32–37]. Polzin and Schwartmann (n 1170) 371–374.

1215 Topi Siniketo, Ulrika Polland and Mikko Manner, 'The Pirate Bay Ruling - When the Fun and Games End' (2009) 20 Entertainment Law Review 12.

1216 Quintais, 'Global Online Piracy Study Legal Background Report' (n 1191) 155–161.

1217 *Nils Svensson and others v Retriever Sverige AB, C-466/12* [2014] EU:C:2014:76 (CJEU) [24].

1218 Quintais, 'Global Online Piracy Study Legal Background Report' (n 1191) 161.

1219 *BestWater International GmbH v Michael Mebes and Stefan Potsch, C-348/13* [2014] EU:C:2014:2315 (CJEU); *GS Media BV v Sanoma Media Netherlands BV, Playboy Enterprises International Inc, Britt Geertruida Dekker, C-160/15,* [2016] EU:C:2016:644 (CJEU); *Stichting Brein v Jack Frederik Wullems, also trading under the name Filmspeler, C-527/15* [2017] EU:C:2017:300 (CJEU).

tive between primary liability and no liability for intermediaries that posted hyperlinks.[1220]

In the *Pirate Bay* case the CJEU extended the jurisprudence on hyperlinking to P2P filesharing services. The Dutch Supreme Court had called on the CJEU to clarify whether by indexing, categorising and linking to copyright protected works on private users' computers *The Pirate Bay* engaged in an unauthorised communication to the public. The claimant, *Stichting Brein*, a rightsholder association, asked the defendants, IAPs *Ziggo* and *XS4ALL*, to block access to *The Pirate Bay* sites. The IAPs had rejected such blocking injunction on the grounds that *The Pirate Bay* by itself was an online intermediary and therefore not engaged in making protected works available to the public. By applying the methodologies developed in the previous cases, the CJEU found that the P2P sites of *The Pirate Bay* engaged in a communication to the public. Moreover, this activity happened in full knowledge of the consequences – a very large number of torrent files made available works without the authors' consent - and for the purpose of obtaining a profit.[1221] As already done in *UPC Telekabel* and *GS Media*, the CJEU did not consider any liability protections that may have applied to this intermediary under the ECD, unlike in some of the national case law mentioned above. The reasoning of the judgement implies that primary liability for copyright relevant acts excludes the application of the safe harbours for intermediaries under the ECD. The erstwhile condition of actual knowledge for secondary infringements was extended to cover constructive knowledge of infringing acts where the platform had primary liability, at least where P2P platforms are concerned.[1222]

Finally, in 2018 the BGH asked the CJEU directly whether the operator of a shared hosting service engaged in an act of communication according to Article 3 (1) Infosoc Directive by making content accessible to users without rightsholders' consent, if: a) the upload process is automated, b) the conditions of use state that copyright infringing use may not be up-

---

1220 Ansgar Ohly, 'The Broad Concept of "Communication to the Public" in Recent CJEU Judgments and the Liability of Intermediaries: Primary, Secondary or Unitary Liability?' (2018) 13 Journal of Intellectual Property Law & Practice 664, 672–673.

1221 *Stichting Brein II* (n 214) paras 36, 43, 46.

1222 Eleonora Rosati, 'The CJEU Pirate Bay Judgment and Its Impact on the Liability of Online Platforms' (2017) 39 European Intellectual Property Review 16. The platform operators could not be unaware that their service provides access to works published without the consent of the rightholders. *Stichting Brein II* (n 214) para 45.

loaded, c) the operator earns revenue with the service, d) the service is used for lawful purposes, but the operator is aware of considerable concurrent illegal use, e) the service has no search function but third parties post searchable link collections online; f) its renumeration structure incentivises illegal uploads; g) the service offers users anonymity, thus facilitating unlawful behaviour.[1223] Considering the line of argument developed through the preceding cases it appears unlikely that the CJEU will come to another conclusion in this preliminary reference by the BGH.

Despite the aggravated legal environment for certain P2P platforms and their users, places like *The Pirate Bay* continue to exist, partly thanks to their distributed nature and partly due to a host of circumvention technologies available to users.[1224] This puts into doubt whether threatening P2P sites with primary liability will seriously deter intentionally infringing P2P business models.

Search engines, hyperlinking and auto-complete functions

The linking controversy did also influence the liability debate over search engines. In fact, the inefficiency to shut down illegal P2P services led copyright owners to pursue other, more essential intermediaries. After IAP's, copyright owners centred their attention on search engines.

The initial years after the enactment of the ECD were characterised by some confusion over the status of search engines. The CJEU's *Google France*[1225] judgement finally established that search engines were to be seen as hosting providers. At the same time, search engines are intermediaries with a specific functional status. They are essential for the functioning of the internet.[1226] Nevertheless, if the provision of hyperlinks, which is the main means used by search engines of making content accessible, consists of an act of communication to the public, then this would affect their business significantly. Initial jurisprudence over search engines' liability for hyperlinks at national level was divergent, much in line with the unclarity over their status as intermediaries. At one extreme, Belgian and Dutch

1223 *uploaded* [2018] BGH DE:BGH:2018:200918BIZR53.17.0, BeckRS 2018, 26223. Registered as CJEU Referral C-683/18 (Cyando) on 6 Nov 2018

1224 Nicolas P Suzor, *Lawless: The Secret Rules That Govern Our Digital Lives* (Cambridge University Press 2019) 98–101; Schmitz (n 30) 556–565.

1225 *Google France v Louis Vuitton* (n 155) para 110.

1226 see Chapter 2

courts found *Google's* search engine directly liable for copyright breaches by posting links to infringing material.[1227] On the other side of the spectrum, a landmark 2003 ruling by Germany's *BGH* freed a news search engine from liability for posting hyperlinks to infringing content. It even significantly limited the service's secondary liability by saying that facilitating the access to works by hyperlinks did not contribute to unlawful behaviour of the party that had made the content available originally.[1228] To complete the disparate picture, a Spanish court in 2007 judged somewhere in between the above extremes. It found that the display of content in search results did breach the copyright of the owners of the referenced website, but that this use was minimal, ephemeral and therefore exempted.[1229] Meanwhile, French courts have ruled conversely. One court accorded *Google's* search engine the protections of the ECD, while yet another one deprived it of these protections.[1230]

As stated above, the CJEU has since had the opportunity to harmonise the interpretation of copyright law regarding hyperlinks. At least the most important search engines by market share as of today, *Google* and *Bing*,[1231] are commercial undertakings that operate for profit. Applying the criteria established in *GS Media* would mean that commercial search engines have duties of care with regards to preventing the publication of hyperlinks to unauthorised content. Any failure to do so would make them primarily liable for making a communication to the public. However, no specific case on commercial search engine liability for copyright content has been escalated to the CJEU as yet. The general uncertainty in this matter is confirmed by Advocate General (AG) *Szpunar's* remark in his Opinion in the *Pirate Bay* case. AG *Szpunar* doubted whether the presumption of knowledge imposed in *GS Media* regarding commercial hyperlink providers

---

1227 *Copiepresse et al v Google Inc* (n 555). *Technodesign v Stichting Brein* [2004] Court of Haarlem 85489 HA ZA 02-992; Verbiest and others (n 315) 86–90.

1228 *Paperboy* [2003] BGH I ZR 259/00, MMR 2003, 719.

1229 *Audiencia Provincial de Barcelona* [2007] Jurisdiction in: Cédric Manara, 'Le droit d'auteur contre l'accès à l'information mondiale ?' (2011) t.XXV Revue internationale de droit economique 143, para 30.

1230 Manara (n 1228) paras 28–29.

1231 With Google taking 93.2% (91.2%) of the market share in Europe (and worldwide) in April 2020 and Bing 2.9% (2.8%) according to: 'Search Engine Market Share Europe' (*StatCounter Global Stats*) <https://gs.statcounter.com/search-engine-market-share/all/europe> accessed 27 May 2020.

could be applied to indexing sites of P2P networks, which work akin to a search engine.[1232]

The *BGH* may have missed an opportunity for clarification at EU level in the 2017 *Vorschaubilder III* case.[1233] Instead, it went ahead and applied its own modifications to the copyright and hyperlinking jurisprudence of the CJEU. The case concerned the image search functionality of *Google's* search engine. A search service that linked its results to *Google's* image search was accused of making a communication to the public by posting freely accessible thumbnail images (with hyperlinks) on its website. The images were owned by the claimant, a website operator for erotic images. Certain areas of their site could only be accessed and images downloaded by paying users. The *BGH* admitted that in order to avoid primary liability according to the *GS Media* criteria, the search service would need to apply duties of cares by checking whether the targeted material was published without authorisation. However, the *BGH* found that the specific importance of search engines for the functioning of the internet exempted it from these duties.[1234] The operation of commercial search engines would be impossible or seriously hampered if they were obliged to verify the legality of targeted content *ex ante*, given the fully automated nature of internet referencing.[1235] This ties in with the *BGH's* line on search engines in other areas of not manifestly unlawful content, such as defamation and hate speech.[1236] The search service in *Vorschaubilder III* could only be held liable for direct copyright infringement if it failed to act following a notification, which had not been the case. This assessment also appears to make secondary liability for linking intermediaries in copyright superfluous. At least it blurs the borders between secondary and primary liability for search engines, or any hosting providers that post hyperlinks. It confirms a trend of replacing or incorporating secondary or "interferer" liability du-

---

1232 *Opinion of Advocate General Szpunar, Stichting Brein v Ziggo BV, XS4ALL Internet BV, C-610/15* [2017] EU:C:2017:99 (CJEU) [52].

1233 Ohly, 'The Broad Concept of "Communication to the Public" in Recent CJEU Judgments and the Liability of Intermediaries' (n 1219) 669.

1234 *Vorschaubilder III* [2017] BGH I ZR 11/16, GRUR 2018, 178 [59–60].

1235 ibid 61–62.

1236 *Zur Prüfungspflicht des Betreibers einer Internet-Suchmaschine bei Persönlichkeitsrechtsverletzungen.* (n 949) para 34.

ties into primary copyright, e.g. the communication to the public, at least in German law.[1237]

In France, by contrast, the line on primary liability of search engines in copyright seems to be less clear. *Google Search*, and a number of IAPs, were pursued for the availability of numerous links to streaming sites offering unauthorised content in 2018.[1238] The rightsowners claimed that *Google Search* went beyond the merely passive role that would offer it liability protections under the LCEN. They asked for dynamic de-referencing injunctions that would order *Google* to identify and de-refence on an ongoing basis URLs that led to certain streaming websites with illegal content. The court avoided to go down the thorny route of deciding whether *Google Search* was an active or passive host. Unlike in Germany, it did not find the hyperlinking practices liable for copyright infringement either. Instead it judged that the search engine was merely an intermediary in the sense of Article 8(3) Infosoc Directive. The dynamic de-referencing injunctions were, however, accorded, as they met the proportionality and efficacy criteria demanded of both IPRED and the Infosoc Directive, according to the court.

This judgement was preceded by a 2012 ruling of France's Supreme Court,[1239] which ceded to the demands of the *National Association of Phonographic Publishers (SNEP)* that *Google's Suggest* application stop proposing terms like *Torrent*, *Megaupload* or *Rapidshare* when users searched for certain artists. The Supreme Court struck down a ruling by the Paris appeals court. *Google's Suggest* tool, it said, oriented users systematically to unauthorised copies of works by associating the searches with the disputed terms. This affected the copyright of the authors. *SNEP* had not attempted to engage intermediary or direct copyright liability but rather restricted it-

1237 Ansgar Ohly, 'Keine Urheberrechtsverletzung Bei Bildersuche Durch Suchmaschinen - Vorschaubilder III - Anmerkung von Ansgar Ohly' [2018] GRUR 2018 178, 188 Para 7.

1238 *FNDF et al v Orange, Google et al)* [2018] Tribunal de grande instance de Paris, 3ème chambre 2ème section N° RG 18/10652, (Unreported). See also : 'White Paper Search Engines - Time to Step Up' (Incopro 2019) 63 <https://www.incoproip.com/reports/how-and-why-search-engines-must-take-responsibility-for-tackling-counterfeiters/>.

1239 *SNEP v Google France* [2012] Cour de cassation, Première chambre civile N° 11-20358. See also : 'White Paper Search Engines - Time to Step Up' (n 1237) 64.

self to using intermediary injunctions granted under Article 336-2 of the French IP law.[1240]

Industry analysis has shown that (dynamic) de-referencing injunctions may lead to a significant reduction in traffic to websites that host mainly infringing content. Following a de-referencing injunction against Google in 2011, traffic to sites grouped under the *AllowStreaming* name lost 48.7% of traffic within 5 months.[1241] In France, de-referencing injunctions against search engines have therefore become established practice, with dynamic de-referencing on the line of outcome injunctions being also accepted more recently.[1242] This is of course not withstanding the known means of circumvention, such as the use of VPNs, site mirroring or the use of proxy services, which remain widely effective. Rightsholders in general have also voiced concerns over the administrational burdens and timeliness of injunctions ordered via a court.[1243] Meanwhile, de-referencing injunctions have generally not been granted against IAPs in France.[1244]

There is scarce evidence in the UK of any orders in copyright cases against search engines.[1245] Instead, the Intellectual Property Office (UK IPO) has facilitated a Voluntary Code of Practice on Search and Copyright between *Google*, *Bing* and *Yahoo!* and rightsowner associations.[1246] The parties agree to the delisting of notified URLs leading to infringing content and to focus on automated demotion following notifications. Further technical measures and KPIs to achieve the objectives of reducing the availability of infringing content are to be discussed confidentially between rightsowners and search engines. The agreement also includes work on preventing autocomplete suggestions which lead to infringing material and remove ads from advertisers that profit from linking to this kind of content. The UK IPO supports best practice sharing, research and assessment on

1240 LOI n° 2006-961 du 1er août 2006 relative au droit d'auteur et aux droits voisins dans la société de l'information.

1241 'White Paper Search Engines - Time to Step Up' (n 1237) 44–47.

1242 *FNDF et al. v Orange, Google et al.).* (n 1237). Outcome injunctions were accepted by the court as proportionate and efficient, while in *APC et autres v Auchan Telecom, Google France et autres* (2013) Unreported (Tribunal de grande instance de Paris). Five years earlier the same court rejected these measures as their proper execution could not be verified by the court and therefore lacked the necessary judicial oversight.

1243 European Commission, 'Summary Response - IPR Enforcement' (n 173) 36.

1244 'White Paper Search Engines - Time to Step Up' (n 1237) 65.

1245 ibid 81.

1246 UK Intellectual Property Office, 'Search Engines and Creative Industries Sign Anti-Piracy Agreement' (*GOV.UK*, 20 February 2017) .

progress. The agreement appears to promote the kind of forward-looking risk assessment needed to effectively fight copyright piracy online. Its significant drawback lies in the fact that it does not appear to be transparent and accountable. It has the hallmarks of a clubby arrangement between dominating industry players to enforce private law provisions, which nevertheless touch on important public interest areas, as provided for in the copyright exception and limitations. It also remains silent on any counterclaims procedures. Although the code allows for the government to impose regulatory action should its objectives not be achieved, there has so far been no official report on its performance.

To cite yet another example of a diverging approach, Spain has created a special safe harbour provision for search engines, outside of, but still similar, to the hosting provider protections of the ECD.[1247]

Whether it concerns primary copyright liability or dynamic (intermediary) injunctions, it appears that search engines enjoy special considerations with courts and legislators due their central status as gatekeepers to internet information. They are thus treated differently to other hosting providers mentioned below. The overall picture is, however, still inconsistent and heterogenic. This is due to, by now, familiar factors: different national legal cultures, uncertainty surrounding both online copyright and online intermediary provisions and different views on how the prevailing problem of infringing material online can be tackled most effectively and proportionally. Overall, the intermediary liability status of search engines remains uncertain to this day.

At the same time, it should not be forgotten that *Google*, which has been dominating the search engine market for years, has continued to operate its own NTD system. According to its obligations under both the US DMCA and the ECD, *Google* has to date delisted over 4.6 billion URLs following notifications by rightsowners.[1248] Until recently, the mechanisms and algorithms that lead to the promotion and listing of certain content, be it sponsored or not, have been hidden deep within the company's realm. This is understandable, on the one side, as this trade secret is key to *Google's* success. On the other side, it leaves users in the dark about why, for example, infringing content is consistently indexed and available through search results. The EU has only very recently introduced regula-

---

1247 Quintais, 'Global Online Piracy Study Legal Background Report' (n 1191) 49.

1248 Google, 'Content Delistings Due to Copyright – Google Transparency Report' <https://transparencyreport.google.com/copyright/overview?hl=en_GB> accessed 28 May 2020.

tions aimed at bringing more transparency for both business clients[1249] and consumers[1250] into the mechanisms that influence the ranking and display of search results. Maybe enlightenment in this area can also progress our understanding of how search engines can help prevent the display of infringing material in a better way. At the very least, these regulations are proof that commercial search engines are much more than neutral information intermediaries. By imposing these transparency obligations, the regulator has clearly caught on to the fact that these gatekeepers influence, determine and control the appearance of search results.[1251] It will be interesting to see whether and how this helps in defining new responsibilities of search engines in future EU legislation, like the proposed Digital Services Act.

Content sharing platforms

UGC websites and social media platforms have increasingly been in the centre of rightsholders' attention over the last 10 years. The different conclusions over the passive or active role of these intermediaries have been mainly played out in the area of IP rights. In addition to the mounting challenges to the passive status of platforms like *YouTube* or *Facebook*, and the scope of their prospective duties, rightsowners have questioned the role that these actors play in the process of communication to the public. This appears to be in line with the challenges mounted against P2P services or search engines. Actions against P2P platforms were motivated by the massive scale of infringements, the permissive attitude of some of these actors and the evolving jurisprudence on hyperlinking. Search engines were in the line of fire for their central position and the ongoing availability and promotion of links to sites that illegally shared protected material.

1249 Regulation (EU) 2019/1150 of the European Parliament and of the Council of 20 June 2019 on promoting fairness and transparency for business users of online intermediation services (Text with EEA relevance) 2019 (OJ L).

1250 Directive (EU) 2019/2161 of the European Parliament and of the Council of 27 November 2019 amending Council Directive 93/13/EEC and Directives 98/6/EC, 2005/29/EC and 2011/83/EU of the European Parliament and of the Council as regards the better enforcement and modernisation of Union consumer protection rules (Text with EEA relevance) 2019 (OJ L 328). To be discussed in more detail in the sections on trademarks and product safety in this chapter

1251 Pasquale (n 19) 497–503.

For content sharing platforms, rightsholders' motivation can be seen in a more complex set of factors, all related to the characteristics of Web 2.0 interactivity: social media and UGC platforms have increasingly become vertically integrated service providers that compete with established media companies. They profit significantly from content uploaded by users, including unauthorised content.[1252]

It should by now come as no surprise that Member States have tackled this issue in different ways. In Italy, courts have recently charged social media and UGC sites with primary copyright liability. *Facebook* was held liable for communication to the public in 2019 by posting links to content the publication of which was not authorised by the rightsholder. Although the court more specifically considered the lack of due diligence on *Facebook's* side to remove the notified links, it still concluded primary liability by applying the CJEU jurisprudence on hyperlinking.[1253] The same Rome court found the VSP *Dailymotion* directly responsible for infringing material uploaded by its users. The VSP's active role situated it outside the safe harbour of the ECD. *Dailymotion's* ability as an active provider to control content meant it could prevent the publication of unauthorised material, the existence of which it was aware of.[1254]

In Germany, the BGH referred a case to the CJEU that has been pitting a music producer against *YouTube* for over a decade.[1255] The case relates to music works and live performances that were made accessible unlawfully via *YouTube* in 2008. The rightsowner asked *Google* and *YouTube* to remove the files and refrain from publishing any works of its licensee in the future. Months later, works of the artist were again accessible via *YouTube*, which led to the start of proceedings. The case escalated through the German court instances right up to the highest national level. The BGH stayed the case and asked the CJEU whether the defendant, *YouTube*, on whose sys-

---

1252 Susy Frankel and others (eds), 'After Twenty Years: Revisiting Copyright Liability of Online Intermediaries', *The evolution and equilibrium of copyright in the digital age* (Cambridge University Press 2014) 39–45. Gillespie, 'Platforms Are Not Intermediaries' (n 175) 206; Suzor (n 1223) 19–25.

1253 Rosati, 'Facebook Found Liable for Hosting Links to Unlicensed Content' (n 624).

1254 *Mediaset v Dailymotion* (n 623); Akshat Agrawal, 'THE COPYKAT' (*The 1709 Blog*, 30 July 2019) <https://the1709blog.blogspot.com/2019/07/the-copykat_30.html> accessed 29 May 2020.

1255 *Request for a preliminary ruling from the Bundesgerichtshof (Germany) lodged on 6 November 2018 — LF v Google LLC, YouTube Inc., YouTube LLC, Google Germany GmbH (Case C-682/18)* (n 632).

tems copyright protected works were made publicly accessible by users, engaged in an act of communication according to Article 3 of the Infosoc Directive. The *BGH* ties the liability question to VSPs that fulfil a number of criteria that essentially read like definitions of contemporary Web 2.0 platforms: the platform operator earns ad revenue; the upload process is automated and not subject to *ex ante* controls; the VSP receives a worldwide, non-exclusive and royalty-free licence for the uploaded videos; the operator indicates in its terms and conditions that infringing content may not be uploaded; rightsholders are provided with technical tools to block infringing content; for registered users search results are categorised and ranked and certain content is recommended based on past viewing behaviour; after being made aware the VSP removes notified infringing content expeditiously.[1256]

In essence, these questions want to establish whether the characteristics of the new UGC platforms imply a direct involvement in the economic right of communication the public. This direct involvement would then imply the unavailability of the ECD protections. The *BGH* itself is of the opinion that *YouTube* did not have the necessary active knowledge of the availability of the infringing materials.[1257] This is line with German jurisprudence on the role of VSPs and social networks in copyright cases so far, which is by some seen as problematic.[1258] However, in view of the CJEU's broadening interpretation of communication to the public in the hyperlinking cases, especially in *Pirate Bay* case, the *BGH* is unsure whether its view on the liability of the VSP would be in conflict with the lines established by the CJEU. As a side note, it should be pointed out that a Berlin court has recently found the *Amazon* marketplace directly infringing the copyright of product images. The marketplace had assigned product pictures from a perfume brand for which the exclusive license had been given to just one seller, to another seller's offers. This decision by *Amazon* conferred on it the role of a direct infringer, regardless of whether

1256 *Opinion of Advocate General Saugmandsgaard Øe, Frank Peterson v Google LLC, YouTube LLC, YouTube Inc, Google Germany GmbH and Elsevier Inc v Cyando AG, Joined Cases C-682/18 and C-683/18* [2020] EU:C:2020:586 (CJEU) [38].

1257 *Haftung von YouTube für Urheberrechtsverletzungen* [2018] BGH I ZR 140/15, GRUR 2018, 1132 [34].

1258 Matthias Leistner, 'Copyright Law on the Internet in Need of Reform: Hyperlinks, Online Platforms and Aggregators' [2017] Journal of Intellectual Property Law & Practice jpw190, 4–5.

the picture allocation mechanism was automated or not, or whether the pictures were just stored on behalf of a third party.[1259]

With regards to the *BGH's YouTube* referral it should also be noted that, in contrast to the judgement in *The Pirate Bay*, the wilful blindness or permissive attitude towards infringement is not part of the argument.[1260] As will be shown below, *YouTube*, especially, has been spearheading the development of infringement detection software. In its second referred question the BGH asks, whether, if *YouTube* was not engaged in an act of communication, it could still avail itself of the protections of the ECD's Article 14. It seeks more authoritative guidance of the active or passive role of Web 2.0 VSPs. However, CJEU jurisprudence has shown that this assessment is likely to be handed back to the national court.[1261] It should be kept in mind that this reference happened in parallel to the draft and eventual adoption of the DSMD, which created a *fait accompli* of direct liability for content sharing providers for unauthorised uploads by users.[1262] At the final stage of writing this work, the AG published his Opinion on this case on 16 July 2020.[1263] Without going into further detail, AG *Saugmandsgaard Øe* refused to see the activities of *YouTube*, and *Cyando*, the defendant in the second, joined case, as causing primary liability for interference with the right of communication to the public. *YouTube* and *Cyando's* activities consisted of providing mere physical facilities.[1264] The Opinion seems to be critical of the case law developed by the CJEU in *GS Media, Filmspeler* and *The Pirate*

1259 *Wiederholungsgefahr, 16 O 103/14* (n 588) para 88. See also Chapter 3

1260 Jurriaan JH van Mil, 'German Federal Court of Justice Asks CJEU If YouTube Is Directly Liable for User-Uploaded Content' (2019) 14 Journal of Intellectual Property Law & Practice 355.

1261 Ansgar Ohly, 'EuGH-Vorlage Zur Haftung Einer Internetvideoplattform Für Urheberrechtsverletzungen - YouTube - Anmerkung von Ansgar Ohly' [2018] GRUR beck-online 1132, 1140.

1262 DSM Directive 2019/790 Article 17 (1).

1263 *Opinion of Advocate General Saugmandsgaard Øe, Frank Peterson v Google LLC, YouTube LLC, YouTube Inc., Google Germany GmbH and Elsevier Inc. v Cyando AG, Joined Cases C-682/18 and C-683/18* (n 1255).

1264 ibid 80–88.

Bay.[1265] The AG also rejected a retroactive application of the DSMD to the cases, which would have led to a different outcome.[1266]

The CJEU jurisprudence may have caused uncertainty over the future availability of secondary liability provisions to online UGC platforms and social networks in copyright cases in other EU countries. A 2018 study on global online piracy by *Quintais* indicated that at least for the Netherlands, Poland and Sweden the CJEU rulings may have put into questions previously upheld protections for VSPs and social networks against primary liability for copyright breaches[1267] In Spain, a new law of 2014 introduced new indirect liabilities for copyright infringing acts on online platforms, which may spell out more far reaching liabilities akin to primary infringement.[1268]

To summarise, the interpretations of the availability of the intermediary liability protections in copyright cases has been characteristic of the disparate approaches of EU Member States towards the ECD. National courts showed the same disunity when it came to assessing the role of interactive Web 2.0. hosts in the act of communication to the public. By bypassing the application of the ECD in favour of the Infosoc Directive, the path of secondary liability has been consistently narrowed down for P2P services. Meanwhile, the CJEU has so far provided little clarity with regards to UGC, social media platforms and search engines.

IV. Industry developments: enforcement by private actors

With litigation by copyright owners becoming a constant threat, especially content sharing platforms like *YouTube* became pioneers in developing systems that helped them proactively identify infringing content. Content identification and removal can happen at two stages, during upload by the users, and retroactively, by screening existing content on the site. *Google*

1265 Eleonora Rosati, 'The AG Opinion in YouTube/Cyando: A Regressive Interpretation of the Right of Communication to the Public' (*The IPKat*, 27 July 2020) <https://ipkitten.blogspot.com/2020/07/the-ag-opinion-in-youtubecyando.html> accessed 14 October 2020.

1266 *Opinion of Advocate General Saugmandsgaard Øe, Frank Peterson v Google LLC, YouTube LLC, YouTube Inc., Google Germany GmbH and Elsevier Inc. v Cyando AG, Joined Cases C-682/18 and C-683/18* (n 1255) paras 247–250.

1267 Quintais, 'Global Online Piracy Study Legal Background Report' (n 1191) 131, 144, 183.

1268 ibid 49–50, 158.

was the first company that started to develop its own content recognition software. Before discussing *Content ID* and other systems in more detail a short overview over the content identification technologies currently in use on platforms to detect copyright violations will be given. These technologies and systems are, however, not restricted to the detection of copyright infringements. The below discussion will therefore also be exemplary for the general state of play on the use of recognition technologies for the variety of unlawful content discussed throughout this chapter.

a. Content recognition and identification technologies

Fingerprinting

Digital fingerprinting means that a file provided by a rightsowner will be analysed for some defining and unique characteristics using a specific algorithm. The unique characteristics identified by the algorithm may relate to melody lines, frequency or image patterns. The defining features will then be coded into a digital fingerprint which will be deposited in a reference database. For any newly uploaded content files, a digital fingerprint will be created using the same algorithm.[1269] The new fingerprint will then be compared against matches in the reference database. At the same time, existing content on the site may also be screened for matches. Digital fingerprinting, which is at times also referred to as perceptual hashing,[1270] is today the most commonly used technology for copyright motivated content recognition on platforms. It is perceived to be more robust and lighter in its use than other technologies, such as hashing or watermarking.[1271] However, the act of comparison is not perfect. Like any content recognition sys-

1269 'MISSION REPORT: Towards More Effectiveness of Copyright Law on Online Content Sharing Platforms : Overview of Content Recognition Tools and Possible Ways Forward' (Conseil Supérieur De La Propriété Littéraire Et Artistique, Centre National Du Cinéma Et De L'image Animée, Haute Autorité Pour La Diffusion Des Œuvres Et La Protection Des Droits Sur Internet 2020) 12–14 <https://perma.cc/4L8X-PBQH> accessed 2 June 2020.

1270 Alper Koz and RL Lagendijk, 'Distributed Content Based Video Identification in Peer-to-Peer Networks: Requirements and Solutions' (2017) 19 IEEE Transactions on Multimedia 475, 475–476. Gorwa, Binns and Katzenbach (n 1066) 4, 7.

1271 'MISSION REPORT: Towards More Effectiveness of Copyright Law on Online Content Sharing Platforms : Overview of Content Recognition Tools and Possible Ways Forward' (n 1268) 14.

tem, digital fingerprinting has had difficulties in context sensitive scenarios, where content is subject to exceptions offered by copyright law, such as criticism or parody. In addition, it may be prone to produce errors where content is altered. Its use is further restricted by the fact that a specific fingerprinting method (relying on an algorithm that targets specific content characteristics) will only operate on the particular media to which it has been tailored.[1272]

Several content identification solutions that rely on fingerprinting have been emerging over the last twenty years. Some are proprietary systems developed or bought up by UGC and social media platforms, such as *Google's Content ID*, *Facebook's Rights Manager* tool or *Apple's Shazam*. Prominent free-standing solutions include *Gracenote* in the area of music and audio recognition, and *Audible Magic, Signature (by the French National Audiovisual Institute (INA))* or *Vobile* in the area of video and image recognition. As discussed in the section on terrorist content, *Microsoft's PhotoDNA* image and video recognition fingerprinting, or perceptual hashing software, has been mainly deployed to detect child pornographic and terrorist content.[1273] Latest versions of fingerprinting technology also enable the detection of live streaming content.

Hashing

Hashing technology assigns a unique, compressed alphanumerical code to each content file. This technology emerged in the 1950s and has since been available open source.[1274] Contrary to fingerprinting, the algorithm does not analyse features or traits but processes the computational value in its entirety, using cryptography. The result is a unique reference that can only

1272 Engstrom and Feamster (n 741) 14–15.

1273 'How PhotoDNA for Video Is Being Used to Fight Online Child Exploitation | Microsoft On The Issues' (*On the Issues*, 12 September 2018) <https://news.microsoft.com/on-the-issues/2018/09/12/how-photodna-for-video-is-being-used-to-fight-online-child-exploitation/> accessed 3 June 2020.

1274 'MISSION REPORT: Towards More Effectiveness of Copyright Law on Online Content Sharing Platforms : Overview of Content Recognition Tools and Possible Ways Forward' (n 1268) 26; Hallam Stevens, 'Hans Peter Luhn and the Birth of the Hashing Algorithm - IEEE Spectrum' (*IEEE Spectrum: Technology, Engineering, and Science News*, 30 January 2018) <https://spectrum.ieee.org/tech-history/silicon-revolution/hans-peter-luhn-and-the-birth-of-the-hashing-algorithm> accessed 25 August 2020.

be matched by exactly the same file.[1275] The need for such systems arose during the 2000s when, thanks to the Web 2.0 architecture, file storage started to migrate from individual copies for each user towards distributed storage. The technology has also been used for content identification on P2P networks, although it is increasingly replaced by more adaptable fingerprinting technology.[1276] Platforms and cloud operators increasingly store several copies of a piece of content, by replicating it throughout their architecture. This is done in order to scale access and downloading for a growing number of geographically distributed users.[1277] Hash-matching is useful to enforce stay-down systems that aim to suppress the re-emergence of notified content, be it through re-uploads from outside a platform's ecosystem or by reactivation through (new) links from within its distributed architecture. However, the hash technology cannot deal with variations, however slight they may be. Today it is used by some UGC platforms, like *Dailymotion* and *YouTube*, for stay-down systems following a notice-and-takedown request and in order to supplement existing fingerprinting technology.[1278]

Watermarking

In watermarking, a piece of content is enriched with a digital mark or stamp that will help prevent or track its (unauthorised) use or replication. Different kinds of digital watermarks exist; they may be visible or hidden, embedded in the pixel structure of the file or added as encrypted metainformation that may, for example, identify the creator.[1279] Watermarking is used for a variety of purposes. In the area of copyright protection, it can be used to detect and measure illegal distribution of content. Apart from that,

1275 Engstrom and Feamster (n 741) 12–13.

1276 Koz and Lagendijk (n 1269) 475.

1277 Urban, Karaganis and Schofield (n 661) 56–57.

1278 'MISSION REPORT: Towards More Effectiveness of Copyright Law on Online Content Sharing Platforms : Overview of Content Recognition Tools and Possible Ways Forward' (n 1268) 26. 'Copyright Protection On Digital Platforms: Existing Tools, Good Practice And Limitations - Report By The Research Mission On Recognition Tools For Copyright-Protected Content On Digital Platforms' (n 734) 17.

1279 Ashish M Kothari, Vedvyas Dwivedi and Rohit M Thanki, *Watermarking Techniques for Copyright Protection of Videos* (Springer Science + Business Media 2018) 4–9.

it is also used to audit the transmission of broadcast content, facilitate document retrieval and for authentication, access and change-tracking of documents.[1280] With regards to IP rights management, watermarking has traditionally been applied by the content creators or rightsowners to ensure that protected content is not replicated, shared or modified without authorisation. In the film industry, the addition of individualised, copy-specific watermarks would allow the tracking of illegally distributed copies back to the original user, thus serving as a deterrent for unlawful distribution or copying. The technique is also used to protect, discover and trace pirated live streams. For example, session-based watermarks that are added by content owners or broadcasters to images or music transmitted during live events, or in a dynamic way during the live stream itself, will help a platform to automatically detect and trace live pirated streams.[1281] Meanwhile, forensic watermarking technology may help protect against screen grabbing from UGC and social media websites by showing visible watermarks to deter this activity or by injecting metadata that helps identify and track the originator.[1282] Online content sharing platforms use watermarking mainly in conjunction with other techniques. For example, fingerprint analysis during an image search enriched with watermark detection adds a second level of security should the former fail to identify a match. However, as a pure content recognition technology, watermarking is not frequently used outside the area of still image recognition.[1283]

Metadata analysis

Metadata is any data that accompanies or surrounds the content in question. The time an image or video was created, its location, version numbers, names of the creator, performers or artists, the file type, file

1280 ibid., Sinha Roy S, Basu A and Chattopadhyay A, Intelligent Copyright Protection for Images, *Intelligent Copyright Protection for Images* (CRC Press 2019) 1–2.

1281 'MISSION REPORT: Towards More Effectiveness of Copyright Law on Online Content Sharing Platforms : Overview of Content Recognition Tools and Possible Ways Forward' (n 1268) 28–29. Cleeng, Live Streaming Piracy: Are We Winning This Epic Battle? (2017) 14. <https://cleeng.com/resources> accessed 30 June 2020

1282 Cleeng (n 1280) 15.

1283 'MISSION REPORT: Towards More Effectiveness of Copyright Law on Online Content Sharing Platforms : Overview of Content Recognition Tools and Possible Ways Forward' (n 1268) 143.

name, its format, the sample rate etc. are all part of metadata. This data is collected by platforms when content is uploaded to their sites. Usually, certain metadata is required during content upload while other may be optional. Content platforms will require bulk uploaders to include metadata in a structured way in a CSV or XML format during the upload process. The metadata can be normally stored and arranged in various ways.[1284] It would eventually be integrated into the platform's backend data warehouse systems which the company relies on when performing data and business analytics and reporting. Initially, the metadata helps the platform to categorise and structure content. As part of the content or product catalogue, it may also be displayed online. The importance of the catalogue metadata will also be touched upon in the context of due diligence of e-commerce marketplaces in the area of trademark protection and product safety.

For rightsowners, metadata is useful for conducting manual or script-based, automated searches on the database of an online platform or its internal search engine when searching for infringing content.[1285] Platforms may offer rightsholders special access to search their databases by metadata. The results of these searches usually inform NTD request. This technique is ideal when large reams of data need to be analysed quickly, i.e. without the need to compare or analyse the content files themselves. On the downside, this method is prone to inaccuracy. Trivial problems, such as misspellings, shared names, or lacking information may produces false positives or false negatives.[1286] If rightsholders include metadata search results unchecked in notice requests it may result in erroneous takedowns.

1284 Carlos Pacheco, 'YouTube Content ID Handbook - Google' (14 March 2013) 18 <https://www.slideshare.net/carlospacheco74/you-tube-content-id-handbook?from_action=save> accessed 16 April 2021.

1285 This technique was, for example, used by a market surveillance authority in the area of product safety, discussed as part of the interviews in Chapter 5. They had access to the API of the search engine of a major e-commerce marketplace and conducted regular searches for certain illegal products. See also: Engstrom and Feamster (n 741) 11–12.

1286 Bryan Lee, Margarete Arno and Daniel Salisbury, 'Searching for Illicit Dual Use Items in Online Marketplaces: A Semi-Automated Approach' (James Martin Center for Nonproliferation Studies, Middlebury Institute of International Studies 2017) 27 7–8. Although this study relates to a different content area, with broader search criteria, it serves as a useful example to demonstrate the high potential error rate when trying to search by metadata on online platforms.

Nevertheless, metadata analysis is in standard use across a variety of platforms, across various content formats.

Predictive analysis

Predictive analysis has already been mentioned in the sections on hate speech and terrorist content. Predictive systems rely on highly automated, sophisticated user and content data analysis that increasingly employ artificial intelligence and machine learning in order pre-empt and prevent unlawful content. This technique incorporates the use of metadata analysis and the data gained through the other analytic techniques described above, as well as the vast amount of data constantly collected by the platform from its users. Predictive analysis also increasingly informs automated detection systems used by online marketplaces to identify trademark infringements and may be key in any system that uses risk-based content analysis and online transaction monitoring, as will be shown in the next section. Due to their central position in the content and, increasingly, infrastructural ecosystem of the internet, the large UGC and social media platforms funnel an ever-growing stream of user, content and infrastructural data through their systems. However, in the area of copyright, predictive analysis has so far been used to a lesser extent compared to other areas. For example, while *YouTube* confirms that the vast majority of its copyright takedowns are automated and detected though its *Content ID* system, this is less due to predictive analysis or artificial intelligence. Their systems rely rather on matching decisions from a reference database, based on advanced fingerprinting technology.[1287]

Predictive analysis centres on the prevention of the first appearance of unlawful content, which is usually difficult if a rightsowner has not officially registered its intellectual property with the platform. Current predictive analysis in the area of copyright violations centres mainly on prioritising processes, such as dispute resolution, automated content analysis or manual decision making in content removal.[1288] For example, predictive analysis can help to focus rightsholder and platform engagement on the most critical cases by concentrating on certain high risk or "red flag" crite-

1287 Gorwa, Binns and Katzenbach (n 1066) 3.

1288 'MISSION REPORT: Towards More Effectiveness of Copyright Law on Online Content Sharing Platforms : Overview of Content Recognition Tools and Possible Ways Forward' (n 1268) 52–53.

ria, such as user accounts with sanction histories, certain type of contents (streams), or highly popular and monetised videos.[1289] This is in line with wider fraud prevention activities, which normally use risk-based approaches and also rely on predictive analysis in order to detect and prevent new fraud patterns.[1290]

b. Platform activities addressing copyright infringements – the rise of automated prevention

This more technical explanation has shown that despite their neutral and merely technical hosting functions, modern social media and UGC hosts have at their disposal a sophisticated and wide arsenal of technologies to identify and eventually remove infringing content.

There are several reasons for the rise of automated, preventive copyright enforcement on major platforms today. First, the spectacular growth of content sharing platforms was accompanied by the emergence of major litigations with large rightsholders, such as the *Viacom* challenge in the US, which lasted from 2007 to 2013,[1291] or the previously mentioned battle that pitted *GEMA* against *YouTube* in Germany for over 10 years. Automated enforcement was meant to pre-empt these risks by demonstrating the commitment of the platform to rightsowners concerns, giving them an operational system that allowed them to manage unauthorised content.[1292] Secondly, NTD requests have been growing in line with the amount of content shared through UGC websites. But the automated NTDs that most large platforms have put in place to address this growth rely mainly on metadata searches by rightsholders and are notorious for their inaccuracy and the opportunity they give for abuse.[1293] In addition, their largely unregulated nature in the EU provides for further legal uncertainty. Thirdly,

1289 Wang (n 504) 285.

1290 Tricia Phillips, Avivah Litan and Danny Luong, 'Begin Investing Now in Enhanced Machine-Learning Capabilities for Fraud Detection' [2017] Gartner 12; Markus Ruch and Stefan Sackmann, 'Customer-Specific Transaction Risk Management in E-Commerce', *Value creation in e-business management* (Springer 2009).

1291 *Viacom 2013* (n 688).

1292 Gorwa, Binns and Katzenbach (n 1066) 6–7; Leron Solomon, 'Fair Users or Content Abusers? The Automatic Flagging of Non-Infringing Videos by Content ID on YouTube' (2015) 44 Hofstra Law Review 33, 255.

1293 Urban, Karaganis and Schofield (n 661).

automated recognition systems are more scalable to the increasing number of content uploaded. In fact, they will improve as more material is uploaded and the software is trained to learn from mistakes and circumvention attempts. Fourthly, automated recognition tools are fully under the control of the platforms, which can adjust and improve them without outside interference. Notice systems, due to their mandatory nature, are more immediately subject to judicial and regulatory scrutiny. It should come as no surprise, that reporting on the scale and nature of these preventive systems is very limited. Most platforms' copyright transparency reports focus on the content removals that are based on NTD requests.[1294] Lastly, as large online platforms now comprise of extensive information infrastructures, they have access to vast amounts of data. This lends itself to the deployment, training and constant adjustment of content moderation systems. Monitoring and filtering algorithms for unlawful content are but one variety of these encompassing content moderation and information management systems.[1295]

Google's *Content ID* program, rolled out successively since 2007, has probably been one of the most commented and most visible efforts in this area. The system is at the heart of *Google's* copyright management tools. It comprises solutions aimed at more high-volume identifications and takedowns (*Content ID*, *Content Verification Program*), frequent removals (*Copyright Match Tool*) and occasional actions (notice-and-takedown webforms).[1296] Under the *Content ID* program, rightsowners will upload their works to *YouTube* as reference files against which a unique digital fingerprint will be created by *Google* and stored in their database.[1297] The company will screen newly uploaded and existing content for matches with the fingerprint stored in its reference database. If a match is assigned, the rightsowner will be notified and offered to claim the matched content. The uploader will also be informed in case they want to contest the decision made by the fingerprinting technology. By claiming the content, rightsowners have the option of blocking, monetising (gain revenue from ads placed against the content) or simply tracking the use of their content.[1298] The

1294 For example: 'Intellectual Property' <https://transparency.facebook.com/intellectual-property> accessed 8 May 2020.

1295 Gillespie, *Custodians of the Internet* (n 1010) 180–182; Klonick (n 1000) 1664; Sartor (n 236) 19–20.

1296 'Copyright Management Tools - YouTube Help' <https://support.google.com/youtube/topic/9282364?hl=en&ref_topic=2676339> accessed 2 June 2020.

1297 Gorwa, Binns and Katzenbach (n 1066) 6.

1298 Carlos Pacheco (n 1283).

Content Verification Program allows rightsowners to search manually for content that infringes their rights through a metadata search and then submit (bulk) notices. Meanwhile, the *Copyright Match Tool* allows uploaders to perform the functions of the *Content ID* system on an ad-hoc basis. They will need to choose individually the course of action if an allegedly infringing video is identified (do nothing & track, block or monetise).

As of today, the *Content ID* database has over 80 million reference files deposited by those rightsowners who cooperate with the world's largest VSP.[1299] Meanwhile, *YouTube* has continuously improved the performance of its tool, adapting its technology, amongst others, to the hosting of live streams, exclusive broadcasting or music channels. It also diversified its service offers to rightsowners. For example, rightsowners may create reference files without uploading the actual content to the platform. In conjunction with the monetisation offer, which has aptly been identified as a stroke of genius,[1300] the company could cash in on additional ad revenue where rightsholders choose to keep content online. In the end it is against *YouTube's* commercial interest to remove content, as it is the broad selection of videos that drives traffic and generates revenue. At the same time, *YouTube* managed to pacify and buy-in rightsowners by offering quick and effective, although possibly less lucrative IP exploitation, in exchange for the bitter pill of them relinquishing some of their rights to the platform. This difference in compensation between what rightsowners have gained through the monetisation and copyright enforcement programs from platforms, and what they allegedly could have earned through traditional licensing agreements, is also called the "value gap." The "value gap" has become a major argumentation tool of rightsowners to push regulators into imposing more far reaching responsibilities on platforms when it comes to policing infringing content online.[1301]

As of 2018, 98% of *YouTube's* copyright claims had been made via its *Content ID* system. In 2017, 98% of *Content ID* claims were fully automated, which means the works were automatically identified and the rightsholders' preferred actions automatically applied to the claimed content. In 90% of cases the rightsowners chose to monetise the content, therefore

1299 'How Google Fights Piracy' (Google 2018) 25 <http://services.google.com/fh/files/newsletters/how_google_fights_piracy.pdf> accessed 2 June 2020.

1300 Edwards, 'With Great Power Comes Great Responsibility?: The Rise of Platform Liability' (n 661) 275.

1301 European Commission, 'COM(2016) 288 Final' (n 223) 8–9.

leaving it on the site.[1302] Considering that to date over 800 million videos[1303] were claimed through *Content ID*, and this represents 98% of all copyright issues, then the company has still had to process over 16 million (i.e. 2%) non-automated requests in the form of notices since 2007. This also means that the statutory NTD procedures, anchored in the US American DMCA) and the European ECD, although sizeable, account for but a small part of copyright motivated content removals. Major rightsowners are now the trusted flaggers (called partners under the *Content ID* program) and notice providers whose requests are expedited. *YouTube* claims to have handed out $3 billion worth of revenue from content monetisation to rightsowners over the last 5 years under this program.[1304] The automated processes that have emerged out of the cooperation between (global) entertainment and media industry players and major platforms rule the world of copyright enforcement today. *YouTube* set the pace for similar efforts of other content sharing providers in this area.

The VSP *Dailymotion* employs automated content recognition since 2007. France-based *Dailymotion*, one of the few European UGC platforms with a global significance, has also been involved in a number of litigations concerning copyright infringements, chiefly in Europe. It has, however, relied mainly on external market solutions, using *Audible Magic* for music recognition and *INA-Signature*, developed by the French *National Audiovisual Institute (INA)*, for video recognition. It has recently also been developing its own content protection system that scans content uploaded by participating rightsowners against the database of its two external providers.[1305] In addition, it allows qualifying rightsowners ("Partners"), to monetise claimed content, similar to *YouTube*.

The *AudibleMagic* fingerprinting technology for audio and video is reportedly also used by *Facebook, Twitch, TikTok, Vimeo or Vkontake*, with notably *Facebook/Instagram* and *Vimeo* developing their own tools for rightsowners to manage (block or monetise) content for which they have claimed copyright.[1306]

1302 'How Google Fights Piracy' (n 1298) 24–25.

1303 'Press - YouTube' (n 668).

1304 'How Google Fights Piracy' (n 1298) 25.

1305 'Protect Your Copyright with Fingerprints' (*Dailymotion Help Center*) <http://faq.dailymotion.com/hc/en-us/articles/203921173> accessed 4 June 2020.

1306 'MISSION REPORT: Towards More Effectiveness of Copyright Law on Online Content Sharing Platforms : Overview of Content Recognition Tools and Possible Ways Forward' (n 1268) 30-31,; Urban, Karaganis and Schofield (n 661)

Music sharing platform *Soundcloud* has been using *Audible Magic's* sound recognition services, but developed its own solution as of 2012. Again, uploaded content will be screened against a fingerprint database during upload and at a number of intervals thereafter.[1307]

For other larger players, such as *LinkedIn*, *Twitter* or *Snapchat* it is not known whether they use fingerprinting recognition tools in the fight against copyright infringements.[1308] Meanwhile, the market for content recognition technologies and services has seen a constant growth and diversification in providers and service offers.[1309] This is not only owed to platform demand but also due to increasing demand from rightsholders to protect their IP assets on the internet.

Little is, however, known of the practices of smaller content sharing platforms in the market. A 2016 study conducted in the US has shown that smaller platforms that rarely receive copyright claims would run manual NTD processes initiated by rightsowners through webforms. Medium-sized players were gradually moving towards automated webforms that allow for bulk notice submissions. They would eventually feel pressurised by rightsholders to move into automated recognition systems that allow for privileged access by larger content owners.[1310] But these systems require substantial investment and architectural choices that go beyond just integrating an API for rightsowners. *Google* spent reportedly up to USD100 million in developing and maintaining its *Content ID* solution.[1311] *SoundCloud*, a much smaller player, invested between EUR5 – 10 million for developing (just) its sound recognition tools. It employs 12 full time staff

---

59; 'Copyright Management | Facebook' <https://rightsmanager.fb.com/> accessed 4 June 2020; Gorwa, Binns and Katzenbach (n 1066) 6.

1307 European Commission, 'Commission Staff Working Document - Impact Assessment - Assessment on the Modernisation of the EU Copyright Rules Accompanying the Documents Proposal for a Directive of the European Parliament and of the Council on Copyright in the Digital Single Market and Proposal for a Regulation of the European Parliament and of the Council Laying down Rules on the Exercise of Copyright and Related Rights Applicable to Certain Online Transmissions of Broadcasting Organisations and Retransmissions of Television and Radio Programmes - SWD(2016) 301 Final - Part 3/3' (European Commission 2016) 166.

1308 'MISSION REPORT: Towards More Effectiveness of Copyright Law on Online Content Sharing Platforms : Overview of Content Recognition Tools and Possible Ways Forward' (n 1268) 32.

1309 ibid 16–19; European Commission, 'Impact Assessment 3/3 - DSM Directive' (n 1306) 167–172. for an overview of current service providers.

1310 Urban, Karaganis and Schofield (n 661) 71–73.

1311 'How Google Fights Piracy' (n 1298) 27.

consisting of engineers, product managers and NTD agents to run the system.[1312]

Overall, the landscape of copyright enforcement on platforms is still uneven. However, there is a marked trend of large UGC and social media platforms to move towards automated enforcement through the deployment of content recognition.[1313] The pressure of rightsholders in this game is not negligible. The trend indicates a move clearly beyond the obligations that are currently required by the intermediary liability provisions in the ECD (and the DMCA). In fact, it has been argued that

> *"in a technical sense the law still governs, but over the last decade sites like YouTube have begun using software (named "Content ID") to intelligently and proactively take down copyrighted works. This understanding, implemented in code, was undertaken in the shadow of the law, but it is not compelled by it, and the decisions made by the software are now more important than the law."*[1314]

Meanwhile, smaller players are less likely to be able to support nor necessarily require these automated tools.

While content recognition technologies may become increasingly robust and accurate,[1315] there remain problems.[1316] First, while the technology maybe good at identifying matches, it may be less so when deciding on infringements.[1317] A video or song that is matched to a fingerprint on a

1312 European Commission, 'Impact Assessment 3/3 - DSM Directive' (n 1306) 166.

1313 'MISSION REPORT: Towards More Effectiveness of Copyright Law on Online Content Sharing Platforms : Overview of Content Recognition Tools and Possible Ways Forward' (n 1268) 3; Urban, Karaganis and Schofield (n 661) 71–73.

1314 Tim Wu, 'Will Artificial Intelligence Eat the Law? The Rise of Hybrid Social-Ordering Systems' (2019) 119 Columbia Law Review 2001, 2007.

1315 'MISSION REPORT: Towards More Effectiveness of Copyright Law on Online Content Sharing Platforms : Overview of Content Recognition Tools and Possible Ways Forward' (n 1268) 3.

1316 European Commission, 'Commission Staff Working Document - Impact Assessment - Assessment on the Modernisation of the EU Copyright Rules Accompanying the Documents Proposal for a Directive of the European Parliament and of the Council on Copyright in the Digital Single Market and Proposal for a Regulation of the European Parliament and of the Council Laying down Rules on the Exercise of Copyright and Related Rights Applicable to Certain Online Transmissions of Broadcasting Organisations and Retransmissions of Television and Radio Programmes - SWD(2016) 301 Final - Part 1/3' (European Commission 2016) 140–141.

1317 Gorwa, Binns and Katzenbach (n 1066) 8. Engstrom and Feamster (n 741) 18–19.

platform's internal database may still legitimately be shared due to copyright exceptions. It may be a parody, scientific citation, criticism or part of a news report. Automated systems are (still) notoriously imperfect in detecting these often context-sensitive scenarios. Artificial intelligence and predictive analysis, although used for hate speech and terrorist content, and heavily researched, are not yet developed enough to make these decisions with a high level of accuracy in the area of copyright.[1318] Failure to respect these exceptions has been widely commented on and is a major drawback of these systems as of today. It may negatively affect cultural diversity, user rights and freedom of expression.[1319] Secondly, the decision-making procedures and appeals processes are unclear and deeply hidden within the organisational structure of these platforms. Transparency on NTD procedures is already a challenge, but detailed transparency reporting in the area of automated content decision-making is even harder to come by. This is not surprising, since the automated tools deployed by platforms rely on agreements with rightsowners and their associations, which may have an interest to conceal their engagement with platforms from public scrutiny. If, for example, automated tools pick up *en masse* on uploads subject to legitimate copyright exceptions, then Google notifies the rightsowner and it is eventually up to them to 'choose' whether they respect or violate these exceptions. At the same time, users often remain unaware of their rights to oppose takedowns or simply fear litigation by major rightsholders.[1320] Thirdly, this means that the original copyright wars between rightsholders changed into an "accommodation between dominant incumbents."[1321] This, however, may create entry barriers on both sides: smaller platforms that may not be able to attract content from larger rightsholders due the inability to guarantee the same level of automated rights protection; smaller, individual artists may not get access to the same protection

---

1318 'MISSION REPORT: Towards More Effectiveness of Copyright Law on Online Content Sharing Platforms : Overview of Content Recognition Tools and Possible Ways Forward' (n 1268) 48–58.

1319 See for example: Solomon (n 1291) 257–259; Sabine Jacques and others, 'The Impact on Cultural Diversity of Automated Anti-Piracy Systems as Copyright Enforcement Mechanisms: An Empirical Study of YouTube's Content ID Digital Fingerprinting Technology' 287–288 <http://rgdoi.net/10.13140/RG.2.2.14443.54560> accessed 5 June 2020; Erickson and Kretschmer (n 1134).

1320 Solomon (n 1291) 253.

1321 Urban, Karaganis and Schofield (n 661) 125.

measures as large rightsowners,[1322] while UGC uploaded by individuals may face a higher risk of being flagged for infringements.[1323]

Nevertheless, automated copyright enforcement, for all of its problems, is not only going to stay, but to grow further in importance. Courts have already been pricing this into their judgements when ruling on the obligations of intermediaries. As an example, German judges in the *GEMA v YouTube* court saga have successively obliged *YouTube* to use its *Content ID* software, supplemented by word filters, where needed, to prevent the re-upload of previously notified infringing content.[1324] In a previously mentioned recent Italian case against *Dailymotion*, a Rome court took the existence of filtering software on the part of the platform as a justification for imposing an obligation to use that technology for preventive monitoring.[1325] In that context, the constant advance in automated filtering and content identification technologies implicitly raises the minimum knowledge standards that can be applied to evaluate the liabilities of intermediaries. This may eventually bring it in conflict with the ECD's Article 15, which imposes a ceiling by prohibiting general monitoring obligations, which in itself is an unclear concept and has been differently interpreted.[1326] For example, some have argued that online platforms have for some time been able to monitor and surveil virtually everything a user does on their platforms and the internet in general.[1327] The picture is further complicated in copyright by the fact that primary liability has been brought into play for intermediaries, which will only spur the use of automated content filtering.

V. EU legal initiatives – the Digital Single Market Directive (DSMD)

The European Commission had identified copyright early on as an area where intermediary liability provisions led to differing legal interpreta-

1322 ibid 139.
1323 Solomon (n 1291) 238–239.
1324 *GEMA v YouTube* (n 264) 407. This line was confirmed in various successive cases opposing the two parties in Germany, See also: Angelopoulos (n 30) 158.
1325 *Mediaset v Dailymotion* (n 623); Gentile (n 623).
1326 Angelopoulos (n 30) 278–279.
1327 For example: Friedmann (n 16); Zuboff (n 5).

tions, and disparate and ineffective enforcement.[1328] Although it did not see a need to amend the horizontal framework of the intermediary liability exemptions under its 2015 Digital Single Market policy, it still identified a number of content areas that required special attention. As part of its new "sectoral, problem driven approach to regulation" it announced a copyright package aimed at a "fairer allocation of value generated by the online distribution of copyright-protected content by online platforms."[1329]

This resulted in the DSMD,[1330] which came into force in June 2019, following a lengthy, passionate and highly publicised negotiation process. Member States will need to transpose it into national law by 7 June 2021. The debate during the drafting phase of the DSMD exposed the substantial lobbying efforts of the various stakeholder groups - the entertainment and music industry, online intermediaries and civil society - in the law-making process. This is a vivid expression of the immense commercial and public interest that digital copyright musters in today's information society. The original draft of the Commission, first presented in 2016, was changed several times in intense discussions between the Commission, the Council and the European Parliament.[1331]

The finally adopted version, still highly criticised,[1332] attempts to solve the intermediary liability problem of online OCSSPs by making them directly liable for copyright relevant acts of communication to the public or

1328 Van Eecke and Truyens (n 316) 20–26. European Commission, 'SEC(2011) 1641 Final' (n 11) 40; European Commission, 'Summary Response - IPR Enforcement' (n 173) 45–48.

1329 European Commission, 'COM(2016) 288 Final' (n 223) 9. Apart from copyright The European Commission also announced to review the AVMSD in the area of hate speech and child protection, the need for formal NTD procedures and to provide guidance on voluntary measures of platforms.

1330 DSM Directive 2019/790.

1331 For summary overview of the different positions of the EU negotiating parties and their evolvement see: Cole, Etteldorf and Ullrich (2020) (n 17) 140–143. Also: João Quintais, 'The New Copyright in the Digital Single Market Directive: A Critical Look' [2020] European Intellectual Property Review 2–3. CREATe, 'EU Copyright Reform: Timeline of Developments & Comparison Table' (*UK Copyright and Creative Economy Centre University of Glasgow*) <https://www.create.ac.uk/policy-responses/eu-copyright-reform/#table> accessed 5 October 2020.

1332 For example by: Gerald Spindler, 'The Liability System of Art. 17 DSMD and National Implementation – Contravening Prohibition of General Monitoring Duties?' (2020) 10 JIPITEC <https://www.jipitec.eu/issues/jipitec-10-3-2019/5041>; Quintais, 'The New Copyright in the Digital Single Market Directive' (n 1330).

of making available to the public.[1333] It leaves, however, open the still existing ambiguities regarding search engines, and to some extent, P2P platforms. To dispel any doubt over the primary liability imposed on OCSSPs, the DSMD clarifies that these services would lose the intermediary immunities offered in Art. 14 (1) ECD. This appears to be a continuation of the CJEU's jurisprudence in hyperlinking, which introduced the view that intermediaries could be directly liable for copyright relevant acts.[1334] As for the type of providers concerned, OCSSPs are defined as ISSPs which store and give public access to a large amount of copyright-protected works uploaded by its users.[1335] In addition, these services organise and promote the protected content for profit-making purposes. Promotion in this sense would not refer to the promotion of the content in question, but rather the placing of advertisements next to protected content.[1336] This wording implicitly acknowledges the active role of OCSSPs, which makes their removal from the ECD's Article 14 (1) immunities logic. The bulk of UGC platforms, *YouTube*, *Dailymotion, Vimeo* and *Facebook*, which have been in the line of fire of rightsholders, would find themselves outside the intermediary liability privileges of the ECD. This follows the argument that, as primary infringers that make works publicly available, they have clearly departed from being passive and merely technical intermediaries. The DSMD is therefore different from the AVMSD and the TERREG proposal, which maintain the application of the intermediary liability exemption conditions of the ECD and therefore the assumption of neutral intermediaries. Instead, these latter provisions attempt to establish enhanced responsibilities within the framework of the ECD.

The analysis could stop here, because under the DSMD, OCSSPs are not part of the current intermediary liability framework any longer, and potential primary infringers. But this view would stop short of the fact that even though active, they remain intermediaries in that they share content originally uploaded by a third party, the originator, and the user who downloads and accesses it. As this work will attempt to explore an alternative intermediary liability framework which does away with the active/passive distinction of the current ECD, the DSMD remains of interest. The DSMD

1333 DSM Directive 2019/790 Article 17 (1).

1334 Rosati, 'The CJEU Pirate Bay Judgment and Its Impact on the Liability of Online Platforms' (n 1221) 15. Nordemann (n 1160) 26.

1335 DSM Directive 2019/790 Article 2 (6).

1336 Spindler, 'The Liability System of Art. 17 DSMD and National Implementation – Contravening Prohibition of General Monitoring Duties?' (n 1331) 346.

also acknowledges this special intermediary (liability) situation[1337] by imposing specific obligations that would protect OCSSPs from being liable as primary infringers. This has led to controversy over the status of Article 17 DSMD, notably whether this Article is *lex specialis* to both the ECD and the Infosoc Directive or not.[1338]

OCSSPs have two alternative obligations. First, the platforms concerned will need to get the authorisation from rightsholders for sharing copyright-protected content. This could be done through the conclusion of licensing agreements.[1339] As stated above, the relations between incumbent OCSSPs and major content owners have been warming up over the last decade, with notably *YouTube* and *Facebook*[1340] signing major licensing deals in this area. The large OCSSPs are therefore in a markedly more comfortable position than smaller players. The DSMD may even entrench their dominant market position.[1341] Licensing agreements, especially where it concerns multi-territorial rights, can be lengthy and complicated to negotiate. It remains open, whether smaller platforms would have enough leverage to attract the interest of large rightsholders to step into such agreements. Even larger platforms may not be able to obtain authorisation for each and

1337 DSM Directive 2019/790 Recital 66.

1338 The view that Article 17 is *lex specialis* is held by: Martin Husovec and João Quintais, 'How to License Article 17? Exploring the Implementation Options for the New EU Rules on Content-Sharing Platforms' (Social Science Research Network 2019) SSRN Scholarly Paper ID 3463011 <https://papers.ssrn.com/abstract=3463011> accessed 1 September 2020. Nordemann & Waiblinger oppose this viewpoint: 'Art. 17 DSMCD: A Class of Its Own? How to Implement Art. 17 into the Existing National Copyright Acts, Including a Comment on the Recent German Discussion Draft - Part 2' (*Kluwer Copyright Blog*, 17 July 2020) <http://copyrightblog.kluweriplaw.com/2020/07/17/art-17-dsmcd-a-class-of-its-own-how-to-implement-art-17-into-the-existing-national-copyright-acts-including-a-comment-on-the-recent-german-discussion-draft-part-2/> accessed 5 October 2020.

1339 DSM Directive 2019/790 Article 17 (1).

1340 Chris Welch, 'Facebook Now Has Music Licensing Deals with All Three Major Labels' (*The Verge*, 9 March 2018) <https://www.theverge.com/2018/3/9/17100454/facebook-warner-music-deal-songs-user-videos-instagram> accessed 9 June 2020; Brad Spitz, 'France: YouTube, Universal and SACEM Enter into a New Agreement' (*Kluwer Copyright Blog*, 16 April 2013) <http://copyrightblog.kluweriplaw.com/2013/04/16/france-youtube-universal-and-sacem-enter-into-a-new-agreement/> accessed 9 June 2020.

1341 'Why Tech Giants Have Little to Lose (and Lots to Win) from New EU Copyright Law – Maurizio Borghi' (*Inforrm's Blog*, 19 September 2018) <https://inforrm.org/2018/09/20/why-tech-giants-have-little-to-lose-and-lots-to-win-from-new-eu-copyright-law-maurizio-borghi/> accessed 8 June 2020.

every piece of content considering the sheer volume of works on their systems. On the other side, smaller rightsowners, such as independent artists, labels or producers, may just not be a priority of large platforms for negotiating an agreement, although this could be a litmus test for assessing best effort of platforms to obtain such an authorisation.

This leads to the second option for avoiding liability. OCSSP are required to demonstrate that they have undertaken best efforts in: obtaining an authorisation from rightsowners; preventing the availability of unauthorised content by applying "high industry standards of professional diligence" after having received information on specific protected works by rightsowners; remove works expeditiously after receiving a notice from a rightsholder and ensure removed works are not uploaded again (stay-down obligation).[1342] The best efforts are to be assessed in view of the OCCSP's size, its particular business model, the type of works uploaded by users and the resources at its disposal in order to prevent unlicensed content.[1343] Although not mentioned explicitly, the passage requiring preventive efforts based on high professional diligence standards implies that platforms will likely need to use automated filtering systems, or upload filters, in order to prevent unauthorised content on their sites. As demonstrated, most large OCSSP now use these automated recognition systems. The DSMD's impact assessment and other public studies have been eager to demonstrate that the market for content recognition has diversified, with a variety of technology providers emerging over the recent years.[1344] This could be interpreted as furnishing a justification that, first, OCSSPs have the choice to acquire such technology as part of their best efforts, and, secondly, the technology constitutes a high industry standard of professional diligence. The fact that the Commission tries to establish best practices with regards to these standards through industry stakeholder fora by considering market developments in the technology only reinforces this view.[1345]

1342 DSM Directive 2019/790 Article 17 (4).

1343 ibid Article 17 (5).

1344 European Commission, 'Impact Assessment 1/3 - DSM Directive' (n 1315) 140–142; European Commission, 'Impact Assessment 3/3 - DSM Directive' (n 1306) 164–172 Annex 12A; 'MISSION REPORT: Towards More Effectiveness of Copyright Law on Online Content Sharing Platforms : Overview of Content Recognition Tools and Possible Ways Forward' (n 1268); 'Copyright Protection On Digital Platforms: Existing Tools, Good Practice And Limitations - Report By The Research Mission On Recognition Tools For Copyright-Protected Content On Digital Platforms' (n 734).

1345 DSM Directive 2019/790 Recital 71.

The DSMD introduces an exemption, by which start-up platforms will wholly or partly be exempted from these requirements.[1346] In addition, assessing best efforts in the context of the OCSSP's business model, the type of content hosted and the resources available, makes for a certain degree of flexibility that would allow smaller OCSSP to scale their efforts by e.g. using a risk-based approach: an OCSSP could identify the content categories or types of content that are at the highest risk of being used for copyright infringements and concentrate its efforts on these. The DSMD also enshrines respect for copyright exceptions into OCSSPs best efforts and obliges them to put in place effective complaints and redress mechanisms. Whether, however, the general monitoring prohibition, taken over from Article 15 ECD will provide additional protection is questionable, especially since that term remains undefined.[1347] Courts and experts may still discuss in years to come whether "best effort" content recognition results in general monitoring or not, while a more useful discussion would rather define criteria for a proportional use of such technology.

Article 17 DSMD essentially requires that OCSSPs act as diligent economic operators. Compared to the ECD, these are the kind of enhanced responsibilities that maybe justified considering the activities and functionalities of today's UGC and social media platform and their effect on copyright. However, the DSMD lacks a solid procedural and supervisory framework to ensure a proportionate and accountable implementation of the enhanced obligations imposed by Article 17. The determination of OCSSP's best efforts must be made according to transparent criteria, especially where it concerns the use of content recognition technology and respect of user rights. Facilitating discussions on best practices through stakeholder dialogues and issuing guidance notes are unlikely to be enough to achieve adequate respect of copyright exceptions, rights of redress and complaints as part of OCSSPs best efforts.[1348] Concerns over the respect of these rights during implementation and operation of Article 17 are therefore more than justified.[1349] These concerns also play a role in the ongoing judicial challenge of the DSMD brought by the Republic of Poland, which is cur-

1346 ibid Article 17 (6).
1347 ibid Article 17 (8).
1348 ibid Article 17 (7), recital 70.
1349 João Pedro Quintais and others, 'Safeguarding User Freedoms in Implementing Article 17 of the Copyright in the Digital Single Market Directive: Recommendations from European Academics' (2020) 10 JIPITEC.

rently pending before the CJEU.[1350] Poland seeks to annul Articles 17 (4) (b) and (c) of the DSMD, because it thinks that the best efforts required from OCSSPs that have failed to get an authorisation from rightsowners will inevitably lead to the use of upload filters. This would result in an undue interference with the rights to freedom of expression and to receive and impart information as guaranteed by Article 13 CFREU.

While the AVMSD tasks ERGA with overseeing and facilitating the implementation of proportionate and transparent proactive measures and provide technical expertise and advice on platforms' preventive obligations towards hate speech,[1351] such a co-regulatory setup is missing in the DSMD. As has been demonstrated previously, purely self-regulatory best practice sharing initiatives have so far created little momentum towards achieving transparent and equilibrated outcomes in respect of due process, especially for users. They are ill suited to shed light on both the mandated licensing practices between market incumbents and the largely opaque content filtering and takedown responsibilities.

VI. Summary and outlook

In copyright, the enforcement of intermediaries' liability framework evolved in the patchwork manner that is characteristic of the various national secondary liability (exemption) approaches, different sanction regimes under national copyright, ordinary law rules and, at times, supplementary sectoral legislation. None of the regimes that have emerged did manage to contain the widespread occurrence of copyright infringements that accompanied the rise of Web 2.0 intermediaries and user interactivity. Due to the particular nature of copyright, the activities of modern online platforms increasingly raised questions on substantive copyright aspects, such as the communication to the public. Many national courts, incensed by the CJEU, have concluded that primary liability is a justifiable verdict where it concerns P2P file sharing services, UGC sites and social media platforms that share large amounts of content. The situation is still less clear for search engines, due to their essential role in the working of the internet.

1350 *Action brought on 24 May 2019 — Republic of Poland v European Parliament and Council of the European Union, C-401/19* (CJEU). The judgement in this case is not expected before spring 2021.

1351 AVMSD 2018/1808 Article 30b, Recital 58.

The imposition of primary liability on OCSSPs through the recent DSMD means that the ECD will now cease to be applicable for an important group of online platforms in the future, at least where it concerns copyright. Direct liability will undoubtly provide a larger stick against platforms to prevent unlawfully shared content. The enhanced responsibilities formulated by the EU lawmaker may arguably be proportionate to the role these actors play in the exchange of protected content and in user interaction. Many of the large and dominating actors are already monitoring and filtering content systematically. In fact, most of their content takedowns happen according to proactive, automated systems. They have stepped into licensing agreements with major rightsowners or their licensing organisations. However, the way the new obligations are being formulated may reinforce relationships between incumbent rightsholders and dominant platforms, and eventually throttle competition, freedom of speech and variety of content. Meanwhile, the best efforts in preventing unauthorised content, which platforms need to demonstrate where they did not receive an authorisation, are fraught with potential pitfalls. They lack solid regulatory oversight and transparency requirements that would ensure respect of user rights and public interest copyright exceptions during the use of filtering technologies and notice-and-stay-down procedures.

As regards P2P sites, despite the clamp down on these intermediaries, there remain ample circumvention and avoidance techniques available for determined infringers. Here, the answer against unlawful activities in the area of copyright would probably lie more in the creation of viable, affordable and widely accessible legal offers as well as better global coordination.

The aggravating stance against intermediaries has even gripped more unlikely jurisdictions. The US Government recently published the results and recommendations of its multi-year study on the intermediary liability framework under the DMCA.[1352] These recommendations hint at a significant rethink of intermediary liability protections for copyright infringements. They confirm that the critical elements of the ECD outlined in this work are also a concern for the policymakers of the DMCA's section 512. The US Copyright office suggests a review of the eligibilities of the safe harbour defence for today's hosting providers, with a possibility to create specific passages for P2P systems and payment service providers. Other recommendations include legislation to make repeat infringer policies mandatory, provide legal clarifications of the actual knowledge and wilful blindness standards, impose higher penalties for abusive notices, clarify the

1352 'Section 512 of Title 17 - A Report of the Register of Copyrights' (n 409).

timeframes for expeditious removal and facilitate voluntary initiatives in infringement prevention by supporting the development of technical standards.[1353] It even states that the progress made in fingerprinting technology may make this technology ubiquitous and feasible for all online service providers in the future.[1354]

5. Trademarks

I. Trademarks, counterfeiting and e-commerce

The rise of online marketplaces on the commercial web has opened new opportunities for consumers to choose from an unprecedented variety of goods, at a global level, and often at competitive prices. It has also created new business opportunities for small and innovative businesses around the world, transformed supply chains and uprooted traditional retail markets. Like in any other area of the internet, this rise has also opened the door for unlawful and criminal activities. The sale of trademark infringing goods, be they counterfeits, unlawful imitations or grey goods, but also illegal or unsafe products, although an ancient phenomenon, has been facilitated by online marketplaces and the internet in general.[1355] Estimates show that already in 2003, the value of counterfeit goods traded online amounted to $25 billion.[1356] More recent data is hard to come by due to the evasive nature of this illicit activity. Evidence remains therefore largely anecdotal. The pharmaceutical company *Pfizer* reported that between 2015 and 2018

1353 ibid 2–7.

1354 ibid 178.

1355 Agreement On Trade-Related Aspects Of Intellectual Property Rights (TRIPS) 1994 Article 51, fn 14. Defines counterfeited goods as "*…any goods, including packaging, bearing without authorization a trademark which is identical to the trademark validly registered in respect of such goods, or which cannot be distinguished in its essential aspects from such a trademark…*" Counterfeit goods are also more colloquially referred to as fake goods. Grey goods are goods that although authorised for sale, are marketed through distribution channels for which the rightsholder has not provided an authorisation to the distributor. Grey or parallel imports refers to products for which the rightsowner has given no authorisation that they be imported into the jurisdiction.

1356 'The Economic Impact of Counterfeiting and Piracy OECD - Executive Summary' (OECD 2007). In: Peggy Chaudhry and Alan Zimmerman, *Protecting Your Intellectual Property Rights* (Springer New York 2013) 27.

it had identified over 10,000 accounts or users on *Facebook*, and 1,000 accounts on *Instagram* that sold counterfeits of its medicines.[1357]

The OECD has estimated the value of overall trade in counterfeit and pirated tangible goods at $250 billion in 2007, or 1.95% of worldwide trade.[1358] By 2016, this activity had grown to $509 billion, or 3.3% of global trade. For the EU, the value of counterfeit goods imports was estimated to have risen from EUR85 billion, or 5 % of total imports in 2013, to EUR121 billion (6.8% of total imports) in 2016.[1359] The social impact of these activities is manifold. Beyond the obvious economic loss to trademark owners and the dampening effect on innovation, this activity displaces legitimate employment, causes loss in public tax revenue and social security contributions, contributes to environmental pollution and may impact the health and safety of consumers.[1360]

Online marketplaces play an increasingly important role in the rise of counterfeit sales in general. They are even seen to be a key distribution channel.[1361] Fraudsters and innocent consumers alike use the characteristics of the internet, anonymity, flexibility and global reach for selling and

1357 OECD and European Union Intellectual Property Office, *Trade in Counterfeit Pharmaceutical Products* (OECD 2020) 48 <https://www.oecd-ilibrary.org/governance/trade-in-counterfeit-pharmaceutical-products_a7c7e054-en> accessed 12 June 2020.

1358 'Magnitude of Counterfeiting and Piracy of Tangible Products – November 2009 Update' (OECD 2009) 1 <https://www.oecd.org/sti/ind/magnitudeofcounterfeitingandpiracyoftangibleproductsnovember2009update.htm> accessed 12 June 2020.

1359 OECD and European Union Intellectual Property Office, *Trade in Counterfeit and Pirated Goods: Value, Scope and Trends* (OECD 2019) 11–14 <https://www.oecd-ilibrary.org/trade/trends-in-trade-in-counterfeit-and-pirated-goods_g2g9f533-en> accessed 12 June 2020. It should be noted that these results rely on customs seizure observations and do not include domestically produced and consumed counterfeit and pirated products; nor do they include pirated digital content on the Internet. The latter remains notoriously difficult to assess, although it can be assumed that a rising proportion of this trade is facilitated through online markets.

1360 'The Economic Impact of Counterfeiting and Piracy OECD - Executive Summary' (n 1355) 16–21; Frontier Economics (n 1133) 46–53. This report estimates that in 2013 between 2.0 and 2.6 million jobs and between $96 - 130 billion in tax revenue were lost due to counterfeiting worldwide. For the OECD region the loss in economic growth was valued between $30 - $54 billion in 2017.

1361 Europol and EU Intellectual Property Office, '2017 Situation Report on Counterfeiting and Piracy in the European Union' (2017) 53; Publications Office of the European Union, 'European Union Serious and Organised Crime Threat

buying counterfeit goods. The sheer market size and variety of offerings, the ability to deceive and attract customers with look-a-like sites and products, are additional reasons that have made online marketplaces a main target for counterfeiters.[1362] They are now joined by social media platforms, UGC sites and electronic messaging services that are either opening their own marketplaces or are being used to initiate transactions that are then conducted through other channels.[1363] Social media influencers are reported to unwittingly promote the sale of counterfeit items. The amount of active accounts identified as offering and selling counterfeits on sites such as *Instagram* is increasing constantly.[1364]

Counterfeiters have over the recent years infiltrated or bypassed traditional supply chains by using small consignments that enable shipments to customers directly from illicit warehouses or marketplaces in overseas locations. The proliferation of electronic payment services and electronic currencies, such as Bitcoin, has also helped this along. As more supply chain actors and intermediaries, from manufacturers, sellers and shippers to parcel delivery companies work digitally, the opportunities for fraud have moved to a new level.[1365] Although the Darknet is also being used for

---

Assessment : Crime in the Age of Technology.' (2017) Website 46 <https://publications.europa.eu/en/publication-detail/-/publication/a0c983b4-1db0-11e7-aeb3-01aa75ed71a1/language-en/format-PDF> accessed 17 August 2018. 'Roles and Responsibilities of Intermediaries: Fighting Counterfeiting and Piracy in the Supply Chain' (n 223) 48–50.

1362 Chaudhry and Zimmerman (n 1355) 28. Roudaut, Mickaël R., 'From Sweatshops to Organized Crime: The New Face of Counterfeiting' in Christophe Geiger (ed), *Criminal enforcement of intellectual property: a handbook of contemporary research* (Edward Elgar 2012) 86–88. Jay Greene, 'How Amazon's Quest for More, Cheaper Products Has Resulted in a Flea Market of Fakes' *Washington Post* (14 November 2019) <https://www.washingtonpost.com/technology/2019/11/14/how-amazons-quest-more-cheaper-products-has-resulted-flea-market-fakes/> accessed 19 June 2020.

1363 Union (n 1360) 22–23. Andrea Stroppa and others, 'Instagram and Counterfeiting in 2019: New Features, Old Problems' (Ghost Data 2019) <https://ghostdata.io/report/Instagram_Counterfeiting_GD.pdf> accessed 20 October 2020.

1364 'How Social Media Behavior Influences Counterfeit Purchases' (*INCOPRO*, 25 February 2020) <https://www.incoproip.com/how-social-media-behavior-influences-counterfeit-purchases/> accessed 30 June 2020. In: 'Combating Trafficking in Counterfeit and Pirated Goods - Report to the President of the United States' (US Department of Homeland Security 2020) 22–23 <https://www.dhs.gov/publication/combating-trafficking-counterfeit-and-pirated-goods> accessed 30 June 2020.

1365 Europol and EU Intellectual Property Office (n 1360) 53–54; EUIPO and Europol (n 1130) 37–39.

counterfeit sales, the legal or surface web remains the favoured channel as counterfeiters target the customer base of major consumer brands. Consumers, on the other hand, more often than not, are fully aware that they buy fake products. Research by the EU Intellectual Property Office (EUIPO) and the OECD has shown that almost 60% of consumers knowingly buy counterfeit products, a fact which doubtlessly helps sustain this activity. But the potential for deception is equally significant. Another study found that 39% of unwitting counterfeit purchases happen through online marketplaces, where it is more difficult for consumers to distinguish fakes from legitimate products.[1366] In any of these cases, the risk to people's health from buying counterfeits produced at substandard safety and quality is significant: unsafe electronic equipment, contaminated apparel, fake toys or jewellery containing dangerous substances, imitation car parts and counterfeit protective equipment are just some of the examples of products that can be found on online marketplaces and that can pose significant risks to consumers.

Meanwhile, the link between counterfeiting and organised crime, including the financing of terrorism, has become more and more publicised.[1367] In fact, online marketplaces are increasingly in the focus of law enforcement and regulators over the possibilities they open up to criminal activity and money laundering.[1368] Given the societal and economic impact, and the continued prevalence of this problem, trademark infringements conducted via online marketplaces have also moved into the focus the European Commission.[1369] The scale of the problem has even moved Amazon, the world's leading online marketplace operator, to spell this out in its 2018 and 2019 Annual Reports filed with the U.S. Securities and Exchange Commission. It stated that its policies and processes to prevent the

---

1366 'Combating Trafficking in Counterfeit and Pirated Goods - Report to the President of the United States' (n 1363) 15.

1367 UNIFAB, 'Counterfeiting & Terrorism, Edition 2016' (2015) <https://www.unifab.com/wp-content/uploads/2016/06/Rapport-A-Terrorisme-2015_GB_22.pdf> accessed 14 November 2019.

1368 Anton Moiseienko, 'Understanding Financial Crime Risks in E-Commerce' [2020] Royal United Services Institute for Defence and Security Studies 21.

1369 European Commission, 'Commission Staff Working Document Online Platforms Accompanying the Document Communication on Online Platforms and the Digital Single Market SWD(2016) 172 Final' (n 54) 21; European Commission, 'COM (2017) 555 Final' (n 69) 3, 7; European Commission, 'C(2018) 1177 Final' (n 8) Recitals 5, 10. European Commission, 'Report on the Protection and Enforcement of Intellectual Property Rights in Third Countries - SWD(2019) 452 Final/2' (2020) 19.

sale of counterfeit, pirated and unlawful products by its sellers may be circumvented or operate insufficiently and that the company is at risk of being held liable for this.[1370]

Consequently, major online marketplaces have all been embroiled in high profile court cases brought by trademark owners. The prolific nature of many of these cases and their sheer number indicate the powerful economic interests involved.[1371] Deep pocketed global brand owners, mainly from luxury goods sectors, such as *L'Oréal*, *LVMH*, *Tiffany*, *Coty* or *PVH*, have sought to classify online marketplaces as direct infringers of their brands. Failing that, they sought to impose far reaching duties to prevent counterfeit sales. While at the beginning most of the defending platforms were small and more fragile players, many have now become major technology firms, horizontally and vertically integrated, often exceeding the size of their erstwhile opponents.

II. EU Trademark protection, its widening scope and the internet

Trademarks are one of the oldest intellectual property rights. The concept of trademark protection goes back to the time of the Industrial Revolution and the emergence of factory production. The increasing division of labour disconnected people from the production chain. It intensified competition through wider choice and fostered the circulation of goods and international trade.[1372] This also made it more difficult for producers and traders to distinguish their products from those of their competitors. Protection was sought against imitations and straightforward copying of products and brand names. Trademark law therefore originally aimed to a) indicate the origin of a branded good, and b) avoid confusion for the con-

---

1370 'Amazon 2018 Annual Report' (Amazon) 14 <https://ir.aboutamazon.com/annual-reports-proxies-and-shareholder-letters/default.aspx> accessed 19 June 2020; 'Amazon 2019 Annual Report' (Amazon) 14–15 <https://ir.aboutamazon.com/annual-reports-proxies-and-shareholder-letters/default.aspx> accessed 19 June 2020.

1371 See for example: *Tiffany (NJ) Inc. v. eBay Inc.* (n 599); *Google France v Louis Vuitton* (n 155); *L'Oréal v eBay* (n 463). *Coty v Amazon (FBA)* (n 590).

1372 WR Cornish, David Llewelyn and Tanya Frances Aplin, *Intellectual property: patents, copyright, trade marks and allied rights* (7. ed, Sweet & Maxwell [u.a] 2010) 640–642.

sumer, or any other ultimate user.[1373] Confusion may arise where a trademarked good is identical or similar to an already existing, earlier, or senior mark.[1374] The period after World War II saw the economic value of branded goods and trademarks rise exorbitantly, thanks to mass consumerism and globalisation, and aided by the sophistication of marketing and advertising. Brands have become commercially significant as intangible assets on companies' balance sheets. They are subject to substantive investments and even takeover battles.[1375]

Trademark law in the EU, similar to copyright, is founded on international agreements, notably the TRIPS Agreement and the 1883 Paris Convention for the Protection of Industrial Property.[1376] In the EU, a dual regime exists. Trademark owners may file for a Community Trademark which applies throughout the internal market and is enforced in a unitary way by the European Trademark Regulation (EUTMR).[1377] Alternatively, they may opt for national protection in one or several Member States of their choice, by registering their marks with national trademark offices, a right regulated under the EU Trademark Directive (EUTMD).[1378] The national trademark rights under the EU Trademark Directive are largely harmonised. Apart from the geographic scope, the substantial rights and protections and the conditions of use and revocation are largely the same as for the fully harmonised unitary EU Trademark (EUTM).[1379]

1373 *Hoffmann-La Roche & Co AG v Centrafarm Vertriebsgesellschaft Pharmazeutischer Erzeugnisse mbH, C-102/77* [1978] EU:C:1978:108 (CJEU) [7].

1374 The origin function, however, would only protect earlier registered marks against a later registration attempt of an identical mark, under Regulation (EU) 2017/1001 on the European Union trade mark 2017 (OJ L 154) Article 9 (2) (a), termed by Griffiths as "core zone" protection. Andrew Griffiths, 'The Trade Mark Monopoly: An Analysis of the Core Zone of Absolute Protection under Art. 5(1)(a)' [2007] Intellectual Property Quarterly 312, 314.

1375 Gordon V Smith, 'Brand Valuation: Too Long Neglected' (1990) 12 European Intellectual Property Review 159.

1376 TRIPS Articles 15-21; Paris Convention for the Protection of Industrial Property 1883.

1377 EUTMR.

1378 Directive (EU) 2015/2436 of the European Parliament and of the Council of 16 December 2015 to approximate the laws of the Member States relating to trade marks (Text with EEA relevance) 2015 (OJ L 336).

1379 ibid Recitals 5 & 8.Although it has been noted that some Member States, notably the UK, have made use of the option provided for in TRIPS Article 1.1 to afford a higher level of protection through their national laws, but this is only of limited relevance here. See for more detail: Althaf Marsoof, *Internet Intermediaries and Trade Mark Rights* (Routledge 2019) 47–50.

In line with the rise in commercial value of consumer brands, their owners have sought to expand the protection of trademarks beyond their essential functions. The arrival of the internet, notably e-commerce and online advertising, have only reinforced this trend.

Today, EU trademark law offers an "additional zone of protection"[1380] for well-known, or trademarks with a reputation,[1381] that goes beyond the core function of origin and the protection against confusion. The rationale behind this is, that reputed trademarks are at an additional risk of being taken unfair advantage of, or of being detrimentally affected by traders that use similar or identical marks for non-similar goods and services. This can be further broken down into acts that take unfair advantage of the distinctive character of a well-known mark (free-riding), are detrimental to the distinctive character of a well-known mark (dilution or blurring) and are to the detriment of the reputation of such a mark (tarnishment).[1382] This CJEU explored this in its *Interflora* ruling concerning trademark use in e-commerce. The UK retailer *Marks & Spencer's (M&S)* had purchased the search keyword "*Interflora*" and some variants on *Google's AdWords* referencing service. Customers typing these words into *Google's* search engines were led through sponsored links to *M&S's* own flower shop and delivery service. *Interflora* successfully complained that this use of its mark amounted to dilution and free-riding of its well-known mark, in addition to affecting the core function of origin protected under Article 5 (1) (a) of the previous version of the EUTMD.[1383]

The last 15 years have also seen a *de facto* extension of the unfair advantage protections for reputed marks to the core origin function of other than well-known marks. The CJEU did this by introducing the concept of the communicative functions of a trademark in *L'Oréal v Bellure*. The referring English court in this case had explicitly stated that the use of defendant *Bellure's* "smell-alike" perfumes did not lead to confusion with the consumer over the origin of its products. It wanted to establish, however, whether comparative advertising could still be considered as affecting the core and supplementary rights protected by trademark law. The CJEU

1380 Griffiths (n 1373) 314.

1381 EUTMR Article 9 (2) (c).

1382 *Interflora Inc, Interflora British Unit v Marks & Spencer plc, Flowers Direct Online Ltd, C-323/09* [2011] EU:C:2011:604 (CJEU) [73–95]; Ilanah Simon Fhima, 'Trademark Law and Advertising Keywords', *Research Handbook on EU Internet Law* (Edward Elgar 2014) 161.

1383 Directive 2008/95/EC to approximate the laws of the Member States relating to trade marks 2008. Equivalent to Article 9 (1) (a) of the EUTMR

took the view that a trademark owner also deserves protection for other than the core function of the trademark, namely that of guaranteeing the quality of the goods or services in question and those of communication, investment or advertising.[1384] This reasoning was then adopted by the CJEU in *Google France*,[1385] which confirmed the expanding scope of trademark protection. Keyword advertisers have since been more readily found to be primary liable for trademark infringements.[1386]

III. Enforcement: primary infringers or intermediaries with responsibilities?

a. Online intermediaries as primary infringers

The expanding protections afforded to trademarks, on the one hand, and the widening use of trademarks for advertising and marketing on e-commerce sites, on the other, are two trends that were bound to lead to legal conflict. While keyword purchasers[1387] and traders are more at risk of being seen as primary infringers, search engines or e-commerce marketplaces themselves have so far largely escaped liability for trademark infringements. Trademark law itself does not provide for remedies against contributory infringements. This means that intermediaries would need to meet the high bar of primary infringements if they were to be held liable under

---

1384 *L'Oréal SA, Lancôme parfums et beauté & Cie SNC, Laboratoire Garnier & Cie v Bellure NV, Malaika Investments Ltd, trading as 'Honey pot cosmetic & Perfumery Sales', Starion International Ltd, C-487/07* [2009] EU:C:2009:378 (CJEU) [58]. The court referred to its deliberations in *Arsenal* and developed the Opinion of the AG in that case. *Arsenal Football Club plc v Matthew Reed, C-206/01* [2002] EU:C:2002:651 (CJEU) [51]; *Opinion of Advocate-General Ruiz-Jarabo Colomier, Arsenal Football Club plc v Matthew Reed, C-206/01* [2002] EU:C:2002:373 (CJEU) [46, 47].

1385 *Google France v Louis Vuitton* (n 155) para 102.

1386 Fhima (n 1381) 164.

1387 The CJEU confirmed in its rulings in *Google France* and *BergSpechte* that an advertiser who selects (search) keywords that are identical with a trademark in order to display advertising links that direct consumers to a website where its goods and services are offered, uses the sign in the course of trade. The advertiser can therefore be prevented by the trademark owner from using the disputed keywords: *Google France v Louis Vuitton* (n 155) paras 51, 52. *Die BergSpechte Outdoor Reisen und Alpinschule Edi Koblmüller GmbH v Günter Guni, trekking.at Reisen GmbH, C-278/08* [2010] CJEU EU:C:2010:163 [18].

trademark law. It is not that trademark owners have not tried to construe the activities of online intermediaries as directly affecting the protection of their marks, on the contrary. But in order to be found liable for confusing consumers over the origin of goods, affecting the communicative functions or taking unfair advantage of a reputed mark, a trader must first be making use of the sign in the course of trade.[1388] The concept of use is closer defined by a non-exhaustive list of actions, which includes for example the affixing of the sign to the goods, putting them on the market, importing and exporting, or using the signs in advertising.[1389] Since trademark law is a unitary right (where its concerns the EUTM), and significantly harmonised (where it concerns the national marks), any doubts over the interpretation of 'use' have ended up at CJEU level.

The three cases that deal with trademark infringement claims against online intermediaries (*Google France*, *L'Oréal v EBay* and *Coty v Amazon)* have so far all absolved these e-commerce marketplace and search engine operators from using the trademarks in the course of trade. In *L'Oréal v eBay*, defendant *eBay* was qualified as an infringer solely where it concerned its activity as a keyword purchaser for *Google AdWords*. Where it displayed trademarks in advertisings and online offers that belonged to third party sellers it was not found to use the trademark in a way that infringed the rights of the brand owners *L'Oréal*.[1390] In view of the vertically integrated nature of today's online platforms this concept can be challenged in itself, as will be seen from the *Coty v Amazon* ruling. The ruling in *L'Oréal v eBay* goes back to the *CJEU's* approach developed in *Google France*. French luxury group *LVMH,* and owner of the *Louis Vuitton* mark, brought infringement proceedings against *Google France.* The use of its trademark in the *AdWords* program, they claimed, had an adverse effect on the essential function of indicating origin and confused customers over the identity of its goods. Under the *AdWords,* program third parties could purchase the terms that made up its trademark in combination with other words, such 'imitation' or 'copy'. When users entered the keyword combinations into *Google's* search engine, sponsored links appeared on the results list, which led to offers that contained imitations of *Vuitton's* products. While the CJEU found that Google did indeed make use of the signs for which it

1388 EUTMR Article 9 (2).

1389 ibid Article 9 (3).

1390 *L'Oréal v eBay* (n 463) paras 89–95.

offered keyword search terms to third parties, it did not do this as part of its own commercial communications.[1391]

The commercial communications concept was a new element introduced into EU Trademark law, which the CJEU however failed to define more clearly, nor has this new requirement been identified by anyone else in more detail.[1392] It can be presumed that the CJEU wanted to express the fact that although *Google* used the signs for its own economic activity, that economic activity merely consisted of providing the technical facility for others to make use of the sign. That facilitation, however, had to be examined outside of the realms of EU trademark law.[1393] Consequently, the CJEU examined the role of *Google* under the ECD which led to the landmark ruling on the criteria of an active role of an intermediary referred to previously. Others have argued that *LVMH* may have had more success if it had asked whether *Google's* use took unfair advantage (free-riding) or happened to the detriment (dilution) of the distinctive character of its marks under the protection afforded to reputed marks. As it stands, search advertising platform operators' activities have so far not met the commercial communication requirement at the highest EU instance, and avoided being seen as engaging in infringing trademark use.[1394] The CJEU applied this methodology in *L'Oréal v EBay*, where it found that an e-commerce marketplace operator does not engage in infringing use of trademarks displayed on its site as part of product offerings and advertisements by its sellers.[1395]

In *Coty v Amazon*, perfume manufacturer *Coty (owner* of the *Davidoff* brand*)* brought an action against the American e-commerce giant's marketplace platform. *Coty* claimed that Amazon's activities were more than neutral due to its logistics service *Fulfillment by Amazon (FBA)*.This service allows sellers to not only sell through the platform's marketplace, but also have their products stored, shipped to customers, and, if needed, returned. *FBA* also offers other services to the seller, such as stock management and sales analytics. Not preventing and sanctioning the sales of counterfeits, *Coty* argued, made the marketplace directly liable for trademark violations. *Amazon* argued that its marketplace and logistics services had to be seen in separation, and that neither of the activities gave the company any active

1391 *Google France v Louis Vuitton* (n 155) para 56.
1392 Marsoof (n 1378) 37 fn 61.
1393 *Google France v Louis Vuitton* (n 155) 57.
1394 Marsoof (n 1378) 36–37.
1395 *L'Oréal v eBay* (n 463) para 102.

role in the intermediation process between sellers and buyers that amounted to use of the signs in the course of trade.

The referring *BGH* tentatively agreed with the previous instances,[1396] which had ruled that *Amazon's FBA* service was a merely neutral transportation and storage service that gave no rise to possession of the goods for the purposes of putting them on the market, i.e. causing a trademark infringement.[1397] However, the *BGH* still had doubts and asked the CJEU to clarify whether *FBA's* activity of storing goods on behalf of a third party constituted trademark use.[1398] First, the AG acknowledged in his Opinion the narrow reading of the *BGH*, which had evaluated the marketplace and the logistics operations of *Amazon* separately. As a mere storage facility that ignored the infringing nature of the stored goods, the marketplace operator would indeed not be liable. However, he also offered an alternative reading of the case. By examining the *FBA* activities in conjunction with the marketplace operations, he found that *Amazon's* vertically integrated service gave it a level of knowledge and control over the activities of its sellers that amounted to use of trademarks in the course of trade.[1399] *Amazon* engaged in an active and coordinated participation in the distribution of products, which not only amounted to a use of the trademark, but even gave it further duties to prevent infringements. It would be contrary to the economic realities of *Amazon's* business model to accept the company's fictitious separation of its activities into different (independent) distribution stages.[1400]

The CJEU, however, did not follow this assessment. Instead it underlined that it was obliged to stick closely to the referring court's questions, which had just asked for guidance on an intermediary that was stocking infringing goods without knowledge of such infringement.[1401] The admittedly unsatisfactory and reductionist qualification of the *BGH's* assessment of *Amazon's* role[1402] resulted in a rather sombre ruling in which the CJEU

1396 *Versand durch Amazon* [2016] OLG München 29 U 745/16, GRUR-Prax 2017 380.

1397 *Davidoff Hot Water III, I ZR 20/17* - [2018] BGH DE:BGH:2018:260718BIZR20.17.0, BeckRS 2018, 19562 [22].

1398 EUTMR Article 9 (3) (b).

1399 *AG Opinion, Coty v Amazon (FBA)* (n 591) para 51.

1400 ibid 59 fn 42.

1401 *Coty v Amazon (FBA)* (n 590) 20–24.

1402 Carina Gommers and Eva De Pauw, 'Liability for Trade Mark Infringement of Online Marketplaces in Europe: Are They "Caught in the Middle"?' (2020) 15 Journal of Intellectual Property Law & Practice 276, 285–286.

applied *Google France* by finding that a mere technical facility provider like *Amazon* did not engage in use of a trademark.[1403] The CJEU still left a backdoor open to the *BGH* by saying that *Amazon's* activities could only qualify as stocking for the purposes of offering or putting the goods on the market where it did itself pursue this aim. This was done in context of the fact that Amazon conceded during the proceedings that it could not clearly identify the original sellers of all of the branded products in question, which theoretically opened the possibility that some of these products were marketed on its own behalf.[1404]

This is in contrast to some recent, but still isolated, rulings at national level, where courts have been more assertive in finding vertically integrated Web 2.0 online marketplaces directly liable for trademark infringements. In the previously discussed UK case of *Cosmetic Warriors,*[1405] Amazon was found to be engaging in commercial communications of the *Lush* sign. Its internal search engine offered the term "*Lush*" to advertisers. The search results displayed a list of product offers by, a) third-party sellers using their own fulfilment services, b) third-part sellers using Amazon's FBA service and c) *Amazon* itself. However, none of the offers were *Lush* products. For the latter two categories *Amazon* clearly engaged in commercial communications to promote its own activities and was found liable.

In 2017, a French court found *Alibaba* guilty of counterfeiting acts according to the French intellectual property code.[1406] The company had offered on its website advertisements leading to counterfeit goods of the French outdoor brand *Lafuma*. The Paris court examined the integrated activities of the Chinese e-commerce giant, which consisted of, amongst others, special advertising services and account statuses offered to its sellers and the integration of payment and logistics services. This, in combination with an explicit intellectual property protection policy, gave the marketplace a level of control over the offers hosted for its sellers that conferred on it an active, editor role, that made use of the disputed sign in the course of trade. This was despite the fact that *Lafuma* was denied damages, because it could not prove financial losses due to this activity. Nevertheless, the court found *Alibaba* had also engaged in acts of unfair commercial practices, as the offers also deceived customers by selling counterfeit prod-

1403 *Coty v Amazon (FBA)* (n 590) para 43.
1404 ibid 48.
1405 *Cosmetic Warriors v Amazon* (n 560).
1406 *Lafuma Mobilier v Alibaba et autres* (n 580).

ucts.[1407] An indication of the criteria for the active role of marketplaces can also be gleaned from a 2017 ruling by France's Supreme Court.[1408] Although the claimant distributor was unsuccessful in its complaints against a selective distribution agreement, the court indicated *orbiter dictum* that the active role of an e-commerce marketplace like *Amazon* could be established from several factors: offering sellers to market their products internationally; payment services, notably cheque and bank card payments processing; product delivery, and solving problems that arise during order fulfilment.

Finally, in 2019 luxury shoe brand *Louboutin* successfully brought infringement claims against *Amazon* in Belgium.[1409] By examining the rulings of the CJEU, namely in *Daimler*,[1410] *Google France* and *L'Oréal v EBay* the Brussels Commercial Tribunal found that *Amazon* did use the *Louboutin* sign as part of its own commercial communications. The court did even go further than its UK counterpart in the *Cosmetic Warrior* case, which only found that *Amazon* used a sign as part of its commercial communication where it concerned *Amazon's* own offers (displayed as part of *Louboutin* keyword searches) and those of third-party sellers using *FBA*. The Belgian court ruled that *Amazon* also made use of the *Louboutin* sign where it displayed offers that were sold and fulfilled by third party sellers. By listing those offers and counting them towards "our selections" and "our fashion crushes" on its website, Amazon used the *Louboutin* sign to promote its own marketplace operations.[1411]

These judgements seem to indicate that the integrated and complex business models of current online marketplaces start to be seen legally for what they have been designed for commercially: controlling and monetis-

---

1407 The link between unfair commercial practices (UCPs) and sales of unlawful products under EU law will be explored in more detail in the next section. For a more detailed treatise of the link between UCPs and counterfeit sales under EU law see: Ansgar Ohly, 'Counterfeiting and Consumer Protection' in Christophe Geiger (ed), *Criminal enforcement of intellectual property: a handbook of contemporary research* (Edward Elgar 2012).

1408 *Concurrence v Amazon Services Europe, Samsung Electronics France* (n 585).

1409 *Christian Louboutin v Amazon Europe Core sarl* [2019] Chambre des actions en cessation du tribunal de l'entreprise francophone de Bruxelles A/19/ 00918. As discussed in : Nick Aries and Louise Vaziri, 'Online Intermediary Liability and TM Infringement: Stuck in the Middle With You' (2020) 9 Trade Marks 2020 A practical cross-border insight into trade mark work 1.

1410 *Daimler AG v Együd Garage Gépjárműjavító és Értékesítő Kft, C-179/15* [2016] CJEU EU:C:2016:134.

1411 Aries and Vaziri (n 1408).

ing to a maximum degree the content and interactions derived from users, be they customers, content creators, sellers, advertisers or others. If the sale of counterfeit products continues as it does on these data-driven super marketplaces, courts rightly appear to be readier in assigning primary liability. This tendency may be supported by the readiness of the EU legislator to assign primary copyright liability to large OCSSPs. It will be interesting to follow whether this trend materialises itself further and whether solid criteria for a primary liability approach will emerge. Meanwhile, less sophisticated platform models may only be subject to the various secondary liability avenues offered by EU and national laws. Search engines also appear to be out of scope for being found directly liable for trademark infringing use, except where it concerns the internal search functionalities of large online marketplaces.

b. Secondary liability trends and consumer law

With trademark law not providing direct legal tools for assessing the role of intermediaries, rightsholders will have to look to other enforcement tools offered by the law. As in other legal subject matter areas that relate to content, rightsholders in the area of trademarks have a wide arsenal of options at their disposal. This does not necessarily make for legal consistency, equality and efficacy across Member States when it comes to enforcing trademark rights and the fight against counterfeits. First, Articles 9 (1) (a) and 11 of IPRED give rightsholders the option to apply for injunctions against intermediaries. IPRED lays down general requirements of proportionality and efficacy for those injunctions, but leaves their execution to national laws. The result is similar to the findings detailed in the previous section on copyright: different national interpretations and legal traditions on the scope of these injunctions and the role and definition of intermediaries under IPRED vary. This makes for an inconsistent enforcement landscape across the EU.[1412] The ECD, the complimentary enforcement tool to the IPRED that sets the liability framework for online intermediaries, has also led to differing interpretations and inconsistent application. It shall suffice to note that, for example, the interplay between Article 11 IPRED

1412 European Commission, 'A Balanced IP Enforcement System Responding to Today's Societal Challenges, COM(2017) 707 Final' (European Commission 2017) 4; European Commission, 'Summary Response - IPR Enforcement' (n 173) 5, 15, 36–37.

and the liability conditions of the ECD in Articles 12 – 15 is not sufficiently clear, as can be seen from the unclarity over if and when injunctions imposed under IPRED would result in a violation of the general monitoring prohibition.[1413] Moreover different NTD requirements mean that some countries have imposed more detailed notification systems for IP related infringements on platforms and others have not.

Member States such as Germany have developed detailed and elaborate duty of care obligations for intermediaries from their jurisprudence in the area of trademark violations, which treat the question of the availability of the hosting defence as secondary.[1414] The UK has had more difficulties in adapting common law concepts to the area of secondary liability for trademark infringements, trying to explore concepts of accessory liability that are based on aiding or assisting in infringements.[1415] French jurisprudence on the availability and scope of secondary liability defences has been much more divergent. A recent comparison of the enforcement practices *vis-à-vis* intermediaries in Belgium, France, Germany and the UK testifies to the continuing heterogeneity in this area.[1416] The review noted the differences that existed in judicial practice when it came to defining the extent and nature of obligations of online hosts in terminating and preventing trademark infringements. This is despite the fact that trademark violations on online marketplaces have been an area of predilection at CJEU level for defining the reactive and preventive duties of search engines,[1417] online marketplaces[1418] and intermediaries in general.[1419]

1413 European Commission, 'Synopsis Report on the Regulatory Environment for Platforms' (n 539) 39.

1414 *Internetversteigerung I (Rolex v Ricardo.de), Az. I ZR 304/01* (n 567); *Internetversteigerung II (Rolex v Ricardo.de)* (n 568); *Internetversteigerung III (Rolex v Ricardo.de), Az. I ZR 73/05* (n 568); *Kinderhochstühle im Internet, I ZR 139/08* (n 722); *Kinderhochstühle im Internet II, I ZR 216/11* (n 584); *Kinderhochstühle im Internet III* (n 584).

1415 Marsoof (n 1378) 47–77.

1416 ibid 78–103.

1417 *Google France v Louis Vuitton* (n 155).

1418 *L'Oréal v eBay* (n 463).

1419 *Tommy Hilfiger Licensing LLC, Urban Trends Trading BV, Rado Uhren AG, Facton Kft, Lacoste SA, Burberry Ltd v Delta Center a.s, C-494/15* [2016] EU:C:2016:528 (CJEU); *Coöperatieve Vereniging SNB-REACT U.A. v Deepak Mehta - C-521/17* (n 276).

An additional enforcement dimension is introduced by the provisions of the Unfair Commercial Practices Directive (UCPD),[1420] which aims to protect consumers against traders that engage in misleading or aggressive marketing and sales practices. With e-commerce on the rise, the internet has also become an area were these unfair practices have been witnessed, be it through misrepresentation of goods, insufficient information or transparency about the products and services offered, or about the traders themselves.[1421] The sale of IP infringing goods, notably in the area of trademarks, would fall under such practices, where a trader confuses the consumer over the origins of a product.[1422] In that respect, both trademark and unfair competition rules go in the same direction. It has been unclear until recently, however, whether online marketplaces could qualify as traders under the UCPD. This would normally be assessed on a case-by-case basis.[1423] The new Omnibus Directive, passed in 2019, appears to solve this question in the affirmative by providing a definition of online marketplaces which would qualify them as traders both under the UCP and the Consumer Rights Directive.[1424] At the same time, this does not appear to deprive online marketplaces from the intermediary liability protections of the ECD. They can therefore be traders and ECD style information hosts at the same time. This creates a potential conflict between the rules of professional conduct imposed under the UCPD on traders hosting offers of unlawful products and the liability exemptions for these traders as online intermediaries.[1425] With regards to the sale of counterfeit goods, which can also be classified as an unfair commercial practice, the UCPD lacks any specific enforcement tools apt to deal with the role of marketplace traders that act solely as intermediaries. This remedy does however exist under IP legislation, namely through IPRED's Article 11. This exposes a gap in enforcement tools, which gives trademark rightsowners better protection

1420 Directive 2005/29/EC of 11 May 2005 concerning unfair business-to-consumer commercial practices in the internal market 2005 (OJ L 149).

1421 ibid Articles 5 - 9, and Annex I.

1422 ibid Article 6 (2) (a) & Recital 14. Ohly, 'Counterfeiting and Consumer Protection' (n 1106) 27–30.

1423 European Commission, 'UCP Directive Guidance' (n 57) 122–126. Valentina Moscon and Reto M Hilty, 'Digital Markets, Rules of Conduct and Liability of Online Intermediaries—Analysis of Two Case Studies: Unfair Commercial Practices and Trade Secrets Infringement' [2020] Max Planck Institute for Innovation and Competition Research Paper 27, 9–11.

1424 Omnibus Directive 2019/2161 (n 1249) Articles 3 & 4, Recital 25.

1425 Moscon and Hilty (n 1422) 13.

than consumers against the sale of IP infringing goods.[1426] Again, it should be kept in mind that the determination of liabilities and duties, and the enforcement mechanisms under these three regimes are to be settled by Member States according to their national interpretations and laws.

IV. Private enforcement

In response to global pressure from rightsowners, uncertainties in the application of intermediary legislation and a desire to bolster consumer trust, some online marketplaces started to implement more proactive voluntary mechanisms to prevent the occurrence of counterfeit products. NTD processes were the obvious, mandatory first line of defence. It should be noted here, that the detection and prevention of counterfeits and trademark infringing goods in general poses specific challenges that cannot easily be compared to fighting copyright infringements or unlawful speech. First, the sale of tangible goods, which is the most common area for trademark infringements on online platforms, is more difficult to analyse and intercept by a marketplace than it is for digital content.[1427] Often enough, product images and word filters have been the only elements available to an online marketplace operator to identify and assess potentially infringing products. A notice may give additional information and assurance from the side of the rightsholder. However, this is fraught with difficulties where the prevention of repeat infringements or voluntary proactive measures are concerned. Marketplaces would need to rely on specific brand and product knowledge and invest in investigative capabilities were they to effectively determine and fight counterfeits. Given the huge number of products and sellers on today's larger marketplaces this becomes an even greater challenge. The tools available to marketplaces have for a long time therefore been more basic than in the area of digital content recognition, relying more on ad-hoc, human verification. Once an infringing offer is removed, little stands in the way of the seller to offer the same products, which remains in its inventory, on other platforms, or through other distribution channels.[1428]

1426 ibid 15–16.

1427 Ullrich, 'Standards for Duty of Care?' (n 1137) 119–121.

1428 Content recognition technologies, such as watermarking or fingerprinting, are of limited use in this area.

Secondly, trademark law is complex and infringements are not restricted to counterfeiting. Counterfeits are usually double identity cases that are more straightforwardly illegal: the infringer imitates a trademark and the goods related to it. This is notwithstanding the fact that sophisticated counterfeits have become notoriously difficult to identify in some product areas.[1429] In light of the expanded protection afforded to trademark owners, determining infringing offers may become more complex, for example, where it concerns issues of free-riding, tarnishment or blurring of reputed marks. The international and even global nature of many online marketplaces also opens the door to grey market sales, parallel imports or violations of selective distribution agreements.[1430] Added to this are various other problems, for example with sales of generic replacement or accessory parts for OEM products, such as printer cartridges, mobile phone chargers or cables etc. Many of these problems can overlap with other legal problems, such as product compliance, product safety or unfair commercial practices, like misrepresentation.[1431] The latter borderline issues are far from easy to determine, even for rightsowners. Not in every case do they necessarily restrict the rights of a brand owner. In effect, they may even be subject to abusive notices, aimed at removing legitimate competitors.[1432]

The flood of NTDs that accompanied the rise of online marketplaces has been processed largely manually until recently. The amount of counterfeit notices that online marketplaces receive from rightsowners is however difficult to establish. Unlike in the areas of hate speech or copyright, the leading online marketplaces remain remarkably nontransparent about their NTD practices. Of the pure online marketplaces, only *Etsy*, a significantly smaller competitor to *Amazon*, *Alibaba*, *eBay* or *JD.com*, has published a transparency report, albeit only until 2016. According to the report, it received 18,857 notices, which resulted in the removal of 235,201 listings from 59,131 sellers. Altogether, the company saw an increase in IP related takedowns by 70% compared to the previous year. Measured by seller gross merchandise value (GMV, the total value of goods sold), the company was about 20 times smaller than *Amazon's* marketplace and 18 times smaller

---

1429 EUIPO and Europol (n 1130) 8–19.

1430 *Coty Germany GmbH v Parfümerie Akzente GmbH, C-230/16* [2017] CJEU EU:C:2017:941.

1431 Robert W Payne, 'Unauthorized Online Dealers of "Genuine" Products in the Amazon Marketplace and beyond: Remedies for Brand Owners' [2014] J Internet Law 3.

1432 Greene (n 1361).

than eBay in 2016.[1433] Other detailed counterfeit or trademark removal data is only available from the Transparency Report of *Facebook*.[1434]

The complexity of assessing trademark infringements and managing NTD requests together with the looming threat of legal conflict with brand owners was accompanied by emerging diligent economic operator responsibilities principles through case law.[1435] This created strong incentives to operationalise and pre-empt the sale of counterfeits and trademark infringements by using technology and by fostering cooperation with rightsowners. Online marketplaces initially launched programs that gave brand owners specific means to identify, flag and have listings removed. *EBay* was the pioneer in this regard with its *Verified Rightsowner Program* (*VeRo*), launched in 1998. This program had 31,000 rightsowner members in 2014. In 2008, the company removed 2.1 million listings through this program and another 2 million proactively.[1436] Both *Amazon* and *Alibaba* have also started similar programs, albeit almost more than 15 years after *eBay*.[1437] This happened often after serious pressure from brand owners. However, here again, the mechanisms and takedown modalities, including counterclaims, remain opaque and generally inaccessible to outsiders. These programs appear to forge deeper relationships, mainly with large brand owners. The latter will be able to liaise directly by exchanging product and brand information with the internal teams at these platforms that are responsible for identifying and taking down allegedly infringing offers. At *Amazon*, these special relationships have gone even further. In 2016 the company started to "gate" certain brands on its sites.[1438] This means brand

1433 According to the following resources: 'Research' (*Marketplace Pulse*) <https://www.marketplacepulse.com/research> accessed 19 June 2020; 'Etsy Annual GMV 2019' (*Statista*) <https://www.statista.com/statistics/219412/etsys-total-merchandise-sales-per-year/> accessed 19 June 2020.

1434 Facebook, 'Intellectual Property' <https://transparency.facebook.com/intellectual-property/jan-jun-2017> accessed 5 June 2020.

1435 E.g. in *L'Oréal v eBay* (n 463). And national case law mentioned Chapter 3

1436 'EBay Drives Commitment to Fight Counterfeiting and Piracy' (28 October 2014) <https://www.eBayinc.com/stories/press-room/uk/eBay-drives-commitment-to-fight-counterfeiting-and-piracy/> accessed 19 June 2020.

1437 'Amazon Brand Registry: Help Protect Your Brand on Amazon' <https://brandservices.amazon.com/> accessed 19 June 2020; 'Alibaba Group - Intellectual Property Protection Platform (IPP Platform)' < https:////ipp.alibabagroup.com/index.htm> accessed 19 June 2020.

1438 Gordon Mcconnell, 'Amazon Starts "Brand Gating" to Stop Counterfeits' (1 September 2016) <https://blog.redpoints.com/en/amazon-plans-to-combat-counterfeits> accessed 19 June 2020.

owners may restrict the sale of their brands on the *Amazon* marketplace either to themselves or to a select number of sellers. Those sellers would either be pre-authorised by the brand owner and/or they would need to provide a proof of authenticity for the products they intend to sell. This happens mainly were large manufactures have opened customised brand shops on the *Amazon* website.[1439] On the one hand, it makes sense to engage brand owners more proactively in the fight against counterfeit products. On the other hand, this privileged relationship is relatively obscure and may lead to a predominance of already large and established brands on these marketplaces, potentially imposing a disproportionally high burden of proof on smaller sellers.[1440]

Apart from these relationship programs, many online marketplaces have been ramping up their automated counterfeit identification technologies. As stated above, *eBay* has worked on proactive removals as early as 2008. French online marketplace *PriceMinister* has been using automated software to detect counterfeits, supported by manual checks, since 2006.[1441] *Etsy* also confirms the use of automated tools in conjunction with community flagging and manual investigations to protect the integrity of its marketplace. Meanwhile the two dominating players, *Alibaba* and *Amazon*, use their brand owner relationship programs, *Brand Registry (Amazon)* and the *IP Protection Platform (Alibaba)*[1442] to fast-track the development of proactive, automated identification tools for rightsowners. The idea here is that interaction and information exchange with brand owners will help to improve automated tools developed to proactively identify and remove suspected counterfeit listings. In the case of *Alibaba*, this includes "image recognition algorithms, including optical character recognition (OCR) technology, product intelligence learning algorithms, a product information library, counterfeit screening models, semantic recognition algorithms, and a real-time interception system."[1443]

1439 See for example: 'Olay' (*Amazon.co.uk*) <https://www.amazon.co.uk/stores/Olay/Olay/page/3BBAE664-6ADE-4D62-86AD-A052F323E900> accessed 19 June 2020.

1440 Mcconnell (n 1437).

1441 *L'Oreal SA v. eBay International AG* (n 563) paras 267–276.

1442 'Alibaba's Enhanced IP Protection Platform Now Eliminates Fake Listings in Less than 24 Hours' (10 August 2017) <https://alibabagroup.com/en/news/article?news=p170810> accessed 19 June 2020. 'Amazon Brand Gating Increases Merchant Suspension Risk' (*TameBay*, 22 February 2019).

1443 'AACA Practices' (*Alibaba Anti-counterfeiting Alliance*) <https://aaca.alibabagroup.heymeo.net/> accessed 25 June 2020.

Amazon took this a step further in 2019 with its *Project Zero*, by allowing selected brand owners of their *Brand Registry* program to remove listings through "self-service counterfeit removals". This information will feed into its proactive tools that already scan the five billion listings updates that are registered every day on its platform, presumable by using a similar array of methods and technologies as *Alibaba*.[1444] The company stated that in 2018 it had spent $400 million, and in 2019 $500 million on efforts to combat fraud, which includes counterfeiting on its platform. It employed 8,000 people in the fraud detection space and blocked 6 billion fraudulent listings and 2.5 million "bad actors."[1445]

There is no self-organised industry initiative, as for example the GIFTC in the area of terrorist content, where online marketplaces join forces on a technical level and exchange best practices. On the other hand, industry associations such as the *International Chamber of Commerce (ICC)*, which represent the interests of many of the large trademark owners have been more proactive. The ICC's initiative *Business Action to Stop Counterfeiting and Piracy (BASCAP)*, has, for example, issued more detailed guidance, setting out best practices and concrete measures that platforms should take in the fight against trademark infringements.[1446] These suggestions, although purely voluntary, could provide useful reference points in formulating enhanced legal responsibilities for online marketplaces. An example for such a duty of care standard for e-commerce platforms, developed as part of the research for this work, is presented in Chapter 6 and ANNEX III.

Online marketplaces appear to be individually developing and employing their prevention systems and technologies, based on the proprietary transaction and user data and the brand intelligence harvested through

---

1444 'Amazon Project Zero: Empowering Brands against Counterfeits' <https://brandservices.amazon.com/projectzero> accessed 25 June 2020; Stephanie Condon, 'Amazon's Project Zero Lets Brands Take down Counterfeits' (*ZDNet*, 28 February 2019) <https://www.zdnet.com/article/amazons-project-zero-lets-brands-take-down-counterfeits/> accessed 25 June 2020.

1445 Kiri Masters, 'The One Change That Would Drastically Reduce Counterfeiting On Amazon's U.S. Marketplace' (*Forbes*) <https://www.forbes.com/sites/kirimasters/2019/11/13/the-one-change-that-would-drastically-reduce-counterfeiting-on-amazons-us-marketplace/> accessed 25 June 2020; 'Amazon Ramping Up Efforts To Take Down Counterfeiters' <https://finance.yahoo.com/news/amazon-ramping-efforts-down-counterfeiters-173702229.html> accessed 25 June 2020.

1446 'Roles and Responsibilities of Intermediaries: Fighting Counterfeiting and Piracy in the Supply Chain' (n 223); BASCAP, 'Best-Practices-for-Removing-Fakes-from-Online-Platforms' (BASCAP 2016).

their systems. Like in other areas, law enforcement and authorities have had difficulties in establishing working contacts and information exchanges with these marketplaces. The preferred practice has been to suspend or ban offending actors (sellers, consumers, advertisers) from their sites and close the case. This practice seems to be under review, however. *Alibaba* and *Amazon* have recently indicated that they intend to work more closely with authorities and law enforcement in this area.[1447]

Both, larger and smaller e-commerce platforms may already have extensive seller data, including VAT numbers, payment details, business addresses, detailed sales and product records, which may even include manufacturer data, or customer data on shopping behaviour and shipping addresses.[1448] The number of other intermediaries that vertically integrate their services into online marketplaces is usually higher than in other areas. Payment services, logistics providers, advertisers may also provide additional data and leverage. Compared to other areas of online interactions – e.g. speech and digital content sharing – users in e-commerce are also more deeply integrated with the platform. Sellers need to provide product data and banking details, and consumers may need to provide verified credit card and address details. This, combined with existing transparency and due diligence obligations under other statutes, for example for food sellers,[1449] online pharmacies[1450] or anti-money-laundering laws,[1451] make for a powerful amalgam of intelligence. The increasingly vertically and horizontally integrated online marketplaces and other platforms have therefore ample data on which sophisticated automated infringement prevention tools, based on predictive analysis, can be built. These would usually be in-

---

1447 Rich and Ho (n 602) 10–11; Todd Bishop, 'Amazon Forms "Counterfeit Crimes Unit," under Pressure to Escalate Fight against Fake Products' (*GeekWire*, 24 June 2020) <https://www.geekwire.com/2020/amazon-forms-counterfeit-crimes-unit-pressure-escalate-fight-fake-products/> accessed 25 June 2020.

1448 Nizan Geslevich Packin and Yafit Lev-Aretz, 'Big Data and Social Netbanks: Are You Ready to Replace Your Bank?' (2016) 53 Houston Law Review 1211, 1223–1242.

1449 Regulation (EC) 852/2004 of 29 April 2004 on the hygiene of foodstuffs 2004 (OJ L 139) Article 6 (2)

1450 Directive 2011/62/EU of 8 June 2011 amending Directive 2001/83/EC on the Community code relating to medicinal products for human use, as regards the prevention of the entry into the legal supply chain of falsified medicinal products 2011 (OJ L 174, 172011) Article 85 c.

1451 Directive 2015/849/EU of 20 May 2015 on the prevention of the use of the financial system for the purposes of money laundering or terrorist financing 2015 (OJ L 141, 562015) Articles 13, 14, Recital 18.

tegrated into wider (online) fraud detection programs. Larger platforms may, however, be in a privileged position to develop and deploy effective anti-counterfeiting technologies due to their superior data collection activities, financial power and special relationship with large brand owners.

Amazon, for example has started to develop its own fraud detection product, based on machine learning, to predict and spot fraudulent online activities. The service is offered to any e-commerce business and is run from its own *AWS* cloud system.[1452] It is understandable that fraud detection mechanisms cannot be disclosed liberally for public scrutiny. Nevertheless, as of now the mechanisms, and broader criteria and outcomes of the blocking, removal and seller sanction processes are secretive and inaccessible. This would need to be considered when solutions for any enhanced duties of care obligation that rely on state-of-the-art prevention tools are being designed.[1453] First, it would be essential that competing (smaller) platforms have access to an array of market solutions that are not dominated by proprietary systems of the current incumbents. Secondly, transparency obligations would need to be established that allow at least for scrutiny on the side of regulators and public authorities, in order to address risks relating to data protection, privacy, competition, consumer protection and freedom of expression.

V. EU policy development

Despite the prominence that the fight against counterfeits and the protection of IP rights via the internet has received, EU policy action has remained relatively subdued in this particular area. As stated, intermediary liability cases concerning trademark infringements have been a common feature since the early days of the ECD.[1454] The European Commission acknowledged in its 10-year review of the ECD that counterfeit sales continued to be a problem for the development of e-commerce and the Single

1452 'Amazon Fraud Detector - Amazon Web Services' (*Amazon Web Services, Inc.*) <https://aws.amazon.com/fraud-detector/> accessed 25 June 2020.

1453 DSM Directive 2019/790 Article 17 (4 b); European Commission, 'Impact Assessment 3/3 - DSM Directive' (n 1306) 167–172. The DSM Directive, for example, prescribes the use of industry standard prevention methods in the area of copyright and was accompanied by a market review of available content recognition tools outside *Google's Content ID* product.

1454 Verbiest and others (n 644) 36–38, 91–93.

Market.[1455] It announced that, apart from promoting self-regulatory initiatives in this area, it would address the problem through a review of IPRED[1456] under its Intellectual Property Strategy.[1457] The persistence of the problem was confirmed in 2016 in the Commission's DSM communication.[1458] The European Commission's strategy paper on online platforms and the DSM of 2016, however, put the focus of legislative action on copyright and the fight against harmful content on VSPs under the AVMSD.[1459] Trademark infringements and intermediary liability also occupied a less prominent space in both the 2017 Communication and the 2018 Recommendations on tackling illegal content online. These documents focussed more prominently on the area of copyright, hate speech and terrorist content. Meanwhile, the IPRED review resulted in a Guidance document that sought to clarify, amongst others, the scope of injunctions available against intermediaries. Voluntary agreements between stakeholders are at this stage the only tangible policy action at EU level.

a. Memorandum of Understanding on the Sale of Counterfeit Goods over the Internet

The 2011 Memorandum of Understanding (MoU), initiated by the Commission, brought major rightsholders, trade associations and online marketplaces to the table.[1460] The aim of the MoU was to achieve closer cooperation and develop a consensus on standards and measures relating to: NTD systems, the exchange of information regarding infringements, proactive measures, dealing with repeat infringers and cooperation with law enforcement and customs authorities. The MoU also committed to the development of key performance indicators (KPIs) to measure implemen-

1455 European Commission, 'SEC(2011) 1641 Final' (n 11) 72.
1456 ibid 74. European Commission, 'E-Commerce Action Plan 2012-2015, State of Play 2013, SWD(2013) 153 Final' (n 537) 18–19.
1457 European Commission, 'A Single Market for Intellectual Property Rights - Boosting Creativity and Innovation to Provide Economic Growth, High Quality Jobs and First Class Products and Services in Europe, COM(2011) 287 Final' (2011).
1458 European Commission, 'Commission Staff Working Document Online Platforms Accompanying the Document Communication on Online Platforms and the Digital Single Market SWD(2016) 172 Final' (n 54) 21.
1459 European Commission, 'COM(2016) 288 Final' (n 223) 8–9.
1460 'Memorandum of Understanding on the Sale of Counterfeit Goods over the Internet, 2011' (n 665).

tation of the agreed commitments.[1461] The commitments are, however, relatively loose, abstract and do not more than reflect the status quo of operational procedures and legal requirements of the ECD. For example, marketplaces commit to efficient and swift reactions to NTD requests, the implementation of commercially reasonable and available proactive and preventive measures, or to implementing repeat infringer policies. Swift reactions to notifications are already required by Article 14 (1) ECD. Secondly, all the three platforms which signed the MoU initially were engaged in some way in proactive measures to detect trademark infringing goods, although the degree of this activity remained largely unknown. The MoU does not provide any additional clarification or commitment in this matter. Finally, the need to act against repeat infringers had been voiced by the CJEU's AG in its Opinion in the *L'Oréal v eBay* case,[1462] which was later confirmed in the CJEU's ruling.[1463] The agreement can be seen as an important, but rather symbolic step,[1464] aimed principally at getting the various stakeholder talk to each other. The progress report on the MoU[1465] two years later showed mixed success. The tenor of the report implies that information sharing, the agreement on KPIs and the transparency on proactive measures by platforms were problematic areas. On the positive side, it appears to have strengthened at least bilateral links between stakeholders, leading to more efficient counterfeit identification and removal processes in specific situations.

The MoU was renewed in 2016,[1466] albeit without making any changes to the 2011 text, except for some new, high level KPIs. These rather basic performance metrics, which were inherently difficult to reach agreement on, as can be seen from the five years it took to agree to them, are: the

1461 ibid. Apart from major consumer brands the MoU was also signed by *Amazon*, *eBay* and *Rakuten (PriceMinister)*

1462 *Opinion of Advocate General Jääskinen, L'Oréal (UK) Ltd v eBay International AG, eBay Europe SARL, eBay (UK) Ltd and others, C-324/09* [2010] EU:C:2010:757 (CJEU) [168, 182].

1463 *L'Oréal v eBay* (n 463) 141.

1464 L Smith, 'European Commission Publishes Memorandum of Understanding on the Sale of Counterfeit Goods over the Internet' (2011) 6 Journal of Intellectual Property Law & Practice 770.

1465 European Commission, 'Report on the Functioning of the Memorandum of Understanding on the Sale of Counterfeit Goods via the Internet /COM/ 2013/0209 Final' (2013) COM/2013/0209 final <http://eur-lex.europa.eu/legal-content/EN/TXT/?uri=CELEX:52013DC0209> accessed 17 March 2017.

1466 'Memorandum of Understanding on the Online Sale of Counterfeit Goods, 2016' (n 542).

number of search results that lead to counterfeit listings;[1467] the number of listings removed following proactive measures by platforms and rightsowner NTD requests; the number of restrictions imposed on sellers. The 2017 report on the functioning of the MoU attests to the ongoing problems of counterfeit sales via marketplaces. According to the first KPI, brand owners that searched marketplace platforms between May to June 2017 reported that on aggregate 14.3% of the top 100 listings of their searches were counterfeits. The report also notes that 97.4% of removals on the participating online marketplaces were made through proactive and preventive systems, which were, however, prone to false positives.[1468] Despite the success of closer and better cooperation on NTD procedures and information exchange, there remained room for improvement. A lack of transparency in how KPIs are collected by platforms remained an issue, according to the report, as did more detailed information on NTD and proactive procedures applied by platforms.

The report concluded that common standards on repeat infringer sanctions and content removals would further improve efficiencies in identifying infringers on the side of rightsowners.[1469] The 2020, more detailed Report on the Functioning of the MoU, seems to indicate that the problems reported in 2017 have not gone away.[1470] The Commission notes that the reporting of the KPIs is of limited value due to methodological inconsistencies in data collection and disagreements between signatories about the interpretation of the numbers obtained from these exercises.[1471] The first KPI (% of search results leading to counterfeit offers) is not reported any longer. Instead, just an indication is given about the oscillating trend in this KPI over the last three years.[1472] The number of listings removed following proactive measures by platforms remained high and varied between 90% and 98% during the six data collection exercises since 2017. Da-

1467 In % of the top 100 listings in a certain product category of a certain brand.

1468 European Commission, 'Overview of the Functioning of the Memorandum of Understanding on the Sale of Counterfeit Goods via the Internet, SWD(2017) 430 Final' (European Commission 2017) 7. Alibaba and Allegro had also joined the MoU by 2017.

1469 ibid 11–13.

1470 European Commission, 'Report on the Functioning of the Memorandum of Understanding on the Sale of Counterfeit Goods via the Internet, SWD(2020) 166 Final/2' (2020) SWD(2020) 166 final/2 <https://ec.europa.eu/docsroom/documents/42701> accessed 27 August 2020.

1471 ibid 7, 11–13.

1472 ibid 8–9.

ta on the third KPI, the number of restrictions imposed on sellers, also remained inconclusive, due to only half of the participating platforms providing feedback on this indicator and one platform not providing data on repeat infringer sanctions.[1473] The feedback on the KPI collection process appears to demonstrate a continuing rift between online platforms and rightsowners over methodologies, readiness to report, the interpretation of the numbers and how to address efficiency gaps in the working of the MoU. On the positive side, the recurring meetings seem to have strengthened relationships between rightsholders and platforms and have led to some bilateral cooperation. Most platforms that participate in the MoU use automated and proactive systems for identifying and removing counterfeit goods. While decision accuracy and false positives remain problems, rightsowners and platforms work increasingly together to define criteria that help platforms in risk profiling for the application of automated tools. However, platforms note that these measures are resource-intensive and would need to remain proportionate and reasonable.[1474] Meanwhile, the use of brand protection programs by platforms is on the rise.[1475] It is endorsed by and large by platforms and rightsowners as an effective means to identify counterfeits.

There remain, however, significant differences about the state of repeat infringer enforcement measures. Rightsholder denied that any significant progress has been made in this matter, thus throwing doubts on the seller vetting and onboarding processes of platforms. Online platforms, however, insisted on the need to remain flexible in the application of these policies.[1476] The European Commission and rightsholders see the recent Platform-to Business Regulation (P2B) as a useful tool for bringing more transparency into operational practices of online platforms, especially where it concerns setting out and implementing sanctioning policies for repeat infringers.[1477] Rightsholders also called up the recent Market Surveillance Regulation 2019/1020 (MSR) in the area of product regulation, which im-

1473 ibid 9–10.
1474 ibid 20–21.
1475 ibid 22.
1476 ibid 27–30.
1477 Platform-to-business (P2B) Regulation 2019/1150 (n 1248) Articles 3 & 4; European Commission, 'MoU Progress Report - SWD(2020) 166 Final/2' (n 1469) 23, 26. Articles 3 and 4 requires that online intermediation services, which includes search engines and e-commerce marketplaces, have clear terms and conditions in place, as well as transparent sanction processes for repeatedly infringing business users.

poses an obligation on ISSPs to cooperate with authorities in the fight against products that pose compliance and safety risks.[1478] Meanwhile, three rightsholders from the luxury sector withdrew from the MoU in January 2020 due to insufficient progress. In 2019, *Facebook (Marketplace)* joined the MoU bringing the total number of participating online platforms to six.

Looking at the technological progress in proactive measures, expedited NTD procedures and private information sharing over the last 10 years, it is surprising that the 2016 MoU is based on the exact loose and basic criteria as its previous version of 2011. There would have been a chance to commit to more ambitious principles and standards both on the side of platforms and rightsholders, but this was expressly rejected in the last 2020 progress report.[1479] Despite the creation of doubtlessly useful KPIs, there is no further evidence of common standards emerging in the fight against trademark infringements committed via online intermediaries. Arguably, the best practices shared in the 2020 Report are too little considering that the MoU goes into its tenth year of existence.

Transparency on the enforcement procedures remains a major problem not only where it concerns relations with the owners of the trademark rights, but also where cooperation with authorities is concerned. With the intricacy and complexity of trademark law and the rise of automated takedowns, there is a clear need to protect against the risk of abusive notices and faulty decisions in the many possible borderline cases.[1480] Platforms' self-styled enforcement mechanisms may have a significant effect on sellers and consumers. The current situation of private agreements between platforms and rightsholders, and the rise in automated tools, may eventually have an anti-competitive effect and restrict consumer choice. There is a real risk that these private ordering style arrangements benefit only the economically powerful stakeholders and preclude the dynamic adaption of

1478 Regulation (EU) 2019/1020 of the European Parliament and of the Council of 20 June 2019 on market surveillance and compliance of products and amending Directive 2004/42/EC and Regulations (EC) No 765/2008 and (EU) No 305/2011 (Text with EEA relevance.) 2019 (OJ L 169) Article 7 (2); European Commission, 'MoU Progress Report - SWD(2020) 166 Final/2' (n 1469) 34.

1479 European Commission, 'MoU Progress Report - SWD(2020) 166 Final/2' (n 1469) 38.

1480 Marsoof (n 1378) 150, 168; Frederick W Mostert and Martin B Schwimmer, 'Notice and Takedown for Trademarks 100th Anniversary Issue' (2011) 101 The Trademark Reporter 249, 278–279.

the responsibilities of intermediaries.[1481] However, despite of the persisting problem of counterfeit sales through online marketplaces and the opacity of the rapidly evolving private enforcement processes, there appears to be no intention of further policy action on the side of the European Commission. Yet, public scrutiny is needed more than ever.[1482]

b. Other EU policy initiatives

Compared to digital content and copyright, the policymaker has more alternatives when it comes to disrupting the supply chain of counterfeit products. To that effect, the European Commission has been more active in neighbouring policy areas. It strengthened, for example, the enforcement powers of EU customs authorities relating to the seizure and prosecution of IPR infringements.[1483] In addition, the "follow the money" approach aims to limit the means of fraudsters and other economic actors to profit from the sales of infringing goods via the internet. In 2018, the European Commission brought advertising intermediaries into the game by forging an MoU by which these actors commit to avoiding the placement of adverts on websites that sell and share counterfeit and copyright infringing goods and content.[1484] Anti-money laundering obligations imposed on online platforms, which integrate payment services into their operations, would provide an additional way to freeze assets of counterfeiters and pursue them criminally. Currently, authorities are only starting to look at this enforcement channel.[1485] Most of the larger online platforms own financial service entities that are regulated by EU Member States' financial supervision authorities.[1486] Other intermediaries that interact with online platforms are transportation or logistics service providers, or payment in-

1481 Dinwoodie (n 312) 471.

1482 ibid.

1483 Regulation (EU) No 608/2013 concerning customs enforcement of intellectual property rights 2013 (OJ L 181).

1484 European Commission, 'Memorandum of Understanding on Online Advertising and Intellectual Property Rights' (n 542).

1485 Moiseienko (n 1367) 14.

1486 The following online platforms have subsidiaries that are registered and regulated as financial services in the EU: *Google* – as electronic money institution (EME) and payment institution (PI) in Lithuania and Ireland, respectively; *Facebook* – as PI and EME in Ireland; *Microsoft* – as PI in Ireland; *Amazon* and *AliExpress* - as EMEs in Luxembourg; *eBay* and *AirBnb* - as PIs in Luxembourg; *Rakuten* - as a bank in Luxembourg; *Uber* – as an EME in the Netherlands;

termediaries.[1487] Apart from the concrete responsibilities of platforms discussed above, diligently operating (multi-sided) marketplaces should be aware of the opportunities and threats that these various supply chain intermediaries present in the fight against unlawful products and content.

Lastly, the draft DSA now appears to partly address the enforcement gaps with regards to trademark infringements on online marketplaces through the imposition of traceability requirements and onboarding due diligence requirements for traders.[1488] These know-your-customer (KYC) style obligations had been demanded by brand owners and other commentators for some time as a means to force due diligence on platform operators in the fight against counterfeits and non-compliant products.[1489]

VI. Summary and outlook

The sale of counterfeits and other trademark infringing products via online platforms has been a significant problem, causing economic damage to rightsholders and important risks to consumer trust and safety. While trademark law provides unitary protection in the EU against primary infringers, secondary liabilities are outside of its scope. The enforcement of the latter has, however, often been frustrated by the disparate national interpretations and applications of the remedies provided by IPRED against intermediaries. Meanwhile, the intermediary liability provisions of the ECD have met the same unsatisfactory patchwork applications as in many other content areas. CJEU guidance on the duties and liabilities of Web 2.0. online marketplaces and search engines have not brought the clarification sought, although they created cornerstone responsibility concepts, such as the diligent economic operator.[1490]

---

searches conducted in the Public Supervision Register of *De Nederlandsche Bank* on 27.08.2020: 'Public Register - De Nederlandsche Bank'

1487 J Bruce Richardson, 'With Great Power Comes Little Responsibility: The Role of Online Payment Service Providers with Regards to Websites Selling Counterfeit Goods' (2014) 12 Canadian Journal of Law and Technology <https://ojs.library.dal.ca/CJLT/article/view/6607> accessed 20 March 2017.

1488 European Commission DSA proposal (n 10) Article 22, Recital 49.

1489 European Commission, 'Summary Response - IPR Enforcement' (n 173) 17, 44; Ullrich, 'Standards for Duty of Care?' (n 1137) 125; Ullrich, 'A Risk-Based Approach towards Infringement Prevention on the Internet' (n 747) 243–245.

1490 *L'Oréal v eBay* (n 463) paras 120–124.

In the by now familiar battle to seize primary infringers on the internet, online marketplaces as middlemen have moved into the focus of rightsowners when it comes to the enforcement of their economic rights. Rightsowners have sought relief by imposing primary liabilities on the likes of *Google Search*, *EBay* and *Amazon*. These efforts, too, have until recently been fruitless. Courts refused to attribute to online marketplaces and search engines any part in the use of trademarks in the course of trade. In some Member States, however, things appear to be changing. This has certainly been aided by the constant expansion of trademark protection during a time of globalisation and consumer focus on brands. But it is also a signal that the manifold ancillary services of integrated online platforms, such as advertising, search, payment services, order fulfilment, complaints handling, sales and fraud analytics, or even fincial services,[1491] make these intermediaries appear in a changing light: they actively and selectively promote third party commerce and derive data and financial benefits from the commercial services they provide to sellers and consumers.

In the shadow of this dispersed and unclear legal picture, online marketplaces have started to build their own private enforcement processes. First, obligatory NTD processes have been enriched with expedited and customised removal processes granted to economically powerful rightsholders. Secondly, rightsholders are hauled into the enforcement efforts of platforms by being involved in the authorisation and removal of products sold by sellers or by providing brand-specific intelligence. Third, most online marketplaces have been developing their own automated prevention tools for spotting and removing trademark infringing goods. These processes are, however, buried in obscurity. Consequently, it is not clear how the risk of abusive notices and potential anti-competitive behaviour by major brands is being contained.

Policy action on the side of the EU lawmaker has been limited to self-regulatory codes of practice. Two successive MoUs produced high level KPIs, that, once implemented, testified to the ongoing problem of counterfeit sales and the rise of automated enforcement systems by platforms. Apart from better cooperation between rightsholders and platforms, and anecdotal evidence of better enforcement against infringers, the Commission repeatedly noted a clear need for further improvement over the almost 10 years of existence of the MoU. The self-regulatory efforts have so far not brought the transparency sought by rightsholders over the manda-

---

1491 'Amazon Lending' <https://sell.amazon.com/programs/amazon-lending.html> accessed 29 June 2020.

tory NTD processes and proactive measures. More importantly, this transparency is also amiss for sellers and consumers. The P2B Regulation[1492] and the Omnibus Directive[1493] will help improve transparency to business users and consumers on the underlying ranking and display mechanisms of internal search results. They will also raise due diligence standards of platforms to some extent, by obliging them to ensure sellers clearly state whether they act as professional traders or private individuals.[1494] This obligation has been carried over into the DSA proposal as a condition for an exemption from consumer law liabilities.[1495] However, clearer positive obligations for platforms when it comes to creating an environment that discourages the sale of counterfeit products are still wanting. The traceability due diligence obligations proposed by the new DSA may be a useful first step in this direction.[1496]

Meanwhile, the US Government completed its more comprehensive review of intermediary liability in 2020 by announcing that it would investigate legislative means to pressure online marketplace into doing more against the phenomenon of counterfeits sold via their services. It would look into the possibility of expanding contributory trademark infringement standards to online platforms.[1497] Given the US tradition so far to absolve online marketplaces from even less onerous duties than stipulated elsewhere in the world, this is a remarkable step. It is further proof of the mounting policy pressures on online intermediaries to become more responsible actors.

D. *Product and food safety regulation*

6. Product safety (non-food products)

I. Background – product safety in e-commerce and online platforms

The sale of unsafe or non-compliant products via online marketplace and other intermediaries has received much less public policy attention than

---

1492 Platform-to-business (P2B) Regulation 2019/1150 (n 1248) Article 5.

1493 Omnibus Directive 2019/2161 (n 1249) Article 6a (1) (a).

1494 ibid Article 6a (1) (b).

1495 European Commission DSA proposal (n 10) Article 5 (3).

1496 ibid Article 22.

1497 'Combating Trafficking in Counterfeit and Pirated Goods - Report to the President of the United States' (n 1363) 33.

for example the issues of hate speech or copyright infringements. However, the fight against the sale of unsafe consumer products is an affirmed part of the Commission's broader initiative to tackle illegal content online and enhance the responsibilities of online platforms. According to this, the violation of product safety rules is part of the array of unlawful content that falls under the ECD's horizontal liability framework and for which online intermediaries should take more responsibility.[1498] Data from the OECD testifies to this growing problem, which correlates with the rise in e-commerce and its expansion into almost any retail category. A 2016 OECD study found that banned, recalled or incorrectly labelled products sold online are more likely to be found on e-commerce platforms than on online retailer websites.[1499] For example, in a sweep of 291 banned or recalled products in 17 OECD jurisdictions (of which 11 in the EU) the OECD found that 86% were still available via e-commerce marketplaces. This concerned safety equipment, sports products, personal care and children's products. Meanwhile, 50% of the 62 products investigated by the study did not meet safety standards, but were nevertheless available via online marketplaces.[1500] Incorrect product labelling is another frequent problem on online marketplaces. It concerned 92% of products targeted by the OECD exercise. The UK consumer association *Which?* found that unsafe children's car seats, smoke alarms, toys, USB chargers and travel adapters where routinely available via marketplaces like *eBay*, *Amazon*, *AliExpress* or *Wish.com*. Moreover, once delisted, many of these offers reappeared within days on these sites. The report also quotes research from the *Danish Consumer Council* highlighting problems with unsafe cosmetics sold via online marketplaces.[1501] Within the EU, national market surveillance authorities (MSAs) like the German *Bundesnetzagentur* (Federal Networks Agency), for example, which is responsible for enforcing compliance with consumer electronics, had identified 3.5 million products sold online that violated EU product standards. This authority routinely sweeps the sites of both e-retailers and online marketplaces. Its 2019 annual report indicates that the availability of illegal products such as frequency jammers or other formally

1498 European Commission, 'COM (2017) 555 Final' (n 69) 3, 6.

1499 OECD, 'OECD' (n 173).

1500 ibid 18–19.

1501 Which?, 'Online Marketplaces and Product Safety' (2019) Policy Paper November 2019 <https://www.which.co.uk/policy/consumers/5234/onlinemarketplaces> accessed 3 July 2020.

non-compliant radio equipment, like mobile phones, Bluetooth speakers or drones is a persistent problem. [1502]

Like in the area of trademark infringement via online marketplaces, the reasons for this can be seen in the ground-breaking change in the supply chain and consumer behaviours caused by the internet and globalisation. Online marketplaces have become the window through which consumers can access a sheer endless variety of products from anywhere in the world and have them delivered home. All this happens through bypassing traditional import and shipping routes through the use of small postal consignments or FSPs, which are difficult to control. In this context, there is a strong link between counterfeits and product safety issues: infiltration of the supply chain happens though the same methods. In addition, counterfeit products are also more prone to carry safety and health risks. This has been described abundantly.[1503] According to the *Which?* survey mentioned above, 70% of marketplace users would support legislative changes that see online marketplaces take over a legal responsibility for overseeing the safety of products sold through their platforms.[1504]

In July 2017, the Commission acknowledged in its Notice on the market surveillance of products sold online[1505] that e-commerce posed mounting challenges to the protection of consumers. The document highlights a number of developments that pose challenges to the effective enforcement of product safety laws. It expresses a number of concerns, such as: difficulties of MSAs to trace products sold online and identify responsible economic operators; a rise in sales from e-commerce business, including marketplaces, that are located outside the EU; market surveillance authorities' problems to get access to products for testing and risk assessments; difficulties in coordinating online market surveillance activities across the EU; low consumer awareness when it comes to e-commerce purchases.[1506]

1502 Stephan Winkelmann, 'Statistik Der Marktüberwachung 2019' (Bundesnetzagentur 2020) 10–15

1503 Ohly, 'Counterfeiting and Consumer Protection' (n 1406) 35–36; European Commission, 'Summary Response - IPR Enforcement' (n 173) 10, 41; 'Combating Trafficking in Counterfeit and Pirated Goods - Report to the President of the United States' (n 1363) 16–17; Koch (n 173) 353–355; OECD and European Union Intellectual Property Office (n 1356); Union (n 1360) 36; Market Surveillance Regulation Recital 17.

1504 Which? (n 1500) 17.

1505 European Commission, 'Commission Notice on the Market Surveillance of Products Sold Online (2017/C 250/01)' (European Commission 2017).

1506 ibid 2.

II. EU product safety law and e-commerce

a. The New Approach and the New Legislative Framework

The large majority of non-food consumer products are regulated by the *New Legislative Framework (NLF)*[1507] Directives, which evolved out of the *New Approach*. This regulatory area is different from the previous fields of intellectual property, which concerned mainly economic rights, enforced chiefly through private law. Likewise, defamation and hate speech[1508] are essentially private law areas that have personality rights at their centre. In that respect, only the fight against terrorism shares its public law focus with the area of product (and food) safety, where both the substantive law and its enforcement provisions are regulated by EU or national public law.

The General Product Safety Directive (GPSD)[1509] and Regulation 765/2008[1510] on market surveillance are the two centrepieces of product regulation in the EU. The GPSD sets out the safety requirements of products and the responsibilities and obligations of economic operators and Member States to meet these requirements. This includes provisions on how to deal with dangerous products and product recalls. The GPSD is complemented by *lex specialis* in certain product sectors. These specific directives set out additional, harmonised technical safety requirements in order to address risks that these products pose to consumer and public health. For example, toys need to meet certain enhanced requirements when it comes to the chemical composition of products, product design (such as detachable small parts), or warning labels etc. Regulation 765/2008 deals mainly with the enforcement of the provisions laid down in the GPSD and the sector specific product laws. It provides more detailed definitions of economic operators (manufacturers, importers, distributors)[1511] and spells out the responsibilities of national MSAs in the enforce-

1507 European Commission, 'New Legislative Framework - Growth' (n 22).

1508 With the notable exception where hate speech impacts the public safety and security interests at national level and for the EU under the area of 'freedom, security and justice'. Council Framework Decision 2008/913/JHA of 28 November 2008 on combating certain forms and expressions of racism and xenophobia by means of criminal law Recital 2.

1509 Directive 2001/95 (GPSD).

1510 Regulation (EC) 765/2008 of 9 July 2008 setting out the requirements for accreditation and market surveillance relating to the marketing of products 2008 (OJ L 218).

1511 ibid Article 2.

ment of product sector laws.[1512] This Regulation was supplemented in 2019 by the Market Surveillance Regulation 2019/1020[1513] (MSR). It was passed as part of the EU Goods Package, which aims to strengthen the horizontal enforcement of EU product safety rules in the face of e-commerce and the fragmentation of national MSAs' activities.[1514]

In order to understand the more structural problems of the enforcement of product regulation with regards to e-commerce and online intermediaries a brief overview of the history of the *NLF* and the *New Approach* is appropriate. The *New Approach* was instigated in 1985[1515] as a consequence of the CJEU's *Cassis de Dijon* ruling.[1516] In this decisive case a German retailer wanted to market French fruit liqueur in its German retail outlets. The German authorities refused the retailer to market the product because domestic legislation required that fruit liqueurs have a minimum alcohol content of 25%. The French product had between 15 – 20% of alcohol content. The German Government cited the general interest reasons of public health and consumer protection against unfair commercial practices[1517] for imposing these restrictions. The CJEU, however, found that these general interest reasons had been unjustly applied, leading to an undue restriction in the free movement of goods. The ruling had two consequences that led to the emergence of the *New Approach* to product legislation.

1) The general interest exemptions that allow for a restriction to the free movement of goods must be applied in a proportional way. As a result, the EU legislator started to define the general interest, or essential requirements, through legislation in various product areas. The idea behind the harmonisation of these essential requirements was to remove any possibility that Member States unilaterally apply restrictions on products on the ba-

---

1512 For a more detailed overview of the interplay between *lex specialis* and the framework legislation of the GPSD and Regulation 765/2008 see: Lauren Sterrett, 'Product Liability: Advancements in European Union Product Liability Law and a Comparison Between the EU and U.S. Regime' (2015) 23 Michigan State International Law Review 885, 42.

1513 Market Surveillance Regulation.

1514 European Commission, 'The Goods Package: Reinforcing Trust in the Single Market, COM(2017) 787 Final' (2017).

1515 Council Resolution of 7 May 1985 on a new approach to technical harmonization and standards 1985 (OJ C 136).

1516 *Rewe-Zentral AG v Bundesmonopolverwaltung für Branntwein, Case 120/78* [1979] EU:C:1979:42 (CJEU).

1517 ibid 9.As provided for in: Treaty on the Functioning of the European Union (Consolidated versions of the Treaty on European Union and the Treaty on the Functioning of the European Union 2016) Article 36.

sis of their general interest. The essential requirements relate mainly to health and safety risks of certain products. Meeting the essential requirements means that the products can be freely marketed across the EU.[1518] Under this kind of approach, the EU has, for example, put in place legislation that fixes essential technical (safety) requirements for electronic products (e.g. electromagnetic compatibility[1519], wireless communication[1520]), toys[1521], protective equipment[1522] or medical devices.[1523] The EU uses Article 114 TFEU, which gives it competence to approximate laws in the interest of the functioning of the single market, as a legal basis for these initiatives.[1524]

2) *Cassis de Dijon* laid the foundations for the principle of mutual recognition.[1525] Goods which can legally be marketed in one Member State will automatically be accepted across all other Member States and the European Economic Area (EEA).[1526] If goods meet the essentially requirements spelled out in the relevant product legislation, then it does not matter where they are first placed on the market for them to be accepted throughout the Community area.

These principles gave rise to EU standardisation and the *CE* sign, the hallmarks of the *New Approach*. Essential requirements are relatively high-

---

1518 For more detail on the interplay of product legislation with the Treaty provisions: European Commission, 'Commission Notice, The "Blue Guide" on the Implementation of EU Products Rules 2016, (2016/C 272/01)' (European Commission 2016); European Commission (ed), *Free Movements of Goods: Guide to the Application of Treaty Provisions Governing the Free Movement of Goods* (Publ Off of the Europ Union 2010); Schepel (n 34) 63–66.

1519 Directive 2014/30/EU of 26 February 2014 on the harmonisation of the laws of the Member States relating to electromagnetic compatibility (recast) 2014 (OJ L 96).

1520 Directive 2014/53/EU of 16 April 2014 on the harmonisation of the laws of the Member States relating to the making available on the market of radio equipment 2014 (OJ L 153).

1521 Directive 2009/48.

1522 Regulation (EU) 2016/425 of the European Parliament and of the Council of 9 March 2016 on personal protective equipment and repealing Council Directive 89/686/EEC (Text with EEA relevance) 2016 (OJ L 081).

1523 Regulation (EU) 2017/745 of 5 April 2017 on medical devices 2017 (OJ L 117, 552017).

1524 Other product areas, such as furniture or tableware, are not subject to specific legislation, but may still be wholly or in part covered by European Norms (standards). In any case, they are still subject to the provisions of the GPSD.

1525 Friedl Weiss and Clemens Kaupa, *European Union Internal Market Law* (Cambridge Univ Press 2014) 69–71.

1526 *Cassis de Dijon* (n 1515) para 14.

level iterations that address the specific health and safety concerns of certain products groups. Meeting them involves, however, more complex technical product design considerations. Inserting these technical specifications into legislation was deemed unpractical and too inflexible given technological and market developments. The European Commission decided to put the responsibility for defining these more detailed technical specifications to standardisation bodies. These private, industry-run organisations were tasked with drawing up harmonised technical standards which incorporate the technical specifications. Meeting such technical standards provided a presumption of compliance for manufacturers that their products complied with the essential requirements spelled out in sector *lex specialis.*[1527] The standards remain largely voluntary, which means that manufacturers may, in theory, design their products to their own technical product specifications and then provide proof that they meet the essential requirements. Under the *New Approach* Directives, manufacturers need to create a declaration of conformity for their products and affix a *CE* Mark. The declaration of conformity needs to list the product directives or regulations that the product complies with. The *CE* mark serves as a demonstration to the consumer and other actors along the supply chain that the product meets the essential requirements and can be marketed in the EU.[1528]

The EU standardisation policy of the *New Approach* is seen as a success that made an important contribution to EU integration.[1529] It has been continuously reformed, formalised and expanded,[1530] covering more products and spreading into the area of services.[1531] As of today, there are over

1527 Decision No 768/2008/EC of the European Parliament and of the Council of 9 July 2008 on a common framework for the marketing of products 2008 (OJ L 218) Article R8.

1528 Jean-Pierre Galland, 'The Difficulties of Regulating Markets and Risks in Europe through Notified Bodies' (2013) 4 European Journal of Risk Regulation 365.

1529 Rob Van Gestel and Hans-W Micklitz, 'European Integration through Standardization: How Judicial Review Is Breaking down the Club House of Private Standardization Bodies' (2013) 50 Common Market L. Rev. 145, 156–157.

1530 Regulation 765/2008 765; Decision 768/2008 768; Regulation (EU) 1025/2012 of 25 October 2012 on European standardisation 2012 (OJ L 316, 14112012).

1531 Jean-Christophe Graz, *The Power of Standards: Hybrid Authority and the Globalisation of Services* (1st edn, Cambridge University Press 2019) 96–97 <https://www.cambridge.org/core/product/identifier/9781108759038/type/book> accessed 2 July 2020.

4,000 technical standards referenced in 30 directives or regulations.[1532] Three large EU standardisation bodies exist that continuously design new or update existing technical standards. This co-regulatory approach, whereby the public interest requirements on products are defined by legislation, but the technical details and procedures of compliance with requirements is handed over to private and society actors, has been seen as a success benefitting companies and the position of the EU as a global standard setter.[1533] This is despite potential problems and rising criticism over transparency and democratic accountability and accessibility of private standards that have ascended to become to quasi law.[1534] Within this system, enforcement lies firmly in the hands of public authorities at Member State level. This will be briefly described further below.

b. Responsibilities and liabilities of economic actors

EU product legislation has traditionally allocated the obligations for compliance with product legislation to the economic actors involved in the making available of the products on the EU market.[1535] Under the GPSD, the primary responsibility for ensuring that products are safe, lies with the person that places a product on the market, usually the producer. The producer is defined as the manufacturer, if situated within the EU, its authorised representative or any other person that affects the safety properties of the product.[1536] These economic actors would incur primary liability for any failure to comply with product safety rules. In that respect, placing on the market refers to the first time a product is made available on the EU market.[1537]

Secondly, those persons that make products available that have been placed on the market, defined as distributors, have to exercise due care when handling and marketing products. This means they need to ensure products have the required signs affixed and carry necessary documentation. They also have specific duties in reacting to any suspicions over when a product may breach compliance requirements. Once their activities affect

1532 ibid 90.
1533 ibid 95.
1534 Van Gestel and Micklitz (n 1528) 150–156.
1535 Directive 2001/95 (GPSD) Article 3 (1).
1536 ibid Article 2 (e).
1537 Regulation 765/2008 Article 2 (2). Market Surveillance Regulation Article 3 (2).

the safety of a product directly, through handling, storage or by changing its labelling, they are considered producers and primary liable.

All these requirements are fleshed out in more detail through Decision 768/2009[1538] and in sector specific legislation. For example, the Toys Safety Directive includes more detailed obligations on manufacturers regarding the traceability of toys, such as the affixation of serial or batch numbers.[1539] All actors have an obligation to cooperate with MSAs in cases where dangerous products have been identified and recalled by manufacturers and authorities. In the time following the GPSD, which was enacted in 2001, there has been a marked shift in the assignment of product compliance obligations from the type of economic actor towards specific activities, such as placing on the market. This can be seen at least partly as a result of the rise of e-commerce. The GPSD had for example not defined the concept of placing or making available on the market. But with the rise of online retail an increasing number of products where in fact placed on the market without an economic operator that resided within the EU, or by EU actors that were traditionally not seen as economic operators, such as fulfilment service providers (FSPs)[1540] or online marketplaces.

As an answer to this problem, the recent Market Surveillance Regulation (MSR) included FSPs as economic actors, with specific responsibilities. It also attempted to clarify the role of online marketplaces (referred to as ISSPs in the regulation). Finally, it stipulated that a product can only be placed on the market if there is an economic operator established in the EU.[1541] This will be analysed below.

III. Enforcement and e-commerce

a. Tackling the challenges of enforcement in e-commerce

Enforcement of product legislation is in the hands of Member States, who allocate their tasks to MSAs. Different product sectors are allocated to specific MSAs. Given the highly technical nature of standards, market surveil-

1538 Decision 768/2008 Chapter R2.

1539 Directive 2009/48 Article 4 (5).

1540 The activities of FSPs will be explained in more detail further below in this chapter.

1541 Market Surveillance Regulation Articles 3 (11, 13, 14, 15), 4, 6, 7 (2), 14 (4) (k), recitals 13, 16, 41.

lance and enforcement are often also distinctly technical exercises. In many Member States, MSAs are made up to a large part of engineers or scientists. The compliance of products often needs to be assessed and technical test reports examined and evaluated. The enforcement picture is therefore a distinctly technical and sectoral one, that may also be delegated to different administrational levels depending on the constitutional and administrational set up of Member States. This verticality has been reinforced by technological complexity and product innovation, which resulted in more complex safety risk assessments and certification requirements.

The need to improve horizontal coordination in order to achieve a level playing field when enforcing product laws and fighting non-compliant products was already recognised before the rise of e-commerce by the European Commission.[1542] Regulation 765/2008 attempted to address this through formulating general requirements on the organisation of market surveillance programs and common measures that MSAs must adopt when assessing products and dealing with economic operators.[1543] However, the rise of e-commerce quickly turned out to be a further challenge with a high impact on enforcement.[1544] A new proposal to strengthen the horizontal cooperation between MSAs, the '2013 Goods Package'[1545], failed, however, due to Member States disagreeing over the content of a proposed consumer product safety regulation.

The Commission's ex-post evaluation report of Regulation 765/2008 of 2016 initiated a new effort towards upgrading the enforcement framework. The report found that the application of the existing product safety framework under the *NLF* was adversely affected by two developments: e-commerce and budget constraints on MSAs.[1546] Regulation 765/2008 did not sufficiently address the problems caused by a fragmented and complicated market surveillance and enforcement system in the EU. MSAs have varying

---

1542 Technopolis Group and others, 'Ex-Post Evaluation of the Application of the Market Surveillance Provisions of Regulation (EC) No 765/2008' (2017) 7–8.

1543 Carsten Ullrich, 'New Approach Meets New Economy: Enforcing EU Product Safety in e-Commerce' (2019) 26 Maastricht Journal of European and Comparative Law 558, 565–566.

1544 European Commission, '20 Actions for Safer and Compliant Products for Europe: A Multi-Annual Action Plan for the Surveillance of Products in the EU, COM/2013/076 Final' (European Commission 2013) Action 12.

1545 European Commission, Proposal for a Regulation on consumer product safety and repealing Council Directive 87/357/EEC and Directive 2001/95/EC, COM(2013) 78 final 2013 [2013/0049/COD].

1546 Technopolis Group and others (n 1541) 102–103, 142–143.

degrees of competencies and resources across Member States. This leads to disparities when it comes to access to product testing or sanctioning powers. Cross-border cooperation between MSAs on EU level, as well as cooperation with economic actors was seen as unsatisfactory.[1547] As a purely illustrative example, there are about 500 different MSAs across the EU that enforce the *NLF* product safety laws. In some Member States, especially those with federal structures, like Germany or Spain, enforcement competencies may be at different administrational levels (Federal, regional state, or even local).[1548] If this is added to the existing funding challenges, then it becomes clear that the enforcement system is broadly inapt to deal with the many unsafe products sold online. Effective market surveillance of e-commerce requires extra close intra-EU cooperation and swift action. Existing informal networks of cooperation such as the Administrative Cooperation Groups (AdCos),[1549] or the Information and Communication System on Market Surveillance (ICSMS)[1550] have witnessed a mixed degree of adoption by Member States, leading to suboptimal efficacy. Even the RAPEX system for notification of dangerous products is used inconsistently by MSAs.[1551] The emerging picture shows the difficulties MSAs face when dealing with product safety issues online, where sellers may delete offerings; change or re-introduce them through other platforms, supply chain channels or Member States; simply disappear or are out of the jurisdictional reach of EU MSAs. These problems will be illustrated in more detail in the case studies in the next Chapter.

1547 ibid 36–72, 11–113.

1548 ibid 82–84; European Commission, 'Commission Staff Working Document -Impact Assessment - Proposal for a Regulation of the European Parliament and of the Council Laying down Rules and Procedures for Compliance with and Enforcement of Union Harmonisation Legislation on Products - SWD(2017) 466 Final - Part 2/4' (European Commission 2017) 401–458.

1549 'Administrative Cooperation Groups (AdCos)' (*Internal Market, Industry, Entrepreneurship and SMEs - European Commission*, 5 July 2016) <https://ec.europa.eu/growth/single-market/goods/building-blocks/market-surveillance/organisation/administrative-cooperation-groups_en> accessed 3 July 2020.

1550 'ICSMS - European Commission' <https://webgate.ec.europa.eu/icsms/?locale=en> accessed 3 July 2020. It is telling that that page prominently states in of its headings that "Current market surveillance practice is desperately in need of improvement."

1551 'Safety Gate: The Rapid Alert System for Dangerous Non-Food Products' <https://ec.europa.eu/consumers/consumers_safety/safety_products/rapex/alerts/repository/content/pages/rapex/index_en.htm> accessed 3 July 2020. For a detailed account of these problems see: Technopolis Group and others (n 1541) 66–78.

The EU aims to address these shortcomings through the creation of a Union Product Compliance Network under the new MSR. This new network is supposed to expand and strengthen the existing regulatory networks, namely the AdCos, ICSMS and RAPEX by backing them up with a centralised administrational structure.[1552] All this will be supported by an improved, binding framework for coordination of surveillance, more EU funding and enhanced powers for MSAs.[1553] In the context of the highly heterogenic state of enforcement, institutional differences and ongoing public funding crises, the EU has a Herculean task ahead.

b. Online intermediaries and product safety law

E-commerce meant that new intermediaries have entered the supply chain of consumer products. These were either entirely new actors, like FSPs or e-commerce marketplaces, or existing providers that adapted to the online environment, such as payment services or advertising intermediaries.

Fulfilment Service providers

Fulfilment service providers (FSPs) have emerged thanks to the demands of e-commerce. FSPs have answered to the demand of customised B2C order fulfilment, helping smaller, brick and mortar or online businesses to scale their e-commerce operations. They offer shipment, storage and stock management solutions, order preparation and may even handle customer returns and complaint handling or sales analytics.[1554] These services are used by sellers that operate their own websites and those selling on online marketplaces. FSPs have helped to democratise e-commerce by enabling small shops to sell potentially worldwide, by offering affordable and easy-to-manage shipping and storage solutions.[1555] On the more controversial side, FSPs have often been identified by MSAs as fulfilling goods on behalf of sellers based outside the EU. However, they were not identified as economic operators under the existing product safety rules prior to the MSR.

1552 Market Surveillance Regulation Articles 29 - 35.

1553 ibid Articles 13 - 16.

1554 C Dwight Klappich and others, 'Warehousing and Fulfillment Vendor Guide' (Gartner 2018) Research Note.

1555 Ullrich, 'Déjà vu Davidoff – The German Federal Court of Justice Refers Another Case Brought by Coty Dealing with Trade Marks in e-Commerce to the CJEU' (n 593) 6.

Both the EU Blue Guide and the Commission Notice concluded that, depending on the activities of the FSP, they could be categorised as distributors, importers or authorised representatives under Regulation 765/2008 and the GPSD.[1556] The Commission noted the legal uncertainty relating to FSPs when it came to enforcing product safety rules and recommended that they be included as economic actor during the drafting phase of the MSR.[1557]

The MSR now includes FSPs as a new category of economic operators if they are engaged in at least two of the following four activities: warehousing, packaging, addressing and dispatching. It is noteworthy that the definition in the MSR clearly distinguishes them from pure postal, parcel or freight delivery services.[1558] It offers therefore a more realistic characterisation than the one accepted in the trademark infringement case *Versand durch Amazon* by the BGH mentioned previously. An FSP would have primary, manufacturer style obligations, if they are the sole economic operator for that product within the EU, i.e. they are placing it on the market. Apart from that, they would in any case have distributor due care obligations of: verifying the existence of applicable product compliance documentation, being at the disposal of MSAs for information and cooperation requests, and informing MSAs where they suspect that a product presents a risk.[1559] The MSR therefore allocates clear obligations to FSPs and gives MSAs a legal basis to enforce product safety rules.[1560] The solution found for online marketplaces differs somewhat in that respect.

Online intermediaries as economic actors prior to the Market Surveillance Regulation

Online marketplaces have seen a phenomenal rise. From global operators *Amazon, Alibaba* and *eBay*, sector specific or emerging sites like *Asos, Etsy*

1556 European Commission, 'Blue Guide' (n 1517) 36; European Commission, '2017/C 250/01' (n 1504) 7.

1557 European Commission, 'Commission Staff Working Document -Impact Assessment - Proposal for a Regulation of the European Parliament and of the Council Laying down Rules and Procedures for Compliance with and Enforcement of Union Harmonisation Legislation on Products - SWD(2017) 466 Final - Part 1/4' (European Commission 2017) 22–25, 125.

1558 Market Surveillance Regulation Article 3 (11).

1559 ibid Article 4.

1560 Whether this will happen effectively in reality depends on the MSA in question and their ability to cooperate with other MSAs and economic operators.

or *Wish*.com, to regional or national players, such as *CDiscount, PriceMinister, Allegro, Frubit, Emag* or *Shopping24*, an impressive variety of online marketplaces exist today. In addition, social media companies like *Facebook* or *Google* have also forayed into e-commerce, founding their own marketplaces, while other social media or messaging networks like *WhatsApp, Instagram, Twitter or Snapchat* offer in-app product purchases. Entirely new technologies, such as voice-based retail, will further change the face of e-commerce.[1561] The EU's ex-post evaluation of Regulation 765/2008 highlighted the problems of MSAs when attempting to enforce product regulation *vis-à-vis* these channels. It is increasingly difficult to pin down the role that online marketplaces play within a supply chain that has become more and more complex.[1562]

As has been seen from the area of trademarks, online marketplaces are habitually classed as online intermediaries under the ECD. The Commission Notice acknowledges that e-commerce platforms cannot be obliged to check on a general basis their marketplaces for unlawful products, because they are protected by the liability exemptions of the ECD.[1563] Consequently, they have also not been classed as economic operators under both the GPSD or Regulation 765/2008. Since they are merely required to remove and prevent specific infringing content after being notified, MSAs face the almost impossible job of seeking out infringing products on e-commerce marketplaces and file NTD requests. While in the area of unlawful speech or IP rights the damaged party or rightsholders will normally do this, this task rests almost entirely on the shoulders of MSAs, or possibly, consumer associations. As an additional complexity, violations in the area of product safety compliance are often difficult to assess. While some MSAs in Europe have been cooperating with large e-commerce platform operators, these kinds of initiatives are entirely voluntary and do normally not cover the variety of smaller or specialised marketplace operators. Still, even this proactive cooperation remains patchy, as will also be shown in the case studies.

As a result, the debate over more proactive responsibilities of these platforms has squarely entered the area of product safety. Both the ex-post evaluation and the Impact Assessment of the MSR show that some MSAs had asked for more incisive enforcement tools to penalise uncooperative online platforms that continuously sold unlawful products. They also pushed for including online platforms in the list of economic operators in the MSR,

1561 'How Conversational Commerce Is Changing E-Commerce' (n 212).
1562 Technopolis Group and others (n 1541) 90.
1563 European Commission, '2017/C 250/01' (n 1504) 10.

with the view to making them more accountable for product safety, and also argued for an amendment of the ECD on these lines.[1564]

Some Member States have attempted to formulate obligations for online intermediaries in their national product sector laws. In the national transpositions of the Radio Equipment Directive (RED) and the Electromagnetic Compatibility Directive (EMCD), Germany gave its MSA powers to demand information and support in the exercise of its duties from any economic actors that "facilitates the distribution" of products falling under the scope of these laws.[1565] The MSA is authorised to enter the premises of the economic actor and temporarily seize products for the purpose of having them tested. While this may be useful *vis-à-vis* FSPs, a more generally worded obligation to support MSAs in their work would be useful where e-commerce marketplaces resist information requests.

No EU case law has, however, been identified to this date that addresses the availability of unsafe or non-compliant products on online marketplaces.[1566] Two cases in the US indicate that marketplaces could be found liable for the sale of unsafe products under certain circumstances. In May 2019, *Amazon* made a legally binding agreement to sell only children's schools supplies and jewellery on its marketplace for which sellers had provided lab test reports and other proof that their products are not toxic. This followed an investigation that revealed over 18,000 purchases of products with unlawful levels of lead and cadmium on its US marketplace, including children's school lunch boxes and pencil cases.[1567] In another 2019

1564 Technopolis Group and others (n 1541) 165–167; European Commission, 'Goods Package Proposal - Impact Assessment 2/4' (n 1547) 125, 447.

1565 Gesetz über die elektromagnetische Verträglichkeit von Betriebsmitteln (EMVG) 2016 Article 29; Gesetz über die Bereitstellung von Funkanlagen auf dem Markt (FuAG) 2017 Article 31. The competent MSA for these two directives in Germany is the Bundesnetzagentur (BNetzA) (Federal Networks Agency).

1566 Apart from complaints by a consumer association, which has not reached the courts so far: '"Eau et Rivières de Bretagne" porte plainte suite à la vente de pesticides aux particuliers par Amazon et eBay' (*France 3 Bretagne*) <https://france3-regions.francetvinfo.fr/bretagne/ille-et-vilaine/rennes/eau-rivieres-bretagne-porte-plainte-suite-vente-pesticides-aux-particuliers-amazon-eBay-1748271.html> accessed 3 July 2020.

1567 Washington State, Office of the Attorney General, 'AG Ferguson: Amazon Must Remove Toxic School Supplies, Kid's Jewelry from Marketplace Nationwide | Washington State' (19 May 2019) <https://www.atg.wa.gov/news/news-releases/ag-ferguson-amazon-must-remove-toxic-school-supplies-kid-s-jewelry-marketplace> accessed 3 July 2020.

case, an US Appeals court denied *Amazon* the protections of the CDA.[1568] The judge found that the marketplace's role in the transaction was more than mere editorial, due to the fact it charges a commission, and offers storage, packaging and delivery services to sellers against an extra fee. It could therefore be held liable. A woman had bought a retractable dog leash from a seller. The dog leash had recoiled, permanently blinding the woman in one eye. The seller subsequently disappeared from the site without a trace.

However, the case studies in Chapter 5 will also show that there is normally little appetite on the side of MSAs to bring marketplace operators to court for a lengthy test case when they need to rely on cooperation to get their daily issues of unsafe products addressed. MSAs routinely approach e-commerce platforms for details of sellers that sell unsafe or non-compliant products, a task which can easily drag out if there are no informal and well working arrangements with platforms. In addition, the ex-post evaluation report of Regulation 2008/765 also shows that MSAs have widely varying enforcement powers when it comes to taking off illegal content from a website. In Spain, Germany, Italy, Belgium, Austria, Ireland, Poland or Sweden, MSAs have virtually no or very few powers to remove unlawful content from websites. As per the ex-post evaluation report, only Slovenian MSAs had the power to remove illegal product offers from websites throughout all of the 33 non-food product sectors surveyed.[1569] Even where they exist, the enforcement options via online sales channels is fragmented and fraught with practical difficulties.[1570] This was confirmed by the case studies in the next chapter. This piecemeal approach is clearly ineffective.

The Market Surveillance Regulation 2019/1010 (MSR)

The MSR includes ISSPs for the first in a piece of product safety legislation.[1571] Recital 16 clarifies that the EU lawmakers had online platforms in mind "which offer intermediary services by storing third party content, without exercising control over that content, and therefore not acting on behalf of an economic operator." Unlike FSPs, ISSPs are, however, not defined as economic operators in the MSR. Moreover, the application of the intermediary liability exemptions of the ECD is confirmed by the MSR,

1568 *Oberdorf v Amazon.com Inc* [2019] Third Circuit Court of Appeals 18-1041.
1569 Technopolis Group and others (n 1541) 74, 210–211.
1570 ibid 74, 159–167.
1571 Market Surveillance Regulation Article 3 (14).

with a special emphasis being put on the actual knowledge criterium.[1572] This does, however, not answer the question over the status of online marketplaces under product safety law, if they are found to fall foul of the ECD protection criteria, by e.g. not acting on actual knowledge along the due diligent economic criteria established in *L'Oréal v eBay*. In such a scenario, the current definitions of economic operators would still exclude them from any further reaching responsibilities. It should nevertheless be mentioned that in contrast to Regulation 765/2008 and Decision 268/2008 the definition of economic operators in the MSR is an open one. Apart from manufacturers, authorised representative, importers, distributor and FSPs, it now also includes "any other natural or legal person who is subject to obligations in relation to the manufacture of products, making them available on the market or putting them into service in accordance with the relevant Union harmonisation legislation."[1573] Whether this could potentially cover ISSPs will be discussed further below.

MSAs are now explicitly authorised to make use of the possibilities offered by the ECD to restrict access to an 'online interface'[1574] operated by a trader that did not comply with an order to remove infringing content or display warnings to end users.[1575] This provides wider enforcement tools to MSAs, but given their limited experience and reluctance in this area so far, it remains to be seen how fast and how efficient this can be implemented. In addition, it would potentially require these 500+ MSAs to engage with online marketplaces directly and, if needed, with the national authorities responsible for enforcing the ECD according to the country-of-origin principle. To complicate things further, courts may also be brought into the picture if content removal orders are deemed to be applied disproportionately. The doubts over the efficacy of content blocking and the possibilities of sellers to market their products elsewhere throws further shadows over this new enforcement opportunity.

The second, arguably more important obligation of ISSPs, is that they need to work together with MSAs in specific cases and facilitate action to

1572 ibid Article 2 (4), Recitals 16, 41, 42.

1573 ibid Article 3 (13). Which refers to any additional requirements imposed by requirements

1574 The definition of online interface has been carried over from the Geo-Blocking Regulation. It offers a technology neutral definition of a website, which is operated by or on behalf of a trader and that gives customers access to its products or service. In the context of the Market Surveillance Regulation this appears to refer mainly to the online shopfronts of retailers.

1575 Market Surveillance Regulation Article 14 (3) (k).

eliminate or mitigate risks presented by a product offered for sale through their sites.[1576] The language here is clearly kept to specific, singular circumstances, so as to disperse any suspicion that online marketplaces could be harnessed by MSAs for broader proactive measures aimed at preventing unsafe products, which could violate the ECD's Article 15. Article 7 (2) of the MSR will nevertheless help MSAs to get online marketplaces to cooperate more readily where it concerns information requests on products, sellers, or conduct test purchases. It could also be used to help MSAs engage marketplace operators to display online warning messages to consumers where it concerns risky product offers. The MSR, however, merely mentions the tools that already exist under the ECD against online marketplaces.

As stated in the section on trademarks, EU regulation in the area of consumer protection against uncommercial practices (UCPD) appears to go further. The Guidance Note of the UCPD gives a useful indication of the direction that accountability for the integrity of products sold via marketplaces could take. It reiterates the fact that the ECD applies without prejudice to the level of protection of interests relating to public health and consumer protection. It therefore serves as a complement to the EU consumer acquis.[1577] Online platforms that fall under the definition of a trader under the UCPD would therefore need to apply standards of professional diligence that correspond to the activity of the platform/trader.[1578] According to the UCPD, the definition of trader includes anyone who acts in the name of or on behalf of a trader.[1579] Meanwhile, B2C commercial practises under the directive include any act "directly connected with the promotion, sale or supply of a product to consumers."[1580] This, it could be argued, is similar to the commercial communication requirement in trademark law. It is hardly questionable that today's online marketplaces are not conducting activities that would qualify them as such traders. This could mean they are held to "designing their web-structure in a way that enables third-party traders to present information to platform users in compliance with EU marketing and consumer law."[1581] According to the

1576 ibid Article 7 (2).
1577 European Commission, 'UCP Directive Guidance' (n 57) 126.
1578 ibid 126–127.
1579 Directive 2005/29/EC Article 2 (b).
1580 ibid Article 2 (d).
1581 European Commission, 'UCP Directive Guidance' (n 57) 126.

UCPD guidance, platforms that fail to comply with this requirement could forfeit their intermediary liability exemption.[1582]

The 2019 Omnibus Directive appears to settle this ambiguity. It clarifies that online marketplace are considered as traders in their own right, and therefore subject to professional diligence standards.[1583] While professional diligence as per the UCPD's definition is dependent on more fluid criteria of good faith and/or honest market practices, it is nevertheless tied to "a standard of special skill and care which a trader may reasonably be expected to exercise."[1584] It is submitted here, that the professional diligence of online marketplace operators could extend towards online labelling and information or registration requirements under certain product or food laws. Online marketplaces are not only (essential) technical facilitators for third-party product offerings, but also increasingly provide additional value added services to sellers or non-professional traders. They are in a central and powerful position and, at a minimum, able to provide sellers with the technical tools to adhere to information requirements and verify compliance with these rules on their sites. This information link between third-party sellers and marketplace operators is also acknowledged by the fact that under the Omnibus Directive marketplaces need to clearly indicate to customers whether a third party acts as a (professional) trader or not.[1585] This confirms a trend of both legislators and the CJEU to take an expansive view of the concept of trader when it comes to protecting consumers. This dates back to at least the 2016 CJEU judgement in *Sabrina Wathelet v. Garage Bietheres*.[1586] The CJEU found that failure by a commercial intermediary to indicate to a customer that the party offering a good for sale was an individual, meant that the intermediary could be seen as the seller under the terms of the Consumer Sales Directive.[1587] This included liabilities for any failure to comply with the terms of the sales contract.[1588] Beyond this, however, the interplay between the UCPD and the ECD in the area of product safety is as unconfirmed as in the area of IPRs,

1582 ibid 126–127.

1583 Omnibus Directive 2019/2161 (n 1249) Article 3.

1584 Directive 2005/29/EC Article 2005/29.

1585 Omnibus Directive 2019/2161 (n 1249) Article 3 (4).

1586 *Sabrina Wathelet v Garage Bietheres & Fils SPRL, C-149/15* [2016] ECLI:EU:C:2016:840 (CJEU).

1587 Directive 1999/44/EC of 25 May 1999 on certain aspects of the sale of consumer goods and associated guarantees 1999 (OJ L 171).

1588 *Wathelet* (n 1585) para 34.

especially trademarks.[1589] The current review of the GPSD, which will be discussed below, may provide an opportunity to lay down more adequate responsibilities for online marketplaces and other platforms that facilitate the marketing and sale of products.

Whether the MSR's open definition of economic operators may provide flexibility for *lex specialis* to include online marketplaces is unclear. The Toys Safety Directive, as one example of the 70 product rules under the MSR's scope,[1590] requires that statutory warning labels be displayed in a clearly visible way online before the consumer makes a purchase decision.[1591] Under EU energy-labelling regulation, a dealer would have to make the energy label and a product information sheet available to customers, including in online distance sales.[1592] Although these obligations apply to manufacturers, distributors, or dealers, online marketplace undeniably have a special role in providing the technical infrastructure so that sellers can comply with these labelling and display requirements. Modern enforcement of product safety regulation should account for the fact, that today's online marketplaces provide virtually all information displayed on their website in a structured and measurable way. Sellers or non-professional traders are already required to upload product information, including photos and product data, in structured formats onto many marketplaces.[1593] Online marketplaces employ site merchandising teams and sophisticated analytics to maximise revenue from the displays on their websites. Where products are subject to mandatory labelling requirements, online platforms should at least have some due care requirements similar to what can be expected from dealers (e.g. under the Energy-labelling Regulation) or distributors. This would mean stretching some of the *lex specialis* economic operator categories, but this does not seem unrealistic given the integrated functionalities of online marketplaces. As stated above, these kinds of possibilities do exist already under the UCPD's and the Omnibus Directive's professional diligence requirements.

To summarise, while providing little direct enforcement means against online marketplaces, there are still some improvements under the new MSR that may help MSAs. First, the open economic operator definition

1589 Moscon and Hilty (n 1422) 12–15.

1590 Market Surveillance Regulation Annex I.

1591 Directive 2009/48 Article 11 (2); European Commission, 'Toy Safety Directive 2009/48/EC - An Explanatory Guidance Document Ref. Ares(2016)1594457' (n 441) 42.

1592 Regulation 2017/1369 Article 5 (1).

1593 Ullrich, 'New Approach Meets New Economy' (n 1542) 576.

may give room for drawing online platforms into its scope in product sectors covered by *lex specialis*. Secondly, MSAs can require that online marketplaces cooperate in specific cases to eliminate or mitigate product safety risks. Third, MSAs have received clarification that they can approach ISSPs to block access to infringing offers. A more ambitious consideration of the role online marketplaces play in the supply chain and the impact they have on product safety, as was done for FSPs, would have been appropriate, however. Marketplaces that are not protected under the ECD due to their active role would currently be in a grey zone between these two legal frameworks.

IV. Private enforcement

Little is publicly known about online marketplaces' voluntary activities in the area of product safety. The reactive duties under the ECD restrict their obligations to removals and possibly stay-downs following an NTD request. They are theoretically not even obliged to act on public product recalls unless they are notified of recalled products on their sites. The websites of the large marketplaces as of today only refer to their terms and conditions, which forbid sellers to list products that are non-compliant, unsafe or recalled.[1594] Larger marketplaces may have monitored or checked whether public recalls are being complied with by sellers on their sites, or whether sellers are subject to product safety escalation from customers, but again, little is known on this.

On 25 June 2018, the European Commission and online marketplaces *AliExpress, Amazon, eBay* and *Rakuten France* initiated the Product Safety Pledge.[1595] Under the Product Safety Pledge, online marketplaces made voluntary commitments to consult public recalls websites from the EU and MSAs and remove recalled products from their sites. The platforms also commit to react to MSA notices within two days, and to customer notifications of product safety issues within 5 days. For that, they vow to put in place effective NTD systems for unsafe products, where not done so already. The commitments also include sanction processes for repeat offenders and the prevention of relistings of removed product offers. On the

---

1594 For example: 'Product Safety Policy' (*eBay*) <https://www.eBay.co.uk/help/policies/prohibited-restricted-items/product-safety-policy?id=4300> accessed 6 July 2020.

1595 European Commission, 'Product Safety Pledge' (n 542).

proactive side, marketplaces will nominate single points of contact for MSAs, and inform and train sellers on EU product safety rules. They also agreed to explore the potential of using technologies to detect unsafe products. Although the last point remains vague, the Pledge may illustrate the rising pressure on platforms to take more responsibility. Two KPIs will measure the processing times of MSA notices and the number of removals of unsafe products spotted by platforms through monitoring the EU RAPEX System (now the Product Safety Gate). The initiative follows the models of other voluntary codes of conduct in the areas of hate speech or counterfeiting.

The latest progress report on the Pledge, covering the period from April to September 2019, showed that the original signatories had complied with the 2-day removal deadline of identified and notified unsafe products in approximately 95% of cases.[1596] Two of the participating platforms shared that they had messaged and trained sellers on product safety rules, albeit without providing any more data on this activity. The platforms indicated that they use a mix of proactive technologies to identify and block unsafe and non-compliant products, which included block filters, internal risk analysis and machine learning tools based on historic, internal data. Two additional marketplaces (*Allegro* and *CDiscount)* have since joined the agreement.

Despite its general wording, the initiative demonstrates that online marketplaces are in a key position to affect product safety on their platforms. The commitments of the Product Safety Pledge understate, however, the role of platforms. Seller education, seller onboarding due diligence and sanctioning can be key processes to limit the sale unsafe and non-compliant products. Risk analysis and proactive identification mechanisms have the potential to be effective if used holistically, e.g. by incorporating data gathered by platforms on sellers, product characteristics, customer reviews and product returns or complaints records. The measures taken by platforms remain largely in the dark. This maybe partly because online marketplaces fear being held liable under the ECD for gaining actual knowledge from any proactive analysis and outreach to sellers. On the other hand, it can be argued that the current responsibilities and voluntary measures are far below what online marketplaces can and should be doing in

1596 European Commission, '2nd Progress Report on the Implementation of the Product Safety Pledge' (2019) <https://ec.europa.eu/info/business-economy-euro/product-safety-and-requirements/product-safety/product-safety-rules_en> accessed 6 July 2020.

order to stem the flood of unsafe and unlawful products sold. More transparency and accountability would also mean that MSAs provide input and assess the measures taken by platforms. The public market surveillance and enforcement system that is characteristic of the *New Approach* and product regulation means that MSAs retain valuable technical information and surveillance expertise that may benefit platforms in their risk assessments. In addition, while the Pledge includes major European online marketplaces, it still misses a number of important market players and also does not consider the rising importance of social media marketplace activities. It covers therefore only the most visible players, but misses business models that are increasingly coming into the focus of MSAs.[1597]

V. EU legislative initiatives

On 23 June 2020, the European Commission launched an initiative to review the GPSD by opening a public consultation. The inception impact assessment outlines two major reasons for the review: 1) the 20-year-old directive does not sufficiently address the fact that new technologies, such as artificial intelligence or the Internet of Things influence product safety; 2) new challenges to product safety that are posed by e-commerce need to be tackled. In addition, the GPSD is not fully in line with the new market surveillance rules established by the MSR.[1598] This overview will focus on point 2). The Commission notes the emergence of new online business models, such as marketplaces, and states that the product safety rules applicable to them are unclear. It refers to the ECD and the Commission's 2018 Recommendation, which calls for enhanced responsibilities of online platforms.[1599] It also hints at the unsatisfactory progress under the voluntary Product Safety Pledge, to which many actors have not participated and which has not been effective enough in addressing product safety concerns. Apart from the obvious public health concerns, this also creates an uneven playing field between economic operators. It also cites the ongoing

1597 Winkelmann (n 1501) 22–25, 29. In this report, marketplace www.wish.com was mentioned as an actor that violated a number of product laws in Germany. The interviews in Chapter 5 show that social media and messaging apps pose rising problems to MSAs.

1598 European Commission, 'Combined Evaluation Roadmap/Inception Impact Assessment - Revision of Directive 2001/95/EC on General Product Safety - Ref. Ares(2020)3256809' (2020) 1.

1599 ibid 2; European Commission, 'C(2018) 1177 Final' (n 8).

purchase of goods online from non-EU operators as an issue that needs to be addressed more effectively.[1600] The legal basis for the initiative is provided by Article 114 TFEU. Achieving better consumer protection and a level playing field for businesses requires better cooperation of MSAs across the EU, which, because of its scale is best done at Union level. The European Commission foresees to coordinate the GPSD review with the proposed Digital Services Act.[1601]

The Commission charts out 4 policy options. With regards to action relevant for online platforms, the first Option would reinforce the current Product Safety Pledge and increase funding for joint market surveillance activities. The second and third options are scaled variants of a partial or full revision of the GPSD. They would result in making some voluntary provisions of the Pledge legally binding (Option 2), or add new obligations that go beyond the current Pledge (Option 3). Market surveillance would either be more strongly aligned across Member States, while keeping different legal instruments, or Member States would be given stronger enforcement powers, with the Commission being enabled to arbitrate in cases where risk assessments diverge. Finally, Option 4 would see an entirely new legal instrument that would incorporate Option 3 and merge the GPSD with the MSR into one set of rules.

The initiative follows the familiar procedure that was also witnessed in the area of terrorist content or copyright. Where progress based on voluntary and self-regulatory codes of conduct is not deemed sufficient, the EU wields the stick of legislative intervention. The concurrence of the GPSD review with the DSA will provide for an interesting policy making process. Enhanced responsibilities for online platforms beyond the Pledge's commitments are, it is submitted here, options that lie within the technically and morally justifiable realm. As stated before, these obligations will need to be accompanied by solid procedural rules and supervisory powers of MSAs. The area of product safety, with its strong expertise in public enforcement and standard development, could be predestined to achieve such a transparent and accountable responsibility structure for online platforms.[1602]

1600 European Commission, 'Combined Evaluation Roadmap/Inception Impact Assessment - Revision of Directive 2001/95/EC on General Product Safety - Ref. Ares(2020)3256809' (n 1597) 2.

1601 ibid 3.

1602 Ullrich, 'Standards for Duty of Care?' (n 1137) 126–127.

The DSA proposal appears to have seized on the enhanced enforcement powers created by the MSR by laying down specific requirements and due diligence obligations for online marketplaces. For one, Article 22 on the traceability of traders, in conjunction with Article 9, allows authorities to request the disclosure of information on specific service recipients (traders). This would provide MSAs with long-sought powers to gain information on traders selling non-compliant products.[1603] The fact that compliance with information orders is directly linked to the availability of the liability exemption may add additional weight to MSAs activities, as any failure to follow these orders could expose marketplaces to direct liabilities under national rules. Secondly, the requirement that marketplaces shall design their online interfaces (e.g. web pages) in a way that allows traders to comply with statutory pre-contractual information and with product safety rules[1604] imposes additional responsibility on marketplace operators. It was shown above, that online marketplaces do provide the essential technical infrastructure that can be harnessed to enable traders to comply with product safety labelling and information requirements. Under the new proposal, they would need to acquire a more in-depth understanding of product-specific safety and compliance labelling requirements online, such as on toy safety, eco-labels, chemical ingredients or food allergen warnings, in order to give traders the technical means to display this mandatory information. This appears to be more than appropriate given the key position that these actors occupy in facilitating the availability of products at a massive scale. The language in Article 22 (7) could be enhanced further by imposing specific non-compliance identification and reporting requirements on marketplace operators, similar to Regulation 2019/1148 on the marketing and use of explosives precursors,[1605] at least were it concerns areas susceptible to higher public health and safety risks. It remains to be seen whether the current GPSD review and product *lex specialis*, both in the area of food and non-food regulation, will venture further with specific obligations for online marketplaces and other online intermediaries. Under the current DSA draft, due diligence operations come closer to viewing online marketplace as economic operators with their own due diligence obligations in the supply chain of products.

1603 This is one of the main enforcement gaps reported by MSAs in the case studies in Chapter 5.

1604 European Commission DSA proposal (n 10) Article 22 (7).

1605 Regulation (EU) 2019/1148 of the European Parliament and of the Council of 20 June 2019 on the marketing and use of explosives precursors Articles 7 - 9.

VI. Summary and outlook

The rise of e-commerce and online marketplaces has also led to an increase in unsafe and non-compliant products sold by sellers via online marketplaces. The phenomenon is global and poses important risks for consumer trust and safety. Like in all the other sector treated beforehand, online intermediaries occupy a special role in this process. An increase of control of and commercial gain driven from the activities of third parties stands in contrast to the wide-reaching exemption from legal responsibilities for the content and products offers hosted and marketed through their systems. Product safety touches on public health and safety interests. Its regulatory set up differs from the private, personality law focussed-areas of defamation and hate speech and the economic and contractual rights impacted by intellectual property. Product safety law, like terrorism provisions, are enforced by public authorities. In the case of product safety law, MSAs operate in a highly technical and fragmented enforcement environment that was largely unprepared for the new problems caused by e-commerce and the rise of online marketplaces. MSAs in the EU have had marked problems to enforce product safety rules in e-commerce. Wide-reaching liability exemptions protect the only actors they often can get hold of when pursuing infringing sellers. The purely reactive duties of online marketplaces mean MSAs are facing the daily uphill struggle of searching for unsafe products on marketplaces and social media, while these powerful actors have virtually no duties.

The MSR has addressed this vacuum of responsibility only marginally, by enhancing marketplaces' obligations to cooperate with MSAs and by offering the possibility to suspend websites with unlawful products. The voluntary Product Safety Pledge has done little to alleviate regulatory concerns over consumer health and safety in e-commerce. The GPSD review, in conjunction with the DSA proposal, may finally lead to a readjustment of responsibilities for online intermediaries in this area. It is submitted here that, at least for sectors that carry higher product safety risks (e.g. toys), and where online labelling obligations exist, online intermediaries should be seen as economic actors with adequate primary or distributor liabilities. The DSA proposal has ventured to address this responsibility gap by obliging online marketplace to enable traders to display statutory product safety information. This, in conjunction with enhanced traceability requirements for traders, is an important step in bringing the responsibilities of online marketplace more in line with their economic significance and their impact on consumer safety.

The *New Approach* is based on a co-regulatory system that uses harminsed technical standards as a means to protect public interests in complex technical and dynamic market sectors.[1606] EU product regulation could be a valuable model for a new intermediary responsibility system. Chapter 6 will explore how online intermediaries could be brought into such a regulatory system.

7. Food safety

I. Background – food in e-commerce and on online platforms

Online food retail took off somewhat later than e-commerce in general. Since 2010, online food retail has, however, also started to become mainstream. The ascendance of e-commerce marketplaces can be seen as a catalyst for this trend. A 2012 survey shows that the number of unique food items offered on the german *eBay* site grew from 2,000 in 1999 to 150,000 in 2012. Amazon launched its grocery category in 2010 with 42,000 unique products, which grew to a selection over 175,000 within two years.[1607] Today, online marketplaces offer millions of food products online. In 2019, 36% of Dutch, 32% of British consumers and 25% of German consumers had shopped for grocery online.[1608] Although online grocery sales made up only 2%[1609] of the total food retail market in Europe in 2018, the sector is set to continue with double digit annual growth rates over the foreseeable future and will represent USD22 billion in the UK and USD17 billion in France by the year 2023.[1610]

The unique nature of e-commerce means that product selection online is vast and can be shipped to virtually anywhere in the world. This has given have given rise to a number of problems that are exacerbated by the techni-

1606 Jacob Rowbottom, 'If Digital Intermediaries Are to Be Regulated, How Should It Be Done?' (*Media Policy Project*, 16 July 2018) <http://blogs.lse.ac.uk/mediapolicyproject/2018/07/16/if-digital-intermediaries-are-to-be-regulated-how-should-it-be-done/> accessed 7 August 2018; Ullrich, 'A Risk-Based Approach towards Infringement Prevention on the Internet' (n 747) 226.

1607 Dirk W Lachenmeier and others, 'Does European Union Food Policy Privilege the Internet Market? Suggestions for a Specialized Regulatory Framework' (2013) 30 Food Control 705, 706.

1608 'Europe: Online Grocery Market, by Country 2006-2019' (*Statista*)

1609 In advanced markets like the UK this share 10%.

1610 'Grocery Sales by Channel in Europe 2018' (*Statista*).

cally complex, tightly regulated and diverse landscape of food retail. EU food safety authorities (FSAs) have become alert to the problems of online food retail since at least 2007. A German study of that year found that of 300 slimming products test-purchased via the internet, 50% were not compliant with EU legislation.[1611] Nutritional supplements (e.g. slimming pills, sports nutrition), novel foods[1612] or foods with ingredients not authorised in the EU are of particular concern in online retail.[1613] In its 2017 Coordinated Food Control Plan on the official control of certain foods marketed through the internet, the European Commission singled out these product categories for a targeted controls exercise. During an EU wide check of 1077 websites, it found altogether 779 non-compliant supplements and novel foods from 734 traders based within and outside the EU. Many of these acted merely as intermediaries (i.e. brokers) that initiated sales through other channels.[1614] This is confirmed by a study of the German Federal Office of Consumer Protection and Food Safety (BVL), which found that sales brokered through messages on sites like *Facebook, Pinterest* or *Instagram* are more and more frequent.[1615] Other commonly identified problems relate to unrestricted sales of alcoholic beverages, incorrect or insufficient food labelling, unlawful health claims and microbiological risks relating to the sale of perishable or cold-chain products.[1616]

This phenomenon has led experts to claim that food regulation in online commerce is less rigorously enforced than in traditional supermarkets

---

1611 Bundesamt für Verbraucherschutz und Landwirtschaft (BVL), 'BVL/FLEP Conference on European Approaches to Risk Based Official Controls in Food Businesses, Including e- Commerce'

1612 European Commission, 'Novel Food' (*Food Safety - European Commission*, 17 October 2016) <https://ec.europa.eu/food/safety/novel_food_en> accessed 9 July 2020.

1613 'Amazon Warns Customers: Those Supplements Might Be Fake' *Wired* <https://www.wired.com/story/amazon-fake-supplements/> accessed 9 July 2020.

1614 European Commission, 'The First EU Coordinated Control Plan on Online Offered Food Products - Analysis of the Main Outcome of the Implementation of the Commission Recommendation on a Coordinated Control Plan on the Official Control of Certain Foods Marketed through the Internet, Ref. Ares(2018)893577' (2018) 2. See also Lachenmeier and others (n 1606) 709.

1615 Bundesamt für Verbraucherschutz und Landwirtschaft (BVL), 'Gemeinsame Zentralstelle "Kontrolle Der Im Internet Gehandelten Erzeugnisse Des LFGB Und Tabakerzeugnisse" - Jahresbericht 2018' (2019) 8 <https://www.bvl.bund.de/DE/Aufgaben/06_Onlinehandel/onlinehandel_node.html> accessed 16 July 2020.

1616 Lachenmeier and others (n 1606) 707–710.

and offline high street retail. Food safety levels risk therefore being lower in online shopping.[1617]

II. Food safety and its enforcement in EU and national law

a. EU food safety law – responsible economic actors

EU food safety constitutes a separate regulatory regime.[1618] The EU Hygiene package[1619] is a comprehensive, technically complex and diverse regulatory system that exists since 2006. It is mainly based on regulations, which underlines the centralised and relatively unitarian character of EU food law.[1620] The responsibility for food safety spreads throughout the entire food supply chain, starting at the manufacturer and ending at the retailer. Like in the area of non-food products, the EU's regulatory choice has led to the establishment of co-regulatory practices.

The Regulation on general food law[1621] and the Regulation on the hygiene of foodstuffs[1622] set out the framework conditions by stipulating responsibilities and quality management principles, such as the mandatory use of Hazard Analysis and Critical Control Points (HACCP) or Good Hygiene Practice (GHP).[1623] The private sector manages the compliance with these principles by designing standards and certifications, an activity that is encouraged by the EU.[1624] Food safety authorities are predominantly

1617 ibid 706.

1618 'General Food Law - Food Safety - European Commission' (*Food Safety*) <https://ec.europa.eu/food/safety/general_food_law_en> accessed 6 July 2018.

1619 European Commission, 'Food Hygiene' (*Food Safety - European Commission*, 17 October 2016) <https://ec.europa.eu/food/safety/biosafety/food_hygiene_en> accessed 9 July 2020.

1620 Agnieszka Bilska and Ryszard Kowalski, 'Food Quality and Safety Management' (2014) 10 Scientific Journal of Logistics 351, 351–353.

1621 Regulation (EC) 178/2002 of 28 January 2002 laying down the general principles and requirements of food law, establishing the European Food Safety Authority and laying down procedures in matters of food safety 2002 (OJ L 31).

1622 ibid.

1623 Regulation 852/2004 Recital 11, Article 1 (d) (e).

1624 ibid Recital 44; Regulation 178/2002 Article 5 (3). Such standards are for example provided by ISO 9000 Quality Management or ISO 22000 Food management systems norms, International Food Standard (IFS), or the British Retail Consortium (BRC) Global Standard. All global food safety standards and norms are collected in the *Codex Alimentarius*, a compendium managed by the UN's Food and Agriculture Organisation (FAO)

tasked with market surveillance and enforcement. This happens through audits and official controls of the procedures developed by industry, and a harmonised system of official controls and registrations, established through Regulation 2017/625.[1625] They are conducted by applying a risk-based approach[1626] by which high risk areas, be they specific food product sectors, economic actors or supply chain activities, receive more frequent and intense controls. With the rise in e-commerce, Member States, which remain in charge of enforcement, have also started to control online sales channels. Enforcement activity may be less fragmented than in the area of non-food products, but as of now there is still a lack of coordination across the EU and expertise in checking and pursuing unlawful sales and operators online.[1627]

The Hygiene Package also lays down rules for areas where more direct regulatory invention was deemed more appropriate. Food Labelling requirements or sector specific provisions relating to e.g. novel foods, or organic products, as well as animal feedstuffs, are points in case. For example, in 2011 the EU adapted its laws on food information for consumers to the online environment. Food labelling requirements for online shops were aligned to those of physical shops. As a consequence, ingredients' lists, allergen warnings and certain nutritional information all need to be displayed online to give consumers information before they make a purchase decision.[1628] Online food retailers also need to register with national authorities[1629] and, depending on the nature of their business, may even need to ask for an authorisation to operate.

1625 Regulation (EU) 2017/625 of 15 March 2017 on official controls and other official activities performed to ensure the application of food and feed law, rules on animal health and welfare, plant health and plant protection products (OJ L 95) Chapter II, Articles 9 - 27. Regulation 852/2004 Article 6. For more detail on the co-regulatory character of EU food law see: Marian Garcia Martinez, Paul Verbruggen and Andrew Fearne, 'Risk-Based Approaches to Food Safety Regulation: What Role for Co-Regulation?' (2013) 16 Journal of Risk Research 1101.

1626 Regulation 2017/625 Article 9.

1627 This will be treated in more detailed in the case study within the following chapter.

1628 Regulation (EU) 1169/2011 of 25 October 2011 on the provision of food information to consumers 2011 (OJ L 304) Article 14 (1).

1629 Peter Kranz, Hannes Harms and Claudia Kuhr, 'Kontrolle der im Internet gehandelten Erzeugnisse des LFGB und Tabakerzeugnisse (G@ZIELT)' (2015) 10 Journal für Verbraucherschutz und Lebensmittelsicherheit 13, 14; Regulation 852/2004 Article 6 (2), Recital 19.

The European Food Safety Authority (EFSA) is a central scientific EU body that supports Member States with risk assessments, communications and enforcement decisions. The protection of human life and health and consumer interests are the general objectives of EU food law.[1630] The main regulatory tools used are harmonised risk management and the precautionary principle.[1631] Food is probably one of the most tightly regulated sectors in the EU, with a higher degree of harmonisation than in the non-food product area.[1632]

Primary responsibility for food safety lies with all food business operators. A food business is defined as "any undertaking, ..., carrying out any of the activities related to any stage of production, processing and distribution of food."[1633] Food business operators have the obligation to ensure that all food under their control satisfies the relevant hygiene requirements. Depending on the kind of foods, specific requirements, like microbiological characteristics, temperature control or cold chain maintenance need to be met.[1634]

The Commission confirmed in 2016 that it deemed food regulation and online food retail to be adapted to the DSM.[1635] Online food traders are covered by the definition of food business operators. They will therefore need to follow food safety rules under general food law, including labelling and information requirements.[1636] On the enforcement side, the new Official Controls regulation empowers FSAs, amongst others, to anonymously purchase samples of products or suspend for an 'appropriate period of time' the web sites of marketplace operators that do not comply with their obligations.[1637] As forward looking actions, the Commission stated that, apart from reinforcing training of enforcement officers in e-

1630 Regulation 178/2002 Article 5 (1).
1631 ibid Articles 5 - 7.
1632 Luis González Vaqué, 'The Proposed EU Consumer Product Safety Regulation and Its Potential Conflict with Food Legislation.' (2014) 9 European Food & Feed Law Review 161, 161.
1633 Regulation 178/2002 Article 3 (2). The food business operator is the natural or legal person under whose control the food business is situated. (Article 3 (3))
1634 Regulation 852/2004 Articles 3 & 4.
1635 European Commission, 'E-Commerce Control of Food - EU Action Plan' (Advisory Group of the food chain, animal and plant health, 25 November 2016) 8 .
1636 ibid 4–5.
1637 ibid 6–7; Regulation 2017/625 Articles 36, 138 (2) (i).

commerce.[1638] it would look into establishing contact with major e-commerce platforms (*Alibaba, Amazon, eBay*).[1639]

b. Online intermediaries and food safety

The European Commission's includes the sale of food products in its broad initiative aimed at tackling unlawful content on online platforms.[1640] The above mentioned 2017 coordinated controls initiative of food sold online, which centred on nutritional supplements and novel foods, concludes that the following actions need to be taken: establishing contacts with major e-commerce platforms, including social media; seeking cooperation with payment service providers; adjusting legislation to the needs of e-commerce controls. It also admits that more needs to be done to "remind the main players of e-commerce such as platforms, payment services and the traders themselves of their responsibilities, to ask for their contributions to increase the safety of online offered foods and to reduce offers which mislead consumers."[1641]

The EU has not undertaken any official legal assessment as to what extent online marketplaces could potentially be held accountable under EU food law when allowing sellers to market food products on their platforms. Given the rising importance of online food sales, via online platforms in particular, this is surprising. Like in any other content area treated beforehand, marketplaces play an essential role in enabling the wide availability of food products to consumers. Labelling, safety and registration requirements are complex under EU food law. As mentioned in the previous section, the likes of *Alibaba* or *Amazon* provide a technical facility for the upload of products and sales offers. That facility is enriched by a wide array of other services from which the platforms derives money. A seller that has to comply with intricate online labelling requirements, would benefit from a marketplace that provides them also with the ability to display ingredients, warnings and other regulatory information in a structured way. It is submitted here that a diligent marketplace operator

1638 'Better Training for Safer Food (BTSF) - Food Safety - European Commission' (*Food Safety*) <https://ec.europa.eu/food/safety/btsf_en> accessed 19 April 2021.

1639 European Commission, 'E-Commerce Control of Food - EU Action Plan' (n 1634) 13.

1640 European Commission, 'COM (2017) 555 Final' (n 69) 3, 6 (fn 28).

1641 European Commission, 'Main Outcome Analysis - EU Internet Control Plan' (n 1613) 5.

would need to be aware of these specific requirements, if they chose to allow the listing of food product offers on their marketplace. This would include allowing the seller to comply with food legislation in a way that is transparent to the consumer. It would entail awareness and knowledge of the information that needs to be displayed in a given product category, and requirements to structure the layout of their sites in a way that enables a legally conform display of product information. This requirement should be commensurate to the health and safety risk related to selling food products, thus translating into an enhanced level of duty of care.[1642] Platforms would also be in a unique position to manage that risk by other due diligence measures, such as seller verification processes to check, for example, food business registrations of sellers, or online product information audits.

At the very least, today's online intermediaries have an impact on the supply chain and a certain level of control over the marketing of these products. As will be seen in the case studies in the next chapter, the view of enforcement authorities on the role of online marketplaces in e-commerce is divided. Some authorities would tend to define these actors as food business operators, where they derive a service fee or commission from sales conducted through their platforms. This ties in with the 'commercial communication' concept in trademark law.

Apart from the enhanced controls programs on the enforcement side, no further EU legal initiatives have so far been launched, and no specific private enforcement initiatives are known. It can be assumed, however, that online marketplace would cover food safety in any of the self-adopted measures that cover product safety of non-food products, like the Product Safety Pledge. Like in the area of non-food product regulation, the recent DSA proposal would enhance the enforcement options for food safety authorities in the fight against illegal and unsafe food online. Given the extensive and very specific requirements on the labelling of food sold online, Article 22 of the DSA proposal on the traceability of traders would be a welcome component for holding online marketplaces to account where they decide to enable the sale of food products. The existing registration requirements for food traders could also be directly linked to the traceabil-

1642 nutraingredients.com, 'How Responsible Is Amazon for the Supplements Sold on Its Sites?' (*nutraingredients.com*) <https://www.nutraingredients.com/Article/2015/10/09/Amazon-s-supplement-responsibility> accessed 9 July 2020.

ity obligations in the new DSA, which requires that marketplaces obtain proof that traders have registered in a public register.[1643]

III. Summary and outlook

The sale of unsafe food online belongs to the EU's broad horizontal strategy to address unlawful content via enhancing online platforms' responsibilities. The current EU Food Law framework has been adapted to some aspects of e-commerce, namely where it concerns the legal status and the responsibilities of online retailers. Labelling and registration requirements apply to these actors as much as general obligations relating to the safety of food products. The food law system itself relies on co-regulatory measures. The broad food law objectives and safety management principles are set up through regulations. These are implemented through standards and norms developed by industry. FSAs at national level, supported by an European scientific agency, EFSA, audit and control food business operators both on the ground and online. E-commerce marketplaces have, however, fallen somewhat between the cracks of this system. There is no clear view of their exact responsibilities under food law outside of the liability exemptions imposed by the ECD. The European Commission and national authorities see a need to involve platforms stronger in the fight against unsafe food products. Their essential functions are recognised, but no concrete policy action has been taken. It is suggested here, that the increasingly integrated involvement of these actors in the facilitation and promotion of food products should confer on them responsibilities that are in line with the consumer health and safety risks related to their activity, especially where it concerns online product labelling and seller registration requirements. Online platforms are certainly in a position to take on these roles. Online food labelling, consumer information and seller registration requirements could be formidable risk management tools, because they can harness the technical facility role of platforms. The EU appears to have seized, at least partly, on this opportunity in its DSA proposal.

1643 European Commission DSA proposal (n 10) Article 22 (1) (e).

E. Summary: Sectoral frameworks and intermediary liability

1. The multilevel regulatory picture of EU intermediary liability

The sectoral analysis of intermediary liability has demonstrated the intricate differences that exist in the regulatory environment for unlawful content and the enforcement options available against intermediaries.

First, in certain content areas, the substantive, normative law provisions differ between Member States (hate speech, defamation, copyright). Some national laws incorporate specific intermediary consideration into their frameworks, as was demonstrated for the 1881 French Press Law, or the 2013 UK Defamation Act. This affects the way the content management practices and the duties of intermediaries are being evaluated on a purely normative way. A prime example here are the different degrees to which certain content is seen as manifestly illegal. These kinds of differences could, arguably, be ironed out by a further increase in competencies at EU level, through further harmonisation of hate speech or even defamation laws,[1644] or copyright exemptions. The enlargement of EU competencies is in itself, however, a highly contentious policy issue. It is not sure whether the usual justifications provided by the internal market and fundamental rights will achieve such harmonisation in the face of pronounced national interests and national competencies, as for example for media law[1645] or national security.

Secondly, the enforcement regimes of each content area vary significantly. In the public law dominated areas of terrorist content and product regulation, there is a marked engagement of law enforcement and surveillance authorities with intermediaries. In private law areas concerning personality and economic rights, enforcement happens mainly through courts.

Thirdly, the free-standing national secondary intermediary liability rules, principles and legal traditions vary across Member States. They also interact to different degrees with sector specific laws.[1646]

Fourthly, the relatively plain and general ECD intermediary liability framework is superimposed on the rich national secondary liability rules and sectoral law. This has a led to disparate interpretations and applications of these rules across the EU. The ECD may be used as an additional

---

1644 Savin (n 384) 142.

1645 Cornils (n 481) 80–81.

1646 For example, as could be seen in the area of defamation and hate speech, the French Press Law excludes the application of the secondary liability provisions of the Code Civil.

option to existing national liability provisions, in conjunction with them[1647] or by being replaced almost exclusively with local secondary liability concepts. The limited arsenal of secondary liability and intermediary sanctions offered through EU laws (ECD, IPRED and the Infosoc Directive)[1648] is eclipsed by a rich repertoire at Member State level.

Fifth, the minimum harmonisation approach of the ECD also means that some Member States have developed their own NTD procedures through law or self-regulatory arrangements, while others have not regulated this at all. This in turn has had an influence on the definition of the knowledge standard by jurisdiction and by content area, as well as on procedural obligations.

All this makes each content sector a distinct multi-level regulatory space, with particular enforcement practices. This landscape is complicated by the fact that within these vertical regulatory spaces, enforcement approaches vary on a horizontal level between countries.

Lawmakers at both EU and national level from various regulatory areas have reacted differently to harmful content management practices of online platforms. Initial attempts to foster self–regulatory initiatives through e.g. codes of conduct, as provided for by the ECD[1649] have been partially followed up by more decisive policy action in selected areas. The EU's regulatory choice of new legislative initiatives is, however, different. In the area of copyright, the DSM has now removed OCSSPs from the scope of the ECD by making them primarily liable for unauthorised content. To protect against direct infringement, OCSSPs will need to strike licensing agreements with rightsholders or show that they have made best efforts to prevent any unauthorised acts. The resulting obligations are to be put in place through self-regulatory arrangements between intermediaries and the rightsholder industry. The AVMSD deploys a slightly different model in the fight against hate speech and content harmful for minors on VSPs. Secondary liability would ensue where VSPs fail to adequately deploy a set of defined preventive measures. The regulatory setup is rounded off by charging ERGA with a coordinating function, which is a first step in the direction of a co-regulatory structure. The proposed anti-terrorism regulation follows a more traditional, rule-making approach by imposing fixed removal deadlines and potential obligations for proactive removal and identification of content. In the area of product and food safety, EU legis-

1647 Oster (n 816); Benabou (n 334).

1648 Leistner (n 336) 78–89.

1649 Directive 2000/31 (ECD) Article 16.

lative initiatives have so far not allocated enhanced responsibilities to online platforms, except for an obligation to cooperate with MSAs in specific cases concerning safety risks of non-food products. The picture is completed by national initiatives such as the *NetzDG* or the now defunct *Loi Avia*, which have pursued either self- or co-regulatory solutions.

2. Summary: Common trends in sectoral online intermediary liabiliy

> *"The problem with many current cyberlaw texts is that questions of intermediary liability are scattered throughout chapters focusing on specific kinds of tortious liability--copyright, trademark, defamation, etc. This organization tends to discourage a focus on the central question involving the rights and obligations of intermediaries across discrete subject matter areas."*[1650]

The analysis in this chapter has exposed a heterogeneric enforcement landscape across different content sectors, which currently seems to develop even further apart. The abandonment of horizontal principles of online intermediary responsibility could seem a plausible solution for accommodating pragmatic, effective and flexible content specific solutions. It is certainly important to respect differences in normative aspects, regulatory specificities and technical details across content sectors. However, this chapter also demonstrated that today's Web 2.0 platforms display essential commonalties that call for horizontal principles of unlawful content prevention on online platforms.

First, in all areas covered, there is a marked push of damaged parties, legislators and enforcers to allocate enhanced responsibilities on intermediaries that are commensurate with their business models in general, and their content management practices in particular. The driver for this appears to be less the degree of manifest illegality of content, but rather more the deep involvement and integration of these platforms in the act of information intermediation. Apart from a push towards enhanced secondary liabilities, this has also led to forays into the area of primary liability allocation, e.g. in copyright. In that context, the distinction between neutral and active intermediaries is by now hopelessly outdated and should be replaced by less rigid criteria that are applied horizontally. Secondly, many of the large integrated platforms straddle different legal content areas, be they copyright, hate speech, trademarks or unsafe products. Common horizontal responsibility

1650 Lipton (n 287) 1346.

principles make therefore for more legal certainty for both users and platform operators themselves. Third, online platforms work according to similar underlying business models and architectural design decisions. They are focussed on exploiting user data, or behavioural surpluses. Content moderation is primarily based on commercial interests.[1651] Fourthly, at least the large, dominating platforms have expanded their automated content management practices to create systems that detect and remove unlawful content. They enforce mainly along their own private content policies, with a secondary regard for the applicable laws. Whether it concerns terrorist speech, copyright violations or unsafe product identification, the procedures and criteria that govern these decisions are mainly driven by commercial objectives. However, they remain largely inaccessible to those parties most concerned by their application. These private content management practices have a significant impact on fundamental rights, such as privacy or human dignity, freedom of expression, economic rights, or public health and safety. The ubiquity and power of online platforms on the internet means that these private norms have become quasi law, and intermediaries akin to parallel states,[1652] that override the public interest criteria formulated and enforced by democratically elected governments. This tendency is observed in each of the content sectors covered above.

This all calls for more wide-reaching responsibility criteria and systemic harm prevention approaches that go beyond content type specific considerations.[1653] A horizontal, principles-based framework would allow for addressing these commonalities in a holistic way by also exploiting synergies between the different, already existing approaches. Finally, such a system would facilitate an easier interlinkage with other legal domains that have become crucial when addressing critical issues of online platform power, such as competition law, data protection, consumer law or IT security.[1654]

1651 Zuboff (n 5). Sarah Jeong, *The Internet of Garbage* (1.5, Vox Media, Inc 2018) Ln 1084 - 1384.

1652 Tambini and Moore (n 232) 406; Natali Helberger, 'Challenging Diversity - Social Media Platforms and a New Conception of Media Diversity' in Damian Tambini and Martin Moore (eds), *Digital dominance: the power of Google, Amazon, Facebook, and Apple* (Oxford University Press 2018) 167.

1653 Taddeo and Floridi (n 120) 1598; Burk (n 295) 452. Lipton (n 23) 155–157.

1654 Tambini and Moore (n 232) 399–406; Peggy Valcke, Inge Graef and Damian Clifford, 'IFairness – Constructing Fairness in IT (and Other Areas of) Law through Intra- and Interdisciplinarity' (2018) 34 Computer Law & Security Review 707, 710–711. Vassilis Hatzopoulos, 'Vers un cadre de la régulation des plateformes?' (2019) XXXIII Revue internationale de droit économique 399, 414.

Chapter 5 - Enforcement case studies

A. *Introduction*

1. Rationale and objectives

This chapter presents two case studies that are meant to demonstrate the challenges market surveillance authorities (MSAs) face when confronted with the issue of unlawful non-food and food products on online platforms. The enforcement of product regulation online is a relatively underexplored area compared to research in e.g. online copyright enforcement or hate speech. Nevertheless, the previous sections have demonstrated that this is a persisting and growing problem, which European MSAs have been trying to tackle for the last 15 years. Unlike IP rights and unlawful speech, which are governed mainly by private law and often contractual arrangements, product regulation boasts a well-established public enforcement structure. In the former areas such a structure does not exist and enforcement of rights has happened mainly through courts, which have significantly shaped the current regime that applies to intermediaries under the ECD.

The case studies aim to capitalise on the fact that a fully operational enforcement structure has been in existence in the area of product regulation well before the rise of commerce through online platforms. The impact of the rise of e-commerce marketplaces and intermediaries on sector specific primary law and its enforcement can therefore be demonstrated tangibly.

The objective of the case studies is twofold:

1) To investigate how enforcement authorities in the area of non-food and food safety detect and prevent unlawful content on platforms, how they work together with online intermediaries and which national and EU legal basis they use for their activities. The survey also tries to establish the intensity of regulatory cooperation between national surveillance authorities at different levels (national, local, EU, international) and whether that cooperation has led to more formalised policy or regulatory initiatives. The rationale is, to test the practical applicability of the ECD liability regime in this area and the regulatory response of highly specialised, technical enforcement bodies to the horizontal challenge of e-commerce.

2) Product and food regulation are part of co-regulatory system. This system relies on both institutionalised and informal cooperation between private and public actors, be it through normative standard setting by industry bodies or through market surveillance and controls by specialist enforcers at operational level.[1655] The results of these surveys will help to establish whether the approaches of enforcement authorities *vis-à-vis* new economic actors in e-commerce are informed by the co-regulatory practices that have prevailed in these sectors. These practices are characterised by a mix of informal cooperation, enforcement using a risk-based approach and precautionary principles.[1656] The results, it is hoped, could inform the debate over a new governance framework for online intermediaries.[1657]

2. Survey structure

The rationale behind the qualitative, pre-structured survey has been explained in the Chapter 1. The surveys in the area of product and food regulation were both structured around five sections. Each section consists of a mix of questions allowing for fixed (binary or multiple) choices, or open answers. ANNEX I contains a model version of the survey.

Section A, the largest section, captured data about the authorities' activities. This includes general information about the authority's foundation, resourcing, the legal scope of the enforcement activity (by EU Regulation/ Directive), the product areas covered and the specific online market surveillance activities and their evolvement over the past five years. This was meant to establish and compare the degree to which different MSAs

1655 LAJ Senden and others, *Mapping Self-and Co-Regulation Approaches in the EU Context": Explorative Study for the European Commission, DG Connect* (European Commission 2015) 37–39 <https://dspace.library.uu.nl/handle/1874/327305> accessed 19 September 2017.

1656 European Commission, '2017/C 250/01' (n 1504) 6, 8, 12. Garcia Martinez, Verbruggen and Fearne (n 1624).

1657 A view also generally supported in: Cristie Ford, *Innovation and the State: Finance, Regulation, and Justice* (Cambridge University Press 2017) 69–73, 188–190. Cohen (n 19) 23–34; Woods, 'The Carnegie Statutory Duty of Care and Fundamental Freedoms' (n 698). Florian Saurwein, Natascha Just and Michael Latzer, 'Governance of Algorithms: Options and Limitations' (2015) 17 info 35. Ullrich, 'A Risk-Based Approach towards Infringement Prevention on the Internet' (n 747).

(and FSAs) have focussed and developed their expertise in the area of online market surveillance.

Section B sought to elicit information about the authorities' awareness of and interaction with the intermediary liability provisions of the ECD. Online platforms have developed in a way that their activities affect more directly the substantive laws that govern the content they host. Enforcers have grappled with that new ambiguity of platforms' activities. One solution would be for subject matter enforcers to develop and exploit means offered in both secondary and primary law areas to deal with the changing role of online intermediaries. This section attempts to test whether MSAs in the areas of product and food safety are making use of the current enforcement tools provided by intermediary regulation in any way, and whether they have developed views on how to improve enforcement efficacy.

Section C asked the authorities about their interaction with ISSPs as part of their market surveillance and controls activities. The co-regulatory structure of product and food safety regulation has traditionally resulted in a more collaborative approach between economic operators and enforcers. This section tried to establish whether this collaborative approach has been expanded to online platforms. It also attempts to establish whether this has shown any success, despite the fact that no legal basis existed for such cooperation at the time the interviews were conducted.[1658]

The penultimate Section D tries to establish the degree of regulatory cooperation with other public authorities, both within the Member State and across the EU. This section aimed to establish strengths and weaknesses of cooperation mechanisms when it comes to enforcement on safety risks *vis-à-vis* online platforms.

Finally, Section E captured the date of the interview and the names of the participating market surveillance officers. Details from this section will, however, not be disclosed.

The two case studies rest on 13 survey answers, of which seven were based on in-person or phone-based interviews. Six authorities filled in the survey independently and sent the responses by e-mail or handed them in personally (see Table 2). One MSA had overarching responsibilities for product and food safety. The interview with that MSA was conducted for both non-food products and foodstuffs and counted as such as well, which resulted in a total of 14 responses.

1658 The obligation to cooperate with MSAs was created in the new MSR, albeit only for specific cases: Market Surveillance Regulation Article 7 (2).

	Product safety	Food safety
Interviews	4	4
Survey completion	6	0
TOTAL	10	4

Table 2 - Number of surveys conducted

Response levels from Food Safety Authorities (FSAs) were markedly lower than in the area product regulation. The low response in the area of food safety betrays a lack of perceived relevance of the topic. As will be shown, for many authorities, e-commerce marketplaces, though essential actors, remained beyond reach for regulatory or resource reasons. Those authorities interviewed in the area of food safety were arguably those most proactively involved, most knowledgeable and most interested in the role of online intermediaries in food safety.

In the following, the terminology of "small" and "large" Member States is being used. The survey results indicated, that, not surprisingly perhaps, there was a marked difference between smaller and larger Member States at the level of resourcing and specialisation of enforcement work across the sectors covered. The term "large" Member States refers to France, Germany, Italy, Spain and the UK, although the interviews did not cover MSAs from all of these countries.

3. Confidentiality

Most of the authorities surveyed objected to the interviews being recorded. Most of them also indicated their preference of not being identified during the evaluation phase. This confidentiality was, however, happily traded off against greater frankness and detail in the discussions on enforcement and policy challenges that many of the authorities face in their daily work.

B. Case study 1: Online market surveillance in product regulation

1. Overview

The area of *New Approach* product regulation spans 29 product sectors, each covered by specific legislation in the form of directives.[1659] In the interest of coherence, it was appropriate to focus on a narrow range of product sectors, given the vast variety of MSAs that operate across the *New Approach* product directives. For this reason, the interviews and surveys conducted focussed on authorities that were responsible for market surveillance under the Radio Equipment Directive (RED)[1660] and the Electromagnetic Compatibility Directive (EMCD).[1661] In theory, these directives cover any consumer electronics that transmit radio waves and whose operation may interfere with that of other devices. The potential area of product coverage is vast, ranging from mobile handsets, PCs, diverse consumer electronics, electronic toys, to electronic household equipment, drones and many more electronic devices. RED, but also the EMCD, will become more relevant with the growth of the IoT and the forecast proliferation of inter-connected radio equipment, be it through wearable connected devices, smart homes or equipment tagged with radio-frequency identification devices (RFID).[1662] RED, for example, also includes technical equipment requirements to protect against data privacy violations and fraudu-

---

1659 European Commission, 'Blue Guide' (n 1517) 13–15. The term product sector is ambiguous if considered in its more commonplace meaning. For example, many consumer electronics products such as mobile phones or laptops would be covered by several *New Approach* 'product sectors': the Low Voltage Directive (2014/35), the Radio Equipment Directive (2014/53) and the Electromagnetic Compatibility Directive (2014/30). If targeted at children, additional compliance with the Toys Safety Directive (2009/48) may be needed.

1660 Directive 2014/53 (RED) 53; Anonymous, 'Radio Equipment Directive (RED)' (*Internal Market, Industry, Entrepreneurship and SMEs - European Commission*, 5 July 2016) <https://ec.europa.eu/growth/sectors/electrical-engineering/red-directive_en> accessed 13 July 2020.

1661 Directive 2014/30 (EMCD); Anonymous, 'Electromagnetic Compatibility (EMC) Directive' (*Internal Market, Industry, Entrepreneurship and SMEs - European Commission*, 5 July 2016) <https://ec.europa.eu/growth/sectors/electrical-engineering/emc-directive_en> accessed 13 July 2020.

1662 Centre for Strategy & Evaluation Services LLP, 'Impact Assessment on Increased Protection of Internet-Connected Radio Equipment and Wearable Radio Equipment - Annex 5 - Annex 5 – Radio Equipment Forecasts' (European Commission 2020) <https://ec.europa.eu/docsroom/documents/40763> accessed 14 July 2020.

lent use.[1663] Typical non-compliant or unlawful products sold via e-commerce and online marketplaces include radio jammers, wireless headsets, detectors, mobile radio sets, drones, security cameras, smartwatches or radio transmitters[1664] or unsafe and recalled products falling under these directives.

The choice of this focus was mainly motivated by the author's previous work and existing contacts with enforcement authorities in this area. The interviews and survey collection took place between December 2017 and March 2019. The research project and the survey were presented at the EMCD AdCo meeting in Edinburgh (UK) on 18 October 2018 and at the RED AdCo meeting in Sophia Antipolis (France) on 28 October 2018. These sessions were also used to garner feedback and discuss common challenges in e-commerce enforcement. The feedback received during these meetings will be added to the discussions below.

2. Survey results – Online market surveillance - RED and EMC Directives

I. Section A: Market surveillance and enforcement

a. Enforcement scope: sector coverage

Of the 10 MSAs that responded to the survey or took part in an interview four had exclusive enforcement competencies for the EMCD and RED. Three of these authorities were from larger Member States and one from a smaller one. One of the lager Member State authorities was not an MSA in itself but a regulatory agency that provided enforcement support and representation at EU level for the responsible MSA, which in itself had enforcement competencies for a wider scope of directives and products.

One MSA had just competency to enforce on the EMCD. Of the remaining five smaller states (four EU members, one EEA member), two had competencies to enforce a selection of five, and respectively six, Directives. Of the other three smaller Member State MSAs, two covered the entire area of the *New Approach*/or CE marking Directives, while the remaining one had overarching responsibility for all consumer products, including food and plant health products, but not pharmaceuticals. That latter authority acted as an enforcement agency, but subject matter policy compe-

1663 Directive 2014/53 (RED) Article 3 (3).
1664 Winkelmann (n 1501) 11–12.

tency for EMCD and RED was devolved to the national radiocommunications agency. This shared responsibility mode was applied throughout a number of other sectors as well for this MSA. In the interview, this MSA also said that its government was thinking of giving it an even broader scope by allocating regulatory competency for pharmaceuticals, competition, telecoms and transportation under one roof.

b. Enforcement vis-à-vis ISPs

In this subsection MSAs were asked whether they had already engaged in enforcement action against ISPs, and if yes, under which legal provision. Although enforcement *vis-à-vis* ISPs would be expected to happen chiefly through the ECD and its national implementation, the previous chapter disclosed the parallel existence and interlinkage of national secondary provisions in ordinary and sector specific laws. This question sought to elicit whether MSAs had used any provisions available through their national laws to enforce against ISPs.

Of 10 MSAs, three from smaller Member States indicated that they had enforced against ISPs in the past. Two of these MSAs had enforced on issues relating to RED, and one under the Low Voltage Directive (LVD).[1665] None of them provided further detail on the exact issue(s) or the ISP concerned. The three responses were captured from MSAs that filled in the survey individually and it was not possible to get further detail.

Of the remaining seven MSAs, two said their preferred approach was to cooperate with ISPs, especially where this concerned larger marketplaces. These two MSAs did in general not consider it appropriate to launch enforcement actions following e.g. non-responsiveness to NTD requests or failure to prevent the re-appearance of notified offers. One of the interlocutors from these two authorities stated that their internal guidelines saw enforcement as the last resort and that cooperation with economic operators was the preferred way of ensuring compliance with the law. They also said that the situation had not been tested where the concerned marketplace also operated as FSPs, such as *Amazon*.[1666] Here, technically, action could

1665 Directive 2014/35/EU of 26 February 2014 on the harmonisation of the laws of the Member States relating to the making available on the market of electrical equipment designed for use within certain voltage limits 2014 (OJ L 96).

1666 *Amazon* operates its *Fulfillment by Amazon* service as an FSP for sellers on its platforms. See also Chapter 4.

be taken but the situation would be unprecedented and not clear. The other MSA stated that they had started to focus on consumer education rather than going after marketplaces. This was also partly due to resource constraints as the MSA covered a broad range of consumer products (outside the area of RED and EMCD).

One other MSA indicated that it did only enforce against smaller internet shops, which acted as distributors. That MSA also indicated that it had received requests for assistance from other EU MSAs to gain information on sellers and products from an online marketplace that was registered in their country. However, since that marketplace had communicated its contact details EU wide, its scope of assistance was limited. They had only contacted the marketplace's offices directly in a limited number of escalated cases, where the enquiring MSA had received no feedback. Another MSA indicated that the EMCD, the RED and Regulation 765/2008 on market surveillance only gave it powers to enforce against producers (and distributors), but not ISPs, which were not covered under the definition of economic operator for any of the directives for which they surveilled the market. Competencies to pursue action under the ECD was devolved to other authorities at different administrational levels (regional and local), with none of which any direct contact had ever been established on this matter.

The three other MSAs did not provide any further detail on why they had not enforced against ISPs.

c. Online market surveillance activity

In this subsection MSAs were asked about the type of online market surveillance they conducted. They were asked to rank the frequency of their screening activity for non-compliant products by type of ISP. They were then asked to indicate the nature of their surveillance activity (Table 3), and provide detail on whether they use automated means for this activity.

Of the 10 MSAs from which responses were received, all engaged in some sort of online surveillance activity. One MSA noted that it did only screen the sites of e-commerce marketplace on a purely reactive basis, when it received indications from other MSAs of economic operators with non-compliant products. Only four of the 10 MSAs screened three or more different types of ISPs as part of their regular surveillance work. There was no clear correlation between the size or subject matter scope of MSAs and the breadth of their surveillance activity.

As can be seen in Table 3, e-commerce marketplaces are most frequently screened by MSAs for non-compliant products and sellers. Meanwhile, two MSAs stated that they focussed their online surveillance activity more on social media networks or search engines than on e-commerce marketplaces. Only one authority from a smaller Member State covered the entire range of ISPs. One MSA noted that it had started to establish contact with payment service providers (PSP), notably *PayPal*. It engaged with this PSP in order to pressure sellers to withdraw non-compliant products or face sanctions. However, it had not been successful with other payment service providers as yet. One MSA stated it used search engines exclusively to generate leads for non-compliant products. Apart from that, it only looked at e-commerce marketplaces and social networks and did not intend to widen its online surveillance to other types of ISPs. However, it did not contact the search engines with any dereferencing or other requests. Another MSA indicated that it planned to start monitoring social media networks, which it recognised as a growing problem regarding the sale of non-compliant products. This was confirmed by one other MSA, which noted the sale of illegal products, such as radio jammers, notably through the *Facebook Marketplace*. None of the MSAs looked at messenger services such as *WhatsApp*, or UGC sites like *YouTube*. One interlocutor stated that they had in the past tracked videos featuring non-compliant products on *YouTube*. However, they had stalled this activity.

	Number of MSAs monitoring			
ISP Category	**most frequently**	**2nd most frequently**	**3rd most frequently**	**also monitored**
E-commerce Platform	**8**	**1**	**1**	-
Social Network	**1**	**2**	**1**	-
UGC platforms	-	-	-	**1**
OTT Services / Messenger	-	-	-	**1**
Search engines	**1**	**2**	**1**	-
Meta search engine/aggregators	-	-	**1**	**1**
Others, please specify	-	-	-	-

Table 3 - Type Online surveillance activity, frequency – non-food

Almost all of the MSAs searched websites of ISPs manually for non-compliant products and a majority also searched proactively for sellers with non-compliant products (Table 4). One MSA indicated that, once it had identified a seller that sold unlawful products on one platform, they also searched for it on other marketplaces. That MSA also stated that it had a team of officers who searched the internet on a 24-hour basis for infringing products. They received alerts form *Google* and *eBay* based on keywords and other search criteria for typical infringing products. Following an identification on *eBay*, the MSA had an expedited access to receive more detailed data on the seller, subject to a reasonably founded request.

The majority of MSAs also contacted ISPs to request information on sellers and products. Six out of 10 MSAs issued NTD requests to ISPs, mainly e-commerce marketplaces.

Two MSAs deployed software to search for non-compliant products online. One MSA had purchased licenses of two pieces of software to monitor the availability of products on selected online marketplaces. They had also seized on the opportunity of *eBay* making its product search interface public and developed a system to filter the platform's product range for potentially non-compliant products. In addition, they did automated image searches for known non-compliant products. The other MSA did not make any statements over their use of software.

Seven of 10 MSAs conducted online test purchases. One MSA, which did not do this, said it had no legal basis to engage in test purchases or mystery shopping. That legal basis would only be created under the new MSR.[1667]

One MSA stated that they engaged with customs authorities where it concerned dropship[1668] or remotely fulfilled orders through e-commerce sites from outside the EU. One MSA listed as part of their other surveillance methods the fact that it invited ISPs to a meeting to educate and inform them on the legal obligations and the general regulatory environment of the product sectors that it covered. This was not listed in the below table as these activities will be treated in a separate section.

1667 Market Surveillance Regulation Article 14 (3) (j), Recital 40.

1668 Dropshipping is a practice whereby retailers (that may sell via online marketplaces) do not hold stock of goods, but commission third parties, such as the manufacturer, other retailers or FSPs, to deliver directly to customers. This practice has also been related to the sale of fake or unlawful products. Nadina Iacob and Felice Simonelli, 'How to Fully Reap the Benefits of the Internal Market for E-Commerce?: New Economic Opportunities and Challenges for Digital Services 20 Years after the Adoption of the e Commerce Directive.' (European Parliament 2020) <https://data.europa.eu/doi/10.2861/47017> accessed 20 April 2021.

Surveillance methods	**Number of MSAs**
Issuing takedown notices	**6**
Conducting test purchases	**7**
Searching the website for unlawful products/ content manually	**9**
Searching the website for non-compliant sellers manually	**7**
Searching the website for unlawful products/ content with software	**2**
Searching the website for non-compliant sellers with software	**0**
Requesting information on products/content	**7**
Requesting information about sellers	**7**
Other, please specify:	Customs cooperation (1)

Table 4 - Surveillance methods - non-food

d. Online market surveillance resources

Five out 10 MSAs had started their online market surveillance activities before 2010. One MSA has engaged since 2000 in online market surveillance. Three MSAs had only started after 2010 (in 2012, 2015 and 2017), while the remaining two did have not have any information about the start of their online market surveillance.

Only two MSAs had dedicated internet market surveillance staff. One of them, a large Member State MSA, had a team of five officers. The other MSA had a team of two officers dedicated to online market surveillance. Although other MSAs had indicated that they had internet market surveillance officers, it could not be verified whether these teams were exclusively looking at the internet or did this as part of their overall market surveillance work. For example, one MSA from a smaller Member State indicated that it had an internet surveillance team of 11 officers, which if cross-checked against the interview conducted with larger MSAs appears to be highly unlikely. Two MSAs indicated that their teams of 13 and 12 market surveillance officers were working in both on- and offline market surveillance. Another MSA, which was responsible for a broad variety of product sectors, noted that it employed 55 market surveillance officers that covered both on- and offline activity. Of these, 40 were dedicated to general product safety, and 15 to food and food supplements. That MSA mentioned that it was currently planning to create a dedicated team of internet market surveillance experts. Other MSAs reported teams of between one and 11 officers that presumedly conducted their activities concurrently on- and offline. One authority did not give any indication about its internet surveillance resources.

Four out of 10 MSAs had increased their internet market surveillance activities over the last five years, either through an increase in staff numbers or a general increase in activities focussed on e-commerce. Of these four MSAs, three belonged to large Member States, and consequently concerned authorities with already higher staff numbers. Another four MSAs recorded no change in the extent of their internet market surveillance, with one MSA stating they nevertheless saw the need for getting more funding as the country extended its focus to become an international logistics hub with a potential increase in small e-commerce consignments. Two MSAs noted a decrease in their funding over the last five years, which translated into less resources with regards to online enforcement activities. Of these authorities, one said it was in a phase of restructuring and considered the creation of a special internet investigation unit, with the funding details however not officially confirmed as yet.

None of the MSAs consulted employed any subcontractors from the private sector for their online market surveillance activities.

II. Section B: Enforcement activity and the ECD

a. Use of the ECD by MSAs

This first question in this section asked whether MSAs had already made use of the ECD intermediary liability provisions (Articles 12 – 15) in any form when engaging with ISPs. This may appear to be similar to the question in Section A (b) on whether MSAs had already enforced against ISPs. However, in this section MSAs were implicitly asked about their awareness of the ECD's enforcement toolset.

Three of the 10 MSAs stated that they had made use of the means offered by the ECD. One larger authority stated, however, that their interpretation of that use was the issuance of NTD requests. The authority stated, that it could not pursue non-responsive platforms because the competencies for this activity were with other authorities, at regional or local levels (see I. Section A. b) The two other MSAs gave no further detail about their use of the ECD. Seven MSAs stated they had not made use of the means offered by the ECD to pursue non-responsive platforms through e.g. injunctions or administrative orders.

The three MSAs that had made use of the ECD in their online surveillance activity stated that they saw specific problems with the liability provisions of Articles 12 – 15. One MSA did not further substantiate their view. Another MSA stated that the liability exemptions were too broad and general in order to be applied effectively. The remaining MSA said that the liability exemptions were outdated. This latter MSA had the view that although NTD was an effective tool, the split of enforcement competencies *vis-à-vis* products and platforms resulted in a loss of efficiency.

One authority that had not made use of the ECD in their work nevertheless stated that it found the liability exemptions too broad and general to be applied effectively. That MSA said, platforms should be obliged to do more to prevent the occurrence of unlawful products and cooperate better with authorities.

b. The relation between product safety laws and the ECD

The next question asked more specifically whether MSAs thought that the liability exemption provisions of the ECD are of any relevance for the enforcement of product regulations. The objective of this question was to elucidate whether enforcement authorities saw the hosting of offers and marketing of unlawful products as illegal information/activity as per the hosting provider liability provisions of the ECD.[1669] Seven MSAs said they were not sure. Of these, one added that platforms did also not qualify as distributors which made any enforcement action under product legislation futile. The only way forward currently was to form voluntary agreements. Two MSAs saw the ECD and product laws as separate from one another. One of these two MSAs added that product regulation was only enforceable against producers that placed products on the market. Only one MSA saw the provisions of the ECD as relevant for the enforcement of sector specific laws.

MSAs were divided over whether online marketplaces could be considered as economic operators (with responsibilities) under product legisla-

---

1669 As stated in Directive 2000/31 (ECD) Article 14 (1) (a).

tion.[1670] Three stated that they would see platforms generally as economic operators for product law purposes, while another three saw them generally not as economic operators. One MSA, which had not been asked this particular question during an early version of the interview, had however proposed in the 2017 MSR Impact Assessment that it was worth considering to include e-commerce platforms under the definition of economic operator.[1671]

MSAs were also divided over whether the ECD and its liability conditions had been discussed during the AdCo meetings of the EMCD and the RED. While four Member States answered in the negative, two other ones said the issues were discussed, with one clarifying that this happened in the context of FSPs. Furthermore, five MSAs were unsure on whether the proposed MSR would provide better tools to enforce product legislation *vis-à-vis* platforms. One MSA was of the opinion that it would, because it broadened the enforcement powers of MSAs.

The Product Safety Pledge of 25 June 2018 could not be covered in three of the four in-person interviews that were conducted prior to June 2018. Three MSAs that were asked about the Product Safety Pledge (as part of the survey) welcomed this initiative saying that the assistance of online platforms in identifying dangerous products and helping in the enforcement against non-compliant seller would be key and result in a significant contribution. Although e-commerce marketplaces are not liable, they provided online space to other sellers. One MSA thought the Pledge will be useful in helping MSAs establish contact and develop relationships with platforms.

III. Section C: Cooperation with ISPs

This section sought to establish the nature and level of contacts that MSAs had established with online marketplaces and other ISPs. As stated above, the co-regulatory product regulation system relies on public-private cooperation both when drafting technical standards and when enforcing and

1670 This was question was added to the survey prior to the AdCo meetings in October 2018 and did therefore not feature during the in-person interviews, which took place prior to this.

1671 European Commission, 'Goods Package Proposal - Impact Assessment 2/4' (n 1547) 447. Note that some survey questions were introduced at a later stage based on feedback from earlier interviews.

addressing product safety issues. These principles are rooted in the GPSD and Decision 768/2008. They were reinforced by the MSR, with a dedicated cooperation chapter and new obligations of cooperation imposed on ISSPs.[1672]

a. Nature of cooperation between MSAs and ISPs

Of the 10 MSAs, four stated they had established working contacts with ISPs which were outside the surveillance activities mentioned in Section A (i.e. NTD, information requests, product searches etc). Two of these MSAs belonged to larger Member States. Of the latter two, one MSA shared that they had participated in workshops and information meetings organised by major online marketplaces in their country. As part of this, they had agreed with some platforms that they would filter for certain unlawful products (by keywords) and display online warning messages (agreed ad hoc) related to certain dangerous products. These agreements were achieved thanks to specific language in the national product sector laws implementing the EMCD and RED, which gave the MSA powers to request support from intermediaries, such as e-commerce marketplaces (see also Chapter 5). Meanwhile, the same MSA took part in annual information exchanges between national regulators to which online platforms were invited. No further detailed was shared on the nature of these events. The second MSA from a larger Member States had entered into bilateral MoUs with two major e-commerce marketplaces, which remained however confidential. It had also struck agreements with another international online marketplace and a major payment services provider. In general, these agreements and MoUs contained agreed standards and policies relating to the identification and prevention of unlawful products and sellers. The MSA had also organised and attended policy meetings together with online platform operators to discuss future cooperation.

Of the two remaining MSAs from smaller Member States which had established contact with ISPs, one said it held regular information exchange and educational meetings with international search engine operators and social media platforms, as well as other local platforms. The other MSA had reached out to two national marketplaces in a quest to get agreements on NTD procedures and ask for the instalment of internal filters that

1672 Directive 2001/95 (GPSD) Article 5 (4); Decision 768/2008 Recital 48; Market Surveillance Regulation Chapter III (Articles 8 & 9); Article 7 (2).

would screen for certain illegal products. The latter request was unsuccessful. Nevertheless, the MSA had passed on a list of keywords and regulatory product information in the hope that the marketplaces would install internal filters and also educate their sellers. The MSA managed to agree a deadline for the removal of unsafe products and advertisements, following a notification by its officers to the marketplace. An expedited deadline was agreed for removal of offers and ads of unsafe products that posed a high risk.

This MSA remained, however, subdued over the success of the agreements struck. It did not have any data to judge whether the measures agreed did indeed help in the fight against unsafe and non-compliant products. The other three MSAs were more positive, stating that the cooperation measures had helped significantly, notably by establishing working contacts and initial processes that could serve as a basis for further cooperation. However, it should be noted that these improvements happened from a low base of virtually no previous contact or exchange between these MSAs and platforms.

b. Obstacles to effective surveillance and enforcement

MSAs were asked about the existence of specific obstacles that stood in the way of effective surveillance and enforcement of e-commerce conducted via online platforms.

Resource constraints on the side of MSAs were the most frequently cited obstacles (seven MSAs) that hindered better and more effective online surveillance and enforcement work. As stated above, one MSA was faced with a 25% budget cut over the last five years. Another MSA said their resource constraints meant they were working strictly on the surveillance of high-risk product areas (risk based approach), which currently included, for example, radio jammers, solar panel inverters and LED lights. The jurisdictional barriers, both with regards to platforms based within and outside the EU, were also seen as enforcement problems. The two MSAs that complained over the unwillingness of platforms to cooperate belonged to the group of MSAs that had entered into agreements and regular contact with online marketplaces.

Number of MSAs finding that…	
Platforms are not willing or do not see any legal obligation to cooperate.	**2**
Platforms have no time/resources to cooperate.	**1**

Number of MSAs finding that...	
Lack of resources on the side of my authority.	7
Platforms are outside of our national jurisdictional reach.	5
Platforms are outside of EU jurisdictional reach.	5
Other, please specify:	4

Table 5 - Obstacles to surveillance and enforcement work – non-food

Regarding the other obstacles, one MSA mentioned that the legal definition of platform operators did not allow for a level of enforcement that would be adequate given the market position of these platforms. This concern was supported by another MSA, which found the existing legal framework not clear where it concerned the role of online marketplaces in the supply chain. In addition, it was hard to identify the responsible person when contacting an ISP. Another smaller MSA stated that, given that no online marketplace operator or online sellers on these marketplaces was based in its country, it was virtually impossible to enforce product legislation on its territory. Meanwhile, another MSA stated that cooperation between EU MSAs was still too ineffective to deal with e-commerce problems. This might eventually be improved by the new MSR and its new system of national single liaison offices for market surveillance.[1673]

IV. Section D: Regulatory cooperation between MSAs

The fragmented nature of market surveillance activity has been commented on before. The disadvantages of the highly specialised sectoral enforcement system were only brought further to the fore by the rise in e-commerce. This subsection aimed at getting the perspective of MSAs regarding the level of cooperation in online market surveillance.

Seven out of 10 MSAs stated that there were other authorities within their countries whose activity overlapped or with theirs. The number of other authorities with overlapping responsibilities varied depending on the scope of activities of the MSA in question and the size of the Member State. Only one Member State cited that its activities were affected by the enforcement authorities of the ECD within its country. Most commonly, the other authorities with overlapping or complementary tasks were medical or pharmaceutical agencies (3 MSAs), consumer protection agencies (3

1673 Market Surveillance Regulation Article 10.

MSAs), customs (3 MSAs), transportation agencies (3 MSAs), Food Safety Authorities (FSAs) (2 MSAs); other authorities included tax inspections, environmental authorities or postal and telecoms regulators. Seven out of the ten MSAs had some level of coordination between national surveillance authorities. One large and one small Member State reported on bi-annual meetings where enforcement work on all *New Approach* directives was coordinated. One smaller Member State said that these kinds of meetings took place on a bi-monthly basis and included discussion on online market surveillance. This was supplemented by bilateral meetings between MSAs. Another MSA from a large Member State said that a central commission coordinated between all authorities that were involved in market surveillance. Three MSAs, of which one from a larger Member State, reported that meetings took place on an ad-hoc and uncoordinated basis.

The question on EU level cooperation was only asked during the four in-person or telephone interviews. The context of EU cooperation was obvious from the surveys gathered after the AdCo meetings. The interviewed MSAs all confirmed AdCos, the ICSMS and the RAPEX system as main channels of interaction between MSAs at EU level. One MSA mentioned bilateral cooperation with MSAs in China, Canada, the US and India. Of the four MSAs interviewed, all said that the EU coordination consisted of best practice sharing and joint surveillance initiatives. Other activities, less frequently mentioned, included sharing of statistics and data, proposing or amending EU legislations, and setting common surveillance and enforcement standards. Eight out of 10 MSAs found that the coordination activity had intensified somewhat over the last five years; two found it had intensified significantly. One MSA qualified this by saying that while cooperation had intensified, output had not improved significantly. Some Member States had even withdrawn from some AdCos.

Asked on the most notable initiatives that came out of MSAs' EU cooperation, three MSAs stated that the best practice sharing on agreements and codes of conducts with online marketplaces had been useful. One other MSA mentioned best practice sharing in general as beneficial. Other initiatives mentioned were the input into the Commission Notice on market surveillance for products sold online,[1674] input into the MSR, especially the designation of FSPs as economic operators and mandatory powers of MSAs to conduct anonymous test purchases.[1675]

1674 European Commission, '2017/C 250/01' (n 1504).
1675 Market Surveillance Regulation Article 14 (3) (j).

C. Case study 2: Online market surveillance in food safety regulation

1. Overview

The sectors covered by food safety regulation cover more regular food and beverages, but also fringe sectors like nutritional supplements, or novel foods and animal feeds. In addition, food that is subject to certain production methods, such as organic products, are also regulated by food safety law. The scope of the food framework encompasses the entire supply chain, from agricultural producers, importers, logistics and distribution companies to retailers. While food safety in Europe is managed and implemented on a co-regulatory basis, enforcement and controls remain solidly in the hands of public authorities.[1676] Food safety is considered one of the most tightly regulated areas in the EU.[1677]

Usually, Member States have one central authority that carries responsibility for general food safety matters. However, other authorities may still be involved in food safety enforcement. For example, nutritional supplements regulation may overlap with responsibilities of pharmaceutical or medicinal product authorities. Food safety issues may also play a role in authorisation and control of plant protection products or affect the area of intellectual property and cultural heritage, for example through Geographic Indications. Despite the existence of these neighbouring enforcement areas, it was relatively straightforward to identify and focus on the central FSAs and their work. The FSAs were selected following a consultation meeting with DG Health and Food Safety at the European Commission, which took place on 6 March 2018. During this meeting, the results of which also fed into this case study, a number of FSAs were identified that, according to indication from the European Commission, played a more proactive role in the area of online food safety surveillance. Of seven authorities that were originally selected, in-person or telephone interviews with four authorities took place eventually. One of these authorities was from a larger Member State. One FSA with particularly wide horizontal surveillance powers was interviewed for both case studies (product regulation and food safety). The interviews were conducted between September 2018 and March 2019.

1676 Garcia Martinez, Verbruggen and Fearne (n 1624) 11.
1677 Vaqué (n 1631) 166.

2. Survey results – Online market surveillance in the area of food safety

I. Section A: Market surveillance and enforcement

a. Enforcement scope: sector coverage

Of the four FSAs interviewed, one had broad sectoral competencies that covered food and feedstuffs, food supplements, cosmetics and chemicals, but also general non-food consumer products. This authority was also interviewed in Case Study 1, where it said that its government was currently looking into further broadening its scope, adding pharmaceuticals, competition, telecoms and transportation to its remit. The other three authorities all also had responsibilities for food supplements. The authority from the larger Member State was also the competent authority in the area of animal feedstuffs, plant protection products, veterinary drugs, toy safety, textiles, food contact materials and tobacco products. One of the smaller FSAs was also responsible for tobacco products and food services, while the fourth FSA looked after seeds and live animals in addition to food and food supplements. Consequently, all of the four FSAs were the lead authorities in their Member States for the application of the EU Food Law *acquis*.

b. Enforcement vis-à-vis ISPs

In this subsection FSAs were asked whether they had taken direct enforcement measures against ISPs, and if yes, under which legal provision. Like in Case Study 1, action against ISPs would normally be taken through the ECD and its national implementation. However, the previous chapter had shown that national secondary intermediary provisions existed in Member States' ordinary laws. This question sought to elicit whether FSAs had used any of these provisions against ISPs.

Three out of the four FSAs had not taken any enforcement action against ISPs so far. One authority stated that they favoured a cooperative approach, especially where it concerned online marketplaces. They did not pursue ISPs, but went mainly after the sellers on these platforms. Another FSA said that, although they had inspected online marketplaces, i.e. verified the legality of offers, they had not acted against marketplaces. They would only have a legal basis for enforcement where a marketplace operator acted also as an FSP, which had not yet happened in their jurisdiction.

One authority stated that it had acted against ISPs under the national laws that implemented the EU Food law *acquis*. It did, however, not provide any further detail. This FSA implied later that the particular way in which the ECD was implemented in its country may have provided for the option to take direct action against a marketplace for not reacting to requests from authorities. The European Commission (DG Health) noted that there was very low appetite on its part to enhance responsibilities and liabilities for platforms in this area, due to fear over a negative impact on the digital business environment.[1678]

c. Online market surveillance activity

In this subsection, FSAs were asked about the type of online market surveillance they conducted. They were asked to rank the frequency of their screening activity for non-compliant products by type of ISP (see Table 6). They were then asked to indicate the nature of their surveillance activity (Table 7), and provide detail on whether they use automated means for this activity.

All of the four FSAs interviewed engaged in some sort of online market surveillance activity. One smaller FSA regularly screened all six types of ISPs given as an option in the survey, while another two screened four different types of ISPs.

Table 6 shows that e-commerce marketplaces are most frequently screened by MSAs for non-compliant food products and sellers. One FSA surveils social networks more frequently than e-commerce marketplaces. One FSA/MSA, also covered in Case Study 1, stated it used search engines exclusively to generate leads for non-compliant products. However, it did not contact the search engines with any dereferencing or other requests. Apart from that, it only looked at e-commerce marketplaces and social networks and did not intend to widen its online surveillance to other types of ISPs. Another MSA indicated that it used *Google's* search engines to identify non-compliant products elsewhere but then tried to reach out to *Google* to block access to these listings and post warning messages next to certain offers. However, this was fraught with problems as the FSA needed to engage the Irish regulator and this was taking too long and too bureaucratic. The FSA from the larger Member State indicated that it planned to start

1678 As a reminder: the interview with DG Health took place in early March 2018.

monitoring UGC platforms and OTT services in the near future. Only one FSA looked at OTT services currently.

	Number of MSAs monitoring			
ISP Category	**most frequently**	**2nd most frequently**	**3rd most frequently**	**also monitored**
E-commerce Platform	3	1	-	-
Social Network	1	1	1	1
UGC platforms	-	-	1	1
OTT Services / Messenger	-	-	-	1
Search engines	-	1	-	1
Meta search engine/aggregators	-	1	1	1
Others, please specify	-	-	-	1

Table 6 - Type Online surveillance activity, frequency – food

Overall, the authorities interviewed engaged in a relatively broad variety of surveillance activities. All of the four FSAs searched websites of ISPs manually for non-compliant products and sellers, conducted test purchases and requested information on non-compliant sellers. However, only two FSAs said they also asked the ISP for information on products. One FSA stated that, although it did test purchases online, it had no proper legal basis. It also lacked the means, such as corporate credit cards.

Three FSAs had issued NTD requests to platforms. However, one FSA remarked that the level of response was unsatisfactory and that some platforms had to be approached repeatedly before they acted. Moreover, the FSA had experienced difficulties in getting contact details from some marketplace operators. That FSA was not fully aware of the obligations of platforms under the ECD to react to NTD requests. One FSA stated that it did not issue NTD requests. However, it emerged during the wider discussion that they did approach platforms with requests to block access or remove content (e.g. *Google Search*). DG Health, by contrast, noted in its interview that the NTD process was generally working well and that there was little need to put additional obligations on platforms.

Two FSAs deployed software to search for non-compliant products and/or sellers online. The FSA from a large Member States operated two pieces of software. One software product was deployed by the tax authorities to identify tax evading businesses selling via online platforms. The FSA uses data from this web crawler to identify businesses that sell food products and then double checks whether these had registered as food business operators, a requirement of the Regulation on the hygiene of foodstuffs.[1679] The software version used is a modification by the national tax authorities of a privately developed product. Secondly, it has taken part in the development of software to identify unlawful food products sold via the internet. This project focuses on identifying food products with prohibited ingredients or misleading declarations. This software was developed in conjunction with a national university and as part of a public research project. The other MSA also used software, developed by its tax authorities to identify online food sellers that had failed to register as a food business.

One FSA had created their own account and page and on a social media network and used this to flag unlawful products to the platform operator and to post warnings to users.

Surveillance methods	**Number of MSAs...**
Issuing takedown notices	3
Conducting test purchases	4
Searching the website for unlawful products/content manually	4
Searching the website for non-compliant sellers manually	4
Searching the website for unlawful products/content with software	1
Searching the website for non-compliant sellers with software	2
Requesting information on products/content	2
Requesting information about sellers	4
Other, please specify:	Own social media page to issue warnings (1)

Table 7 - Surveillance methods - food

d. Online market surveillance resources

Two FSAs had no recollection of when they started their online market surveillance activities. One FSA started in 2007. It said it belonged to the group of five or so EU Member States that pioneered online market surveillance for food safety within the network of European Food Law Enforcement Practitioners (FLEP).[1680] The other, from the larger Member State, started its activities in 2011 as a pilot project before formally establishing an internet surveillance unit in 2013. That unit employed currently

---

1679 Regulation 852/2004 Article 6 (2).

1680 PJ Byrne, 'FLEP - Food Law Enforcement Practitioners' <http://www.flep.org/what.html> accessed 17 July 2020.

six people entirely dedicated to internet market surveillance. It was financed by regional food safety authorities, which retained the main competencies for enforcing the food safety *acquis*, but was assembled under the roof of the central consumer protection and food safety agency. While the number of staff (six officers) had not changed since the beginning of the operations in 2013, the FSA said that there was a public recognition that internet surveillance was becoming more important. This FSA also started in April 2020 to host another unit that looks exclusively at the online sale of plant protection products. It was not disclosed how many people work in this new unit. This FSA also said that apart from its own staff of 32, many of the large number of local food safety inspectors were also looking at e-commerce as part of their daily controls work.

The smaller FSA that started its online market surveillance in 200,7 said that it had 30 staff that had received special training for online controls and enforcement. These officers, although not exclusively looking at e-commerce, were predestined to work on internet market surveillance. This number had not changed over the last five years. Meanwhile, the entire number of food safety inspectors stood at over 550 for the entire country.

Another FSA said that of its total staff of between 400 to 500 local food safety inspectors that worked nationwide, a group of 32 specialists were assembled who were fighting food fraud, part of which also concerned e-commerce activities. In addition, the authority employed 2.5 full-time resources looking exclusively at online market surveillance. Their activities covered food and food supplements. This number had stayed the same over the last five years.

The FSA/MSA already covered in Case Study 1, which engaged in a broad variety of product sectors, noted that of its 55 market surveillance officers, 15 worked in the area of food and food supplements and 40 on other product safety issues. It should be assumed that this is supplemented by a considerable number of local food safety inspectors. All of its officers were conducting both on- and offline market surveillance. The authority had experienced budget cuts of 25% over the last five years. As part of ongoing restructuring it was currently planning to create a dedicated team of internet market surveillance experts.

None of the FSAs consulted or employed any subcontractors from the private sector for their online market surveillance activities.

The DG Health interlocutor from the European Commission confirmed that there were marked differences between Member States' focus on online market surveillance.

II. Section B: Enforcement activity and the ECD

a. Use of the ECD by FSAs

The first question in this section asked whether FSAs had already made use of the ECD intermediary liability provisions (Articles 12 – 15) in any form when engaging with ISPs. This question appears to be similar to the one in Section A (b) on whether FSAs had already enforced against ISPs. However, in this section, FSAs are implicitly asked about their awareness of the ECD's enforcement toolset.

None of the four FSAs stated that they had made use of the means offered by the ECD *vis-á-vis* online platforms. The FSA from a larger Member State remarked that ECD enforcement was under the competencies of other authorities within the country and could therefore not be handled via its service.

There was a general hesitancy amongst the four FSAs to make any pronounced statement on the ECD's liability provisions. The authority interviewed already in the first case study repeated that platforms should probably be more cooperative and that the ECD liability provisions may be too broad in order to be effective. However, it did not take action against online platforms on the basis of the ECD because it preferred not to antagonise them in the interest of future cooperation. This latter view was echoed by the FSA from the larger Member State. It did not want to comment on any issues with the ECD's liability provisions. The two other FSAs were similarly evasive. One FSA broadly stated that online marketplaces should do more to assist FSAs in their work, but did not make any more specific statements on exactly how or whether this was related to the ECD. The remaining FSA voiced in the following discussion that the ECD liability provisions may be outdated, as the kind of information hosts covered under the ECD's Article 14 may not exist anymore today. Online platforms were more active today and maybe a new definition was needed.

The DG Health representative, however, stated that the ECD in its current form was perceived as working well due to FSAs' use of NTD procedures. They also doubted that more proactive monitoring on the side of platforms was adequate due to the complex and specialised nature of food law. This finding is relativised by the interviews with the FSAs, which clearly found that the use of NTD was not without problems. Meanwhile, the FSAs interviewed had a more mixed view on the ECD's liability protections for online marketplaces and the role of these actors.

b. The relation between food safety laws and the ECD

The next question asked more specifically whether FSAs thought that the liability provisions of the ECD are of any relevance for the enforcement of food safety law. The objective was to elucidate whether FSAs saw the hosting of offers and marketing of unlawful products as illegal activity as per the hosting provider liability provisions of the ECD.

Two of the four FSAs said they were not sure. One of them added that platforms did also not qualify as distributors or food business operators, which made any enforcement action under food safety legislation pointless.

The other FSA said that normally online marketplaces were not considered food business operators. However, this could change where the platform takes a commission from the sellers and charges other fees. This, it said, would make it an active participant in the transaction and potentially responsible. The FSA from a larger Member State had a clear view that the ECD was not relevant for the enforcement of food safety laws. Meanwhile, online marketplaces themselves were also not covered by food law under the Regulation on the Hygiene of foodstuffs, which applied only to "undertakings, the concept of which implies a certain continuity of activities and a certain degree of organization." [1681]

Finally, the fourth FSA was affirmative that the ECD's liability provisions were relevant for the enforcement of food law. In its view, unlawful food products were included under the definition illegal information or activity. However, the ECD was not well transposed in its national law and no authority had been allocated with clear enforcement competency. This made the imposition of injunctions, such as cease-and-desist of certain offers, placement of online warning messages, or the imposition of keyword filters, difficult. The FSA was currently trying to exploit this enforcement vacuum by gaining competencies to enforce on the basis of the ECD, i.e. through placing injunctions against online marketplace operators. This FSA also had a pronounced view on the responsibilities of online marketplaces under food safety law. The CJEU's ruling in *L'Oréal v eBay,* it said, opened up the possibility of qualifying active platforms as food business operators. However, setting a legal precedent would be a difficult and time-consuming undertaking and the FSA preferred to place injunctions under the ECD.

1681 Regulation 852/2004, Recital 9.

DG Health view was that it was unlikely that enforcement under food safety law would be expanded towards platforms. However, it was likely to be applied towards FSPs in the future. Nevertheless, the representative said that there was development in the position of the European Commission towards platforms, with a general push for more responsibilities and regulation of platforms. Recent terrorist attacks and hate speech were responsible for a marked shift of the European Commission's position on this matter.

III. Section C: Cooperation with ISPs

This section sought to establish the nature and level of contacts that FSAs had made with online marketplaces and other ISPs. The co-regulatory structure of food safety law is based on industry designing and implementing food safety management systems according to private standards. FSAs takes these industry standards into account when conducting official controls of food businesses.

a. Nature of cooperation between FSAs and ISPs

All of the four FSAs said they had established working contacts with ISPs which were outside the surveillance activity established in Section A (i.e. NTD, information requests, market surveillance). The FSA from the larger Member State said that this cooperation consisted mainly of ad-hoc activities. For example, the FSA had distributed information material concerning the legal provisions on the sale of certain food products and supplements to online platforms. They had also asked ISPs to nominate contact points to the FSA for enquiries and removal requests. In addition, they tried to interest marketplaces and other e-commerce sites to gain trust mark certifications for safe shopping experiences. Although the authority was not able to recommend or endorse specific certificates, it worked together with industry associations to drive adoption of certification in this area. Another FSA also engaged mainly in ad hoc initiatives to inform marketplaces about applicable product legislation, with a view to have this passed on to their sellers. They engaged technical intermediaries that provide, e.g. product data, to inform marketplaces on gaps in their online product labelling and sales information, provided lists of forbidden ingredients and products for possible filtering and distributed regulatory information for seller education. They had also met with one marketplace operator in another Member States to discuss issues of obvious non-compliance with applicable food safety laws and basic due diligence, but had made no progress with this operator.

One of the FSAs had taken part in a workshop organised by another authority in their Member State to which online marketplaces had been invited. During that workshop they reached an agreement with a national marketplace operator to establish mutual points of contact for NTD requests and other enquiries. Prior to this, the exchange of information had happened exclusively through the legal team of that e-commerce marketplace. They were also in the process of establishing contact with the national e-commerce business association to get a better understanding of the business models of certain national ISPs.

The FSA already interviewed in Case Study 1 had reached out to two national marketplaces in a quest to get agreements on NTD procedures and ask for the instalment of internal filters that would screen for certain illegal products. Although that request was unsuccessful, the FSA noted that platforms were slightly more forthcoming in their cooperation in matters of food safety than in non-food products. The FSA had passed on a list of keywords and regulatory information in the hope that the marketplaces would install internal filters and educate sellers, but had received no feedback as yet. The FSA also managed to agree a deadline for the removal of unsafe products and advertisements, which included food supplements and alcoholic beverages following NTD requests by its officers. An expedited deadline was agreed for removal of offers and ads of unlawful products that posed a high risk.

This FSA was gloomy over the success of the agreements struck. So far it did not have any data to judge whether the measures agreed did indeed help in the fight against non-compliant food products. The other three FSAs were more positive, stating that the cooperation measures had helped significantly, notably by establishing working contacts. One authority valued the fact that operational contacts between authorities and platforms were established, which was an improvement on the previously more formal exchange of communication via lawyers. However, another FSA also mentioned that the positive change happened from a very low basis and that there was room for improvement.

According to the DG Health interlocutor, the European Commission had established regular contacts with the major marketplace operators *Amazon, eBay, Alibaba* and *Facebook*. It was currently working on a list of obviously unlawful ingredients and products that it intended to circulate among online marketplaces. The aim was to get a non-bonding commitment from marketplaces to monitor and filter for relevant products.

b. Obstacles to effective surveillance and enforcement

MSAs were asked about the existence of specific obstacles that stood in the way of effective surveillance and enforcement in e-commerce conducted via online platforms.

The jurisdictional barrier, both with regards to platforms based within and outside the EU was seen as an enforcement problem by three of the four interviewed FSAs. One FSA mentioned that efficiency of cooperation between FSAs in Europe was lacking. Speed of action was a major problem in this context.

Two FSAs cited resource problems on their side as an obstacle to enforcement. As was mentioned before, one FSA was faced with a 25% budget cut over the last five years. Another FSA had not seen any increase in the 2.5 headcount accorded to its internet market surveillance of food and food supplements despite a growth in workload.

Two FSAs saw the unwillingness of platforms to cooperate as an obstacle to effective enforcement against unsafe and unlawful food products.

Number of MSAs finding that...	
Platforms are not willing or do not see any legal obligation to cooperate.	**2**
Platforms have no time/resources to cooperate.	-
Lack of resources on the side of my authority.	**2**
Platforms are outside of our national jurisdictional reach.	**3**
Platforms are outside of EU jurisdictional reach.	**3**
Other, please specify:	

Table 8 Obstacles to surveillance and enforcement work – food

IV. Section D: Regulatory cooperation between FSAs

This subsection asked for the perspective of FSAs regarding the level of regulatory cooperation in online market surveillance.

All FSAs stated that there were other authorities within their countries whose activity overlapped with theirs. The work of the national pharmaceutical regulator had an impact on all four FSAs. Further overlaps existed with tax authorities (2 FSAs), plant protection agencies (1 FSA), customs (1 FSA) and a number of trade, technical and labour inspections services. All four FSAs had some level of coordination between their national surveillance authorities. The FSA from a large Member State was the only one where no formal coordination between other MSAs existed. Meetings between authorities took place on an ad-hoc and uncoordinated basis. This authority also criticised that e-commerce enforcement still happened too much in silos with in its own country. Among the three FSAs where cooperation between national surveillance authorities was more institutionalised, one reported that this took place between all MSAs (food and non-food) on a bi-monthly basis and included discussions of online market surveillance. This was supplemented by bilateral meetings between MSAs. Another FSA stated that its authority has had regular quarterly meetings on internet market surveillance with the national pharmaceutical regulator for the last 10 years. Since 2018, the FSA also took part in best practice sharing on internet market surveillance with national non-food MSAs. In addition, bilateral contacts existed with the national tax authorities.

The fourth MSA has been taking part in an interdepartmental working group on e-commerce, which exists since 2017 and which meets on an annual basis. Apart from that, it had a bilateral cooperation with national trade inspection services.

The interviewed FSAs all stated that the EU level cooperation happened mainly via the Food Law Enforcement Practitioners (FLEP) working group, which was established after the first EU Directive on official controls in 1990. Its main objective is the exchange of information, learning and cooperation in the area of European food law enforcement.[1682] FLEP participants also discuss e-commerce food safety surveillance. Apart from that, two FSAs mentioned the European Commission's initiative on online food offered, which exists since 2017 and which coordinates e-commerce controls, but also formulates policy recommendations.[1683] One FSA mentioned that it had formed a special bilateral cooperation with the FSA of another Member State, which was also part the FSAs interviewed.

All of the four FSAs interviewed stated that EU coordination consisted of best practice sharing. FSAs were exchanging their practical experience in enforcement work, such as for example conducting test purchases. Three

---

1682 Byrne (n 1679).

1683 'Online Offered Food (2017) - Food Safety - European Commission' (*Food Safety*) <https://ec.europa.eu/food/safety/official_controls/eu-coordinated-control-plans/online-offered-food-2017_en> accessed 20 April 2021.

FSAs said that joint surveillance activities and the formulation of policy recommendations were other features of their EU cooperation. Setting common market surveillance standards and exchange of data and statistics was mentioned by one FSA as an additional activity. This FSA said that this latter activity should ideally be intensified. One FSA mentioned the Better Training for Safe Food Initiative as an additional activity.[1684] All FSAs found that coordination had intensified over the last five years; two found it had intensified significantly and two noticed that it had increased somewhat. One FSA stated that participation in the FLEP e-commerce working group had grown from eight Member States in 2011 to 18 in 2017. Another FSA stated that a new enforcement case management system had been brought in place, which was good, but, at a turnaround time of 3 months, still too lengthy.

Three FSAs noted that the input of the FLEP working group into the recent official controls regulation had been one of the most notable initiatives that came out of FSAs EU cooperation. They cited the possibility of conducting online test purchases and the new provisions relating to the closure of websites as main achievements. Other initiatives included the Better Training for Safe Food Initiative and a guide for maintenance of the cooling chain in food e-commerce.

The DG Health representative confirmed the intensified cooperation between EU FSAs, which manifested itself also through improved use and functioning of the EU's Food and Feed Safety Alerts (RASFF) system, a notification tool for unsafe food that posed high health risks.[1685]

D. Summary of MSA/FSA case studies

The case studies confirmed that the availability of unsafe products online via online platforms, be they food or non-food, is a problem that is in the policy focus of the EU and of Member States. The interviews conducted, however, also confirm the disparate set up, funding, knowledge and experience when it comes to online market surveillance and the enforcement of the relevant provisions.

1684 'Better Training for Safer Food (BTSF) - Food Safety - European Commission' (n 1637).

1685 European Commission, 'RASFF - Food and Feed Safety Alerts' (*Food Safety - European Commission*, 17 October 2016) <https://ec.europa.eu/food/safety/rasff_en> accessed 17 July 2020.

A number of observations concerning the online market surveillance and enforcement system in the area of food and product safety can be made.

1. Enforcement hesitation and unclarity over the relevance of the ECD

Considering that online marketplaces and ISPs in general have been identified as a major channel through which unsafe, non-compliant or straightforwardly illegal products are being offered to EU consumers, it is astonishing how little the enforcement has been adapted to this phenomenon. This is not meant to be a criticism of the work of MSAs (or FSAs). These authorities work in an area of highly complex, technical regulation which requires expert knowledge. Their enforcement work involves technical risk assessment and cooperation with economic operators in the withdrawal of products. This kind of market surveillance is tried and tested when it comes to traditional, physical sales and supply chain activities. With regards to online intermediaries, the ECD offers a conceptually and structurally different regulatory framework, with its reliance on knowledge creation through notices and the imposition of injunctions. This corresponds more to the private regulation areas of speech and economic (IP) regulation. In addition, product and food safety regulation have until recently not envisaged obligations for intermediaries that are not economic actors. This has only recently happened with the MSR (in 2019), some national product rules, like the German implementations of the EMCD and RED, and, to a limited extent, in official controls for food safety. It comes therefore as no surprise that none of the authorities interviewed had seized on the use of preventive injunctions offered by the ECD's Article 14 (3). Only one FSA appeared to be aware of that possibility. Nor is it clear whether the MSAs have been allocated the competency to do so under their national rules. As it is, MSAs have been remarkedly cautious when approaching platforms in order to get assistance in the identification and removal of unlawful product offers. Only those MSAs and FSAs that have been more proactive in their online market surveillance have demanded that platforms be more cooperative in the fight against unsafe products. The use of NTD also seems to be generally underexploited. Many MSAs/FSAs have only since recent been able to establish points of contacts to achieve takedowns for the removal of unlawful product. In that respect, some of the achievements in the Product Safety Pledge merely commit online marketplaces to actions that they have been obliged to take under the ECD for the last 20 years. This hesitation to enforce in grey areas of sectoral and territorial competency has also been pointed out by consumer protection experts. They suggest that more guidance is needed for MSA/FSAs. However, they also note that authorities may feel hesitant because of the risk of being challenged by large, global players in courts,[1686] an assertion which was confirmed through some of the feedback gathered in the surveys.

2. The technical role and legal classification of online platforms

Secondly, like across other sectors discussed above, MSAs and FSAs have a limited understanding about the functioning of online platforms, such as their business models, or content management practices. The assessment by MSAs/FSAs of the role of online marketplaces and social media platforms in the supply chain of these products varies. For example, while many authorities interviewed underlined the platform character of online marketplaces, they did not pick up on the fact that much of the relevant and sometimes regulated product information (product title, description, ingredients, pictures, etc.) is displayed through structured fields. The data in these field is provided by uploaders/sellers and exploited by platforms for various commercial purposes, but less so, it seems for harm prevention. Some of the MSAs/FSAs saw the fact that platforms charged a commission for the intermediation services or played an otherwise active role as a factor that influences their legal exposure and obligations. This could extend to making these marketplaces primary liable for the safety of the products offered. Others did not share this view or had no view at all. Enforcement authorities appear to be in dire need of an updated legal clarification of the role and responsibilities of the new Web 2.0 intermediaries in e-commerce. The MSR (for non-food products) and the Official Controls regulation (in the area of food safety) only partly help in addressing this problem. The upcoming review of the GPSD, in conjunction with the envisaged Digital Services Act, provide for a unique chance to fill his gap.

1686 M Goyens, 'Effective Consumer Protection Frameworks in a Global and Digital World' (2020) 43 Journal of Consumer Policy 195, 201.

3. Product and food safety enforcement expertise as a chance

Thirdly, FSAs and MSAs are prepared to proactively search for and assess unlawful products online. This is in line with the nature of product and food safety regulation, which puts market surveillance and enforcement solidly in the hands of public authorities. This technical expertise in assessing the lawfulness of product offers is a precious asset. In other content areas there are currently no or few public actors with the same resource and expertise to make such decisions. If online marketplaces were obliged to work more proactively with MSAs and FSAs in order to identify and prevent unlawful products on the basis of the technical expertise shared with them, this could lead to a new risk management system. Online marketplaces, whose activities are capable of amplifying harms to consumer health and safety through the listing and promotion of certain products, would need to meet certain essential requirements to contain these risks. These essential requirements could consist of processes of regulatory cooperation and/or due diligence measures relating to the onboarding and display of products in question and their sellers. Such essential requirements of platforms could be either incorporated into existing technical and industry standards for food and product safety, or set up through a new intermediary responsibility framework and linked to existing legislation. This will be elaborated on in the next chapter.

4. Horizontal cooperation

One current drawback is the fragmented and slow cooperation between MSAs/FSAs at EU level. The interviews have demonstrated that although authorities value increased cooperation in the area of online market surveillance, more can be done. This is also broadly in line with the sectoral analysis of product and food safety law enforcement in the previous chapter. Rather than a threat, e-commerce could be an opportunity to rekindle horizontal cooperation. The European Commission could expand its facilitative role and intensify common activities through working groups such as RAPEX (now the Product Safety Gate), RASFF, AdCos, the coordinated control programs and training and best practice sharing in online market surveillance. The gradual shift in the European Commission's policy position on platforms' responsibilities since 2017 needs to be backed up by more tangible support when it comes to joint surveillance and enforcement. A first step in the right direction is the research planned by the EU into challenges and opportunities for MSAs in relation to new technologies and the digital supply chain.[1687] An enhanced co-regulatory support structure at EU or national level could be a useful start for creating synergies of enforcement expertise across Member States and content sectors.

1687 European Commission, 'Assessing the Challenges and Opportunities for Market Surveillance Activities in Relation to New Technologies and Digital Supply Chain - Call for Tenders N° 834/PP/GRO/PPA/20/11848 - 2020/S 116-280777' <https://ted.europa.eu/udl?uri=TED:NOTICE:280777-2020:TEXT:EN:HTML> accessed 31 July 2020.

Chapter 6 - A new framework for online intermediary responsibility

This work has so far outlined various problems with unlawful content propagated through online intermediaries. Chapter 2 sketched the stellar rise and evolution of online platforms as essential facilitators of information exchanges and gatekeepers to the internet over the last two decades. Chapter 3 provided the backdrop of a broad horizontal legal framework of liability exemptions that has been resting on essentially unchanged premises for 20 years. It demonstrated that three main liability conditions – neutrality, actual knowledge and the scope of (preventive) obligations – are outdated and would need to be replaced by new criteria that allocate responsibilities that are in line with the commercial and technical involvement of platforms in the intermediation process. Chapter 4 outlined the specific problems of the interaction between the outdated horizontal liability framework and content specific laws both in national and EU contexts. The avenues explored in response to unlawful information shared through online platforms ranged from primary liability, enhanced secondary liabilities based on duty of care obligations, the formulation of new offenses specific to information intermediaries to the use of ordinary law secondary liability doctrines. The regulatory choices included various self-regulatory arrangements, solutions that went into the direction of co-regulation and more straightforward rule and command style interventions. All this has been accompanied by ample jurisprudence, which partly served as a blueprint for the new regulatory advances.

Academics, industry representatives and think tanks have not been standing by idly. Various intermediary liability (exemption) reform proposals have seen the light since 2007. The frequency with which these proposals appeared has increased markedly over the last five years. Some focus on specific violations, others on particular types of platforms. Yet others are more occupied by the type of regulatory intervention or the specific liability standard. Almost all grapple with the question of how enhanced public interest responsibilities can be implemented in a way that protects the precarious balance of fundamental rights that will inevitably be affected when regulating information gatekeepers' content management practices.

In the following, a number of reform approaches and proposals will be outlined and evaluated. This overview will serve as a basis for a more theoretical discussion. It will first be used to critically assess the regulatory choices of a new intermediary responsibility framework. The particular characteristics of the internet, its intermediaries and the broad nature of unlawful activity and content call for a carefully gauged level of regulatory intervention. Secondly, the discussion will move to the type of responsibility that would be more adequate given the developments and challenges discussed throughout this work. For example, can a primary liability approach be reconciled with certain types of intermediary responsibility, such as duty of care? Lastly, a reform proposal will be put forward that advocates for a move away from liability towards a broader responsibility framework. The suggested solution will also advocate for closer state involvement in the form of co-regulation. This would allow for better oversight and enforcement of the adherence to public interests and fundamental rights that are affected by online platforms' content management practices.

A. *Intermediary responsibility reform proposals – an overview*

The overview of intermediary liability reform proposals discussed below does not claim to be exhaustive. The proposals were selected according to their comprehensiveness and to the degree to which they inspired the approach suggested later in this chapter, either because of corresponding assessments or by providing conceptual demarcations. Many of the proposals analysed below advocate for enhanced responsibilities of online platforms through obliging them to apply duties of care that are proportional to their involvement in the intermediation process. This commonly results in online intermediaries needing to a) be aware of and evaluate the possible harms and ensuing risks of their business model with regards to unlawful content or activity, b) design and implement measures to address these risks *ex ante* and *ex post*, c) ensure the risk responses are transparent and accountable and comply with legal standards.

1. Systemic approaches

As early as 2007, less than 10 years after the enactment of the ECD, *Verbiest et al* saw a need for an overhaul of the intermediary liability system.[1688] They started from the observation that the ECD did not create any incentives for intermediaries to prevent future similar infringements of those notified to them. However, they rejected a negligence-based approach that would task courts with developing such standards. Already at the time, courts across the EU diverged in their interpretation of liability (exemption) standards towards intermediaries. The fear was that asking courts to create negligence standards would result in widely different outcomes. Secondly, waiting for court-made law would simply take too long. In addition, this depended on relevant cases being brought before judges. Instead, *Verbiest et al* looked to the example of the *New Approach*, used in product safety regulation.[1689] EU legislators would ask European standardisation committees (CEN) to develop technical standards of filtering that would apply to specific content sectors. Intermediaries, rightsholders and other stakeholders would take part in such a standard creation. The standard could be adapted to evolving technologies and would be considered by courts in their assessments. In content sectors where such standards existed, providers could be ordered to use them in order to stop repeat infringements. Like under the *New Approach*, the adoption of these standards would be voluntary. ISPs could deploy their own solutions, but would need to demonstrate that these are equivalent to the relevant technical standard. Finally, failure to comply with such a standard would result in comprehensive filtering obligations. Non-profit ISPs would be exempt.[1690]

Helman and Parchomovsky (2011) pursued a similar idea for copyright infringements by proposing a "best available technology safe harbour." This standard would replace the current DMCA liability provisions and exempt online intermediaries from liability where they had used the best available technology to prevent infringements.[1691] Government agencies would determine which technologies and solutions were considered as best filtering technology. Their proposal is motivated by the fact the US intermediary

1688 Verbiest and others (n 315) 20–23.

1689 ibid 22.

1690 This proposal was repeated in 2016: Gerald Spindler and Christian Thorun, 'Die Rolle Der Ko-Regulierung in Der Informationsgesellschaft' (2016) 6 MMR-Beil. 1, 24.

1691 Helman and Parchomovsky (n 309).

framework of the DMCA disincentivised information hosts to filter and monitor for infringing content, except for very narrowly construed "red flag" content. They use cheapest cost avoider, economic reasoning for tasking online intermediaries with stronger obligations to participate in the prevention of copyright infringements.[1692] Not only are online intermediaries technically and infrastructurally best placed to monitor, prevent and remove infringing content. Their activity would also alleviate the need for content owners to engage in duplicate efforts.[1693] *Helman and Parchomovsky* advocate for collaboration between intermediaries, content owners and technology providers in the operation of prevention technology. While webhosts would perform the filtering, their analysis would be based on technology developed by copyright clearinghouses, which would rely on one central, government-held copyright database. They note that independent clearinghouses would have the highest incentive to strive for accurate technology, e.g. with regard to determining fair use exceptions.[1694] In contrast to *Verbiest et al*, this approach does not just apply to the prevention of repeat infringements, but to any copyright infringements, as deemed fit by the best technology standards.

Busch (2018) has adopted the use of *New Approach* technical standards to online reputation systems. Although the focus of his work is not on unlawful content, the proposal suggests the application of such a co-regulatory system to the entire 'platform ecosystem'.[1695] Technical standardisation may be more apt than traditional command and control regulation on the one hand, and codes of conduct on the other, to provide flexibility in the fast-changing and highly technical setting of the internet, while at the same time providing procedural transparency.[1696] In addition, the technical standards approach fits within the EU's strategy to expand the use of technical standards as a soft law instruments and apply it notably in the

1692 ibid 1202, 1212.

1693 ibid 1203.

1694 ibid 1215–1223.

1695 Christoph Busch 'Towards a "New Approach" for the Platform Ecosystem: A European Standard for Fairness in Platform-to-Business Relations' 3.

1696 Research Group on the Law of Digital Services, 'Discussion Draft of a Directive on Online Intermediary Platforms' [2016] Journal of European Consumer and Market Law 164, 165; Christoph Busch, 'Crowdsourcing Consumer Confidence - How to Regulate Online Rating And Review Systems in the Collaborative Economy' in Alberto De Franceschi (ed), *European Contract Law and the Digital Single Market: The Implications of the Digital Revolution* (Intersentia 2016) 231–232.

area of information and communication technologies (ICT).[1697] The eventual solution showcased by *Busch* refers to an ISO standard for online consumer reviews.[1698] A European Commission study by *van Eecke* (2009) proposed the creation of sector specific technical standards for the interaction between rightsowners and online platforms in the identification of infringing material. This concept could also be applied to NTD mechanisms, including counterclaims procedures.[1699]

Kempel and Wege (2010) explore the establishment of a risk management system that would help internet intermediaries determine reasonable duties of care that were starting to be formulated in intermediary liability jurisprudence at the time. They note that courts had come to different interpretations of what could be considered reasonable efforts for ISPs.[1700] This created legal uncertainty for ISPs and imposed incalculable liability risks. Any risk mitigation through excessive content monitoring could lead to the ISP gaining actual knowledge, while no or insufficient control could lead to courts finding the ISP had neglected its duties of care. They suggest that ISPs use a risk management methodology to adequately identify, analyse, evaluate and control risks related to unlawful content on their systems. Regulations, they argue are not suited to provide detailed and pragmatic risk management duties. By contrast, technical norms or standards are suitable instruments for defining adequate duties of care based on a risk management approach. Technical norms under the European standardisation approach are capable of defining state of the art requirements while establishing proportionality (reasonableness), due to their stakeholder approach.[1701] Once defined, these technical standards can be referenced as a legally binding standard in legislation. The ECD's Recitals 40 and 41 underline the intention of the EU to promote the creation of such standards. This proposal mirrors suggestions by *Verbiest et al* who made use of *New Approach* style regulation. For *Kempel and Wege* technical norms have the

1697 European Commission, 'Communication: ICT Standardisation Priorities for the Digital Single Market COM(2016) 176 Final' <https://ec.europa.eu/digital-single-market/en/news/communication-ict-standardisation-priorities-digital-single-market> accessed 29 August 2018.

1698 Technical Committee : ISO/TC 290 Online reputation, 'ISO 20488:2018 - Online Consumer Reviews — Principles and Requirements for Their Collection, Moderation and Publication' <https://www.iso.org/standard/68193.html> accessed 21 July 2020.

1699 Van Eecke and Truyens (n 316) 42.

1700 Kempel and Wege (n 16) 107–108.

1701 ibid 116–118.

advantage of being adaptable to the fast technological development of the internet. They are international and respond to the cooperative character of internet content by allowing for an allocation of responsibilities to different stakeholders.[1702] By contrast, they may not be of particular use for adapting to different business models or for defining prospective responsibilities, they argue. The latter is based on the fact that their proposed system is mainly looking at the management of the risk of unlawful content and therefore existing user behaviour. The degree to which a platform operator may profit, intentionally or unintentionally, from the unlawful behaviour of third parties would best be established by law.[1703] However, later proposals by e.g. *Woods and Perrin* or *Helberger*, described below, argue that co- or self-regulatory systems may well be capable of incorporating prospective responsibility criteria, such as "by-design" concepts into responsibility frameworks.

One of the most detailed and comprehensive proposals for a statutory duty of care for online platforms has been made by *Woods and Perrin* (2018).[1704] This proposal has been adopted by the UK Government's White Paper to deal with the harms caused by unlawful and harmful content on social media.[1705] *Woods and Perrin* see social media platforms as quasi-public spaces on which significant parts of the population convene, communicate or look for goods and services to buy. This 'utility' approach to modern day online intermediaries has also been supported by others, such as *Pasquale, Wagner* or *Helberger.*[1706] This quasi-public character of online platforms entails certain duties of care to protect the public against harms that could be caused by the use of these digital spaces. They point to equivalent legal obligations in more traditional areas:[1707] employers need to protect their workers against damage to health and safety; under environmental protection regulations entities handling, producing or disposing of waste have particular duties that depend on the type of activity and the

---

1702 See also Herberger et al' s concept of cooperative responsibility: Helberger, Pierson and Poell (n 68).

1703 Kempel and Wege (n 16) 120.

1704 William Perrin and Lorna Woods, 'Reducing Harm in Social Media through a Duty of Care' (*Carnegie UK Trust*, 8 May 2018); Lorna Woods, 'Duty of Care' (2018) 46 InterMEDIA. Woods and Perrin (n 799).

1705 Great Britain and Department for Culture (n 197).

1706 Pasquale (n 19) 297–300; Wagner, 'Free Expression? Dominant Information Intermediaries as Arbiters of Internet Speech' (n 83) 235–236; Helberger (n 1651) 167.

1707 Woods and Perrin (n 799) 21–28.

type of waste involved; the GDPR makes entities that collect and process personal data accountable to do this according to specific principles. Under the GDPR, data controllers need to secure and protect personal data according to the level of risk.[1708] Entities with high risk personal data processing activities need to perform impact assessments. The common theme is, that companies are tasked with duties to assess the risk of harms facilitated or caused by their business activity and put appropriate measures in place to address them.

Focussing on social media platforms, *Woods and Perrin* define harms which may arise from content and intermediation practices and which trigger the public interest. These harms correspond broadly to the sectors touched on in Chapter 4. Economic harms include copyright and trademark violations; terrorist speech would fall under national security harms; hate speech and defamation would fall under harmful threats, emotional harms or harms to minors.[1709] Social media service operators would then be tasked to assess the risk of each harm in the context of their business model and architecture. They would need to devise and implement measures to address and prevent the most significant harms and risk. The regulator would provide guidance on the risk assessment approach for social media service operators and assess the outcomes of the measures taken by platforms. *Woods and Perrin* propose that successful common approaches to harm reduction and risk management be set out by industry codes of practice, which are endorsed by regulators. This would allow for flexibility and customisation given the fast pace of innovation in this sector.[1710] These codes would also allow for the establishment of forward looking or prospective responsibility criteria such as safety-by-design.[1711] The regulator would also set out basic procedural and "structural requirements" for regulated platforms. Platforms would need to provide proof of their risk assessment procedures (for example risk rating and new service review mechanisms), parental control systems, complaints handling procedures or any other broad requirements established by the law. Under this co-regulatory structure, the regulator would have a set of broad guidance and approval functions such as publishing transparency reports, guidance notes,

1708 Regulation (EU) 2016/679 of 27 April 2016 on the protection of natural persons with regard to the processing of personal data and on the free movement of such data 2017 (OJ L 119, 452016) Articles 5, 25, 32 (1), 35.

1709 Woods and Perrin (n 799) 35–42.

1710 ibid 46.

1711 ibid 47.

model policies, approve codes of practice and facilitate society stakeholder dialogue and research.[1712] In that sense, this proposal is not dissimilar from the role attributed to the *CSA)* under the recently failed *Loi Avia* in France. *Woods and Perrin* do not foresee, however, specific exemptions for smaller players.[1713] They also apply their principles in an overarching way for each platform at 'system level', and would not create different regimes for different content sectors or types of activities.[1714] However, it remains unclear how current sectoral provisions, some of which have now extended primary liability towards online platforms, i.e. in copyright, could be (re)integrated into this framework. It appears obvious from the iterations of *Woods and Perrin* that they propose to create a specific responsibility regime for platforms, thus excluding the allocation of primary liabilities under substantive law, such as copyright or defamation.

Valcke et al. (2017) have also argued for the necessity of a new duty-of-care standard that online platforms adopt in order to remove and prevent unlawful activity and content. They base their approach on the diligent economic operator standard, first formulated in the CJEU case *L'Oréal v eBay*, and subsequently refined in *GSMedia*, *UPC Telekabel* and *Delfi (ECtHR)*. They liken these responsibilities to the Roman law doctrine of *bonus pater familias*. Industry self-regulatory codes of ethics or conduct, such as those drawn up by national press or journalism councils, could serve as a blueprint for similar standards and principles for internet intermediaries. Under these codes, behaviour would be seen as unethical or irresponsible where a platform failed to take steps that could be reasonably expected of it under such codes in order to prevent unlawful content or behaviour. In *Delfi's* case this was the failure to take sufficient account of the risk that the comments function it provided could be abused for hate speech. Courts could use these standards as a yardstick when confronted with liability disputes over unlawful content.[1715] In a similar vein, *Leistner* (2014) suggests a broad analysis of EU national case law on intermediary liability.[1716] The focus would be on an evaluation of cases where preventive measures were imposed on ISPs. The idea is to extract new common principles that would be developed into an EU wide reasonable duty of care standard. The proposal focusses on the area of IP infringements. However, he rejects the use

1712 ibid 48–49.
1713 ibid 35.
1714 ibid 12.
1715 Valcke, Kuczerawy and Ombelet (n 551).
1716 Leistner (n 336) 89.

of self-regulatory industry standards, as proposed by *Valcke et al.* Such standards, if developed by present market actors (large intermediaries and rightsowners), bear the risk of being biased towards their interests, to the detriment of less economically powerful users.[1717]

The concept of reasonableness has also been exploited by *Waisman et al* (2011), who propose a flexible standard of duty of care for search engines.[1718] Like *Leistner* and *Valcke et al*, they trace the evolving duty of care concept through European case law and suggest the allocation of flexible, reasonable duties. The degree of reasonable care would follow the consideration of certain criteria, such as the scope, cost, harm and impact on fundamental rights of any duties of care applied to search engines. Reasonableness with regards to the costs of a duty of care would, for example, take into account whether this prevents the provision of socially valuable services or poses a market entry barrier. A further threshold of reasonableness would be the undue restriction of freedom of expression.[1719]

Finally, *Lavi* (2015) explores a context-based liability regime for social media and UGC platforms.[1720] Focussing on speech acts under the CDA in the US, he starts form the by now familiar argument that the active/passive dichotomy and the far-reaching liability immunities facilitate the development of technology that promotes behaviour that society normally prohibits. In addition, it discourages intermediaries from designing safer systems.[1721] *Lavi* advocates for a scaled liability system that imposes gradually increasing penalties allocated under inducement liability at the beginning of the spectrum, to contributory liabilities at the extreme side.[1722] The severity of the liability and the ensuing penalties would depend on the strength of intent, actual knowledge and the effect of the platform's nudges, i.e. the way in which architectural and design choices promote unlawful and harmful user behaviour.[1723] Courts would allocate these penalties. This would serve as a deterrent for online platforms to engage in biased and opaque nudging practices. *Lavi* sees the reliance on transparency obligations for intermediaries that engage in biased nudging practices as

---

1717 ibid.
1718 Waisman and Hevia (n 313).
1719 ibid 799–802.
1720 Michal Lavi, 'Content Providers' Secondary Liability: A Social Network Perspective' (2015) 26 Fordham Intell. Prop. Media & Ent. LJ 855, 888.
1721 Lavi (n 199) 62.
1722 ibid 82–84.
1723 ibid 79–82.

problematic, because of many users' proven disinterest and incomprehension of disclosure statements.[1724]

2. Procedural approaches

A number of researchers focus on the application of due process requirements on online intermediaries. *Wielsch* (2019) argues that it would be reasonable to charge online intermediaries with the protection of fundamental rights through procedure. He justifies this with the quasi role of online intermediaries as speech regulators.[1725] This is part of a wider societal trend to charge multinational corporations with the protection of fundamental rights, at least where it concerns communication infrastructure providers. The CJEU had already confirmed this in *UPC Telekabel*.[1726] Duties of care would constitutionalise internal standards of speech regulation when it comes to unlawful content, leading to the development of 'public standards of legality'.[1727] The German *NetzDG* is a case in point of institutionalising these procedural requirements. In the *NetzDG*, failure to delete unlawful content is not a punishable act, while failure to have effective and transparent complaints handling systems in place is.[1728] *Gillespie* (2018) suggests that online platforms be obliged to follow public standards on how content is moderated, rather than standards on what content to remove.[1729] These public standards could be formulated through: transparency reporting obligations; minimum moderation standards, such as response times or appeals processes; data sharing practices with researchers; the involvement of external expert advisory panels; labour protection standards for moderators; data portability obligations.[1730] This view is supported by *Laidlaw*, who calls for a codification of rules on how platforms moderate content based on due process principles.[1731] *Bambauer* (2018) de-

1724 ibid 90.

1725 Dan Wielsch, 'Private Law Regulation of Digital Intermediaries' [2019] SSRN Electronic Journal 14–20 <https://www.ssrn.com/abstract=3369592> accessed 3 May 2019.

1726 *Telekabel* (n 757) para 55. In: Wielsch (n 1724) 17.

1727 Wielsch (n 1724) 17.

1728 ibid 19.

1729 Gillespie, 'Platforms Are Not Intermediaries' (n 175) 213; Gillespie, *Custodians of the Internet* (n 1010) 44.

1730 Gillespie, 'Platforms Are Not Intermediaries' (n 175) 213–216.

1731 Laidlaw (n 494) 23–24.

mands that online platforms be brought to shed light on the internal processes and mechanisms that lead to the decisions on which content removal, amplification or restoration are based.[1732] This goes somewhat deeper than the previous proposals because it requires platforms to disclose their normative choices in content moderation. This, in turn, would allow for adjustments where public interest and fundamental rights criteria are not sufficiently met. He points to the fact that most online platforms do document their (internal) content moderation guidelines and should therefore be able to explain the rationale of their decision-making when moderating content.[1733]

Helberger et al (2018) focus on the governance mechanisms of online platforms. Traditional legal systems tend to allocate main responsibility and liability to a single actor. The active/passive dichotomy of information hosts under the ECD is a case in point.[1734] In reality, however, content creation and moderation on today's platforms is a more participatory exercise that relies on three groups of actors. Online platforms 'manage' user activity in this process. Users, on the other hand, can only act responsibly if the platform architecture is shaped in a way that is conducive to this, such as, for example, by providing training and education, reporting and flagging tools, or clear policies.[1735] This means online platforms are in a position to take prospective responsibilities to design their systems in a way that allows for responsible interaction of users.[1736] Regulators, the third type of actors, should be responsible for providing adequate frameworks for risk and responsibility sharing, by promoting public debates on the balancing of public values in content management. None of the three actors alone, it is argued, should bear the brunt of responsibility. *Helberger et al* propose four steps for building such a cooperative responsibility framework: First, the public values of the various intermediation activities should be defined. Secondly, responsibilities should be attributed to each actor in the protection of the public values of each sector, type of intermediary etc. Thirdly, stakeholders should agree on how they can fulfil their responsibilities. Fourthly, this should result in more formal codifications, either through regulations, codes of conduct or best practices.[1737] This frame-

1732 Bambauer (n 297) 421–423.
1733 ibid 422–423.
1734 Helberger, Pierson and Poell (n 68) 2.
1735 ibid 5.
1736 ibid 2–4.
1737 ibid 10.

work provides a useful conceptual and moral approach to allocating responsibilities and positive obligations on users, platforms and public actors. However, it leaves open the question of the regulatory choice of the risk management framework.

3. Common and divisive features of current intermediary liability reform proposals

Most of the proposals presented here have a number of things in common. First, they eschew the traditional distinction between active and neutral hosts. There is an increasingly broad consensus, that at least as information hosts are concerned, it is a futile exercise to tie liability, or the availability of immunities, to the allegedly neutral status of an online platform.[1738] Even more, none of today's Web 2.0 online platforms are absolutely neutral, because the business models rely on the exploitation of content and user behaviour, and they design their technical architectures accordingly. Secondly, the participatory nature of online platforms in the intermediation process justifies enhanced, but at the same time, nuanced responsibilities that are proportionate to the riskiness of a platform's ecosystem. Thirdly, there is an acknowledgement that today's Web 2.0 platforms significantly influence user behaviour and control access to information and commercial transactions. As quasi-public utilities they now affect the public interest in many ways, of which the harms caused by unlawful content are just one, yet high profile, aspect.[1739] Fourth, the proposed regulatory tools focus on duties of care, risk management approaches and procedural obligations (due process, transparency, fairness).

Yet, the approaches for regulating online intermediaries' liability conditions or responsibilities discussed here also vary in important aspects. For one, there are different views about the regulatory model that such a new intermediary responsibility framework should follow. While almost none of the commentators advocate for traditional command and control regulation, differences about the depth of public intervention remain. Systemic

1738 Lavi (n 199) 14; Chander and Krishnamurthy (n 883); Zuboff (n 5) l 2042; Martens (n 53) 33–35; Helberger, Pierson and Poell (n 68) 2; Sylvain (n 795) 59.

1739 Competition, data protection or consumer protection are other public interest areas where EU and national legislators have been intervening or have considered legislative action.

approaches of *Verbiest et al*, *Kempel and Wege*, *Helman and Parchomovsky*, or *Woods and Perrin*, which advocate for more defined risk management frameworks, appear to favour more or less co-regulatory solutions. The broad parameters of public interest criteria would be set through regulation. Industry is then commissioned to devise tools, mechanisms and methodologies to comply with these criteria. Regulators would have more closely defined oversight and sanctioning powers with regards to compliance with the values and principles set down by law.[1740] The co-regulatory approaches show different shades of state involvement. While *Verbiest et al* and *Kempel and Wege* favour the use of technical standards as a co-regulatory tool, *Woods and Perrin* look at codes of conduct and industry practices in order to implement regulatory provisions. They see the latter as more suited because of their flexibility and adaptability to specific risks, business models and technological change than standards.[1741] Proponents of procedural approaches that look more to jurisprudence as an inspiration of new duties of care are more divided. While some favour self-regulatory approaches (*Valcke et al*), others have voiced no pronounced view. Overall, a preference for self-regulatory solutions is, however, visible.

It should also be said that the approaches discussed here vary widely in scope. While some propose overarching frameworks and methodologies (*Woods and Perrin*, *Helberger*), others focus on specific types of platforms or contents (*Lavi*, *Waisman et al*), specific processes, like content moderation (*Bambauer, Laidlaw, Gillespie*) or consider retrospective responsibility aspects such as duties of care for prevention, detection and removal of unlawful content (*Verbiest et al*, *Kempel and Wege*, *Helman and Parchomovsky)*. Proposals that concentrate on retrospective responsibilities belong to earlier reform attempts. The inclusion of prospective, "by-design" responsibilities has only happened more recently, after 2015.

For completeness, it should be mentioned that there are also commentators that see less of a need to change the current intermediary framework.[1742] Some point out that the trend towards "responsibilisation" of intermediaries might lead to more opaque private speech regulation on the

1740 For a more detailed definition of co- and self-regulation see the next section.

1741 Woods and Perrin (n 799) 27.

1742 Savin (n 384) 173; 'Open Letter on Intermediary Liability Protections in the Digital Single Market' (*EDRi*, 28 April 2015) <https://edri.org/open-letter-on-intermediary-liability-protections-in-the-digital-single-market/> accessed 28 October 2019. Savin (n 482).

Internet.[1743] However, it should be underlined that it is the aim of a functional and adequate new responsibility framework to improve due process, accountability and transparency standards. If left as is, online platforms will continue in opaque content moderation practices that follow entirely commercial objectives, without facing significant liabilities for the harm to public interests and fundamental rights caused.

B. *The regulatory choice of a new intermediary responsibility system*

1. The current regulatory choice

The diversity of regulatory approaches towards new platform responsibilities is also reflected in the regulatory initiatives put forward at EU and Member State level. The European Commission's facilitation of industry-driven, voluntary codes of conduct and memoranda of understanding[1744] betrays its initial penchant for self-regulatory arrangements. This style of regulatory interventions is explicitly supported by the ECD.[1745] The EU saw self-regulation as a more flexible tool than Directives or Regulations[1746] to deal effectively with the rapid market and technological changes introduced by the internet. But even with its latest legislations, such as the DSMD, the EU does not seem to have departed from its self-regulatory path. The best efforts of OCSSP to prevent copyright infringing content in the absence of any licensing agreements, will be judged, amongst others, on the use of high industry standards of professional diligence.[1747] However, the definition of such standards is merely facilitated by the European Commission and Member States, who are supposed to bring together industry and user stakeholders to exchange best

1743 Belli and Sappa (n 42) 183; Giancarlo Frosio F, 'Reforming Intermediary Liability in the Platform Economy: A European Digital Single Market Strategy' [2017] Northwestern University Law Review Online 20.

1744 See the initiatives at EU and national level mentioned in Chapter 4: 'Code of Conduct on Countering Illegal Hate Speech Online' (n 542); European Commission, 'EU Internet Forum' (n 1061); European Commission, 'Memorandum of Understanding on Online Advertising and Intellectual Property Rights' (n 542); 'Memorandum of Understanding on the Online Sale of Counterfeit Goods, 2016' (n 542); Bundesministeriums der Justiz und für Verbraucherschutz (n 953).

1745 Directive 2000/31 (ECD) Article 16.

1746 Lodder and Murray (n 448) 54.

1747 DSM Directive 2019/790 Article 17 (4) (d), Recital 66.

practices.[1748] Public authorities or regulators do not appear to have any more formal role in the approval or audit of best efforts.

The AVMSD, by contrast ventures more into co-regulation by tasking ERGA with coordinating and providing technical advice in regulatory matters in the area of hate speech. Admittedly, merely providing advice may be considered as not sufficient to count as proper co-regulation. On the other hand, the mere existence of a formal regulatory body that has been appointed with a defined role and tasks, although these are more informal in nature, can be considered as a first step away from self-regulation into the area of co-regulation.[1749] The now failed *Loi Avia* is similar in that respect. It established an overarching regulatory agency, the *CSA*, with defined powers of overseeing ISPs' efforts in the fight against hate speech and other unlawful content. The TERREG proposal goes even further. Like the DSMD and the AVMSD, it asks hosting providers to put specific preventive measures in place that are commensurate to the risk of unlawful activity. However, providers subject to a high risk of terrorist content sharing will need to report on their specific preventive measures to competent public authorities. Authorities have then the power to evaluate the measures taken by the platforms with regards to their proportionality and effectiveness. That assessment should consider the general risk level, the size of the platform and its resources, as well as the safeguards in place for the respect of fundamental rights.[1750]

As this work attempts to propose its own regulatory proposal to intermediary responsibility, a brief excursion into different regulatory models that are employed in the EU, and in internet regulation in general, will be discussed. The concepts of co- and self-regulation shall be elaborated on in more detail.

1748 ibid Recital 71.

1749 Taking Marsden's *Beaufort* scale of self- and co-regulation as a yardstick this could be considered a first step in the realm of co-regulation, i.e. probably Step 7. Marsden, *Internet Co-Regulation* (n 275) 227.

1750 European Commission Proposal for a Regulation to prevent terrorist content online, EP resolution (n 1122) Articles 4 , 5, Recitals 16 & 17.

2. Regulatory approaches for the internet

Wu, *Castells* and others[1751] have convincingly argued that today's connected information society is just the latest culmination of a consistent trend of industrialisation, globalisation and successive revolutions in information and communication technologies. The rise of new regulatory models that straddle the border between private and state actors is intricately linked with this trend. The theoretical explanation for this phenomenon was first provided by *Durkheim*. Living around the turn of the 20th century, *Durkheim* observed the profound social and economic changes caused by the second industrial revolution. Mass-production, urbanisation, internationalisation and technological innovation led to an upheaval in social relations and economic organisation.[1752] Modern society became more complex and removed from traditional, more communal and religious values. As traditional moral values were uprooted, they left a void, which Durkheim called *anomie*.[1753] Durkheim found that new societal relations were characterised by a specialisation and the division of labour, not just in the economic sphere but also in politics, administration and the legal system.[1754] This new division of labour, which resulted in more dense and complex interrelations within society, would eventually generate new values and rules, and displace the state of *anomie*. For *Durkheim*, the nation state was less apt to regulate complex economic and social relations and interactions of individuals in this new society. This would be done through private professional associations and through corporations. Public law would become more and more broad, stipulating mainly what was to be done, but not how it was to be achieved. Meanwhile, contracts would become more important in everyday life. In effect, the division between private and public law had already become increasingly blurred by this division of labour in *Durkheim's* time.[1755]

1751 Castells (n 3); Wu, *The Master Switch* (n 1). Naughton (n 6) 390–392. Chris Marsden, 'Prosumer Law and Network Platform Regulation: The Long View towards Creating Offdata' (2018) 2 Georgetown Law Technology Review 376, 379–381. Vincenzo Zeno-Zencovich and Giorgio Giannone Codiglione, 'Ten legal perspectives on the "big data revolution"' in Fabiana Di Porto (ed), *Big data e concorrenza* (A Giuffrè editore 2016) 30.

1752 Anthony Giddens and Philip W Sutton, *Sociology* (6. ed, Polity Press 2009) 13–15.

1753 Durkheim (n 31) ll 7043–7072.

1754 ibid 697.

1755 ibid 1182.

Durkheim's theory has influenced a variety of contemporary approaches and critiques of governance and regulation. *Schepel* sees him as a precursor to governance, deregulation and privatisation, as he explains the state's shift of specialist regulatory tasks towards the private sector, while itself assuming broader, coordinative roles.[1756] Meanwhile, *Zuboff*, picks up on *Durkheim's* warnings that certain types of unchecked division of labour may lead to inequalities and injustices in society. She compares this to predatory practices of online platforms, which perpetuate divisions of learning by producing inequalities in the way people are able to access and evaluate information and knowledge in the information society.[1757] Indeed, *Durkheim* himself saw the necessity of government or the state to oversee the respect of basic principles and norms of social solidarity and justice in order to ensure social coherence in a specialised and changing society.[1758]

Blommaert points to the breath-taking development of new social media platforms and the *Durkheimian anomies* they present for interaction between users.[1759] Users are filling these gaps with ad hoc rules and new norms rapidly. However, it is unclear how much users' actions are down to deliberate, individual choice and how much happens through the agency of algorithms managed by social media platforms.[1760] In that respect social media platforms exercise new forms of power. With their algorithms and big data analytics, they shape communities and digital user identities.[1761] The new social norms on the internet may therefore be steered and manipulated by those globally operating companies for their own purposes, which creates new inequalities. Competing norm-setting organisations, such as multinational enterprises, international organisations, globally operating professional and civil society organisations and technical standards bodies have led to a world of legal pluralism, according to *Teubner*.[1762] Public governance is made difficult, because the global internet's social processes operate at a transnational stage, while governments regulate social processes at a state level. In addition, the inertia that characterises governments and bureaucracies, often makes their regulatory actions appear

1756 Schepel (n 34).
1757 Zuboff (n 5) ll 3400–3438.
1758 Durkheim (n 31) 6220–6509.
1759 Blommaert (n 63) ll 463–478.
1760 ibid 911–924.
1761 ibid 1438, 1547.
1762 Gunther Teubner, 'Global Bukowina: Legal Pluralism in the World-Society', *Global Law Without a State* (1997).

anachronistic.[1763] The difficulties of courts and governments to adapt to the international nature of unlawful content on the internet, and the speed with which these challenges manifest themselves, have been demonstrated in the previous chapters. These anachronisms determine also the regulatory choice of measures taken to combat unlawful content online.

The following, non-hierarchical account outlines some of the main regulatory approaches and concepts that have been applied to the internet. They all represent more general attempts to tackle the legal challenges in a diversifying and increasingly complex, international economic and social order of which the internet and its information intermediaries are just one vivid expression. Given the nature of the challenges outlined beforehand, it is suggested that a new intermediary responsibility framework should adopt these policy approaches and tools.

I. Self and co-regulation on the internet

Various definitions of self-regulation exist. For the purposes here, the definition in the EU's 2003 Interinstitutional Agreement on Better Law-making[1764] shall be used as a reference. This agreement was a follow-up to the European Governance White Paper, in which the European Commission vowed to improve trust in and support for the EU project through more accountable, participative and flexible policy-making. Self- and co-regulation were identified as new approaches that would help to achieve more effective, simpler and faster regulation.[1765] According to the 2003 Interinstitutional Agreement on Better Law-making self-regulation is defined as:

> *"...the possibility for economic operators, the social partners, non-governmental organisations or associations to adopt amongst themselves and for themselves common guidelines at European level (particularly codes of practice or sectoral agreements)."*[1766]

The definition at hand is useful because it provides a clear demarcation line to co-regulation. Some commentators have classed co-regulation as a

---

1763 Blommaert (n 63) ll 708, 1406.

1764 Interinstitutional agreement on better law-making, OJ C 321/01 2003.

1765 European Commission, 'European Governance - A White Paper, COM(2001) 428 Final' (European Commission 2001) 18–21. See also: Senden and others (n 1654) 5.

1766 Interinstitutional agreement on better law-making, OJ C 321/01 para 22.

self-regulatory approach,[1767] while for others the dividing line seems to be less clear or relevant.[1768] For *Senden*, the determination of co-regulation versus self-regulation depends on the state, nature and intensity of public involvement in the policy cycle.[1769] A majority of experts, however, draw a methodological and conceptual line between co- and self-regulation, especially where it concerns more complex areas of technology regulation.[1770] For *Marsden*, co-regulation consists of a complex interaction of general (state) legislation and self-regulation, which gives a sense of shared responsibilities between private actors and the state authorities.[1771]

The 2003 Interinstitutional Agreement on Better Law-making defines co-regulation as:

> *"...the mechanism whereby a Community legislative act entrusts the attainment of the objectives defined by the legislative authority to parties which are recognised in the field (such as economic operators, the social partners, non-governmental organisations, or associations)."*[1772]

A variety of commentators have offered typologies of self- and co-regulation which chart regulatory approaches according to the degree of state involvement. This shall not be discussed further here.[1773] It shall be sufficient for the purposes discussed here that the difference between self- and co-regulation is that in the latter the state sets binding policy objectives

---

1767 Weber (n 265) 18–19.

1768 Cohen (n 19) 395–402. Cohen portrays the risks and disadvantages of self- and co-regulation in the information age in an almost interchangeable way.

1769 Senden and others (n 1654) 35–36.

1770 Cornils (n 481) 38–40. Cornils describes a scaled approach by which self-regulatory industry commitments, which failed regulators' expectations, are formalised and imposed by law. Economic actors are still left to organise compliance with the provisions. Irene Kamara, 'Co-Regulation in EU Personal Data Protection: The Case of Technical Standards and the Privacy by Design Standardisation "Mandate"' (2017) 8 24, 6–7. Kamara identified differences of self- and co-regulatory approaches in European standardisation. See for a more general discussion: Michèle Finck, 'Digital Co-Regulation: Designing a Supranational Legal Framework for the Platform Economy' <https://papers.ssrn.com/abstract=2990043> accessed 3 August 2020. Marsden, *Internet Co-Regulation* (n 275) 51–70. Dimitrios Koukiadis, *Reconstituting Internet Normativity: The Role of State, Private Actors, Global Online Community in the Production of Legal Norms* (First edition., 2015) 63–64.

1771 Marsden, 'Guaranteeing Media Freedom on the Internet' (n 280) 82–86.

1772 Interinstitutional agreement on better law-making, OJ C 321/01 para 18.

1773 For examples see: Marsden, *Internet Co-Regulation* (n 275) 51–63; Senden and others (n 1654) 35–39; Saurwein, Just and Latzer (n 1656) 38.

through legislation. Private industry actors are then given the task to develop systems and measures to comply with these objectives. The state will finally be involved in approving, implementing, monitoring and enforcing the solutions drawn up by private actors. This is slightly distinct from the enforced self-regulation concept developed first by *Braithwaite*, where the state would have a mere approval, but no enforcement, and only limited monitoring duties.[1774] However, this "extension and individualisation of co-regulatory theory"[1775] is not considered substantial for the purposes discussed below and could be adjusted at a later stage if needed.

The following section gives a brief account of commonly voiced supportive and critical points of self- and co-regulation and their application to the internet.

a. Self-regulation

The prevalence of self-regulation on the internet has already been remarked on in Chapter 2. The tendency of the US Government to put the internet's infrastructural regulation to ICANN, a privately organised stakeholder organisation that relies on contractual arrangements, is just one aspect. It reflected a traditional cultural preference of self-regulation in the US. Through the influence of the cyberlibertarians of the 1990s, these self- or even autoregulatory structures have been extended to content regulation. This was certainly aided by the fact that the internet cuts across different jurisdictions with ease and determination. As a result, states have so far relied widely on private regulatory arrangements to address public interests when it comes to unlawful content online.[1776] Today, these structures are entrenched further by the private contractual arrangements between platforms and users. Content regulation, as shown in Chapter 4, has become predominantly a privately enforced matter in which the state has but limited power and influence. Current internet regulation emphasises freedom from the state, claiming that public interference into its contractual architecture is less efficient and not adapted to the needs of the contracting parties.[1777]

1774 Ayres and Braithwaite (n 39) 102–108.

1775 ibid 102.

1776 Wagner, *Global Free Expression - Governing the Boundaries of Internet Content* (n 136) 128–129.

1777 Koukiadis (n 1769) 284–285.

Yet, there are additional reasons for the reliance on self-regulatory models in today's internet and content governance. For one, today's regulators and enforcers face a capability challenge in enforcing against unlawful activity on the internet. This capability gap has been demonstrated in the sectoral analysis and case studies in Chapters 4 and 5. Regulators may not be prepared, staffed or budgeted to deal with the sheer amount of content, and the technical skills required to supervise and audit the automated decision-making procedures of online platforms.[1778] The supposed subjects of regulation are therefore readily brought back into the frame in order to help addressing concerns over unlawful content. Secondly, the internet introduces a new horizontal challenge that cuts across legal domains and nation states. The new nature of multi-sided global online platforms calls for innovative and interdisciplinary approaches, which often goes against the sectoral and specialised realm of traditional regulators.[1779] This has become apparent in the case studies on product and food safety enforcement. Specialised food scientists and technical engineers are not well set up to deal with assessing product risks and taking enforcement action on products sold online via marketplaces or social media platforms. Thirdly, public authorities can rarely match the 'discursive capacities'[1780] of (the internet) industry to assemble different stakeholders and shape policy debates and perceptions on a societal level. The extensive lobby activities of the internet's largest actors have been prominently noted.[1781] As a result, self-regulatory proposals and initiatives receive more coverage and thought than other policy approaches. Lastly, many European countries and varieties of capitalism have traditionally been embracing self-regulatory and other collaborative structures between state and industry. This is especially the case for

1778 Jason Freeman, 'Consumer Legislation and E-Commerce Challenges' (2015) 2 Rivista Italiana di Antitrust/Italian Antitrust Review 2 <http://iar.agcm.it/article/view/11380> accessed 19 September 2017; Cohen (n 19) 383–397; Leighton Andrews, 'Algorithms, Regulation, and Governance Readiness' in Karen Yeung and Martin Lodge, *Algorithmic regulation* (2019) 214–216. Spindler and Thorun (n 1689) 6. Deirdre K Mulligan and Kenneth A Bamberger, 'Saving Governance-By-Design' (2018) 106 California Law Review 697, 768–770. Cohen shows how regulator's capacities are being outpaced by "infoglut" and rapid technological change. Andrews describes a shortfall in governance readiness with regards to states' delivery and regulatory capacities where it concerns algorithmic regulation.

1779 Cohen (n 19) 375–387; Andrews (n 1777) 215. Goyens (n 1685) 202.

1780 Andrews (n 1777) 216.

1781 See for example: Tambini and Moore (n 232) 405. Zuboff (n 5) ll 2271–2343.

new and emerging industry sectors.[1782] *Marsden* states that self-regulation, together with state regulation, is as old as markets.[1783]

Self-regulation may therefore appear to be a natural choice for the internet. The European Commission's various initiatives and the marked preference for this kind of regulation in the ECD and the DSMD seem to support this. But self-regulatory models for the internet have also received mounting controversy.[1784] The previous sectoral chapters have outlined some of the flaws of self-regulation when it comes to content regulation and unlawful activity. One main criticism refers to a loss of democratic control, accountability and transparency where online intermediaries are left to regulate content under self-imposed rules and processes.[1785] This is of particular concern when public interests collide with private commercial objectives. Restricting unlawful content or risky, harmful behaviour will more often than not conflict with the business objective of maximising user traffic and data generation, and steer interaction. The less precise public interests are being articulated, the less likely self-regulation will achieve its objectives. Industry codes of practice, for example, are often too vague, with few tangible accountability and transparency provisions.[1786] In this game, commercial interests have so far prevailed, as the ongoing availability of unlawful content and the inefficacy of the self-regulatory initiatives discussed in Chapter 4 have shown. The far-reaching liability immunities for online intermediaries and the persisting ambiguities in this area make self-regulatory initiatives, which are already difficult to enforce legally, even less likely to be respected.[1787]

The efficacy of self-regulation is further dented by the gatekeeping powers of today's information intermediaries.[1788] Dominant market players have enhanced means to obscure irresponsible content management and risky design features of their services. They are able to exercise discreet

1782 Senden and others (n 1654) 20–30; Marsden, *Internet Co-Regulation* (n 275) 67–70. Senden describes marked self- and co-regulatory traditions in Germany, Italy, the Netherlands and the UK. Marsden identified Scandinavian and 'Rhinish' varieties of capitalism as conducive to co- and self-regulatory structures.

1783 Marsden, *Internet Co-Regulation* (n 275) 54.

1784 Spindler and Thorun (n 1689). Saurwein, Just and Latzer (n 1656) 42.

1785 Weber (n 265) 22; Wagner, 'Free Expression? Dominant Information Intermediaries as Arbiters of Internet Speech' (n 83) 223–225.

1786 Kleinsteuber (n 282) 66.

1787 Pasquale (n 19) 496. Saurwein, Just and Latzer (n 1656) 40–42.

1788 Helberger, Kleinen-von Königslöw and van der Noll (n 120) 50.

powers on platform participants because of the network effects they have created. Meanwhile, their considerable discursive capabilities and technological superiority infiltrate and influence the thinking and policy making of regulators, leading to "deep capture."[1789]

The current oligopolistic market structure, in which one or two major platforms hold sway over certain online service sectors (*Facebook* for social media and instant messaging, *YouTube* for video-sharing, *Amazon* and *Alibaba* for e-commerce, *Google* for search) means that self- or auto-regulatory 'solutions' by these players become the quasi-standard. There is little chance for regulatory competition, or a true, more open multi-stakeholder exchange.[1790] As self-regulation is not legally binding, it leaves the door open for black sheep to undermine standard practices.[1791] The weakest link argument is a particularly powerful one in the context of the global nature of the internet. It is supported by analysis made in Chapter 4 in the area of terrorist content or unsafe products. Smaller or less prominent platforms have attracted an increasing amount of unlawful activity as regulators focus on the dominant players. Meanwhile, the non-binding character of current industry agreements gives the state only limited room for effective enforcement. The general lack of transparency and democratic accountability of self-regulatory arrangements is only exacerbated by current market structures, fast-moving information technologies and the amount and speed with which online content is shared globally. The criticism of "privatised censorship" is therefore intrinsically linked to the self-regulatory practices of online platforms today.[1792]

b. Co-regulation

Co-regulation has been one proposed solution to counter the trend of freewheeling private content regulation. The reliance on state-imposed regulatory objectives, on the one hand, and the freedom granted to platforms to devise adequate and accountable technical solutions, on the other, have been seen as an answer to the regulatory capability challenge while ensuring accountability and compliance with public interests. The above-men-

1789 Cohen (n 19) 376–378, 395.

1790 Wagner, 'Free Expression? Dominant Information Intermediaries as Arbiters of Internet Speech' (n 83) 222.

1791 Weber (n 265) 22.

1792 Cornils (n 481) 42.

tioned systemic approaches to online intermediaries, which rely on co-regulation, shall serve as examples for how a variety of experts have proposed to address this regulatory conundrum. For *Kleinsteuber*, a more appropriate term would be "regulated self-regulation." Compared to traditional "command and control" state regulation and to self-regulation, co-regulation is a relatively recent phenomenon.[1793] Originating in Australia, it has been discussed and subsequently adopted by national governments in Europe since the 1980s and 1990s. The EU has continued to support the use of self- and co-regulatory models as part of their better law-making agenda.[1794] This can, for example, be seen by the Principles for better self- and co-regulation as part of the EU's digital agenda.[1795]

Examples of co-regulatory approaches adopted by the EU include the previously discussed EU Food Safety and *New Approach* product regulation framework,[1796] or the REACH chemicals and environmental framework.[1797] In areas driven more by digital technologies, the media sector (AVMSD) [1798] or data protection (GDPR)[1799] are prominently cited examples for co-regulation. In all these areas, structured regulatory oversight authorities are in place at national and/or EU level, that monitor, enforce and audit compliance of industry's efforts to meet public interest objectives set by law.[1800] Co-regulation is seen as a more flexible and 'decentred' approach compared to command and control legislation, and a more struc-

1793 Kleinsteuber (n 282) 62–63; Marsden, *Internet Co-Regulation* (n 275) 54.

1794 European Commission, 'Communication: Better Regulation for Better Results - An EU Agenda - COM/2015/0215 Final' (2015) s 3.1. Colin Scott, 'Integrating Regulatory Governance and Better Regulation as Reflexive Governance' in Sacha Garben and Inge Govaere (eds), *The EU better regulation agenda: a critical assessment* (Hart 2018) 17–18.

1795 European Commission, 'The "Principles for Better Self- and Co-Regulation"' (*Shaping Europe's digital future - European Commission*, 22 August 2014) <https://ec.europa.eu/digital-single-market/en/best-practice-principles-better-self-and-co-regulation> accessed 4 August 2020.

1796 See also: Mark Dawson, 'Better Regulation and the Future of EU Regulatory Law and Politics' (2016) 53 Common Market Law Review 1209, 1231–1233.

1797 Carolyn Abbot, 'Bridging the Gap – Non-state Actors and the Challenges of Regulating New Technology' (2012) 39 Journal of Law and Society 329, 354.

1798 Cornils (n 481) 38–39. AVMSD 2018/1808 Recitals 12 - 14.

1799 Kamara (n 1769).

1800 Regulation (EU) 1025/2012 of 25 October 2012 on European standardisation 2012 (OJ L 316, 14112012) Article 5. With a possible qualification that the AVMSD supports co-regulation mainly in the area of traditional media regulation, while the measures for VSPs in Article 28 (b) would not (yet) squarely sit within that category.

tured and accountable solution compared to self-regulation. It answers to the demand for a more responsive regulation.[1801] This demand is created by new challenges in regulating in a world characterised by diverse, fast-changing business and social environments, information asymmetries as to the expertise needed to regulate effectively and various social actors that control and participate in regulation.[1802] Co-regulation is connected to other concepts commonly associated with responsive regulation, such as risk regulation, standardisation, corporate social responsibility or regulatory governance.[1803]

Co-regulatory solutions have several strengths that make them particularly suitable for addressing the challenges posed by new markets and technologies.[1804] First, the state and private actors share power in the regulatory process.[1805] Ideally, this power sharing acknowledges and exploits the intrinsic controls that these actors already have. A co-regulatory arrangement would install additional independent oversight mechanisms where there is a danger of conflict of interest and where public interests or fundamental rights are involved, e.g. ethical concerns in algorithmic content selection.[1806] Secondly, regulators can make use of the resources and the subject matter expertise of the regulated subjects.[1807] Moreover, the regulator will be able to acquire technical expertise through its involvement in monitoring and auditing compliance. This is one of the major obstacles today for embedding public values into technology design.[1808] Meanwhile, industry actors may get insight into the rationales and objectives that drive policy making. This process helps mitigate existing information asymmetries. Thirdly, co-regulatory systems are more flexible. Public – private ar-

1801 Ayres and Braithwaite (n 39) 102–109. It should be noted that Ayres and Braithwaite's distinction between co-regulation and enforced self-regulation is not followed here. For the purposes of this work, internal company compliance frameworks which are based on industry standards are treated as co-regulatory solutions.

1802 J Black, 'Decentring Regulation: Understanding the Role of Regulation and Self-Regulation in a "Post-Regulatory" World' (2001) 54 Current Legal Problems 103, 106–110.

1803 Marsden, 'Prosumer Law and Network Platform Regulation: The Long View towards Creating Offdata' (n 1750) 395. Ford (n 1656) 69–73. Koukiadis (n 1769) 66.

1804 Abbot (n 1796) 347.

1805 Koukiadis (n 1769) 63.

1806 Saurwein, Just and Latzer (n 1656) 41.

1807 Abbot (n 1796) 348.

1808 Mulligan and Bamberger (n 1777) 740–741.

rangements, such as standards, and regular contact between industry actors and regulators allow for adaptability to fast-paced technological and business environments. Regulatory disconnects can be detected in a timely manner.[1809] This flexibility extends also to the diversity of economic actors. A co-regulatory solution could for example allow for tailored content risk management solutions depending on online platform's business models, while respecting the underlying horizontal public interest principles.[1810] Fourth, the flexibility and adaptability allow for experimentation and the application of innovative policy solutions. This could be particularly useful in the diverse and multi-level regulatory space of intermediary responsibility. The rich experience from various best practices, national regulatory initiatives or industry solutions, is a fertile ground for policy experimentation[1811] and could be exploited through a co-regulatory approach. Fifth, enforcement is made easier and cheaper.[1812] Co-regulatory arrangements often lead to companies themselves establishing or being required to establish their internal oversight functions in the form of compliance officers or teams.[1813] This means the private sector will bear the majority of costs, while internal compliance functions still need to answer to public regulators. Lastly, co-regulation allows for the inclusion of various society stakeholders in the rule making process. Apart from industry and regulators, civil society, consumers or adjacent regulators can be brought into decision-making and oversight functions.[1814] At EU level, it may therefore be used to address allegations of democratic deficit or legitimacy gaps with which EU policy making has been plagued.[1815]

However, where the regulator tries to regain control, it needs to counter the pressures that have led to the emergence of self-regulatory models in

1809 Abbot (n 1796) 348.

1810 Finck (n 1769) 20.

1811 Wolfgang Kerber and Julia Wendel, 'Regulatory Networks, Legal Federalism, and Multi-Level Regulatory Systems' (2016) 13–2016 5–6 <http://ssrn.com/abstract=2773548> accessed 6 April 2017.

1812 Finck (n 1769) 21.

1813 The GDPR requires data protection officers, various health and safety regulations require the creation of health and safety officers, while in financial regulation compliance departments are responsible for various regulatory requirements such as anti-bribery, money-laundering or Ayres and Braithwaite (n 39) 105–107; Sean J Griffith, 'Corporate Governance in an Era of Compliance' (2015) 57 Wm. & Mary L. Rev. 2075.

1814 Marsden, 'Prosumer Law and Network Platform Regulation: The Long View towards Creating Offdata' (n 1750) 394–395.

1815 Finck (n 1769) 26–27.

the first place. How will the state design and structure a co-regulatory system that: formulates clear public policy objectives; introduces accountability into the secretive design decisions of private content governance systems; gives regulators technical and multidisciplinary expertise to effectively evaluate and verify responsible technology designs; and that re-introduces public legitimacy into the policymaking process?

These are questions that lead beyond the more structural connotations of the term co-regulation. Indeed, co-regulation calls up a whole host of other concepts of responsive regulation, such as governance,[1816] legal pluralism, compliance,[1817] standardisation, corporate social responsibility (CSR),[1818] duty of care[1819] or risk regulation.[1820]

II. Corporate (social) responsibility for online platforms

There is no authoritative or commonly agreed on definition of corporate social responsibility (CSR). Leaving the differences between national or international CSR commitments aside,[1821] it can generally be said that it means that companies take responsibilities for their impact on society, by ensuring that social, environmental, ethical and consumer concerns are incorporated in their business operations and strategy.[1822] The demand that online platforms act more responsibly with regards to the fight against unlawful content is increasingly linked to them embracing wider principles of CSR.[1823] Many of the popular platforms have become globally operating corporate actors. Even where they operate only out of one jurisdiction, their content is exposed to users worldwide. Their content management practices, however, are often competing with state regulation. This had led to calls for including internet intermediaries into international corporate responsibility frameworks to ensure their content management, informa-

1816 Marsden, *Internet Co-Regulation* (n 275) 55.
1817 Finck (n 1769) 17, 24.
1818 Spindler and Thorun (n 1689) 8–9, 22.
1819 Ullrich, 'A Risk-Based Approach towards Infringement Prevention on the Internet' (n 747) 236–238.
1820 ibid 243–244; Favro and Zolynski (n 1015) 4.
1821 John Gerard Ruggie, 'Multinationals as Global Institution: Power, Authority and Relative Autonomy: Multinationals as Global Institution' (2018) 12 Regulation & Governance 317, 317.
1822 European Commission, 'UCP Directive Guidance' (n 57) 63.
1823 Taddeo and Floridi (n 120) 1578.

tion access and privacy practices comply with (international) fundamental rights standards.[1824] Other have argued that the social responsibilities of platforms under local intermediary liability and data protection laws should be seen in conjunction with forward looking responsibilities to create conditions for responsible usage. This would result in a system of cooperative or organisational responsibilities that takes account of the gatekeeping and infrastructural powers of online platforms to enable responsible behaviours by their users.[1825]

CSR could be a tool that may guide internet intermediaries in the development of systems that safeguard users' fundamental rights.[1826] Others point to the fact that co-regulatory systems should be seen as a chance for online platforms to demonstrate their commitment to CSR principles.[1827] The above-mentioned Principles for better self- and co-regulation under the EU's digital agenda have arisen out of the EU's strategy on CSR. CSR could therefore be seen as one means to fill the *Durkheimian anomic space* created by the new Web 2.0 information intermediation practices and their wide reaching intermediary liability immunities. Active and transparent cooperation between state institutions and socially responsible enterprises,[1828] in this case, online intermediaries, along CSR principles could be a step to fill the current void of responsibility with new values when it comes to combating unlawful activity.

1824 Taddeo and Floridi (n 1014) 1579. Agnes Callamard, 'The Human Rights Obligations of Non-State Actors' in Rikke Frank Jørgensen (ed), *Human Rights in the Age of Platforms* (The MIT Press 2019) 211–212 <https://direct.mit.edu/books/book/4531/Human-Rights-in-the-Age-of-Platforms> accessed 28 May 2020. Such as in the Council of Europe, 'Recommendation CM/Rec(2014)6 of the Committee of Ministers to Member States on a Guide to Human Rights for Internet Users (Adopted by the Committee of Ministers on 16 April 2014 at the 1197th Meeting of the Ministers' Deputies)'.

1825 Helberger, Pierson and Poell (n 68) 3–4.

1826 Tarlach McGonagle, 'The Council of Europe and Internet Intermediaries' in Rikke Frank Jørgensen (ed), *Human Rights in the Age of Platforms* (The MIT Press 2019) 247 <https://direct.mit.edu/books/book/4531/Human-Rights-in-the-Age-of-Platforms> accessed 28 May 2020.

1827 Spindler and Thorun (n 1689) 22.

1828 Senden and others (n 1654) 10–11. European Commission, 'Communication: A Renewed EU Strategy 2011-14 for Corporate Social Responsibility, COM/2011/0681 Final' (2011) para 4.3. <https://eur-lex.europa.eu/legal-content/EN/TXT/?uri=CELEX:52011DC0681> accessed 6 August 2020.

III. Duties of care

The tendency towards formulating new duties of care for online platforms has been mentioned throughout the preceding chapters. Apart from being already an explicit policy option for Member States when regulating the responsibilities of online intermediaries under the ECD, it has been increasingly suggested by policymakers and academics. Duties of care are directly linked to obligations that platforms have as diligent economic operators. This has been confirmed by CJEU and national case law mentioned throughout this work. They may be a particularly useful tool for imposing an obligation responsibility[1829] on online platforms because of their link to negligence principles under various secondary liability doctrines in both civil and common law systems.[1830] It should be pointed out that the duties of care advocated here refer to the negligence, tort-based duties that some Member States already draw on from their ordinary law areas, or which are established through statutes in national and EU law. They should be distinguished from the methodological approaches developed by the CJEU when examining institutions' use of discretionary powers and compliance with the principle of proportionality.[1831]

Duty of care as a concept has been applied both by courts and as a principle in regulation. In both contexts the focus is decidedly procedural. Under a duty of care approach, courts will not look at the quality of a business decision but at the quality of the decision-making process.[1832] The principle of duty of care lends itself particularly well to proportionality assessments and the rights balancing exercises involved in these acts. It is helpful when evaluating whether the different factors involved in the decision-making process were adequately considered.[1833] This means a court will need to review facts, knowledge and the public and private interests at

1829 Naughton (n 6) 389.

1830 See Chapter 3

1831 Herwig CH Hofmann, 'Delegation, Discretion and the Duty of Care in the Case Law of the Court of Justice of the European Union' [2018] SSRN Electronic Journal 15–19 <https://www.ssrn.com/abstract=3169744> accessed 28 August 2018. Nevertheless, both notions of duty of care share the focus on procedural aspects, the consideration of (technical) facts and risk management principles.

1832 Robert J Rhee, 'The Tort Foundation of Duty of Care' (2013) 88 NOTRE DAME LAW REVIEW 61, 1147.

1833 Hofmann (n 1830) 18.

stake.[1834] Duty of care is therefore particularly well suited to more complex, highly technical situations which may not be solved by using traditional legal means, such as judicial review. However, it has also been shown that in the high volume, fast-changing and diverse area of intermediary liability courts may not be the most effective and best suited institutions to engage in duty of care reviews and establish standards of responsibility.[1835]

The advantage of statute-based duties of care is that they can bypasses potentially diverging, and even contradictory interpretations of national and ordinary law concepts of secondary liability or torts. They lend themselves to more complex technical areas where risks are dynamic and where prescriptive, rules-based requirements may fail to take account of the variety of possible threat scenarios. *Woods* describes the historical process of incorporating duty of care into statutes of common law jurisdictions, using the example of UK Health and Safety legislation.[1836] Duty of care principles, based on reasonableness or the Roman law concept of *bonus pater familias,* have also been applied in civil law countries[1837] and in EU law contexts in general. For example, under EU product safety law distributors have certain defined due care obligations with regards to products placed on the market by manufacturers.[1838] The duty of care is not always specifically indicated as such but often referred to as 'due care', 'reasonable measures', 'reasonable care', 'diligent behaviour' or ' professional diligence' related to certain threats or risks. This, however, also entails that parties with responsibilities engage in risk assessment exercises or demonstrate that they have sufficient knowledge and adequate processes in place to address risks. The GDPR,[1839] AVMSD,[1840] REACH[1841] or the EU Framework Di-

1834 ibid 16.

1835 Frederick Mostert, 'Free Speech and Internet Regulation' (2019) 14 Journal of Intellectual Property Law & Practice 607, 610; Finck (n 1769) 18. Ullrich, 'A Risk-Based Approach towards Infringement Prevention on the Internet' (n 747) 232.

1836 Woods, 'The Duty of Care in the Online Harms White Paper' (n 794) 7–10.

1837 Valcke, Kuczerawy and Ombelet (n 551) 111.

1838 Decision 768/2008 Article R5.

1839 Regulation 2016/679 (GDPR) Article 35.

1840 AVMSD 2018/1808 Article 28b (3).

1841 Regulation 907/2006 concerning the Registration, Evaluation, Authorisation and Restriction of Chemicals (REACH 2006 (OJ L 396) Recitals 17 - 19.

rective on Health and Safety at Work[1842] establish such ongoing, dynamic responsibilities for economic actors. These responsibilities entail risk management procedures against broadly formulated public interest objectives or fundamental rights of employees or users. The AVMSD provides an example where these principles have been applied to VSPs, a certain type of hosting providers. The DSMD also relies to a certain extent on these principles by requiring OCSSPs to demonstrate that they have made best efforts in the prevention of unlicensed content on their platforms. When fixed in statutes, duty of care needs to be moulded into more structured frameworks. This is also necessary in order to reduce ambiguity and differences in interpretation and application that would ensue from tying duties of care to ordinary law principles. As has been shown in Chapters 2 and 3, the negligence-based duty of care concept is not equally recognised and applied in Member States legal systems. Risk regulation and standardisation provide more neutral and generic structural and procedural frameworks that are capable of ironing out these kinds of differences. These concepts shall be explored in more detail below.

IV. Risk regulation and compliance

The formulation of duty of care responsibilities through statutes is closely linked to risk (based) regulation. Risk regulation focusses on the control of risks, with a priority given to high risk activities of regulated entities. Compliance with set rules is of lesser importance.[1843] Risk regulation has emerged since the 1990s as part of a drive towards flexible regulation and regulatory governance.[1844] Regulators tried respond to the new challenges posed to state authority in a globalised, information society system in which policy-relevant knowledge is distributed throughout society (industry, technical experts, regulators) and held in epistemic communities. The state loses its central character as an epistemic authority[1845] as the focus of

1842 Council Directive 89/391/EEC on the introduction of measures to encourage improvements in the safety and health of workers at work 1989 (OJ L 183) Articles 5, 6, 9.

1843 Robert Baldwin, Martin Cave and Martin Lodge, *Understanding Regulation: Theory, Strategy, and Practice* (2nd ed, Oxford University Press 2012) 281.

1844 Ford (n 1656) 60–74.

1845 Schepel (n 34) 25.

public policy changes from politics to technical expertise.[1846] Risk regulation addresses the state of uncertainty on the part of the regulator by requiring the firm to comply with regulatory objectives through defined risk management processes. It acknowledges that economic actors are best placed due to the control and ownership they have over their internal data and business processes to assess the risks related to their activities. Regulators have little knowledge initially of how disruptive innovations, such as the internet or digital technology, will affect public values. They also have no reference to assess the impact of regulation,[1847] nor have their functions traditionally required that they use ('big') data to measure compliance, or establish liability and conformity.[1848]

If a regulatory objective were that an e-commerce online platform does not facilitate the sale of trademark infringing goods while respecting sellers' freedom to conduct a business, then it would need to demonstrate whether and how its business model and technical architecture promote responsible seller behaviour. Secondly, the platform would need to demonstrate that is has internal controls in place to contain high risk activities that occur on the platform (such as seller onboarding due diligence, NTD systems, risk-based monitoring).[1849] Modern approaches to risk regulation would aim to produce decisional accountability, whereby economic actors will need to be able to demonstrate to regulators and other stakeholders that public values and interests are being respected and how this is done.[1850] For that to happen, regulatory risk management or risk-based approaches will be individualised at the firm level. They will need to be embedded in the technology and, for platforms, in the technical architecture and the algorithms that make content decisions. The regulated company would need to show that its design choices were done with public interest obligations in mind and with a view to contain any activities that pose a high risk to public values.[1851] That demonstration would entail technical

1846 Haas (n 38) 4–7. Nupur Chowdhury and Ramses A Wessel, 'Conceptualising Multilevel Regulation in the EU: A Legal Translation of Multilevel Governance?' (2012) 18 European law journal 335, 337.

1847 Ford (n 1656) 186–191. Marsden, *Internet Co-Regulation* (n 275) 231–234.

1848 Zeno-Zencovich and Codiglione (n 1750) 54.

1849 Baldwin, Cave and Lodge (n 1842) 282.

1850 Bamberger (n 37) 684–685.

1851 Baldwin and Black note the move away of regulators from process/based controls to a focus on high risk activities or key problems. Robert Baldwin and Julia Black, 'Driving Priorities in Risk-based Regulation: What's the Problem?' (2016) 43 Journal of Law and Society 565, 568.

documentation, records of risk management procedures (risk identification, assessment and control), impact assessments and internal tests and audits of the internal processes. Risk regulation has been widely applied in the financial sector, in environmental management, but also in biotech, food and product safety regulation.[1852] In the digital technology area the GDPR[1853] and the Security of Network and Information Systems (NIS) Directive[1854] are prime examples for such risk regulation.

The demands of risk regulation have led to the emergence of compliance functions within companies. For one, statute may require such a function within a company. EU Anti-Money laundering legislation, the GDPR or Health and Safety legislations are cases in point that foresee 'responsible persons' or compliance officers for companies that engage in high risk activities. Secondly, large companies will not be able to run efficient regulatory risk management functions simply as part of their normal business teams. Compliance teams often need functional, financial and hierarchical independence within the company and develop their own technical expertise.[1855] However, the rise of automated compliance systems has somewhat worked against the fully independent compliance function.[1856] For Griffith "compliance is a de facto government mandate imposed upon firms."[1857] "It does what corporate laws' duty of care might have done."[1858] Thirdly, due to the complexity and the variety of risks, regulators often encourage or mandate the development of standards and automated reporting systems in order to effectively regulate firms. As a result, a whole new governance, risk and compliance (GRC) service industry has developed that offers the entire lifecycle of regulatory risk management, auditing and controls, and statutory reporting.[1859] For example, the best available technology safe harbour approach offered by *Helman and Parchomovsky*[1860] above would likely lead to the emergence of such a GRC system for compliance with copyright by online platforms.

1852 Cohen (n 19) 374, 393–394; Ford (n 1656) 103.
1853 Woods and Perrin (n 799) 23–24.
1854 Directive 2016/1148 concerning measures for a high common level of security of network and information systems across the Union 2016 (OJ L 194) Articles 14 (1), 16 (1), Recitals 44, 46. 49.
1855 Griffith (n 1812) 2099–2103.
1856 Bamberger (n 37) 686–687.
1857 Griffith (n 1812) 2073.
1858 ibid 2113.
1859 Bamberger (n 37) 673–674, 689–702.
1860 Helman and Parchomovsky (n 309).

Another (optional) feature of risk regulation is the application of a precautionary approach. This principle was originally formulated in environmental legislation of the 1970s, but the practice of precautionary interventions dates further back.[1861] Under the precautionary approach a regulator should err on the side of caution if it cannot gain sufficiently reliable data or evidence in order to assess a risk. The approach is employed where certain activities may pose systemic risks that would cause irreversible damage, such as in the area of environmental and climate protection. On the downside, this approach may be highly costly and prevent innovation.[1862] *Woods and Perrin* suggest that it may be an appropriate approach in the regulation of social media platforms' content management systems. Evaluating the impact of certain harms is made difficult by constant change in algorithms and the fast proliferation of new features. However, the danger of significant damage to people and society calls for a precautionary application of regulation to these social media platforms.[1863]

In summary, risk regulation attempts to provide a framework for containing harmful practices in situations of uncertainty and rapid change. Responsible actors would need to put systems in place to identify and control the worst risks to public interests. Regulators, meanwhile, provide the public policy objectives and the risk management framework for economic operators. The interactions and the task sharing between regulator and industry make this predominantly an example of co-regulation.[1864]

Risk regulation still requires substantial investment and a culture change on the side of the regulator. For a start, regulators themselves need to acquire technical expertise and capabilities in order to be able to audit and assess risk management processes, control software or algorithms.[1865] Chapters 4 and 5 have exposed marked gaps in the analytical and delivery capacities[1866] of regulators in the areas of product and food safety and terrorist content. Meanwhile, as regards IP rights and hate speech such regulators are just emerging or not yet existent. Secondly, the mandate of (risk) regulators in the area of platform liability needs to be broadened and deepened. They should be empowered to seek cooperation with other regula-

1861 Mike Feintuck, 'Precautionary Maybe, but What's the Principle? The Precautionary Principle, the Regulation of Risk, and the Public Domain' (2005) 32 Journal of Law and Society 371, 374–375.

1862 Cohen (n 19) 394; Ford (n 1656) 190.

1863 Woods and Perrin (n 799) 10–11.

1864 Abbot (n 1796) 353–354; Marsden, *Internet Co-Regulation* (n 275) 232.

1865 Mulligan and Bamberger (n 1777) 768–770.

1866 Andrews (n 1777) 215–17.

tory agencies, solicit multi-stakeholder input from society and deepen their regulatory charge. The latter would include research, discursive capacities, legislative input, wider review powers and being subjected to judicial review.[1867] As will be described below, prominent failures in risk regulation are due mainly to regulators' inadequate oversight and misjudgement of their regulatory methods where complex, highly-automated compliance systems are being employed.[1868]

V. Standardisation

Technical standards, in the following referred to simply as standards, can be traced back over the last 150 years. As a response to the new complexity and diversity in production, the acceleration in technical innovation and the internationalisation of economies, both industry and governments sought to bring about more compatibility. Compatibility of products and processes was needed to accelerate industrialisation, innovation and efficiency gains in production.[1869] Standards arose out of bottom-up processes driven by industry. They are typically voluntary, but have also been imposed from above through legislation. Governments can, for example, lay down mandatory standards for certain products in order to meet requirements of public safety, security or other general interests.[1870] In the US, standards development is largely left to industry and market conditions, with minimum government oversight. Europe has traditionally favoured a more interventionist approach towards standards development by which governments may exert an oversight function and lay down regulatory objectives.[1871] However, entirely industry driven standards do also exist in Europe. As a purely industry driven exercise standards fulfil self-regulatory goals. Where the government is involved in setting the regulatory frame-

1867 For an excellent detailed account see Mulligan and Bamberger (n 1777) 760–768. and Andrews (n 1777).

1868 Cohen (n 19) 372–373.

1869 Stefan Timmermans and Steven Epstein, 'A World of Standards but Not a Standard World: Toward a Sociology of Standards and Standardization' (2010) 36 Annual Review of Sociology 69, 75–76.

1870 ibid 76.

1871 Jane K Winn, 'Globalization and Standards: The Logic of Two-Level Games' (2009) 5 I/S: A Journal of Law and Policy for the Information Society 34, 190.

works for standards development, this will result in co-regulatory structures.[1872]

The initial role of standards in ensuring interoperability and safety has expanded with globalisation and the above-mentioned normative competition exerted by transnational companies[1873] and their global value chains.[1874] Standards today still assure the seamless operation of globalised economic activity, but they have also taken on more social functions. Independent, third party certification of products and supply chains demonstrate compliance of private, transnational actors with wider ecological, social, human rights or technical values.[1875] For consumers, standards address the information asymmetries that exist in complex supply and information value chains by providing for traceability and transparency. For companies, they have become a substantial element of CSR efforts.[1876] As of today, standards are a pervasive feature of our societies that, whilst not easily visible to people in their daily actions, structure how they communicate, work or consume. Standardisation is a decidedly social act, and "an integral element of modern national political, economic and legal systems."[1877] At a global level, transnational standards have been described as the "hidden normative backbone of complex societies."[1878] This is in line with *Durkheim's* prediction that the division of labour and the internationalisation of industries and markets would itself form the basis for new rules and normative values.[1879] The state maintains a coordinative role as private actors from industry and civil society create consensual rules and technical requirements through standards. Standards can therefore be seen as filling the normative void created by increasingly specialised, knowl-

1872 Marsden, *Internet Co-Regulation* (n 275) 67–70; Finck (n 1769) 17–19.

1873 Teubner, 'Self-Constitutionalizing TNCs? On the Linkage of "Private" and "Public" Corporate Codes of Conduct' (2011) 18 Indiana Journal of Global Legal Studies 617, 633.

1874 Klaas Hendrik Eller, 'Private Governance of Global Value Chains from within: Lessons from and for Transnational Law' (2017) 8 Transnational Legal Theory 296, 315–316.

1875 Some of the numerous examples of certification schemes and standards, without commenting on their normative effect on supply chains and markets, are: the Forest Stewardship Council (FSC), EU energy consumption labels (Eco/labelling), organic product certifications, fairtrade certifications, CE product labelling.

1876 Eller (n 1873) 316–320.

1877 Winn (n 1870) 189.

1878 Eller (n 1873) 311–312.

1879 Durkheim (n 31) l 7029; Schepel (n 34) 14–15.

edge-based, global societies in which the state has lost its epistemic authority and needs to draw on social and economic actors.

Standards have some distinctive advantages over traditional command and control regulation, which would make them predestined as a regulatory and enforcement tool for a new intermediary responsibility system. First, efficient administrative rule-making in modern societies (in both the industrialised and the post-industrial information society) relies on technical and scientific expertise. Expertise resides outside government, with private actors in industry or civil society.[1880] In the area of intermediary responsibility, adopting a standards approach would take account of the fact that, across all content sectors discussed above, online platforms alone maintain the technical expertise to design responsible systems. Secondly, standards are flexible and can be modified according to technological and market changes. They can also be adapted to different platform business models and content areas.[1881] Although standards may still be not dynamic enough to keep pace with technology changes in the platform economy, some have argued that ICT standards development is generally nimbler than elsewhere.[1882] Thirdly, their cooperative character provides for opportunities of wide stakeholder inclusion. This is particularly the case where standards incorporate more procedural elements that can be linked to wider CSR efforts of companies.[1883] Given the wide societal interests served by online platforms, it is submitted here that a wide multi-stakeholder approach should be a decisive element of any standard developed in this field. However, it should also be pointed out that insufficient transparency and democratic legitimacy remain a significant critical point of standardisation. This is especially the case where this process relies on bottom-up, highly technical, self-regulatory arrangements that may be subject to regulatory capture.[1884] Fourthly, standards make it easier, cheaper and more predictable for economic operators to comply with more complex

---

1880 Van Gestel and Micklitz (n 1528) 154; Teubner (n 1872).

1881 Verbiest and others (n 315) 22–23.

1882 Winn (n 1870) 189.

1883 Eller (n 1873) 317.

1884 Abbe Brown and Rónán Kennedy, 'Regulating Intersectional Activity: Privacy and Energy Efficiency, Laws and Technology' (2017) 31 International Review of Law, Computers & Technology 340, 358; Van Gestel and Micklitz (n 1528) 152, 177–179; Herwig CH Hofmann, 'A European Regulatory Union - The Role of Agencies and Standards' in Panos Koutrakos and Jukka Snell (eds), *Research Handbook on the Law of the EU's Internal Market* (Edward Elgar Publishing 2017) 18.

technical requirements. Their unified nature also eases enforcement in an international environment.[1885] Lastly, in the EU, standardisation is already a tried and tested regulatory approach across a wide area of technical and economic fields and beyond.[1886] It has been prominently applied in two content areas that are affected by unlawful content online. Product and food safety regulation provide a chance to incorporate intermediary responsibility provisions and experiment with an already existing enforcement network.

In the EU, technical standardisation, and the use of harmonised technical standards in particular, has become a widely adopted regulatory approach of choice for a wide area of economic regulation since the 1980s. A procedural infrastructure in the form of standardisation and accreditation bodies has been in existence for over 20 years. In 2001, the EU confirmed that standardisation was seen as an effective way of achieving EU objectives.[1887] Since then, standardisation has been extended to a wide field of sectors, including service sectors and more horizontal areas with broader public interests, such as occupational health and safety. The EU solidified the procedural and political basis of standardisation in Regulation 1025/2012. It laid down transparency, participation and accessibility requirements for civil society and SMEs to account for the extension of standardisation into wider areas of CSR and social norms.[1888] In addition, it established an annual work programme for standardisation and vowed to expand it across other areas.[1889]

Standardisation received a further policy boost with the EU's 2016 Joint initiative on standardisation under the Digital Single Market. In this policy document, which is part of the EU's standardisation package, the EU commits to improving, amongst others, transparency and accountability of the standard setting process, the development cycle of standards and a push to use standards to support digitisation in Europe.[1890] The focus of European standards on ICT was confirmed in 2016 by the Communication on ICT

1885 Schepel (n 34) 67–70.
1886 ibid 71–72.
1887 European Commission, 'European Governance - A White Paper, COM(2001) 428 Final' (n 1764) 21.
1888 Regulation 1025/2012 Articles 5, 6; Schepel (n 34) 66–68.
1889 Regulation 1025/2012 Article 8.
1890 'Joint Initiative on Standardisation: Responding to a Changing Marketplace - Growth - European Commission' (*Growth*) <https://ec.europa.eu/growth/content/joint-initiative-standardisation-responding changing-marketplace_en> accessed 29 August 2018 Actions 8, 9, 14.

Standardisation Priorities for the Digital Single Market.[1891] The EU acknowledged the increasingly fast change of digital technologies and the need for standards creation to adapt to this. It noted the new challenges that many new technologies, such as mobile apps or IoT pose on a horizontal level to security, privacy and user safety. It also noted the potential impact of standards on fundamental rights and the increasing controversy of access rights to standards.[1892] The annual work programmes on standardisation would adapt to the priorities set for the Digital Single Market. As an illustrative example, the EU requested the European standards organisations in 2015 to create a standard that would allow economic operators to develop, implement and execute privacy-by-design approaches demanded under the then proposed GDPR.[1893] The Commission asked that existing international standards such as ISO 9001 on quality management systems, ISO 27001/2 on information security management[1894] and European privacy risk management methodologies be considered in this process.[1895] It is suggested here that the EU could follow a similar approach if a new duty of care responsibility standard was to be made mandatory for online intermediaries.

The reliance of the functioning of the internet on standards needs no further mentioning. These standards have always been highly technical in nature. Standard setting bodies, such as the Internet Engineering Task Force (IETF) or the World Wide Web Consortium (W3C) were dominated by engineers and other technical experts. Butn as infrastructure regulation is being subsumed by content regulation, internet standard setting has also been increasingly invaded by content issues. Digital rights management, data protection and fears of censorship are more socially based, normative concerns that have found their way into these predominantly technical cir-

---

1891 European Commission, 'Communication: ICT Standardisation Priorities for the Digital Single Market COM(2016) 176 Final' (n 1696).

1892 ibid 3.

1893 Regulation 2016/679 (GDPR) Articles 25 (3), 42, 43.

1894 'ISO - ISO 9000 Family — Quality Management' (*ISO*) <https://www.iso.org/iso-9001-quality-management.html> accessed 11 August 2020; 'ISO - ISO/IEC 27001 — Information Security Management' (*ISO*) <https://www.iso.org/isoiec-27001-information-security.html> accessed 11 August 2020.

1895 Commission Implementing Decision on a standardisation request to the European standardisation organisations as regards European standards and European standardisation deliverables for privacy and personal data protection management - C(2015) 102 final 2015 (M/530) 5–6.

cles of internet standard making bodies.[1896] The debate over the involvement of ICANN, the infrastructural guardian of the internet, in copyright enforcement is just one proof of this tendency.[1897] Technical standards of the internet, however, are able to address the increasing policy attentions and accommodate forum shifts. Yet, the balance needs to be carefully managed. As shown by *Harcourt et al* the work of technical standards bodies has been influenced through participation by society. Digital rights activists have been involved in protocol management to address the issue of user tracking and state surveillance, although their influence remains constrained.[1898] Overall, states have progressively ceded more formal involvement in policy matters to more informal participation in international standards fora without however relinquishing influence, which may pose additional challenges for democratic accountability.[1899] Despite these risks, this shows that a technical standardisation approach in the area of intermediary responsibility would fit into the wider regulatory structure of the internet. In addition, if the EU were to drive a wide stakeholder approach, this could go some way in addressing the current imbalances of making public interests and fundamental rights heard more equitably in standards development.

3. Application to a new intermediary responsibility framework

The approaches and policy tools outlined above will be an integral part of the online intermediary responsibility framework for unlawful content proposed hereafter. The suggested model will rely on co-regulation. The regulator would outline responsibilities through the definition of key harms or threats that touch on the public interest and fundamental rights. The responsibilities would translate into more defined duties of care that follow a risk-based approach. Compliance with these responsibilities would be certified through voluntary, harmonised standards.

1896 Alison Harcourt, George Christou and Seamus Simpson, *Global Standard Setting in Internet Governance* (First edition, Oxford University Press 2020) 5–6, 87–88. They describe how copyright protection has found its way into the World Wide Web Consortium (W3C) standard body. Efforts to use ICANN as an enforcer in the area of copyright are another example: Bridy (n 276).

1897 Bridy (n 276).

1898 Harcourt, Christou and Simpson (n 1895) 175–188.

1899 ibid 211, 236–237.

In the below summary the interaction between the different tools will be briefly outlined. Self-regulatory approaches have until now not been effective in fighting the ongoing problem of unlawful content on online platforms and intermediaries. This has been demonstrated for all content sectors above throughout Chapter 4. It is therefore appropriate to step up public involvement, as was done for example though the AVMSD. Co-regulation provides a more robust structure that gives the public sector necessary leverage. Lawmakers will set clear public policy and fundamental rights objectives through law and put regulators in charge of coordinating, supervising, auditing and enforcing compliance with these goals. The more structured and mandated cooperation that is characteristic of co-regulation is also better suited to answer to the demands for a cooperative responsibility of all stakeholders in the process of online intermediation.[1900] This reflexive process goes also a long way in addressing the current governance readiness gaps of public authorities when it comes to complex technological problems, and algorithmic systems in particular.[1901] It is also capable of being more accountable and transparent than pure self-regulation. Finally, the European technical standardisation process favoured here takes place in a co-regulatory setting. Meanwhile, both co-regulation and standards have the potential to address the diversity in the platform economy and the fast pace of technological change.

The proposed model will define responsibilities that follow the formulation of precise harms or threats to public interests and fundamental rights that are caused by various types of unlawful content on online platforms. The gradual move away from intermediary liabilities towards responsibilities has been in the making for several years.[1902] This was initiated by courts through e.g. the diligent economic operator principle, or the application of various negligence standards of secondary liability at Member State level. EU and national lawmakers have increasingly embraced this move over the last five years. The EU Communication and the subsequent Recommendation on enhanced responsibilities for online platforms attest to this.[1903] The responsibility framework also lends itself to wider incorporation into the CSR principles that acknowledge certain fundamental

1900 See for example: Helberger, Pierson and Poell (n 68).

1901 Andrews (n 1777) 210–223. Governance readiness comprises the delivery, regulatory, coordinative, analytical and discursive capacities of regulators.

1902 Frosio, 'Reforming Intermediary Liability in the Platform Economy: A European Digital Single Market Strategy' (n 1742).

1903 European Commission, 'COM (2017) 555 Final' (n 69) 2; European Commission, 'C(2018) 1177 Final' (n 8).

rights obligations of transnational corporations, of which the leading online intermediaries are prominent examples. Finally, both risk regulation and standards put an emphasis on proactive, responsible conduct by online platforms. The formulation of responsibilities directly shapes the definition and structuring of risks and risk management approaches.[1904] In addition, responsibility is more adapted to the multilevel and multi-actor field of intermediary liability, which is characterised by uncertainties. As a framework it is better suited to enable the emergence of standards and duty of care obligations than the more reactive and rigid ordering model of liability.[1905]

Duties of care are a fitting concept to structure and circumscribe the responsibilities of internet intermediaries. They are rooted in a more defined legal setting which is linked to negligence, although certain ordinary law differences remain at national level. Duty of care lends itself to highly technical and complex activities that are difficult to monitor with traditional legal tools.[1906] However, in order to prevent resorting to different national negligence approaches of secondary liability it is important to construct an independent duty of care and responsibility system. Risk management and technical standards could provide the frame for such a system that bypasses the risk of national divergence.

Like duty of care, risk regulation and risk-based approaches correspond to situations that deal with a high amount of uncertainty and that require a flexible and reflexive approach.[1907] Standards, on the other hand, formalise and structure risk management approaches, technical specifications and requirements based on multi-stakeholder input.

These concepts, applied to a new intermediary responsibility approach, all fit into the wider context of responsive or flexible regulation, that is associated with regulatory governance. They answer to the multi-level regulatory nature of the EU and the particular challenges in the area of intermediary responsibility. The gravity of potential harms and rights at stake necessitates multi-stakeholder involvement as well as more robust means for public intervention and goals setting. At the same time, a certain level of flexibility is required to account for the diversity of economic platform models and the types of harms or threats at stake.

1904 Baldwin and Black (n 1850) 578–579.
1905 Eller (n 1873) 324–327.
1906 Hofmann (n 1830) 18.
1907 Ford (n 1656) 69–73.

I. Risks and pitfalls of flexible regulatory tools

However, the tools and approaches mentioned above also share some common criticisms, which shall be discussed here. First, the lack of democratic legitimacy and procedural transparency are commonly voiced criticisms of co-regulatory arrangements. This extends to those systems that involve risk regulation and standard setting through highly technical and closed committees of specialists. This has been partly demonstrated in the above section on standardisation. Although this is an even larger problem in self-regulation, where public oversight is even less pronounced, it remains a real risk in co-regulation.[1908] This is particularly true where standards are driven through a bottom up approach and where government involvement remains limited.[1909] While *Marsden* suggests that this legitimacy gap is inherent in internet regulation, where technology and globalisation heavily favour the influence of corporations,[1910] co-regulation could also provide the answer to the problem. As regulators oversee the standard making process they could impose regular public reporting and disclosure requirements and actively promote the participation of civil society.[1911]

Secondly, the legitimacy problem is closely linked to the phenomenon of regulatory capture. As regulators work in close cooperation with industry during standard-setting and also in defining risk-based approaches, they may be drawn in by the latter's preoccupations and concerns. As a result, the regulatory responses risk being more tilted towards the interests of industry than public interests or fundamental rights. This is a particular problem in networked and technology-oriented settings[1912] and could therefore be a risk of the regulatory framework proposed here. Although this, too, may be a dilemma inherent in any co-regulatory standard devel-

1908 Marsden, 'Guaranteeing Media Freedom on the Internet' (n 280) 219; Regulation 1025/2012 Articles 5 - 8. This problem was implicitly addressed through these articles, which set the path for broader society stakeholder involvement in standard making and in the accessibility to standards. Spindler and Thorun (n 1689) 12.

1909 Brown and Kennedy (n 1883) 358.

1910 Marsden, 'Guaranteeing Media Freedom on the Internet' (n 280) 11–12.

1911 Finck (n 1769) 27. Spindler and Thorun (n 1689) 17. A first step was made with the Technical Standards Regulation, which requires that standardisation organisations encourage and facilitate participation of society stakeholders in the standardisation process.

1912 Cohen (n 19) 395.

opment process, one answer could be to decentre policy making and involve civil society groups in third party monitoring.

Remedying the two above risks through transparency, disclosure and third-party oversight are however no trivial tasks in the area of internet content regulation. More often than not, transparency and reporting requirements are executed as a lip service, resulting in disclosures that are politically invisible or insufficiently clear and convoluted. The disparate nature and selective detail of many transparency reports has been shown in the sections on hate speech or IP infringements in Chapter 4. The perceived irrelevance for users may then result in a subversion of public values.[1913] This is particularly true in the area of algorithmic regulation and machine learning systems. To address this risk, standard setting in this area should include requirements of disclosure, for example of information about data that was used to train algorithms. This would allow researchers to reproduce the programming of machine learning systems used by platforms for content moderation.[1914]

Third, regulators need to close the capacity or governance readiness gaps that currently hinder effective participation in policymaking, supervision and enforcement.[1915] Past failure of regulators to follow up and adequately audit technical systems, software and risk management processes have led to spectacular failures in self- and co-regulatory systems. One of the more recent prominent examples of failure in regulation through technology was the 2015 *Volkswagen* emissions software scandal.[1916] Regulators simply did not have the capabilities to detect and prove the fraudulent manipulation of the company's emission testing software that gamed regulatory requirements during a span of 6 years. This underlines the risks of compliance technologies, where compliance certification is left primarily to private entities. A powerful and technologically savvy company like *Volkswagen* was able to influence the control technologies. The fraud was eventually proven by independent researchers.[1917] On the one hand, the danger here would be, for example, that, first, a *New Approach* style certification system for algorithmic software that is supposed to mitigate the risks of unlawful content propagation could be gamed by one or several of the few, large platforms. Secondly, the manipulation is then missed or acquiesced

1913 Mulligan and Bamberger (n 1777) 776–780.
1914 ibid 780–782.
1915 ibid 759–768; Andrews (n 1777) 214–217.
1916 Mulligan and Bamberger (n 1777) 718–719.
1917 Cohen (n 19) 372–373.

to by the private entity that is appointed to audit or certify the software or system. On the other hand, if a regulator is not capable of understanding, evaluating and auditing software for the various algorithmic harms that content management systems may present, the regulatory objectives may be missed. Evidence of these harms is, however, emerging more strongly.[1918] While, aside from algorithm review, investigative techniques exist to identify and evaluate these harms (e.g. black box tinkering[1919] or the above-mentioned computational reproducibility[1920]), regulators need to be able to understand and apply them. There is a clear need for regulators and policy makers to go beyond their traditional remit and understand algorithmic decisions, because the data analytics behind them, are, in the end, inherently value-ridden.[1921] Regulators need to be able to decipher and evaluate these values against public interest principles.

This also means that regulators need to be able to function in true networks. Assembling different public actors in the multi-level sectoral structure of certain content sectors within the EU may not be enough. Horizontal, more holistic cooperation is also required. Pulling together experience from fields in hate speech, economic rights, consumer and data protection and competition law may produce useful synergies. This kind of cooperation through regulatory networks is particularly useful where, as in the area of platform responsibility, regulators and enforcers may have strong sectoral competencies, but where operational capacities are limited.[1922] This regulatory gap has been shown in the area of product and food safety enforcement. Here, a more holistic and diagonal exchange of information and training would arguably help regulators in their regulatory delivery capacities *vis-à-vis* online platforms. It would also help address the challenge of the 'diagonal integration' of today's leading online platforms.[1923]

Fourth, standardisation and co-regulatory arrangements may pose competition problems. If private standard setting bodies are dominated by

1918 Andrews (n 1777) 210–213.

1919 Maayan Perel and Niva Elkin-Koren, 'Black Box Tinkering: Beyond Disclosure in Algorithmic Enforcement » Florida Law Review' (2017) 69 Florida Law Review <http://www.floridalawreview.com/2017/black-box-tinkering-beyond-disclosure-algorithmic-enforcement/> accessed 11 April 2019.

1920 Mulligan and Bamberger (n 1777) 782.

1921 Vincenzo Zeno-Zencovich, 'Legal Epistemology in the Times of Big Data' in Ginevra Peruginelli and Sebastiano Faro (eds), *Knowledge of the law in the big data age* (IOS Press 2019) 4.

1922 Kerber and Wendel (n 1810) 6.

1923 Tambini and Moore (n 232) 399–401.

large, oligopolistic market players, there is a risk that standards are designed in such a way that they pose entry barriers for smaller, new competitors.[1924] This would be a real risk, if dominating platforms were, due to their technical and economic capacities, able to dictate discussions in standard setting fora. The Chapter 4 sections on copyright and trademarks have demonstrated that *Google* has, for example, become a leader in the development of content filtering technologies for copyright. *Amazon* is currently becoming a major (holistic) fraud detection service provider in the platform economy. The leading online platforms have superior capacities in this regard due to the fact that they can rely on vast amounts of user and traffic data, have formidable analytical and software development capacities and huge financial resources. Care would need to be taken that their technical and economic superiority does not lead to the development of standards that entrench their power further. Meanwhile, it is a fact that co- and self-regulatory institutional arrangements work most smoothly and are most stable when they rely on cooperation by oligopolistic market players.[1925] The temptation is that regulators become complacent with such seemingly steady and well-oiled arrangements.

Fifth, co-regulatory set ups, and *New Approach*, or *NLF* style, harmonised standards have faced more recent challenges regarding their constitutionality and the impossibility of judicial review.[1926] Harmonised standards, even under the current European approach, are still privately drawn up norms that enact public interest principles. Taken to the extreme, states could set up *Potemkin* regulators that pretend to perform regulatory supervision and enforcement of privately set up mandatory standards.[1927] Meanwhile, courts would find it difficult to review standards, first, due to their private nature and, secondly, because of their highly technical features.[1928] Until recently, the legal nature of technical standards and the institutional framework surrounding them was unclear. Since standards are not part of the public law body, the decisions of certification bodies had not been sub-

1924 Graz (n 1530) 79–80; Eller (n 1873) 327.

1925 Marsden, *Internet Co-Regulation* (n 275) 225.

1926 ibid 224; Galland (n 1527) 372–374. Spindler and Thorun (n 1689) 21. Van Gestel and Micklitz (n 1528) 151. LAJ Senden, 'The Constitutional Fit of European Standardization Put to the Test' (2017) 44 Legal Issues of Economic Integration 337, 342–348.

1927 Marsden, *Internet Co-Regulation* (n 275) 224–225.

1928 Harm Schepel, 'The New Approach to the New Approach: The Juridification of Harmonized Standards in EU Law' (2013) 20 Maastricht Journal of European and Comparative Law 521, 533.

ject to judicial scrutiny. Moreover, access to technical standards documentation is not free. Their location in "legal no man's land"[1929] has, however, been increasingly challenged. As harmonised standards have become an important part of the European regulatory space, they have ascended to become quasi law, but without sufficient constitutional safeguards attached to it.[1930] In *Fra.bo* the CJEU found that a private certification body of a widely applicable industry standard for water systems exercised *de facto* powers to regulate market access. Its decision affected therefore the economic freedoms under the EU Treaties.[1931] The tendency of submitting private regulation of the *New Approach* style to EU fundamental rights principles found its continuation in the more recent rulings in *Schmitt* and *James Elliott.*[1932] In *Schmitt*, the CJEU found that a consumer, who had been damaged through fraudulent breast implants, could have legal recourse against a private national certification body *(TÜV Rheinland)* because the latter owed a duty of care to consumers.[1933] In *James Elliott*, the CJEU judged that an European harmonised standard for construction products, in this case the composition of asphalt, was part of the EU body of law. Although a private law instrument, the harmonised standard enacted EU law. Harmonised standards have a public legal effect under the *New Approach* and they are published in the EU's Official Journal.[1934] This trend of the constitutionalisation of EU private regulation[1935] just outlines the democratic legitimacy and accountability challenges that this regulatory instrument has been facing.[1936] On the other side, increased constitutionalisation may also risk annihilating the distinct advantages of this type of regulation and reduce its appeal to industry and regulators.[1937]

1929 Van Gestel and Micklitz (n 1528) 150.

1930 Senden (n 1925) 351–352.

1931 *Fra.bo SpA v Deutsche Vereinigung des Gas- und Wasserfaches eV (DVGW) — Technisch-Wissenschaftlicher Verein, C-171/11* [2012] EU:C:2012:453 (CJEU) [26–31].

1932 Paul Verbruggen and Barend Van Leeuwen, 'The Liability of Notified Bodies under the EU's New Approach: The Implications of the PIP Breast Implants Case' (2018) 43 European Law Review 394, 407–408.

1933 *Elisabeth Schmitt v TÜV Rheinland LGA Products GmbH,* [2017] EU:C:2017:128 (CJEU) [47].

1934 *James Elliott Construction Limited v Irish Asphalt Limited, C-613/14* [2016] EU:C:2016:821 (CJEU) [34–42].

1935 Verbruggen and Leeuwen (n 1931) 408.

1936 see also: Senden (n 1925).

1937 Schepel (n 1927) 533.

C. Primary and secondary responsibility and the sanctions regime

Chapter 4 has shown that sectoral attempts at reforming the current intermediary liability system have brought differing results. In copyright, non-diligent OCSSPs will be directly liable for copyright infringements. In trademark law, national courts have started to develop arguments for finding vertically integrated online marketplaces primary liable. Meanwhile, in speech related acts primary liability has been widely rejected by both courts and legislators, in favour of broader negligence-based duty of care approaches. Likewise, in product and food safety law, online intermediaries are generally not defined as economic operators with direct responsibilities. It is not immediately clear how a new approach towards platform responsibility can reconcile these different tendencies, nor whether it should.

The moral difficulties of making third parties directly responsible for the unlawful actions of others have been outlined in Chapter 3. This work sides with those that argue that *in principle* intermediaries should not be made primary liable for the action of others. Responsibilities, whose breach result in negligence-based, secondary liability would therefore be the preferred policy option. On the other hand, it has also been shown that some of the vertically integrated and intrusive business practices of platforms do indeed affect the substantive provision of the legal acts that regulate certain content. Apart from copyright, the commercial communication criterium in trademark law is one such example. Where platform intermediation affects the substantive law of the content/service that has been made accessible, primary liability would therefore appear to be a justifiable option. This could even be extended to product law, where failure on the side of online marketplaces to provide traders with the technical facilities to comply with statutory labelling and information requirements could result in direct liability. Meanwhile, for speech acts, the platform's activity of distribution or amplification does not affect the (il)legal nature of the content. Therefore, primary liability for defamatory and hate speech acts or terrorist offences would seem excessive.

It is submitted here that it would be too rigid in the context of the diversity of content and related laws to mandate either a full secondary or a full primary liability approach. The fluid lines between primary and secondary liability are likely to continue as business models and technologies evolve.[1938] Instead, this work argues for a special regime based on negli-

1938 Lipton (n 287) 1347; Assaf Hamdani (n 304) 106–107.

gence (linked to duty of care obligations). Negligence could, however, trigger (harmonised) primary liability where EU sectoral law provides for this, i.e. the DSMD. As shown in the copyright section in Chapter 4, the DSMD may well lend itself to a negligence-based duty of care assessment. In fact, the "best efforts" concepts can be applied to a risk-based duty of care standard).[1939] Where sectoral provisions do not foresee primary liability, a separate sanctions regime would be applied. The GDPR could serve as an example for the imposition of administrative fines and penalties.[1940] Alternatively, the regime would trigger secondary liability which would fall back to the provisions provided in national laws of Member States. In view of the disparate nature of the secondary liability regimes and their enforcement, this solution is, however, considered counterproductive.

D. A co-regulatory duty of care based on harmonised technical standards

1. Introduction

The following proposal sketches out a mandatory duty of care responsibility that follows a risk-based approach and relies on the (technical) standards system used under the *New Approach*. The focus of this proposals is on a) structuring the risk-based approach and b) how a risk management standard should be tied to a horizontal duty of care in legislation.

First, the methodological reliance on the *New Approach* and technical standard is influenced by the early elaborations of *Verbiest and Spindler* in their 2007 Study on the Liability of Internet Intermediaries for the European Commission, and the risk management approach first proposed by *Kempel and Wege* in 2010.[1941]

1939 Directive (EU) 2019/790 of the European Parliament and of the Council of 17 April 2019 on copyright and related rights in the Digital Single Market and amending Directives 96/9/EC and 2001/29/EC (Text with EEA relevance.) 2019 (OJ L 130) Article 17 (3), Recital 66.Chapter 4 C 4

1940 Regulation 2016/679 (GDPR) Articles 83, 84.

1941 Verbiest and others (n 315); Kempel and Wege (n 16). This was initially picked up by this author in his LLM Dissertation, written in 2012 at the University of Edinburgh: Ullrich, 'Online Intermediaries' Liability 2012' (n 17) 28–29 and subsequently refined by applying the principles of Transaction Risk Management in anti-money laundering: Ullrich, 'A Risk-Based Approach towards Infringement Prevention on the Internet' (n 747).

Secondly, *Helman and Parchomovsky's* suggestion of a best available technology safe harbour for copyright infringements has been inspirational.[1942] The flexibility of such an approach, coupled with the best available technology standard that would be vetted and approved by a public body, has much in common with the standardisation solution offered here. The idea of creating a market for independent filtering service providers and the creation of a centrally managed copyright database also go a long way in pushing for public accountability and the respect of fundamental rights.[1943]

Thirdly, the more recent proposal of *Woods and Perrin*[1944] for a statutory duty of care has helped to validate and further improve on the framework suggested below. The definition of distinct harms by *Woods and Perrin* has helped to solve the question whether a framework should be structured by content area or type of intermediary. The harms-based approach will help platforms covered by the regulation to focus on the most important question: how to design their business models and technologies in a responsible way that pre-empts and eliminates the most egregious harms that users still risk to encounter on many online platforms today. In addition, *Helberger et al's*[1945] distinction of prospective and retrospective (cooperative) responsibilities have led to an adjustment of the risk assessment framework.

2. Changes to the ECD's online intermediary liability framework

The proposed scheme would radically change the current ECD intermediary liability provisions. First, the distinction between passive and active intermediaries would be removed. It has been shown throughout this dissertation that this distinction is outdated for today's information hosts. Courts have been grappling with the concept and a wide array of stakeholders have likewise questioned its relevance in the era of Web 2.0. Secondly, the actual knowledge standard, which is connected to the reactive concept of liability, would not be carried over into the new framework. Uncertainty (of knowledge and information) is a central element in risk as-

1942 Helman and Parchomovsky (n 309).
1943 ibid 1221–1226.
1944 Woods and Perrin (n 799).
1945 Helberger, Pierson and Poell (n 68).

sessment.[1946] Responsible platforms should do everything that can be reasonably expected of them to attain knowledge and data to assess the risk of the harms defined in legislation. Where such knowledge is not available, the risk assessment should lead the platform to take appropriate mitigation or precautionary measures. Thirdly, the new framework eschews the general monitoring prohibition of Article 15 ECD. It has been demonstrated that the definition of general monitoring remains unclear. It is suggested that this ambiguity will not go away with the ongoing evolution in technology. On the other hand, the protection of privacy, freedom of expression and other fundamental rights, can and should be effectively ensured through (algorithmic) governance, risk management and due process measures that are attuned to the particular harm in question and incorporated in the duty of care standard. In escalated cases, courts would conduct the balancing exercises and provide further guidance. It has been demonstrated and argued here that courts are able to conduct these balancing exercises without having to resort to the blanket prohibition of Article 15 ECD. This is supported by the view that the current use of Article 15 ECD presents an over-emphasis of free speech over other fundamental rights and harms, which sits uncomfortably with the European tradition of more equitable fundamental rights balancing.[1947] Lastly, the framework moves away from a liability to a responsibility regime. This also means that a "Good Samaritan" protection, as demanded by some for the EU,[1948] does not fit into such a new framework, which rests on positive responsibilities and does not see online platforms as neutral bystanders whose proactive measures are caritative acts that soften the harmful impact of their own systems.[1949] There is no single argument for broader responsibilities of online platforms. This work should have demonstrated that besides the purely

---

1946 European Commission, 'EU General Risk Assessment Methodology (Action 5 of Multi-Annual Action Plan for the Surveillance of Products in the EU (COM(2013)76))' (European Commission 2015) 14.

1947 Smith, 'Enforcement and Cooperation between Member States' (n 684) 33.

1948 Joan Barata, 'Positive Intent Protections: Incorporating a Good Samaritan Principle in the EU Digital Services Act' (*Center for Democracy and Technology*, 29 July 2020) <https://cdt.org/insights/positive-intent-protections-incorporating-a-good-samaritan-principle-in-the-eu-digital-services-act/> accessed 14 October 2020; Sartor (n 236) 31. Tambiama Madiega, 'Reform of the EU Liability Regime for Online Intermediaries: Background on the Forthcoming Digital Services Act : In-Depth Analysis.' (European Parliament 2020) 18 <https://op.europa.eu/publication/manifestation_identifier/PUB_QA0420239ENN> accessed 14 October 2020.

1949 Smith, 'Enforcement and Cooperation between Member States' (n 684) 32–33.

economic reasons of the cheapest cost avoider, online platforms have become gatekeepers that occupy critical positions in the internet's informational and physical architecture. This, and their role as quasi-public spaces for large swathes of the world's population, confer on them also positive moral responsibilities to prevent harms that impact public interests and fundamental rights.

This is the suggested definition of online intermediaries to which this regime would apply:

> *Any information society service providers whose activity consists of the storage of information provided by a recipient of the service, whereby the recipient of the service is acting not under the authority or the control of the provider.*

It should also be noted this regime would not apply to IAPs. It is suggested that the current regime of the ECD's Article 12, which has been progressively re-interpreted and adapted by courts, is fit for purpose. Likewise, the caching provision in Article 13 would also be left untouched by the new framework. In addition, the special position of search engines should be considered and result in a modified, regime that takes account of the essential functions that these intermediaries have for the functioning of the internet.

Finally, the exponential impact of large, dominant platforms and intermediaries (*GAFAM*) in the area of content management has been repeatedly stressed. Due to time and space limitations, this work does not venture to develop a special regime of stricter duties of care for these players. Nevertheless, the creation of such an extra regime, which is considered by an increasing number of scholars and has also been included in the proposals of the Commission's Digital Service Act package, is expressly endorsed.[1950] The approach presented here could thus be adapted in order to enhance certain risk management and transparency obligations of these dominant platforms.

1950 Wagner, 'Free Expression? Dominant Information Intermediaries as Arbiters of Internet Speech' (n 83) 232 236; De Streel and Husovec (n 83) 45–46; Molly K Land, 'Regulating Private Harms Online: Content Regulation under Human Rights Law' in Rikke Frank Jørgensen (ed), *Human Rights in the Age of Platforms* (The MIT Press 2019) 304–305 <https://direct.mit.edu/books/book/4531/Human-Rights-in-the-Age-of-Platforms> accessed 28 May 2020.

3. Sectoral flexibility – the harms under a horizontal framework

In a previous version of the system proposed here specific duties of care were tied to different platform business models.[1951] The idea was that certain types of platforms were subject to specific 'sectoral' violations. UGC platforms were linked to specific duties in the area of copyright; online marketplaces to trademark violations; social media to hate speech and violence, and news portals (with comment functions) also to hate speech and propagation of violence. This system was open ended for new types of platforms and harms.

The harms approach suggested by *Woods and Perrin*,[1952] provides a simpler and at the same time more encompassing solution. The harms would be picked up through existing or future sectoral legislation. For example, in the area of hate speech the AVMSD Article 28b already sets out duty of care style obligations for VSPs. This could be complemented or replaced by reference to a duty of care standard for the harms addressed by this directive. This standard could then also be picked up by other sectoral provisions that address hate speech or the protection of minors, and which do not specifically address VSPs. The same could be done in the area of copyright for OCSSPs, where the best efforts mentioned in Article 17 DSMD could be supplemented or replaced by reference to a duty of care (technical) standard. In the same vein, IPRED could be amended to reference this standard for intermediaries in areas of IP law not covered by the DSMD. Likewise, the TERREG proposal and Regulation 2019/1148 on marketing and use of explosive precursors could reference a duty of care (technical) standard designed to address the specific harms caused by terrorist content or activity. The same goes for the MSR in the area of product safety, and selected regulations within the EU Hygiene package for the area of food safety. An illustration of such a sectorally adaptable system can be found in ANNEX II.

Meanwhile, the reformed ECD or a future DSA would serve as a framework directive or regulation. A framework directive/regulation is an EU instrument that establishes general (usually minimum) principles and policy

1951 Ullrich, 'A Risk-Based Approach towards Infringement Prevention on the Internet' (n 747) 249.

1952 Woods and Perrin (n 799) 35–40. Saurwein, Just and Latzer (n 1656) 38. are also proposing a harms based approach, but focus mainly on the governance of algorithms.

objectives for a broader legal area.[1953] However, it leaves flexibility to EU or national lawmakers to define stricter or deviating standards in *lex specialis* for specific sectors of the wider area covered by the framework legislation. As an example, the E-Privacy Directive (2002/58) is *lex specialis* to the GDPR in that it specifies the data protection rules applying to electronic communications.[1954] The GPSD and the MSR are framework provisions in the area of product safety and its enforcement, while sectoral provisions, such as the Toy Safety Directive, would lay down *lex specialis* where it concerns the specific obligations of manufacturers or distributors for the making available of toys on the EU market. Under this approach, the new EU act on digital services would establish the kind of harms and principles that a new duty of care responsibility system for online intermediaries would address. It could mention the kind of harms to which duty of care standards for information host would apply. The harms would then be linked to the sectoral acts, which contain reference to specific duty of care standards.

Below is a non-exhaustive proposal of overarching harms and some specific sub-categories, which overlap to some extend with the harms proposed by *Woods and Perrin*[1955]:

- Harms to personality rights, incl. protection of minors
  This category would cover, for example, defamation, hate speech, child pornography. The AVMSD would be one current EU law which could reference a duty of care standard that targets this harm. The problem here is that defamation is subject to national rules, which makes the creation of an overall standard problematic, if not impossible currently. One possibility could be to require Member States to incorporate reference to the duty of care standard in their local laws on defamation. This would likely preclude primary liability for this kind of harm because of the exclusive competency of Member States over substantive law in this area. However, as outlined above, primary lia-

1953 Pauline Westerman, 'Arguing About Goals: The Diminishing Scope of Legal Reasoning' (2010) 24 Argumentation 211, 212.

1954 Mark D Cole and Teresa Quintel, '"Is There Anybody out There?" – Retention of Communications Data. Analysis of the Status Quo in Light of the Jurisprudence of the Court of Justice of the European Union (CJEU) and the European Court of Human Rights (ECtHR)' in Russell L Weaver, Jane Reichel and Steven I Friedland (eds), *Comparative perspectives on privacy in an Internet era* (Carolina Academic Press 2019) 81. Regulation 2016/679 (GDPR) Recital 173.

1955 Woods and Perrin (n 799) 35–41.

bility may not be a justified option in this field. It would also mean that explicit reference to the country-of-origin principle of such a duty of care would need to be made, although such a standard would likely harmonise substantive negligence based duties fully.

- Economic harms
  This covers mainly intellectual property rights, such as copyright and trademarks, but could also comprise online fraud. The substantive aspects of both IP rights are harmonised. It is perceivable that reference to this duty of care standard could also be inserted into IPRED, the Infosoc Directive and the DSMD.
- Harms to public security, order and democracy
  This category covers harms that threaten the stability of society, democracy, the environment or the functioning of the state. Terrorist content, the sale of prohibited products, such as trafficking in wildlife and protected species, weapons or drugs, are types of unlawful content that are contained in this section. The proposed TERREG could have a reference to a specific duty of care standard in this area. Other sector specific EU legislation would need to be identified that is suitable to carry references to this duty of care standard.[1956]
- Consumer protection
  This area covers, for example, products and services that are non-compliant, unsafe or prohibited. This area has a strong link to economic harms. Duty of care risk management considerations would likely be similar. In addition, they normally affect the same kind of platforms, such as online marketplaces or social media and messaging apps. A duty of care standard could be referenced in the recent MSR or in applicable *lex specialis* such as the Toys Safety Directive, and cross-referenced in the UCPD. This may entail classifying online marketplaces as economic operators under certain product safety *lex specialis*, but not in others.[1957] For food safety, the Official Controls regulation, the Hygiene of Foodstuffs regulation or the Food Labelling Regulation[1958] could be suitable places where such standards are referenced. Again, online platforms may need to be classified as food business operators

1956 Such as: Directive 2001/62. or the Directive 2008/99/EC on the protection of the environment through criminal law 2008 (OJ L 328) 99.
1957 This would depend on whether online platforms' business models potentially directly affect the essential requirements of these products. In that case the specific product safety standards (European Norms) could even contain obligations for online intermediaries.
1958 Regulation 2017/625; Regulation 852/2004; Regulation 1167/2011.

for this. It has been shown above, that food safety authorities could justify this classification where these intermediaries charge a commission or derive other revenue from the intermediation activity, i.e. through advertising.

The sectoral framework should also include specific protections for small or emerging platform operators. Such sandboxing requirements are known from other areas, such as financial regulation, where FinTech start-ups are given space to evolve and experiment without onerous compliance requirements at a crucial initial stage of development.[1959] Such requirements could, for example, be applied for the use of automated content recognition technologies or compliance with a technical, duty of care standard. The German *NetzDG* provides another example of how smaller platforms could be addressed. It frees social networks with less than two million domestic users from certain requirements relating to identification and removal of unlawful content.[1960]

4. The duty of care risk management system

At the heart of this proposal is a technical compliance framework in which platforms have to follow a risk-based approach in order to prevent and combat unlawful use of their systems. The division into prospective and retrospective duties of care is needed, because it is acknowledged that not all abusive uses of online platforms can be foreseen and pre-empted, even if prospective care was taken in an exemplary manner. Platforms launch new business models, algorithms and architectures on a frequent basis. They often experiment with new features or launch beta versions, which is part of agile software project management methods. This means that minor defects or lacking features may be fixed after launch. In this scenario, it is important that the intermediary has effective retrospective technologies in place that filter and monitor high risk activities and content areas, effective NTD procedures and other processes that involve stakeholders. This

---

1959 Dirk A Zetzsche and others, 'Regulating a Revolution: From Regulatory Sandboxes to Smart Regulation' (2017) 23 Fordham Journal of Corporate & Financial Law 31, 64–65; European Commission, 'Fintech: A More Competitive and Innovative European Financial Sector, Consultation Document' (European Commission 2017) 16–17 <https://ec.europa.eu/info/sites/info/files/2017-fintech-consultation-document_en_0.pdf> accessed 9 January 2018.

1960 NetzDG para 1 (2).

would also be part of the continuous improvement that is part of a proper risk management approach.[1961] Prospective responsibilities relate therefore mainly to *ex-ante* measures that a platform should take in order to address harms that are reasonably foreseeable from its technology, architecture and business model. Retrospective measures would focus on *ex-post* measures that address unlawful content or activity as it occurs or happened in the past.[1962] Content filtering, which is often seen as a preventive measure, would, in its strictest sense be a retrospective measure.

The approach below seeks to mould risk management into a duty of care standard for online platforms by using the methodology laid out in the ISO 31000 risk management standard.[1963] This standard enjoys a wide applicability throughout the corporate world. It has been incorporated into other standards and is referenced in the EU risk assessment methodology.[1964] It is likely that most companies are familiar with its application, as well as with similar globally used 'societal' standards such as social responsibility (ISO 26000), anti-bribery management (ISO 37000),[1965] quality management (ISO 9001), or information security management (ISO 27001). A future duty of care standard could make us of this. In the following, the duty of care for online platforms will be broken down into the procedural steps of risk management (Risk identification, risk analysis and evaluation, and risk control). This is meant to demonstrate how a duty of care could be 'made concrete' within a platform business. For a broad concept like duty of care to work in an operational environment, it needs to be broken down into steps that can be directly applied to business planning, processes and systems. Such a lateral and structured approach will also give regulators and courts the means to verify whether the intermediary applied the required duty of care.

1961 Grant Purdy, 'ISO 31000:2009-Setting a New Standard for Risk Management: Perspective' (2010) 30 Risk Analysis 881, 883.

1962 Yeung and Expert Committee on human rights dimensions of automated data processing and different forms of artificial intelligence (MSI-AUT) (n 293) 48–49.

1963 'ISO - ISO 31000 — Risk Management' (*ISO*) <https://www.iso.org/iso-31000-risk-management.html> accessed 14 August 2020.

1964 European Commission, 'EU General Risk Assessment Methodology (Action 5 of Multi-Annual Action Plan for the Surveillance of Products in the EU (COM(2013)76))' (n 1945) 5. 'ISO - ISO/IEC 29100:2011(E) - Information Technology — Security Techniques — Privacy Framework' 18 <https://standards.iso.org/ittf/PubliclyAvailableStandards/c045123_ISO_IEC_29100_2011.zip> accessed 11 April 2020.

1965 Graz (n 1530) 47.

I. Risk assessment

According to standard methodology, risk assessment relies on three key steps: risk identification, risk analysis and risk evaluation. Analysis and evaluation are intricately linked and have been summarised under one section for simplicity here. An eventual technical standard would be expected to be more detailed and take account of various risk assessment techniques and formalities relating to the documentation and follow-up of risk assessments.[1966]

a. Risk identification

Risk identification will be done first in context of the particular statutory harms defined by law. This simplifies the process as the platforms will need to focus first and foremost on the public interests and fundamental rights. This does not mean that other risks should not also be picked up during the risk identification process. They may have knock-on effects on the wider risk environment the platforms operate in. For example, by considering the risk of counterfeit in the area of economic harms, an online marketplace or social messaging app may be able to identify additional risks related to money-laundering, product safety or fraud. Risk identification can be done in various ways. A platform could convene project and business teams on a regular basis, or engage in risk identification prior to the launch of major new features, such as a new content sharing feature, an algorithm update, or a new ad feature. As stated above, risk identification of platform design features, business models, architectures or algorithms is something that platforms will not always necessarily get right from the start. It lies in the entrepreneurial nature of many of these businesses that they launch new features or services, experiment with them and then decide whether to keep or discontinue them. This is why it is important that platforms have the procedural and organisational means in place to document these processes and review them regularly.

It is suggested here that an online intermediary first define clearly the most prominent (statutory) harms that may typically occur on their platform. They are expected to understand the wider risk environment in which they operate. This should be done by looking at internal data, escalations from outside users and other stakeholders and by consulting wider

1966 'ISO - ISO 31000 — Risk Management' (n 1962) para 5.4.

interdisciplinary research and feedback from society. This requirement could be adjusted to the size of the regulated entity. Certain platform models attract certain types of harms more than others. This should be documented when identifying risks of new design or business feature launched by the platform.

Secondly, online platforms should identify and understand the risk drivers related to their platform models. Risk drivers take account of the fact that the occurrence of unlawful content in itself is difficult to contain. However, platforms' architecture is capable of creating a framework that leads to an amplification of the risks related to the harms caused by unlawful content and behaviour.[1967]

For example, social media and UGC sites have been in the focus with regards to harms to personality rights and public security. Research in this area has shown that anonymity[1968] and nudging mechanisms for content propagation[1969] can be risk drivers for these harms. This does not mean that anonymity should be impossible. However, it should have consequences for the user and the way their content is (algorithmically) handled on the platform. In addition, adequate verification techniques should be in place. The way recommendation algorithms are structured and designed, the choice that is given to users to share or comment on content, or to whom it can be distributed, all influence the harms that can be caused.

For online marketplaces, typical risk drivers can relate to the provenance and legal status of sellers; or the type of product categories that the platforms offer to their sellers. This is also closely connected to anonymity or the ease with which a seller can start to sell on an online market platform. The sale of medicines, nutritional supplements or toys may pose a higher risk to consumers, and is generally regulated in a stricter way.

Following stakeholder dialogues a more complete example list of common risk drivers could be stablished for each harm and then incorporated

1967 Lavi (n 199) 54–56.

1968 David Babbs, 'New Year, New Internet? Why It's Time to Rethink Anonymity on Social Media' (*Inforrm's Blog*, 31 January 2020) <https://inforrm.org/2020/01/31/new-year-new-internet-why-its-time-to-rethink-anonymity-on-social-media-david-babbs/> accessed 14 August 2020; Kinsella (n 917). Jesse Fox, Carlos Cruz and Ji Young Lee, 'Perpetuating Online Sexism Offline: Anonymity, Interactivity, and the Effects of Sexist Hashtags on Social Media' (2015) 52 Computers in Human Behavior 436.

1969 Lavi (n 199) 18–35.

into a standard.[1970] This would necessitate empirical research and evidence gathering and broader stakeholder dialogues in order to get agreement of common risk drivers that impact harms on online platforms. This research is increasingly taking place,[1971] but the need to get even more data should be facilitated by obligations to allow independent researchers access to content data and propagation mechanisms on online platforms. The list of typical risk drivers can be continuously assessed and updated via regulatory guidance notes and eventual standard revisions. Platforms could brainstorm risk drivers before new business features are being launched or consult researchers, industry specialists or regulators on a confidential basis to help identify additional risk drivers.

b. Risk analysis and evaluation

Risk analysis means that each risk is examined in detail with regards to the impact of the harm caused and the likelihood of it occurring. Companies will need to have adequate and robust analytical capabilities and organisational structures in place that allow them to generate and apply internal data and intelligence for these purposes.

Platforms are also expected to understand the wider risk environment in which they operate, be it through participation in industry dialogues or by being in regular contact with regulators, researchers and user associations. It is obvious that, for example, periods of heightened terrorist risk or economic instability should be considered when platforms analyse risks that emanate from certain drivers. This can be supported through guidance and research from a regulator.[1972] This is also why many regulatory regimes require the existence of a structural nexus within a company, often in the form of a compliance function, in order to ensure specific regulatory risks

1970 This has been done in the next section's example case for online marketplaces, and in ANNEX III.

1971 See for example: Birgit Stark and Daniel Stegmann, 'Are Algorithms a Threat to Democracy? The Rise of Intermediaries: A Challenge for Public Discourse' (Algorithm Watch 2020) .

1972 For example, the European Food Safety Authority (EFSA) or the European Agency for Health and Safety at Work (EU-OSHA) provide this analytical support on changing risk environments. 'Emerging Risks - Safety and Health at Work - EU-OSHA' <https://osha.europa.eu/en/emerging-risks> accessed 18 August 2020.

are being managed.[1973] In anti-money laundering law, regulated institutions need to appoint a compliance officer and, potentially, a specific internal audit function;[1974] the GDPR requires a data protection officer for certain entities.[1975] The duty of care regime for online intermediaries could require the establishment of a "safety officer" or another function that regulators can turn to for regulatory obligations, such as proof of risk assessments that the platform has to perform.

The risk analysis should lead to an evaluation and ranking of the risks by their seriousness. For example, if a new feature on a social media platform allows users to post or stream live video clips, then the platform would need to assess and evaluate whether this poses a serious, medium or low risk to: personality rights of privacy, personal integrity or harm to minors; economic harms related to copyright violations; public security harms related to terrorist content. It is also appropriate to ask platforms that allow users total anonymity to provide a risk assessment of specific harms. Again, a company would need to be able to have the analytical and organisational capacity to measure this risk. The sections on terrorist content, hate speech and copyright have shown that through initiatives like the GIFTC, or through NTD data, online platforms have the means to gather this information. It is submitted that even smaller platforms that are not part of industry initiatives or wider stakeholder groups should be able to capture and analyse escalations from users or regulators.[1976] Here, regulators in conjunction with industry associations, could provide support in helping these platforms in putting risk analysis and evaluation methods in place.

It is more difficult to verify the application of risk assessments when it comes to content management algorithms, especially where they rely on artificial intelligence. However, here too, the parameters and weightings that determine content decisions follow certain values and business objectives. A risk assessment would inevitably need to disclose these objectives as their impact on certain harms will need to be measured. Risk assessment could involve playing with these parameters to measure their impact on unlawful behaviour and content. Some methods how to address responsibility in this area have been mentioned in the previous section of this chapter.

1973 Griffith (n 1812) 2093–2095.

1974 Directive 2015/849 Article 8 (4).

1975 Regulation 2016/679 (GDPR) Section 4.

1976 This is supported by the fact that they have to be able to assess and react to notices of unlawful content or activity received by users.

Likewise, if an online marketplace were to launch a new product category, such as for example nutritional supplements, or allow sellers from a new geographic area to operate on their platform, then the economic risks to trademark rights or consumer protection risks to product safety could be assessed through different tools. First, a platform could look at the regulatory requirements of a new product area, such as (online) labelling, information requirements, risks to product integrity and the wider market environments (consumer and brand trends, counterfeit risks etc). It could then assess the risks related to letting unverified sellers from across the world list products in this area. It could also test the propensity of mistakes, such as incorrect labelling, or erroneous product information. After careful analysis it would then need to decide whether the activity or feature presents a high risk. As demonstrated in Chapter 3, courts in China have, for example, incorporated "red flag" (knowledge) tests into their duty of care regimes. A platform would automatically need to apply enhanced due diligence measures on content that is subject to high popularity or that goes viral, simply due to the size of the harm caused if that kind of content was indeed unlawful. In the area of copyright, the idea is that certain popular music or videos may be more susceptible to fraudulent practices.[1977] Likewise, viral content may create more opportunities for fraudsters. Chapter 4 has shown that red flags are also being used in predictive analysis by online platforms. A technical standard could provide indicative examples of typical red flags that would have to be considered in a risk assessment and evaluation.

A platform could also be required to score the risk of each legally defined harm when launching a new business, design feature or basic algorithms. Again, these mandatory risk assessments exist in other areas: the GDPR obliges data controllers whose activities pose a high risk to the privacy rights of individuals to perform a data protection impact assessment prior to starting their operations.[1978] Under anti-money laundering legislation, financial institutions need to identify and assess the risks of money laundering and terrorist financing;[1979] EU health and safety legislation[1980] requires that employers perform an assessment of the risks to safety and health at work. There are many more examples. The EU has provided am-

1977 Wang (n 504) 284–286.

1978 Regulation 2016/679 (GDPR) Article 35.

1979 Directive 2015/849 Article 8.

1980 Council Directive 89/391/EEC on the introduction of measures to encourage improvements in the safety and health of workers at work Article 9.

ple policy and procedural guidance to economic actors in these areas. Regulators could provide similar guidance and host best practice sharing and trainings to facilitate a consistent approach to risk assessment

II. Risk control measures

Risk controls are aimed at modifying the severity of a risk to an acceptable level. There are a number of possible risk responses that can be taken to address or control a risk. These shall not be covered in detail here.[1981] However, not all risk responses are appropriate to any type of risk. For example, risk assurance or risk sharing would not alleviate the harmful impact on users but just spread the punitive impact on the risk taker. In the context of the statutory harms and their risks discussed here, two risk responses would seem appropriate to address prospective responsibility: risk mitigation and risk avoidance. These responses would be broadly in line with the precautionary principle.[1982] If a platform was to launch a new feature or activity that it has classed as high risk with regards to certain harms then risk avoidance would see it refrain from deploying this feature or activity at least until it has brought in place proper safeguards. Bringing in place safeguards, such as user verification and restrictions on anonymity, or charging user fees, would in turn be counted as risk mitigation. In this case the platform would have taken a prospective responsibility to create a safer user environment.

Under its retrospective responsibility the platform would bring in place targeted monitoring and filtering, NTD or user flagging processes. These risk responses could be classed as contingency or fall-back measures because they deal with the risk once it materialises and becomes an actual harm. Although filtering systems do prevent unlawful content appearing on the site, this also means that a user was still able to access the site and (try to) upload this kind of content. Both prospective and retrospective measures should complement each other. An entirely prospective ap-

1981 For more detail see: 'ISO - ISO 31000 — Risk Management' (n 1962) s 5.5. Risk Treatment.

1982 Heidi Tworek, 'How Platforms Could Benefit from the Precautionary Principle' (*Centre for International Governance Innovation*, 19 November 2019) <https://www.cigionline.org/articles/how-platforms-could-benefit-precautionary-principle> accessed 17 August 2020. This author also suggests the risk assessment methodology as part of a precautionary principle approach for online platforms.

proach may throttle speech and content, while overreliance on retrospective measures may end up in frequent removals and sanctions without giving users an incentive to behave responsibly. Meanwhile, the ideal balance between both approaches may be different depending on the type of harm. It should be stressed that under this model, the risk identification and risk evaluation processes that feed into prospective and retrospective responsibility (control) measures are the same.

a. Risk control: prospective responsibility for empowering safe platform use

Prospective responsibility relies on the governance-by-design approach, which has become a wider policy approach with regards to technology driven businesses. This principle refers to "the purposeful effort to use technology to embed values."[1983] It has become prominent largely thanks to the endorsement by the GDPR's privacy-by-design approach. For the purposes targeted here, the principle imposed on platforms should be one of safety-by-design, by which platforms would need to embed online safety values into their services throughout the product development life cycle, including product updates.[1984] They do not just extend to architecture and processes but also to the way content moderation algorithms are designed by platforms, and the values and priorities they apply to suppression or amplification.[1985]

The platform would be required to address high risks related to statutory harms. As of now platforms have responded in a seemingly haphazard and reactive way to address high risk situations of certain harms by reacting to regulatory or public pressure. *Twitter* for example implemented a feature in August 2020 to give users more options over who can reply to their tweets. The measure is aimed at limiting trolls and the possibility of

---

1983 Mulligan and Bamberger (n 1777) 697. Florian Saurwein and others, 'Algorithmische Selektion im Internet: Risiken und Governance automatisierter Auswahlprozesse' [2017] kommunikation @ gesellschaft 22, 8.

1984 As suggested by: Woods, 'Duty of Care' (n 1703) 20–21. Woods and Perrin (n 799) 11–12, advocated, in principle, by: Helberger, Pierson and Poell (n 68) 6–8; Lavi (n 199) 19–30 and applied by: Great Britain and Department for Culture (n 197) 80–81.

1985 Gillespie, *Custodians of the Internet* (n 1010) 197–214.

hate speech and abusive comments.[1986] Other sites have started to impose enhanced user verification processes for participation, or consent mechanisms from other users when uploading images of them in a bid to ensure trust in more sensitive environments.[1987] Anonymity and user verification remain key design features that influence the riskiness of platforms and the content circulating on them. Linking different verification and anonymity levels to the way users can engage on a social media or UGC platform would be one way to control such risks.[1988]

Online marketplaces that integrate their own payments services will already need to ask sellers to undergo specific identity verification under existing anti-money laundering legislation. Additional risk control measures could foresee that sellers that want to sell in certain high-risk categories undergo additional due diligence or verification processes.

The 'best efforts' prescribed in the DSMD Article 17 (4)) relate to retrospective measures of filtering and NTD. They would be applied when the OCSSP failed to follow prospective duties of concluding licensing agreements with rightsowners for the content shared on its sites. Here, the additional question would be how an environment could be created that prospectively encourages users to refrain from sharing infringing content, where this poses a high-risk exposure to economic harms.

The AVMSD in Article 28b (3) also mentions possible prospective risk control measures that platforms may need to take in order to prevent unlawful hate speech or content that harms minors. These measures foresee technical features that allow users to report and flag content or implement parental controls.

Online platforms have ample mechanisms or risk control measures at their disposal to create user environments that allow for safe interaction. The exact detail of prospective (and retrospective measures) that are available, feasible and reasonable or proportionate for online platforms requires significant additional research and more formal discussions and negotiations between the various stakeholders. It is beyond the frame of this work to define the nature, scope and technical design of measures and processes for such a platform responsibility system. This would be at the heart of a safety-by-design standards creation process. Standardisation is a com-

---

1986 'Twitter Rolls out New Reply Controls to Combat Trolls' (*VentureBeat*, 11 August 2020) <https://venturebeat.com/2020/08/11/twitter-rolls-out-new-reply-controls-to-combat-trolls/> accessed 17 August 2020.

1987 Suzor (n 1223) 217–218.

1988 Babbs (n 1967).

plex and, unfortunately, lengthy process in which technical experts and other stakeholders from industry, technical bodies, the public sector, academia and civil society should engage. It normally takes several years before an initial standard emerges. However, once this onerous legwork is done, future updates and adaptions to changing technology and business realities can be done flexibly, while relying on established structures and resources.

For illustrative reasons, a non-exhaustive list of some important prospective design criteria shall be mentioned here. These rely on other research done in this area and on indicative case law where prospective or preventive duties have been endorsed by courts as part of reasonable due diligence measures. Some of these points have also been included in the example of a duty of care standard portrayed in the next section and described in more detail in ANNEX III.

- Anonymity management, user identification and verification measures (KYC)[1989]
  The effect of anonymity as a risk driver for unlawful behaviour has been described above in this section and in the sectoral analysis in Chapter 4. A platform would need to assess how much anonymous posting or uploading of content encourages the creation of harms. Some have suggested linking the degree of anonymity and user identification and/or verification by a platform to the kind of interactions the user is allowed to engage in.[1990] Minimum standards of identification or verification could be established in the duty of care standard, depending on the type and the severity of harms caused by anonymity and the fundamental rights affected. A scaled approach by type of harm appears to be also supported by case law. In *Delfi* the ECtHR underlined the importance of anonymity for freedom of expression in the context of user comments enabled on a news portal.[1991] In *Mc Fadden*,

1989 Ullrich, 'A Risk-Based Approach towards Infringement Prevention on the Internet' (n 747) 243–245. Niombo Lomba and Tatjana Evas, 'Digital Services Act - European Added Value Assessment' (European Parliament 2020) EPRS_STU(2020)654180_EN 283 <www.europarl.europa.eu/RegData/etudes/STUD/2020/654180/EPRS_STU(2020)654180_EN.pdf> accessed 23 October 2020. Suzor (n 1223) 217–218.

1990 Anna Vamialis, 'Online Defamation: Confronting Anonymity' (2013) 21 International Journal of Law and Information Technology 31, 56–62. Babbs (n 1967).

1991 *Delfi* (n 777) paras 147–149.

the CJEU ruled that password protection of a publicly accessible Wi-Fi network, which resulted in a disclosure of the identity of the user to the network operator, was a proportionate measure to prevent harms caused by copyright infringements.[1992] In the area of e-commerce, even more onerous KYC and identification processes may be adequate due to the potential harm of counterfeiting to a combination of consumer safety, economic interests and financial transactions. The latter may already require platforms to apply enhanced identity verification of sellers under EU anti-money laundering legislation where they offer payments services.[1993] Similar provisions exist in the area of food safety, which requires online sellers of food products to register their activity with national food safety authorities. Online intermediaries that facilitate the sale of food products by third parties could be obliged to verify this registration with sellers before allowing them to sell on their platforms.

Solid processes for user identification may create a trustful environment simply because of their deterrent effect to abusive users, but also because they enable a better administration of retrospective measures, such as sanction processes. In this context, *Zeno-Zencovich* argues that anonymity rules on the internet can and should be adapted to who communicates, what, where, with whom and how, and the competing interests at stake.[1994] Concerning the who, individuals, groups of individuals and business entities could be given differentiated anonymity options,[1995] or verification procedures. Regarding the 'with whom', the circle of addressees (public/defined groups/individual) could trigger different anonymity requirements, depending, for example, on the speech context, the frequency of engagement, or the interests and rights at stake.[1996] This typology could provide a useful base for risk controls that finetune anonymity with the aim of mitigating harms. This leads to the next point.

1992 *Mc Fadden* (n 139) para 96.

1993 Ullrich, 'A Risk-Based Approach towards Infringement Prevention on the Internet' (n 747) 239–240. Directive 2015/849 Articles 13 - 18.

1994 Vincenzo Zeno-Zencovich, 'Anonymous Speech on the Internet' in András Koltay (ed), *Media Freedom and Regulation in the New Media World* (Wolters Kluwer Kft 2014) 107.

1995 ibid 107–109.

1996 ibid 110–113.

- Providing benign user engagement options (in reply, sharing, creation, commenting or flagging content);
  As noted at various points in this work and by many other commentators, content moderation on digital platforms is steered by economic interest. This also determines the choice that users have in their interactions with each other and with content. More benign interaction opportunities would, however, limit or abolish those architectures or technical features that cause or amplify harm.[1997] The recent example of *Twitter* (see above), by which users are given more options in determining who can reply to their posts is one example that appears to follow the line of argument developed by *Zeno-Zencovich* above. Another solution could be to define and bolster the roles of independent, institutional trusted flaggers or community managers from civil society, regulators or other institutions. They could intervene preventively in certain harms, not only by flagging content but also by plugging their own software into platforms' APIs in order to identify, monitor and evaluate harmful content and behaviour.[1998] *Woods and Perrin* suggest that for certain contexts user interaction could be deliberately slowed down. This could be done to motivate users to engage more thoroughly with some contents before simply reposting them.[1999] It would eventually be the work of the standardisation process to evaluate and consolidate the ample research that is currently going on in this area and define some key mechanisms and tools as state of the art against the use of which platforms' duty of care would be measured.

- Allowing for computational reproducibility and independent assessment of content management and filtering algorithms[2000]
  Given the opacity and complexity of content moderation and the continuation of unlawful content, this transparency requirement is a crucial first step towards for creating the independent oversight needed to control harms.[2001] The duty of care and responsibility of platforms should therefore, at least during an initial phase, be measured by how

---

1997 Lavi (n 199) 26, who calls these feature 'evils nudges'.
1998 Gillespie, *Custodians of the Internet* (n 1010) 125–136.
1999 Woods and Perrin (n 799) 14–15.
2000 Mulligan and Bamberger (n 1777) 782.
2001 Gillespie, *Custodians of the Internet* (n 1010) 198–199; Gorwa, Binns and Katzenbach (n 1066) 10–11; Karen Yeung, 'Why Worry about Decision-Making by Machine?' in Karen Yeung and Martin Lodge, *Algorithmic regulation* (2019) 28.

transparent platforms are in providing the data behind harms. This could include obligations written down in the standard on: providing researchers and regulators access to databases and algorithms, e.g. through APIs and testing interfaces that allow for simulation or replication of content moderation processes;[2002] providing information on the data used to train algorithms; disclosing the parameters and methodologies that influence algorithms; detail about the human involvement in decision-making; an account and explanation of the updates made to content management and filtering algorithms.[2003] All these requirements could follow or draw on current and emerging open standards and mechanisms for the accountability of algorithmic and AI systems, that are more transparent than voluntary self-regulatory codes.[2004]

- Content management algorithms that incorporate considerations of harms and fundamental rights;
  Research on this issue has been gathering in breadth and depth.[2005] The principles that should underpin architectures and algorithms practices will likely need to follow broad ethics principles. The normative objectives of such impact assessments could be tied to principles set down in sectoral legislation. An example is provided in the sample duty of care standard in ANNEX III. Similar to requirements in the GDPR, platforms could be required to perform harms impact assessments of their systems for harms that pose high risks. Platforms would need to disclose these assessments to regulators and report on the use of the measures from the toolboxes described in the previous bullet points to address these harms. Multidisciplinary expert teams[2006] assembled by regulators, including for example engineers, psychologists, sociologists and lawyers would be required to review the risk control measures pro-

2002 Perel and Elkin-Koren (n 1918); Mulligan and Bamberger (n 1777) 253.

2003 Mulligan and Bamberger (n 1777) 781; Ioanna Miliou and Dino Pedreschi, 'Artificial Intelligence (AI): New Developments and Innovations Applied to e Commerce.' (European Parliament 2020) 13–14 <https://data.europa.eu/doi/10.2861/2605> accessed 27 October 2020.

2004 Yeung and Expert Committee on human rights dimensions of automated data processing and different forms of artificial intelligence (MSI-AUT) (n 293) 67–69. Brown and Kennedy (n 1883) 357–361.

2005 Yeung and Expert Committee on human rights dimensions of automated data processing and different forms of artificial intelligence (MSI-AUT) (n 293) 68–72. *Andrews* provides a useful typology of algorithmic harms that pose challenges for public policy. Andrews (n 1777) 210–211.

2006 Gillespie (n 1010) 198.

posed by platforms. All this assumes, that achieving and maintaining fair content management and platform systems is an ongoing process, whose intensity will depend on the measurable presence and impact of harms.

Transparency on the design and use of algorithmic content management and filtering systems, even where the latter are part of retrospective responsibility measures, are a distinct feature of a prospective responsibility. Transparency signals a commitment on the part of a platform to be scrutinised by stakeholders and to be open to improvements and adjustments when it comes to managing harms. It therefore promotes a wider culture of cooperative responsibility. However, transparency should not only apply to complex algorithmic and architectural decisions. More straightforward aspects, such as simple and easily accessible terms and conditions on e.g. prohibited content and behaviour, and the possible sanction mechanisms will also go a long way to creating a culture of trust and safety.

Some commentators have argued that in order for a substantial shift to happen, the underlying business rationale of today's digital platforms needs to be changed. *Gillespie* argues that, if the revenue basis were to move away from advertising (maximised through excessive user attention grabbing), complementary regulatory tools may be needed. Competition, data protection and consumer protection tools such as data portability, interoperability, transparency and a right to an explanation may steer the industry towards subscription based systems that value more long–term and equitable user interaction.

b. Risk control: retrospective responsibility to contain unlawful content

Although retrospective responsibility is more difficult to be attributed to actors that are not the originators of unlawful information and harm caused, the previous sections have shown that failure to take on prospective responsibilities also facilitates the occurrence of harm. Therefore, there is a link between prospective and retrospective responsibilities in deontological argumentation.[2007] In addition, there are clear consequentialist reasons,[2008] e.g. the cheapest cost avoider argument, that justify retrospective responsibility.

However, were prospective safety-by-design principles applied in a perfect way, there would be no need for retrospective risk management. That perfect situation is unlikely to happen. First, uncertainty is one characteristic of risk, and not all risks can always be adequately predicted and evaluated. The particular nature of technology, project and software management means that some risks may only appear during or after launch of a new business feature. Some risks may have been simply misjudged or the controls were not adequate.

Secondly, low or medium risks may become high risks, for example when regulation, technology or user habits change, or seemingly unrelated factors impact on online platform ecosystems.

Lastly, depending on the type of harm, prospective responsibilities may be more difficult to take on. In the area of copyright, it may be more difficult to steer responsible behaviour if a UGC platform is unable to gain authorisations from rightsowners. Other prospective risk control measures do not appear to be realistic given the complexity of limitations and exemptions in copyright. For example, user verification measures would do little in discouraging a user from uploading infringing content if they are not aware of the licenses the platform holds or if they are unaware of the intricacies of copyright. Therefore, the best efforts stipulated in Article 17 (4) of the DSMD focuses more extensively on retrospective measures of content filtering and NTD.

Retrospective measures in the context discussed here are aimed at limiting the impact of unlawful content or activity. Content monitoring and filtering, enhanced control measures for red flag events, NTD processes, as well as effective sanction policies and procedures would be the most common retrospective responsibility measures.

2007 Vedder (n 292) 73.
2008 ibid.

Retrospective risk control measures should focus on instances of high-risk content and behaviour where they occur on the platform. Apart from that, they would also serve to monitor and measure the efficacy of prospective tools. For example, high risks to consumer protection harms emanating from the launch of a category of new sellers or products on a marketplace could be addressed by advanced due diligence during seller onboarding and *ex ante* product verification requirements. However, the platform would still put in place retrospective measures of enhanced transaction and listings monitoring in order to measure the impact of the prospective measures and spot potential gaps in the process. Once the risk is classed as medium or low, it would still continue monitoring, albeit on a less intensive basis. This continuous monitoring of the risk environment through retrospective measures also helps to stay alert of any changes in the risk environment. This should also be included as a requirement in a duty of care standard. This kind of approach is also used in other areas. Under anti-money laundering legislation, financial institutions have to have prospective measures of due diligence in place for lower and high risk clients. At the same time, they also need to have systems in place to identify potentially unlawful behaviour, for example through monitoring for suspicious transactions and behaviour according to established criteria.[2009]

III. Example of a duty of care standard for economic harms

ANNEX III provides a possible approach and format of a risk-based duty of care standard. This standard was developed in 2019 together with *React*, a global anti-counterfeiting industry association, based in Amsterdam. A fact-finding exercise conducted by *React* as part of this project in autumn 2018[2010] revealed a wide variety of different policies, processes and capabilities of online marketplaces globally, but also within Europe, when it came to fighting and preventing counterfeit products. For example, within Europe the survey found that the reaction to notices varied significantly between marketplaces. While many operators responded within one to three

2009 Directive 2015/849 Articles 13 (1) (d), 15 (3), 18 (2).

2010 REACT had contacted 11 nationally operating European marketplaces (of which one in Russia), one regional operator based in South America, 22 Asian marketplaces, of which nine were operating internationally, and seven North American based marketplaces, of which five operated globally. This survey is not included in the duty of care standard document of ANNEX III.

days to notices, some could take up to one or two weeks to action these requests. A majority did not have any counterclaims processes in place nor did they state any service level agreements (SLAs) to notice filers. This disparate picture was mirrored on a global level. This is of relevance since a number of these operators, while not having any subsidiary in the EU, may still target EU consumers. The majority of European marketplaces contacted appeared to have no solid sanctioning or suspension processes in place against infringing sellers. Consequently, the re-appearance of previously notified and removed products and sellers remained an endemic problem on all but one platform contacted. This was also a problem in many of the marketplaces contacted outside of Europe, including large, global players. None of the marketplaces contacted by *React* in Europe had any transparency reports about their NTD activity, counterclaims or sanction processes in place. A minority engaged in more proactive communication and education of sellers regarding the compliance requirements with regards to IP rights on the platform. None of the platforms contacted in Europe confirmed the existence of voluntary proactive measures to identify and prevent counterfeits. In North America, only one player had such processes in place, while in Asia the large majority of platforms contacted had voluntary proactive measures in place. This may reflect the more hawkish stance of courts and legislation on intermediary liability in countries like China or India mentioned in Chapter 3. However, the actual detail of these proactive measures remains unclear. In Europe, four of the 11 marketplaces contacted had a dedicated IP program in place that allowed brand owners expedited access when it came to identifying and notifying trademark violations. In North America, the majority of platforms had such programs in place, while in Asia seven out of the 22 marketplaces contacted offered this service to brand owners.

Taking these disparate situations as a departing point, the project undertook to define standard processes and capabilities that e-commerce platforms should have in place in order to identify and address the highest risks of counterfeit and the sale of unsafe and illegal products. The aim of this exercise was to establish common, reasonable measures that can be expected from online marketplaces worldwide when it comes to acting responsibly towards the risk of counterfeit and non-compliant products. For one, this solution aims to establish a platform responsibility level that is higher, and according to this opinion, more adequate, than the current minimum requirements in EU (and US) legislation. Secondly, this unified approach would level expectations of all platform stakeholders and provide better predictability, transparency and accountability. Thirdly, the standard approach provides also for flexibility, as it is an adaptable system. In addition, the risk management process itself allows platforms to respond to risk drivers that are specific to their business model.

It should be noted that this exercise did not take any existing legislation in Europe or elsewhere as a limiting reference. It has been shown in Chapters 3 and 4 that the current liability exemptions framework in the EU (and elsewhere) limits the mandatory actions that platforms need to take to combat unlawful content and products to mere reactive duties and a tightly circumscribed set of proactive obligations. In reality, however, most platforms, even smaller ones, have today access to substantial data and can exert a certain degree of control over offers and advertisements on their systems. Data and fees generated from online transactions and advertisements generate the bulk of their revenue. In addition, platforms increasingly integrate a number of other remunerated services. They may offer payment transactions and related services, logistics, promotional or optimisation services.[2011]

Based on these considerations, the proposed duty of care standard in ANNEX III assembles the most common features of online marketplaces today and sketches out a risk management approach that platforms could reasonably be expected to apply when conducting their business. The system is centred on the recognition and management of two types of harms that may be facilitated by e-commerce marketplaces today: 1) economic harms related to the offer of products and advertisements that constitute trademark violations, and 2) harms to the public interest of consumer protection caused by the sale of unlawful (unsafe, non-compliant, illegal) products.

The standard incorporates principles of existing common risk management systems that are widely applied throughout the corporate world and that may already be familiar to platforms and their stakeholders: ISO 31000:2009 Risk Management, ISO 29100:2011 Information Technology – Security Techniques – Privacy Framework, ISO 20488:2018 Online consumer reviews. Following a risk management approach, the standard identifies common risk drivers related to three larger categories from which harms may be caused: sellers, product (categories) and the platform's business model (e.g. architectural design, service integration). The standard provides more detailed operational risk drivers relating to each category. A

2011 The proposal also draws on the professional experience of the author as a fraud detection, compliance and audit manager at a global online marketplace and retailer.

(future) standard could specify that, at a minimum, some or all of these drivers must be covered in a risk assessment exercise, or alternatively, leave this list as an entirely indicative and non-exhaustive guidance.

As part of the risk assessment, the drivers would need to be analysed and quantified. Online marketplaces would need to have capabilities and resources in place in order to conduct such a risk analysis. A number of these organisational and structural pre-requirements have been provided as part of the standard. It is clear that smaller players may not have the same capabilities as larger players. However, the proposal suggests that a minimal risk analysis based on internal data and awareness of the external risk environment should be imposed on all platforms. This ties into the argument that the actual knowledge standard is not any longer adequate as a liability standard for current online marketplaces, or any of the online platform business models covered here. The voluntary choice to engage in (Web 2.0.) platform business models requires a parallel build-up of knowledge and risk assessment methods to address potential harms. Actual knowledge of unlawful acts is a reactive concept that does not befit today's online platforms. It needs to be supplanted by an approach whereby the platform is required to become knowledgeable and aware of the risks of its business. An online marketplace needs to have tools and structures in place that help it deal with uncertainty, by establishing the potential impact of the harm caused by certain risk drivers and the likelihood of them occurring through its platform (the core of the risk assessment). These capabilities can also be relied on when establishing transparency and reporting obligations for these actors. Example of such internal tools would be the capability to capture and analyse notice and takedown data, the establishment and analysis of seller sanctions, or internal (documented) brainstorming and review processes when launching new platform features or services. This could tie in with the methodology of established ISO standards and industry practices. External capabilities would consist of the integration of brand owner or industry intelligence. Where an online marketplace qualifies as a trader, this could link in with the standards of professional diligence referred to in the UCPD.[2012]

The capabilities will be essential for measuring and rating the risks of the harms that emanate from the risk drivers. The risk rating procedure would need to be documented internally, with a potential obligation to conducting it in regular intervals or every time a significant change hap-

2012 Directive 2005/29/EC Article 5 (2) (a), Recital 20; European Commission, 'UCP Directive Guidance' (n 57) 123–132.

pens in one of the broader risk driver categories. Regulators could be given powers to consult these procedures on request. The platform would need to put measures in place to address identified high risks. The proposed standard lists a number of such measures. They correspond to both the prospective and retrospective duties discussed in this chapter. For example, high risks relating to certain product categories or seller profiles would necessitate enhanced onboarding or verification procedures prior to these products or sellers going live on the platform. Retrospective measure would include enhanced monitoring of transactions in specific, high risk product categories or for specific, high risk (gropus of) sellers. A non-exhaustive list of control measures for high risks is given in the standard in ANNEX III. The management of high risks necessitates enhanced analytical, organisational and structural capabilities on the side of the platform.

The standard also proposes procedural requirements for NTD on online marketplaces. The disparate nature of NTD processes was one of the problematic areas identified in the survey conducted by *React*. Unified standards will go a long way in establishing a level playing field across platforms and producing procedural transparency and predictability for the various platform stakeholders.

Finally, the standard suggests measures that aim to instil more transparency into the content management activities of online marketplaces. Some of these, like the requirements to provide clear terms and conditions and actions taken *vis-à-vis* stakeholders that violate platform policies, would feed into prospective responsibility measures. On the other hand, transparency reporting obligations, possibly separated into publicly accessible reports and into confidential reports for regulators or defined stakeholder groups, aim at helping to fill the accountability and transparency gaps that have been a central criticism against platforms. Secondly, these reporting requirements may also help platforms to identify the capacities needed to detect, measure and control high risks.

5. Transparency and accountability obligations

I. Transparency

The need for platforms to be more transparent about almost everything that negatively affects users has been repeated by many commentators and for many years.[2013] Transparency in the way information is managed on platforms would be essential in order to understand how and why, for example, unlawful content is spread and remains accessible. This does not require complex disclosure statements or technical reports, which may be protected by trade secrets of companies or are simply not intelligible for the average user.[2014] Alternative solutions are live visualisations and explanations of *why* certain content pieces are repeated or exposed. *Gillespie* argues that platforms could empower users and civil society associations to identify abusive and unlawful content, which would directly help other users to make decisions on whether they want to access this kind of content.[2015] A co-regulatory standard could list such prospective transparency systems that allow users to create safe and responsible online platform spaces.

Secondly, there should be minimum standards of transparency when it comes to automated content filtering systems.[2016] Again, the detail required may differ when looking at the target audience. But given the high degree of automation in content filtering and takedowns, more transparency goes a long way in addressing how platforms act responsibly and consider all stakeholders' interests and rights. As of today, some platforms have given a certain degree of insight into their moderation processes and decision criteria. But this varies by area. In the areas of hate speech and copyright some transparency reporting has been put in place by platforms. However, concerning terrorist speech, counterfeiting, defamation or unsafe products there are virtually no detailed reports available. In addition, details on the accuracy of removal decisions, appeals processes and detailed management of take down decisions remain widely inaccessible. In effect, these systems remain out-of-control systems, that are highly automated and opaque.[2017] This throws into the dark the risk management procedures that have been applied by these platforms. It is not clear, for example, whether automated systems favour commercial over legal criteria, which is an allegation made frequently and which goes against a responsible duty of

2013 Gillespie, *Custodians of the Internet* (n 1010) 198–199; Citron (n 914) 31; OECD, 'The Economic and Social Role of Internet Intermediaries - DSTI/ICCP(2009)9/FINAL' (n 46) 10–12, 88. Bamberger (n 37) 727–730.

2014 Yeung (n 2000) 28.

2015 Gillespie, *Custodians of the Internet* (n 1010) 199–200.

2016 Gorwa, Binns and Katzenbach (n 1066) 11.

2017 Christian Katzenbach and Lena Ulbricht, 'Algorithmic Governance' [2019] Internet Policy Review 10–11 <http://policyreview.info/node/1424> accessed 28 January 2020.

care approach.[2018] The current obligations of transparency reports in national legislation, such as in the German *NetzDG* are a good start but they do not go far enough. The main idea is that, far from just throwing data at the public that is sorted in a way that appears to give meaningful information, regulators need to come up with requirements that expose the risk assessments and control measures for each harm and that show how fundamental rights have been respected in this process. The way in which humans are being involved during automated content-decision-making, harmonised metrics on decision accuracy, the number of appeals and content reinstatements, should be publicly accessible. Meanwhile, regulators should have insight into the detailed design parameters that determine control measures. The regulator should still require platforms to report on a regular basis on the operation of their NTD systems. NTD systems are still a crucial retrospective responsibility measure for smaller platforms.[2019]

II. Accountability

Transparency on its own is of limited use. But it is a means to hold internet intermediaries accountable for the content management decisions they are taking on a daily basis and that *de facto* regulate our information access to the internet today. Since the 1980s, there has been an accelerating trend in software development of relying on empirical techniques to the detriment of theory and systemic reasoning. According to *Clarke and Wigan*, big data, machine learning and algorithmic decision-making represent the current pinnacle of systems that do not need to be logically justified any longer, in contrast to earlier principles of software development.[2020] Online platforms of today are the embodiment of such empiricism. This initially naïve and now fervent application of computing power has led to a lack of ethical responsibility for harm caused by decisions delegated to machines;[2021] it has by now become high-jacked by purely commercial motivations.

2018 Sylvain (n 795) 59; Pasquale (n 19) 496; Damian Tambini, 'Social Media Power and Election Legitimacy' in Damian Tambini and Martin Moore (eds), *Digital dominance: the power of Google, Amazon, Facebook, and Apple* (Oxford University Press 2018) 289.

2019 Urban, Karaganis and Schofield (n 661) 59.

2020 Clarke and Wigan (n 84) 693–694.

2021 ibid 694.

Transparency will help regulators and civil society to ask online platforms the right questions about the ethical parameters, focussed on harm, that have or have not gone into content management and platform design decisions. The focus on transparency would aim to reinstall procedural accountability.[2022] That procedural accountability will be structured through the duty of care risk management standard. That standard provides a guideline of how the ethical values – embodied by the harms and fundamental rights that need to be balanced – are being incorporated into platform design and content management. For example, the privacy-by-design standard pursued in the GDPR has been explicitly endorsed as an appropriate means to achieve accountability for compliance of operational procedures with data protection principles and values.[2023] The eventual measurement of the effectiveness of the duty of care standard would be part of a more outcomes-based accountability.[2024] This would be achieved through regular transparency reporting, independent stakeholder dialogues and reports and assessments by the regulator.

III. Complementary regulatory approaches towards online platforms

It has been argued by a wider circle of commentators that an online intermediary responsibility framework would be most effective if supplemented by more holistic regulatory initiatives in other contentious area of digital platform power.[2025] While the delimitations offered in the introduction have made clear that neighbouring substantive law areas that affect the digital platform economy cannot be treated here, a brief overview of these complementary measures shall still be given.

Some key regulatory advances have been made recently in neighbouring areas of intermediary responsibility. The GDPR gives data subjects new

2022 Bunting (n 66) 21–22.

2023 European Data Protection Supervisor, 'Opinion of the European Data Protection Supervisor' paras 101–117 <https://edps.europa.eu/data-protection/our-work/publications/opinions/comprehensive-approach-personal-data-protection_en> accessed 19 August 2020.

2024 Bunting (n 66) 22.

2025 Pasquale (n 19) 489; Edwards, 'With Great Power Comes Great Responsibility?: The Rise of Platform Liability' (n 661). Damian Tambini, 'Platform Dominance' in Damian Tambini and Martin Moore (eds), *Digital dominance: the power of Google, Amazon, Facebook, and Apple* (Oxford University Press 2018) 62–63.

and enhanced rights. It allows for data portability, the right to object to and obtain an explanation on fully automated decision-making procedures, including profiling, and to rectification and erasure of personal data.[2026] Meanwhile the privacy-by-design principle and the data protection impact assessments impose more procedural and architectural responsibilities on data controllers (and processors). Because user and content data (exemplified by 'big data') have moved to the heart of the business model of most online platforms today, the GDPR may be one tool to curtail the unchecked collection and processing of user data. It is still too early to tell what influence the GDPR will have on the activities of online platforms. Experts are, however, divided.[2027] Some estimate that the GDPR may well help break the monopolistic tendencies of digital platforms. A stronger move towards subscription-based business models may well help address the anonymity challenge and break some of the more vicious nudging practices.[2028] Others, however, are less optimistic and see that the GDPR does not provide adequate tools to address the reality of the current pervasive data gathering and processing practices on digital platforms. It may even be wishful thinking.[2029]

The 2019 Omnibus Directive strengthens the positions of consumers *vis-à-vis* online marketplaces by imposing stronger transparency requirements on the latter. It adds to the trend of defining platform business models and establishing specific responsibilities for these actors. The AVMSD and the DSMD have already introduced definitions for VSPs and OCSSPs. The Omnibus Directive does the same for online marketplaces.[2030] This definition, updated from previous EU Acts, clearly classifies these actors as traders under the UCPD and confers professional due diligence obliga-

2026 Regulation 2016/679 (GDPR) Articles 16 - 22.

2027 Shoshana Zuboff, '"We Make Them Dance": Surveillance Capitalism, the Rise of Instrumentarian Power, and the Threat to Human Rights' in Rikke Frank Jørgensen (ed), *Human Rights in the Age of Platforms* (The MIT Press 2019) 33–34 <https://direct.mit.edu/books/book/4531/Human-Rights-in-the-Age-of-Platforms> accessed 28 May 2020.

2028 Edwards, 'With Great Power Comes Great Responsibility?: The Rise of Platform Liability' (n 661) 289.

2029 Joris van Hoboken, 'The Privacy Disconnect' in Rikke Frank Jørgensen (ed), *Human Rights in the Age of Platforms* (The MIT Press 2019) <https://direct.mit.edu/books/book/4531/Human-Rights-in-the-Age-of-Platforms> accessed 28 May 2020; Tal Z Zarsky, 'Incompatible: The GDPR in the Age of Big Data.' (2017) 47 Seton Hall Law Review 995, 1003.

2030 Omnibus Directive 2019/2161 (n 1249) Article 3.

tions on them.[2031] Online marketplaces will need to disclose the parameters that influence search rankings to consumers and also call out any rankings that are influenced by advertisements.[2032] They also have to provide clear information regarding the legal status of third parties that are offering goods and services on their platform.

In a similar vein, the Platform to Business (P2B) regulation obliges platforms to disclose ranking parameters behind search results to business users, and disclose where and why differentiated treatment exists that may bias the display of search results.[2033] This regulation is in itself a valuable testimony to the fact that online search intermediaries do determine how content is displayed to users and that this is influenced by commercial priorities. This questions yet again the active/neutral dichotomy of the current liability regime. Any lessons drawn from the disclosure of ranking and differentiated treatment parameters may, arguably, be important when drawing up transparency obligations for other content management practices under a new online platform responsibility framework. Under both the P2B Regulation and the Omnibus Directive search intermediaries are, understandably, not required to disclose publicly the detailed functioning of their ranking mechanisms and the algorithms behind it.[2034] However, experience from the operation of these requirements may still help to gauge a possible requirement to disclose public interest and fundamental rights criteria of content management algorithms under a duty of care standard for online platforms.

6. The regulatory institution

Chapter 4 has demonstrated that the commonalities of the technological operations, legal challenges with content and responsibilities, and the convergence of content specific laws call for an overarching, principles-based

2031 Directive 2005/29/EC 29 Article 5.

2032 Omnibus Directive 2019/2161 (n 1249 Article 3. This follows initiatives taken at Member State level, such as in France – see: Élise Poillot, Natacha Sauphanor-Brouillaud and Hélène Aubry, 'Droit de la consommation' [2018] Recueil Dalloz 583.

2033 Platform-to-business (P2B) Regulation 2019/1150 (n 1248) Articles 5, 7; Omnibus Directive 2019/2161 (n 1249) Recital 23.

2034 Omnibus Directive 2019/2161 (n 1249) Recital 27.

approach. This is supported by various other commentators.[2035] Given the influence of online intermediary regulation on the internal market's free movement principles and its impact on fundamental rights it would appear appropriate to create regulatory powers that are, at a minimum, strongly coordinated at EU level by Member States and their competent regulatory authorities. The AVMSD has already allocated some responsibilities in this matter to the European Regulators Group for Audiovisual Media Services (ERGA), which exists since 2014. However, ERGA currently acts simply as an advisory body, representing Member States' national regulatory authorities for audiovisual media services. France had broadened the powers of the *CSA* for intermediary regulation in several areas. *Woods and Perrin*[2036] have argued for the UK that a horizontally focussed regulatory institution that takes on issues of platform responsibilities would be an adequate way forward. Since this work proposes a co-regulatory approach, it does support the view that a more enhanced degree of regulatory supervision than is currently the case is necessary. Given the need for managing society stakeholder dialogues, conducting additional research, overseeing the creation, supervision and auditing of compliance with and the effectiveness of a new technical standard for duty of care, a broad regulatory mandate will be needed. The new regulatory institution, whatever form it may take, will need to recruit technical and research expertise, policy capacities, as well as judicial competences. With the immense gaps in governance readiness that exist today in this area[2037] the new institution could become an important building block towards supporting and coordinating the construction of the necessary regulatory capacities in policymaking and in enforcement. Further intense policy dialogue and research would be needed to establish the status of such a new regulatory set-up.

One option could consist of a council or other body of national regulators and agencies that is supported by a scientific agency on the lines of the European Food Safety Authority (EFSA) or the EU Agency for Safety and Health at Work (EU-OSHA). The EU's current Observatory on the Online Platform Economy could, for example, be the nucleus for such an institution. Alternatively, a more centralised, broad and powerful regulatory authority on the lines of the European Banking Authority (EBA) could be an-

---

2035 Lipton (n 23) 155-157; Taddeo and Floridi (n 120) 1598; Burk (n 295) 452; Valcke, Graef and Clifford (n 1653) 710–711.

2036 Woods and Perrin (n 799) 55–57.

2037 Andrews (n 1777); Freeman (n 1777) 79–81. Cohen (n 19) 383–397.

other option. The creation of a strong regulator with more epistemic authority may, however, go against the demands of responsive and flexible regulation that maybe more appropriate in the area of platform responsibility.

Given the complex, multi-layered and vertical structures of content law regimes and the need for a strong horizontal framework of overarching principles and responsibilities, a looser structure could be more effective. The complex regulatory structures outlined in Chapter 4 reflect the distribution of competencies under the various legal and content areas between the EU and Member States. Any overly centralised solution is likely to bring to the fore the (substantial) overlap and conflict of competencies that exist when regulating platform responsibility relating to unlawful content. It would include aspects as diverse as media policy, product regulation, personality rights, property rights, public security and consumer protection. It is outside the frame of this work to engage in further analysis of the most appropriate regulatory setup to regulate platform responsibility. To give just one example, however, *Kerber and Wendel et al* have shown that in the area of telecoms regulation, the EU relies on a regulatory network that is held together by a central body (BEREC) with specific tasks and powers. Despite the retention of competencies by national telecoms regulators, BEREC initiated the vast majority of regulatory activity, such as issuing guidance notes, reports or setting standards.[2038] Because of its decision-making structure, its specialist working groups and its influence in conflict resolution, it has become a key governance instrument that impacts rule-making in this area.[2039]

Any solution would most likely be the result of intense political compromise between Member States and the European Commission. More detailed suggestions and possible avenues, that take on board the challenges of enforcing new responsibility provisions in the context of the diversity of content on platforms today, are being currently explored. All of these acknowledge the cross-border challenge of the issues and call for enhanced regulatory cooperation at EU level.[2040] This could provide a basis for further research.

2038 Kerber and Wendel (n 1810) 10–13.

2039 ibid 12.

2040 Cole, Etteldorf and Ullrich (2020) (n 17) 45–48, 258–261; 'ERGA Position Paper on the Digital Services Act' (European Regulators Group for Audiovisual Media Services (ERGA) 2020) <https://erga-online.eu/?page_id=14> accessed 5 November 2020.

7. Brief of evaluation of the Commission's DSA proposal of December 2020

As stated in the introduction, the completion of this work coincided with the European Commission's own, long awaited publication of its proposal to adapt the responsibilities of online intermediaries. A brief analysis that focusses on main common points and differences from the solution proposed here shall therefore be appropriate.[2041]

The Commission chose to treat the question of liability exemptions and that of additional responsibilities as separate issues. That structure, however, is implicitly self-imposed by the Commission's choice to transplant the current ECD intermediary liability exemptions regime almost unchanged into the new DSA. The retention of controversial concepts of neutrality, actual knowledge, expeditious removal and the addition of a "Good Samaritan" provision are unlikely to provide for more clarity for courts and legislators in the future, as the intermediary landscape evolves. This is despite the clarifications, derived from EU case law, that Recitals 18 and 22 of the DSA proposal are supposed to provide on the neutrality and the actual knowledge conditions. In addition, the DSA proposal, predictively, keeps the prohibition of general monitoring due to its significance for fundamental rights protection. However, whether Recital 28, which states that general monitoring does not mean monitoring obligations in specific cases, provides the clarification that was widely demanded on this issue, is doubtful.[2042] Meanwhile, the scope of the liability exemption has been narrowed by obliging intermediaries to comply with illegal content removal and information disclosure orders. While the unchanged insistence on the intermediary liability exemptions can be seen as somewhat surprising, given the persistent criticism of its design, the issue is relegated to second stage by the imposition of free-standing, due diligence obligations. These due diligence obligations would apply regardless over whether or not an intermediary qualifies for the exemption conditions outlined in Articles 3 – 9 of the proposal and regardless of whether and what kind of liabilities it would incur under national rules. The Commission decided against exclusive, free-standing positive obligations, as advocated in this work, due to

2041 For a more detailed analysis see: Cole, Etteldorf and Ullrich (2021) (n 548).
2042 ibid 139-140 (81–82).

doubts over a potential conflict with the proportionality and subsidiarity principles of such a solution.[2043]

The creation of harmonised positive due diligence obligations, on the other hand, are to be welcomed. Again, this is not the place for an in-depth analysis. The DSA proposes staggered obligations that increase with the degree of involvement of the intermediary in the intermediation processes and its potential to create harm.[2044] The due diligence obligations accumulate successively, starting from intermediaries at the lowest level (Articles 10 – 13), all hosting providers (Articles 14 – 15), online platforms (Articles 16 – 24) and, finally, very large online platforms (VLOPs) (Articles 25 – 33). Similar to the proposal put forward in this work, the DSA aims to set these obligations at a horizontal level and without prejudice, or as complimentary provisions, to existing or future sectoral provisions. The AVMSD, the proposed TERREG, the Regulation on the marketing and use of explosives precursors, the P2B Regulation, consumer protection, product safety rules and provisions on copyright would therefore all apply as *lex specialis*.[2045] Common transparency reporting obligations, the nomination of contact points or legal representatives for all intermediaries, as well as detailed notice and action (NTD) and counterclaims procedures for hosting providers are new obligations that do not come as a surprise. Notice and action, counterclaims and transparency reporting procedures can be seen as baseline requirements that have been widely demanded. Online platforms are subject to additional, largely procedural, obligations relating to complaints handling, dispute resolution, the use of trusted flaggers, repeat infringements and sanction processes, law enforcement cooperation and transparency reporting on automated content moderation and advertising display. This will doubtlessly help creating additional internal processes, structures and systems which force platforms to build and organise their awareness and knowledge of potential illegal content and activity, and incorporate this into the wider corporate epistemology which informs decision making. The additional requirements for marketplace operators to put KYC-style verification processes of traders in place (Article 22) has

2043 European Commission, 'Commission Staff Working Document - Impact Assessment - Annexes - Accompanying the Document Proposal for a Regulation of the European Parliament and the Council on a Single Market For Digital Services (Digital Services Act) and Amending Directive 2000/31/EC - Part 2' (2020) 161–162 <https://ec.europa.eu/digital-single-market/en/digital-services-act-package> accessed 8 January 2021.

2044 Cole, Etteldorf and Ullrich (2021) (n 548) 186–200.

2045 European Commission DSA proposal (n 10) Article 1 (5), Recitals 9 - 11.

been positively commented on in Chapter 4's sections on trademarks and product and food safety. This ties in with existing due diligence obligations that already exist in the area of consumer law and anti-money laundering compliance. For online marketplaces, this bolsters the general due diligence obligations that are imposed on all online platforms against the misuse of their services (Article 20). However, given that content management processes of other online platforms, such as social media networks or UGC platforms are also capable of posing significant harms, such enhanced verification measures may also be appropriate for these types of platforms, for example when addressing the risks related to user anonymity.[2046]

It is also positive that the DSA takes up the idea of risk management due diligence obligations, data access and compliance scrutiny rights by external, academic researchers, and additional transparency and consumer empowerment options relating to recommender systems, advertising and reporting.[2047] However, requiring these measures only from VLOPs may be a missed opportunity, in particular where it concerns the risk management obligations. For one, it has been shown that the identification of systemic or high risks to public interest and fundamental rights should be a practice embedded into the business planning of every corporate actor. These are basic features of socially responsible and sustainable business management. Secondly, it has been shown that systemic risks may also arise from platforms that are not "very large." Content dissemination happens at a fast and almost uncontrollable speed, making smaller online platforms also prone to causing harms and damages to public interests. This has, for example, been an observation in the area of terrorist content online.[2048] The new audit obligations (Article 28) in conjunction with the risk management obligations and the requirements to appoint compliance officers will likely lead to the emergence of a future GRC system for VLOPs. Large international audit and compliance service providers can be expected to jump on the opportunity to incorporate these kind of systems into their existing service offers. However, the risks of removed technical compliance systems, whereby the private sector audits the private sector, have been outlined above. This should not absolve the regulator from building their own capacities to perform technical and systemic oversight and enforce-

2046 Cole, Etteldorf and Ullrich (2021) (n 548) 182–183.

2047 European Commission DSA proposal (n 10) Articles 25 - 33.

2048 OECD, 'Current Approaches to Terrorist and Violent Extremist Content among the Global Top 50 Online Content-Sharing Services' (n 1090) 6–7.

ment functions. The solutions proposed by the DSA in Articles 28 should therefore be only be a first, transitory step that helps regulators in the acquisition of their own technical auditing skills and capacities.[2049]

Finally, the DSA proposal continues to rely on self-regulatory codes of conduct and best practice sharing as a means of implementing the provisions of the DSA (Articles 34 to 37). However, as has been shown throughout this work, the success of these kind of arrangements has been questionable, at least. If this approach is to be maintained, it would have to be accompanied by more solid regulatory coercive powers, with the option to move towards co-regulatory structures. The use of (technical) standards, as largely advocated for in this work, is limited to more technical areas in the DSA proposal, i.e. to notice-and-action, audits and external information access and exchange requirements. However, little stands in the way of basing complaints handling, sanctions and abuse prevention systems, trader traceability requirements, recommender system due diligence or general systemic risk assessment and control on (harmonised) technical standards. In addition, the multitude of sectoral, national regulators that are likely to be involved in the horizontal supervision of the due diligence obligations spelled out in the proposal, calls for more incisive powers than promotion of best practice sharing and codes of conduct.

2049 Cole, Etteldorf and Ullrich (2021) (n 548) 199.

Chapter 7 - Conclusion

As this work was written the COVID-19 pandemic crisis hit the world. The consequences of this global emergency, which cost the lives of many people, deprived millions across the world of their livelihoods and ruined many businesses, will be felt over years to come. One immediate effect was that it demonstrated the dependence of our societies on the internet and its intermediaries. More than that, the crisis further increased this dependence as companies replaced business trips and conferences with online meetings, as schools and universities moved their teaching online, as people resorted to online shopping and online social gatherings instead of visiting each other, or going to restaurants, concerts or cinemas. In the face of the world's crisis, "big tech" reaped in record revenues and bolstered its corporate power further. The market capitalisation of the *GAFAM* jumped by over 53% between June 2019 and July 2020 reaching USD6.4 trillion. This was massively boosted by society's turn to the internet and the services of online intermediaries.[2050]

Without these services, to be sure, the disastrous impact of the pandemic would have been even greater, on a medical, social and economic scale. The internet has been essential for many people and their families, businesses and public services in a time of isolation and disruption.

Yet, the increasing reliance of people on online intermediaries like social media and online marketplaces has reinforced the serious challenges of unlawful content online. Dis- and misinformation, hate speech, extremist propaganda and counterfeit products have surged on the internet to unseen levels.[2051] They have reinforced general concerns about the stability of

---

2050 Richard Waters, Hannah Murphy and Patrick McGee, 'Big Tech Defies Global Economic Fallout with Blockbuster Earnings' (31 July 2020); 'Big 5 US Tech Giants Hit $6.4 Trillion in Market Cap, a 53% Jump in a Year – 24/7 Wall St.' <https://247wallst.com/technology-3/2020/07/21/big-5-us-tech-giants-hit-6-4-trillion-in-market-cap-a-53-jump-in-a-year/> accessed 20 August 2020; Peter Eavis and Steve Lohr, 'Big Tech's Domination of Business Reaches New Heights' *The New York Times* (19 August 2020)

2051 Hannah Murphy, Dave Lee and Siddharth Venkataramakrishnan, 'Facebook Groups Trading Fake Amazon Reviews Remain Rampant' *FT.com* (12 August 2020); Sylvain Rolland, 'Coronavirus : Internet infesté par les arnaques et les fake news' *La Tribune* (20 February 2020)<https://www.latribune.fr/technos-m

democratic societies.[2052] Traditional media, like newspapers and public television, which are bound to standards of fact-based research and integrity, have been displaced as news sources. The new information sources, however, do not subscribe to the same standards. They derive money from people uploading, reading, watching, sharing and commenting. The more users interact, the more money is gained through advertisements. The problem is that news distribution models which prioritise content that receives the most attention do not do well when it comes to promoting quality and unbiased information, which is essential in times of crisis.[2053] It does well, however, for the profit revenues of social media giants and other online platforms. The additional efforts of *Facebook, Twitter, Amazon, Google* and others to counter the tide of harmful and unlawful content were a start, but not more than that. They have not led to a significant change in the availability of unlawful content.[2054]

At the same time, the debate on the role and responsibilities of online intermediaries also shows a public change of mind. The neutral and merely technical nature of the early internet intermediaries of the 1990s and the Web 1.0 is largely seen as a thing of the past. Chapter 2 demonstrated that today internet intermediaries are not just essential for facilitating our access to the internet and information. They have also become the world's

---

edias/internet/coronavirus-internet-infeste-par-les-arnaques-et-les-fake-news-840839.html> accessed 20 August 2020; Deutscher Ärzteverlag GmbH Ärzteblatt Redaktion Deutsches, 'Onlinespiele und soziale Medien: Corona verstärkt die Sucht' [2020] *Deutsches Ärzteblatt* <https://www.aerzteblatt.de/archiv/214932/Onlinespiele-und-soziale-Medien-Corona-verstaerkt-die-Sucht> accessed 20 August 2020. Zoe Thomas, 'Misinformation on Coronavirus Causing "Infodemic"' *BBC News* (13 February 2020) <https://www.bbc.com/news/technology-51497800> accessed 20 August 2020.

2052 Jennifer Cobbe and Elettra Bietti, 'Rethinking Digital Platforms for the Post-COVID-19 Era' (*Centre for International Governance Innovation*, 12 May 2020) <https://www.cigionline.org/articles/rethinking-digital-platforms-post-covid-19-era> accessed 20 August 2020.

2053 Ben Scott and Taylor Owen, 'Governing Platforms after COVID-19' (*Centre for International Governance Innovation*, 18 August 2020) <https://www.cigionline.org/articles/governing-platforms-after-covid-19> accessed 20 August 2020.

2054 Dave Lee and Hannah Murphy, 'Facebook Fails to Curb Spread of Medical Misinformation, Report Finds' *FT.com* (19 August 2020). Hannah Murphy, Judith Evans and Alistair Gray, 'Facebook Accused of Failing to Deliver on Advertisers' Boycott Demands' *FT.com* (2 August 2020). Laura Urquizu, 'Counterfeiting Is a Bn-Dollar Problem. COVID-19 Has Made It Far Worse' (*Fast Company*, 4 May 2020) <https://www.fastcompany.com/90500123/counterfeiting-is-a-bn-dollar-problem-covid-19-has-made-it-far-worse> accessed 20 August 2020.

most powerful corporate actors. This happened on the back of a digital transformation instigated by Web 2.0 and its new interactivity. Online intermediaries evolved from technical facilities that hosted and enabled access to information of third parties to true information management systems. Third party information and the traffic resulting from it is a treasure trough of valuable marketing data. This means that platforms, far from being neutral, actively manipulate user interaction and take decisions on what content is seen by whom, and in which order. Even more so, they now own significant parts of the internet's infrastructure, making them systemically relevant for many essential services.[2055]

Chapter 3 outlined the challenges of adapting the law to these sweeping changes, which have caused a surge in unlawful content and harms that users are exposed to on a daily basis. Law, however, is known to be lagging behind. Considering the lightning changes that the internet has introduced, this is a major concern. The EU regulatory framework that regulates the liability exemption conditions of today's online platforms is based on assumptions that started to change already 15 years ago. At the time, the utilitarian policy view was that the budding internet sector needed to be protected against looming liabilities.

This work suggests that the three key challenges that courts and policymakers have grappled with, and which were analysed in Chapter 3, need to be resolved through a new responsibility framework. First, the neutrality condition that guarantees wide ranging exemptions from liability for the content hosted, sounds like an outlandish concept judged by today's realities. It is remarkable that companies like *Facebook* are to this day still seen as neutral, passive and mere technical facility providers by both national courts and the CJEU.[2056] National courts are, however, increasingly seeing online platforms as active parties. They even allocate primary or enhanced liabilities to these actors. Overall, however, the ECD liability exemption condition of neutrality is still interpreted in different ways across the EU.

Secondly, the definition of actual knowledge of unlawful activity or content has been problematic from the outset. For a start, NTD processes are not harmonised by the ECD. Yet, since actual knowledge for neutral hosts is tied to receiving a notification, courts have often had to go back and de-

2055 Stephan Bohn, Nicolas Friederici and Ali Aslan Gümüsay, 'Too Big to Fail Us? Platforms as Systemically Relevant' (*Internet Policy Review*, 11 August 2020) <https://policyreview.info/articles/news/too-big-fail-us-platforms-systemically-relevant/1489> accessed 20 August 2020.

2056 *Eva Glawischnig-Piesczek v Facebook Ireland Limited, C-18/18* (n 463) para 22.

fine when a notice, where it was not regulated by national law, would confer that knowledge. More importantly, the CJEU broke ground by defining the diligent economic operator duties for online intermediaries. This exploded the narrow concept of actual knowledge. Again, however, national courts indulged in varying interpretations even after *L'Oréal v eBay*. This is due to a variety of factors: different approaches to the question of neutrality, varying interpretations of due care, different intermediary business models, the concrete circumstances of the case at hand and courts' varying technical understanding and willingness to go deeper. It is also heavily determined by national secondary liability approaches. The actual knowledge standard concept, it is suggested, should be merged into a wider corporate responsibility standard in which a diligent economy operator would be assumed to know about certain activities that take place within its infosphere.[2057] Again, today's intermediaries are almost omniscient and highly sophisticated content governors. Exploiting and analysing data is at the very heart of their business model. It should also be at the heart of their efforts to prevent unlawful behaviour.

The third controversy concerns the scope of obligatory proactive infringement prevention efforts. This is intimately related to the above two issues. Again, the ECD is ambiguous here, because it gives courts and authorities the possibility to prevent specific infringements while forbidding the imposition of general monitoring. The concept of general monitoring, however, is not clearly defined. As content monitoring and filtering techniques have been making continuous progress, while details about their true use by major platforms remain unclear, this is a moving target for courts. It took courts considerable time to acknowledge more generally that stay-down orders did not result in general monitoring obligations where identical information is concerned. When it comes to similar kinds of content courts made varying assessments. The latest ruling by the CJEU on this matter seems to suggest that the decision could depend on the type of violation, with IP infringements being less likely to justify an expansion of proactive monitoring duties to similar violations. The semantic complexity of hate speech or defamation, by contrast, may justify a broader interpretation of proactive duties towards similar content, as long it does not involve human reassessment.[2058] The impact of broad monitoring duties for intermediaries on fundamental rights, such as freedom of speech, priva-

2057 Floridi (n 801).

2058 *Opinion of Advocate General Szpunar on Eva Glawischnig-Piesczek v Facebook Ireland Limited, C-18/18* (n 264) paras 68–69.

cy and the freedom to conduct a business is undisputed. This analysis suggests, however, that Article 15 ECD is an inappropriate tool in today's fast moving and diverse internet that will continue to cause more conflicting interpretations. Even more, the quest over finding the dividing line between general and specific monitoring duties has impeded the more important task of defining proportional and effective obligations for online intermediaries in the fight against unlawful content. Any decision over the proportionality of preventive measures, such as risk-based content filtering and monitoring, should be made on a more differentiated, sectoral basis. Different violations trigger different fundamental rights and call for specific balancing exercises. This could be done through a duty of care standard which allows for different scopes of responsibilities depending on the harm, or nature of violation.

Another realisation from Chapter 3 is that the patchwork of different liability assessments and outcomes is closely related to different national secondary liability approaches. If a future intermediary responsibility framework wants to drive legal predictability and uniform approaches in the EU digital single market, it would need to go down the politically thorny road of finding a solution that bypasses the application of national laws on intermediaries. The complexity of this issue becomes even more apparent in the sectoral analysis of Chapter 4.

This analysis has demonstrated the intricate differences that exist in the regulatory environment for unlawful content and the enforcement options available against intermediaries. In fact, the vertically layered, multi-level regulatory structure of the EU is enriched by sector specific rules with different vertical layering structures. In addition, many courts have been applying laws in a diagonal fashion,[2059] by borrowing from other content areas' intermediary concepts. Several atomising trends have been identified. First, the unharmonised nature of substantive law provisions, such as defamation, hate speech or the exceptions and limitations of copyright have made a unified application of the ECD almost impossible. The 1881 French Press Law or the 2013 UK Defamation Act are two examples where national laws impose specific intermediary rules. This ultimately affects the way online platforms' content management practices and duties are being seen on a normative level. For example, the difference in substantive law affects whether infringing content is seen as manifestly illegal, which, in

2059 Sophie Stalla-Bourdillon, 'Uniformity v. Diversity of Internet Intermediaries' Liability Regime: Where Does the ECJ Stand?' (2011) 6 Journal of International Commercial Law and Technology 51, 52, 57.

turn, plays into the assessment of the liability exemption conditions. This would need to be solved through further harmonisation at EU level, which in the case of defamation law appears improbable. It was attempted, for example, in the area of copyright through the recent DSMD. More harmonised areas, such as trademark law, product and food safety regulation and, to some extent, terrorist content and hate speech, promise to be more adapted to an EU wide intermediary responsibility framework.

Secondly, the limited and more general arsenal of secondary liability exemptions offered through EU law[2060] is eclipsed by a rich repertoire at Member State level. The ECD framework is superimposed on an elaborate national secondary liability landscape that exists in ordinary national law as well as in sectoral law. Next to the intrinsic problems and ambiguities of the ECD, this is probably the second most important factor for the disparate interpretation and application of the intermediary liability exemptions framework across the EU. As of today, legislators and courts use the ECD as an additional option to existing national intermediary provisions, in conjunction with them[2061] or by replacing them almost exclusively with local secondary liability approaches.

Third, regarding enforcement regimes, there are significant differences in the options available against intermediaries. In the public law dominated areas of terrorist content and product regulation, there is a marked engagement of law enforcement and surveillance authorities with intermediaries. In private law areas, concerning personality or economic rights, enforcement happens mainly through courts. Although this work did not address the sanctions regimes tied to intermediary obligations, it is suggested here that a specific framework that punishes non-compliance with a duty of care standards should be imposed by a new Digital Services Act, similar to the GDPR.[2062]

Lastly, the minimum harmonisation approach of the ECD also means that some Member States have developed their own NTD procedures, through law or self-regulatory arrangements, while others have not regulated this at all. This in turn has had an influence on the definition of the knowledge standard in the jurisdiction and in the content area concerned, as well as procedural obligations. A new duty of care standard would need to harmonise NTD procedures.

2060 Leistner (n 336) 78–89.

2061 Oster (n 816); Benabou (n 334).

2062 Regulation 2016/679 (GDPR) Articles 83 & 84, Recital 129.

Lawmakers at both EU and national level have reacted differently to these challenges. Many policy makers started off with self–regulatory initiatives that are explicitly supported through the ECD. With traction from online platforms lacking, some have followed this up with more interventionist policy action. The regulatory choices of these initiatives differ. In the area of copyright, the DSMD has now removed OCSSPs from the scope of the ECD. The new obligations of OCSSPs are to be put in place through self-regulatory arrangements between intermediaries and the rightsholder industry. The AVMSD uses a tentatively co-regulatory model in the fight against hate speech and content harmful for minors on VSPs. The proposed TERREG anti-terrorism online regulation ventures further into a more traditional rule-making approach. Amongst the national initiatives, the *NetzDG* favours a more self-regulatory approach, while the now largely defunct *Loi Avia* deployed co-regulatory measures.

Chapter 4 has shown that intermediary liability provisions and their enforcement appear to disintegrate into specific sectoral and even national practices. This work, however, warns against giving in to this seemingly more flexible and pragmatic approach. Abandoning horizontal principles of online intermediary responsibility risks ignoring essential commonalties that relate to the practices of today's online platforms. First, the pressure to allocate enhanced responsibilities to intermediaries is a common feature across all sectors analysed here. They all call for moral responsibilities that are commensurate with the intrusive and encompassing business models and their deep involvement and integration into the act of information intermediation. In some areas, such as copyright or trademarks, this has pushed legislators and courts even to allocating primary liability, thus breaking a regulatory paradigm. Whether this is justified or not, the analysis here supports the view that the distinction between neutral and active intermediaries is outdated and should be abandoned across all content sectors. Secondly, many of the large integrated platforms operate across different content areas and potentially give rise to several harms: platforms like *Facebook, YouTube* or *Twitter* may facilitate economic, personality, consumer protection and public security related harms. Common horizontal responsibility norms would make therefore for more legal certainty for both users and platform operators themselves. Third, online platforms work according to similar underlying business models and architectural design decisions. They are focussed on exploiting user data, or behavioural surpluses. Fourthly, at least the large, dominating platforms have expanded their automated content management practices to create systems that detect and remove unlawful content. They enforce mainly along their own private content policies, which are driven by commercial concerns, with a secondary regard for the applicable laws. However, these policies remain largely hidden to those stakeholders most concerned by their application. These private content management practices have a significant impact on fundamental rights. The ubiquity and power of online platforms on the internet means that these private norms have become quasi law and the intermediaries akin to parallel states. They override the public interest criteria formulated and enforced by democratically elected governments. This tendency was observed in each of the content sectors analysed.

Chapter 5 showcased the problems authorities face when confronted with unlawful and unsafe products and food sold via online marketplaces. The case studies are exemplary for the capability gaps of enforcers and courts when confronted with the role of new actors that are regulated through a different regime. Regulators are either not familiar with or do not have the competencies to make use of the possibilities offered by the ECD. When, in addition, that regime provides generous liability exemptions to actors that play an essential role in the wide availability of regulated products, it has left MSAs at a loss to address the surge of non-compliant products on the internet. The main obstacles for an effective enforcement are formidable. The sheer amount and speed of unlawful products appearing (disappearing and re-appearing) on marketplaces across various jurisdictions has overwhelmed a system that is highly fragmented, relies on more complex and slower risk assessments and is weakened by budget constraints. Cooperation with online intermediaries appears to improve slowly, albeit from a low basis. It is, however, non-committal and piecemeal. The second problem is that enforcement authorities, although technical experts in their own field, are naturally not aware of the business models and technical functionalities of online platforms. They may therefore misjudge the real impact and influence that integrated online marketplaces have on the distribution of products.

However, the areas of product and food safety also pose unique chances and learnings for a new online intermediary responsibility framework. MSAs in the areas surveyed have knowledge about the legality and illegality of content. These kinds of enforcers do not exist in the area of IP rights or speech. The co-regulatory framework of the *New Approach*, harmonised technical standards and food safety certifications, provide structures that could be conducive to regulating intermediary responsibility.

Chapter 6 has explored the creation of such a *New Approach* style regulatory framework of online platform responsibility. Dissatisfaction with the current regime has generated an increasing number of proposals for a new regulatory system. All of these envisage greater responsibilities of intermediaries for the content they host and exploit. The majority converge on the idea that the distinction between passive and active intermediaries should be a thing of the past. More than that, most agree that today's Web 2.0. platforms steer and manipulate user behaviour. Combined with emerging gatekeeping power to information and the autonomous sway over content management they exercise quasi-public functions. Many proposals advocate for a move from liabilities to responsibilities on the lines of CSR, duty of care and risk management. As much as they agree on these common points, they differ in scope and the regulatory choice. More systemic, horizontal proposals appear to favour public involvement, while sectoral and procedural approaches rely more on self-regulation.

This work proposes a co-regulatory approach that applies a horizontal, principles-based framework that imposes duty of care style responsibility tied to statutory harms. Such a system, it was argued, could exploit synergies between already existing sectoral approaches. It would also facilitate an easier interlinkage with other legal domains that have become crucial when addressing critical issues of online platform dominance, such as competition law, data protection or consumer law.[2063]

Self-regulation, although a 'natural' approach of internet governance may not be appropriate any longer, given the seriousness of the harms caused by unlawful content, the autonomous and elusive content management practices of large online platforms and their gatekeeping powers. Past self-regulatory attempts, it was shown, have also lacked traction and efficacy. Through co-regulation, the state would get a chance to reclaim authority in an area that is essential for the long-term stability of democratic societies and social justice. Imposing responsibilities on private actors to prevent harms that effect public interests and fundamental rights is also in line with wider trends of corporate social responsibility and risk-based management. Most online platforms are now big and sophisticated enough to manage such obligations. It would bring intermediary regulation into line with the way states have been trying to respond to the constant challenge of our modern societies.

Risk regulation, CSR or standardisation are all means, it was shown, to deal with the socio-economic changes brought about by information technology and globalisation. The above chapters have demonstrated the de-

---

2063 Tambini and Moore (n 232) 399–406; Valcke, Graef and Clifford (n 1653) 710–711.

gree to which the state has lost epistemic authority in this area[2064] and needs to rely on private expert networks.[2065] In the area of online platform regulation, expert knowledge and technical expertise is, however, dominated and influenced by online intermediaries. A co-regulatory system, such as proposed here, would keep oversight over public interest principles and fundamental rights under state authority. Such principles and the related harms would be established through a framework regulation that replaces the ECD. That new Act could reference the sectoral EU rules that address the defined harms. The use of technical standards for duty of care for each harm would capture the much-needed expertise of industry stakeholders, such as intermediaries, technology service providers, researchers and civil society stakeholders. This system allows for flexibility, both by allowing for the formulation of harm specific due diligence obligations and by being adaptable to technical developments. The technical (duty of care) standards could be referenced in the sectoral rules that are mentioned in the new framework ECD, such as for example the DSMD, the AVMSD, the MSR or a new TERREG.

Like with any regulatory system there are also risks. Standardisation and risk regulation, if set up without due care and clearly defined procedural safeguards, may be subject to regulatory capture. Regulators are in dire need to improve their governance readiness because they will need to assess and audit compliance with technical standards that impose fairness obligations on content algorithms, technical design principles and business models of online platforms. In the EU, technical standardisation faces some particular problems related to democratic legitimacy and accessibility.

However, this appears to be manageable compared to the profound challenges the EU and many other countries around the world face opposite the societal harms caused by the content intermediation practices of powerful internet platforms. It is time to put in place enhanced responsibilities that are in line with the power and influence these commercial intermediaries exert over expression, information and markets.

2064 Schepel (n 34) 25.
2065 Haas (n 38) 4–7. Chowdhury and Wessel (n 1845) 337.

ANNEX I – Interview Questionnaire (Model)

uni.lu UNIVERSITY OF LUXEMBOURG

RUL | RESEARCH UNIT IN LAW

FACULTY OF LAW, ECONOMICS AND FINANCE

SURVEY SHEET

INTERVIEWS WITH EU MARKET SURVEILLANCE AUTHORITIES

PHD THESIS ON THE EU LEGAL FRAMEWORK FOR ONLINE INTERMEDIARY LIABILITY

CARSTEN ULLRICH

V.9

UNIVERSITY OF LUXEMBOURG

Faculty of Law, Economics and Finance

INTRODUCTION - context

This interview is part of a doctoral thesis in Law conducted at the University of Luxembourg, Faculty of Law, Economics and Finance. This doctoral research project is part of a wider multidisciplinary doctoral research programme at the University of Luxembourg, which focuses on the way enforcement in multi-level regulatory systems functions.

The research context is the current EU regulatory environment of online intermediaries (ISPs), with a focus on liability for unlawful content or activity, as per the Ecommerce Directive 2000/31 ("ECD"), Articles 12 - 15.

The following commonly voiced critical statements of the current ISP liability framework will be explored:

1) The division between "active" and "passive" hosts is increasingly blurred by new types of ISPs and technological advances (e.g. social media, collaborative platforms, the use of big data and content management and recognition technologies). It will be explored whether this is adequate and if yes how this affects the concept of ISPs "actual knowledge" of unlawful content or activity.
2) The growth and sophistication of ISPs may call for a review of the current liability exemptions for internet intermediaries. The dissertation will explore whether more far-reaching proactive duties of care with regards to infringement prevention are justified.
3) Current legislative proposals focus on complementing the ECD with sector specific rules (e.g. copyright or hate speech) and they promote largely self-regulatory solutions. The thesis will critically explore the suitability of self and co-regulatory solutions for a reformed content liability framework by drawing on experience from internet market surveillance in specific areas of product regulation.

What does this survey want to achieve?

As part of this PhD research, a number of product sectors and market authorities have been identified who are engaging in more proactive internet surveillance of unlawful products. These activities have so far been little discussed academically in the context of the above ISP liability framework.

This survey aims to analyse the surveillance and enforcement activities of selected market authorities (MSAs) in the EU in the areas of non-food consumer products and food products sold online. The objective is to understand how MSAs detect and prevent unlawful content on platforms, how and if they work together with ISPs and which national and EU legal basis they use for their activities. In addition, the survey tries to establish the level of regulatory cooperation which exists between national surveillance authorities at different levels (national, local, EU, international) and whether that cooperation has led to more formalised policy or regulatory initiatives.

The results of these survey will help to establish whether these activities bear characteristics of co-regulatory mechanisms, by which state actors are and economic operators (in this case ISPs) define practices, (technical) standards and policies of infringement prevention and enforcement. The results of the survey will help to establish whether more proactive duties of care for removing and preventing unlawful content/products can be imposed on ISPs.

Nature of the surveys

The survey will be conducted as qualitative, structured interviews by conducting meetings with policy officers at selected market surveillance authorities in Europe. The length of the meetings varies depending on the breadth of product areas covered. However, they are envisaged to last 2 - 3 hours with possible follow-up questions by telephone or email as needed. Although the style of the interview style will be conversational, the same survey questions will be asked to all interviewees to ensure comparability of results.

The results of this survey and the discussion will be used for the academic research purposes indicated above only. If you have any questions or concerns please contact carsten.ullrich@uni.lu directly.

A. Market surveillance and enforcement

A.1.	When was your authority founded?

Please state first year of operation

A.2.	In which product area(s) does your authority conduct market surveillance of unlawful products or sellers on the internet.

Please name all:

A.3.	Which national, EU or other laws specific to your product sector are the basis for your surveillance and/or enforcement activity.

Please name the national laws and where applicable corresponding EU legislation. For example, in the area of food several EU Regulations or Directives may apply according to which market surveillance authorities monitor for compliance (such as for example the Regulation on food labelling[2066] *or the Food controls Regulation Organic Food Regulation*[2067]*)*

A.4.	Have you enforced based on any of the above-mentioned legal provisions against information service providers (online platforms)?

1. ☐ Yes
2. ☐ No

If you have answered yes, please state, which laws mentioned in the previous question:
If you have answered no, have you enforced against ISPs on the basis of other legal provisions? If yes, which?

A.5.	Which kind of online intermediaries do you surveil typically?

2066 *Regulation (EU) No 1169/2011 of the European Parliament and of the Council of 25 October 2011 on the provision of food information to consumers 2011*

2067 *Regulation (EU) 2017/625 of the European Parliament and of the Council of 15 March 2017 on official controls and other official activities performed to ensure the application of food and feed law, rules on animal health and welfare, plant health and plant protection products,*

Please rank the below ISPs according to the most frequently surveilled (most frequent = 1, second most frequent = 2, etc.).

ISP Category	Rank
E-Commerce Platform (e.g. eBay, Amazon)	
Social Network (e.g. Facebook, Twitter)	
User generated content platforms (e.g. YouTube, SoundCloud, Flickr)	
Over The Top Communication Services (e.g. WhatsApp, Skype)	
Search engines (e.g. Google, Bing)	
Meta search engine/aggregators (price comparison sites), (e.g. Booking.com, Shopzilla,)	
Others, please specify	

A.6.	What are the main surveillance and enforcement methods used by you.

Multiple choice possible.

1. ☐ Issuing takedown notices
2. ☐ Conducting test purchases
3. ☐ Searching the website for unlawful products/content manually
4. ☐ Searching the website for non-compliant sellers manually
5. ☐ Searching the website for unlawful products/content with software
6. ☐ Searching the website for non-compliant sellers with software
7. ☐ Product/content Information requests
8. ☐ Information requests about sellers
9. ☐ Other, please specify:

A.7.	If you use software please state whether it is:

Multiple choice possible.

1. ☐ Self-developed
2. ☐ Purchased or rented from a specialist provider
3. ☐ Developed in cooperation with service provider.

Please share further detail on the provider and the type of software, if possible:

A.8.	Apart from any annual reports, do you publish any other activity reports or information to the public?

1. ☐ Yes
2. ☐ No

If yes, please share the URL.

Are there any non-public activity reports or data? If possible, please share detail on the kind of information shared and with who.

A.9.	Please state the year in which you started online market surveillance.

A.10.	How many people in your institution are currently engaged in internet market surveillance? How many people work overall in your authority?

Market surveillance:_____
Total – authority:______

A.11.	Has this number changed over the last five years?

1. ☐ Increased
2. ☐ Stayed the same
3. ☐ Decreased

A.12.	Do you employ private sector subcontractors for this work?

1. ☐ Yes
2. ☐ No
3. ☐ Sensitive information, cannot disclose.

A.13.	If you answered *Yes* above, since when do you employ them?

Pease state the year when started.

A.14.	If you answered the above, what exact activity / service do they perform for you?

Multiple choice possible.
1. ☐ Surveillance software provider
2. ☐ Platform surveillance by contractors
3. ☐ Issuing Notice and take down requests
4. ☐ Reporting of enforcement and surveillance activity
5. ☐ Other, please specify:
6. ☐ Sensitive information, cannot disclose.

B. Enforcement activity and the E-Commerce Directive

B.1.	The E-Commerce Directive (2000/31/EC) has put in place conditions for the liability for unlawful content or activity hosted or transmitted by information service providers (ISPs). These are regulated in Articles 12 – 15. Has your authority enforced against ISPs based on these provisions or the equivalent (transposed) national legislation?

1. ☐ Yes
2. ☐ No
3. ☐ I am not sure.

B.2.	If you have answered *Yes* above: do you have any specific problems with these provisions?

1. ☐ Yes
2. ☐ No

B.3.	If you have answered *Yes* above: which of the below statements reflect your view best?

1. ☐ The liability exemptions are too broad and general to be applied effectively.
2. ☐ They are adequate and effective for my work.
3. ☐ They are too restrictive and put an unjustly high burden on ISPs/ internet platforms.
4. ☐ The liability exemptions are outdated.
5. ☐ I do not want to comment.

B.4.	To your knowledge, are the liability conditions of Articles 12 - 15 ECD (or its national implementations) relevant for the enforcement of product sector specific laws mentioned in A.3.)?

1. ☐ Yes
2. ☐ No
3. ☐ I am not sure.

If yes, please share further detail.

C. Cooperation with information service providers

C.1.	Is your authority working with online marketplaces, online platforms, internet access providers or other intermediaries (ISPs) in activities other than the surveillance measures mentioned in A.6?

1. ☐ Yes
2. ☐ No

If you have answered *Yes* above, can you give detail about the nature of this activity?

Examples of such activities could be:

- *Defining policies. (technical) criteria and standards for preventing unlawful products, content and sellers*
- *Taking part in workshops and trainings organized by the platforms/ISPs.*
- *Workshops and trainings organized by your authority for platforms/ISPs.*
- *Organizing and attend policy meetings together with platforms/ISPs*
- *Others:*

C.2.	If you have answered *Yes* above, would you say that these activities have brought success?

1. ☐ Yes, it has helped significantly
2. ☐ Yes, somewhat.

3. ☐ No, there is no difference to before.
4. ☐ On the contrary, it is now more difficult to surveil and enforce.

Please provide more detail if possible:

C.3.	What are the main obstacles that you face in your surveillance and enforcement work?

1. ☐ Platforms are not willing or do not see any legal obligation to cooperate.
2. ☐ Platforms have no time/resources to cooperate.
3. ☐ Lack of resources on the side of my authority.
4. ☐ The platforms are outside of our national jurisdictional reach.
5. ☐ The platforms are outside of EU jurisdictional reach.
6. ☐ Other, please specify:

C.4.	In your view, do e-commerce platforms have specific supply chain responsibilities which could qualify them as economic operators or food businesses under EU food law?

1. ☐ Yes
2. ☐ No
3. ☐ I am not sure

Please provide further explanation, if possible:

D. Regulatory Cooperation

D.1.	Are they any other authorities in your country, which work in your area of activity, for example at regional or local level or in a neighbouring product sector?

4. ☐ Yes
5. ☐ No

Please name these authorities.

D.2.	If you have answered *Yes* above, do you coordinate your activities with these authorities from your country?

Please share further detail on the kind of cooperation (e.g. frequency, kind of co-operation, which authority, etc.).

D.3.	Do you coordinate your activities with enforcement authorities from other EU Member States or non-EU countries

1. ☐ Yes
2. ☐ No

D.4.	If you answered yes above, please state with which authorities in which Member States you are working together. Include any EU agencies and authorities.

D.5.	What is the nature of this cooperation?

Multiple choice possible.
1. ☐ Sharing or creation of statistics
2. ☐ Sharing best practice
3. ☐ Setting common surveillance and enforcement criteria and standards
4 . ☐ Conducting joint surveillance & enforcement activities
5. ☐ Proposing new or amending EU legislation (EU Policy initiatives)
6. ☐ Other, please specify:

D.6.	How would you say has the frequency and level of international cooperation changed over the last 5 years?

1. ☐ It has intensified significantly
2. ☐ It has intensified somewhat
3. ☐ It has remained unchanged
4. ☐ It has decreased
5. ☐ It has decreased significantly
6. ☐ I am not sure/no comment

Please share further detail you may have:

D.7.	If applicable, which have been the most notable policy initiatives resulting from this international cooperation?

For example, EU legislation (incl. draft proposals), standard setting, best practice, codes of conduct, trust certification, etc.

D.8.	If applicable, do any of the above initiatives include participation by private sector actors, such as platforms or industry associations?

1. ☐ Yes
2. ☐ No

If yes, please share further detail.

E. Additional data (not part of the interview)

E.1.	Date and location of interview (completed by interviewer).

E.2.	Interview conducted with (names and position) - (completed by interviewer).

ANNEX II – A sectorally adaptable, risk-based duty of care standard (model)

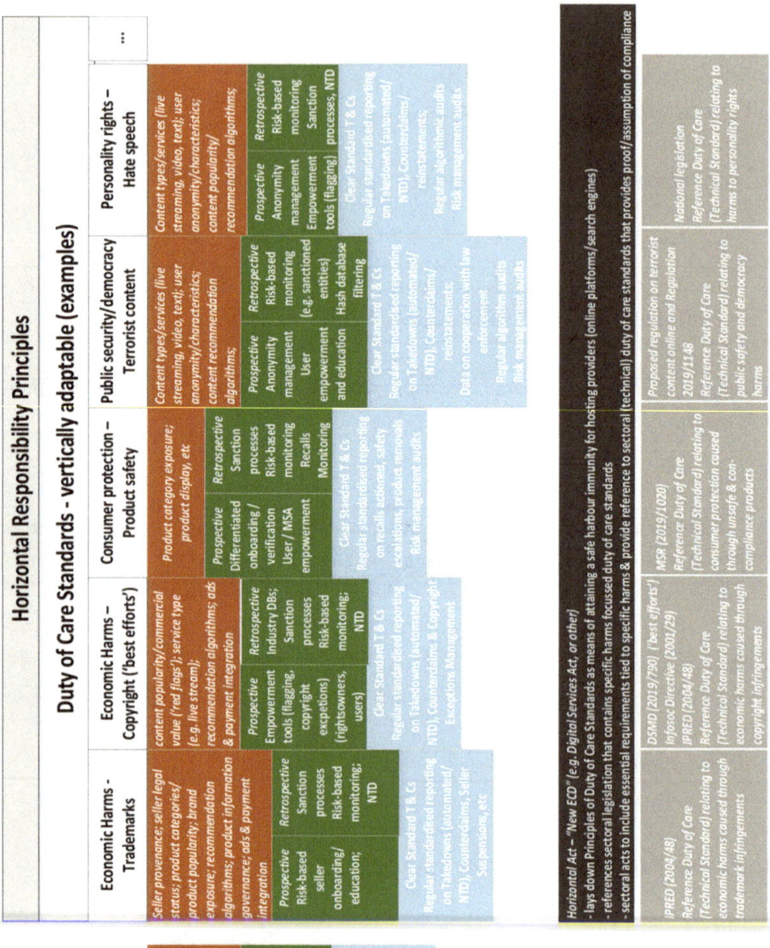

ANNEX III – A duty of care standard for E-Commerce platforms

Duty of Care for E-Commerce platforms
A Standard for Removing and Preventing Counterfeit on E-Commerce Platforms

Carsten Ullrich / REACT
Revised and abridged version – August 2020
For inclusion in PhD Dissertation

A. *Introduction*

This document proposes a standard approach for e-commerce platforms to remove and prevent IP infringing content and unsafe or illegal products. E-commerce platforms worldwide routinely deploy reactive Notice and Takedown (NTD) processes, which allow brand owners to inform platforms of infringing or illegal around the world. In many jurisdictions, the existence of these reactive systems protects platforms against liabilities for unlawful content offered by their parties via their sites. There is, however, considerable legal ambiguity over the scope of proactive measures platforms should take to help stem the continuing flood of IP infringements and unlawful products in e-commerce.

Online platforms, including in e-commerce, have become important gatekeepers, enabling users to interact and sell on the internet. However, their business models increasingly rely not just on intermediating between users but on analysing and monetising massive amounts of traffic and content data left by these users. Their participation in and control over the activity conducted via their systems has therefore increased steadily over recent years.

In the area of e-commerce, where counterfeit sales conducted via online marketplaces remain a serious problem, this provides an economic, technological and moral justification for charging these actors with more responsibilities. These responsibilities should go beyond the current mandatory NTD obligations, and include preventive and transparency responsibilities. These responsibilities should be seen as a duty of care, along the lines of corporate responsibility, in which platforms cooperate in overall efforts to stop the infringement of intellectual property rights.

Section B constitutes the core of this document. This section defines the duties, which an e-commerce marketplace should fulfil in order to identify and mitigate the highest risks of IP infringement on its platform. Using a risk management system, the platform would need to put processes in places to identify, analyse and evaluate the counterfeit risks emanating from sellers, products and its specific business model. A number of non-exhaustive typical risk drivers are being listed for which the platform would need to perform a risk assessment. Subsequently, control measures are being listed which the platform should put in place to mitigate the highest counterfeit risks. Section C provides an overview of the technical and organisation capabilities a platform would need to have in place in order to be seen as a responsible corporate actor. Additional risk drivers and control measures are listed in ANNEX I. For completeness, common criteria for an effective and accountable NTD systems are proposed in Section C.

Section D will summarise the transparency reporting requirements that should be in place so that all users can verify the platforms' efforts. The data reported should be consistent across different all actors so as to ensure comparability. Finally, confidential reports should be made available to brand owners and public authorities. These reports should provide detail about the effectiveness of the duty of care measures put in place by platforms. They should also give detail about the automated removal decisions and provide information on system audits, corrective actions and cooperation with law enforcement.

1. Principles

The following principles should be followed when applying the duty of care measures and risk management actions proposed in this document. They are based on principles which are already applied and widely used in existing international standards.

Create and protect value"

The duty of care standard contributes to the demonstrable achievement of objectives and improvements in legal and regulatory compliance, reputation, governance, public acceptance, health and safety.

Be part of decision-making*

The duty of care measures help decision makers to make informed choices, prioritize actions and identify alternative actions.

Accountability*

Ensure that there is accountability, authority and competence to manage the processes. This includes ensuring risk controls are effective, efficient and adequate. This can be done by identifying risk owners, performance measurement and external/internal reporting, escalation processes and recognition at all levels.

Accuracy, quality & using the best information available*

The duty of care approach is informed by hard data, experience, stakeholder feedback, forecasts and expert judgement. Account should be taken of data and modelling limitations.

Collection limitation / proportionality**

Any personal information should not be collected indiscriminately. Both the amount and the type of personal information collected should be limited to that which is necessary.

Be dynamic, iterative, and responsive to change*

The risk management system continually senses and responds to change. Risks may emerge, change or disappear as external and internal events occur, context and knowledge change. Risks are continuously being monitored and reviewed.

Security/Privacy***

Ensure all systems have anti-fraud mechanisms in place to protect data from internal and external fraud. Ensure all systems protect the personal data of users.

.*ISO 31000:2009 Risk Management

** ISO 29100:2011 Information Technology – Security Techniques – Privacy Framework

*** ISO 20488:2018 Online consumer reviews

B. *Duty of care: risk assessment, prevention and removal*

1. Methodology: risk-based approach

This section proposes a risk-based approach towards the identification and prevention of counterfeit and otherwise infringing sales. According to this, e-commerce platforms have duties of care to effectively address activities and features of their business model that pose a high counterfeit risk. The definition of risk as the *effect of uncertainty on objectives* (ISO 31000) implies a preventive approach. This section will lay down actions which can be reasonably expected of an online marketplace today (duty of care) in order to assess and control the highest risk of counterfeit emanating from its business model.

The risk management actions proposed draw on principles and processes laid down in international standards ISO 31000 (Risk management), ISO 9000 (Quality management). It also draws on the recent ISO 204888 (Online consumer reviews). Given the limited time and scope of this project there will not be any more detailed and structured references to these standards.

The risk-based approach is an ongoing process. It is expected that companies identify and evaluate risk drivers on an ongoing basis and every time a new business or design feature is deployed. As an example, this can include the launch of a new product category, new categories of sellers, new target markets. Other designs and architecture features may relate to the possibility for sellers to provide product information, the way customers are allowed to comment on sellers and products, the way products and services are being recommended, the payment services on offer or the possibility of sellers of buying sponsored listings etc.

2. Risk assessment

I. Harms definition

- Economic harms

Counterfeit products violate the economic rights of trademark owners. [Here empirical data may be inserted about the economic damage caused by the sale of counterfeit products online]. The ongoing and continued violation trademark rights impacts on the exercise of the fundamental right to protection of intellectual property as guaranteed by Article 17 (2) of the Charter of Fundamental Rights of the European Union.

- Consumer protection

Counterfeit products may pose serious risks for consumer health. The sale of unsafe or illegal may also have negative consequences for the health and safety of consumers.

II. Risk identification & definition

This standard addresses the risk of the platform being used for the sale of counterfeit and illicit products. Definition of the risks that this duty of care standard addresses:

- Use of platform for counterfeit sales
- Use of platform for sales of unsafe / illegal products

III. Risk analysis

a. Risk drivers

A platform should be able to establish risk drivers (or risk factors) which impact its exposure to the risks and the causation of harms. These risk drivers are related to three broader categories.

a) The platform needs to establish and document risk drivers related to its **business model**. A non-exhaustive list of optional risk drivers is proposed under ANNEX I.
b) The platform needs to establish and document risk drivers relating to **sellers/advertisers**. A non-exhaustive list of basic (required) and optional risk drivers is proposed under ANNEX I.
c) The platform needs to establish and document risk drivers related to **products.** A non-exhaustive list of basic (required) and optional risk drivers is proposed under ANNEX I.

Figure C1 provides a list of common counterfeit risk drivers (or risk factors) which a responsible e-commerce platform can be expected to manage proactively.

A non-exhaustive overview of basic (duty of care) and additional (best practice) risk drivers, analytical tools and control measures high risks can be found in ANNEX I.

Figure C1: Risk drivers that e-commerce platforms can reasonably be expected to evaluate

Business model related: factors and features which can be indicative of counterfeit risk (non-exhaustive)	
Risk Driver	Problem
Platform architecture / design	Platform architecture, e.g. listings structure, product display, data requirements from sellers / information governance may impact counterfeit risk
Advertising	Advertising may change the exposure to counterfeit risk (money from counterfeit listings pages; advertising for counterfeit products)
Fulfilment service	Offering a fulfilment service may change risk exposure to counterfeit and illicit products.
Payment services	Degree of payment integration (own payment services, third party pay merchants, seller independent) may change exposure to counterfeit risk.
Recommender algorithms	Recommending products from sanctioned sellers or high risk product categories may change risk exposure to counterfeit

Seller related: factors which can be indicative of counterfeit risk (non-exhaustive)	
Risk Driver	Problem
Seller provenance	Different regions may be more susceptible to counterfeit trade than others
Seller legal status (B2C, C2C)	Private individuals and commercial sellers may pose different risks when selling on the platform
Seller sanctions - takedowns	Amount / frequency of product takedowns is correlated to seller counterfeit risk
Seller sanctions - suspensions	Amount / frequency of account suspensions is indicative of seller counterfeit risk; sellers with closed accounts may reopen accounts

Product (category) related: factors which can be indicative of counterfeit risk (non-exhaustive)	
Risk Driver	Problem
Product popularity (Red Flag knowledge)	Sales volume/popularity (e.g. high ranked, fast selling listing) may affect product counterfeit risk.
Product counterfeit exposure	Different product groups maybe more subject to counterfeits than others.
Brand exposure	Different brands may pose different counterfeit risk levels.

b. Platform capabilities

The platform should have robust analytical processes in place that allow them to generate internal data and intelligence for risk analysis and risk classification.

Platforms are expected to understand the wider risk environment in which they operate. They should draw on external intelligence from brand owners, supply chain intermediaries, industry, international organisations, government and law enforcement. Figure C2 lists the analytical tools that e-commerce marketplaces should deploy for risk analysis as part of their duty of care.

Figure C2: Risk analysis tools and capabilities which e-commerce platforms should have in place

Internal data & analytical tools	For risk driver
Takedown data analytics from NTD requests and automated/internal takedowns by: • seller ID • seller provenance • seller legal status • seller size • seller tenure • product group • brand	Seller provenance Seller legal status Seller sanctions (takedowns & account suspensions) Product popularity (red flag knowledge) Product group exposure Brand exposure
Seller sanctions and suspension analytics	Seller provenance Seller legal status Product popularity (red flag knowledge)
Product sales analytics	Product group exposure Product popularity (red flag knowledge)
Price analytics (list price fluctuations, deviation from RRP)	Product popularity (red flag knowledge) Brand exposure
Keyword search tools (for customer reviews, seller ratings, product descriptions, product titles)	Product exposure Brand exposure

External data / intelligence	For risk driver
Intelligence and reports from public authorities, law enforcement, international organizations (for examples see ANNEX VI)	Seller provenance
Legal requirements applying to private and commercial sellers	Seller legal status
Industry and supply chain intermediary	Product popularity (red flag knowledge) Product group exposure Brand exposure
Brand owner information	Product popularity (red flag knowledge) Product group exposure Brand exposure

IV. Risk evaluation

Following the analysis, the counterfeit risks relating to each risk factor should be evaluated (or classified) into high, medium and low risks. The eventual risk evaluation of sellers, products and business model should take into account the risk scores across all factors.

a) **Seller risk:** the platform should establish risk profiles for sellers by taking into account how the sellers scores across different risk drivers.
b) **Product risk:** the platform should establish risk levels for each product group by taking into account the exposure to risk drivers.
c) **Business model risk:** the platform should establish the counterfeit risk levels of specific features of its platform design and business model.

Platforms should have documented and transparent processes in place to evaluate risk and determine high risks. They should establish for each risk driver criteria or thresholds for risk levels (usually low, medium or high risks). The risk evaluation can for example be documented in a risk matrix (see for examples in ANNEX IV).

These processes must be validated by the management and fit into the wider counterfeit and overall risk management strategy of the company. They need to be regularly reviewed and audited.

3. Risk control

Platforms should adopt a graduated approach that corresponds to the risk level.

This standard puts an emphasis on the risk response measures adopted to high counterfeit risks. These should be dealt with as a priority and resources should be concentrated on these risks.

Risks at all levels should be monitored continuously in order to identify trends which could lead to a change in risk level.

A number of risk mitigation and risk avoidance measures are proposed in order to control high counterfeit risks.

For example, sellers, product and brands which display high risk indicators should be subject to enhanced due diligence checks during onboarding (KYC) and enhanced transaction and account review procedures during their tenure and lifecycle on the platforms.

Reviews should be largely automated, but need to be supplemented by regular human reviews. Human reviews are needed in order to verify systems decision accuracy and decide in non-standard situations. They will also be useful to enhance and adjust automated systems based on artificial intelligence.

In order to be able to conduct enhanced controls of high risks the e-commerce platform would need to have in place basic investigative resources and capabilities, listed in Figure C3.

Figure C3: Basic risk analysis tools and capabilities that are needed in order to control high risks

Duty of care: proactive processes – platform capabilities for high risks	Comment
Robust onboarding / KYC procedures, including: • ID / (business) address verification; tax registration	
Automated and manual systems and processes capable of: • managing and analysing seller population • registering and analysing transactions • reviewing and investigating seller accounts (requesting and verifying documents, such as invoices or authorizations) • registering and analysing takedowns and suspensions • detecting and verifying relation to other accounts • conducting and analysing keyword searches of customer reviews, seller ratings, product titles and product descriptions • reviewing and investigating listing authenticity (requesting and verifying documents, such as invoices or authorizations, incorporating feedback from supply chain intermediaries and brand owners)	These actions can be assured through a team of trained reviewers or investigators for example as part of existing fraud / risk management. The processes can be documented through standard operating procedures, or by providing training materials, for example based on brand or industry intelligence.
Regular audit and review of sellers, product group and brands': • risk categorizations • risk evaluation criteria	

With these capabilities in place, platforms are in a position to design control measures in order to address the high risks of counterfeits (Figure C4). These measures would be at the core of the duty of care of on online marketplaces.

Figure C4: Control measures for high risks as part of a duty of care

Duty of care: control measures for high risks	Risk driver	Comment
Onboarding: enhanced due diligence checks / KYC for: • sellers from high risk regions/countries • commercial sellers	Seller provenance Seller legal status	Combine with internal anti-money laundering procedures (KYC, risk profiling) as possible
Onboarding: check new sellers for relations with suspended accounts	Seller sanctions - suspensions	
Onboarding: enhanced authorization requirements for selling in high-risk product groups / categories	Product popularity (red flag knowledge) Product group exposure Brand exposure)	This could include enhanced information and training regarding compliance with applicable laws and T&Cs, sample invoice checks, feedback brand owners.
Enhanced automated and manual monitoring of: • transactions of sellers from high risk regions/ countries • transactions, customer reviews, seller ratings, product titles from sellers with a takedown history • transactions, customer reviews, seller ratings, product titles, account relations of previously suspended sellers • product listings (titles, descriptions, price points) in high risk product categories • listings from high risk brands (keyword searches, price points, images) • popular ("viral") product sales (keyword searches, price points, images) • listings uploads of high-risk sellers, brands, in high-risk product categories product	Seller provenance Seller legal status Seller sanctions - takedowns Seller sanctions – suspensions Product popularity (red flag knowledge) Product group exposure Brand exposure)	Enhanced monitoring would include: reviews for suspicious or unusual transactions, systems to prevent re-upload of blocked listings, reviewing suspicious account movements and alterations, keyword searches in product titles and descriptions, customer reviews and seller ratings, invoice checks, product document reviews, image reviews, price point feedback from brands/ manufacturers.
A documented strike policy for listings takedowns and account suspensions/closures. (example ANNEXII)	Seller sanction –takedowns and suspension.	
Automated or manual processes to detect and enforce private seller legal thresholds for selling.	Seller legal status	

ANNEX I contains a full overview of all drivers for seller, product and business model related counterfeit risks, the processes and data needed to establish risk levels and control measures for high risks.

C. *Duty of care: Notice-and-Takedown*

In most jurisdictions in the world e-commerce platforms' liabilities with regards to unlawful information hosted from third parties is limited to failure to comply with reactive removal obligations. These removal obligations are normally fulfilled by Notice – and Takedown (NTD) processes.

The REACT survey confirmed that NTD systems are in place on most platforms across the globe.

There are, however, significant variations in service levels and in procedural and transparency commitments by platforms which inhibits the effective and consistent enforcement.

The good management of NTD is an essential part of the platform's entire commitment to help fight the use of its system for unlawful activities, such as counterfeit and unsafe or illegal product sales. Following the principles of Openness and Accountability responsible and effective NTD processes should be set up in the following way.

Notice and Takedown: Duty of care requirements
Make notice forms easily available to users and brand owners
Provide clear and easy notification systems
Provide the possibility to file notices for all kinds of IP violations: trademarks (counterfeit), copyright, designs, patents.
Provide the possibility to attach additional information and proof.
Provide the possibility to notify links, including advertising) leading to infringing products or content.
Provide for the possibility to file bulk notices
Provide service level agreements (SLAS) for the decision-making on notices (removal or stay-up) - this should not exceed 48 hours.
Explain the process of notice appeals, including for automated for takedowns and provide SLAs.
Provide noticing parties information on the completion of their NTD request.

See also: BASCAP, 'Best-Practices-for-Removing-Fakes-from-Online-Platforms', 2016

D. *Duty of care: transparency*

1. Terms & Conditions

Platforms should make a clear and unambiguous statement of their intolerance towards the use of their platform for IP infringing and other unlawful activities in their terms and conditions (T&Cs).

Terms & Conditions: company commitments
Have a clear statement that prohibits the sale of IP infringing and other unlawful products
Clear commitment towards removing and sanctioning sellers violating this prohibition.
Inform users of the NTD process and, where appropriate, provide a separate link to relevant NTD service conditions and NTD form(s)
Inform users of the type of infringements sanctioned, including for example advertising or other links to infringing products or content, incorrect but similar product names, image violations, etc.
Inform sellers of the platform's right to cooperate with law enforcement authorities.
Inform sellers of the platform's policy on discontinuing accounts and withholding of funds in the case of illegal activity.

2. Transparency reporting

An e-commerce platform should publish a regular account of its activities in the fight against IP theft. Many platforms already publish accounts of notices and content removals, albeit in other content areas (such as hate speech). Transparency reports will ensure that the platform's commitment is visible to all stakeholders, provide accountability and help evaluate the effectiveness of the duty of care measures put in place.

Transparency reporting should be published bi-annually, but be separated into publicly available and confidential reports.

Public Transparency Reports (Bi-annual) – content
Number listing removals: NTD requests, automated removals
NTD requests: number, % of appeals, % of successful appeals, listing removals, % invalid notices
NTD requests: by type of infringement
NTD requests: by source - brand owner, seller, public authority
NTD requests: processed outside SLA (%)
Automated removals: number, % appeals, % successful appeals
Number of seller accounts closed

Confidential Transparency Reports (Bi-annual) (rightsholders/government) - content
Number of listing removals: by product category, top brands (total/product category)
Seller accounts closed by provenance (country), seller size (turnover/listings)
The number of cases referred/reported to law enforcement authorities
Activity report on: staff training, cooperation with brand owners, process audits/reviews incl. automated systems

Annex I - Management of risk drivers

Risk	Seller related: establish, analyse and control factors which can be indicative of counterfeit risk (non-exhaustive)					
Risk	Risk Driver	Problem	Prerequisite: Internal Data	Prerequisite: External data	Evaluation	Controls for high risks
Counterfeit	Seller provenance	Different regions may be more susceptible to counterfeit trade than others	Takedown data analytics by location/provenance (from NTD requests and automated/internal takedowns), Seller suspension/ sanctions analytics	Official reports: US Notorious Markets Lists, EU Sanction Lists, EU Anti-Counterfeiting Intelligence Support Tool (ACIST), EU Customs reports, industry reports (BASCAP, UNIFAB)	Ranking of countries/regions' exposure to counterfeit risk	Enhanced automated and manual monitoring and review of transactions and listings of sellers from high risk countries/regions.
						Enhanced due diligence checks / KYC for sellers from high risk regions during onboarding
	Seller legal status (B2C, C2C)	Private individuals and commercial sellers may pose different risks when selling on the platform	Takedown data analytics by legal status, Seller suspension/sanctions analytics	Local legal requirements (VAT, definition of private seller, etc)	Establish to what extend counterfeit risk level depends legal status	Differentiated due diligence checks during onboarding, including ID verification for commercial sellers. Automated controls / limits for private sellers.
	Seller sanctions - takedowns	amount / frequency of product takedowns is correlated to seller counterfeit risk	Takedown data analytics by seller		Establish quantitative criteria (number of takedowns) for different risk levels	Enhanced automated transaction and seller reviews (customer reviews, seller ratings, product titles, product image checks, etc). Establish strike process for takedowns.
	Seller sanctions - suspensions	Amount / frequency of account suspensions indicative of seller counterfeit risk; sellers with closed accounts may reopen accounts	Seller suspension/sanctions analytics		Establish quantitative criteria for different risk levels regarding suspensions	Enhanced automated transaction and seller reviews. Strike policy for account suspension. Check for accounts relations to sanctioned accounts during new seller on-boarding
	Seller size (turnover/listings)	Different size sellers may pose a different risk of counterfeit	Takedown data analytics by seller size, seller sales data analytics		Determine the way seller size (turnover, volume sales) influences the counterfeit risk	Differentiated monitoring and seller checks depending on size. Additional due diligence / reviews of sellers when risk level thresholds.
	Seller product portfolio (I)	Different product groups maybe more subject to counterfeits than others	Takedown data analytics by product	brand owner intelligence, industry reports, supply chain intelligence	Determine counterfeit risk levels of different product groups	Enhanced information and authorisation procedures during onboarding for selling in high risk product groups. Enhanced automated transaction and seller
Unsafe or illicit product	Seller product portfolio (II)	Different product groups may pose different regulatory requirements	Customer reviews, regulatory authority escalations, NTD request analysis	Regulatory product requirements	Determine compliance implications of products and platform risk exposure levels of sellers.	Enhanced information and authorisation procedures during onboarding for selling in high risk product groups.
Counterfeit / Unsafe or Illicit products	Seller tenure	sellers with recent tenure may pose different risks than those with a track record	Sanctions history, seller analytics		Determine whether tenure confers different levels of exposure to counterfeit risks.	Enhanced monitoring of new sellers.
	Seller rating	Sellers with negative customer rating may pose higher counterfeit / product compliance risk	Customer feedback, sanctions and takedown data analytics		Determine the degree to which negative customer feedback is related to counterfeit risk	Automated checks of seller ratings, enhanced reviews for negatively rated sellers. Keyword searches in seller reviews (counterfeit, fake, unsafe, etc.).

	Product (category) related: establish, analyse and control factors which can be indicative of counterfeit risk (non-exhaustive)					
Risk	Risk Driver	Problem	Internal Data	External data	Evaluation	Controls for high risks
	Product popularity (red flag knowledge)	sales volume/popularity (high ranked listing) may change product counterfeit risk	Sales analytics, price analytics, Takedown data analytics	Brand information, industry reports	Determine whether and which popularity (per product group/brand) confers higher counterfeit risk "(red flag knowledge").	Enhanced automated monitoring of fast selling products (enhanced keyword searches of product title and customer reviews, enhanced manual reviews), enhanced price analytics (diversion from RRP)
	Product group exposure	Different product groups maybe more subject to counterfeits than others.	Takedown data analytics, Sales analytics, keyword search analytics	Brand information, industry reports	Determine the counterfeit risk levels of different product groups	Enhanced automated monitoring of high risk product (groups) (keyword searches of customer reviews, product title, product description reviews), enhanced price analytics (diversion from RRP)
	Brand exposure	Different brands may face different counterfeit risk levels	Takedown data analytics, price analytics, keyword search analytics	Brand information, supply chain intelligence	Determine brands that are subject to high counterfeit risks.	Enhanced automated monitoring of high risk brands) (keyword searches of product title, product description reviews, customer feedback, enhanced automated product image checks), enhanced price analytics (diversion from RRP) for high risk brands, Establish IP program with enhanced NTD and monitoring.
	Product regulatory requirements	Different product groups may pose different regulatory requirements impacting the risk of non-compliant/unsafe offers.	Takedown data analytics, customer reviews, notices, regulatory authority escalations	Regulatory requirements analysis	Determine compliance implications and platform risk exposure levels from allowing sales of certain products.	Enhanced information and authorisation procedures during onboarding for selling in high risk product groups. Require enhanced listing information requirements and audit completion.

	Business model: establish, analyse and control factors of platform design and business services which can be indicative of counterfeit risk (non-exhaustive)					
Risk	Risk Driver	Problem	Internal Data	External data	Evaluation	Controls for high risks
Counterfeit / Unsafe or Illicit products	Payment services	Degree of payment integration (own payment services, third party pay merchants, seller independent) may change exposure to counterfeit risk.	own payment services: internal AML checks and KYC procedures	pay service merchants : analysis of risk intelligence and AML information.	Determine the risk levels posed by current payment solutions.	own payment services: integrate AML processes and risk profiling in seller verification (KYC) and onboarding procedures, disrupt disbursements and payments for suspended accounts.
						Pay service merchants: establish information exchange on high risk/suspended sellers, disrupt disbursements and payments for suspended accounts.
	Fulfilment service	Offering a fulfilment service may change risk exposure to counterfeit and illicit products..	NTD analysis, seller sanctions/suspension history	supply chain information (customs, transportation)	Determine whether own fulfilment service changes risk level of counterfeit.	Enhanced counterfeit and document checks for high risk products, brands and sellers (see above) during receive, storage, shipment preparation.
	Advertising	Advertising may change the exposure to counterfeit risk (money from counterfeit listings pages; advertising for counterfeit products)	Takedown analysis for adverts/sponsored links; ad revenue analytics		Determine to what degree advertising on product offer pages changes counterfeit risk	NTD requests for ads/sponsored links, on-boarding checks, counterfeit risk scores strike processes for advertisers
	Platform architecture / design	Platform architecture: e.g. listings structure, product display / information governance may impact counterfeit risk	NTD analysis, fraud detection data, IT security audit data	Industry sources, external audit data	holistic risk analysis of architecture (using e.g. IT security, fraud, risk and/or quality management standards)	FOR EXAMPLE: limit product listing edit rights to low/medium risk sellers, provide structured product data upload fields with compulsory information requirements, automated review and audit of: product information data/edit logs

Annex II - IP Infringement Strike Policy (Example)

Confirmed counterfeit takedowns (NTD/automated)	Trusted seller	Seller	Private individual
1	warning	warning	warning
2	warning	warning	warning
3	account suspension/ plan of action*	permanent closure	permanent closure
4	Final warning		
5	Permanent closure		

**Plan of Action/account suspension: the seller is contacted by the platform and asked to provide reasons for the occurrence of counterfeit (infringing) products. They would need to commit to actions in order to prevent the sale of counterfeit. A temporary account suspension would be imposed (e.g. 1 month) during which the seller will have to implement these actions.*

Annex III – Risk Matrix (examples)

Legal status (example)		Impact (litigation, reputation, volume,...)		
		Low	Medium	High
Liklihood of Ctf in %	Low			
	Low			
	Medium	private		
	Medium			commercial
	High			
	High			

Provenance (example)		Impact (litigation, reputation, volume,...)		
		Low	Medium	High
Liklihood of Ctf in %	Low			EU
	Low		US	
	Medium			
	Medium			
	High			China
	High			

Product group (example)		Impact (regulatory, reputation, volume,...)		
		Low	Medium	High
Liklihood of Ctf in %	Low	Furniture		
	Low			
	Medium			Cosmetics
	Medium		Fashion	Food
	High		CE	Toys
	High			Luxury Fashion

Annex IV – Public Reports and Data Sources

Europol and EU Intellectual Property Office, '2017 Situation Report on Counterfeiting and Piracy in the European Union' (2017)

Frontier Economics, 'The Economic Impacts of Counterfeiting and Piracy - Report Prepared for BASCAP and INTA'.
Office of the United States Trade representative, '2017 Out-of-Cycle Review of Notorious Markets'w

Bibliography

A. *Books, book sections, journal articles and public reports*

Abbot C, 'Bridging the Gap – Non-state Actors and the Challenges of Regulating New Technology' (2012) 39 Journal of Law and Society 329

Abdel-Khalik J, 'Is EBay Counterfeiting?' in Hannibal Travis (ed), Cyberspace law: censorship and regulation of the Internet (Routledge 2013)

Akdeniz Y, Internet Child Pornography and the Law: National and International Responses (Taylor & Francis Group 2008)

Andrews L, 'Algorithms, Regulation, and Governance Readiness' in Karen Yeung and Martin Lodge, Algorithmic regulation (2019)

Angelopoulos C, 'Filtering the Internet for Copyrighted Content in Europe' (2009) 4 iris plus 12

——, European Intermediary Liability in Copyright: A Tort-Based Analysis (Kluwer Law International BV 2017)

Angelopoulos C and others, 'Study of Fundamental Rights Limitations for Online Enforcement through Self-Regulation' (Institute for Information Law (IViR), University of Amsterdam 2015)

Apa E and Bassini M, 'Court of Rome Rules Vimeo Liable for Copyright Infringement' [2019] iris Newlsetter 50

Ardia DS, 'Free Speech Savior or Shield for Scoundrels: An Empirical Study of Intermediary Immunity under Section 230 of the Communications Decency Act' (2010) 43 Loyola of Los Angeles Law Review 373

Aries N and Vaziri L, 'Online Intermediary Liability and TM Infringement: Stuck in the Middle With You' (2020) 9 Trade Marks 2020 A practical cross-border insight into trade mark work 1

Arnold D (ed), Handbuch Logistik (3., neu bearb Aufl, Springer 2008)

Assaf Hamdani, 'Gatekeeper Liability' (2003) 77 Southern California Law Review 53

Australian Government, Attorney-General's Department, 'Sharing of Abhorrent Violent Material Act - Fact Sheet' <https://www.ag.gov.au/Crime/federal-offenders/Documents/AVM-Fact-Sheet.pdf> accessed 3 January 2020

Autenne A and De Ghellinck É, 'L'émergence et le développement des plateformes digitales : les enseignements de la théorie économique de la firme' (2019) t.XXXIII Revue internationale de droit économique 275

Avia L, Amellal K and Taïeb G, 'Renforcer La Lutte Contre Le Racisme et l'antisémitisme Sur Internet - Rapport à Monsieur Le Premier Ministre' (2018) <https://www.gouvernement.fr/rapport-visant-a-renforcer-la-lutte-contre-le-racisme-et-l-antisemitisme-sur-internet> accessed 24 April 2021

Ayres I and Braithwaite J, Responsive Regulation: Transcending the Deregulation Debate (Oxford University Press 1992) <http://site.ebrary.com/id/10087207> accessed 19 February 2019

Baldwin R and Black J, 'Driving Priorities in Risk-based Regulation: What's the Problem?' (2016) 43 Journal of Law and Society 565

Baldwin R, Cave M and Lodge M, Understanding Regulation: Theory, Strategy, and Practice (2nd ed, Oxford University Press 2012)

Ballegooij W van and Bakowski P, The Cost of Non-Europe in the Fight against Terrorism: Study (European Parliament, European Parliamentary Research Service 2018)

Bambauer DE, 'From Platforms to Springboards' (2018) 2 Georgetown Law Technology Review 15

Bamberger KA, 'Technologies of Compliance: Risk and Regulation in a Digital Age' (2009) 88 Tex. L. Rev. 669

Bartolini C, Santos C and Ullrich C, 'Property and the Cloud' (2018) 34 Computer Law & Security Review 358

Barwise P and Watkins L, 'The Evolution of Digital Dominance' in Damian Tambini and Martin Moore (eds), Digital dominance: the power of Google, Amazon, Facebook, and Apple (Oxford University Press 2018)

Becker M, 'When Public Principals Give up Control over Private Agents: The New Independence of ICANN in Internet Governance' [2019] Regulation & Governance rego.12250

Bednarz T, 'Keyword Advertising before the French Supreme Court and beyond - Calm at Last after Turbulent Times for Google and Its Advertising Clients?' (2011) 42 International Review of Intellectual Property and Competition Law 641

Belli L and Sappa C, 'The Intermediary Conundrum' (2017) 8 JIPITEC 183

Benabou VL, 'Quelle(s) responsabilité(s) des intermédiaires techniques sur Internet?' (2006) 61 Annales des télécommunications 865

Benkler Y, 'From Consumers to Users: Shifting the Deeper Structures of Regulation Toward Sustainable Commons and User Access' (2000) 52 Fed. Comm. L. J. 561

Bermejo F, 'Online Advertising as a Shaper of Public Communication' in Rikke Frank Jørgensen (ed), Human Rights in the Age of Platforms (The MIT Press 2019) <https://direct.mit.edu/books/book/4531/Human-Rights-in-the-Age-of-Plat forms> accessed 28 May 2020

Bertolini E, Franceschelli V and Pollicino O, 'Analysis of ISP Regulation under Italian Law' in Graeme B. Dinwoodie (ed), Secondary liability of internet service providers (Springer Berlin Heidelberg 2017)

Bilić P, 'Search Algorithms, Hidden Labour and Information Control' (2016) 3 Big Data & Society 1

Bilska A and Kowalski R, 'Food Quality and Safety Management' (2014) 10 Scientific Journal of Logistics 351

Black Julia, 'Decentring Regulation: Understanding the Role of Regulation and Self-Regulation in a "Post-Regulatory" World' (2001) 54 Current Legal Problems 103

Blázquez FJC, 'User-Generated Content Services and Copyright' (2008) 5 iris plus 1

Blocman A, 'Pas d'obligation générale de surveillance du réseau, rappelle la Cour de cassation' [2013] iris plus

Blommaert J, Durkheim and the Internet: On Sociolinguistics and the Sociological Imagination. (Bloomsbury Publishing Plc 2018)

Bohn S, Friederici N and Gümüsay AA, 'Too Big to Fail Us? Platforms as Systemically Relevant' (Internet Policy Review, 11 August 2020) <https://policyreview.info/articles/news/too-big-fail-us-platforms-systemically-relevant/1489> accessed 20 August 2020

Boldrin M and Levine DK, Against Intellectual Monopoly (Cambridge Univ Press 2010)

Bonadio E and Santo M, 'Court of Milan Holds Video Sharing Platforms Liable for Copyright Infringement' (2012) 7 Journal of Intellectual Property Law & Practice 14

Bosher H and Yeşiloğlu S, 'An Analysis of the Fundamental Tensions between Copyright and Social Media: The Legal Implications of Sharing Images on Instagram' (2019) 33 International Review of Law, Computers & Technology 164

Boudreau KJ and Hagiu A, 'Platforms Rules: Multi-Sided Platforms as Regulators' in Annabelle Gawer (ed), Platforms, markets and innovation (Paperback edition reprinted, Edward Elgar 2014)

Brey P, Gauttier S and Milam P-E, Harmful Internet Use. Study Part II, Part II, (European Parliament, European Parliamentary Research Service 2019) <http://www.europarl.europa.eu/RegData/etudes/STUD/2019/624269/EPRS_STU(2019)624269_EN.pdf> accessed 6 April 2020

Bridy A, 'Notice and Takedown in the Domain Name System: ICANN's Ambivalent Drift into Online Content Regulation.(Internet Corporation for Assigned Names and Numbers)' (2017) 74

Brown A and Kennedy R, 'Regulating Intersectional Activity: Privacy and Energy Efficiency, Laws and Technology' (2017) 31 International Review of Law, Computers & Technology 340

Büllesbach A (ed), Concise European IT Law (2nd ed, Kluwer Law International 2010)

Bundesamt für Verbraucherschutz und Landwirtschaft (BVL), 'Gemeinsame Zentralstelle "Kontrolle Der Im Internet Gehandelten Erzeugnisse Des LFGB Und Tabakerzeugnisse" - Jahresbericht 2018' (2019) <https://www.bvl.bund.de/DE/Aufgaben/06_Onlinehandel/onlinehandel_node.html> accessed 16 July 2020

Bundesministeriums der Justiz und für Verbraucherschutz, 'Together against Hate Speech - Ways to Tackle Onl Ine Hateful Content Proposed by the Task Force against Illegal Online Hate Speech' (2015)

Bunting M, 'Keeping Consumers Safe Online: Legislating for Platform Accountability for Online Content' (Communication Chambers 2018)

Burk DL, 'Toward an Epistemology of ISP Secondary Liability' (2011) 24 Philosophy & Technology 437

Busch C, 'Crowdsourcing Consumer Confidence - How to Regulate Online Rating And Review Systems in the Collaborative Economy' in Alberto De Franceschi (ed), European Contract Law and the Digital Single Market: The Implications of the Digital Revolution (Intersentia 2016)

——, 'Towards a "New Approach" for the Platform Ecosystem: A European Standard for Fairness in Platform-to-Business Relations' 3

Calabresi G, The Costs of Accidents: A Legal and Economic Analysis (Yale University Press 1970)

Callamard A, 'The Human Rights Obligations of Non-State Actors' in Rikke Frank Jørgensen (ed), Human Rights in the Age of Platforms (The MIT Press 2019) <https://direct.mit.edu/books/book/4531/Human-Rights-in-the-Age-of-Platforms> accessed 28 May 2020

Carbonara E, Guerra A and Parisi F, 'Sharing Residual Liability: The Cheapest Cost Avoider Revisited' (2016) 45 The Journal of Legal Studies 173

Carisimo E and others, 'Studying the Evolution of Content Providers in IPv4 and IPv6 Internet Cores' (2019) 145 Computer Communications 54

Castells M, The Rise of the Network Society (2nd ed, Blackwell Publishers 2000)

Castets-Renard C, 'Online Surveillance in the Fight Against Terrorism in France' in Tatiana-Eleni Synodinou and others (eds), EU internet law: regulation and enforcement (Springer Berlin Heidelberg 2017)

Centre for Strategy & Evaluation Services LLP, 'Impact Assessment on Increased Protection of Internet-Connected Radio Equipment and Wearable Radio Equipment - Annex 5 - Annex 5 – Radio Equipment Forecasts' (European Commission 2020) <https://ec.europa.eu/docsroom/documents/40763> accessed 14 July 2020

Chander A and Krishnamurthy V, 'The Myth of Platform Neutrality' (2018) 2 Georgetown Law Technology Review 17

Chaudhry P and Zimmerman A, Protecting Your Intellectual Property Rights (Springer New York 2013)

Chowdhury N and Wessel RA, 'Conceptualising Multilevel Regulation in the EU: A Legal Translation of Multilevel Governance?' (2012) 18 European law journal 335

Citron DK, 'Extremist Speech and Compelled Conformity' (2018) 93 NOTRE DAME LAW REVIEW 43

Citron DK and Wittes B, 'The Internet Will Not Break: Denying Bad Samaritans Section 230 Immunity' (2017) University of Maryland Francis King Carey School of Law Legal Studies Research Paper No. 2017-22 <https://papers.ssrn.com/sol3/papers.cfm?abstract_id=3007720> accessed 18 September 2017

——, 'The Problem Is Not Just Backpage: Revising Section 230 Immunity' (2018) 2 Georgetown Law Technology Review 21

Clark D and Claffy K, 'Platform Models for Sustainable Internet Regulation' (2014) 4 Journal of Information Policy 463

Clarke R, 'Web 2.0 as Syndication' (2008) 3 Journal of theoretical and applied electronic commerce research <http://www.scielo.cl/scielo.php?script=sci_arttext&pid=S0718-18762008000100004&lng=en&nrm=iso&tlng=en> accessed 22 July 2019

Clarke R and Wigan M, 'The Information Infrastructures of 1985 and 2018: The Sociotechnical Context of Computer Law & Security' (2018) 34 Computer Law & Security Review 677

Coase RH, 'The Problem of Social Cost' (1960) 3 The Journal of Law and Economics 1

Cobbe J and Bietti E, 'Rethinking Digital Platforms for the Post-COVID-19 Era' (Centre for International Governance Innovation, 12 May 2020) <https://www.cigionline.org/articles/rethinking-digital-platforms-post-covid-19-era> accessed 20 August 2020

Cohen JE, 'The Regulatory State in the Information Age' (2016) 17 Theoretical Inquiries in Law 369

Cole MD, Etteldorf C and Ullrich C, Cross-Border Dissemination of Online Content: Current and Possible Future Regulation of the Online Environment with a Focus on the EU E-Commerce Directive, vol 81 (1st edn, Nomos 2020) <https://www.nomos-elibrary.de/10.5771/9783748906438/cross-border-dissemination-of-online-content> accessed 21 April 2021

Cole MD, Etteldorf C and Ullrich C, Updating the Rules for Online Content Dissemination: Legislative Options of the European Union and the Digital Services Act Proposal, vol 83 (1st edn, Nomos 2020) https://www.nomos-elibrary.de/10.5771/9783748925934/updating-the-rules-for-online-content-dissemination> accessed 13 May 2021

Cole MD and Quintel T, '"Is There Anybody out There?" – Retention of Communications Data. Analysis of the Status Quo in Light of the Jurisprudence of the Court of Justice of the European Union (CJEU) and the European Court of Human Rights (ECtHR)' in Russell L Weaver, Jane Reichel and Steven I Friedland (eds), Comparative perspectives on privacy in an Internet era (Carolina Academic Press 2019)

Collins R, Three Myths of Internet Governance: Making Sense of Networks, Governance and Regulation (Intellect Books 2009)

'Combating Trafficking in Counterfeit and Pirated Goods - Report to the President of the United States' (US Department of Homeland Security 2020) <https://www.dhs.gov/publication/combating-trafficking-counterfeit-and-pirated-goods> accessed 30 June 2020

Common MF, 'Fear the Reaper: How Content Moderation Rules Are Enforced on Social Media' [2020] International Review of Law, Computers & Technology 1

Constantinides P, Henfridsson O and Parker GG, 'Introduction—Platforms and Infrastructures in the Digital Age' (2018) 29 Information Systems Research 381

'Copyright Protection On Digital Platforms: Existing Tools, Good Practice And Limitations - Report By The Research Mission On Recognition Tools For Copyright Protected Content On Digital Platforms' (Conseil Superieur de la Propriete Litteraire et Artistique (CSPLA), Ministère de la Culture 2017)

Coraggio G, 'Internet Litigation.' (2015) 21 IP Litigator 25

Cornils DM, 'Designing Platform Governance: A Normative Perspective on Needs, Strategies, and Tools to Regulate Intermediaries' (Algorithm Watch 2020)

Cornish WR, Llewelyn D and Aplin TF, Intellectual property: patents, copyright, trade marks and allied rights (7. ed, Sweet & Maxwell [u.a] 2010)

Council of Europe, 'Recommendation CM/Rec(2014)6 of the Committee of Ministers to Member States on a Guide to Human Rights for Internet Users (Adopted by the Committee of Ministers on 16 April 2014 at the 1197th Meeting of the Ministers' Deputies)'

Craig JDR, 'Invasion of Privacy and Charter Values: The Common-Law Tort Awakens' (1997) 42 McGill Law journal 355

Crémer J, de Montjoye Y-A and Schweitzer H, 'Competition Policy for the Digital Era - Final Report' (European Commission 2019) <http://ec.europa.eu/competition/publications/reports/kd0419345enn.pdf> accessed 31 July 2019

Dam CC van, European Tort Law (Second edition, Oxford University Press 2013)

Dara R, 'Intermediary Liability in India: Chilling Effects on Free Expression on the Internet' [2011] SSRN Electronic Journal <http://www.ssrn.com/abstract=2038214> accessed 2 January 2020

Davies L, 'Internet and the Elephant' (1996) 24 Int'l Bus. Law

Davis BJ, 'Comment: Untangling the "Publisher" versus "Information Content Provider" Paradox of 47 u.s.c. § 230: Toward a Rational Application of the Communications Decency Act in Defamation Suits against Internet Service Providers' (2002) 32 New Mexico Law Review 75

Dawson M, 'Better Regulation and the Future of EU Regulatory Law and Politics' (2016) 53 Common Market Law Review 1209

Derieux E and Granchet A, Lutte Contre Le Téléchargement Illégal: Lois Dadvsi et Hadopi (Lamy 2010)

Determann L, 'Case Update: German CompuServe Director Acquitted on Appeal' (1999) 23 Hastings International and Comparative Law Review 17

Diakopoulos N and others, 'I Vote For—How Search Informs Our Choice of Candidate' in Damian Tambini and Martin Moore (eds), Digital dominance: the power of Google, Amazon, Facebook, and Apple (Oxford University Press 2018)

Dinwoodie GB, 'Secondary Liability for Online Trademark Infringement: The International Landscape' (2014) 37 Columbia Journal of Law & the Arts 463

——, 'A Comparative Analysis of the Secondary Liability of Online Providers' in Graeme B. Dinwoodie (ed), Secondary liability of internet service providers (Springer Berlin Heidelberg 2017)

Dixit P, 'Liability of Indian E-Commerce Websites for Trade Mark Infringement by Sellers' (2019) 14 Journal of Intellectual Property Law & Practice 424

Durkheim É, De la division du travail social (1873) (Presses Électroniques de France 2013)

Dyson E, 'Cyberspace and the American Dream: A Magna Carta for the Knowledge Age (Release 1.2, August 22, 1994)' (1996) 12 The Information Society 295

Edwards L, 'The Changing Shape of Cyberlaw' (2004) 1 SCRIPT-ed 363

——, 'The Fall and Rise Of Intermediary Liability Online', Law and the Internet (3rd ed, Hart Pub 2009)

——, 'With Great Power Comes Great Responsibility?: The Rise of Platform Liability' in Lilian Edwards (ed), Law, policy, and the Internet (Hart 2019)

Edwards L and Veale M, 'Slave to the Algorithm? Why a 'Right to Explanation'Is Probably Not the Remedy You Are Looking For' (2017) 16 Duke Law & Technology Review 18

Edwards L and Waelde C, 'Online Intermediaries and Liability for Copyright Infringement', WIPO Workshop Keynote Paper (2005) <https://papers.ssrn.com/sol3/papers.cfm?abstract_id=1159640> accessed 15 October 2019

Elkin-Koren N and Salzberger EM, 'Law and Economics in Cyberspace' (1999) 19 International Review of Law and Economics 553

Eller KH, 'Private Governance of Global Value Chains from within: Lessons from and for Transnational Law' (2017) 8 Transnational Legal Theory 296

Eltis K, 'Can the Reasonable Person Still Be "Highly Offended" - An Invitation to Consider the Civil Law Tradition's Personality Rights-Based Approach to Tort Privacy' [2008] University of Ottawa Law & Technology Journal 199

Engstrom E and Feamster N, 'The Limits of Filtering: A Look at the Functionality & Shortcomings of Content Detection Tools' (Engine 2017) <https://www.engine.is/the-limits-of-filtering> accessed 3 March 2020

Epstein R, 'Manipulating Minds' in Damian Tambini and Martin Moore (eds), Digital dominance: the power of Google, Amazon, Facebook, and Apple (Oxford University Press 2018)

'ERGA Position Paper on the Digital Services Act' (European Regulators Group for Audiovisual Media Services (ERGA) 2020) <https://erga-online.eu/?page_id=14> accessed 5 November 2020

Erickson K and Kretschmer M, 'Analyzing Copyright Takedown of User-Generated Content on YouTube' [2018] JIPITEC 75

Etteldorf C, 'Bill to Combat Right-Wing Extremism and Hate Crime' [2020] iris Newlsetter <http://merlin-int.obs.coe.int/article/8802> accessed 16 April 2020

European Commission, 'Communication from the Commission: Illegal and Harmful Content on the Internet, COM(96) 487 Final' (1996) <https://core.ac.uk/reader/5078710> accessed 9 October 2019

——, 'Communication from the Commission on" Europe at the Forefront of the Global Information Society: Rolling Action Plan", COM(96) 607 Final' (1996)

——, 'Communication from the Commission: A European Initiative in Electronic Commerce, COM(97) 157 Final'(1997)

——, 'European Governance - A White Paper, COM(2001) 428 Final' (2001)

——, 'First Report on the Application of Directive 2000/31/EC of the European Parliament and of the Council of 8 June 2000 on Certain Legal Aspects of Information Society Services, in Particular Electronic Commerce, in the Internal Market' (2003) COM(2003) 702 final

——, 'Communication: A Renewed EU Strategy 2011-14 for Corporate Social Responsibility, COM/2011/0681 Final' (2011) <https://eur-lex.europa.eu/legal-content/EN/TXT/?uri=CELEX:52011DC0681> accessed 6 August 2020

——, 'A Single Market for Intellectual Property Rights - Boosting Creativity and Innovation to Provide Economic Growth, High Quality Jobs and First Class Products and Services in Europe, COM(2011) 287 Final' (2011)

——, 'A Coherent Framework for Building Trust in the Digital Single Market for E-Commerce and Online Services, COM(2011) 942 Final' (2011)

——, 'Bringing E-Commerce Benefits to Consumers - Accompanying Document SEC2011_1640' (2011)

——, 'Online Services, Including e-Commerce, in the Single Market, A Coherent Framework to Boost Confidence in the Digital Single Market of e-Commerce and Other Online Services, Accompanying the Document , SEC(2011) 1641 Final' (2012)

——, '20 Actions for Safer and Compliant Products for Europe: A Multi-Annual Action Plan for the Surveillance of Products in the EU, COM/2013/076 Final' (2013)

——, 'E-Commerce Action Plan 2012-2015, State of Play 2013, SWD(2013) 153 Final' (2013)

——, 'The European Agenda on Security - COM(2015) 185 Final' (2015)

——, 'EU General Risk Assessment Methodology (Action 5 of Multi-Annual Action Plan for the Surveillance of Products in the EU (COM(2013)76))' (2015)

——, 'Synopsis Report on the Public Consultation on the Regulatory Environment for Platforms, Online Intermediaries and the Collaborative Economy' <https://ec.europa.eu/digital-single-market/en/news/results-public-consultation-regulatory-environment-platforms-online-intermediaries-data-and> accessed 29 March 2017 (2016)

——, 'Communication: A European Agenda for the Collaborative Economy - COM(2016) 356 Final' (2016)

——, 'Toy Safety Directive 2009/48/EC - An Explanatory Guidance Document Ref. Ares(2016)1594457' (2016)

——, 'Communication: ICT Standardisation Priorities for the Digital Single Market COM(2016) 176 Final' (2016) <https://ec.europa.eu/digital-single-market/en/news/communication-ict-standardisation-priorities-digital-single-market> accessed 29 August 2018

——, 'Commission Staff Working Document Online Platforms Accompanying the Document Communication on Online Platforms and the Digital Single Market SWD(2016) 172 Final' (2016)

——, 'Guidance on the Implementation/Application of Directive 2005/29/EC on Unfair Commercial Practices SWD(2016) 163'(2016)

——, 'Online Platforms and the Digital Single Market Opportunities and Challenges for Europe COM(2016) 288 Final' (2016)

——, 'Commission Notice, The "Blue Guide" on the Implementation of EU Products Rules 2016, (2016/C 272/01)' (2016)

——, 'Commission Staff Working Document - Impact Assessment - Assessement on the Modernisation of the EU Copyright Rules Accompanying the Documents Proposal for a Directive of the European Parliament and of the Council on Copyright in the Digital Single Market and Proposal for a Regulation of the European Parliament and of the Council Laying down Rules on the Exercise of Copyright and Related Rights Applicable to Certain Online Transmissions of Broadcasting Organisations and Retransmissions of Television and Radio Programmes - SWD(2016) 301 Final - Part 1/3' (2016)

——, 'Commission Staff Working Document - Impact Assessment - Assessment on the Modernisation of the EU Copyright Rules Accompanying the Documents Proposal for a Directive of the European Parliament and of the Council on Copyright in the Digital Single Market and Proposal for a Regulation of the European Parliament and of the Council Laying down Rules on the Exercise of Copyright and Related Rights Applicable to Certain Online Transmissions of Broadcasting Organisations and Retransmissions of Television and Radio Programmes - SWD(2016) 301 Final - Part 3/3' (2016)

——, 'Summary of Responses to the Public Consultation on the Evaluation and Modernisation of the Legal Framework for IPR Enforcement' (2016) <http://ec.europa.eu/DocsRoom/documents/18661> accessed 17 March 2017

——, 'E-Commerce Control of Food - EU Action Plan' (Advisory Group of the food chain, animal and plant health, 25 November 2016) <https://ec.europa.eu/food/sites/food/files/safety/docs/adv-grp_plenary_20161125_pres_04.pdf> accessed 30 November 2018

——, 'Commission Notice on the Market Surveillance of Products Sold Online (2017/C 250/01)' (2017)

——, 'Communication: Tackling Illegal Content Online Towards an Enhanced Responsibility of Online Platforms', COM (2017) 555 final (2017)

——, 'Fintech: A More Competitive and Innovative European Financial Sector, Consultation Document' (2017) <https://ec.europa.eu/info/sites/info/files/2017-fintech-consultation-document_en_0.pdf> accessed 9 January 2018

——, 'Overview of the Functioning of the Memorandum of Understanding on the Sale of Counterfeit Goods via the Internet, SWD(2017) 430 Final' (2017)

——, 'A Balanced IP Enforcement System Responding to Today's Societal Challenges, COM(2017) 707 Final' (2017)

——, 'Guidance on Certain Aspects of Directive 2004/48/EC of the European Parliament and of the Council on the Enforcement of Intellectual Property Rights, COM(2017) 708 Final' (2017)

——, 'Commission Staff Working Document -Impact Assessment - Proposal for a Regulation of the European Parliament and of the Council Laying down Rules and Procedures for Compliance with and Enforcement of Union Harmonisation Legislation on Products - SWD(2017) 466 Final - Part 1/4' (2017)

——, 'Commission Staff Working Document -Impact Assessment - Proposal for a Regulation of the European Parliament and of the Council Laying down Rules and Procedures for Compliance with and Enforcement of Union Harmonisation Legislation on Products - SWD(2017) 466 Final - Part 2/4' (2017)

——, 'The Goods Package: Reinforcing Trust in the Single Market, COM(2017) 787 Final' (2017)

——, 'Commission Recommendation of 1.3.2018 on Measures to Effectively Tackle Illegal Content Online, C(2018) 1177 Final' (2018)

——, 'The First EU Coordinated Control Plan on Online Offered Food Products - Analysis of the Main Outcome of the Implementation of the Commission Recommendation on a Coordinated Control Plan on the Official Control of Certain Foods Marketed through the Internet, Ref. Ares(2018)893577' (2018) <https://ec.europa.eu/food/sites/food/files/oc_oof_analysis_main_outcome_en.pdf> accessed 8 October 2018

——, 'Commission Staff Working Document - Impact Assessment - Proposal for a Regulation of the European Parliament and of the Council on the Marketing and Use of Explosives Precursors - SWD(2018) 104 Final' (2018)

——, 'Memorandum of Understanding on Online Advertising and Intellectual Property Rights' (2018) <https://ec.europa.eu/docsroom/documents/30226> accessed 26 June 2020

——, 'Product Safety Pledge Voluntary Commitment of Online Marketplaces with Respect to the Safety of Non-Food Consumer Products Sold Online by Third Party Sellers' (2018)

——, 'Commission Staff Working Document - Impact Assessment - Proposal for a Regulation of the European Parliament and of the Council on Preventing the Dissemination of Terrorist Content Online - SWD(2018) 408 Final' (TERREG) (2018)

——, '2nd Progress Report on the Implementation of the Product Safety Pledge' (2019) <https://ec.europa.eu/info/business-economy-euro/product-safety-and-requirements/product-safety/product-safety-rules_en> accessed 6 July 2020

——, 'Report on the Functioning of the Memorandum of Understanding on the Sale of Counterfeit Goods via the Internet, SWD(2020) 166 Final/2' (2020) SWD(2020) 166 final/2 <https://ec.europa.eu/docsroom/documents/42701> accessed 27 August 2020

——, 'Code of Conduct on Countering Illegal Hate Speech Online - Results of the 3rd Monitoring Exercise - Fact Sheet | January 2018' <https://ec.europa.eu/newsroom/just/document.cfm?doc_id=49286> accessed 23 August 2018

——, 'Communication: Better Regulation for Better Results - An EU Agenda - COM/2015/0215 Final' (2015)

——, 'Commission Staff Working Document - Impact Assessment - Annexes - Accompanying the Document PROPOSAL FOR A REGULATION OF THE EUROPEAN PARLIAMENT AND THE COUNCIL on a Single Market For Digital Services (Digital Services Act) and Amending Directive 2000/31/EC - Part 2' (2020) <https://ec.europa.eu/digital-single-market/en/digital-services-act-package> accessed 8 January 2021

EUIPO and Europol, 'Intellectual Property Crime Threat Assessment' (2019)

European Commission (ed), Free Movements of Goods: Guide to the Application of Treaty Provisions Governing the Free Movement of Goods (Publ Off of the Europ Union 2010)

——, Assessment of the Application and Impact of the VAT Exemption for Importation of Small Consignments Final Report. (European Commission 2015)

——, 'Communication on the on the Mid-Term Review on the Implementation of the Digital Single Market Strategy - A Connected Digital Single Market for All COM(2017) 228 Final' COM(2017) 228 final (2017)

——, A Multi-Dimensional Approach to Disinformation: Report of the Independent High Level Group on Fake News and Online Disinformation (2018)

——, 'Communication From The Commission To The European Parliament, The Council, The European Economic And Social Committee And The Committee Of The Regions Tackling Online Disinformation: A European Approach COM(2018) 236 Final' (2018) <https://eur-lex.europa.eu/legal-content/EN/TXT/?uri=CELEX:52018DC0236> accessed 19 July 2019

——, 'Assessment of the Code of Conduct on Hate Speech on Line - State of Play (Information Note) - 12522/19' (2019)

——, 'Report on the Protection and Enforcement of Intellectual Property Rights in Third Countries - SWD(2019) 452 Final/2' (2020)

——, 'Commission Launches Consultation to Seek Views on Digital Services Act Package' (European Commission - European Commission, 2 June 2020) <https://ec.europa.eu/commission/presscorner/detail/en/ip_20_962> accessed 21 August 2020

——, 'Combined Evaluation Roadmap/Inception Impact Assessment - Revision of Directive 2001/95/EC on General Product Safety - Ref. Ares(2020)3256809' (2020)

European Council, 'European Counter-Terrorism Strategy - 14469/4/05 REV 4' (2005)

European Data Protection Supervisor, 'Opinion of the European Data Protection Supervisor' (2014) <https://edps.europa.eu/data-protection/our-work/publications/opinions/comprehensive-approach-personal-data-protection_en> accessed 19 August 2020

European Parliament, 'REPORT on the Proposal for a Regulation of the European Parliament and of the Council on Preventing the Dissemination of Terrorist Content Online - A8-0193/2019' (2019) PE 632.087v02-00 <https://www.europarl.europa.eu/doceo/document/A-8-2019-0193_EN.html> accessed 30 April 2020

European Union Agency for Law Enforcement Cooperation, European Union Terrorism Situation and Trend Report 2019. (2019)

European Union Council, 'Progress Report - E-Commerce Directive - 8891/99' (1999)

Europol and EU Intellectual Property Office, '2017 Situation Report on Counterfeiting and Piracy in the European Union' (2017)

Evans DS, 'Competition and Regulatory Policy for Multi-Sided Platforms with Applications to the Web Economy' [2008] SSRN Electronic Journal <http://www.ssrn.com/abstract=1090368> accessed 30 July 2019

Evans DS and Schmalensee R, 'Network Effects: March to the Evidence, Not to the Slogans' [2017] SSRN Electronic Journal <https://www.ssrn.com/abstract=3027691> accessed 31 July 2019

Favro K and Zolynski C, 'De la régulation des contenus haineux à la régulation des contenus (illicites)' [2019] Legipresse 461

Feintuck M, 'Precautionary Maybe, but What's the Principle? The Precautionary Principle, the Regulation of Risk, and the Public Domain' (2005) 32 Journal of Law and Society 371

Féral-Schuhl C, Cyberdroit 2018/19 - 7e ed.: Le droit à l'épreuve de l'internet (Edition 2018-2019, Dalloz 2018)

Fhima IS, 'Trademark Law and Advertising Keywords', Research Handbook on EU Internet Law (Edward Elgar 2014)

Finck M, 'Digital Co-Regulation: Designing a Supranational Legal Framework for the Platform Economy' <https://papers.ssrn.com/abstract=2990043> accessed 3 August 2020

Floridi L, 'Information Ethics: On the Philosophical Foundation of Computer Ethics' (1999) 1 Ethics and Information Technology 33

Ford C, Innovation and the State: Finance, Regulation, and Justice (Cambridge University Press 2017)

Fox J, Cruz C and Lee JY, 'Perpetuating Online Sexism Offline: Anonymity, Interactivity, and the Effects of Sexist Hashtags on Social Media' (2015) 52 Computers in Human Behavior 436

Francois T, 'Terrorist Content Online' (European Parliament 2020) Members' Research Service PE 649.326

Frankel S and others (eds), 'After Twenty Years: Revisiting Copyright Liability of Online Intermediaries', The evolution and equilibrium of copyright in the digital age (Cambridge University Press 2014)

Freeman J, 'Consumer Legislation and E-Commerce Challenges' (2015) 2 Rivista Italiana di Antitrust/Italian Antitrust Review <http://iar.agcm.it/article/view/11380> accessed 19 September 2017

Frieden R, 'A Primer on Network Neutrality' (2008) 43 Intereconomics 4

Friedmann D, 'Sinking the Safe Harbour with the Legal Certainty of Strict Liability in Sight' (2014) 9 Journal of Intellectual Property Law & Practice 148

Frontier Economics, 'The Economic Impacts of Counterfeiting and Piracy - Report Prepared for BASCAP and INTA'

Frosio GF, 'Reforming Intermediary Liability in the Platform Economy: A European Digital Single Market Strategy' [2017] Northwestern University Law Review Online

——, 'The Death of No Monitoring Obligations' (2017) 8 J. Intell. Prop. Info. Tech. & Elec. Com. L. 199

——, 'Why Keep a Dog and Bark Yourself? From Intermediary Liability to Responsibility' (2018) 26 International Journal of Law and Information Technology 1

Frosio GF and Mendis S, 'Monitoring and Filtering: European Reform or Global Trend?' [2019] Center for International Intellectual Property Studies Research Paper No. 2019-05 29

Gadinis S and Mangels C, 'Collaborative Gatekeepers' (2016) 73 Wash. & Lee L. Rev. 797

Gagliardone I and others, Countering Online Hate Speech (UNESCO 2015)

Galland J-P, 'The Difficulties of Regulating Markets and Risks in Europe through Notified Bodies' (2013) 4 European Journal of Risk Regulation 365

Garcia LD, 'The Evolution of the Internet: A Socio-Economic Account' in Johannes M Bauer and Michael Latzer (eds), Handbook on the economics of the internet (Paperback edition, EE, Edward Elgar Publishing 2017)

Garcia Martinez M, Verbruggen P and Fearne A, 'Risk-Based Approaches to Food Safety Regulation: What Role for Co-Regulation?' (2013) 16 Journal of Risk Research 1101

Garland J and Chakraborti N, 'Divided by a Common Concept? Assessing the Implications of Different Conceptualizations of Hate Crime in the European Union' (2012) 9 European Journal of Criminology 38

Geiger C, 'The Rise of Criminal Enforcement of Intellectual Property Righs...and Its Failure in the Context of Copyright Infringements on the Internet' in Susy Frankel, Daniel J Gervais and New Zealand Centre of International Economic Law (eds), The evolution and equilibrium of copyright in the digital age (Cambridge University Press 2014)

Geiger C and Izyumenko E, 'The Role of Human Rights in Copyright Enforcement Online: Elaborating a Legal Framework for Website Blocking' (2016) 3 American University International Law Review 45

Geiger C and Schönherr F, 'Limitations to Copyright in the Digital Age' in Andrej Savin and Jan Trzaskowski (eds), Research Handbook on EU Internet Law (Edward Elgar Publishing 2014)

Geschke D and others, '#Hass Im Netz - Der schleichende Angriff auf unsere Demokratie' (Institut für Demokratie und Zivilgesellschaft (IDZ) 2019) <http://www.das-nettz.de/publikationen/hass-im-netz-der-schleichende-angriff-auf-unsere-demokratie> accessed 3 April 2020

Giblin R, 'Beyond Graduated Response' in Susy Frankel, Daniel J Gervais and New Zealand Centre of International Economic Law (eds), The evolution and equilibrium of copyright in the digital age (Cambridge University Press 2014)

Giddens A and Sutton PW, Sociology (6. ed, Polity Press 2009)

Gillespie AA, 'Hate and Harm: The Law on Hate Speech' in Andrej Savin and Jan Trzaskowski (eds), Research Handbook on EU Internet Law (Edward Elgar Publishing 2014)

Gillespie T, Custodians of the Internet: Platforms, Content Moderation, and the Hidden Decisions That Shape Social Media (Yale University Press 2018)

——, 'Platforms Are Not Intermediaries' (2018) 2 Georgetown Law Technology Review 198

Giovanella F, 'Online Service Providers' Liability, Copyright Infringement, and Freedom of Expression: Could Europe Learn from Canada?' in Mariarosaria Taddeo and Luciano Floridi, The responsibilities of online service providers (Springer Berlin Heidelberg 2016)

Gommers C and De Pauw E, 'Liability for Trade Mark Infringement of Online Marketplaces in Europe: Are They "Caught in the Middle"?' (2020) 15 Journal of Intellectual Property Law & Practice 276

Gorwa R, 'The Platform Governance Triangle: Conceptualising the Informal Regulation of Online Content' (2019) 8 Internet Policy Review

——, 'As Platforms Rely Less on Human Content Moderators, What's at Stake?' (Centre for International Governance Innovation, 31 March 2020) <https://www.cigionline.org/articles/platforms-rely-less-human-content-moderators-whats-stake> accessed 22 April 2020

Gorwa R, Binns R and Katzenbach C, 'Algorithmic Content Moderation: Technical and Political Challenges in the Automation of Platform Governance' (2020) 7 Big Data & Society 205395171989794

Goyens M, 'Effective Consumer Protection Frameworks in a Global and Digital World' (2020) 43 Journal of Consumer Policy 195

Granchet A, 'Réseaux sociaux, médias en ligne et partage de contenus : le temps de la responsabilité et de la régulation' [2020] Legipresse 93

Graz J-C, The Power of Standards: Hybrid Authority and the Globalisation of Services (1st edn, Cambridge University Press 2019) <https://www.cambridge.org/core/product/identifier/9781108759038/type/book> accessed 2 July 2020

Great Britain and Department for Culture M and S, Online Harms White Paper. (2019)

Griffith SJ, 'Corporate Governance in an Era of Compliance' (2015) 57 Wm. & Mary L. Rev. 2075

Griffiths A, 'The Trade Mark Monopoly: An Analysis of the Core Zone of Absolute Protection under Art. 5(1)(a)' [2007] Intellectual Property Quarterly 312

Groupe Les Republicains, 'Saisine CC – PPL Avia lutte contre les contenus haineux sur internet' (2020) <https://www.conseil-constitutionnel.fr/sites/default/files/as/root/bank_mm/decisions/2020801dc/2020801dc_saisine.pdf>

Guibault L, 'Why Cherry-Picking Never Leads to Harmonisation: The Case of the Limitations on Copyright under Directive 2001/29/EC' (2010) 1 JIPITEC 55

Haas PM, 'Introduction: Epistemic Communities and International Policy Coordination' (1992) 46 International Organization 1

Harcourt A, Christou G and Simpson S, Global Standard Setting in Internet Governance (First edition, Oxford University Press 2020)

Hatzopoulos V, The Collaborative Economy and EU Law (Hart Publishing 2018)

——, 'Vers un cadre de la régulation des plateformes?' (2019) XXXIII Revue internationale de droit économique 399

Hatzopoulos V and Roma S, 'Caring for Sharing? The Collaborative Economy under EU Law' (2017) 54 Common Market Law Review 81

Haucap J and Stühmeier T, 'Competition and Antitrust in Internet Markets' in Johannes M Bauer and Michael Latzer (eds), Handbook on the economics of the internet (Paperback edition, EE, Edward Elgar Publishing 2017)

Hegarty C and Cameron E, 'Case for Minimal Regulation of Electronic Network Communications' 10th BILETA Conference Electronic Communications (1995) <https://www.bileta.org.uk/conference-papers/10th-annual-conference-1995/> accessed 3 January 2017

Helberger N, 'Challenging Diversity - Social Media Platforms and a New Conception of Media Diversity' in Damian Tambini and Martin Moore (eds), Digital dominance: the power of Google, Amazon, Facebook, and Apple (Oxford University Press 2018)

Helberger N, Kleinen-von Königslöw K and van der Noll R, 'Regulating the New Information Intermediaries as Gatekeepers of Information Diversity' (2015) 17 info 50

Helberger N, Pierson J and Poell T, 'Governing Online Platforms: From Contested to Cooperative Responsibility' (2018) 34 The Information Society 1

Helman L and Parchomovsky G, 'The Best Available Technology Standard' [2011] Columbia Law Review 1194

van Hoboken J, 'The Privacy Disconnect' in Rikke Frank Jørgensen (ed), Human Rights in the Age of Platforms (The MIT Press 2019) <https://direct.mit.edu/books/book/4531/Human-Rights-in-the-Age-of-Platforms> accessed 28 May 2020

Hodwitz O, 'Rule-of-Law and Respect for Human Rights Considerations' in John R Vacca (ed), Online terrorist propaganda, recruitment and radicalization (2020)

Hoecke M van, 'Legal Doctrine: Which Method(s) for Which Kind of Discipline?' in Mark van Hoecke (ed), Methodologies of Legal Research: which kind of method for what kind of discipline? (Hart 2011)

Hoeren T and Bensinger V (eds), Haftung Im Internet: Die Neue Rechtslage (De Gruyter 2014)

Hoffman B, Inside Terrorism (Columbia University Press 2017)

Hoffmann A and Gasparotti A, 'Liability for Illegal Content Online - Weaknesses of the EU Legal Framework and Possible Plans of the EU Commission to Address Them in a "Digital Services Act"' (cep | Centre for European Policy 2020)

Hofmann HCH, 'A European Regulatory Union - The Role of Agencies and Standards' in Panos Koutrakos and Jukka Snell (eds), Research Handbook on the Law of the EU's Internal Market (Edward Elgar Publishing 2017)

——, 'Delegation, Discretion and the Duty of Care in the Case Law of the Court of Justice of the European Union' [2018] SSRN Electronic Journal <https://www.ssrn.com/abstract=3169744> accessed 28 August 2018

Holbrook D, 'Designing and Applying an "Extremist Media Index"' (2015) 9 (5) Perspectives on Terrorism 57

Holt TJ, Freilich JD and Chermak SM, 'Legislating Extremism and Cyberterror' in John R Vacca (ed), Online terrorist propaganda, recruitment and radicalization (2020)

Holznagel B, 'Das Compliance-System Des Entwurfs Des Netzwerkdurchsetzungsgesetzes' [2017] ZUM 2017 615

House of Commons, Home Affairs Committee, 'Hate Crime: Abuse, Hate and Extremism Online' (2017) Fourteenth Report of Session 2016–17 <https://publications.parliament.uk/pa/cm201617/cmselect/cmhaff/609/60902.htm> accessed 14 April 2020

'House of Representatives - Digital Millennium Copyright Act of 1998' (1998) Rept. 105–551

Hugenholtz PB, 'Why the Copyright Directive Is Unimportant and Possibly Invalid Hugenholtz' (2000) 22 European Intellectual Property Review 499

Husovec M, 'Injunctions against Innocent Third Parties': (2013) 4 JIPITEC 14

——, 'General Monitoring of Third-Party Content: Compatible with Freedom of Expression?' (2016) 11 Journal of Intellectual Property Law & Practice 17

Huston G, 'A Quick Look at QUIC' (2019) 22 The Internet Protocol Journal 2

Iacob N and Simonelli F, 'How to Fully Reap the Benefits of the Internal Market for E-Commerce?: New Economic Opportunities and Challenges for Digital Services 20 Years after the Adoption of the e Commerce Directive.' (European Parliament 2020) <https://data.europa.eu/doi/10.2861/47017> accessed 20 April 2021

Jackson BA and others, Practical Terrorism Prevention: Reexamining U.S. National Approaches to Addressing the Threat of Ideologically Motivated Violence (RAND 2019)

Jacob R, Heinz A and Décieux JP, Umfrage: Einführung in die Methoden der Umfrageforschung (3., überarb. Aufl, Oldenbourg 2013)

Jacques S and others, 'The Impact on Cultural Diversity of Automated Anti-Piracy Systems as Copyright Enforcement Mechanisms: An Empirical Study of YouTube's Content ID Digital Fingerprinting Technology' <http://rgdoi.net/10.13140/RG.2.2.14443.54560> accessed 5 June 2020

Jansen H, 'The Logic of Qualitative Survey Research and Its Position in the Field of Social Research Methods' (2010) 11 Forum Qualitative Sozialforschung / Forum: Qualitative Social Research <http://www.qualitative-research.net/index.php/fqs/article/view/1450> accessed 6 August 2019

Johnson DR and Post D, 'Law And Borders- The Rise of Law in Cyberspace' (1996) 48 Stanford Law Review 1367

jugendschutz.net, 'Löschung rechtswidriger Hassbeiträge bei Facebook, YouTube und Twitter - Ergebnisse des Monitorings von Beschwerdemechanismen jugendaffiner Dienste' (Bundesministerium für Justiz und Verbraucherschutz, Bundesministerium für Familie, Senioren, Frauen und Jugend 2017) <https://www.fair-im-netz.de/SharedDocs/Downloads/DE/News/Artikel/03142017_Monitoring_jugendschutz.net.pdf?__blob=publicationFile&v=3> accessed 22 September 2020

——, 'Stellungnahme von jugendschutz.net zum Entwurf eines Gesetzes zur Verbesserung der Rechtsdurchsetzung in sozialen Netzwerken (NetzDG)' <https://www.bmjv.de/SharedDocs/Gesetzgebungsverfahren/Stellungnahmen/2017/Downloads/03172017_Stellungnahme_jugendschutz.net_RefE_NetzDG.html> accessed 22 September 2020

Jougleux N, 'The Role of Internet Intermediaries in Copyright Law Online Enforcement' in Tatiana-Eleni Synodinou and others (eds), EU internet law: regulation and enforcement (Springer Berlin Heidelberg 2017)

Julià-Barceló R and Koelman KJ, 'Intermediary Liability in the E-Commerce Directive: So Far so Good, but It's Not Enough' (2000) 16 Computer Law & Security Review 231

Jütte BJ, 'The EU's Trouble with Mashups: From Disabling to Enabling a Digital Art Form' (2014) 5 JIPITEC 172

——, Reconstructing European Copyright Law for the Digital Single Market: Between Old Paradigms and Digital Challenges (1. edition, Nomos ; Hart Publishing 2017)

Kaczorowska A, European Union Law. (Taylor and Francis 2013)

Kamara I, 'Co-Regulation in EU Personal Data Protection: The Case of Technical Standards and the Privacy by Design Standardisation "Mandate"' (2017) 8 24

Katz ML and Shapiro C, 'Systems Competition and Network Effects' (1994) 8 Journal of Economic Perspectives 93

Katzenbach C and Ulbricht L, 'Algorithmic Governance' [2019] Internet Policy Review <http://policyreview.info/node/1424> accessed 28 January 2020

Kempel L and Wege P, 'Die Haftung von Plattformbetreibern für „eigene Inhalte" – Welchen Einfluss hat ein Managementsystem auf den Umgang mit Haftungsrisiken?' in Nadine Klass, Silke von Lewinski and Henning Große Ruse-Khan, Nutzergenerierte Inhalte als Gegenstand des Privatrechts: Aktuelle Probleme Des Web 2.0. (Springer 2010)

Kerber W and Wendel J, 'Regulatory Networks, Legal Federalism, and Multi-Level Regulatory Systems' (2016) 13–2016 <http://ssrn.com/abstract=2773548> accessed 6 April 2017

Khan LM, 'Amazon's Antitrust Paradox' [2017] The Yale Law Journal 96

——, 'Amazon—An Infrastructure Service and Its Challenge to Current Antitrust Law' in Damian Tambini and Martin Moore (eds), Digital dominance: the power of Google, Amazon, Facebook, and Apple (Oxford University Press 2018)

Kleinsteuber HJ, 'The Internet between Regulation and Governance', Self-regulation, Co-regulation, State Regulation (OSCE 2004) <https://www.osce.org/fom/13844?download=true>

Klonick K, 'The New Governors: The People, Rules, and Processes Governing Online Speech' (2018) 131 Harvard Law Review 1599

Knieps G and Bauer JM, 'The Industrial Organization of the Internet' in Johannes M Bauer and Michael Latzer (eds), Handbook on the economics of the internet (Paperback edition, EE, Edward Elgar Publishing 2017)

Koch H-G, 'Strategies against Counterfeiting of Drugs: A Comparative Criminal Law Study' in Christophe Geiger, Criminal enforcement of intellectual property: a handbook of contemporary research (Edward Elgar 2012)

Koenig TH and Rustad M, Global Information Technologies: Ethics and the Law (West Academic 2018)

Kohl U, 'The Rise and Rise of Online Intermediaries in the Governance of the Internet and beyond – Connectivity Intermediaries' (2012) 26 International Review of Law, Computers & Technology 185

——, The Net and the Nation State - Multidisciplinary Perspectives on Internet Governance (Cambridge University Press 2017)

Kohl U and Fox C, 'Introduction: Internet Governance and the Resilience of the Nation State' in Uta Kohl (ed), The Net and the Nation State Multidisciplinary Perspectives on Internet Governance (2017)

Kothari AM, Dwivedi V and Thanki RM, Watermarking Techniques for Copyright Protection of Videos (Springer Science+Business Media 2018)

Koukiadis D, Reconstituting Internet Normativity : The Role of State, Private Actors, Global Online Community in the Production of Legal Norms (First edition., 2015)

Koz A and Lagendijk RL, 'Distributed Content Based Video Identification in Peer-to-Peer Networks: Requirements and Solutions' (2017) 19 IEEE Transactions on Multimedia 475

Kranz JJ and Picot A, 'Internet Business Strategies' in Johannes M Bauer and Michael Latzer (eds), Handbook on the economics of the internet (Paperback edition, EE, Edward Elgar Publishing 2017)

Kranz P, Harms H and Kuhr C, 'Kontrolle der im Internet gehandelten Erzeugnisse des LFGB und Tabakerzeugnisse (G@ZIELT)' (2015) 10 Journal für Verbraucherschutz und Lebensmittelsicherheit 13

Ku RSR and Lipton JD, Cyberspace Law: Cases and Materials (2nd ed, Aspen Publishers, Inc 2006)

Kuczerawy A, Intermediary Liability and Freedom of Expression in the EU: From Concepts to Safeguards (Intersentia 2018)

Kumar S, 'The Algorithmic Dance: YouTube's Adpocalypse and the Gatekeeping of Cultural Content on Digital Platforms' [2019] Internet Policy Review <http://policyreview.info/node/1417> accessed 26 July 2019

Lachenmeier DW and others, 'Does European Union Food Policy Privilege the Internet Market? Suggestions for a Specialized Regulatory Framework' (2013) 30 Food Control 705

Laidlaw E, 'Notice-and-Notice-Plus: A Canadian Perspective Beyond the Liability and Immunity' in Giancario F Frosio (ed), The Oxford Handbook of Intermediary Liability Online (Oxford University Press 2019) <https://ssrn.com/abstract=3311659> accessed 6 August 2019

Lametti D, 'The Cloud: Boundless Digital Potential or Enclosure 3.0?' [2012] Virginia Journal of Law & technology

Larrieu J, Le Stanc C and Tréfigny-Goy P, 'Droit Du Numérique Juillet 2010 - Août 2011' Recueil Dalloz 2011 2363

Lavi M, 'Content Providers' Secondary Liability: A Social Network Perspective' (2015) 26 Fordham Intell. Prop. Media & Ent. LJ 855

——, 'Evil Nudges' (2018) 21 Vanderbilt Journal of Entertainment and Technology Law

Lee B, Arno M and Salisbury D, 'Searching for Illicit Dual Use Items in Online Marketplaces: A Semi-Automated Approach' (James Martin Center for Nonproliferation Studies, Middlebury Institute of International Studies 2017) 27

Lehrer A, 'Tiffany V. EBay: Its Impact And Implications On The Doctrines Of Secondary Trademark And Copyright Infringement' (2012) 18 Boston University Journal of Science & Technology Law 32

Leistner M, 'Structural Aspects of Secondary (Provider) Liability in Europe' (2014) 9 Journal of Intellectual Property Law & Practice 75

Leistner M, 'Copyright Law on the Internet in Need of Reform: Hyperlinks, Online Platforms and Aggregators' [2017] Journal of Intellectual Property Law & Practice jpw190

Leonard P, 'Safe Harbors in Choppy Waters Building a Sensible Approach to Liability of Internet Intermediaries in Australia.' (2010) 3 Journal of International Entertainment & Media Law 221

Lessig L, 'The Zones of Cyberspace' (1996) 48 Stanford Law review 1403

——, Code and Other Laws of Cyberspace (Basic Books 1999)

——, Code: Version 2.0 (2. ed., Basic Books 2006)

Levinson NS and Marzowski M, 'International Organizations and Global Internet Governance: Interorganizational Architecture' in Derrick L Cogburn and others (eds), Turn to Infrastructure in Internet Governance (Springer Nature 2016)

Lewandowski D, 'Is Google Responsible for Providing Fair and Unbiased Results?' in Mariarosaria Taddeo and Luciano Floridi, The responsibilities of online service providers (Springer Berlin Heidelberg 2016)

Lim PH and Longdin L, 'P2P Online File Sharing: Transnational Convergence and Divergence in Balancing Stakeholder Interests' (2011) 33 European Intellectual Property Review 2011 690

Lipton J, 'Law of the Intermediated Information Exchange' (2012) 64 Florida Law Review 33

——, Rethinking Cyberlaw: A New Vision for Internet Law (Edward Elgar Publishing 2015)

Lodder AR and Murray AD (eds), EU Regulation of E-Commerce: A Commentary (Edward Elgar Publishing 2017)

Lomba N and Evas T, 'Digital Services Act - European Added Value Asessment' (European Parliament 2020) EPRS_STU(2020)654180_EN <www.europarl.europa.eu/RegData/etudes/STUD/2020/654180/EPRS_STU(2020)654180_EN.pdf> accessed 23 October 2020

Mac Síthigh D, 'The Mass Age of Internet Law' (2008) 17 Information & Communications Technology Law 79

Mackey TK, Aung P and Liang BA, 'Illicit Internet Availability of Drugs Subject to Recall and Patient Safety Consequences' (2015) 37 International Journal of Clinical Pharmacy 1076

MacQueen HL and others, Contemporary Intellectual Property: Law and Policy (2nd ed, Oxford University Press 2011)

Madiega T, 'Reform of the EU Liability Regime for Online Intermediaries: Background on the Forthcoming Digital Services Act : In-Depth Analysis.' (European Parliament 2020) <https://op.europa.eu/publication/manifestation_identifier/PUB_QA0420239ENN> accessed 14 October 2020

Maistre R-O, 'Point d'étape Vers Un Nouveau Modèle de Régulation Des Plateformes' [2019] Legipresse 459

Manara C, 'Le droit d'auteur contre l'accès à l'information mondiale ?' (2011) t.XXV Revue internationale de droit economique 143

Marcellino JJ and Blakeslee M, 'Fair Use in the Context of a Global Computer Network--Is a Copyright Grab Really Going On?' (1997) 6 Information & Communications Technology Law 137

Mariez J-S and Godfrin L, 'Censure de La « loi Avia » Par Le Conseil Constitutionnel : Un Fil Rouge Pour Les Législateurs Français et Européens ?' [2020] Dalloz actualité 29 juin 2020

Marsden C, 'Prosumer Law and Network Platform Regulation: The Long View towards Creating Offdata' (2018) 2 Georgetown Law Technology Review 376

——, 'Co- and Self-Regulation in European Media and Internet Sectors: The Results of Oxford University's Study Www.Selfregulation.Info', Self-regulation, Co-regulation, State Regulation (OSCE 2004) <https://www.osce.org/fom/13844?download=true>

——, 'Beyond Europe: The Internet, Regulation, and Multistakeholder Governance—Representing the Consumer Interest?' (2008) 31 Journal of Consumer Policy 115

——, Internet Co-Regulation: European Law, Regulatory Governance and Legitimacy in Cyberspace (Cambridge University Press 2011)

Marsoof A, Internet Intermediaries and Trade Mark Rights (Routledge 2019)

Martens B, 'An Economic Policy Perspective on Online Platforms' (Institute for Prospective Technological Studies 2016) Digital Economy Working Paper 2016/05 JRC101501

Martinez Mata Y, 'Bolkestein Revisited in the Era of the Sharing Economy' [2017] Revista Electrónica de Estudios Internacionales <http://www.reei.org/index.php/revista/num33/notas/bolkestein-revisited-in-the-era-of-the-sharing-economy> accessed 12 September 2017

Mayer-Schönberger V and Foster TE, 'A Regulatory Web: Free Speech and the Global Information Infrastructure' (1997) 3 Mich. Telecomm. Tech. L. Rev 17

McGonagle T, 'The Council of Europe and Internet Intermediaries' in Rikke Frank Jørgensen (ed), Human Rights in the Age of Platforms (The MIT Press 2019) <https://direct.mit.edu/books/book/4531/Human-Rights-in-the-Age-of-Platforms> accessed 28 May 2020

Medienanstalt Hamburg/Schleswig-Holstein, 'MA HSH - Auswertung von Transparenzberichten Nach NetzDG' (Medienanstalt Hamburg/Schleswig-Holstein 2019) <https://www.ma-hsh.de/infothek/publikationen/ma-hsh-auswertung-der-transparenzberichte-nach-netzdg.html> accessed 16 April 2020

Mehra SK and Trimble M, 'Secondary Liability of Intermediary Service Providers in the United States: General Principles and Fragmentation' in Graeme B. Dinwoodie (ed), Secondary liability of internet service providers (Springer Berlin Heidelberg 2017)

'Memorandum of Understanding on the Online Sale of Counterfeit Goods, 2016' <http://ec.europa.eu/DocsRoom/documents/18023/attachments/1/translations/> accessed 17 March 2017

'Memorandum of Understanding on the Sale of Counterfeit Goods over the Internet, 2011' <https://perma.cc/DF6M-JNJ8> accessed 29 June 2020

Merrill K, 'Domains of Control: Governance of and by the Domain Name System' in Derrick L Cogburn and others (eds), Turn to Infrastructure in Internet Governance (Springer Nature 2016)

Meserole C and Byman D, 'Terrorist Definitions and Designations Lists - What Technology Companies Need to Know' [2019] Royal United Services Institute for Defence and Security Studies

Michaux B and Van Camp S, 'Belgium' in Gerald Spindler and Fritjof Börner (eds), E-commerce law in Europe and the USA (Springer 2002)

Mill JS, On Liberty and Other Essays (Digireads (2010 edition) 1859)

Miller A and Stivachtis YA, 'Investigations of Terrorist Cases Involving the Internet' in John R Vacca (ed), Online terrorist propaganda, recruitment and radicalization (2020)

Miliou I and Pedreschi D, 'Artificial Intelligence (AI): New Developments and Innovations Applied to e Commerce.' (European Parliament 2020) <https://data.europa.eu/doi/10.2861/2605> accessed 27 October 2020

Mills A, 'The Law Applicable to Cross-Border Defamation on Social Media: Whose Law Governs Free Speech in "Facebookistan"?' (2015) 7 Journal of Media Law 1

'MISSION REPORT: Towards More Effectiveness of Copyright Law on Online Content Sharing Platforms : Overview of Content Recognition Tools and Possible Ways Forward' (Conseil Supérieur De La Propriété Littéraire Et Artistique, Centre National Du Cinéma Et De L'image Animée, Haute Autorité Pour La Diffusion Des Œuvres Et La Protection Des Droits Sur Internet 2020) <https://perma.cc/4L8X-PBQH> accessed 2 June 2020

Moiseienko A, 'Understanding Financial Crime Risks in E-Commerce' [2020] Royal United Services Institute for Defence and Security Studies 34

Montero E, 'La responsabilité des prestataires intermédiaires sur les réseaux' in Mireille Antoine, Le commerce électronique européen sur les rails?: analyse et proposition de mise en oeuvre de la directive sur le commerce électronique (Bruylant 2001)

Moore M and Tambini D (eds), Digital Dominance: The Power of Google, Amazon, Facebook, and Apple (Oxford University Press 2018)

Moscon V and Hilty RM, 'Digital Markets, Rules of Conduct and Liability of Online Intermediaries—Analysis of Two Case Studies: Unfair Commercial Practices and Trade Secrets Infringement' [2020] Max Planck Institute for Innovation and Competition Research Paper 27

Mostardini M, Neirotti L and Travostino M, 'Italy' in Gerald Spindler and Fritjof Börner (eds), E-commerce law in Europe and the USA (Springer 2002)

Mostert F, 'Free Speech and Internet Regulation' (2019) 14 Journal of Intellectual Property Law & Practice 607

Mostert F and Schwimmer MB, 'Notice and Takedown for Trademarks 100th Anniversary Issue' (2011) 101 The Trademark Reporter 249

Mulligan DK and Bamberger KA, 'Saving Governance-By-Design' (2018) 106 California Law Review 697

Musiani F, 'Alternative Technologies as Alternative Institutions: The Case of the Domain Name System' in Derrick L Cogburn and others (eds), Turn to Infrastructure in Internet Governance (Springer Nature 2016)

Musiani F and Denardis L, 'Governance by Infrastructure' in Laura Denardis and others (eds), Turn to Infrastructure in Internet Governance (Springer Nature 2016)

Nair A, The Regulation of Internet Pornography Issues and Challenges (Routledge 2019)

Naughton J, 'Platform Power and Responsibility in the Attention Economy' in Damian Tambini and Martin Moore (eds), Digital dominance: the power of Google, Amazon, Facebook, and Apple (Oxford University Press 2018)

Nazzini R, 'Google and the (Ever-Stretching) Boundaries of Article 102 TFUE' (2015) 6 Journal of European Competition Law & Practice 301

Newman N, 'Reuters Institute Digital News Report 2019' (Reuters Institute, University of Oxford 2019)

Nielsen DCK and others, 'Study on the Economic Impact of the Electronic Commerce Directive' (DG Internal Market and Services, European Commission 2007)

Nimmer D, Copyright: Sacred Text, Technology, and the DMCA (Kluwer Law International 2003)

Noam EliM, 'From The Internet of Science to the Internet of Entertainment' in Johannes M Bauer and Michael Latzer (eds), Handbook on the economics of the internet (Paperback edition, EE, Edward Elgar Publishing 2017)

Nolte G and Wimmers J, 'Wer Stört? Gedanken Zur Haftung von Intermediären Im Internet – von Praktischer Konkordanz, Richtigen Anreizen Und Offenen Fragen' (2014) 16 GRUR

Nordemann JB, Liability of Online Service Providers for Copyrighted Content - Regulatory Action Needed?: In-Depth Analysis. (European Parliament ed, 2018) <http://www.europarl.europa.eu/RegData/etudes/IDAN/2017/614207/IPOL_IDA(2017)614207_EN.pdf> accessed 13 May 2020

——, 'Haftung von Providern im Urheberrecht Der aktuelle Stand nach dem EuGH-Urteil v. 12. 7. 2011 – C-324/09 – L'Oréal/eBay' GRUR 2011 977

OECD, 'The Economic and Social Role of Internet Intermediaries - DSTI/ICCP(2009)9/FINAL' (OECD 2010)

——, 'Online Product Safety' (2016) OECD Digital Economy Papers 261 <http://www.oecd-ilibrary.org/science-and-technology/online-product-safety_5jlnb5q93jlt-en> accessed 23 April 2018

——, 'Rethinking Antitrust Tools for Multi-Sided Platforms' (2018) <www.oecd.org/competition/rethinking-antitrust-tools-for-multi-sided-platforms.htm> accessed 30 July 2019

——, 'Current Approaches to Terrorist and Violent Extremist Content among the Global Top 50 Online Content-Sharing Services', vol 296 (2020) OECD Digital Economy Papers 296 <https://www.oecd-ilibrary.org/science-and-technology/current-approaches-to-terrorist-and-violent-extremist-content-among-the-global-top-50-online-content-sharing-services_68058b95-en> accessed 19 March 2021

OECD and European Union Intellectual Property Office, Trade in Counterfeit and Pirated Goods: Value, Scope and Trends (OECD 2019) <https://www.oecd-ilibrary.org/trade/trends-in-trade-in-counterfeit-and-pirated-goods_g2g9f533-en> accessed 12 June 2020

——, Trade in Counterfeit Pharmaceutical Products (OECD 2020) <https://www.oecd-ilibrary.org/governance/trade-in-counterfeit-pharmaceutical-products_a7c7e054-en> accessed 12 June 2020

Ohly A, 'Counterfeiting and Consumer Protection' in Christophe Geiger, Criminal enforcement of intellectual property: a handbook of contemporary research (Edward Elgar 2012)

——, 'EuGH-Vorlage Zur Haftung Einer Internetvideoplattform Für Urheberrechtsverletzungen - YouTube - Anmerkung von Ansgar Ohly' [2018] GRUR beck-online 1132

——, 'Keine Urheberrechtsverletzung Bei Bildersuche Durch Suchmaschinen - Vorschaubilder III - Anmerkung von Ansgar Ohly' [2018] GRUR 2018 178

——, 'The Broad Concept of "Communication to the Public" in Recent CJEU Judgments and the Liability of Intermediaries: Primary, Secondary or Unitary Liability?' (2018) 13 Journal of Intellectual Property Law & Practice 664

'Omer C, 'Intermediary Liability for Harmful Speech: Lessons from Abroad' 28 Harvard Journal of Law & Technology 37

O'Neil C, Weapons of Math Destruction: How Big Data Increases Inequality and Threatens Democracy (Penguin Books 2016)

O'Regan C, 'Hate Speech Online: An (Intractable) Contemporary Challenge?' (2018) 71 Current Legal Problems 403

O'Reilly T, 'What Is Web 2.0: Design Patterns and Business Models for the Next Generation of Software' [2007] Communication & Strategies 17

Oster J, 'Communication, Defamation and Liability of Intermediaries' (2015) 35 Legal Studies 348

Packin NG and Lev-Aretz Y, 'Big Data and Social Netbanks: Are You Ready to Replace Your Bank?' (2016) 53 Houston Law Review 1211

Pappalardo K and Suzor N, 'The Liability of Australian Online Intermediaries' (2018) 40 Sydney Law Review 31

Pasquale F, 'Platform Neutrality: Enhancing Freedom of Expression in Spheres of Private Power' (2016) 17 Theoretical Inquiries in Law 487

Payne RW, 'Unauthorized Online Dealers of "Genuine" Products in the Amazon Marketplace and beyond: Remedies for Brand Owners' [2014] J Internet Law 3

Pellegrini D and De Canio F, The New Social Game: Sharing Economy and Digital Revolution : Into the Change of Consumers' Habit (Bocconi University Press 2017)

Penfold C, 'Nazis, Porn and Politics: Asserting Control Over Internet Content' (2001) 2 The Journal of Information, Law and Technology <http://elj.warwick.ac.uk/jilt/01-2/penfold.html> accessed 2 October 2019

Perel M and Elkin-Koren N, 'Black Box Tinkering: Beyond Disclosure in Algorithmic Enforcement » Florida Law Review' (2017) 69 Florida Law Review <http://www.floridalawreview.com/2017/black-box-tinkering-beyond-disclosure-algorithmic-enforcement/> accessed 11 April 2019

Perrin W and Woods L, 'Reducing Harm in Social Media through a Duty of Care' (Carnegie UK Trust, 8 May 2018) <https://www.carnegieuktrust.org.uk/blog/reducing-harm-social-media-duty-care/> accessed 28 August 2018

Peters J and Johnson B, 'Conceptualizing Private Governance in a Networked Society' (2016) 18 NCJL & Tech. 15

Phillips T, Litan A and Luong D, 'Begin Investing Now in Enhanced Machine-Learning Capabilities for Fraud Detection' [2017] Gartner 12

Poell T, Nieborg D and Van Dijck J, 'Platformisation' (2019) 8 Internet Policy Review <http://policyreview.info/node/1425> accessed 28 January 2020

Poillot É, Sauphanor-Brouillaud N and Aubry H, 'Droit de la consommation' [2018] Recueil Dalloz 583

Pollicino O and Bassini M, 'Free Speech, Defamation and the Limits to Freedom of Expression in the EU: A Comparative Analysis (Ch. 21)' in Andrej Savin and Jan Trzaskowski, Research Handbook on EU Internet Law (Edward Elgar Publishing 2014

Polzin G and Schwartmann R, 'Sharehoster Und Andere Host-Provider' in Thomas Hoeren and Viola Bensinger (eds), Haftung im Internet: die neue Rechtslage (De Gruyter 2014)

Prévost E, 'Study on Forms of Liability and Jurisdictional Issues in the Application of Civil and Administrative Defamation Laws in Council of Europe Member States' (2019) Council of Europe study DGI(2019)04

Purdy G, 'ISO 31000:2009-Setting a New Standard for Risk Management: Perspective' (2010) 30 Risk Analysis 881

Quintais J, 'The New Copyright in the Digital Single Market Directive: A Critical Look' [2020] European Intellectual Property Review

Quintais JP, 'Global Online Piracy Study' (Institute for Information Law (IViR), University of Amsterdam 2018)

——, 'Global Online Piracy Study Legal Background Report' (Institute for Information Law (IViR), University of Amsterdam 2018)

——, 'Safeguarding User Freedoms in Implementing Article 17 of the Copyright in the Digital Single Market Directive: Recommendations from European Academics' (2020) 10 JIPITEC <https://www.jipitec.eu/issues/jipitec-10-3-2019/5042>

Quintais JP and Poort J, 'The Decline of Online Piracy: How Markets – Not Enforcement – Drive down Copyright Infringement' (2019) 34 American University International Law Review 807

Quintel TA, 'Interoperability and Law Enforcement Access to Personal Data. Data Protection Rights of Third Country Nationals in the Light of the CJEU's Case Law' [2018] Europarättslig tidskrift, 2/2018.

Quintel T and Ullrich C, 'Self-Regulation of Fundamental Rights? The EU Code of Conduct on Hate Speech, Related Initiatives and Beyond' in Bilyana Petkova and Tuomas Ojanen (eds), Fundamental rights protection online: the future regulation of intermediaries (Edward Elgar Publishing 2020)

Rahman KS, 'Regulating Informational Infrastructure: Internet Platforms As The New Public Utilities' (2018) 2 Georgetown Law Technology Review 234

Reed C, Internet Law: Text and Materials (2nd ed, Cambridge University Press 2004)

Reidenberg J, 'Governing Networks and Rule-Making in Cyberspace' (1996) 45 Emory Law Journal 911

Reinsel D, Gantz J and Rydning J, 'The Digitization of the World from Edge to Core' (Seagate, IDC 2018)

Renard I and Barberis MA, 'France' in Gerald Spindler and Fritjof Börner (eds), E-commerce law in Europe and the USA (Springer 2002)

Research Group on the Law of Digital Services, 'Discussion Draft of a Directive on Online Intermediary Platforms' [2016] Journal of European Consumer and Market Law 164

Rhee RJ, 'The Tort Foundation of Duty of Care' (2013) 88 NOTRE DAME LAW REVIEW 61

Rich RB and Ho D, 'Sound Policy and Practice in Applying Doctrines of Secondary Liability Under U.S. Copyright and Trademark Law to Online Trading Platforms: A Case Study' (2020) 32 Intellectual Property & Technology Law Journal 15

Richardson JB, 'With Great Power Comes Little Responsibility: The Role of Online Payment Service Providers with Regards to Websites Selling Counterfeit Goods' (2014) 12 Canadian Journal of Law and Technology

Roberts ST, Behind the Screen: Content Moderation in the Shadows of Social Media (Yale University Press 2019)

Robinson G, 'The European Commission's Proposal for a Regulation on Preventing the Dissemination of Terrorist Content Online' [2018] eucrim - The European Criminal Law Associations' Forum <https://eucrim.eu/articles/commission-proposal-regulation-preventing-dissemination-terrorist-content-online/> accessed 6 April 2020

Rosati E, 'The CJEU Pirate Bay Judgment and Its Impact on the Liability of Online Platforms' (2017) 39 European Intellectual Property Review

——, 'Intermediary IP Injunctions in the EU and UK Experiences: When Less (Harmonization) Is More?' (2017) 12 Journal of Intellectual Property Law & Practice 338

Roudaut, Mickaël R., 'From Sweathsops to Organized Crime: The New Face of Counterfeiting' in Christophe Geiger (ed), Criminal enforcement of intellectual property: a handbook of contemporary research (Edward Elgar 2012)

Rowland D, Kohl U and Charlesworth A, Information Technology Law (4th ed, Routledge 2012)

Ruggie JG, 'Multinationals as Global Institution: Power, Authority and Relative Autonomy: Multinationals as Global Institution' (2018) 12 Regulation & Governance 317

Ryan J, A History of the Internet and the Digital Future (Reaktion Books 2013)

Ruch M and Sackmann S, 'Customer-Specific Transaction Risk Management in E-Commerce', Value creation in e-business management (Springer 2009)

Sartor G, 'Providers Liability: From the ECommerce Directive to the Future - IP/A/IMCO/2017-07' (2017)

——, 'The Impact of Algorithms for Online Content Filtering or Moderation. Upload Filters' (European Parliament 2020)

Saurwein F and others, 'Algorithmische Selektion im Internet: Risiken und Governance automatisierter Auswahlprozesse' [2017] kommunikation @ gesellschaft 22

Saurwein F, Just N and Latzer M, 'Governance of Algorithms: Options and Limitations' (2015) 17 info 35

Savin A, 'Regulating Internet Platforms in the EU - The Emergence of the "Level Playing Field"' (2018) 34 Computer Law & Security Review 1215

——, EU Internet Law (Second edition, Edward Elgar Publishing 2017)

Schepel H, The Constitution of Private Governance: Product Standards in the Regulation of Integrating Markets (Hart Pub 2005)

——, 'The New Approach to the New Approach: The Juridification of Harmonized Standards in EU Law' (2013) 20 Maastricht Journal of European and Comparative Law 521

Schmidt W-A and Prieß M, 'Germany' in Gerald Spindler and Fritjof Börner (eds), E-commerce law in Europe and the USA (Springer 2002)

Smith DM, 'Enforcement and Cooperation between Member States' (European Parliament 2020)

Schmitz S and Ries T, 'Three Songs and You Are Disconnected from Cyberspace? Not in Germany Where the Industry May "Turn Piracy into Profit"' (2012) 3 European Journal of Law and Technology 14

Schmitz S and Robinson G, 'Das NetzDG Und Die CPS Guidelines Zur Verfolgung Strafbarer Inhalte In Sozialen Medien', Recht 4.0 - Innovationen aus den rechtswissenschaftlichen Laboren (OlWIR Verlag für Wirtschaft, Informatik und Recht 2017)

Schmitz S, The Struggle in Online Copyright Enforcement: Problems and Prospects (1. edition, Nomos 2015)

Scholte JA, 'Polycentrism and Democracy in Internet Governance' in Uta Kohl (ed), The Net and the Nation State - Multidisciplinary Perspectives on Internet Governance (Cambridge University Press 2017)

Schruers M, 'Copyright, Intermediaries, and Architecture' in Francesca Musiani and others (eds), Turn to Infrastructure in Internet Governance (Springer Nature 2016)

Schulz W, 'Regulating Intermediaries to Protect Privacy Online – the Case of the German NetzDG', Personality and Data Protection Rights on the Internet, Forthcoming (2018) <https://ssrn.com/abstract=3216572> accessed 27 August 2018

Schwemer SF, 'Trusted Notifiers and the Privatization of Online Enforcement' (2019) 35 Computer Law & Security Review 105339

Scott B and Owen T, 'Governing Platforms after COVID-19' (Centre for International Governance Innovation, 18 August 2020) <https://www.cigionline.org/articles/governing-platforms-after-covid-19> accessed 20 August 2020

Scott C, 'Integrating Regulatory Governance and Better Regulation as Reflexive Governance' in Sacha Garben and Inge Govaere (eds), The EU better regulation agenda: a critical assessment (Hart 2018)

'Section 512 of Title 17 - A Report of the Register of Copyrights' (United States Copyright Office 2020) <https://www.copyright.gov/policy/section512/> accessed 29 June 2020

Senden LAJ and others, Mapping Self-and Co-Regulation Approaches in the EU Context": Explorative Study for the European Commission, DG Connect (European Commission 2015) <https://dspace.library.uu.nl/handle/1874/327305> accessed 19 September 2017

——, 'The Constitutional Fit of European Standardization Put to the Test' (2017) 44 Legal Issues of Economic Integration 337

Senftleben M, 'Breathing Space for Cloud-Based Business Models' (2013) 4 JIPITEC < https://www.jipitec.eu/issues/jipitec-4-2-2013/3743/senftleben.pdf>

Sinha Roy S, Basu A and Chattopadhyay A, Intelligent Copyright Protection for Images, Intelligent Copyright Protection for Images (CRC Press 2019)

Siniketo T, Polland U and Manner M, 'The Pirate Bay Ruling When the Fun and Games End' (2009) 20 Entertainment Law Review 12

Smith GV, 'Brand Valuation: Too Long Neglected' (1990) 12 European Intellectual Property Review 159

Smith L, 'European Commission Publishes Memorandum of Understanding on the Sale of Counterfeit Goods over the Internet' (2011) 6 Journal of Intellectual Property Law & Practice 770

Sokol DD and Ma J, 'Understanding Online Markets and Antitrust Analysis' (2017) 15 Northwestern Journal of Technology and Intellectual Property 43

Solomon L, 'Fair Users or Content Abusers? The Automatic Flagging of Non-Infringing Videos by Content ID on YouTube' (2015) 44 Hofstra Law Review 33

Spindler G, 'BGH-Urteil (U. v. 19.4.2007 - I ZR 35/04) Internetversteigerung II - Anmerkung' [2007] MMR 511

——, 'Präzisierungen Der Störerhaftung Im Internet Besprechung Des BGH-Urteils „Kinderhochstühle Im Internet"' [2011] GRUR 101

——, 'Internet Intermediary Liability Reloaded' (2017) 8 JIPITEC 166

——, 'The Liability System of Art. 17 DSMD and National Implementation – Contravening Prohibition of General Monitoring Duties?' (2020) 10 JIPITEC <https://www.jipitec.eu/issues/jipitec-10-3-2019/5041>

Spindler G and Börner F (eds), E-Commerce Law in Europe and the USA (Springer 2002)

Spindler G, Schuster F and Anton K (eds), Recht Der Elektronischen Medien: Kommentar (2. Aufl, CH Beck 2011)

Spindler G and Thorun C, 'Die Rolle Der Ko-Regulierung in Der Informationsgesellschaft' (2016) 6 MMR-Beil. 1

Stalla-Bourdillon S, 'Sometimes One Is Not Enough! Securing Freedom of Expression, Encouraging Private Regulation, or Subsidizing Internet Intermediaries or All Three at the Same Time: The Dilemma of Internet Intermediaries' Liability' (2012) 7 Journal of International Commercial Law and Technology 22

——, 'Internet Intermediaries As Responsible Actors? Why It Is Time to Rethink the E-Commerce Directive as Well.' in Mariarosaria Taddeo and Luciano Floridi, The responsibilities of online service providers (Springer Berlin Heidelberg 2016)

——, 'Uniformity v. Diversity of Internet Intermediaries' Liability Regime: Where Does the ECJ Stand?' (2011) 6 Journal of International Commercial Law and Technology 51

Stark B and Stegmann D, 'Are Algorithms a Threat to Democracy? The Rise of Intermediaries: A Challenge for Public Discourse' (Algorithm Watch 2020)

Sterrett L, 'Product Liability: Advancements in European Union Product Liability Law and a Comparison Between the EU and U.S. Regime' (2015) 23 Michigan State International Law Review 885

Stevens H, 'Hans Peter Luhn and the Birth of the Hashing Algorithm - IEEE Spectrum' (IEEE Spectrum: Technology, Engineering, and Science News, 30 January 2018) <https://spectrum.ieee.org/tech-history/silicon-revolution/hans-peter-luhn-and-the-birth-of-the-hashing-algorithm> accessed 25 August 2020

Stevens WR and Fall KW, TCP/IP Illustrated. Volume 1, Volume 1, (2nd edn, Addison-Wesley 2011)

de Streel A and others, Moderation of Illegal Content Online: Law, Practices and Options for Reform. (EU Publications Office 2020) <https://data.europa.eu/doi/10.2861/831734> accessed 7 October 2020

de Streel A and Husovec M, 'The E-Commerce Directive as the Cornerstone of the Internal Market: Assessment and Options for Reform.' (European Parliament 2020) <https://www.europarl.europa.eu/RegData/etudes/STUD/2020/648797/IPOL_STU(2020)648797_EN.pdf> accessed 2 November 2020

Summers RS, 'The New Analytical Jurists' (1966) 41 New York University Law Review 861

Susser D, Roessler B and Nissenbaum H, 'Technology, Autonomy, and Manipulation' (2019) 8 Internet Policy Review 22

Suzor NP, Lawless: The Secret Rules That Govern Our Digital Lives (Cambridge University Press 2019)

Svantesson DJB, Solving the Internet Jurisdiction Puzzle (First edition, Oxford University Press 2017)

——, 'Internet & Jurisdiction Global Status Report 2019' (Internet & Jurisdiction Policy Network 2019)

Swiss Institute of Comparative Law, 'Study on Filtering, Blocking and Take-down of Illegal Content on the Internet' (Council of Europe 2015) <https://www.coe.int/en/web/cybercrime/news/-/asset_publisher/S73WWxscOuZ5/content/study-on-filtering-blocking-and-take-down-of-illegal-content-on-the-internet> accessed 4 February 2020

Sylvain O, 'Intermediary Design Duties' (2018) 50 Connecticut Law Review 203

Synodinou T-E, 'Copyright Law: An Ancient History, a Contemporary Challenge' in Andrej Savin and Jan Trzaskowski (eds), Research Handbook on EU Internet Law (Edward Elgar Publishing 2014)

——, 'Directive 2001/29/EC on the Armonisation of Certain Aspects of Copyright and Related Rights in the Information Society' in Arno R Lodder and Andrew D Murray (eds), EU regulation of e-commerce: a commentary (Edward Elgar Publishing 2017)

——, EU Internet Law: Regulation and Enforcement (Springer Berlin Heidelberg 2017)

Taddeo M and Floridi L, 'The Debate on the Moral Responsibilities of Online Service Providers', The responsibilities of online service providers (Springer Berlin Heidelberg 2016)

——, 'The Debate on the Moral Responsibilities of Online Service Providers' (2016) 22 Science and Engineering Ethics 1575

Tambini D, 'Platform Dominance' in Damian Tambini and Martin Moore (eds), Digital dominance: the power of Google, Amazon, Facebook, and Apple (Oxford University Press 2018)

——, 'Social Media Power and Election Legitimacy' in Damian Tambini and Martin Moore (eds), Digital dominance: the power of Google, Amazon, Facebook, and Apple (Oxford University Press 2018)

Tambini D and Moore M, 'Dominance, the Citizen Interest and the Consumer Interest (Conclusion)' in Damian Tambini and Martin Moore (eds), Digital dominance: the power of Google, Amazon, Facebook, and Apple (Oxford University Press 2018)

Tao Q, 'The Knowledge Standard for the Internet Intermediary Liability in China' (2012) 20 International Journal of Law and Information Technology 1

Tao Q, 'Legal Framework of Online Intermediaries' Liability in China' (2012) 14 info 59

Technopolis Group and others, 'Ex-Post Evaluation of the Application of the Market Surveillance Provisions of Regulation (EC) No 765/2008' (2017)

Teubner, 'Self-Constitutionalizing TNCs? On the Linkage of "Private" and "Public" Corporate Codes of Conduct' (2011) 18 Indiana Journal of Global Legal Studies 617

Teubner G, 'Global Bukowina: Legal Pluralism in the World-Society', Global Law Without a State (1997)

'The Economic Impact of Counterfeiting and Piracy OECD - Executive Summary' (OECD 2007)

Thompson M, 'Beyond Gatekeeping: The Normative Responsibility of Internet Intermediaries' (2016) 18 Vanderbilt Journal of Entertainment & Technology Law 783

Timmermans S and Epstein S, 'A World of Standards but Not a Standard World: Toward a Sociology of Standards and Standardization' (2010) 36 Annual Review of Sociology 69

Topidi K, 'Words That Hurt (2): National and International Perspectives on Hate Speech Regulation' [2019] SSRN Electronic Journal <https://www.ssrn.com/abstract=3488718> accessed 6 April 2020

Tuch AF, 'Multiple Gatekeepers' (2010) 96 Virginia Law Review 1583

Tworek H, 'How Platforms Could Benefit from the Precautionary Principle' (Centre for International Governance Innovation, 19 November 2019) <https://www.cigionline.org/articles/how-platforms-could-benefit-precautionary-principle> accessed 17 August 2020

UK Parliament, 'Lords Hansard Text for 23 Sep 2013 (Pt 0001)' (2013) <https://publications.parliament.uk/pa/ld201314/ldhansrd/text/130923w0001.htm#wa_st_3> accessed 27 April 2020

Ullrich C, 'Online Intermediaries' Liability 2012: As the Digital Economy Comes of Age, Does the Industry Need to Take On More Responsibilities?' (Social Science Research Network 2012) SSRN Scholarly Paper ID 3594317 <https://papers.ssrn.com/abstract=3594317> accessed 22 July 2020

——, 'Standards for Duty of Care? Debating Intermediary Liability from a Sectoral Perspective' (2017) 8 JIPITEC 111

——, 'A Risk-Based Approach towards Infringement Prevention on the Internet: Adopting the Anti-Money Laundering Framework to Online Platforms' (2018) 26 International Journal of Law and Information Technology 226

——, 'Déjà vu Davidoff – The German Federal Court of Justice Refers Another Case Brought by Coty Dealing with Trade Marks in e-Commerce to the CJEU' (2019) 14 Journal of Intellectual Property Law & Practice 5

——, 'New Approach Meets New Economy: Enforcing EU Product Safety in e-Commerce' (2019) 26 Maastricht Journal of European and Comparative Law 558

UNIFAB, 'Counterfeiting & Terrorism, Edition 2016' (2015) <https://www.unifab.com/wp-content/uploads/2016/06/Rapport-A-Terrorisme-2015_GB_22.pdf> accessed 14 November 2019

Union PO of the E, 'European Union Serious and Organised Crime Threat Assessment : Crime in the Age of Technology.' (2017) Website <https://publications.europa.eu/en/publication-detail/-/publication/a0c983b4-1db0-11e7-aeb3-01aa75ed71a1/language-en/format-PDF> accessed 17 August 2018

Urban JM, Karaganis J and Schofield BL, Notice and Takedown in Everyday Practice (American Assembly 2016)

US Department of Justice's, 'Department of Justice's Review of Section 230 of the Communications Decency Act Of 1996' (2020) <https://www.justice.gov/ag/department-justice-s-review-section-230-communications-decency-act-1996> accessed 7 October 2020

Valcke P, Graef I and Clifford D, 'IFairness – Constructing Fairness in IT (and Other Areas of) Law through Intra- and Interdisciplinarity' (2018) 34 Computer Law & Security Review 707

Valcke P, Kuczerawy A and Ombelet P-J, 'Did the Romans Get It Right? What Delfi, Google, EBay, and UPC TeleKabel Wien Have in Common' in Mariarosaria Taddeo and Luciano Floridi, The responsibilities of online service providers (Springer Berlin Heidelberg 2017)

Vamialis A, 'Online Defamation: Confronting Anonymity' (2013) 21 International Journal of Law and Information Technology 31

van Dam, CC, European Tort Law (Second edition, Oxford University Press 2013)

van der Vegt I and others, 'Shedding Light on Terrorist and Extremist Content Removal' [2019] Royal United Services Institute for Defence and Security Studies

van Eecke P, 'Online Service Providers and Liability: A Plea for a Balanced Approach' (2011) 48 Common Market L. Rev. 1455

van Eecke P and Truyens M, 'Legal Analysis of a Single Market for the Information Society (SMART 2007/0037)' (European Commission 2011) <https://ec.europa.eu/digital-single-market/en/news/legal-analysis-single-market-information-society-smart-20070037> accessed 4 February 2020

van Eijk N a. NM and others, 'Moving Towards Balance: A Study into Duties of Care on the Internet' (Social Science Research Network 2010) SSRN Scholarly Paper ID 1788466 <https://papers.ssrn.com/abstract=1788466> accessed 13 May 2020 van Gestel R and Micklitz H-W, 'European Integration through Standardization: How Judicial Review Is Breaking down the Club House of Private Standardization Bodies' (2013) 50 Common Market L. Rev. 145

van Mil JJH, 'German Federal Court of Justice Asks CJEU If YouTube Is Directly Liable for User-Uploaded Content' (2019) 14 Journal of Intellectual Property Law & Practice 355

van Schewick B, 'Internet Architecture and Innovation in Applications' in Johannes M Bauer and Michael Latzer (eds), Handbook on the economics of the internet (Paperback edition, EE, Edward Elgar Publishing 2017)

Vanberg AD, 'From Archie to Google - Search Engine Providers and Emergent Challenges in Relation to EU Competition Law' (2012) 3 European Journal of Law and Technology 18

Vaqué LG, 'The Proposed EU Consumer Product Safety Regulation and Its Potential Conflict with Food Legislation.' (2014) 9 European Food & Feed Law Review 161

Vedder A, 'Accountability of Internet Access and Service Providers – Strict Liability Entering Ethics?' (2001) 3 Ethics and Information Technology 67

Verbiest T and others, 'Study on the Liability of Internet Intermediaries, Markt 2006/09/E'

——, 'Study on the Liability of Internet Intermediaries, Markt 2006/09/E - Country Report Spain - Executive Summary'

Verbruggen P and Leeuwen BV, 'The Liability of Notified Bodies under the EU's New Approach: The Implications of the PIP Breast Implants Case' (2018) 43 European Law Review 394

Verweyen U, 'Grenzen der Störerhaftung in Peer to Peer-Netzwerken' [2009] MMR 590

Vranken M, 'Duty to Rescue in Civil Law and Common Law: Les Extremes Se Touchent' (1998) 47 International and Comparative Law Quarterly 934

Wagner B, 'Governing Internet Expression: How Public and Private Regulation Shape Expression Governance' (2013) 10 Journal of Information Technology & Politics 389

——, Global Free Expression - Governing the Boundaries of Internet Content (Springer Berlin Heidelberg 2016)

——, 'Free Expression? Dominant Information Intermediaries as Arbiters of Internet Speech' in Damian Tambini and Martin Moore (eds), Digital dominance: the power of Google, Amazon, Facebook, and Apple (Oxford University Press 2018)

Wagner G, 'Haftung von Plattformen Für Rechtsverletzungen (Teil 1)' [2020] GRUR 2020 329

Waisman A and Hevia M, 'Theoretical Foundations of Search Engine Liability' (2011) 42 International Review of Intellectual Property and Competition Law 785

Walker C and Conway M, 'Online Terrorism and Online Laws' (2015) 8 Dynamics of Asymmetric Conflict 156

Wang J, 'Development of Hosting ISPs' Secondary Liability for Primary Copyright Infringement in China – As Compared to the US and German Routes' (2015) 46 IIC - International Review of Intellectual Property and Competition Law 275

Warf B, 'Alternative Geographies of Cyberspace' in Uta Kohl (ed), The Net and the Nation State - Multidisciplinary Perspectives on Internet Governance (Cambridge University Press 2017)

Warwick S, 'Is Copyright Ethical? An Examination of the Theories, Laws and Practices Regarding the Private Ownership of Intellectual Work in the United States' [1999] B.C. Intell. Prop. & Tech. F.

Weber RH, Shaping Internet Governance: Regulatory Challenges (Springer Berlin Heidelberg 2010)

——, 'Future Design of Cyberspace Law' (2012) 5 Journal of Politics and Law 15

Weimann G, Terrorism in Cyberspace: The next Generation (Woodrow Wilson Center Press 2015)

Weiss F and Kaupa C, European Union Internal Market Law (Cambridge Univ Press 2014)

Westerman P, 'Arguing About Goals: The Diminishing Scope of Legal Reasoning' (2010) 24 Argumentation 211

Which?, 'Online Marketplaces and Product Safety' (2019) Policy Paper November 2019 <https://www.which.co.uk/policy/consumers/5234/onlinemarketplaces> accessed 3 July 2020

Wielsch D, 'Private Law Regulation of Digital Intermediaries' [2019] SSRN Electronic Journal <https://www.ssrn.com/abstract=3369592> accessed 3 May 2019

Winkelmann S, 'Statistik Der Marktüberwachung 2019' (Bundesnetzagentur 2020)

Winn JK, 'Globalization and Standards: The Logic of Two-Level Games' (2009) 5 I/S: A Journal of Law and Policy for the Information Society 34

Winner L, 'Cyberlibertarian Myths and the Prospects for Community' (1997) 27 ACM SIGCAS Computers and Society 14

Wischmeyer T, '"What Is Illegal Offline Is Also Illegal Online": The German Network Enforcement Act 2017' in Bilyana Petkova and Tuomas Ojanen (eds), Fundamental rights protection online: the future regulation of intermediaries (Edward Elgar Publishing 2020)

Wood C and others, 'Great Britain' in Gerald Spindler and Fritjof Börner (eds), E-commerce law in Europe and the USA (Springer 2002)

Woods L, 'Duty of Care' (2018) 46 InterMEDIA

——, 'The Carnegie Statutory Duty of Care and Fundamental Freedoms' [2019] Carnegie UK Trust <https://www.carnegieuktrust.org.uk/publications/doc-fundamental-freedoms/> accessed 2 March 2020

——, 'The Duty of Care in the Online Harms White Paper' (2019) 11 Journal of Media Law 6

Woods L and Perrin W, 'Online Harm Reduction – a Statutory Duty of Care and Regulator' (Carnegie UK Trust 2019)

Wright RW, 'Allocating Liability Among Multiple Responsible Causes: A Principled Defense of Joint and Several Liability for Actual Harm and Risk Exposure' 21 UC Davis Law Review 1141

Wu FT, 'Collateral Censorship and the Limits of Intermediary Immunity' (2011) 87 Notre Dame Law Review 293

Wu T, The Master Switch: The Rise and Fall of Information Empires (Atlantic 2012)

——, 'Will Artificial Intelligence Eat the Law? The Rise of Hybrid Social-Ordering Systems' (2019) 119 Columbia Law Review 2001

Yen AC, 'Internet Service Provider Liability for Subscriber Copyright Infringement, Enterprise Liability, and the First Amendment' 88 The Georgetown Law Journal 63

Yeung K, 'Why Worry about Decision-Making by Machine?' in Karen Yeung and Martin Lodge, Algorithmic regulation (2019)

Yeung K and Expert Committee on human rights dimensions of automated data processing and different forms of artificial intelligence (MSI-AUT), 'Responsibility and AI' (2019) Council of Europe study DGI(2019)05 <https://edoc.coe.int/en/artificial-intelligence/8026-responsibility-and-ai.html> accessed 11 November 2020

Yu Y and Wang X, 'E-Commerce Logistics in Supply Chain Management' (2017) 117 Industrial Management & Data Systems 24

Zarsky TZ, 'Incompatible: The GDPR in the Age of Big Data.' (2017) 47 Seton Hall Law Review 995

Zeno-Zencovich V, 'Anonymous Speech on the Internet' in András Koltay (ed), Media Freedom and Regulation in the New Media World (Wolters Kluwer Kft 2014)

——, 'Legal Epistemology in the Times of Big Data' in Ginevra Peruginelli and Sebastiano Faro (eds), Knowledge of the law in the big data age (IOS Press 2019)

Zeno-Zencovich V and Codiglione GG, 'Ten legal perspectives on the "big data revolution"' in Fabiana Di Porto (ed), Big data e concorrenza (A Giuffrè editore 2016)

Zetzsche DA and others, 'Regulating a Revolution: From Regulatory Sandboxes to Smart Regulation' (2017) 23 Fordham Journal of Corporate & Financial Law 31

Zittrain J, Jurisdiction (Foundation Press 2005)

Zuboff S, The Age of Surveillance Capitalism: The Fight for the Future at the New Frontier of Power (Profile Books 2019)

——, '"We Make Them Dance": Surveillance Capitalism, the Rise of Instrumentarian Power, and the Threat to Human Rights' in Rikke Frank Jørgensen (ed), Human Rights in the Age of Platforms (The MIT Press 2019) <https://direct.mit.edu/books/book/4531/Human-Rights-in-the-Age-of-Platforms> accessed 28 May 2020

B. Blog articles, internet news articles and webpages

'2016 W3C Internal Reorganization' <https://www.w3.org/2016/08/2016-reorg.html> accessed 8 August 2019

'AACA Practices' (Alibaba Anti-counterfeiting Alliance) <https://aaca.alibabagroup.heymeo.net/> accessed 25 June 2020

'Administrative Cooperation Groups (AdCos)' (Internal Market, Industry, Entrepreneurship and SMEs - European Commission, 5 July 2016) <https://ec.europa.eu/growth/single-market/goods/building-blocks/market-surveillance/organisation/administrative-cooperation-groups_en> accessed 3 July 2020

Agrawal A, 'THE COPYKAT' (The 1709 Blog, 30 July 2019) <https://the1709blog.blogspot.com/2019/07/the-copykat_30.html> accessed 29 May 2020

Aleksandar S, 'How Much Time Do People Spend on Social Media in 2019?' (Tech Jury, 8 March 2019) <https://techjury.net/blog/time-spent-on-social-media/> accessed 23 July 2019

'Alibaba Group - Intellectual Property Protection Platform (IPP Platform)' < https:////ipp.alibabagroup.com/index.htm > accessed 19 June 2020

'Alibaba's Enhanced IP Protection Platform Now Eliminates Fake Listings in Less than 24 Hours' (10 August 2017) <https://alibabagroup.com/en/news/article?news=p170810> accessed 19 June 2020

'Amazon 2018 Annual Report' (Amazon) <https://ir.aboutamazon.com/annual-reports-proxies-and-shareholder-letters/default.aspx> accessed 19 June 2020

'Amazon 2019 Annual Report' (Amazon) <https://ir.aboutamazon.com/annual-reports-proxies-and-shareholder-letters/default.aspx> accessed 19 June 2020

'Amazon Brand Gating Increases Merchant Suspension Risk' (TameBay, 22 February 2019)

'Amazon Brand Registry: Help Protect Your Brand on Amazon' <https://brandservices.amazon.com/> accessed 19 June 2020

'Amazon Fraud Detector - Amazon Web Services' (Amazon Web Services, Inc.) <https://aws.amazon.com/fraud-detector/> accessed 25 June 2020

'Amazon Leads; Microsoft, IBM & Google Chase; Others Trail | Synergy Research Group' <https://www.srgresearch.com/articles/amazon-leads-microsoft-ibm-google-chase-others-trail> accessed 1 August 2019

'Amazon Lending' <https://sell.amazon.com/programs/amazon-lending.html> accessed 29 June 2020

'Amazon Project Zero: Empowering Brands against Counterfeits' <https://brandservices.amazon.com/projectzero> accessed 25 June 2020

'Amazon Ramping Up Efforts To Take Down Counterfeiters' <https://finance.yahoo.com/news/amazon-ramping-efforts-down-counterfeiters-173702229.html> accessed 25 June 2020

'Amazon Research - Marketplace Pulse' <https://www.marketplacepulse.com/research/amazon> accessed 17 July 2019

'Amazon Warns Customers: Those Supplements Might Be Fake' Wired <https://www.wired.com/story/amazon-fake-supplements/> accessed 9 July 2020

'Amazon.de - Mitteilung an Amazon.de Über Eine Rechtsverletzung' <https://www.amazon.de/report/infringement?> accessed 4 February 2020

'Analysis: ISIS Use of Smaller Platforms and the DWeb to Share Terrorist Content – April 2019 - Tech Against Terrorism' (29 April 2019) <https://www.techagainstterrorism.org/2019/04/29/analysis-isis-use-of-smaller-platforms-and-the-dweb-to-share-terrorist-content-april-2019/> accessed 19 March 2021

Article 19, 'Responding to "Hate Speech": Comparative Overview of Six EU Countries' (2018) <https://www.article19.org/wp-content/uploads/2018/03/ECA-hate-speech-compilation-report_March-2018.pdf> accessed 20 August 2018

'Artikel Bezahlen' (eBay) <https://www.eBay.de/help/buying/paying-items/artikel-bezahlen?id=4009> accessed 26 August 2020

Ärzteblatt DÄG Redaktion Deutsches, 'Onlinespiele und soziale Medien: Corona verstärkt die Sucht' [2020] Deutsches Ärzteblatt <https://www.aerzteblatt.de/archiv/214932/Onlinespiele-und-soziale-Medien-Corona-verstaerkt-die-Sucht> accessed 20 August 2020

Babbs D, 'New Year, New Internet? Why It's Time to Rethink Anonymity on Social Media' (Inforrm's Blog, 31 January 2020) <https://inforrm.org/2020/01/31/new-year-new-internet-why-its-time-to-rethink-anonymity-on-social-media-david-babbs/> accessed 14 August 2020

Ball J, 'How to Cut Big Tech down to Size' (25 January 2019) <https://www.prospectmagazine.co.uk/science-and-technology/how-to-cut-big-tech-down-to-size> accessed 19 August 2020

Barata J, 'Positive Intent Protections: Incorporating a Good Samaritan Principle in the EU Digital Services Act' (Center for Democracy and Technology, 29 July 2020) <https://cdt.org/insights/positive-intent-protections-incorporating-a-good-samaritan-principle-in-the-eu-digital-services-act/> accessed 14 October 2020

Barlow JP, 'A Declaration of the Independence of Cyberspace' (1996) <https://www.eff.org/cyberspace-independence> accessed 24 May 2019

BASCAP, 'Best-Practices-for-Removing-Fakes-from-Online-Platforms' (BASCAP 2016)

Bensinger WHAG, 'L'Oréal, EBay Settle Dispute Over Counterfeit Goods' Wall Street Journal (15 January 2014) <https://www.wsj.com/articles/l8217or233al-eBay-settle-dispute-over-counterfeit-goods-1389816939> accessed 14 January 2020

Berliri M, 'The Court of Appeal of Milan Rules on Yahoo's Liability with Respect to Copyright Infringement' (Global Media and Communications Watch, 25 February 2015) <https://www.hlmediacomms.com/2015/02/25/the-court-of-appeal-of-milan-rules-on-yahoos-liability-with-respect-to-copyright-infringement/> accessed 18 February 2020

'Better Training for Safer Food (BTSF) - Food Safety - European Commission' (Food Safety) </food/safety/btsf_en> accessed 10 August 2018

'BfJ - Pressemitteilungen -Aktuell- - Bundesamt Für Justiz Erlässt Bußgeldbescheid Gegen Facebook' <https://www.bundesjustizamt.de/DE/Presse/Archiv/2019/20190702.html?nn=3451902> accessed 16 April 2020

'Big 5 US Tech Giants Hit $6.4 Trillion in Market Cap, a 53% Jump in a Year – 24/7 Wall St.' <https://247wallst.com/technology-3/2020/07/21/big-5-us-tech-giants-hit-6-4-trillion-in-market-cap-a-53-jump-in-a-year/> accessed 20 August 2020

Bishop T, 'Amazon Forms "Counterfeit Crimes Unit," under Pressure to Escalate Fight against Fake Products' (GeekWire, 24 June 2020) <https://www.geekwire.com/2020/amazon-forms-counterfeit-crimes-unit-pressure-escalate-fight-fake-products/> accessed 25 June 2020

Bottomley J, 'Understanding Caching' [2004] Linux Journal <https://www.linuxjournal.com/article/7105> accessed 8 October 2019

Brett W, 'Defamation Act 2013: A Summary and Overview Six Years on, Part 2, Sections 4 to 14 –' (Inforrm's Blog, 30 January 2020) <https://inforrm.org/2020/01/30/defamation-act-2013-a-summary-and-overview-six-years-on-part-2-sections-4-to-14-brett-wilson-llp/> accessed 13 March 2020

'Browser Statistics' <https://www.w3schools.com/browsers/default.asp> accessed 1 August 2019

Bundesamt für Verbraucherschutz und Landwirtschaft (BVL), 'BVL/FLEP Conference on European Approaches to Risk Based Official Controls in Food Businesses, Including e- Commerce' <http://www.flep.org/downloads/workshops/2010/Risk_based_controls_conf_Berln_day2summary.pdf> accessed 10 August 2018

Byrne PJ, 'FLEP - Food Law Enforcement Practitioners' <http://www.flep.org/what.html> accessed 17 July 2020

Canada E and SD, 'Notice and Notice Regime' (gcnws, 17 June 2014) <https://www.canada.ca/en/news/archive/2014/06/notice-notice-regime.html> accessed 20 December 2019

Carlos Pacheco, 'YouTube Content ID Handbook - Google' (14 March 2013) <https://perma.cc/Y8AB-VCGC> accessed 2 June 2020

'Case Studies & Customer Success - Amazon Web Services (AWS)' (Amazon Web Services, Inc.) <https://aws.amazon.com/solutions/case-studies/> accessed 30 July 2019

'Cdiscount.com Payment' (CDiscount) <https://www.cdiscount.com/payment/paymentinfo.html> accessed 26 August 2020

Cleeng, Live Streaming Piracy: Are We Winning This Epic Battle? (2017) <https://cleeng.com/resources> accessed 30 June 2020

'Code of Conduct on Countering Illegal Hate Speech Online' (2016) <http://ec.europa.eu/justice/fundamental-rights/files/hate_speech_code_of_conduct_en.pdf> accessed 9 March 2017

Condon S, 'Amazon's Project Zero Lets Brands Take down Counterfeits' (ZDNet, 28 February 2019) <https://www.zdnet.com/article/amazons-project-zero-lets-brands-take-down-counterfeits/> accessed 25 June 2020

'Copyright Act 1968 (Cth) | Wilmap' <https://wilmap.law.stanford.edu/entries/copyright-act-1968-cth> accessed 3 January 2020

'Copyright Infringement Notification - YouTube' <https://www.youtube.com/copyright_complaint_form> accessed 4 February 2020

'Copyright Management | Facebook' <https://rightsmanager.fb.com/> accessed 4 June 2020

'Copyright Management Tools - YouTube Help' <https://support.google.com/youtube/topic/9282364?hl=en&ref_topic=2676339> accessed 2 June 2020

Council of the EU, 'Terrorist Content Online: Council Presidency and European Parliament Reach Provisional Agreement' (10 December 2020) <https://www.consilium.europa.eu/en/press/press-releases/2020/12/10/terrorist-content-online-council-presidency-and-european-parliament-reach-provisional-agreement/> accessed 15 March 2021

'Counter-Terrorism:Written Question - 30893' (UK Parliament) <https://www.parliament.uk/business/publications/written-questions-answers-statements/written-question/Commons/2016-03-14/30893/> accessed 27 April 2020

'Data Never Sleeps 2.0' (Domo 2014) <https://www.domo.com/learn/data-never-sleeps-2>

'Data Never Sleeps 3.0' (Domo 2015) <https://web-assets.domo.com/blog/wp-content/uploads/2015/08/15_domo_data-never-sleeps-3_final1.png> accessed 26 July 2019

'Data Never Sleeps 6.0' (Domo 2018) <https://www.domo.com/learn/data-never-sleeps-6> accessed 23 July 2019

'Data Never Sleeps 7.0' (Domo 2019) <https://www.domo.com/learn/data-never-sleeps-7> accessed 23 July 2019

Davis A and Rosen G, 'Open-Sourcing Photo- and Video-Matching Technology to Make the Internet Safer' (About Facebook, 1 August 2019) <https://about.fb.com/news/2019/08/open-source-photo-video-matching/> accessed 29 April 2020

'Digital-Services-Act-Note-DG-Connect-June-2019.Pdf' <https://cdn.netzpolitik.org/wp-upload/2019/07/Digital-Services-Act-note-DG-Connect-June-2019.pdf> accessed 7 January 2020

'"Eau et Rivières de Bretagne" porte plainte suite à la vente de pesticides aux particuliers par Amazon et eBay' (France 3 Bretagne) <https://france3-regions.francetvinfo.fr/bretagne/ille-et-vilaine/rennes/eau-rivieres-bretagne-porte-plainte-suite-vente-pesticides-aux-particuliers-amazon-eBay-1748271.html> accessed 3 July 2020

Eavis P and Lohr S, 'Big Tech's Domination of Business Reaches New Heights' The New York Times (19 August 2020)

'EBay Drives Commitment to Fight Counterfeiting and Piracy' (28 October 2014) <https://www.eBayinc.com/stories/press-room/uk/eBay-drives-commitment-to-fight-counterfeiting-and-piracy/> accessed 19 June 2020

'EBay Research' (Marketplace Pulse) <https://www.marketplacepulse.com/research/eBay> accessed 17 July 2019

'Ecommerce in Europe' (Ecommerce News) <https://ecommercenews.eu/ecommerce-in-europe/> accessed 11 July 2019

'Emerging Risks - Safety and Health at Work - EU-OSHA' <https://osha.europa.eu/en/emerging-risks> accessed 18 August 2020

'Etsy Annual GMV 2019' (Statista) <https://www.statista.com/statistics/219412/etsys-total-merchandise-sales-per-year/> accessed 19 June 2020

'EU Action Needed: German NetzDG Draft Threatens Freedom of Expression' (EDRi, 23 May 2017) <https://edri.org/eu-action-needed-german-netzdg-draft-threatens-freedomofexpression/> accessed 27 August 2018

European Commission, 'Electromagnetic Compatibility (EMC) Directive' (Internal Market, Industry, Entrepreneurship and SMEs - European Commission, 5 July 2016) <https://ec.europa.eu/growth/sectors/electrical-engineering/emc-directive_en> accessed 13 July 2020

——, 'Radio Equipment Directive (RED)' (Internal Market, Industry, Entrepreneurship and SMEs - European Commission, 5 July 2016) <https://ec.europa.eu/growth/sectors/electrical-engineering/red-directive_en> accessed 13 July 2020

——, 'Antitrust: EC Opens Formal Investigation against Amazon' (European Commission - European Commission) <https://ec.europa.eu/commission/presscorner/detail/en/ip_19_4291> accessed 30 July 2019

——, 'Report on the Functioning of the Memorandum of Understanding on the Sale of Counterfeit Goods via the Internet /COM/2013/0209 Final' (2013) COM/2013/0209 final <http://eur-lex.europa.eu/legal-content/EN/TXT/?uri=CELEX:52013DC0209> accessed 17 March 2017

——, 'The "Principles for Better Self- and Co-Regulation"' (Shaping Europe's digital future - European Commission, 22 August 2014) <https://ec.europa.eu/digital-single-market/en/best-practice-principles-better-self-and-co-regulation> accessed 4 August 2020

——, 'EU Internet Forum: Bringing Together Governments, Europol and Technology Companies to Counter Terrorist Content and Hate Speech Online' (European Commission - European Commission, 3 December 2015) <https://ec.europa.eu/commission/presscorner/detail/en/IP_15_6243> accessed 28 April 2020

——, 'Food Hygiene' (Food Safety - European Commission, 17 October 2016) <https://ec.europa.eu/food/safety/biosafety/food_hygiene_en> accessed 9 July 2020

——, 'Novel Food' (Food Safety - European Commission, 17 October 2016) <https://ec.europa.eu/food/safety/novel_food_en> accessed 9 July 2020

——, 'Counter Terrorism and Radicatlisation - Protection' (Migration and Home Affairs - European Commission, 6 December 2016) <https://ec.europa.eu/home-affairs/what-we-do/policies/counter-terrorism/protection_en> accessed 26 August 2020

——, 'Radicalisation Awareness Network' (Migration and Home Affairs - European Commission, 6 December 2016) <https://ec.europa.eu/home-affairs/what-we-do/networks/radicalisation_awareness_network_en> accessed 28 April 2020

——, 'How the Code of Conduct Helped Countering Illegal Hate Speech Online - Factsheet'

——, 'Assessing the Challenges and Opportunities for Market Surveillance Activities in Relation to New Technologies and Digital Supply Chain - Call for Tenders N° 834/PP/GRO/PPA/20/11848 - 2020/S 116-280777' <https://ted.europa.eu/udl?uri=TED:NOTICE:280777-2020:TEXT:EN:HTML> accessed 31 July 2020

——, 'New Legislative Framework - Growth - European Commission' (Growth) </growth/single-market/goods/new-legislative-framework_en> accessed 2 July 2020

——, 'RASFF - Food and Feed Safety Alerts' (Food Safety - European Commission, 17 October 2016) <https://ec.europa.eu/food/safety/rasff_en> accessed 17 July 2020

——, Press Release - Antitrust: Commission Fines Google €2.42 Billion for Abusing Dominance as Search Engine by Giving Illegal Advantage to Own Comparison Shopping Service' <http://europa.eu/rapid/press-release_IP-17-1784_en.htm> accessed 28 August 2018

——, Press Release - Code of Practice against Disinformation: Commission Calls on Signatories to Intensify Their Efforts' <https://europa.eu/rapid/press-release_IP-19-746_en.htm> accessed 2 August 2019

——, Press Release - Digital Single Market: EU Negotiators Agree to Set up New European Rules to Improve Fairness of Online Platforms' Trading Practices' <https://ec.europa.eu/commission/presscorner/detail/en/IP_19_1168> accessed 17 July 2019

——, 'The Digital Services Act Package' (Shaping Europe's digital future - European Commission, 2 June 2020) <https://ec.europa.eu/digital-single-market/en/digital-services-act-package> accessed 4 November 2020

'Europe: Online Grocery Market, by Country 2006-2019' (Statista) <http://www.statista.com/statistics/915391/e-commerce-purchase-rate-of-food-or-groceries-in-europe-by-country/> accessed 7 July 2020

'Europe: Online Grocery Market Sizes 2018-2023' (Statista) <http://www.statista.com/statistics/960484/online-grocery-market-sizes-europe/> accessed 7 July 2020

Facebook, 'Community Standards Enforcement Report - Hate Speech' (2019) <https://transparency.facebook.com/community-standards-enforcement#hate-speech> accessed 16 April 2020

——, 'Community Standards Enforcement Report - Terrorist Propaganda' (2019) <https://transparency.facebook.com/community-standards-enforcement#terrorist-propaganda> accessed 28 April 2020

——, 'Understanding the Community Standards Enforcement Report' (November 2019) <https://transparency.facebook.com/community-standards-enforcement/guide> accessed 28 April 2020

——, 'Intellectual Property' <https://transparency.facebook.com/intellectual-property/jan-jun-2017> accessed 5 June 2020

'Facebook's AI Wipes Terrorism-Related Posts' BBC News (29 November 2017) <https://www.bbc.com/news/technology-42158045> accessed 28 April 2020

FATF, 'What We Do - Financial Action Task Force (FATF)' <https://www.fatf-gafi.org/about/whatwedo/> accessed 24 September 2020

'FSM | About Us' <https://www.fsm.de/en/about-us> accessed 4 February 2020

Gartner, 'The International ISP Market: Evaluation and Selection Criteria (Archived)' (1998) Research Note R-06-3028

——, 'The ISP Market - France' (1998) G0084758

——, 'The ISP Market - Germany' (1998) G0084761

——, 'The ISP Market - UK' (1998) G0084764

'General Food Law - Food Safety - European Commission' (Food Safety) <https://ec.europa.eu/food/safety/general_food_law_en> accessed 6 July 2018

Gentile A, 'Rome Court Finds Videosharing Platform Directly Liable for Content Uploaded by Users' (The IPKat) <http://ipkitten.blogspot.com/2019/07/rome-court-finds-videosharing-platform.html> accessed 24 October 2019

'Germany: Removal of Online Hate Speech in Numbers – Kirsten Gollatz, Martin J Riedl and Jens Pohlmann' (Inforrm's Blog, 23 August 2018) <https://inforrm.org/2018/08/24/germany-removal-of-online-hate-speech-in-numbers-kirsten-gollatz-martin-j-riedl-and-jens-pohlmann/> accessed 27 August 2018

'GifCT' <http://www.gifct.org> accessed 28 April 2020

'Global Digital Report 2018' (Wearesocial 2018) <https://wearesocial.com/blog/2018/01/global-digital-report-2018> accessed 23 July 2019

Google, 'Content Delistings Due to Copyright – Google Transparency Report' <https://transparencyreport.google.com/copyright/overview?hl=en_GB> accessed 28 May 2020

——, 'Removals under the Network Enforcement Law – Google Transparency Report' <https://transparencyreport.google.com/netzdg/youtube?hl=en> accessed 16 April 2020

Greene J, 'How Amazon's Quest for More, Cheaper Products Has Resulted in a Flea Market of Fakes' Washington Post (14 November 2019) <https://www.washingtonpost.com/technology/2019/11/14/how-amazons-quest-more-cheaper-products-has-resulted-flea-market-fakes/> accessed 19 June 2020

'Grocery Sales by Channel in Europe 2018' (Statista) <http://www.statista.com/statistics/1103169/grocery-sales-in-europe-by-channel/> accessed 7 July 2020

'How Conversational Commerce Is Changing E-Commerce' (Content Harmony®, 28 June 2016) <https://www.contentharmony.com/blog/conversational-commerce/> accessed 6 July 2020

'How Google Fights Piracy' (Google 2018) <http://services.google.com/fh/files/newsletters/how_google_fights_piracy.pdf> accessed 2 June 2020

'How PhotoDNA for Video Is Being Used to Fight Online Child Exploitation | Microsoft On The Issues' (On the Issues, 12 September 2018) <https://news.microsoft.com/on-the-issues/2018/09/12/how-photodna-for-video-is-being-used-to-fight-online-child-exploitation/> accessed 3 June 2020

'How Social Media Behavior Influences Counterfeit Purchases' (INCOPRO, 25 February 2020) <https://www.incoproip.com/how-social-media-behavior-influences-counterfeit-purchases/> accessed 30 June 2020

'How to Report Things on Facebook | Facebook Help Center' <https://www.facebook.com/help/181495968648557/> accessed 4 February 2020

Human Rights Watch, 'Germany: Flawed Social Media Law' (Human Rights Watch, 14 February 2018) <https://www.hrw.org/news/2018/02/14/germany-flawed-social-media-law> accessed 16 April 2020

'ICANN Organizational Chart - ICANN' <https://www.icann.org/resources/pages/chart-2012-02-11-en> accessed 8 August 2019

'ICSMS - European Commission' <https://webgate.ec.europa.eu/icsms/?locale=en> accessed 3 July 2020

Institut National de l'Audiovisuel, 'Ina-Signature : Protégez et Gérez Vos Contenus' <https://www.ina-expert.com/content/download/2103/44165/version/latest/file/1> accessed 5 March 2018

INTA Anticounterfeiting Committee China Subcommittee, 'Online Counterfeiting Issues and Enforcement in China (CT20)' (International Trademark Association 2015)

'Intellectual Property' <https://transparency.facebook.com/intellectual-property> accessed 8 May 2020

'International Standard ISO/IEC 29100:2011(E) - Information Technology — Security Techniques — Privacy Framework'

'Internet Users' Preferences for Accessing Content Online - Flash Eurobarometer 437' (European Commission 2016)

'ISO - ISO 9000 Family — Quality Management' (ISO) <https://www.iso.org/iso-9001-quality-management.html> accessed 11 August 2020

'ISO - ISO 31000 — Risk Management' (ISO) <https://www.iso.org/iso-31000-risk-management.html> accessed 14 August 2020

'ISO - ISO/IEC 27001 — Information Security Management' (ISO) <https://www.iso.org/isoiec-27001-information-security.html> accessed 11 August 2020

Jan 21 JY| and 2019, 'Global Ecommerce Sales Grow 18% in 2018' (Digital Commerce 360) <https://www.digitalcommerce360.com/article/global-ecommerce-sales/> accessed 11 July 2019

Jasser C, 'Recent Decisions of the Paris Court of Appeal: Towards an Extra Duty of Surveillance for Hosting Providers?' (Kluwer Copyright Blog, 29 March 2011) <http://copyrightblog.kluweriplaw.com/2011/03/29/recent-decisions-of-the-paris-court-of-appeal-towards-an-extra-duty-of-surveillance-for-hosting-providers/> accessed 17 February 2020

Jeong S, The Internet of Garbage (1.5, Vox Media, Inc 2018)

'Joint Initiative on Standardisation: Responding to a Changing Marketplace - Growth - European Commission' (Growth) </growth/content/joint-initiative-standardisation-responding-changing-marketplace-0_en> accessed 29 August 2018

Kayali L, 'Brussels' Plan to Rein in Big Tech Takes Shape' POLITICO (30 September 2020) <https://www.politico.eu/article/digital-services-act-brussels-plan-to-rein-in-big-tech-takes-shape-thierry-breton-margrethe-vestager/> accessed 4 November 2020

Keller D, 'Filtering Facebook: Why Internet Users and EU Policymakers Should Worry about the Advocate General's Opinion in Glawischnig-Piesczek' (Inforrm's Blog, 7 September 2019) <https://inforrm.org/2019/09/08/filtering-facebook-why-internet-users-and-eu-policymakers-should-worry-about-the-advocate-generals-opinion-in-glawischnig-piesczek-daphne-keller/> accessed 25 October 2019

Kinsella S, 'Twitter Cannot Keep Hiding Behind Blanket Anonymity' (Inforrm's Blog, 6 April 2020) <https://inforrm.org/2020/04/07/twitter-cannot-keep-hiding-behind-blanket-anonymity-stephen-kinsella/> accessed 9 April 2020

Klappich CD and others, 'Warehousing and Fulfillment Vendor Guide' (Gartner 2018) Research Note

Knies B, 'Amazon Haftet Für Urheberrechtsverletzungen Seiner Verkäufer' (new-media-law.net, 9 June 2016) <https://www.new-media-law.net/amazon-haftet-fuer-urheberrechtsverletzungen-seiner-verkaeufer/> accessed 17 January 2020

Ku M, 'Introducing Marketplace: Buy and Sell With Your Local Community' (About Facebook, 3 October 2016) <https://about.fb.com/news/2016/10/introducing-marketplace-buy-and-sell-with-your-local-community/> accessed 11 November 2020

Lee D and Murphy H, 'Facebook Fails to Curb Spread of Medical Misinformation, Report Finds' FT.com (19 August 2020)

'Magnitude of Counterfeiting and Piracy of Tangible Products – November 2009 Update' (OECD 2009) <https://www.oecd.org/sti/ind/magnitudeofcounterfeitingandpiracyoftangibleproductsnovember2009update.htm> accessed 12 June 2020

'Marketplaces Year in Review 2018' (Marketplace Pulse 2018) <https://www.marketplacepulse.com/marketplaces-year-in-review-2018> accessed 17 July 2019

Masters K, 'The One Change That Would Drastically Reduce Counterfeiting On Amazon's U.S. Marketplace' (Forbes) <https://www.forbes.com/sites/kirimasters/2019/11/13/the-one-change-that-would-drastically-reduce-counterfeiting-on-amazons-us-marketplace/> accessed 25 June 2020

Mcconnell G, 'Amazon Starts "Brand Gating" to Stop Counterfeits' (1 September 2016) <https://blog.redpoints.com/en/amazon-plans-to-combat-counterfeits> accessed 19 June 2020

Meeker M, 'Internet Trends 1995' (Morgan Stanley 1996) <https://www.bondcap.com/report/it95/> accessed 14 June 2019

——, 'Internet Trends 2019' <https://www.bondcap.com/report/itr19/> accessed 14 June 2019

'Mobile Operating System Market Share Worldwide' (StatCounter Global Stats) <http://gs.statcounter.com/os-market-share/mobile/worldwide> accessed 31 July 2019

Müller A, 'Wegen Facebook-Likes verurteilt | NZZ' Neue Zürcher Zeitung (29 May 2017) <https://www.nzz.ch/zuerich/aktuell/bezirksgericht-zuerich-wegen-facebook-likes-verurteilt-ld.1298231> accessed 24 March 2020

Murphy H, Evans J and Gray A, 'Facebook Accused of Failing to Deliver on Advertisers' Boycott Demands' FT.com (2 August 2020) <https://www.ft.com/content/752208c1-9d5f-44b5-a3f7-ce2ea6c5dc46> accessed 20 August 2020

Murphy H, Lee D and Venkataramakrishnan S, 'Facebook Groups Trading Fake Amazon Reviews Remain Rampant' FT.com (12 August 2020) <https://www.ft.com/content/d4af6504-924e-4f94-b82e-0f02671faa12> accessed 20 August 2020

nutraingredients.com, 'How Responsible Is Amazon for the Supplements Sold on Its Sites?' (nutraingredients.com) <https://www.nutraingredients.com/Article/2015/10/09/Amazon-s-supplement-responsibility> accessed 9 July 2020

Olay' (Amazon.co.uk) <https://www.amazon.co.uk/stores/Olay/Olay/page/3BBAE664-6ADE-4D62-86AD-A052F323E900> accessed 19 June 2020

'Online Offered Food (2017) - Food Safety - European Commission' (Food Safety) <https://ec.europa.eu/food/safety/official_controls/eu-coordinated-control-plans/online-offered-food-2017_en> accessed 20 April 2021

'Open Letter on Intermediary Liability Protections in the Digital Single Market' (EDRi, 28 April 2015) <https://edri.org/open-letter-on-intermediary-liability-protections-in-the-digital-single-market/> accessed 28 October 2019

Orsi J, Practicing Law in the Sharing Economy: Helping People Build Cooperatives, Social Enterprise, and Local Sustainable Economies. (American Bar Association 2014) <http://public.eblib.com/choice/publicfullrecord.aspx?p=1718422> accessed 25 July 2019

'Our Members' (IWF) <https://www.iwf.org.uk/become-a-member/join-us/our-members> accessed 4 February 2020

'Out of Balance - Defamation Law in the European Union: A Comparative Overview for Journalists, Civil Society and Policymakers' <http://legaldb.freemedia.at/wp-content/uploads/2015/05/IPI-OutofBalance-Final-Jan2015.pdf> accessed 3 December 2020

'Press - YouTube' <https://www.youtube.com/about/press/> accessed 4 June 2020

'Product Safety Policy' (eBay) <https://www.eBay.co.uk/help/policies/prohibited-restricted-items/product-safety-policy?id=4300> accessed 6 July 2020

'Protect Your Copyright with Fingerprints' (Dailymotion Help Center) <http://faq.dailymotion.com/hc/en-us/articles/203921173> accessed 4 June 2020

'Public Register - De Nederlandsche Bank' <https://www.dnb.nl/en/supervision/public-register/index.jsp?naam=> accessed 27 August 2020

Red Points, Millennials and Piracy - Behaviour, Trends and Future Planning (2016) <https://meet.redpoints.com/lp-203-ebook-millennials-and-piracy/> accessed 7 May 2020

'REFIT – Making EU Law Simpler and Less Costly' (European Commission - European Commission) <https://ec.europa.eu/info/law/law-making-process/evaluating-and-improving-existing-laws/refit-making-eu-law-simpler-and-less-costly_en> accessed 7 January 2020

Renieris EM, 'What Google's Privacy Sandbox Means for Internet Governance' (Emerging Technology, Platform Governance - Centre for International Governance Innovation, 19 March 2021) <https://www.cigionline.org/articles/what-googles-privacy-sandbox-means-internet-governance> accessed 1 April 2021

'Research' (Marketplace Pulse) <https://www.marketplacepulse.com/research> accessed 19 June 2020

'Roles and Responsibilities of Intermediaries: Fighting Counterfeiting and Piracy in the Supply Chain' <https://iccwbo.org/publication/roles-responsibilities-intermediaries/> accessed 26 September 2017

——, 'Italian Court Finds Google and YouTube Liable for Failing to Remove Unlicensed Content (but Confirms Eligibility for Safe Harbour Protection)' (The IPKat, 30 April 2017) <https://ipkitten.blogspot.com/2019/03/italian-supreme-court-clarifies.html> accessed 23 January 2020

Rolland S, 'Coronavirus : Internet infesté par les arnaques et les fake news' La Tribune (20 February 2020) <https://www.latribune.fr/technos-medias/internet/coronavirus-internet-infeste-par-les-arnaques-et-les-fake-news-840839.html> accessed 20 August 2020

Rosati E, 'Milan Court Issues Dynamic Blocking Injunction against Italian ISPs - The IPKat' (The IPKat, 25 August 2018) <https://ipkitten.blogspot.com/2018/08/milan-court-issues-dynamic-blocking.html> accessed 18 February 2020

——, 'Facebook Found Liable for Hosting Links to Unlicensed Content' (The IPKat, 21 February 2019) <http://ipkitten.blogspot.com/2019/02/facebook-found-liable-for-hosting-links.html> accessed 23 January 2020

——, 'Italian Supreme Court Clarifies Availability of Safe Harbours, Content of Notice-and-Takedown Requests, and Stay-down Obligations - The IPKat | Diigo' (The IPKat, 20 March 2019) <https://ipkitten.blogspot.com/2019/03/italian-supreme-court-clarifies.html> accessed 23 January 2020

Rowbottom J, 'If Digital Intermediaries Are to Be Regulated, How Should It Be Done?' (Media Policy Project, 16 July 2018) <http://blogs.lse.ac.uk/mediapolicyproject/2018/07/16/if-digital-intermediaries-are-to-be-regulated-how-should-it-be-done/> accessed 7 August 2018

'Safety Gate: The Rapid Alert System for Dangerous Non-Food Products' <https://ec.europa.eu/consumers/consumers_safety/safety_products/rapex/alerts/repository/content/pages/rapex/index_en.htm> accessed 3 July 2020

'Search Engine Market Share Europe' (StatCounter Global Stats) <https://gs.statcounter.com/search-engine-market-share/all/europe> accessed 27 May 2020

'Section 230 of the Communications Decency Act' <https://www.eff.org/issues/cda230> accessed 8 October 2019

'Signaler les comportements inappropriés' <https://help.twitter.com/fr/safety-and-security/report-abusive-behavior> accessed 5 February 2020

'Skype Adds Snapchat-like AI Photo Effects to Its Mobile App' (Engadget) <https://www.engadget.com/2017/11/08/skype-photo-effects/> accessed 31 July 2019

Solomon N, 'Why Amazon's Collaboration With the CIA Is So Ominous – and Vulnerable' HuffPost (34:16 500) <https://www.huffpost.com/entry/why-amazons-collaboration_b_4824854> accessed 10 April 2020

Spitz B, 'France: YouTube, Universal and SACEM Enter into a New Agreement' (Kluwer Copyright Blog, 16 April 2013) <http://copyrightblog.kluweriplaw.com/2013/04/16/france-youtube-universal-and-sacem-enter-into-a-new-agreement/> accessed 9 June 2020

'State of Hate 2020 - Far Right Terror Goes Global' (HOPE not hate 2020) <https://www.hopenothate.org.uk/wp-content/uploads/2020/02/state-of-hate-2020-final.pdf> accessed 9 April 2020

Statista, 'Social Media Usage Worldwide' (2020)

——, 'Online Search Usage' (2020)

——, 'Biggest Companies in the World by Market Cap 2020' <http://www.statista.com/statistics/263264/top-companies-in-the-world-by-market-capitalization/> accessed 11 November 2020

——, 'Most Used Social Media 2021' <http://www.statista.com/statistics/272014/global-social-networks-ranked-by-number-of-users/> accessed 1 April 2021

Stroppa A and others, 'Instagram and Counterfeiting in 2019: New Features, Old Problems' (Ghost Data 2019) <https://ghostdata.io/report/Instagram_Counterfeiting_GD.pdf> accessed 20 October 2020

Technical Committee: ISO/TC 290 Online reputation, 'ISO 20488:2018 - Online Consumer Reviews — Principles and Requirements for Their Collection, Moderation and Publication' <https://www.iso.org/standard/68193.html> accessed 21 July 2020

Thomas Z, 'Misinformation on Coronavirus Causing "Infodemic"' BBC News (13 February 2020) <https://www.bbc.com/news/technology-51497800> accessed 20 August 2020

'Together We're Tackling Online Terrorism' (Counter Terrorism Policing, 19 December 2018) <https://www.counterterrorism.police.uk/together-were-tackling-online-terrorism/> accessed 23 September 2020

'Total Number of Websites - Internet Live Stats' <https://www.internetlivestats.com/total-number-of-websites/> accessed 19 June 2019

'Twitter Rolls out New Reply Controls to Combat Trolls' (VentureBeat, 11 August 2020) <https://venturebeat.com/2020/08/11/twitter-rolls-out-new-reply-controls-to-combat-trolls/> accessed 17 August 2020

UK Intellectual Property Office, 'Search Engines and Creative Industries Sign Anti-Piracy Agreement' (GOV.UK, 20 February 2017)

Urquizu L, 'Counterfeiting Is a Billion-Dollar Problem. COVID-19 Has Made It Far Worse' (Fast Company, 4 May 2020) <https://www.fastcompany.com/90500123/counterfeiting-is-a-billion-dollar-problem-covid-19-has-made-it-far-worse> accessed 20 August 2020

von der Leyen U, 'A Union That Strives for More - My Agenda for Europe. Political Guidelines for the next European Commission 2019 - 2024'

Wakefield J, 'Facebook Internet Cable "Circumference of Earth"' BBC News (15 May 2020) <https://www.bbc.com/news/technology-52676253> accessed 11 June 2020

Washington State, Office of the Attorney General, 'AG Ferguson: Amazon Must Remove Toxic School Supplies, Kid's Jewelry from Marketplace Nationwide | Washington State' (19 May 2019) <https://www.atg.wa.gov/news/news-releases/ag-ferguson-amazon-must-remove-toxic-school-supplies-kid-s-jewelry-marketplace> accessed 3 July 2020

Waters R, 'Facebook's Attempt to Prove Impartiality Looks Doomed to Failure' Financial Times (22 August 2019)

Waters R, Murphy H and McGee P, 'Big Tech Defies Global Economic Fallout with Blockbuster Earnings' FT.com (31 July 2020)

'Website Ranking: Top Websites Rank In The World - SimilarWeb' <https://www.similarweb.com/top-websites> accessed 1 August 2019

Welch C, 'Facebook Now Has Music Licensing Deals with All Three Major Labels' (The Verge, 9 March 2018) <https://www.theverge.com/2018/3/9/17100454/facebook-warner-music-deal-songs-user-videos-instagram> accessed 9 June 2020

'What Is SECONDARY LIABILITY? Definition of SECONDARY LIABILITY (Black's Law Dictionary)' <https://thelawdictionary.org/secondary-liability/> accessed 13 August 2019

'What Is UNLAWFUL? Definition of UNLAWFUL (Black's Law Dictionary)' (The Law Dictionary, 7 November 2011) <https://thelawdictionary.org/unlawful/> accessed 18 February 2019

'White Paper Search Engines - Time to Step Up' (Incopro 2019) <https://www.incoproip.com/reports/how-and-why-search-engines-must-take-responsibility-for-tackling-counterfeiters/>

'Why Tech Giants Have Little to Lose (and Lots to Win) from New EU Copyright Law – Maurizio Borghi' (Inforrm's Blog, 19 September 2018) <https://inforrm.org/2018/09/20/why-tech-giants-have-little-to-lose-and-lots-to-win-from-new-eu-copyright-law-maurizio-borghi/> accessed 8 June 2020

Woods L, 'When Is Facebook Liable for Illegal Content under the E-Commerce Directive? CG v. Facebook in the Northern Ireland Courts' (Inforrm's Blog, 28 January 2017) <https://inforrm.org/2017/01/28/when-is-facebook-liable-for-illegal-content-under-the-e-commerce-directive-cg-v-facebook-in-the-northern-ireland-courts-lorna-woods/> accessed 23 January 2020

C. *Case law*

1. National

I. France

APC et autres v Auchan Telecom, Google France et autres (2013) Unreported (Tribunal de grande instance de Paris)

Carl L v Raphaël M, Thierry M et Réseau Voltaire (2000) Unreported (Tribunal de Grande Instance de Paris 17ème chambre, Chambre de la presse)

Christian, C, Nord Ouest Production v Dailymotion, UGC Images (2007) (Unreported) (Tribunal de Grande Instance de Paris)

Concurrence v Amazon services Europe, Samsung Electronics France [2017] Cour de cassation - Chambre commerciale, financière et économique - 14-16.737, FR:CCASS:2017:CO01027

Décision 2009-580 DC - 10 juin 2009 - Loi favorisant la diffusion et la protection de la création sur internet - Non conformité partielle [2009] Conseil Constitutionnel CSCX0913243S, FR:CC:2009:2009580DC

Décision n° 2020-801 DC du 18 juin 2020, Loi visant à lutter contre les contenus haineux sur internet [2020] Conseil Constitutionnel 2020–801

DWC v eBay France, eBay Europe [2009] Cour de cassation, Chambre commerciale, Paris 08-11.672

eBay Inc, eBay International v LVMH et autres [2012] Cour de cassation (Surpeme Court) Chambre commerciale, financière et économique 11–10.508

eBay International v Burberry Ltd et autres (2012) (Unreported) (Cour d'appel de Paris Pôle 5, Chambre 12)

Google France c/ Syndicat Français de la Literie (2010) (Unreported) (Cour d'appel de Paris Pôle 5)

Google France v Bac films [2012] Cour de cassation, Première chambre civile 11-13.669, FR : CCASS : 2012 : C100831

Google Inc v Les Films de la Croisade, Goatworks Films (2010) (Unreported) (Cour d'appel de Paris Pôle 5, chambre 2)

Groupement des brocanteurs de Saleya, CBA / eBay France et Ing (2012) (Unreported) (Cour d'appel de Paris Pôle 5, chambre 1)

Hermès International v Feitz [2009] Tribunal de Grande Instance de Troyes RG 06/02604

H&M Hennes & Mauritz Logistics GBC France et H&M Hennes & Mauritz AB v Google Inc, Youtube (2013) Unreported (Tribunal de grande instance de Paris)

Jansport Apparel v Cdiscount (2019) (Unreported) (Tribunal de Grande instance, Paris, 3ème chambre - 2ème section)

Jean Yves L dit Lafesse v Myspace (2007) (Unreported) (Tribunal de grande instance de Paris)

Jean-Louis C v Ministère public, la Ligue internationale contre le racisme et l'antisémitisme (Licra), la Ligue française pour la défense des droits de l'homme et du citoyen, le Mouvement contre le racisme et pour l'amitié entre les peuples (Mrap) et l'Union des étudiants juifs de France (Uejf) (1999) Unreported (Cour d'appel de Paris 11ème chambre correctionnelle, section A)

Jean-Yves Lafesse et autres v Google et autres (2009) (Unreported) (Tribunal de grande instance de Paris, 3ème chambre)

Lafuma Mobilier v Alibaba et autres (2017) (Unreported) (Tribunal de Grande instance, Paris)

Les Editions R v Google France, Google Inc (2013) Unreported (Tribunal de grande instance de Paris 17ème chambre civile)

L'Oréal SA c eBay France SA [2009] Tribunal de Grande Instance de Paris RG 07/11365

L'Union des Etudiants Juifs de France (UEJF) v Twitter (2013) (Unreported) (Cour d'appel de Paris Pôle 1, chambre 5)

M X et Nouvelles de l'annuaire Français v Qwant (2020) Unreported (Cour d'appel de Paris, pôle 1, chambre 3)

Maceo v eBay International AG, (2012) (Unreported) (Tribunal de grande instance de Paris, 3ème chambre, 1ère section)

Madame L v les sociétés Multimania Production, France Cybermedia, SPPI, Esterel (1999) (Unreported) (Tribunal de Grande Instance de Nanterre)

Monsieur X et la société Z v Wikimedia France (2014) Unreported (Cour d'appel de Paris, Pôle 2 – Chambre 7)

Olivier M c/ Prisma Presse, Google (2011) (Unreported) (Tribunal de Grande instance, Paris, 17eme chambre)

Roland Magdane et autres v Daily Motion (2010) (Unreported) (Cour d'appel de Paris Pôle 5, chambre 1)

Rose B v JFG Networks (2013) (Unreported) (Cour d'appel de Paris Pôle 1, chambre 2)

SA Louis Vuitton Malletier v eBay Inc and eBay International [2008] 2010 ETMR 10 (Tribunal de Grande Instance de Paris, France)

SARL Zadig Productions, Jean-Robert Viallet et Mathieu Verboud v Sté Google Inc et AFA (2007) (Unreported) (Tribunal de grande instance de Paris)

SNEP v Google France [2012] Cour de cassation, Première chambre civile N° 11-20358

SNEP v Microsoft France et Microsoft Inc (2016) (Unreported) (Tribunal de grande instance de Paris)

UEJF and Licra v Yahoo! Inc and Yahoo France (2000) (Unreported) (Tribunal de Grande Instance de Paris)

II. Germany

Alone in the Dark [2012] BGH I ZR 18/11, GRUR 2013, 370

Auskunftsanspruch über persönliche Daten von Nutzern einer Onlineplattform wegen des Verdachts der Zweckentfremdung von Wohnraum [2017] VG Berlin 6 Kammer 6 L 162.17, DE:VGBE:2017:07206L162170A

Beeinträchtigung der Herkunftsfunktion einer Marke trotz Fälschungshinweises (Parfume Made in China) [2018] LG Stuttgart, 17 Zivilkammer 17 O 928/13, GRUR-RS 2018, 20582

CDBench, 6 U 5475/99 [2000] MMR 2000 617 (OLG München)

CompuServe [1998] AG München 8340 Ds 465 Js 173158/95, MMR 1998, 429

Coty Germany GmbH v eBay International AG (No1), [2011] LG Stuttgart, 17 Zivilkammer 17 O 169/11, [2012] ETMR 19

Davidoff Hot Water III, I ZR 20/17 - [2018] BGH DE:BGH:2018:260718BIZR20.17.0, BeckRS 2018, 19562

Flach Film et autres v Google France, Google Inc (2008) (Unreported) (Tribunal de commerce de Paris 8ème chambre)

FNDF et al vs Orange, Google et al) [2018] Tribunal de grande instance de Paris, 3ème chambre 2ème section N° RG 18/10652, (Unreported)

GEMA v YouTube [2012] LG Hamburg 310 O 461/10, MMR 2012, 404

Haftung der Internetvideoplattform Youtube für rechtswidrige Uploads, 310 O 461/10 [2012] LG Hamburg 310 O 461/10, OpenJur 2012 36010

Haftung des Suchmaschinenbetreibers für geschlossene rechtswidrige Äußerungen [2014] LG Hamburg 324 O 660/12, openJur 2014, 26809

Haftung eines Sharehosters als Störer [2013] BGH I ZR 79/12, ZUM-RD 2013, 565

Haftung eines sozialen Netzwerkes für durch Dritte hochgeladene ehrverletzende Inhalte, 11 O 2338/16 UVR [2017] GRUR-RS 2017 103822 (LG Würzburg)

Haftung für falsche UVP-Angabe bei Amazon [2015] OLG Köln 6 W 29/15, openJur 2016, 3226

Haftung von YouTube für Urheberrechtsverletzungen [2018] BGH I ZR 140/15, GRUR 2018, 1132

Internetversteigerung I (Rolex v Ricardo.de), Az I ZR 304/01 (2004) GRUR 2004, 860 (BGH)

Internetversteigerung II (Rolex v Ricardo.de) [2007] BGH I ZR 35/04, JurPC-Web-Dok. 0108/2007

Internetversteigerung III (Rolex v Ricardo.de), Az I ZR 73/05 [2008] MIR06/2008 (BGH)

Kinderhochstühle im Internet, I ZR 139/08 [2010] MIR 122010 (BGH)

Kinderhochstühle im Internet II, I ZR 216/11 [2013] MIR 2013 Dok 077 (BGH)

Kinderhochstühle im Internet III [2015] BGH I ZR 240/12, 144/2015 JurPC Web-Dok

Marion's Kochbuch [2009] BGH I ZR 166/07, MIR 2010, Dok. 082

Markenrechtsverletzung durch Onlineauktion [2002] LG Düsseldorf 4a O 464/01

Paperboy [2003] BGH I ZR 259/00, MMR 2003, 719

Rapidshare I [2008] OLG Hamburg 5 U 73/07, MMR 2008, 823

RapidShare II [2012] OLG Hamburg 5 U 87/09, MMR 2012, 393

Sharehoster II [2009] OLG Hamburg 5 U 111/08, openJur 2009, 1105

shift.tv, Urteil v 22042009, Az I ZR 216/06 [2009] GRUR 2009 845 (BGH)

Störerhaftung des Webhosters [2007] LG Köln 28 O 15/07, MMR 2007, 806

uploaded [2018] BGH DE:BGH:2018:200918BIZR53.17.0, BeckRS 2018, 26223

Verantwortlichkeit des Betreibers einer Suchmaschine mit Suchwortergänzungsfunktion [2013] BGH VI ZR 269/12, 108/2013 JurPC WebDok

Verantwortlichkeit eines Hostproviders für einen das Persönlichkeitsrecht verletzenden Blog-Eintrag (Blogspot) [2011] BGH VI ZR 93/10, GRUR 2012, 311

Verantwortlichkeit eines Sharehoster-Dienstes für die rechtswidrige Zugänglichmachung urheberrechtlich geschützter Filme [2010] OLG Düsseldorf I-20 U 166/09, ZUM 2010, 600

Versand durch Amazon [2016] OLG München 29 U 745/16, GRUR-Prax 2017 380

Vorschaubilder [2010] BGH I ZR 69/08, MMR 2010 475

Vorschaubilder III [2017] BGH I ZR 11/16, GRUR 2018, 178

Wiederholungsgefahr, 16 O 103/14 [2016] LG Berlin, 16 Zivilkammer DE:LGBE:2016:0126.16O103.14.0A, BeckRS 2016, 10918

Zur Prüfungspflicht des Betreibers einer Internet-Suchmaschine bei Persönlichkeitsrechtsverletzungen [2018] BGH VI ZR 489/16, GRUR 2018, 642

III. Italy

Arnoldo Mondadori Editore SPA, v Fastweb SPA and others [2018] Tribunale di Milano 51624/2017

Delta TV v Google and YouTube [2017] Turin Court of First Instance (Tribunale di Torino) No. 1928, RG 38113/2013

Mediaset v Dailymotion [2019] Rome Court of First Instance 14757/2019

Mediaset v Facebook [2019] Rome Court of First Instance 3512/2019

Order of the Tribunal of Cuneo on 23 June 1997

Order of the Tribunal of Napoli on 8 August 1997

Order of the Tribunal of Roma on 4 July 1998

Order of the Tribunal of Roma on 22 March1999

Reti Televisive Italiane S.p.a (RTI) v Vimeo [2019] Tribunale di Roma 623

Reti Televisive Italiane S.pA v Italia On Line S.r.l [2011] Court of Milan 3821/11

Reti Televisive Italiane SpA v Yahoo! Inc and Reti Televisive Italiane SpA v Yahoo! Inc [2019] Court of Appeal of Milan 7708/19 and 7709/19

Reti Televisive Italiane S.pA v Yahoo! Italia S.r.l and Yahoo! Inc, (2011) (Unreported) (Court of Milan)

Télécom Italia (Tiscali) v Dargaud Lombard, Lucky Comics (2010) (Unreported) (Cour de cassation 1ère chambre civile)

Yahoo! Italia S.r.l and Yahoo! Inc, v Reti Televisive Italiane S.pA (2015) (Unreported) (Court of Appeal of Milan)

IV. UK

Bunt v Tilley & Ors (2006) [2006] EWHC 407 (QB) (England and Wales High Court Queen's Bench Division)

Byrne v Deane [1937] 1 KB 818

Cartier International AG & Ors v British Sky Broadcasting Ltd & Ors [2016] [2106] England and Wales Court of Appeal (Civil Division) A3/2014/3939 & A3/2014/4238, EWCA Civ 658

CG v Facebook Ireland Ltd & Anor [2016] 2016 NICA 54 (Court of Appeal in Northern Ireland)

Galloway v Frazer, Google Inc (YouTube) and Ors [2016] Northern Ireland Queen's Bench Division HOR979, [2016] NIQB 7

Godfrey v Demon Internet Limited [1999] High Court Of Justice Queen's Bench Division 998-G-No 30, EWHC QB 244

Godfrey v Demon Internet Limited [1999] High Court Of Justice Queen's Bench Division 1998-G-No 30, EWHC QB 240

J20 v Facebook Ireland Ltd [2012] High Court Of Justice In Northern Ireland Queen's Bench Division COL10121

L'Oreal SA v eBay International AG (2009) E.T.M.R. 53 (High Court of Justice (Chancery Division))

R v Rock and Overton, [2010] Gloucester Crown Court T20097013,

Sir Elton John and others v Countess Joulebine and others [2001] MCLR 91 (Unreported)

Tamiz v Google Inc [2013] England and Wales Court of Appeal (Civil Division) A2/2012/0691, [2013] EWCA Civ 68

Tamiz v Google Inc Google UK Ltd [2012] England and Wales High Court (Queen's Bench Division) HQ11D03178, [2012] EWHC 449 (QB)

The Football Association Premier League Ltd v British Telecommunications Plc & Ors [2017] 2017 EWHC 480 Ch (England and Wales High Court (Chancery Division))

Totalise Plc v The Motley Fool Ltd & Anor [2001] EWHC 706 (QB) (19 February 2001) (Unreported)

Twentieth Century Fox Film Corp & Ors v British Telecommunications Plc [2011] 2011 EWHC 1981 Ch (High Court of Justice Chancery Division)

V. US

A&M Records, Inc v Napster, Inc [2001] United States Court of Appeals for the Ninth Circuit 00–16401, 00–16403, 239 F.3d 1004

Corbis Corp v Amazon Inc [2004] US District Court, WD Washington (Seattle) No. CV03-1415L., 351 F.Supp.2d 1090

Cosmetic Warriors Ltd & Anor v amazon.co.uk Ltd & Anor (2014) [2014] EWHC 181 (Ch)

Cubby, Inc v CompuServe Inc, (1991) 776 F. Supp. 135 (SDNY)

Hendrickson v eBay [2001] CD Cal CV 01-0495 RJK (RNBx) (C.D. Cal. 2001), 165 F. Supp. 2d 1082

Inwood Laboratories Inc v Ives Laboratories, Inc, (1982) 456 U.S. 844 (United States Supreme Court)

Milo & Gabby LLC v Amazon.com [2017] Fed Cir 2016–1290, 693 F. App'x 879

Oberdorf v Amazon.com Inc [2019] Third Circuit Court of Appeals 18–1041

Perfect 10, Inc v CCBill, LLC [2007] 9th Cir 04–57143, 04–57207, 488 F3d 1102

Playboy Enterprises, Inc v Frena (1993) 839 F. Supp. 1552 (MD Fla)

Randall Stoner v EBay Inc, et al [2000] Sup Ct Ca Civ. No. 305666, (Unreported)

Religious Technology Center v Netcom On-Line Com (1995) 907 F. Supp. 1361 (Dist Court, ND Cal)

Reno v American Civil Liberties Union [1997] US Supreme Court 96–511, 521 US 844

Rosetta Stone Ltd v Google, Inc (2012) 676 F 3d 144 (4th Cir)

Sega Enterprises Ltd v MAPHIA (1994) 857 F. Supp. 679 (Dist Court, ND Cal)

Sega Enterprises Ltd v MAPHIA (1996) 948 F. Supp. 923 (Dist Court, ND Cal)

Stratton Oakmont, Inc v Prodigy Services Co (1995) 1995 WL 323710 (NY Sup Ct)

Tiffany (NJ) Inc v eBay Inc (2010) 600 F. 3d 93 (2nd Cir)

Tiffany (NJ) Inc v eBay Inc (2010) 600 F. 3d 93 93 (2nd Cir)

Viacom International v YouTube [2012] US Court of Appeals for the Second Circuit (Manhattan) 10–03270

Viacom International v YouTube [2013] US District Court for the Southern District of New York No. 07 Civ. 2103, 2013 WL 1689071

Yahoo! Inc v La Ligue Contre Le Racisme Et L'Antisemitisme [2006] 9th Cir 2006 01–17424, 433 F.3d 1199

VI. Other jurisdictions

Audiencia Provincial de Barcelona [2007] Juriscom.net

Christian Louboutin Sas vs Nakul Bajaj & Ors on 2 November, 2018 [2018] High Court of Delhi CS COMM-344/2018

Christian Louboutin v Amazon Europe Core sarl [2019] Chambre des actions en cessation du tribunal de l'entreprise francophone de Bruxelles A/19/ 00918

Copiepresse et al vs Google Inc [2007] Brussels Court of First Instance 7964

Cour d'Appel d'Anvers, 28 février 2002 (2002) (Unreported)

Cour d'Appel de Bruxelles, 13 février 2001 (2001) (Unreported)

Crookes v Newton [2011] Supreme Court of Canada 33412, 3 SCR 269

'CS COMM--344/2018. Case: CHRISTIAN LOUBOUTIN SAS Vs. NAKUL BAJAJ & ORS. Delhi High Court - Case Law - VLEX 744249193' <https://vlex.in/vid/christian-louboutin-sas-vs-744249193> accessed 6 August 2019

Glawischnig-Piesczek v Facebook, [2016] Handelsgericht Wien 11 CG 65/16 w-17

Google Inc v Equustek Solutions Inc [2017] Supreme Court of Canada 36602, 1 SCR 824

Lancôme v EBay, A/07/06032 (2008) (Unreported) (Tribunal de commerce de Bruxelles)

Request for a preliminary ruling from the Bundesgerichtshof (Germany) lodged on 6 November 2018 — LF v Google LLC, YouTube Inc, YouTube LLC, Google Germany GmbH (Case C-682/18) (CJEU)

Request for a preliminary ruling from the Oberster Gerichtshof (Austria) lodged on 1 July 2019 — Puls 4 TV GmbH & Co KG v YouTube LLC and Google Austria GmbH (Case C-500/19) (CJEU)

Stokke Nederland BV v Marktplaats BV [2012] Gerechtshof Leeuwarden 107.001.948/01, NL:RBZLY:2007:BA4950

Technodesign v Stichting Brein [2004] Court of Haarlem 85489 HA ZA 02–992

Vereniging Buma, Stichting Stemra v KaZaA BV (2003) [2004] E.C.D.R. 16 (Hoge Raad)

2. EU and ECtHR

I. EU

Action brought on 24 May 2019 — Republic of Poland v European Parliament and Council of the European Union, C-401/19 (CJEU)

Arsenal Football Club plc v Matthew Reed, C-206/01 [2002] EU:C:2002:651 (CJEU)

Asociación Profesional Élite Taxi v Uber Systems Spain SL, C-434/15 [2017] EU:C:2017:981 (CJEU)

Belgische Vereniging van Auteurs, Componisten en Uitgevers CVBA (SABAM) v Netlog NV, C-360/10 [2012] EU:C:2012:85 (CJEU)

Die BergSpechte Outdoor Reisen und Alpinschule Edi Koblmüller GmbH v Günter Guni, trekking.at Reisen GmbH, C-278/08 [2010] CJEU EU:C:2010:163

BestWater International GmbH v Michael Mebes and Stefan Potsch [2014] EU:C:2014:2315 (CJEU)

Commission Decision relating to proceedings under Article 102 of the Treaty on the Functioning of the European Union and Article 54 of the Agreement on the European Economic Area (AT39740 - Google Search (Shopping)) [2017]

Coöperatieve Vereniging SNB-REACT UA v Deepak Mehta - C-521/17 [2018] EU:C:2018:639 (CJEU)

Coty Germany GmbH v Amazon Services Europe Sàrl and others, C-567/18 [2020] EU:C:2020:267 (CJEU)

Coty Germany GmbH v Parfümerie Akzente GmbH, C-230/16 [2017] CJEU EU:C:2017:941

Daimler AG v Együd Garage Gépjárműjavító és Értékesítő Kft, C-179/15 [2016] CJEU EU:C:2016:134

Elisabeth Schmitt v TÜV Rheinland LGA Products GmbH, C-219/15 [2017] EU:C:2017:128 (CJEU)

Eva Glawischnig-Piesczek v Facebook Ireland Limited, C-18/18 [2019] CJEU EU:C:2019:821

Fra.bo SpA v Deutsche Vereinigung des Gas- und Wasserfaches eV (DVGW) — Technisch-Wissenschaftlicher Verein, C-171/11 [2012] EU:C:2012:453 (CJEU)

Google France, Google Inc v Louis Vuitton Malletier, C-236/08 [2010] EU:C:2010:159 (CJEU)

Google LLC v Bundesrepublik Deutschland, C-193/18 [2019] CJEU EU:C:2019:498

Google Spain v AEPD and Mario Costeja González, C-131/12 [2014] EU:C:2014:317 (CJEU)

GS Media BV v Sanoma Media Netherlands BV, Playboy Enterprises International Inc, Britt Geertruida Dekker, C-160/15, [2016] EU:C:2016:644 (CJEU)

Hoffmann-La Roche & Co AG v Centrafarm Vertriebsgesellschaft Pharmazeutischer Erzeugnisse mbH, C-102/77 [1978] EU:C:1978:108 (CJEU)

Interflora Inc, Interflora British Unit v Marks & Spencer plc, Flowers Direct Online Ltd, C-323/09 [2011] EU:C:2011:604 (CJEU)

J Nold, Kohlen- und Baustoffgroßhandlung v Commission of the European Communities, C-4/73 [1974] EU:C:1974:51 (CJEU)

James Elliott Construction Limited v Irish Asphalt Limited, C-613/14 [2016] EU:C:2016:821 (CJEU)

Johan Deckmyn and Vrijheidsfonds VZW v Helena Vandersteen and Others, C-201/13 [2014] EU:C:2014:2132 (CJEU)

Ker-Optika bt v ÀNTSZ Dél-dunántúli Regionális Intézete, C-108/09 [2010] EU:C:2010:725 (CJEU)

L'Oréal SA, Lancôme parfums et beauté & Cie SNC, Laboratoire Garnier & Cie v Bellure NV, Malaika Investments Ltd, trading as 'Honey pot cosmetic & Perfumery Sales', Starion International Ltd, C-487/07 [2009] EU:C:2009:378 (CJEU)

L'Oréal (UK) Ltd v eBay International AG, eBay Europe SARL, eBay (UK) Ltd and others, C-324/09 [2011] EU:C:2011:474 (CJEU)

Nils Svensson and others v Retriever Sverige AB, C-466/12 [2014], EU:C:2014:76 (CJEU)

Opinion of Advocate General Cruz Villalón UPC Telekabel Wien GmbH v Constantin Film Verleih GmbH, Wega Filmproduktionsgesellschaft mbH, C-314/12 [2011] EU:C:2013:781 (CJEU)

Opinion of Advocate General Jääskinen, L'Oréal (UK) Ltd v eBay International AG, eBay Europe SARL, eBay (UK) Ltd and others, C-324/09 [2010] EU:C:2010:757 (CJEU)

Opinion of Advocate General Szpunar on Eva Glawischnig-Piesczek v Facebook Ireland Limited, C-18/18 [2019] CJEU EU:C:2019:458

Opinion of Advocate General Szpunar on YA, AIRBNB Ireland UC, Hotelière Turenne SAS, Association pour un hébergement et un tourisme professionnel (AHTOP), Valhotel, C-390/18 [2019] ECLI:EU:C:2019:336 (CJEU)

Opinion of Advocate General Szpunar, Stichting Brein v Ziggo BV, XS4ALL Internet BV, C-610/15 [2017] EU:C:2017:99 (CJEU)

Opinion of Advocate-General Ruiz-Jarabo Colomier, Arsenal Football Club plc v Matthew Reed, C-206/01 [2002] EU:C:2002:373 (CJEU)

Opinion of Advocate General Saugmandsgaard Øe, Frank Peterson v Google LLC, YouTube LLC, YouTube Inc, Google Germany GmbH and Elsevier Inc v Cyando AG, Joined Cases C-682/18 and C-683/18 [2020] EU:C:2020:586 (CJEU)

Productores de Música de España (Promusicae) v Telefónica de España SAU, C-275/06 [2008] EU:C:2008:54 (CJEU)

Rewe-Zentral AG v Bundesmonopolverwaltung für Branntwein, C-120/78 [1979] EU:C:1979:42 (CJEU)

Sabrina Wathelet v Garage Bietheres & Fils SPRL, C-149/15 [2016] ECLI:EU:C:2016:840 (CJEU)

Scarlet Extended SA v Société belge des auteurs, compositeurs et éditeurs SCRL (Scarlet Extended), C-70/10 [2011] EU:C:2011:771 (CJEU)

Schlussanträge des Generalanwalts Manuel Campos Sánchez-Bordona, Coty Germany GmbH gegen Amazon Services Europe Sàrl und andere, C-567/18 [2019] EU:C:2019:1031 (CJEU)

Skype Communications Sàrl v Institut belge des services postaux et des télécommunications (IBPT), C-142/18 [2019] EU:C:2019:460 (CJEU)

Stichting Brein v Jack Frederik Wullems, also trading under the name Filmspeler, C-527/15 [2017] EU:C:2017:300 (CJEU)

Stichting Brein v Ziggo BV, XS4ALL Internet BV, C-610/15 [2017] EU:C:2017:456 (CJEU)

Tobias Mc Fadden v Sony Music Entertainment Germany GmbH, C-484/14 [2016] EU:C:2016:689 (CJEU)

Tommy Hilfiger Licensing LLC, Urban Trends Trading BV, Rado Uhren AG, Facton Kft, Lacoste SA, Burberry Ltd v Delta Center a.s, C-494/15 [2016] EU:C:2016:528 (CJEU)

UPC Telekabel Wien GmbH v Constantin Film Verleih GmbH, Wega Filmproduktionsgesellschaft mbH, C-314/12 [2014] EU:C:2014:192 (CJEU)

VCAST Limited v RTI SpA, C-265/16 [2017] EU:C:2017:913 (CJEU)

YA, AIRBNB Ireland UC, Hotelière Turenne SAS, Association pour un hébergement et un tourisme professionnel (AHTOP), Valhotel, C-390/18 [2019] ECLI:EU:C:2019:1112 (CJEU)

II. ECtHR

Delfi AS v Estonia [2015] ECtHR (Grand Chamber) 64569/09

Editorial Board of Pravoye Delo and Shtekel v Ukraine [2011] ECtHR (Fifth Section) 33014/05

Handyside v The United Kingdom [1976] ECtHR (Plenary) 5493/72

KU v Finland [2008] ECtHR (Fourth Section) 2872/02

Magyar Tartalomszolgáltatók Egyesülete and Index.hu zrt v Hungary [2016] ECtHR (Fourth Section) 22947/13

D. Statutes & Bills

Avia L, Proposition de loi visant à lutter contre la haine sur internet

Bundesministerium für Justiz und Verbraucherschutz, Entwurf für ein Gesetz zur Bekämpfung des Rechtsextremismus und der Hasskriminalität 2019

——, Entwurf eines Gesetzes zur Änderung des Netzwerkdurchsetzungsgesetzes 2020

Council of the EU, 'Proposal for a Regulation of the European Parliament and of the Council on Preventing the Dissemination of Terrorist Content Online - Analysis of the Final Compromise Text with a View to Agreement 2018/0331(COD) - 12906/20' <https://data.consilium.europa.eu/doc/document/ST-12906-2020-INIT/en/pdf> accessed 15 March 2021

Counsel P, Malicious Communications (Social Media) Bill 2017 [HC Bill 44]

European Commission, Proposal for a European Parliament and Council Directive on certain legal aspects of electronic commerce in the internal market 1999 [1999/C 30/04]

——, Proposal for a Regulation on consumer product safety and repealing Council Directive 87/357/EEC and Directive 2001/95/EC, COM(2013) 78 final 2013 [2013/0049/COD]

——, Proposal for a regulation on preventing terrorist content online, COM(2018) 640 final 2018 (TERREG)

——, European Parliament legislative resolution of 17 April 2019 on the proposal for a regulation of the European Parliament and of the Council on preventing the dissemination of terrorist content online (COM(2018)0640 – C8-0405/2018 – 2018/0331(COD))

——, Proposal for a Regulation of the European Parliament and of the Council on a Single Market For Digital Services (Digital Services Act) and amending Directive 2000/31/EC, COM(2020) 825 final 2020

European Parliament, Council and the Commission, 'Interinstitutional Agreement on Better Law-Making, OJ C 321/01' (2003)

Lord McNally, Online Harms Reduction Regulator (Report) Bill [HL] 2020 [HL Bill 22]

Additional Protocol to the Convention on Cybercrime, concerning the criminalisation of acts of a racist and xenophobic nature committed through computer systems 2003 (European Treaty Series - No189)

Agreement On Trade-Related Aspects Of Intellectual Property Rights (TRIPS) 1994

Anticybersquatting Consumer Protection Act (ACPA) (15 USC § 1125(d))

Berne Convention for the Protection of Literary and Artistic Works 1886

Broadcasting Services Act 1992

Bürgerliches Gesetzbuch (Germany)

Charter of Fundamental Rights of the European Union 2009

Code Civil (France)

Code Penal (France)

Codice Civile 1942 (Italy)

Council Common Position of 27 December 2001 on the application of specific measures to combat terrorism 2001 (OJ L 344)

Commission Implementing Decision on a standardisation request to the European standardisation organisations as regards European standards and European standardisation deliverables for privacy and personal data protection management - C(2015) 102 final 2015 (M/530)

Copyright Amendment (Digital Agenda) Act 2000 http://www.legislation.gov.au/Details/C2004A00702> accessed 3 January 2020

Communications Decency Act 1996 (47 USC § 230) (US)

Copyright (Amendment) Act, 2012, s. 52 (India)

Copyright, Designs and Patents Act 1988 c.48 (UK)

Copyright Modernization Act 2012 (SC 2012, c 20) (Canada)

Copyright Rules 2013, GSR 172(E) (India)

Council Decision (CFSP) 2020/1132 of 30 July 2020 updating the list of persons, groups and entities subject to Articles 2, 3 and 4 of Common Position 2001/931/CFSP on the application of specific measures to combat terrorism 2020 (OJ L 247)

Council Directive 89/391/EEC on the introduction of measures to encourage improvements in the safety and health of workers at work 1989 (OJ L 183)

Council Framework Decision 2008/913/JHA of 28 November 2008 on combating certain forms and expressions of racism and xenophobia by means of criminal law 2008 (OJ L 328)

Council of Europe - Convention on Cybercrime 2001

Council of Europe - Convention on the Prevention of Terrorism 2005

Council Resolution 85/C 136/01 of 7 May 1985 on a new approach to technical harmonization and standards 2010

Council Resolution of 7 May 1985 on a new approach to technical harmonization and standards 1985 (OJ C 136)

Crime and Disorder Act 1998 (UK)

'Criminal Code Amendment (Sharing of Abhorrent Violent Material) Act 2019' http://www.legislation.gov.au/Details/C2019A00038> accessed 3 January 2020

Decision No 768/2008/EC of the European Parliament and of the Council of 9 July 2008 on a common framework for the marketing of products 2008 (OJ L 218)

Decision No 1151/2003/EC adopting a multiannual Community action plan on promoting safer use of the Internet by combating illegal and harmful content on global networks (OJ L 162)

Defamation Act 1996 c.31 1996 (UK)

Defamation Act 2013 c. 26 (England and Wales)

Directive 95/46/EC of the European Parliament and of the Council of 24 October 1995 on the protection of individuals with regard to the processing of personal data and on the free movement of such data 1995 (OJ L 281)

Directive 98/48/EC of the European Parliament and of the Council of 20 July 1998 amending Directive 98/34/EC laying down a procedure for the provision of information in the field of technical standards and regulations 1998 (OJ L 217)

Directive 1999/44/EC of 25 May 1999 on certain aspects of the sale of consumer goods and associated guarantees 1999 (OJ L 171)

Directive 2000/31/EC of 8 June 2000 on certain legal aspects of information society services, in particular electronic commerce, in the Internal Market 2000 (OJ L 178)

Directive 2001/29/EC of 22 May 2001 on the harmonisation of certain aspects of copyright and related rights in the information society 2001 (OJ L 167, 2262001)

Directive 2001/95/EC of 3 December 2001 on general product safety (OJ L 11)

Directive 2002/58/EC of the European Parliament and of the Council of 12 July 2002 concerning the processing of personal data and the protection of privacy in the electronic communications sector (Directive on privacy and electronic communications) 2002 (OJ L 201)

Directive 2004/48/EC of 29 April 2004 on the enforcement of intellectual property rights

Directive 2005/29/EC of 11 May 2005 concerning unfair business-to-consumer commercial practices in the internal market 2005 (OJ L 149)

Directive 2008/95/EC to approximate the laws of the Member States relating to trade marks 2008

Directive 2008/99/EC on the protection of the environment through criminal law 2008 (OJ L 328)

Directive 2009/48/EC of 18 June 2009 on the safety of toys 2009 (OJ L 170)

Directive 2011/62/EU of 8 June 2011 amending Directive 2001/83/EC on the Community code relating to medicinal products for human use, as regards the prevention of the entry into the legal supply chain of falsified medicinal products 2011 (OJ L 174, 172011)

Directive 2014/30/EU of 26 February 2014 on the harmonisation of the laws of the Member States relating to electromagnetic compatibility (recast) 2014 (OJ L 96)

Directive 2014/35/EU of 26 February 2014 on the harmonisation of the laws of the Member States relating to the making available on the market of electrical equipment designed for use within certain voltage limits 2014 (OJ L 96)

Directive 2014/53/EU of 16 April 2014 on the harmonisation of the laws of the Member States relating to the making available on the market of radio equipment 2014 (OJ L 153)

Directive 2015/849/EU of 20 May 2015 on the prevention of the use of the financial system for the purposes of money laundering or terrorist financing 2015 (OJ L 141, 562015)

Directive 2015/1535/EU of 9 September 2015 laying down a procedure for the provision of information in the field of technical regulations and of rules on Information Society services 2015 (OJ L 241)

Directive 2016/1148 concerning measures for a high common level of security of network and information systems across the Union 2016 (OJ L 194)

Directive (EU) 2015/2436 of the European Parliament and of the Council of 16 December 2015 to approximate the laws of the Member States relating to trade marks (Text with EEA relevance) 2015 (OJ L 336)

Directive (EU) 2017/541 on combating terrorism 2017 (OJ L 88)

Directive (EU) 2018/1808 of the European Parliament and of the Council of 14 November 2018 amending Directive 2010/13/EU on the coordination of certain provisions laid down by law, regulation or administrative action in Member States concerning the provision of audiovisual media services (Audiovisual Media Services Directive) in view of changing market realities 2018 (OJ L 303)

Directive (EU) 2019/790 of the European Parliament and of the Council of 17 April 2019 on copyright and related rights in the Digital Single Market and amending Directives 96/9/EC and 2001/29/EC (Text with EEA relevance.) 2019 (OJ L 130)

Directive (EU) 2019/2161 of the European Parliament and of the Council of 27 November 2019 amending Council Directive 93/13/EEC and Directives 98/6/EC, 2005/29/EC and 2011/83/EU of the European Parliament and of the Council as regards the better enforcement and modernisation of Union consumer protection rules (Text with EEA relevance) 2019 (OJ L 328)

Electronic Communications Act (Estonia) (English Version) 2006

Equality Act 2010 (England and Wales, Scotland)

European Convention for the Protection of Human Rights and Fundamental Freedoms 1950

Gesetz über die Bereitstellung von Funkanlagen auf dem Markt (FuAG) 2017 (Germany)

Gesetz über die elektromagnetische Verträglichkeit von Betriebsmitteln (EMVG) 2016 (Germany)

Gesetz über Urheberrecht und verwandte Schutzrechte (Germany)

Gesetz zur Verbesserung der Rechtsdurchsetzung in sozialen Netzwerken 2017 (BGBl I S 3352 (Nr 61)) (Germany)

Greek Constituion, (Official English language translation of the Greek Constitution, Hellenic Parliament) 2008

Information Technology (Amendment) Act, 2008, s. 79 (India)

Information Technology (Intermediaries Guidelines) Rules, 2011, GSR 314(E) (India)

Joint Action 96/443/JHA to combat racism and xenophobia 1996 (OJ L185)

Loi du 29 juillet 1881 sur la liberté de la presse (France)

Loi n° 82-652 du 29 juillet 1982 sur la communication audiovisuelle 1982 (France)

Loi n° 2004-575 du 21 juin 2004 pour la confiance dans l'économie numérique 2004 (2004-575) (France)

LOI n° 2006-961 du 1er août 2006 relative au droit d'auteur et aux droits voisins dans la société de l'information (France)

LOI n° 2009-1311 du 28 octobre 2009 relative à la protection pénale de la propriété littéraire et artistique sur internet 2009 (2009-1311) (France)

LOI n° 2018-1202 du 22 décembre 2018 relative à la lutte contre la manipulation de l'information 2018 (2018-1202) (France)

LOI n° 2020-766 du 24 juin 2020 visant à lutter contre les contenus haineux sur internet | Legifrance 2020 (2020-766) (France)

Paris Convention for the Protection of Industrial Property 1883

Protection from Harassment Act 1997 (England and Wales, Scotland)

Public Order Act 1986 (UK)

Regulation 907/2006 concerning the Registration, Evaluation, Authorisation and Restriction of Chemicals (REACH 2006 (OJ L 396)

Regulation (EC) 178/2002 of 28 January 2002 laying down the general principles and requirements of food law, establishing the European Food Safety Authority and laying down procedures in matters of food safety 2002 (OJ L 31)

Regulation (EC) 765/2008 of 9 July 2008 setting out the requirements for accreditation and market surveillance relating to the marketing of products 2008 (OJ L 218)

Regulation (EC) 852/2004 of 29 April 2004 on the hygiene of foodstuffs 2004 (OJ L 139)

Regulation (EC) No 864/2007 of the European Parliament and of the Council of 11 July 2007 on the law applicable to non-contractual obligations 2007 (OJ L 199)

Regulation (EU) 1025/2012 of 25 October 2012 on European standardisation 2012 (OJ L 316, 14112012)

Regulation (EU) 1169/2011 of 25 October 2011 on the provision of food information to consumers 2011 (OJ L 304)

Regulation (EU) 2016/425 of the European Parliament and of the Council of 9 March 2016 on personal protective equipment and repealing Council Directive 89/686/EEC (Text with EEA relevance) 2016 (OJ L 081)

Regulation (EU) 2016/679 of 27 April 2016 on the protection of natural persons with regard to the processing of personal data and on the free movement of such data 2017 (OJ L 119, 452016)

Regulation (EU) 2017/625 of 15 March 2017 on official controls and other official activities performed to ensure the application of food and feed law, rules on animal health and welfare, plant health and plant protection products (OJ L 95)

Regulation (EU) 2017/745 of 5 April 2017 on medical devices 2017 (OJ L 117, 552017)

Regulation (EU) 2017/1001 on the European Union trade mark 2017 (OJ L 154)

Regulation (EU) 2017/1369 of 4 July 2017 setting a framework for energy labelling and repealing Directive 2010/30/EU 2017 (OJ L 198)

Regulation (EU) 2019/1020 of the European Parliament and of the Council of 20 June 2019 on market surveillance and compliance of products and amending Directive 2004/42/EC and Regulations (EC) No 765/2008 and (EU) No 305/2011 (Text with EEA relevance.) 2019 (OJ L 169)

Regulation (EU) 2019/1148 of the European Parliament and of the Council of 20 June 2019 on the marketing and use of explosives precursors 2019 (OJ L 186)

Regulation (EU) 2019/1150 of the European Parliament and of the Council of 20 June 2019 on promoting fairness and transparency for business users of online intermediation services (Text with EEA relevance) 2019 (OJ L)

Regulation (EU) No 608/2013 concerning customs enforcement of intellectual property rights 2013 (OJ L 181)

Regulation (EU) No 1215/2012 on jurisdiction and the recognition and enforcement of judgments in civil and commercial matters 2012

Rome Convention for the Protection of Performers, Producers of Phonograms and Broadcasting Organisations 1961

Strafgesetzbuch (Germany)

Telemediengesetz (Germany)

The Digital Millennium Copyright Act 1998 (17 USC § 512) (US)

The Electronic Commerce (EC Directive) Regulations 2002 (UK)

The Lanham (Trademark) Act 1946 (15 USC § 1051 et seq) (US)

Treaty on European Union (2007)

Treaty on European Union (Consolidated versions of the Treaty on European Union and the Treaty on the Functioning of the European Union 2016) 2016

Treaty on the Functioning of the European (Consolidated versions of the Treaty on European Union and the Treaty on the Functioning of the European Union 2016)Union 2016 (OJ C 202)

WIPO Copyright Treaty (WCT) 1996

WIPO Performances and Phonograms Treaty (WPPT) 1996

Index